WOMEN'S FOOTBALL YEARBOOK

2019-20

Published by
Legends Publishing

E-mail david@legendspublishing.net
Website www.legendspublishing.net

Author's note: For team names, competitions, and in general, we have avoided the word 'women' or 'ladies' wherever possible because it seems superfluous in, what is after all, 'The Women's Football Yearbook'. We use it in the case of Cardiff City Ladies (to distinguish them from Cardiff City Women who compete in the Welsh Premier League), Leicester City Women (to distinguish them from grassroots club Leicester City Ladies), and Southampton FC Women and Southampton Women's FC (to distinguish them from each other and to draw a clearer distinction between each of them and Southampton Saints). We also use it where there might otherwise be confusion between whether we are talking about men's or women's football.

CONTENTS

2019-20 (Tier 1)

2019-20 (Tier 2)

2019-20 (Tiers 3-4)
(includes teams relegated from Tier 4 at end of 2018-19)

NIKITA PARRIS HELPED MAN CITY TO A CUP DOUBLE IN 2018-19 BEFORE JOINING LYON

FOREWORD

In 11 years as a Manchester United player Phil Neville won the Champions League, six Premier League titles, and three FA Cups before joining Everton in 2005. At international level he was capped 59 times by England. Appointed England women's head coach in January 2018, Neville led the Lionesses to their first SheBelieves Cup title in March 2019 and to the semi-finals of the World Cup four months later.

I'm sometimes asked what's surprised me most since becoming England manager. When I started this role, I spoke at length with my sister Tracey – who has so much experience as a successful player and coach in international netball – and asked her if I needed to adapt my management style. Her advice was invaluable. She told me all female players want to be treated like elite athletes and want honest appraisal. While I wouldn't necessarily describe it as a surprise, it soon became apparent to me that she was right. My players want to be challenged and treated the same as any other athletes.

I will never forget my first home match against Wales at Southampton's St Mary's Stadium. I felt immense pride that day and have the same feeling every time I set foot in the dugout as England manager. Taking England to the Women's World Cup this summer is the biggest thing that I've ever done in my professional life. Throughout my whole career as a player I dreamed about going to a World Cup. Now, I've had the opportunity to go to one as England manager, with 23 unbelievably talented footballers who played their hearts out and did their country proud. As a coach it's the best job I could ask for, and as a group we are determined to continue to grow and strive for even more.

What makes my job easier is that these players want success so badly. We sit for hours and hours talking through tactics and they want to learn the intricacies of every system.

We must ensure we capitalise on the increased profile the women's game is enjoying. We need to leave a legacy from the World Cup. We want to see as many women and girls playing and engaged with the game as possible. We want women and girls from all over the country, from whatever background, to play, coach, referee and work in the sport. Our players are brilliant ambassadors, great people and their skills and ability to communicate with people will help grow the game, I'm sure of that.

Everyone involved with women's football today takes so much inspiration from the previous generations of players. As a squad we attended The FA Women's Awards in May and it was clear from the award winners how many sacrifices people have made in the distant and recent past. Even present-day internationals like Jill Scott and Karen Carney, who herself retired after the World Cup, have had to fight to grow the game. Jill was still living in the north east, working full-time, while training and playing at Everton part-time in the north west. They made sacrifices and the young players in our ranks look up to those individuals.

The FA/Getty

PHIL NEVILLE: APPOINTED ENGLAND WOMEN'S HEAD COACH IN JANUARY 2018

Women's football has made great strides in recent times, maximising attendances at show-piece matches is a vital part of growing a following at all levels and I think The FA and clubs deserve credit for their hard work when it comes to attracting families and school groups. Our ambassadors and players act as role models for young girls and they are vital. All are playing their part in growing attendances for Cup finals and Lionesses games. There's still work to be done but progress is being made. If you take into consideration the crowds our WSL and Championship sides attract on a weekly basis, we've got a good foundation. Our players deserve to play in front of big crowds. The women's game is more popular than it's ever been.

The standard is improving all the time. I'd encourage anyone who may be thinking of attending a game to do so. The whole experience is fantastic, a real family atmosphere with some quality football on display. It's wonderful to see the profile of the women's game growing from year to year and magnificent that it now has its own Women's Football Yearbook which appears to be going from strength to strength.

I hope you enjoy the book.

Phil

INTRODUCTION

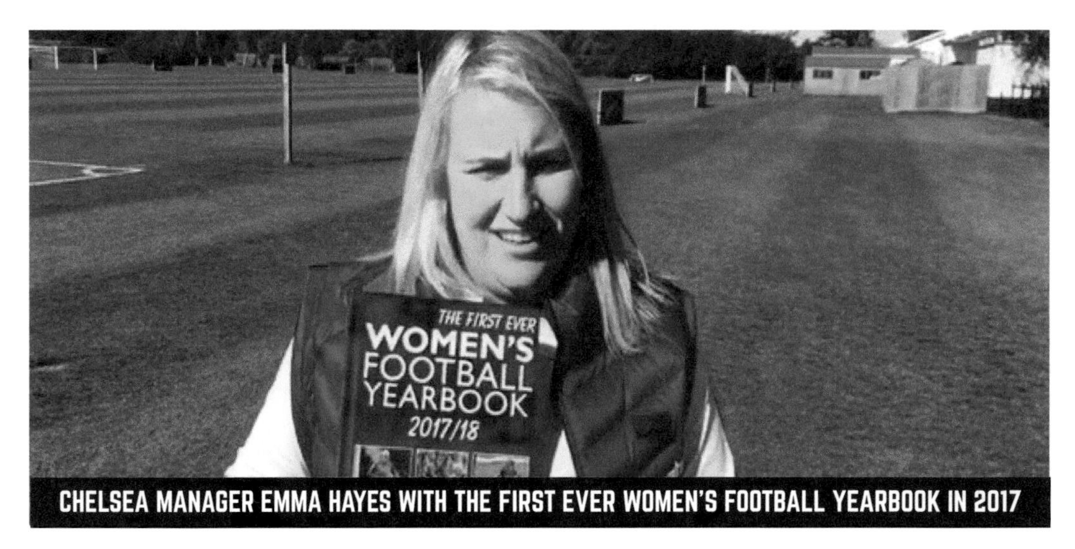

CHELSEA MANAGER EMMA HAYES WITH THE FIRST EVER WOMEN'S FOOTBALL YEARBOOK IN 2017

The inspiration for 'The Women's Football Yearbook' is the (men's) 'Football Yearbook' (sponsored by Rothman's from its launch in 1970-71 until 2002-03, Sky Sports from 2003-04 until 2017-18 and by The Sun since 2018-19). A vital journalistic tool and fans' bible, the men's 'Football Yearbook' is the authority on the game. It occurred to me in 2017 that there had never been a women's football yearbook and so I set about putting together the first one, asking women's football expert Tom Garry to help. I love football at every level and am a firm believer that every game – from World Cup final all the way down to park match – matters to someone, even if only to the 22 players, substitutes and coaching staff involved. It seemed to me a great shame that there wasn't an official printed record of the women's game in England.

I very quickly found a potential sponsor and publisher, but when the sponsor pulled out so did the publisher and, having already done most of the work, Tom and I were left with no option but to self-publish 'The First Ever Women's Football Yearbook 2017-18'. Positive reviews helped us find an established publisher for the second edition. Dave Lane at Legends Publishing did a magnificent job enhancing the look and feel of the book and in 'The Women's Football Yearbook 2018-19' we were able to include colour photos for the first time.

For this, the third edition, we have again been able to incorporate positive changes with a more user-friendly listing of honours won by clubs in the WSL and Championship, greater detail about the WNL sides and even more photos than before.

While putting together the three editions of the book I have continued to learn so much about life at all levels of the game. Outside of the very top clubs, women's football is held together by the extraordinary work of volunteers. Players pay to play; coaches give up their time to coach and so many others do so much to keep their clubs going. Tom and I decided to donate 50% of author royalties received from sales of 'The Women's Football Yearbook 2018-19' to sponsor non-professional players with the intention that every copy sold would therefore play a part in growing the women's game.

Chris Slegg

A TRIBUTE TO PATRICIA GREGORY

British Library

The Women's Football Yearbook 2019-20 is dedicated to Patricia Gregory (left of photo alongside Clare Balding, Kelly Smith and Baroness Sue Campbell) in celebration of the 50th anniversary of The Women's Football Association, co-founded by her in 1969.

Today women's football in England has a professional top division, games are played in Premier League stadiums and England matches draw millions of television viewers. None of this would have been possible if it hadn't been for Gregory's determination to overturn the FA ban on women playing the game which had come into force in 1921.After watching Tottenham win an FA Cup match with her dad in the late 1960s Gregory was curious as to why no women played the game, and so she wrote to her local newspaper to ask that very question. In reply Gregory was sent several letters from interested readers asking her if they could join her team. There was just one problem. Gregory had never played, so didn't have a team. So, she set one up and called it White Ribbon. Her next problem was her discovery that the FA ban prevented her from hiring pitches or qualified referees.

Undeterred, her fight for equality began. In 1967 she placed an advert in a football magazine to find out if there were any women's tournaments taking place. A carpenter from Kent called Arthur Hobbs responded, he was organising just such a competition. Gregory's team visited but did not take part until the following year when the tournament expanded from eight teams to 32. It grew again a year later with 47 teams involved in 1969. That year an agreement was taken between those clubs to set up The Women's Football Association with Hobbs elected as Honourable Secretary and Gregory as Honourable Assistant Secretary. The other officers were Patricia Dunn (Chairman); Pat Gwynne (Vice-Chairman); and Charlie Cooke (Treasurer). The WFA first met in November 1969, and it was under pressure from them that the FA overturned the ban on women's football at the end of that year.

In 1971 Europe's governing body, UEFA, voted to recognise women's football, meaning official matches could now take place. UEFA left it to each national association to determine how women's football should be run. Many countries fully integrated the women's game into their FAs, but in England, The FA left it to Gregory, Hobbs and their fellow board members on the WFA to oversee proceedings.

The WFA created The Women's FA Cup (known as the Mitre Challenge Trophy when it was first held in 1970-71), set up the first England team and oversaw the regional leagues which eventually evolved into the football pyramid we have today.

Despite little financial help, through sheer hard work Gregory and the WFA kept women's football going in England until the time was judged to be right to hand over the organisation and development to The FA in 1993.

The Women's Football Yearbook salutes Patricia Gregory for her invaluable role in the evolution of women's football in England.

FA WOMEN'S SUPER LEAGUE
TIER ONE

Arsenal's 2018-19 title win – their first since 2012 – means English football now has an established Big Three with the Gunners muscling back in alongside more recent champions Manchester City and Chelsea. And what of Manchester United? Could the newly promoted Championship title winners prove a serious force in their first season in the WSL? With Tottenham Hotspur also elevated to the top-flight as Championship runners-up, for the first time the Big Six of the men's game all have teams competing in the elite level of women's football.

Yeovil Town occupied the sole relegation place at the end of 2018-19 (and dropped to Tier 3 after failing in their bid for a Championship licence) meaning that with one going down and two coming up the WSL has now expanded from 11 to 12 teams with the benefit that each match day will bring a full round of fixtures without teams having to take it in turns to sit out. From the end of 2019-20 the FA's intention is that there will be one up, one down between the WSL and the Championship.

The 2019-20 season is the second year of the WSL being a fully professional top-flight following the most recent overhaul of the structure of women's football in the summer of 2018. At that point Tier 2 was renamed as the FA Women's Championship (instead of WSL 2) while the top-flight became the FA Women's Super League (WSL) instead of WSL 1. The renaming was in part to draw a clearer distinction between the divisions, given that the WSL was to now be a fully professional League.

The 11 clubs awarded Tier 1 licences for 2018-19 (namely Arsenal, Birmingham City, Brighton & Hove Albion, Bristol City, Chelsea, Everton, Liverpool, Manchester City, Reading, West Ham United and Yeovil Town) had been required to show they had the financial means to support full-time players and staff. Coaches would be required to deliver a minimum of 16 hours' daytime contact per week (plus matches), increasing to 20 hours by the 2021-22 season.

The 11 clubs awarded Tier 2 licences for 2018-19 (namely Aston Villa, Charlton Athletic, Crystal Palace, Durham, Leicester City Women, Lewes, London Bees, Manchester United, Millwall Lionesses, Sheffield United and Tottenham Hotspur) had been required to appoint full-time general managers and provide a minimum of eight hours' daytime contact per week (plus matches) for semi-professional players. Manchester United (who would go on to become champions) had been controversially allowed to operate as the only full-time team in an otherwise part-time division.

The changes had major repercussions for several clubs. Yeovil Town were eventually able to crowdfund the £350,000 they needed to preserve their top-flight status, but Sunderland were unable to support full-time football and dropped out of the top-flight to begin 2018-19 as a Tier 3 club in the FA Women's National League (WNL) Northern Premier. Other casualties were 2017-18 WSL 2 champions Doncaster Rovers Belles along with Oxford United, Sheffield FC and Watford who all dropped from Tier 2 to Tier 3 because of the new financial demands.

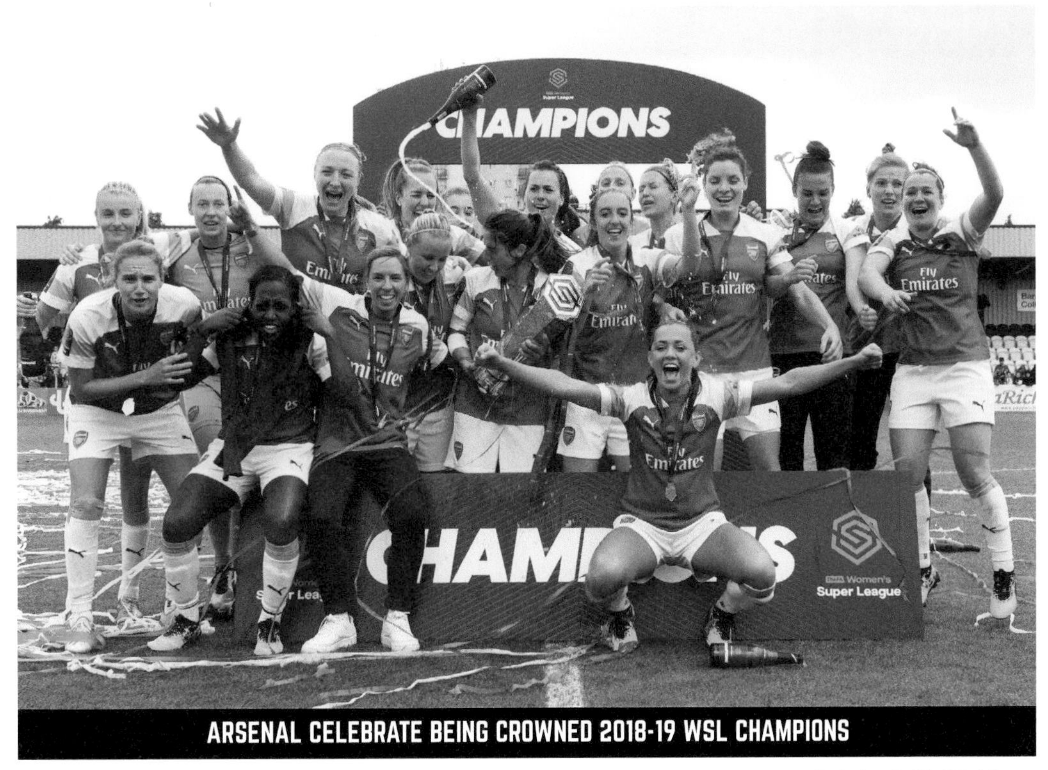

ARSENAL CELEBRATE BEING CROWNED 2018-19 WSL CHAMPIONS

The main beneficiaries were WSL newcomers Brighton (who had finished 2017-18 as WSL 2 runners-up) and West Ham United who were catapulted two divisions (from what had been called the WPL Southern Premier) to the new WSL.

This first club section of The Women's Football Yearbook concentrates on the 12 teams who are competing in the WSL in 2019-20. The clubs appear in alphabetical order: Arsenal; Birmingham City; Brighton & Hove Albion; Bristol City; Chelsea; Everton; Liverpool; Manchester City; Manchester United; Reading; Tottenham Hotspur; and West Ham United.

The stadium listed is the main home ground the club played at in 2018-19 and the manager or managers are those who took charge of the team throughout 2018-19. Some clubs may have changed their stadiums and managers throughout the summer of 2019 after our publishing deadlines.

Results of each team's matches in the Champions League (where applicable), WSL, FA Cup and Continental Cup (which is the League Cup for teams in Tiers 1 and 2) for 2018-19 are listed. Where known the following information has been included for each game: scorers; goal times; penalties; missed/saved penalties; own goals; and attendances. The figure in the column on the far right is the club's League position after all that day's fixtures have been completed. This has been included from the second fixture onwards. Where the home team uses a stadium other than their main home ground this is denoted on the home team's pages.

In the tables showing player appearances, an appearance is any match in which that player started the game or came on as a substitute. Appearances are shown for the Champions League (where applicable), WSL, FA Cup and Continental Cup.

ARSENAL

FOUNDED: 1987 **NICKNAME: THE GUNNERS** **2019-20: WSL (TIER 1)**

Honours:	No.	Competition name & year(s)
European Champions	1	UEFA Cup: 2007
English League Champions	15	3xWSL: 2011, 2012, 2019 12xWPL National Division: 1993, 1995, 1997, 2001, 2002, 2004, 2005, 2006, 2007, 2008, 2009, 2010
English League Runners-up	3	WPL National Division: 1994, 1998, 1999
FA Cup Winners	14	1993, 1995, 1998, 1999, 2001, 2004, 2006, 2007, 2008, 2009, 2011, 2013, 2014, 2016
FA Cup Runners-Up	2	2010, 2018
English League Cup Winners	15	5xContinental Cup: 2011, 2012, 2013, 2015, 2018 10xWPL Cup: 1992, 1993, 1994, 1998, 1999, 2000, 2001, 2005, 2007, 2009
English League Cup Runners-up	5	2xContinental Cup: 2014, 2019 3xWPL Cup: 2003, 2006, 2008
Tier 2 Champions (Regional)	1	WPL Southern Division: 1992

Arsenal are English women's football's most decorated club and they added to their trophy cabinet as they became champions of England for a 15th time in 2018-19, ending their seven-year wait for a WSL crown. The Gunners clinched their third title of the WSL era at Brighton on 28 April, as well as reaching February's Continental Cup final, where they were beaten in a penalty shootout by Manchester City at Bramall Lane in Sheffield.

It was a campaign to be proud of for Australian manager Joe Montemurro and his side, as they lifted the WSL trophy for the first time since the emergence of Chelsea and Manchester City as major challengers in the women's game midway through this decade.

The Gunners had become the dominant force in England after their formation in 1987 by Arsenal men's former kitman Vic Akers, who led them to an extraordinary 32 major trophies in his 22 years as their manager, including 2007's historic European title during their quadruple-winning season. They remain the only British women's side to reach a major European final.

In 2018-19 they rediscovered their ruthless form of old, winning 18 of their 20 League games without drawing any, and enjoying a goal difference of +57. Arguably their most impressive performance saw them beat defending champions Chelsea 5-0 in October, although it was Chelsea who ended the Gunners' hopes in the FA Cup as the Blues beat them 3-0 in the 5th Round.

WSL ERA FINAL LEAGUE POSITIONS (SS = SPRING SERIES)

SEASON	2011	2012	2013	2014	2015	2016	2017ss	2018	2019
TIER	T1	T1	T1	T1	T1	T1	T1	T1	T1
POSITION	1/8	1/8	3/8	4/8	3/8	3/9	3/9	3/10	1/11

2018-19 REVIEW

League:	**WSL (Tier 1): Champions**		
FA Cup:	5th Round	**Stadium:**	Meadow Park, (Boreham Wood FC)
Conti Cup:	Runners-up	**Manager:**	Joe Montemurro (since Nov 2017)

2018-19 STAR PERFORMER – VIVIANNE MIEDEMA

A WSL RECORD 22 GOALS IN 2018-19

Of the Gunners' 70 goals in 20 WSL games in 2018-19, almost a third were scored by Netherlands striker Vivianne Miedema, who was the WSL's top scorer as she netted 22 times, as well as providing 10 assists. Miedema's performances saw her recognised by her peers when she was voted as the PFA Player of the Year for 2018-19 becoming the first Arsenal player to land that honour since Kim Little in 2013.

In all competitions she dispatched 39 goals in 46 appearances throughout the campaign including four hat-tricks. It was perhaps fitting that the former Bayern Munich forward scored the opening goal in the 4-0 win over Brighton at the end of April that clinched the WSL title in front of a competition record crowd of 5,265 at the Amex Stadium.

2018-19 WSL RESULTS

					Att	Pos
09.09	Liverpool (h)	W	5-0	Vivianne Miedema 6, 39, 90, Lisa Evans 14, Kim Little 35	1,173	1
19.09	Yeovil Town (a)	W	7-0	Jordan Nobbs 6, 76, Beth Mead 20, Katie McCabe 52, Vivianne Miedema 54, Dominique Bloodworth 80, Kim Little 89	1,101	1
23.09	West Ham U (h)	W	4-3	Danielle van de Donk 12, 41, 62, Kim Little 73	1,081	1

14.10	Chelsea (a)	W	5-0	Kim Little (pen) 21, Vivianne Miedema 38, 57, Jordan Nobbs 52, 67	2,020	1
21.10	Reading (h)	W	6-0	Vivianne Miedema 3, 49, 85, Jordan Nobbs 7, Beth Mead 45, Danielle van de Donk 76	1,586	1
28.10	Bristol City (a)	W	4-0	Jordan Nobbs 13, Vivianne Miedema 41, 89, Danielle van de Donk 90	658	1
04.11	Birmingham C (h)	W	3-1	Jordan Nobbs 59, 90, Danielle van de Donk (pen) 67	1,431	1
18.11	Everton (a)	W	4-0	Danielle van de Donk 44, Jordan Nobbs 49, Vivianne Miedema 51, 66	367	1
25.11	Brighton & H A (h)	W	4-1	Vivianne Miedema 24, Dominique Bloodworth 33, Danielle van de Donk 39, Beth Mead 80	1,237	1
02.12	Manchester C (a)	L	0-2		2,149	1
06.01	West Ham U (a)	W	4-2	Leah Williamson 26, Janni Arnth 31, Danielle van de Donk 59, 65	913	1
13.01	Chelsea (h)	L	1-2	Vivianne Miedema 80	3,019	2
27.01	Reading (a)	W	3-0	Vivianne Miedema 2, Kim Little (pen) 80, Katie McCabe 90+4	1,619	2
20.02	Yeovil Town (h)	W	3-0	Kim Little 59, (pen), 73, Beth Mead 71	1,107	2
14.03	Bristol City (h)	W	4-0	Vivianne Miedema 11, 59, 78, Katie McCabe 76	1,019	2
24.03	Liverpool (a)	W	5-1	Kim Little 20, Beth Mead 22, 65, Dominique Bloodworth 67, Vivianne Miedema 85	570	1
31.03	Birmingham C (a)	W	1-0	Katie McCabe 79	1,520	1
21.04	Everton (h)	W	2-1	Louise Quinn 5, Vivianne Miedema 28	2,003	1
28.04	Brighton & H A (a)	W	4-0	Vivianne Miedema 6, Katie McCabe 31, Beth Mead 70, Danielle van de Donk 76	5,265	1C
11.05	Manchester C (h)	W	1-0	Emma Mitchell 88	2,200	1C

2018-19 FA CONTINENTAL TYRES LEAGUE CUP: GROUP TWO SOUTH

19.08	West Ham U (h)	W	3-1	Katie McCabe 12, 80, Beth Mead 44	834	
16.09	Lewes (a)	W	9-0	Danielle van de Donk 6, Vivianne Miedema 21, 27, 60, Katie McCabe 26, Kim Little (pen) 37, (pen) 45, 68, Lisa Evans 59	945	
05.12	Charlton A (h)	W	5-0	Vivianne Miedema 6, 74, Katie McCabe 29, 78, Amelia Ritchie (og) 58 *	202	Q
12.12	Millwall L (a)	W	3-1	Vivianne Miedema 55, Ruby Grant 56, Leah Williamson 60	463	
09.01QF	Birmingham C (h)	W	2-1	*Arsenal GK Sari van Veenendaal saved pen 18,* Danielle van de Donk 84, Vivianne Miedema 90+1		
07.02 SF	Manchester Utd (h)	W	2-1	Vivianne Miedema 18, 59	1,836	
23.02 F	Manchester C (n)	D	0-0aet (L2-4p		2,424	

(n) Played at Bramall Lane, (Sheffield United FC)

*Arsenal credit goal to Mead, but FA record as Ritchie (og)

2018-19 FA CUP

03.02 R4	Crawley Wasps (a)	W	4-0	Kim Little 17, Ruby Grant 43, 75, 86	1,550
17.02 R5	Chelsea (a)	L	0-3		2,232

2018-19 AS IT HAPPENS

MIEDEMA AND VAN DE DONK CELEBRATE A GUNNERS GOAL

09.09.18: Vivianne Miedema's hat-trick in the 5-0 home win over Liverpool on the opening day of the WSL season is the first scored by an Arsenal player in the League since Kelly Smith bagged one in September 2014.

14.10.18: Arsenal beat champions Chelsea 5-0, becoming the first team to win against the Blues in the WSL since May 2017 and the first to do so on Chelsea's own patch since July 2016.

04.11.18: Arsenal's 3-1 win at home to Birmingham City sees them equal their best start to a WSL season with seven consecutive wins. They eventually extend the run to nine before losing their 10th match, away to Manchester City on 2 December.

27.01.19: The deflected strike with which Vivianne Miedema puts Arsenal ahead after two minutes of their 3-0 win at Reading is her 16th WSL goal of the season – a new record number of goals for one player within a single WSL season, and set with seven games remaining. She breaks the record of 15 set by Birmingham's Ellen White in 2017-18.

03.02.19: Sixteen-year-old Ruby Grant grabs the headlines as she scores a hat-trick in Arsenal's 4-0 win away to WNL South East 1 (Tier 4) leaders Crawley Wasps in the FA Cup 4th Round.

26.03.19: Republic of Ireland international Katie McCabe signs a new long-term contract extension with Arsenal. The length of the deal is not made public.

31.03.19: Arsenal's1-0 win at home to Birmingham guarantees them a top-two finish and qualification for the 2019-20 Champions League with three games remaining. It marks their return to Europe for the first time since the 2013-14 season.

28.04.19: Arsenal seal the title with a game to spare thanks to a 4-0 win away to Brighton & Hove Albion. It's the Gunners' first League title since 2012, their third of the WSL era and their 15th overall. The match – played at Brighton men's Amex Stadium – is watched by a WSL record crowd of 5,265, beating the previous of 5,052 for Arsenal v Chelsea at The Emirates Stadium in 2012. Vivianne Miedema opens the scoring and ends the day by being named PFA Player of the Year.

ARSENAL PLAYER APPEARANCES AND GOALS 2018-19

				WSL		FAC		CC		Total	
				A	G	A	G	A	G	A	G
Albuquerque, Ana Caterina	M	POR	03.07.02	-	-	1	-	1	-	2	-
Arnth, Janni	D	DEN	15.10.86	5	1	2	-	3	-	10	1
Bailey-Gayle, Paige	F	ENG	12.11.01	3	-	-	-	1	-	4	-
Bloodworth, Dominique	M	NED	17.01.95	19	3	1	-	5	-	25	3
Carter, Danielle	F	ENG	18.05.93	6	-	-	-	-	-	6	-
Dawbarn, Hannah	D	ENG	10.11.01	-	-	1	-	2	-	3	-
Evans, Lisa	F	SCO	21.05.92	19	1	1	-	6	1	26	2
Filis, Melissa	M	ENG	30.07.02	1	-	1	-	2	-	4	-
Grant, Ruby	M	ENG	15.04.02	2	-	1	3	2	1	5	4
Hazard, Amelia	M	ENG	22.10.00	2	-	1	-	2	-	5	-
Kemme, Tabea	D	GER	14.12.91	3	-	-	-	-	-	3	-
Kuyken, Ava	M	ENG	15.06.01	7	-	2	-	3	-	12	-
Little, Kim	M	SCO	29.06.90	14	8	2	1	5	3	21	12
McCabe, Katie	F	IRL	21.09.95	20	5	2	-	7	5	29	10
Mead, Beth	F	ENG	09.05.95	19	7	1	-	6	1	26	8
Miedema, Vivianne	F	NED	15.07.96	20	22	1	-	7	9	28	31
Mitchell, Emma	D	SCO	19.09.92	11	1	1	-	3	-	15	1
Nobbs, Jordan	M	ENG	08.12.92	8	9	-	-	2	-	10	9
Paul, Lachante	M	ENG	06.08.01	-	-	-	-	1	-	1	-
Peyraud-Magnin, Pauline	G	FRA	17.03.92	13	-	1	-	2	-	16	-
Quinn, Louise	D	IRL	17.06.90	19	1	2	-	6	-	27	1
Samuelsson, Jessica	D	SWE	30.01.92	8	-	-	-	2	-	10	-
Schnaderbeck, Viktoria	M	AUT	04.01.91	5	-	-	-	-	-	5	-
Van de Donk, Danielle	M	NED	05.08.91	19	11	2	-	6	2	27	13
Van Veenendaal, Sari	G	NED	03.04.90	7	-	1	-	5	-	13	-
Veje, Katrine	M	DEN	19.06.91	8	-	2	-	3	-	13	-
Walti, Lia	M	SUI	19.04.93	12	-	-	-	5	-	17	-
Williamson, Leah	D	ENG	29.03.97	19	1	2	-	6	1	27	2

BIRMINGHAM CITY

FOUNDED: 1968 **NICKNAME: THE BLUES** **2019-20: WSL (TIER 1)**

Honours:	No.	Competition name & year(s)
FA Cup Winners	1	2012
FA Cup Runners-up	1	2017
English League Runners-up	2	2xWSL: 2011, 2012
English League Cup Runners-up	4	3xContinental Cup: 2011, 12, 16 1xWPL Cup: 2002
Tier 2 Champions (Regional)	1	WPL Northern: 2002
Tier 3 Champions (Regional)	1	Midland Combination: 1999

Birmingham City once again exceeded expectations in 2018-19 with another strong WSL campaign resulting in a 4th place finish. They did so despite having to cope with the upheaval of a mid-season managerial change. Marc Skinner, who had been in charge since 2016, and who led them to the 2017 FA Cup final at Wembley, left the Blues in January 2019 to take up the position of head coach at Florida-based club Orlando Pride in America's NWSL.

Birmingham had been just six points off the top of the table when Skinner made his move, but the club acted swiftly to replace him with the respected former Chile and Peru boss Marta Tejedor.The Spaniard's first game in charge was a trip to 3rd-placed Chelsea and Tejedor oversaw a dramatic 3-2 win, with Ellen White's brilliant stoppage-time volley securing the points in a thrilling game.

After that morale-boosting victory, City won a further five of their remaining eight League games – including their final four in succession – to comfortably secure 4th spot, finishing 13 points clear of 5th-placed Reading and only seven points off a Champions League qualification spot.

The outlook for 2019-20 will depend on how the club rebuilds after the summer departures of a string of first-team stars including England striker White and long-serving defender Aoife Mannion, who both left for Manchester City, and Wales midfielder Hayley Ladd who joined newly promoted Manchester United.

Blues have spent much of the WSL era as one of the main contenders to the now established elite of Arsenal, Chelsea and Manchester City. They were runners-up behind the Gunners in the first two WSL seasons of 2011 and 2012. Also, in 2012 they won the FA Cup, beating Chelsea on penalties after a 2-2 draw at Ashton Gate. City have played in three Continental Cup finals although they lost on all three occasions in 2011, 2012, and 2016. In 2013-14 they became the second British team (after Arsenal) to reach the Champions League semi-finals. They held Tyreso to a goalless draw in the first leg but went down 3-0 in the return leg in Sweden. Their only other Champions League campaign in 2012-13 saw them knocked out in the Round of 32 by Italian side Bardolino Verona.

WSL ERA FINAL LEAGUE POSITIONS (SS = SPRING SERIES)

SEASON	2011	2012	2013	2014	2015	2016	2017ss	2018	2019
TIER	T1	T1	T1	T1	T1	T1	T1	T1	T1
POSITION	2/8	2/8	4/8	3/8	6/8	4/9	7/9	5/10	4/11

2018-19 REVIEW

League: WSL (Tier 1): 4th
FA Cup: 5th Round
Conti Cup: QF

Stadium: Automated Technology Group Stadium
Damson Park, (Solihull Moors FC)
Managers: Marc Skinner (Dec 2016-Jan 2019)
Marta Tejedor (since Jan 2019)

AOIFE MANNION HELPED BLUES KEEP NINE WSL CLEAN SHEETS IN 2018-19

2018-19 STAR PERFORMER – AOIFE MANNION

Former England Under-23 international Aoife Mannion left Birmingham for Manchester City in the summer of 2019 having spent her entire senior career at the club. Only Arsenal and Chelsea conceded fewer WSL goals than the 17 Birmingham let in during 2018-19. A key part of City's solidity was the astute positional awareness of Mannion. The popular defender, born locally in Solihull, played every single minute of the WSL campaign. She also has an eye for the spectacular as her long-range winner in October's 1-0 victory at Bristol City proved, it was one of the goals of the season. She graduated through Aston Villa's Centre of Excellence before joining Birmingham when she was 18 in 2013 and played in the Blues' Champions League campaign that season as they made it to the semi-finals.

2018-19 WSL RESULTS

					Att	Pos
09.09	Everton (h)	W	1-0	Charlie Wellings 1	603	3
19.09	Brighton & H A (h)	W	1-0	Aoife Mannion (pen) 45+1	449	2
23.09	Reading (a)	W	1-0	Meaghan Sargeant 7	693	2
30.09	Manchester C (h)	L	2-3	Abbie McManus (og) 8, Meaghan Sargeant 49	824	2
14.10	Bristol City (a)	W	1-0	*Aoife Mannion missed pen 33 (saved Sophie Baggaley),* Aoife Mannion 75	436	2
21.10	Chelsea (h)	D	0-0	*Birmingham GK Ann-Katrin Berger saved pen 75 (Karen Carney), Hayley Ladd sent off 85*	1,177	2
04.11	Arsenal (a)	L	1-3	Emma Follis 60	1,431	3
18.11	West Ham Utd (h)	W	3-0	Kerys Harrop 19, Emma Follis 40, Lucy Staniforth 79	663	4
25.11	Liverpool (a)	W	2-0	Emma Follis 3, Connie Scofield 40	336	3
02.12	Yeovil Town (h)	W	2-1	Lucy Staniforth 50, Charlie Wellings 76	662	3
09.12	Manchester C (a)	L	0-1		1,157	4
06.01	Reading (h)	W	2-1	Kerys Harrop 72, Meaghan Sargeant 89	606	4
13.01	Bristol City (h)	L	0-1		610	4
27.01	Chelsea (a)	W	3-2	Emma Follis 36, Lucy Quinn 60, Ellen White 90+2	2,053	4
20.02	Brighton & H A (a)	L	1-2	Ellen White 26	358	4
31.03	Arsenal (h)	L	0-1		1,520	4
17.04	Everton (a)	W	3-1	Hayley Ladd 9, Ellen White 34, 67	103	4
21.04	West Ham Utd (a)	W	2-1	Hayley Ladd 44, Chloe Arthur 76	706	4
28.04	Liverpool (h)*	W	2-0	Ellen White 20, 29	1,545	3
11.05	Yeovil Town (a)	W	2-0	Charlie Wellings 59, 64	463	4

*Played at St Andrew's Trillion Trophy Stadium, (Birmingham City FC)

2018-19 FA CONTINENTAL TYRES LEAGUE CUP: GROUP ONE NORTH

19.08	Manchester C (h)	D	0-0 (L 4-5p)		574	
26.08	Aston Villa (h)	W	2-0	Kerys Harrop 71, Charlie Wellings 88	638	
16.09	Sheffield United (a)	W	2-0	Lucy Staniforth 72, Shania Hayles 83	331	
05.12	Leicester City W (a)	W	6-0	Shania Hayles 3, 60, Lucy Staniforth 22, Chloe Arthur 31, Charlie Wellings 37, Aoife Mannion (pen) 73	364	
12.12	Bristol City (h)	D	0-0 (L1-3p)		363	Q
09.01 QF	Arsenal (a)	L	1-2	*Aoife Mannion missed pen 18 (saved Sari van Veenendaal),* Lucy Quinn 61		

2018-19 FA CUP

03.02 R4	Yeovil Town (a)		P-P		
10.02 R4	Yeovil Town (a)	W	3-1	Aoife Mannion (pen) 38, Emma Follis 46, Charlie Wellings 58	523
17.02 R5	Reading (a)	L	1-2	Aoife Mannion (pen) 77	275

2018-19 AS IT HAPPENS

09.09.18: Charlie Wellings scores just 42 seconds into the new WSL season against Everton to give Birmingham the lead on the opening day. It proves to be the only goal of the game.

11.01.19: Birmingham confirm that manager Marc Skinner will leave the club after this Sunday's game against Bristol City. The 35-year-old's final match in charge ends in a 1-0 home defeat. As expected, a few days later Skinner – who became Birmingham boss in December 2016 and led the club to the 2017 FA Cup final – is named manager of Orland Pride in the US.

27.01.19: Marta Tejedor's first match as manager ends in a surprise 3-2 win away to champions Chelsea with Ellen White scoring the winner three minutes into injury-time. It's the second shock result Kingsmeadow has witnessed in 24 hours with League One AFC Wimbledon having beaten Premier League West Ham in the men's FA Cup 4th Round the day before.

21.04.19: Chloe Arthur's first League goal for the club proves to be the winner as the Blues come from behind to win 2-1 at West Ham. Arthur strikes with 14 minutes to go as Birmingham chalk up back-to-back wins for the first time under new manager Marta Tejedor.

28.04.19: Birmingham's final home game of the season is played at St Andrew's, home of Birmingham City men. A crowd of 1,545 sees Blues beat Liverpool 2-0 to climb to 3rd in the WSL, having played a game more than Chelsea who slip to 4th.

11.05.19: With Chelsea having since moved back into 3rd place, a final day 2-0 win away to Yeovil secures 4th place in the table for Birmingham, bettering last season's 5th place finish. Blues' points tally of 40 is also their highest ever return in the WSL.

BIRMINGHAM CITY APPEARANCES & GOALS 2018-19				WSL		FAC		CC		Total	
				A	G	A	G	A	G	A	G
Arthur, Chloe	M	SCO	21.01.95	19	1	2	-	6	1	27	2
Berger, Ann-Katrin	G	GER	09.10.90	8	-	-	-	3	-	11	-
Ewers, Marisa	D	GER	24.02.89	8	-	1	-	2	-	11	-
Follis, Emma	M	ENG	06.01.92	20	4	2	1	3	-	25	5
Hampton, Hannah	G	ENG	16.11.00	12	-	2	-	3	-	17	-
Harrop, Kerys	D	ENG	03.12.90	19	2	2	-	6	1	27	3
Hayles, Shania	M	ENG	22.12.99	5	-	-	-	3	3	8	3
Ladd, Hayley	D	WAL	06.10.93	19	2	2	-	4	-	25	2
Mannion, Aoife	D	ENG	24.09.95	20	2	2	2	6	1	28	5
Mayling, Sarah	M	ENG	20.03.97	17	-	1	-	5	-	23	-
Quinn, Lucy	F	ENG	29.09.93	13	1	2	-	5	1	20	2
Sargeant, Meaghan	D	ENG	16.03.94	19	3	1	-	6	-	26	3
Scofield, Constance	M	ENG	26.05.99	10	1	-	-	4	-	14	1
Scott, Harriet	D	IRE	10.02.93	14	-	2	-	4	-	20	-
Staniforth, Lucy	M	ENG	02.10.92	19	2	2	-	6	2	27	4
Walker, Claudia	M	ENG	10.06.96	7	-	2	-	-	-	9	-
Wellings, Charlie	F	ENG	18.05.98	20	4	2	1	5	2	27	7
White, Ellen	F	ENG	09.05.89	8	6	1	-	2	-	11	6
Williams, Paige	D	ENG	10.03.95	12	-	1	-	6	-	19	-

BRIGHTON & HOVE ALBION

FOUNDED: 1990 **NICKNAME: THE SEAGULLS** **2019-20: WSL (TIER 1)**

Honours:	No.	Competition name & year(s)
English Tier 2 Runners-up	1	WSL 2: 2018
Tier 2 Champions (Regional)	1	WPL Southern: 2001
Tier 3 National Play-off Winners	1	WPL National Play-off: 2016
Tier 3 Champions (Regional)	1	WPL Southern: 2016
Tier 3 Runners-up (Regional)	1	WPL Southern: 2015

Brighton joined England's top-flight for the first time in 2018-19. Some would argue they achieved that status through on-field merit given that they finished the previous campaign as Tier 2 runners-up. Technically though their promotion was based on satisfying the FA criteria for a WSL licence.No-one can deny the club's progress in recent years has been impressive. They won what was then known as the WPL Southern Premier (Tier 3) in 2015-16 before beating Sporting Albion (now West Bromwich Albion) in the play-off to secure promotion to WSL 2 for the 2017 Spring Series. The Seagulls secured a 7th-place finish in that competition before their first full WSL 2 season in 2017-18 resulted in the above-mentioned runners-up spot behind champions Doncaster Rovers Belles.

Former England boss Hope Powell was appointed as manager in July 2017. Powell oversaw the national team for 15 years from 1998, guiding the Lionesses to six major tournaments, including two World Cups and the runners-up place at Euro 2009.

She comfortably steered Albion clear of relegation in their first top-flight campaign of 2018-19 as they recovered from the disappointment of losing their first four WSL games without scoring a goal. As the months wore on Powell's side seemed to grow in strength. After mid-season wins over Yeovil and Liverpool, they claimed a first major scalp when they beat Birmingham in February and then ran out 4-0 winners against FA Cup finalists West Ham on the final day.

The forerunners to Brighton & Hove Albion Women were Brighton GPO who reached the FA Cup semi-finals in 1975-76. The current club do not count the GPO days as part of their history, considering themselves to have been formed in 1990 when linking up with Brighton & Hove Albion men's. They were founding members of the FA Women's Premier League starting life in Division One South (Tier 2) in 1991-92.

WSL ERA FINAL LEAGUE POSITIONS (SS = SPRING SERIES)

SEASON	2011	2012	2013	2014	2015	2016	2017ss	2018	2019
TIER	T3	T3	T3	T3	T3	T3	T2	T2	T1
POSITION	7/10	4/10	4/10	7/11	2/12	1/12	6/10	2/10	9/11

2018-19 REVIEW

League: WSL (Tier 1): 9th
FA Cup: 4th Round
Conti Cup: QF
Stadium: The People's Pension Stadium
Broadfield Stadium, (Crawley Town FC)
Manager: Hope Powell (since Jul 2017)

BHAFC/Paul Hazlewood

AILEEN WHELAN WAS VOTED BRIGHTON'S PLAYER OF THE YEAR 2018-19

2018-19 STAR PERFORMER – AILEEN WHELAN

Former Notts County and Everton forward Aileen Whelan featured in all 20 of Brighton's WSL games in their debut top-flight campaign. Whelan, who turned 28 in mid-August 2019, ended the season by claiming the award for Brighton's Player of the Year. Her work-rate and tenacity were key ingredients in Brighton out-performing many people's pre-season expectations and comfortably avoiding relegation. Whelan started out as a youth player at Rugby Town, a club that had been rebuilt by her dad and his friend to help give girls in the area an opportunity to play. She went on to represent Rushden & Diamonds, Barnet, MK Dons and Nottingham Forest before joining County for whom she was an FA Cup runner-up, coming on as a substitute against Chelsea in the final at Wembley in 2015. A former England Under-23 player, Whelan also won gold with Great Britain at the World University Games in Kazan in 2013 as part of a team including the likes of Danielle Carter, Demi Stokes, Izzy Christiansen and Fran Kirby. She scored a goal in the final as GB beat Mexico 6-2.

2018-19 WSL RESULTS

					Att	Pos
09.09	Bristol City (h)	L	0-1		376	8
19.09	Birmingham C (a)	L	0-1		449	9
23.09	Liverpool (h)	L	0-1		443	9
30.09	Chelsea (a)	L	0-2		1,175	10
14.10	Everton (a)	D	3-3	Danielle Buet 3, Ellie Brazil 75, 78	177	10
21.10	Manchester C (h)	L	0-6		815	10
28.10	Yeovil Town (h)	W	2-1	Jodie Brett 13, Victoria Williams 32, *Brighton GK Marie Hourihan saved Ellie Mason pen 69 (rebound scored)*	562	9
18.11	Reading (h)	L	1-4	Aileen Whelan 61	330	9
25.11	Arsenal (a)	L	1-4	Ini Umotong 9	1,237	9
02.12	West Ham U (h)	L	0-1		376	10
09.12	Chelsea (h)	L	0-4		773	10
06.01	Liverpool (a)	W	2-0	Laura Rafferty 34, Ini Umotong 49	398	9
13.01	Everton (h)	D	0-0		454	9
27.01	Manchester C (a)	L	0-3		1,279	9
10.02	Bristol City (a)	D	0-0		256	9
20.02	Birmingham C (h)	W	2-1	Kayleigh Green 29, Ellie Brazil 72	358	9
13.03	Yeovil Town (a)	D	1-1	Victoria Williams 28	408	9
20.04	Reading (a)	L	0-1		1,119	9
28.04	Arsenal (h)*	L	0-4		5,265	9
12.05	West Ham U (a)	W	4-0	Kayleigh Green 21, Megan Connolly 39, Amanda Nilden 79, Ellie Brazil 90+3	1,412	9

*Played at American Express Community Stadium/Falmer Stadium, (Brighton & Hove Albion FC)

2018-19 FA CONTINENTAL TYRES LEAGUE CUP: GROUP ONE SOUTH

19.08	Chelsea (a)	L	1-3	Aileen Whelan 78	1,095	
26.08	Tottenham H (a)	D	2-2 (L 9-10p)	Victoria Williams 51, Ini Umotong 90+1	144	
16.09	London Bees (h)	W	3-1	Ini Umotong 27, Ellie Brazil 36, Aileen Whelan 88	171	
05.12	Crystal Palace (h)	W	5-1	Sophie Perry 12, Kate Natkiel 38, 64, Jodie Brett 40, Fliss Gibbons 72	204	
12.12	Yeovil Town (a)	W	4-1	Ellie Brazil 15, Danielle Buet (pen) 45, Kayleigh Green 53, Beth Roe 83	224	Q
10.01 QF	Manchester City (a)	L	1-7	Danielle Buet (pen) 9	786	

2018-19 FA CUP

03.02 R4	Manchester Utd (h)	L	0-2	*Danielle Buet missed pen 78 (saved by Siobhan Chamberlain)*	764

2018-19 AS IT HAPPENS

16.10.18: The six goals in Brighton's 3-3 draw away to Everton in the WSL come as something of a surprise given that Brighton have failed to score in their opening four League fixtures, and Everton in their opening three. Ellie Brazil, the daughter of former Preston, Newcastle and Fulham player Gary Brazil, scores two goals – both with her head.

12.12.18: Nineteen-year-old Beth Roe scores her first goal for Brighton within six seconds of play re-starting after coming off the bench in the Continental Cup tie away to Yeovil. Roe takes a throw-in to a team-mate who immediately passes it back to her, she then dribbles into the box and scores with what is her fourth touch of the game (including her throw-in). Roe's goal completes the scoring in a 4-1 win.

27.01.19: Hope Powell gives 16-year-old Ellie Hack her first professional start in the WSL game away to Manchester City. Hack recovers well after giving away the third-minute penalty with which Nikita Parris puts City into the lead before they go on to win 3-0.

28.04.19: A WSL record crowd of 5,265 watches Brighton's 4-0 home defeat to Arsenal, a match which is staged at Brighton men's Amex Stadium. The result seals the title for the Gunners. The attendance breaks the previous record of 5,052 who watched Arsenal v Chelsea at The Emirates Stadium in 2012.

BRIGHTON APPEARANCES & GOALS 2018-19

				WSL		FAC		CC		Total	
				A	G	A	G	A	G	A	G
Barton, Kirsty	M	ENG	29.05.92	15	-	1	-	3	-	19	-
Brazil, Ellie	F	ENG	10.01.99	19	4	1	-	3	2	23	6
Brett, Jodie	M	ENG	09.03.96	10	1	1	-	5	1	16	2
Buet, Danielle	M	ENG	31.10.88	19	1	1	-	5	2	25	3
Connolly, Megan	M	IRE	07.03.97	6	1	1	-	-	-	7	1
Gibbons, Felicity	D	ENG	09.07.94	17	-	1	-	4	1	22	1
Gillett, Lucy	G	USA	23.10.93	2	-	-	-	3	-	5	-
Green, Kayleigh	F	WAL	22.03.88	18	2	1	-	4	1	23	3
Hack, Ellie	D	ENG	12.06.02	1	-	-	-	1	-	2	-
Harris, Sophie	G	ENG	25.08.94	4	-	1	-	4	-	9	-
Hartley, Laura	G	ENG	31.01.01	1	-	-	-	-	-	1	-
Hourihan, Marie	G	IRE	10.03.87	11	-	-	-	-	-	11	-
Le Tissier, Maya	D	ENG	18.04.02	2	-	-	-	1	-	3	-
Legg, Jenna	M	ENG	23.06.97	3	-	1	-	4	-	8	-
Mason, Abigail	D	ENG	28.06.00	-	-	-	-	1	-	1	-
Natkiel, Kate	M	ENG	24.09.92	12	-	-	-	6	2	18	2
Nilden, Amanda	D	SWE	07.08.98	4	1	-	-	1	-	5	1
Peplow, Chloe	M	ENG	03.12.98	16	-	1	-	2	-	19	-
Perry, Sophie	D	IRE	11.11.86	7	-	-	-	6	1	13	1
Rafferty, Laura	D	NIR	29.04.96	13	1	-	-	5	-	18	1
Roe, Bethan	D	ENG	03.11.99	2	-	-	-	2	1	4	1
Simpkins, Emily	M	ENG	25.05.90	6	-	-	-	4	-	10	-
Umotong, Ini-Abasi	F	NGA	15.05.94	20	2	1	-	5	2	26	4
Whelan, Aileen	F	ENG	18.08.91	20	1	1	-	5	2	26	3
Whelan, Fern	D	ENG	05.12.88	7	-	1	-	1	-	9	-
Williams, Victoria	D	ENG	05.04.90	19	2	1	-	6	1	26	3

BRISTOL CITY

FOUNDED: 1998 (AS BRISTOL ROVERS) NICKNAME: THE ROBINS 2019-20: WSL (TIER 1)

Former Names: Bristol Rovers (1998-2005) Bristol Academy (2005-2016)

NB: The current club is not to be confused with a different Bristol City which existed 1990s-2007

Honours:	No.	Competition name & year(s)
FA Cup Runners-up	2	2011, 2013 (both as Bristol Academy)
English League Runners-up	1	WSL: 2013 (as Bristol Academy)
English Tier 2 Runners-up	1	WSL 2: 2016
Tier 2 Champions (Regional)	1	WPL Southern: 2003 (as Bristol Rovers)
Tier 2 Runners-up (Regional)	1	WPL Southern: 2002 (as Bristol Rovers)

Bristol City entered 2018-19 under new management after Tanya Oxtoby was brought in to replace Willie Kirk following the Scot's decision to step down and initially take up the role of assistant manager at the newly reformed Manchester United Women. Kirk's highlights had included 2016's promotion back to the top tier, as well as reaching the 2016-17 FA Cup quarter-finals.

Australian former Doncaster Rovers Belles player Oxtoby left her role as assistant coach at Birmingham City Women to join the Vixens in July 2018, having previously managed Nottingham Forest Ladies before working as part of Perth Glory's backroom coaching team in Western Australia.

As well as a new first-team boss, Bristol City also had a changed squad, after their summer departures included highly rated youngster Lauren Hemp to Manchester City and captain Millie Turner's move to Manchester United. But Oxtoby and her new team hit the ground running, winning their opening WSL game at newly promoted Brighton before earning hard-fought back-to-back draws against title hopefuls Chelsea and Manchester City.

Those results in September led to Oxtoby's name going into the history books as the first winner of the League Managers' Association's WSL Manager of the Month award. Come the end of the season the club's 6th-place finish was their highest in the top tier since they were runners-up during their Bristol Academy days in 2013.

Founded in 1998 as Bristol Rovers Women, the club is not to be confused with a different Bristol City which was formed in the 1990s and folded in 2007. Rovers became Bristol Academy in 2005 and then the current Bristol City in 2016. They have enjoyed their greatest successes under the Bristol Academy name, reaching two FA Cup finals and the 2014-15 Champions League in which they knocked out Barcelona before losing to Frankfurt in the quarter-finals.

Traditionally nicknamed the Vixens, in the summer of 2019 they adopted the Robins moniker to align them with the men.

WSL ERA FINAL LEAGUE POSITIONS (SS = SPRING SERIES)

SEASON	2011	2012	2013	2014	2015	2016	2017ss	2018	2019
TIER	T1	T1	T1	T1	T1	T2	T1	T1	T1
POSITION	5/8	4/8	2/8	7/8	8/8	2/10	8/9	8/10	6/11

2018-19 REVIEW

League: WSL (Tier 1): 6th

FA Cup: 5th Round | **Stadium:** Stoke Gifford Stadium

Conti Cup: Group | **Manager:** Tanya Oxtoby (since Jul 2018)

SOPHIE BAGGALEY WAS NAMED FA WSL PLAYERS' PLAYER OF THE YEAR 2018-19

Bristol City Women via JMPUK

2018-19 STAR PERFORMER – SOPHIE BAGGALEY

Former England youth international goalkeeper Sophie Baggaley was an ever-present member of Bristol City's side in the WSL in 2018-19 and kept six clean sheets in her 20 League appearances. According to Opta she made 84 saves (only Yeovil's Megan Walsh with 144 made more) and completed the season with a saves-to-shots ratio of 71.2%. Baggaley collected a string of awards throughout 2018-19, including the first ever PFA Player of the Month award in September, an accolade she claimed again for her performances in January. She was nominated for the PFA Young Player of the Year, was included in the PFA Team of the Year and was later named the FA WSL Players' Player of the Year and PFA Fans' Player of the Year.

2018-19 WSL RESULTS

					Att	Pos
09.09	Brighton & H A (a)	W	1-0	Lucy Graham 71	376	4
19.09	Chelsea (h)	D	0-0		459	4
23.09	Manchester C (a)	D	2-2	Danique Kerkdijk 15, Juliette Kemppi 49	1,338	4
30.09	Everton (h)		P-P			6
14.10	Birmingham C (h)	L	0-1	*Bristol City GK Sophie Baggaley saved pen 33 (Aoife Mannion)*	436	7
21.10	Yeovil T (a)	W	2-1	Lucy Graham 33, 73	583	5
28.10	Arsenal (h)	L	0-4		658	7
04.11	Reading (a)	L	0-3		482	7
17.11	Liverpool (h)	W	2-1	Lucy Graham 14, Ella Rutherford 21	554	6
25.11	West Ham U (a)	L	0-2		562	6
09.12	Everton (a)	W	2-0	Ella Rutherford 65, Katie Rood 90+1	211	7
06.01	Manchester C (h)	D	1-1	Lucy Graham (pen) 61	812	7
13.01	Birmingham C (a)	W	1-0	Gemma Evans 16	610	6
27.01	Yeovil Town (h)	W	2-1	Lucy Graham (pen) 56, Rosella Ayane 72	616	5
10.02	Brighton & H A (h)	D	0-0		256	5
20.02	Chelsea (a)	L	0-6		1,821	5
14.03	Arsenal (a)	L	0-4		1,019	5
24.03	Everton (h)	W	1-0	Lucy Graham 33	475	5
31.03	Reading (h)	L	0-1	*Bristol City GK Sophie Baggaley saved pen 47 (Fara Williams)*	391	5
21.04	Liverpool (a)	L	2-5	Danique Kerkdijk 34, Niamh Fahey (og) 81	324	6
28.04	West Ham U (h)	L	1-2	Heather Payne 60	602	6

2018-19 FA CONTINENTAL TYRES LEAGUE CUP: GROUP ONE NORTH

19.08	Leicester City W (a)	D	2-2 (L 2-4p)	Lucy Graham (pen) 55, 85	294
26.08	Sheffield Utd (h)	W	3-1	Lucy Graham 26, Loren Dykes 56, Jess Woolley 72	156
16.09	Manchester C (h)	L	0-3		451
05.12	Aston Villa (h)	W	5-2	Lucy Graham 7, 19, Juliette Kemppi 34, 52, Katie Robinson 86	218
12.12	Birmingham C (a)	D	0-0 (W3-1p)		363

2018-19 FA CUP

03.02 R4	AFC Wimbledon (a)	W	3-0	Abi Harrison 1, Katie Robinson 24, Poppy Wilson 36	520
17.02 R5	Durham (h)	L	0-2		

BRISTOL CITY CELEBRATE A GOAL IN THEIR WSL MATCH AGAINST WEST HAM

Bristol City Women via JMPUK

2018-19 AS IT HAPPENS

08.10.18: Tanya Oxtoby wins the first ever League Managers' Association WSL Manager of the Month award with goalkeeper Sophie Baggaley collecting the WSL Player of the Month award.

15.10.18: Goalkeeper Sophie Baggaley adds another honour as she becomes the first winner of the PFA's Player of the Month award for her performances in September, the award is voted for by fans.

17.11.18: Lucy Graham and Ella Rutherford are on target as City secure a crucial 2-1 win at home to Liverpool. It's the team's third win from their opening eight WSL games.

03.02.19: Scotland international Abi Harrison – who signed from Hibernian in the January transfer window – makes her first start for City in the FA Cup 4th Round tie away to WNL South East 1 side AFC Wimbledon. She opens the scoring after just 12 seconds as City go on to win 3-0.

24.03.19: After heavy 6-0 and 4-0 defeats away to Chelsea and Arsenal respectively, City achieve a morale-boosting 1-0 win at home to Everton thanks to Lucy Graham's 33rd minute goal.

31.03.19: Goalkeeper Sophie Baggaley saves a penalty for the second time this season as she thwarts Fara Williams' 47th minute effort for Reading. Unfortunately for her City lose 1-0, just as they did when she kept out Aoife Mannion's spot-kick for Birmingham back in October.

BRISTOL CITY APPEARANCES & GOALS 2018-19

				WSL		FAC		CC		Total	
				A	G	A	G	A	G	A	G
Allen, Florence	D	ENG	13.08.99	2	-	-	-	-	-	2	-
Ayane, Rosella	F	ENG	16.03.96	15	1	2	-	3	-	20	1
Baggaley, Sophie	G	ENG	29.11.96	20	-	1	-	4	-	25	-
Biesmans, Julie	M	BEL	04.05.94	20	-	2	-	5	-	27	-
Brown, Frankie	D	SCO	08.10.87	20	-	2	-	5	-	27	-
Cumings, Eartha	G	SCO	11.06.99	-	-	1	-	1	-	2	-
Dykes, Loren	D	WAL	05.02.88	19	-	1	-	5	1	25	1
Evans, Gemma	D	WAL	01.08.96	19	1	2	-	4	-	25	1
Graham, Lucy	M	SCO	10.10.96	19	7	1	-	4	5	24	12
Harrison, Abi	F	SCO	07.12.97	8	-	2	1	-	-	10	1
Humphrey, Carla	F	ENG	15.12.96	20	-	2	-	5	-	27	-
Johnson, Alicia	D	ENG	24.12.98	3	-	-	-	1	-	4	-
Kemppi, Juliette	F	FIN	14.05.94	14	1	1	-	5	2	20	3
Kerkdijk, Danique	D	NED	01.05.96	19	2	2	-	5	-	26	2
Pattinson, Poppy	D	ENG	30.04.00	19	-	2	-	5	-	26	-
Payne, Heather	F	IRE	20.01.00	9	1	2	-	3	-	14	1
Robinson, Katie	F	ENG	08.08.02	7	-	1	1	2	1	10	2
Rood, Kathryn	F	NZL	02.09.92	4	1	-	-	3	-	7	1
Rutherford, Ella	F	ENG	28.04.00	20	2	1	-	2	-	23	2
Wilson, Poppy	M	ENG	06.08.99	1	-	1	1	2	-	4	1
Woolley, Jess	F	ENG	27.03.01	4	-	1	-	4	1	9	1

CHELSEA

FOUNDED: 1992 **NICKNAME: THE BLUES** **2019-20: WSL (TIER 1)**

Honours:	No.	Competition name & year(s)
English League Champions	3	2xWSL 1: 2015, 2018 1x WSL 1 Spring Series: 2017
English League Runners-up	2	2xWSL 1: 2014, 2016
FA Cup Winners	2	2015, 2018
FA Cup Runners-up	2	2012, 2016
Tier 2 Champions (Regional)	1	WPL Southern: 2005
Tier 2 Runners-up (Regional)	1	WPL Southern: 2001

Under long-serving manager Emma Hayes, Chelsea have become one of the most successful teams of the WSL era, securing League and FA Cup Doubles in 2015 and 2018, as well as winning the 2017 WSL Spring Series. Their entertaining style of football has also helped them continually grow their fanbase reaching a club record average home crowd of more than 2,000 for WSL matches at Kingsmeadow in 2018-19.

While their 3rd-place finish was their lowest in the WSL since 2013, they earned further respect for their performances in Europe, reaching the Champions League semi-finals for a second successive season before being narrowly beaten this time by the all-conquering Lyon.

En route to the last four the Blues enjoyed 11-0 and 7-0 aggregate victories over SFK 2000 Sarajevo and Fiorentina respectively, before Maren Mjelde's last-gasp goal saw them dramatically overcome Paris St-Germain in the quarter-finals. That set up a meeting with holders Lyon and, despite losing the first leg 2-1, midfielder Erin Cuthbert's second half away goal gave Chelsea real hope before the reverse leg in London.

A week later they went close to sending the tie in to extra time after Eugenie Le Sommer's opener for the visitors was followed by South Korea star Ji So-yun's brilliant free-kick for the hosts. Chelsea couldn't find another goal though and lost 3-2 on aggregate. Lyon would go on to win the European title for a fourth consecutive year.

Indeed, Chelsea were knocked out of all three Cups at the semi-final stage by the eventual winners. Manchester City got the better of them in the last four of both the FA Cup and Continental Cup. It was a Nikita Parris brace that put paid to Chelsea's Continental Cup hopes as City beat them 2-0 in January, while a tense FA Cup semi-final was heading into extra-time before Magdalena Eriksson's injury time own goal gave City a 1-0 win.

The women's side is fully integrated into Chelsea FC who bought AFC Wimbledon's Kingsmeadow Stadium for the team to move into ahead of 2017-18. Founded in 1992, they won the WPL Southern (Tier 2) title in 2001 and 2005 but had to wait until 2015 for their first major honour when Ji struck the only goal against Notts County in the first Wembley FA Cup final.

WSL ERA FINAL LEAGUE POSITIONS (SS = SPRING SERIES)

SEASON	2011	2012	2013	2014	2015	2016	2017ss	2018	2019
TIER	T1	T1	T1	T1	T1	T1	T1	T1	T1
POSITION	6/8	6/8	7/8	2/8	1/8	2/9	1/9	1/10	3/11

2018-19 REVIEW

League: WSL (Tier 1): 3rd
CL: SF
FA Cup: SF **Stadium:** The Cherry Red Records Stadium, Kingsmeadow
Conti Cup: SF **Manager:** Emma Hayes (since Aug 2012)

Darren Walsh

ERIN CUTHBERT SCORED 13 GOALS IN ALL COMPETITIONS IN 2018-19

2018-19 STAR PERFORMER – ERIN CUTHBERT

Young attacking midfielder Erin Cuthbert enjoyed an excellent campaign for her club as well as helping Scotland qualify for the World Cup for the first time. Cuthbert's abilities were well illustrated by her exquisitely taken goal in Chelsea's Champions League semi-final first leg away at Lyon, as she superbly tucked away a difficult half-volley with a level of skill and focus that typified her fine season. She started out as a youth player at Rangers, then moved to Glasgow City where she won two SPL titles, two Scottish FA Cups and one SPL Cup before making the switch to Chelsea in 2017.

ERIN CUTHBERT FENDS OFF MANCHESTER CITY'S TESSA WULLAERT

Darren Walsh

2018-19 WSL RESULTS

					Att	Pos
09.09	Manchester C (h)	D	0-0		2,501	5
19.09	Bristol City (a)	D	0-0		459	5
23.09	Everton (a)	D	0-0		213	
30.09	Brighton & H A (h)	W	2-0	Fran Kirby 32, Erin Cuthbert 36	1,175	5
14.10	Arsenal (h)	L	0-5		2,020	5
21.10	Birmingham C (a)	D	0-0	*Karen Carney missed pen 75 (saved by Ann-Katrin Berger)*	1,177	7
28.10	Liverpool (h)	W	1-0	Magdalene Eriksson 27	1,528	4
04.11	West Ham U (a)	W	2-0	Ramona Bachmann 62, 85	962	4
18.11	Yeovil Town (h)	W	5-0	Millie Bright 20, Ji So-yun 27, Erin Cuthbert 42, Ramona Bachmann 45, Bethany England 79	1,484	3
02.12	Reading (h)	W	1-0	Ji So-yun 49	1,741	4
09.12	Brighton & H A (a)	W	4-0	Magdalena Eriksson 65, Bethany England 69, 90+1, Ji So-yun 76	733	3
06.01	Everton (h)	W	3-0	Bethany England 6, Drew Spence 60, Hannah Blundell 69	3,221	3
13.01	Arsenal (a)	W	2-1	Erin Cuthbert 26, 63	3,019	3
27.01	Birmingham C (h)	L	2-3	Erin Cuthbert 13, 83	2,053	3
10.02	Manchester C (a)	D	2-2	Ji So-yun 50, 89	3,078	3
20.02	Bristol City (h)	W	6-0	Fran Kirby 2, 34, (pen) 82, Bethany England (6, 61, 89)	1,821	3
13.03	Liverpool (a)	W	4-0	Fran Kirby 16, (pen) 22, 51, Adelina Engman 90+2	237	3
31.03	West Ham U (h)	D	1-1	Bethany England 43	2,854	3
07.05	Yeovil Town (a)	W	8-0	Bethany England 4, 27, 45+2, Erin Cuthbert 16, 51, Adelina Engman 28, Fran Kirby 84, 87	843	3
11.05	Reading (a)	W	3-2	Ji So-Yun 8, Karen Carney 51, Bethany England 64	612	3

2018-19 FA CONTINENTAL TYRES LEAGUE CUP: GROUP ONE SOUTH

19.08	Brighton & H A (h)	W	3-1	Drew Spence 45, Fran Kirby 69, Bethany England 87	1,095	
26.08	London Bees (a)	W	6-1	Ramona Bachmann 7, 45, Drew Spence 9, 36, Fran Kirby 79, *Drew Spence pen saved by Sarah Quantrill 81*, Bethany England 81 (penalty rebound)	374	
16.09	Crystal Palace (a)	W	4-0	Adelina Engman 10, Bethany England 56, 64, Drew Spence 59	449	
05.12	Yeovil Town (h)	W	7-0	Adelina Engman 2, Drew Spence 18, 63, Bethany England 25, 77, Nicola Cousins (og) 37, Erin Cuthbert 75	916	Q
12.12	Tottenham H (a)	W	5-0	Deanna Cooper 10, Ali Riley 18, Karen Carney 47, Bethany England 60, 72	358	
09.01 QF	Reading (h)	W	4-0	Fran Kirby 3, 87, Anita Asante 37, Ali Riley 90	973	
06.02 SF	Manchester C (h)	L	0-2		1,358	

2018-19 FA CUP

03.02 R4	Everton (a)	W	2-0	Drew Spence 66, Hannah Blundell 90	560
17.02 R5	Arsenal (h)	W	3-0	Bethany England 5, 58, Jonna Andersson 40	2,232
17.03 QF	Durham (a)	W	1-0	Ji So-yun 28	1,629
14.04 SF	Manchester C (a)	L	0-1		1,763

2018-19 CHAMPIONS LEAGUE

12.09 R32 1L	SFK 2000 Sarajevo (BIH) (a)	W	5-0	Millie Bright 6, Drew Spence 22, Maria Thorisdottir 36, *Fran Kirby missed pen 80 (saved Envera Hasanbegovic),* Ji So-yun 87, Adelina Engman 89	2,200
26.09 R32 2L	SFK 2000 Sarajevo (BIH) (h)	W	6-0 Chelsea win 11-0 on aggregate	Drew Spence 4, Fran Kirby 31, 77, Maren Mjelde 50, Hannah Blundell 86, *Fran Kirby missed pen 90 (saved by Envera Hasanbegovic)* Erin Cuthbert 90 (scored from penalty rebound)	667
17.10 R16 1L	Fiorentina (ITA) (h)	W	1-0	Karen Carney (pen) 8	804
31.10 R16 2L	Fiorentina (ITA) (a)	W	6-0 Chelsea win 7-0 on aggregate	Drew Spence 23, Fran Kirby 38, (pen) 53, 63, Erin Cuthbert 57, Ramona Bachmann 67, *Millie Bright sent off 74*	3,015
21.03 QF 1L	PSG (FRA) (h)	W	2-0	Hannah Blundell 73, Erin Cuthbert 88	2,616
27.03 QF 2L	PSG (FRA) (a)	L	1-2 Chelsea win 3-2 on aggregate	Maren Mjelde 90+1	13,220
21.04 SF 1L	Lyon (FRA) (a)	L	1-2	*Fran Kirby missed pen 45 (saved by Sarah Bouhaddi),* Erin Cuthbert 72	22,911
28.04 SF 2L	Lyon (FRA) (h)	D	1-1 Lyon win 3-2 on aggregate	Ji So-yun 34	4,670

2018-19 AS IT HAPPENS

14.10.18: Chelsea suffer their first WSL defeat since May 2017 as they lose 5-0 to Arsenal. It is also the Blues' first home League defeat since July 2016.

31.10.18: Fran Kirby scores the first Champions League hat-trick of her career in the 6-0 win away to Fiorentina. It is also the club's record away win in Europe.

27.01.19: Chelsea's 3-2 defeat at home to Birmingham is the second shock result Kingsmeadow has witnessed in 24 hours with League One AFC Wimbledon having beaten Premier League West Ham in the men's FA Cup 4th Round the day before.

15.02.19: Twenty-five-year-old Norway defender Maria Thorisdottir signs a new contract with the Blues which runs until 2021.

20.02.19: Both Fran Kirby and Beth England score hat-tricks as Chelsea win 6-0 at home to Bristol City in what is Magda Eriksson's first match as captain.

31.03.19: Drew Spence is given a guard of honour before Chelsea's home match against West Ham kicks off to mark her 10 years with the Blues. The match finishes 1-1.

14.04.19: Chelsea's hopes of retaining the FA Cup they won in 2018 end in heart-breaking fashion as they lose 1-0 away to Manchester City in the semi-finals due to an injury-time own goal from Magdalena Eriksson.

21.04.19: A crowd of 22,911 – a record Champions League attendance outside of the final – watches Lyon beat Chelsea 2-1 in the semi-final first leg. The holders go 2-0 up through a Magdalena Eriksson own goal (her second in a week) and Amandine Henry's flick from a corner. Fran Kirby's penalty just before half-time is saved by Sarah Bouhaddi (her third penalty miss in this season's Champions League) but Erin Cuthbert grabs a crucial away goal in the 72nd minute.

29.04.19: Chelsea's Champions League dream ends at the semi-final stage as they are held to a 1-1 draw by defending champions Lyon meaning they exit the competition 3-2 on aggregate. A crowd of 4,670 – the highest for a women's match at Kingsmeadow – sees a Maren Mjelde own goal put Lyon ahead before Ji So-yun equalises just after the half-hour mark.

CHELSEA APPEARANCES & GOALS 2018-19

				WSL		FAC		CC		CL		Total	
				A	G	A	G	A	G	A	G	A	G
Andersson, Jonna	D	SWE	02.01.93	18	-	3	1	5	-	6	-	32	1
Asante, Anita	D	ENG	27.04.85	3	-	-	-	4	1	-	-	7	1
Bachmann, Ramona	F	SUI	25.12.90	16	3	4	-	4	2	7	1	31	6
Bailey, Jade	M	ENG	11.11.95	1	-	-	-	4	-	2	-	7	-
Berger, Ann-Katrin	G	GER	09.10.90	1	-	3	-	-	-	4	-	8	-
Blundell, Hannah	D	ENG	25.05.94	17	1	3	1	3	-	6	2	29	4
Bright, Millie	D	ENG	21.08.93	16	1	4	-	3	-	6	1	29	2
Carney, Karen	M	ENG	01.08.87	14	1	3	-	4	1	8	1	29	3
Carter, Jessica	D	ENG	27.10.97	13	-	2	-	6	-	3	-	24	-
Cooper, Deanna	D	ENG	20.06.93	5	-	-	-	6	1	1	-	12	1
Cuthbert, Erin	F	SCO	19.07.98	19	8	4	-	6	1	7	4	36	13
Durack, Elizabeth	G	ENG	20.05.94	-	-	-	-	3	-	-	-	3	-
England, Beth	F	ENG	03.06.94	18	12	3	2	7	8	7	-	35	22
Engman, Adelina	F	FIN	11.10.94	11	2	2	-	5	2	4	1	22	5
Eriksson, Magdalena	D	SWE	08.09.93	19	2	4	-	5	-	7	-	35	2
Ingle, Sophie	M	WAL	02.09.91	14	-	3	-	4	-	8	-	29	-
Ji, So-yun	M	KOR	21.02.91	17	6	3	1	2	-	8	2	30	9
Kirby, Fran	F	ENG	29.06.93	16	9	4	-	5	4	8	5	33	18
Lindahl, Hedvig	G	SWE	29.04.83	9	-	-	-	2	-	3	-	14	-
Mjelde, Maren	M	NOR	06.11.89	7	-	2	-	2	-	5	2	16	2
Riley, Ali	D	NZL	30.10.87	9	-	2	-	4	2	2	-	17	2
Spence, Drew	M	ENG	23.10.92	17	1	3	1	6	6	7	3	33	11
Telford, Carly	G	ENG	07.07.87	10	-	1	-	2	-	1	-	14	-
Thorisdottir, Maria	D	NOR	05.06.93	5	-	-	-	3	-	2	1	10	1

EVERTON

FOUNDED: 1983 (AS HOYLAKE) **NICKNAME: THE TOFFEES** **2019-20: WSL (TIER 1)**

Former Names:
Hoylake (1983-1987)
Leasowe Pacific (1987-1995)

Honours:	No.	Competition name & year(s)
English League Champions	1	WPL: 1998
English League Runners-up	5	WPL: 2006, 2007, 2008, 2009, 2010
FA Cup Winners	2	1989 (as Leasowe Pacific), 2010
FA Cup Runners-up	3	1988 (as Leasowe Pacific), 2005, 2014
English League Cup Winners	1	WPL Cup: 2008
English League Cup Runners-up	3	WPL Cup: 1997, 1999, 2010
English Tier 2 Champions	1	WSL 2 Spring Series: 2017

Andy Spence's long-serving tenure as Everton boss came to an end in November 2018 after four defeats and two draws from his team's opening six WSL games had seen them languishing at the bottom of the table.

Spence was replaced by former Bristol City Women and Hibernian Ladies boss Willie Kirk, as the Scot opted to leave his role as the assistant manager at Manchester United Women to take the chance of managing a WSL side again as a number one.

A victory in the Merseyside derby followed in December, and the club picked up two more wins – away at West Ham United and at home to Reading – over the remainder of the season, as they went on to finish 10th, four points below 9th placed Brighton. The Toffees exited at the group stage of the Continental Cup, while being eliminated in the 4th Round of the FA Cup by holders Chelsea.

Before the summer 2019 transfer window opened, Kirk revealed that he was set to bring in between six and eight new players, with six or seven players leaving the club, representing a relatively sizeable rebuild as he attempts to improve on 2018-19.

Kirk told The Women's Football Yearbook: "Since taking over midway through the 2018-19 season we experienced a whole host of ups and downs. Each one of those experiences will be used to improve us going into 2019-20.

"We feel we have made some big improvements during the summer in terms of staffing, player recruitment and our way of working. Everyone is excited about the journey that we are now on and we are determined to have a very positive season. Everton have a rich history in the women's game, a great tradition of developing our own players, and we are totally integrated into, and seen as an important part of, Everton FC."

Everton were runners-up to League champions Arsenal in each of the final five seasons before the dawn of the WSL era in 2011 and then finished 3rd in the first two WSL campaigns. They haven't managed to scale those heights since. The club has twice tasted FA Cup glory, winning the famous trophy in their days as Leasowe Pacific in 1989 and again as Everton in 2010.

WSL ERA FINAL LEAGUE POSITIONS (SS = SPRING SERIES)

SEASON	2011	2012	2013	2014	2015	2016	2017ss	2018	2019
TIER	T1	T1	T1	T1	T2	T2	T2	T1	T1
POSITION	3/8	3/8	5/8	8/8	3/10	3/10	1/10	9/10	10/11

2018-19 REVIEW

League:	WSL (Tier 1): 10th		
FA Cup:	4th Rd	**Stadium:**	Merseyrail Community Stadium, (Southport FC)
Conti Cup:	Group	**Managers:**	Dan Spence (Dec 2015-Nov 2018)
			Willie Kirk (since Dec 2018)

2018-19 STAR PERFORMER – SIMONE MAGILL

Emma Simpson

EVERTON CELEBRATE A GOAL FROM SIMONE MAGILL

Northern Ireland forward Simone Magill picked up Everton's Player of the Year award in 2018-19. Magill, who turned 24 in November 2018, is reportedly the first female player for Northern Ireland to play professionally in the modern era. Two of Everton's three WSL victories in 2018-19 were achieved courtesy of winning goals from Magill. Starting out as a youth player at Cookston Youth and then Mid-Ulster Ladies, she joined Everton when she was 19 in 2013 and played in the FA Cup final the following year when Everton were beaten 2-0 by Arsenal at Stadium: mk.

Emma Simpson

SIMONE MAGILL WAS VOTED EVERTON'S PLAYER OF THE YEAR 2018-19

2018-19 WSL RESULTS

Date	Opponent	Res	Score	Scorers	Att	Pos
09.09	Birmingham C (a)	L	0-1		603	9
20.09	Manchester C (h)	L	0-4		296	9
23.09	Chelsea (h)	D	0-0		213	
30.09	Bristol City (a)		P-P			9
14.10	Brighton & H A (h)	D	3-3	Inessa Kaagman 27, Gabby George 45+1, Chloe Kelly 70	177	9
28.10	West Ham Utd (h)	L	1-2	Chloe Walker 5, *Everton GK Kirstie Levell saved pen 54 (Jane Ross)*	143	10
04.11	Yeovil Town (a)	L	0-1		732	11
18.11	Arsenal (h)	L	0-4		367	11
25.11	Reading (a)	L	1-2	Hannah Cain 13	625	11
02.12	Liverpool (h)	W	2-1	Inessa Kaagman 6, Simone Magill 41	258	11
09.12	Bristol City (h)	L	0-2		211	9
06.01	Chelsea (a)	L	0-3		3,221	10
13.01	Brighton & H A (a)	D	0-0		454	10
20.02	Manchester C (a)	L	1-3	Chaney Boye-Hlorkah 12	964	10
13.03	West Ham Utd (a)	W	1-0	Hannah Cain 88	607	10
24.03	Bristol City (a)	L	0-1		475	10
31.03	Yeovil Town (h)	L	0-1		230	10
17.04	Birmingham C (h)	L	1-3	Inessa Kaagman 8	103	10
21.04	Arsenal (a)	L	1-2	Chaney Boye-Hlorkah 61	2,003	10
28.04	Reading (h)	W	3-2	Inessa Kaagman 40, Chaney Boye-Hlorkah 52, Simone Magill 65	174	10
11.05	Liverpool (a)	L	1-3	Abbey Leigh-Stringer 39	1,842	10

2018-19 FA CONTINENTAL TYRES LEAGUE CUP: GROUP TWO NORTH

Date	Opponent	Res	Score	Scorers	Att
26.08	Durham (a)	L	0-1		284
16.09	Reading (h)	W	3-2	Claudia Walker 14, 27, Inessa Kaagman 56	143
05.12	Liverpool (a)		P-P		
13.12	Manchester Utd (h)	L	0-3		267
16.12	Liverpool (a)	W	3-1	Chaney Boye-Hlorkah 2, Simone Magill 10, Elise Hughes 18	207

2018-19 FA CUP

Date	Opponent	Res	Score	Att
03.02 R4	Chelsea (h)	L	0-2	560

2018-19 AS IT HAPPENS

16.10.18: Everton and Brighton play out a thrilling 3-3 draw in the WSL. The six goals come as a surprise given neither team have managed to score in a League fixture so far this season (Brighton 4 games, Everton 3).

07.11.18: Manager Andy Spence is sacked three days after a 1-0 defeat to Yeovil sees the Toffees replace their opponents at the bottom of the WSL. His replacement is former Bristol City manager Willie Kirk who leaves his position as Manchester United assistant to take the job on 1 December. Kirk takes charge of his first match the following day, a 2-1 win over Merseyside rivals Liverpool.

28.03.19: Everton look likely to avoid relegation as Yeovil – the only club below them – announce they are set to go into administration and that they "recognise they will not be a WSL club next season." The Glovers – who are five points behind Everton with just five games of the season remaining – will be docked 10 points with immediate effect.

16.04.19: Yeovil announce they have avoided going into administration but will not appeal the 10-point penalty they were hit with last month when they informed the FA of their intention to appoint an administrator.

17.04.19: Everton's WSL status is secured as Yeovil lose 5-0 at home to Reading meaning the Glovers are guaranteed to finish bottom of the table in the only relegation place.

28.04.19: Everton win their penultimate match of the season as they come from behind to beat Reading 3-2 and secure only their third WSL victory of the campaign. The Toffees trail to Remi Allen's eighth-minute goal but hit back through Inessa Kaagman, Chaney Boye-Hlorkah and Simone Magill before Fara Williams pulls one back for the visitors.

EVERTON APPEARANCES & GOALS 2018-19

				WSL		FAC		CC		Total	
				A	G	A	G	A	G	A	G
Boye-Hlorkah, Chantelle	F	ENG	08.09.95	17	3	1	-	4	1	22	4
Brougham, Georgia	D	ENG	18.03.96	17	-	1	-	4	-	22	-
Brownlie, Emma	D	SCO	04.09.93	7	-	1	-	-	-	8	-
Bruinenberg, Dominique	M	NED	23.01.93	12	-	1	-	4	-	17	-
Bryson, Faye	D	ENG	04.07.97	8	-	-	-	4	-	12	-
Cain, Hannah	F	ENG	11.02.99	13	2	-	-	-	-	13	2
Chance, Olivia	M	NZL	05.10.93	1	-	-	-	-	-	1	-
Doyle, Emma	M	ENG	30.11.99	2	-	-	-	-	-	2	-
Finnigan, Megan	M	ENG	02.04.98	19	-	1	-	3	-	23	-
Flaherty, Rebecca	G	SCO	06.03.98	10	-	-	-	1	-	11	-
George, Gabrielle	D	ENG	02.02.97	16	1	1	-	4	-	21	1
Hinds, Taylor	D	ENG	25.09.99	12	-	-	-	2	-	14	-
Hughes, Elise	F	WAL	15.04.01	12	-	1	-	1	1	14	1
James, Angharad	M	WAL	01.06.94	19	-	1	-	4	-	24	-
Kaagman, Inessa	M	NED	17.04.96	19	4	1	-	3	1	23	5
Kelly, Chloe	F	ENG	15.01.98	11	1	-	-	3	-	14	1
Levell, Kirstie	G	ENG	07.01.97	20	-	1	-	3	-	24	-
Magill, Simone	F	NIR	01.11.94	17	2	1	-	4	1	22	3
Stringer, Abbey-Leigh	M	ENG	17.05.95	15	1	1	-	2	-	18	1
Turner, Danielle	D	ENG	10.09.91	14	-	1	-	3	-	18	-
Walker, Claudia	F	ENG	10.06.96	10	1	-	-	4	2	14	3
Wilson, Olivia	D	ENG	28.04.99	1	-	-	-	-	-	1	-
Worm, Siri	D	NED	20.04.92	13	-	1	-	1	-	15	-

LIVERPOOL

Women

FOUNDED: 1989 (AS NEWTON) **NICKNAME: THE REDS** **2019-20: WSL (TIER 1)**

Former Names:

Newton (1989-1991)

Knowsley United (1991-1994)

Honours:	No.	Competition name & year(s)
English League Champions	2	WSL: 2013, WSL 1: 2014
FA Cup Runners-up	3	1994 (as Knowsley United), 1995, 1996
English League Cup Runners-up	1	WPL Cup: 1993 (as Knowsley United)
Tier 2 Champions (Regional)	3	WPL Northern: 2004, 2007, 2010
Tier 2 Runners-up (Regional)	1	WPL Northern: 2006

Liverpool's 2018-19 season began in extraordinary fashion when manager Neil Redfearn resigned from his post in September after just one WSL game, a 5-0 loss at Arsenal. The club had also seen numerous key players leave during the summer 2018 transfer window, including captain Gemma Bonner, England left-back Alex Greenwood and Scotland star Caroline Weir.

Redfearn, the former boss of Leeds United men and Doncaster Rovers Belles, had only been in his job with the Reds since June, after guiding the Belles to the Tier 2 title in 2017-18.

First-team coach Vicky Jepson and former Liverpool and England goalkeeper Chris Kirkland were placed in co-caretaker charge, and they steadied the ship with three League wins from a possible four, including an away victory at West Ham.

That prompted the appointment of Jepson as Liverpool's new manager in October, with Kirkland as her assistant, and they went on to finish 8th, five points off a place in the top half and 10 points above their Merseyside neighbours, Everton.

Jepson told The Women's Football Yearbook: "There are so many positives that we can take from 2018-19. We were a new group that had to deal with many challenges, and I am so proud of them and what they achieved. In 2019-20 it's time for us to really kick on and climb that table and finish higher, and hopefully win some silverware which is what we are aiming for."

Despite falling well adrift of title front-runners Arsenal, Chelsea and Manchester City in recent seasons, Liverpool remain one of the most successful women's teams of the modern era, and one of only three teams to have been crowned WSL champions more than once. Their back-to-back title wins of 2013 and 2014 – with the latter coming amid the most dramatic final-day conclusion the WSL has seen – are the greatest achievements of their 30-year history.

WSL ERA FINAL LEAGUE POSITIONS (SS = SPRING SERIES)

SEASON	2011	2012	2013	2014	2015	2016	2017ss	2018	2019
TIER	T1	T1	T1	T1	T1	T1	T1	T1	T1
POSITION	8/8	8/8	1/8	1/8	7/8	5/9	4/9	6/10	8/11

2018-19 REVIEW

League:	WSL (Tier 1): 8th		
FA Cup:	QF	**Stadium:**	Prenton Park, (Tranmere Rovers FC)
Conti Cup:	Group	**Managers:**	Neil Redfearn (Jun-Sep 2018)
			Vicky Jepson & Chris Kirkland (joint interim, Sep-Oct 2018)
			Vicky Jepson (since Oct 2018)

COURTNEY SWEETMAN-KIRK SHOOTS IN THE CONTI CUP GAME AGAINST MANCHESTER UNITED

Liverpool FC/ Getty Images

2018-19 STAR PERFORMER – COURTNEY SWEETMAN-KIRK

Former England Under-23 striker Courtney Sweetman-Kirk crossed from the blue half of Merseyside to the red in the summer of 2018. She finished the 2018-19 WSL season as Liverpool's top scorer with 10 goals, including a contender for Goal of the Season in the Reds' 2-2 draw at Reading in December. Sweetman-Kirk – who turned 28 in November 2018 – expertly guided Kirsty Linnett's right-wing cross into the corner of the net and her fantastic finish not only wowed fans but it also crucially helped earn Liverpool a draw that ended a five-game losing streak.

2018-19 WSL RESULTS

					Att	Pos
09.09	Arsenal (a)	L	0-5		1,173	11
23.09	Brighton & H A (a)	W	1-0	Rinsola Babajide 85	443	6
30.09	Reading (h)	L	0-1	*Rhiannon Roberts sent off 56*	382	8
14.10	Yeovil Town (h)	W	2-1	Kirsty Linnett 18, Jessica Clarke 87	423	6
21.10	West Ham Utd (a)	W	1-0	Courtney Sweetman-Kirk 7	1,966	4
28.10	Chelsea (a)	L	0-1		1,528	5
04.11	Manchester C (h)	L	0-3		661	5
17.11	Bristol City (a)	L	1-2	Courtney Sweetman-Kirk 36	554	7
25.11	Birmingham C (h)	L	0-2		336	8
02.12	Everton (a)	L	1-2	Jessica Clarke 12	258	8
09.12	Reading (a)	D	2-2	Courtney Sweetman-Kirk 10, 68	582	8
06.01	Brighton & H A (h)	L	0-2		398	8
13.01	Yeovil Town (a)	W	2-1	Courtney Sweetman-Kirk (pen) 27, 90+3	984	8
28.01	West Ham Utd (h)	W	1-0	Courtney Sweetman-Kirk 49	186	8
13.03	Chelsea (h)	L	0-4		237	8
24.03	Arsenal (h)	L	1-5	Courtney Sweetman-Kirk (pen) 76	570	8
31.03	Manchester C (a)	L	1-2	Courtney Sweetman-Kirk (pen) 53	1,568	8
21.04	Bristol City (h)	W	5-2	Rinsola Babajide 12, 41, 65, Yana Daniels 44, Ashley Hodson 90	324	8
28.04	Birmingham C (a)	L	0-2		1,545	8
11.05	Everton (h)	W	3-1	Courtney Sweetman-Kirk 26, Niamh Charles 31, Amy Rodgers 88	1,842	8

2018-19 FA CONTINENTAL TYRES LEAGUE CUP: GROUP TWO NORTH

19.08	Manchester Utd (h)	L	0-1		829
16.09	Durham (a)	D	3-3 (W 5-4p)	Sophie Bradley-Auckland 2, Rinsola Babajide 71, Courtney Sweetman-Kirk 86	352
05.12	Everton (h)		P-P		
12.12	Reading (a)	D	1-1 (W5-4p)	Courtney Sweetman-Kirk 65	323
16.12	Everton (h)	L	1-3	Niamh Fahey 14	207

2018-19 FA CUP

03.02 R4	MK Dons (h)		P-P		
10.02 R4	MK Dons (h)	W	6-0	Laura Coombs 31, Courtney Sweetman-Kirk 32, Leandra Little 60, Jemma Purfield 61, 86, Ashley Hodson 79	394
17.02 R5	Millwall L (h)	W	2-0	Kirsty Linnett 57, Rinsola Babajide 67	412
17.03 QF	Manchester C (a)	L	0-3		1,366

RINSOLA BABAJIDE SCORED SIX GOALS IN ALL COMPETITIONS IN 2018-19

Liverpool FC/ Getty Images

2018-19 AS IT HAPPENS

14.09.18: Manager Neil Redfearn quits after just one WSL game in charge. Vicky Jepson and goalkeeping coach Chris Kirkland are appointed as interim joint managers.

22.10.18: Liverpool confirm that their home for the season will be Tranmere Rovers FC's Prenton Park ground.

26.10.18: Vicky Jepson is appointed as Liverpool's permanent manager. Chris Kirkland stays on as assistant.

10.02.19: January transfer window signing Jemma Purfield scores twice on her debut in a 6-0 win against Tier 3 MK Dons in the FA Cup 4th Round. The match is also notable for Leandra Little scoring her first goal for the club and for Ashley Hodson netting after coming on as a substitute after nine months out through injury.

16.02.19: The Reds announce that defender Satara Murray is leaving the club after four years in order to return to America to be closer to her family. The 25-year-old plays her final game for the Reds the following day as they beat Millwall Lionesses 2-0 in the FA Cup 5th Round.

13.03.19: Seventeen-year-old Bo Kearns – who has been with Liverpool since the age of eight – is named in the squad for the first time and makes her debut as an 83rd minute substitute in Liverpool's WSL match at home to Chelsea. Unfortunately for the Reds the match ends in a 4-0 defeat.

23.03.19: Chris Kirkland resigns as assisant manager to concentrate on his goalkeeping academy and mental health app.

11.05.19: Liverpool's highest crowd at Prenton Park, 1,842, watches a 3-1 final-day derby win over Everton.

LIVERPOOL APPEARANCES & GOALS 2018-19

				WSL		FAC		CC		Total	
				A	G	A	G	A	G	A	G
Babajide, Rinsola	F	ENG	17.06.98	17	4	3	1	1	1	21	6
Blanchard, Annabel	F	ENG	07.05.01	1	-	-	-	-	-	1	-
Bradley-Auckland, Sophie	D	ENG	20.10.89	20	-	3	-	4	1	27	1
Charles, Niamh	F	ENG	21.06.99	9	1	-	-	1	-	10	1
Clarke, Jessica	F	ENG	05.05.89	12	2	-	-	4	-	16	2
Coombs, Laura	M	ENG	29.01.91	20	-	3	1	4	-	27	1
Daniels, Yana	F	BEL	08.05.92	15	1	2	-	4	-	21	1
Fahey, Niamh	M	IRE	13.10.87	17	-	3	-	3	1	23	1
Hodson, Ashley	F	ENG	05.05.95	6	1	3	1	-	-	9	2
Jhamat, Simran	F	ENG	22.01.01	2	-	-	-	-	-	2	-
Kearns, Missy Bo	M	ENG	14.04.01	3	-	-	-	-	-	3	-
Kitching, Fran	G	ENG	17.02.98	6	-	2	-	2	-	10	-
Linnett, Kirsty	F	ENG	24.09.93	15	1	1	1	3	-	19	2
Little, Leandra	D	ENG	08.11.84	11	-	2	1	2	-	15	1
Matthews, Jasmine	D	ENG	24.03.93	10	-	-	-	4	-	14	-
Murray, Christie	F	SCO	03.05.90	19	-	3	-	4	-	26	-
Murray, Satara	D	ENG	01.07.93	14	-	1	-	3	-	18	-
Preuss, Anke	G	GER	22.09.92	14	-	1	-	2	-	17	-
Purfield, Jemma	F	ENG	21.02.97	6	-	3	2	-	-	9	2
Robe, Leighanne	D	ENG	26.12.93	19	-	2	-	4	-	25	-
Roberts, Rhiannon	D	WAL	30.08.90	8	-	2	-	2	-	12	-
Rodgers, Amy	M	ENG	04.05.00	12	1	3	-	3	-	18	1
Sweetman-Kirk, Courtney	F	ENG	16.11.90	19	10	3	1	4	2	26	13
Thomas, Lauren	M	ENG	10.01.00	2	-	1	-	2	-	5	-

MANCHESTER CITY

FOUNDED: 1988 **NICKNAME: CITY, THE BLUES** **2019-20: WSL (TIER 1)**

Honours:	No.	Competition name & year(s)
English League Champions	1	WSL 1: 2016
English League Runners-up	4	3xWSL 1: 2015, 2018, 2019
		1xWSL 1 Spring Series: 2017
FA Cup Winners	2	2017, 2019
English League Cup Winners	3	Continental Cup: 2014, 2016, 2019
English League Cup Runners-up	1	Continental Cup: 2018
Tier 3 Champions (Regional)	2	WPL Northern: 2012
		Northern Combination: 2001

The fifth and sixth major trophies of Manchester City's history were added to their trophy cabinet in 2018-19 as they completed a domestic Cup Double. City's season had started with a significant disappointment, with their Champions League campaign ending in the Round of 32, as they were beaten 3-1 on aggregate by Atletico Madrid who would go on to win the Spanish League.

However, domestically, Nick Cushing's outfit were formidable, winning the FA Cup at Wembley as they ultimately overpowered West Ham United in front of 43,264 spectators, with second-half goals from a trio of English players: Keira Walsh, Georgia Stanway and substitute Lauren Hemp.

Cushing's team did not concede a single goal in their five-game FA Cup run and they were also dominant in the Continental Cup, which they won for the third time since 2014. City and Arsenal could not be separated after 120 goalless minutes of February's final at Bramall Lane, but Canada forward Janine Beckie's spot-kick settled a tense penalty shootout, after England goalkeeper Karen Bardsley had saved from the Gunners' Leah Williamson and Danielle van de Donk.

In the WSL, it was Arsenal who sealed the title in the penultimate round of fixtures. City though went within two minutes of completing an entire campaign unbeaten in all domestic competitions. Cushing's side had not lost any of the first 19 of 20 League games, before the Gunners beat them 1-0 in the final game of the season thanks to Scotland defender Emma Mitchell's 88th-minute wonder goal.

City's five League draws (Arsenal didn't draw any) were a key factor in them missing out on the title but they remain one of the dominant forces in English football. Cushing arrived in 2013 and they have not finished outside of England's top two since 2014.

Cushing told The Women's Football Yearbook: "It's incredible to be part of a club like Manchester City, who always want to push the boundaries and take the women's game to the next level. Since 2014 we have won six trophies, including the FA Cup and Continental Cup this season, and we'll be in the Champions League again in 2019-20, competing on all four fronts once more. The team continues to grow, and we are incredibly proud of what our players have achieved on the pitch for both club and country."

WSL ERA FINAL LEAGUE POSITIONS (SS = SPRING SERIES)

SEASON	2011	2012	2013	2014	2015	2016	2017ss	2018	2019
TIER	T3	T3	T2	T1	T1	T1	T1	T1	T1
POSITION	4/10	1/10	4/10	5/8	2/8	1/9	2/9	2/10	2/11

2018-19 REVIEW

League: WSL (Tier 1): Runners-up

CL: Round of 32

FA Cup: Winners

Conti Cup: Winners

Stadium: The Academy Stadium

Manager: Nick Cushing (since Nov 2013)

MCWFC OSC and Dave Coop

NIKITA PARRIS IN ACTION FOR MANCHESTER CITY AGAINST YEOVIL

2018-19 STAR PERFORMER – NIKITA PARRIS

City must now adapt to life without Nikita Parris who left for Champions League winners Lyon in May 2019. The England winger – who can also play as a striker – dazzled fans with 19 goals and seven assists in the WSL in 2018-19, scoring once every 84 minutes on average. Only Arsenal's Vivianne Miedema (with 22) scored more WSL goals. In November 2018, at the age of 24, Parris became the WSL's all-time leading scorer when she overtook Eni Aluko's tally of 36. At the point of leaving City she had extended her record to 47. Her on-field talents – coupled with her off-field work to support youngsters from an inner-city region of Merseyside with her academy – saw the former Everton player voted as the Football Writers' Association's Women's Footballer of the Year.

2018-19 WSL RESULTS

Date	Opponent	Res	Score	Scorers	Att	Pos
09.09	Chelsea (a)	D	0-0		2,501	6
20.09	Everton (a)	W	4-0	Georgia Stanway 14, Nikita Parris 64, 68, Claire Emslie 90+2	296	4
23.09	Bristol City (h)	D	2-2	Nikita Parris (pen) 83, Stephanie Houghton 90	1,338	3
30.09	Birmingham C (a)	W	3-2	Caroline Weir 54, Nikita Parris 65, Tessa Wullaert 73	824	3
14.10	West Ham Utd (h)	W	7-1	Caroline Weir 2, Nikita Parris 7, 17, Georgia Stanway 72, 80, Stephanie Houghton 76, Tessa Wullaert 86	1,245	3
21.10	Brighton & H A (a)	W	6-0	Georgia Stanway 21, 64, 68, Caroline Weir 43, Nikita Parris 87, Claire Emslie 90	815	3
26.10	Reading (h)	D	1-1	Georgia Stanway 33	1,015	2
04.11	Liverpool (a)	W	3-0	Niamh Fahey (og) 50, Nikita Parris 59, (pen) 85	661	2
25.11	Yeovil Town (a)	W	4-0	Nikita Parris 17, Caroline Weir 40, Stephanie Houghton 83, Claire Emslie 88	1,153	2
02.12	Arsenal (h)	W	2-0	Georgia Stanway 18, 64	2,149	2
09.12	Birmingham C (h)	W	1-0	Georgia Stanway 12	1,157	2
06.01	Bristol City (a)	D	1-1	Nikita Parris 36	812	2
13.01	West Ham Utd (a)	W	3-1	Caroline Weir 15, Lauren Hemp 39, Nikita Parris 86	640	1
27.01	Brighton & H A (h)	W	3-0	Nikita Parris (pen) 3, 40, Gemma Bonner 31	1,279	1
10.02	Chelsea (h)	D	2-2	Tessa Wullaert 12, Georgia Stanway 24	3,078	1
20.02	Everton (h)	W	3-1	Keira Walsh 47, Janine Beckie 55, Nikita Parris 90	964	1
13.03	Reading (a)	W	4-3	Nikita Parris 15, 36, 39, Demi Stokes 54	449	1
31.03	Liverpool (h)	W	2-1	Claire Emslie 28, Jen Beattie 90+5	1,568	2
28.04	Yeovil Town (h)	W	2-1	Nikita Parris (pen) 30, Lauren Hemp 65	1,369	2
11.05	Arsenal (a)	L	0-1		2,200	2

2018-19 FA CONTINENTAL TYRES LEAGUE CUP: GROUP ONE NORTH

Date	Opponent	Res	Score	Scorers	Att	
19.08	Birmingham C (a)	D	0-0	(W 5-4p)	574	
26.08	Leicester C W (h)	W	4-0	Tessa Wullaert 53, 80, Janine Beckie 72, Nadia Nadim 83	1,609	
16.09	Bristol City (a)	W	3-0	Claire Emslie 52, Nadia Nadim (pen) 65, Caroline Weir 72	451	
05.12	Sheffield Utd (h)	W	6-0	Janine Beckie 7, 24, 48, 78, Jess Park 14, Georgia Stanway (pen) 52	1,079	Q
13.12	Aston Villa (a)	W	4-0	Gemma Bonner 21, Janine Beckie 25, Jess Park 77, Lauren Hemp 84	458	
10.01 QF	Brighton & H A (h)	W	7-1	Nikita Parris 6, Lauren Hemp 23, 86, Caroline Weir 59, Claire Emslie 88, Georgia Stanway 90, Janine Beckie 90+2	786	
06.02 SF	Chelsea (a)	W	2-0	Nikita Parris (pen) 49, 81	1,358	
23.02 F	Arsenal (n)	D	0-0aet	(W4-2p)	2,424	

(n) Played at Bramall Lane, (Sheffield United FC)

MANCHESTER CITY CELEBRATE WINNING THE 2018-19 CONTINENTAL CUP

MCWFC OSC and Dave Coop

2018-19 FA CUP

02.02 R4	Watford (h)	W	3-0	Nikita Parris 62, 69, Pauline Bremer 86	883
17.02 R5	Tottenham H (a)	W	3-0	Stephanie Houghton 37, Lauren Hemp 39, Gemma Bonner 51, *Man City GK Ellie Roebuck saved pen 76 (Angela Addison)*	1,158
17.03 QF	Liverpool (h)	W	3-0	Janine Beckie 25, Georgia Stanway 69, 88	1,366
14.04 SF	Chelsea (h)	W	1-0	Magdalena Eriksson (og) 90+1	1,763
04.05 F	West Ham Utd (n)	W	3-0	Keira Walsh 52, Georgia Stanway 79, Lauren Hemp 87	43,264

(n)Played at Wembley Stadium

2018-19 CHAMPIONS LEAGUE

13.09 R32 1L	Atletico Madrid (ESP) (a)	D	1-1	Gemma Bonner 16	1,671
26.09 R32 2L	Atletico Madrid (ESP) (h)	L	0-2		1,178
			Atletico Madrid win 3-1 on aggregate		

MCWFC OSC and Dave Coop

KAREN BARDSLEY (LEFT) SAVED TWO PENALTIES AS CITY WON THE CONTINENTAL CUP

2018-19 AS IT HAPPENS

04.11.18: When Nikita Parris converts an 84th minute penalty against Liverpool (her second goal of the game) to complete a 3-0 win away, she registers the 37th WSL goal of her career taking her above former Chelsea player Eni Aluko as the competition's all-time leading goal scorer.

23.02.19: Manchester City win the Continental Cup beating Arsenal 4-2 on penalties following a goalless draw. City's 18-year-old substitute Lauren Hemp takes City's second penalty and sees it saved by Sari van Veenendaal, but Arsenal fail to take advantage as City keeper Karen Bardsley then stops successive efforts from Leah Williamson and Danielle van de Donk. Janine Beckie converts the winning kick.

22.03.19: Twenty-year-old England international Georgia Stanway signs a new deal that will keep her at City until 2022.

14.04.19: City beat Chelsea 1-0 in an FA Cup semi-final broadcast live on BBC One. A Magdalena Eriksson own goal in injury-time proves decisive as City knock out the holders.

28.04.19: City's slim chances of catching Arsenal are over as the Gunners seal the title with a game to spare thanks to a 4-0 win away to Brighton in the lunch-time kick-off. City then suffer a nightmare start in their home game against bottom club Yeovil as they find themselves trailing to Olivia Fergusson's goal after just 25 seconds, however they hit back to win 2-1 thanks to a Nikita Parris penalty and Lauren Hemp's header.

29.04.19: Manchester City forward Nikita Parris is named the Football Writers' Association Player of the Year with club-mate Raheem Sterling winning the men's award.

04.05.19: City win the FA Cup for the second time, beating West Ham United 3-0 in the final at Wembley. The match is all-square until seven minutes after the break when Keira Walsh puts City ahead with a long-range strike. Georgia Stanway and Lauren Hemp add gloss to the score line late on.

11.05.19: City come within just two minutes of completing the entire domestic season unbeaten in all competitions but fall 1-0 to a stunning 88th minute effort from Arsenal's Emma Mitchell on the final day of the WSL campaign. Later in the day England forward Nikita Parris confirms on Instagram that she will leave the club this summer. A few days later she joins Champions League winners Lyon.

MAN CITY APPEARANCES & GOALS 2018-19

				WSL		FAC		CC		CL		Total	
				A	G	A	G	A	G	A	G	A	G
Bardsley, Karen	G	ENG	14.10.84	5	-	4	-	6	-	2	-	17	-
Beattie, Jennifer	D	SCO	13.05.91	17	1	4	-	5	-	2	-	28	1
Beckie, Janine	F	CAN	20.08.94	10	1	2	1	6	7	-	-	18	9
Bissell, Emma	F	ENG	21.12.01	-	-	-	-	1	-	-	-	1	-
Bonner, Gemma	D	ENG	13.07.91	17	1	4	1	8	1	2	1	31	4
Bremer, Pauline	F	GER	10.04.96	4	-	2	1	3	-	-	-	9	1
Campbell, Megan	D	IRL	28.06.93	4	-	1	-	-	-	-	-	5	-
Emslie, Claire	F	SCO	08.03.94	14	4	4	-	7	2	1	-	26	6
Hemp, Lauren	F	ENG	07.08.00	10	2	4	2	5	3	1	-	20	7
Houghton, Stephanie	D	ENG	23.04.88	20	3	5	1	6	-	1	-	32	4
Jans, Mie	D	DEN	06.02.94	-	-	-	-	2	-	1	-	3	-
Lawley, Melissa	M	ENG	28.04.94	4	-	1	-	4	-	2	-	11	-
McManus, Abbie	D	ENG	14.01.93	13	-	2	-	5	-	2	-	22	-
Morgan, Esme	D	ENG	18.10.00	6	-	1	-	3	-	-	-	10	-
Nadim, Nadia	F	DEN	02.01.88	3	-	-	-	3	2	2	-	8	2
Park, Jessica	M	ENG	21.10.01	2	-	1	-	3	2	-	-	6	2
Parris, Nikita	F	ENG	10.03.94	19	19	5	2	4	3	2	-	30	24
Roebuck, Ellie	G	ENG	23.09.99	15	-	1	-	1	-	-	-	17	-
Scott, Jill	M	ENG	02.02.87	19	-	4	-	4	-	2	-	29	-
Stanway, Georgia	F	ENG	03.01.99	19	11	5	3	6	2	2	-	32	16
Stenson, Fran	G	ENG	27.04.01	-	-	-	-	1	-	-	-	1	-
Stokes, Demi	D	ENG	12.12.91	11	1	4	-	2	-	-	-	17	1
Walsh, Keira	M	ENG	08.04.97	19	1	5	1	7	-	2	-	33	2
Weir, Caroline	F	SCO	20.06.95	18	5	4	-	6	2	2	-	30	7
Wullaert, Tessa	F	BEL	19.03.93	18	3	4	-	7	2	2	-	31	5

MANCHESTER UNITED

REFORMED: 2018 **NICKNAME: THE RED DEVILS** **2019-20: WSL (TIER 1)**

Honours:	No.	Competition name & year(s)
Tier 2 Champions	1	Championship: 2019

Manchester United's decision to reform a women's side in the summer of 2018 was widely hailed as a major moment for the English game. The Red Devils ended their 13-year absence from the senior divisions when they were successful in applying for a licence to join the Championship for the 2018-19 season, amid the restructuring of the top women's leagues in England.

There was controversy about the FA positioning them in Tier 2. Some felt they should have had to work their way up from lower down the pyramid, others suggested it was not fair on the other Championship sides to allow United to compete as the only full-time club in a part-time division.

Former England, Arsenal and Liverpool centre-back Casey Stoney was installed as the new team's head coach and spent summer 2018 hastily recruiting an entire squad of 21 players. England left-back Alex Greenwood was among the club's high-profile signings, while off the field Stoney added former Bristol City and Hibernian boss Willie Kirk as her assistant manager. Kirk would leave later in the season to become the new first team boss at Everton, but before then, his influence would play a part in the club signing some of those who had played for him in the past, including Scotland's ex-Hibs star Lizzie Arnot and former Bristol City skipper Millie Turner.

Once the season got under way, United began in dominant fashion, beating Aston Villa 12-0 in their first Championship game. They went on to claim the title in style, winning 18 and losing just one of their 20 League matches, scoring 98 goals and conceding just seven. They also proved themselves against top-flight opponents, beating Brighton in the FA Cup and Liverpool, Everton and West Ham in the Continental Cup on their way to reaching the semi-finals.

Stoney told The Women's Football Yearbook: "It's been an incredible season; to bring 21 players together and win the League in our first year is a real testament to the hard work and commitment from the players and staff. Lifting the trophy was a special moment for everyone.

We are under no illusions that it will be tougher in the WSL, but we've shown that we can compete against WSL sides during our FA Cup and Conti Cup campaigns which gives us confidence."

In the 1970s female fans of Manchester United formed their own team, Manchester United Ladies. Many recognized them as Manchester United FC's unofficial women's team. In 2001 they became officially affiliated with Manchester United FC, but in 2005 they were disbanded when United decided to direct resources at girls' football instead of a senior team.

They returned to senior football in 2018 and their 21-player squad for their debut Championship campaign contained seven of their former youth players, among them midfielder Katie Zelem fresh from having won Serie A with Juventus in 2017-18.

WSL ERA FINAL LEAGUE POSITIONS

SEASON	2011	2012	2013	2014	2015	2016	2017	2018	2019
TIER	N/A	N/A	N/A	N/A	N/A	N/A	N/A	N/A	T2
POSITION	N/A	N/A	N/A	N/A	N/A	N/A	N/A	N/A	1/11

2018-19 REVIEW

League: Championship (Tier 2): Champions

FA Cup: QF **Stadium:** Leigh Sports Village

Conti Cup: SF **Manager:** Casey Stoney (since Jun 2018)

KATIE ZELEM HAS WON NATIONAL TITLES WITH LIVERPOOL AND JUVENTUS

2018-19 STAR PERFORMER – KATIE ZELEM

Former Liverpool and Juventus midfielder Katie Zelem picked up United's 2018-19 Player of the Year award, voted for by the fans. Her first goal of the season came from the spot in the opening day 12-0 win over Aston Villa and she went on to net 10 times in 18 Championship appearances. Throughout the campaign she demonstrated she could dictate games with her all-round play and mature performances. Zelem started out in United's youth ranks but in 2013, at a time when the club didn't have a senior women's team, she left to pursue a WSL career with Liverpool before making the switch to Italy in 2017. She has won the WSL title twice with Liverpool (2013 and 2014), Serie A with Juventus (2018) and the Championship with United (2019).

KATIE ZELEM LIFTS THE 2018-19 FA CHAMPIONSHIP TROPHY

2018-19 CHAMP RESULTS

Date	Opponent	Res	Score	Scorers	Att	Pos
09.09	Aston Villa (a)	W	12-0	Jess Sigsworth 25, 33, 35, 49, 62, Lauren James 10, 23, Kirsty Hanson 55, 59, Katie Zelem (pen) 28, Mollie Green 66, Ella Toone 68	1,165	1
20.09	Sheff Utd (h)	W	3-0	Katie Zelem (pen) 12, Kirsty Hanson 35, Lizzie Arnot 64	2,003	1
23.09	London Bees (a)	W	5-0	Mollie Green 17, 55, Lauren James 27, Millie Turner 44, Ella Toone 75	642	1
30.09	Durham (h)	D	0-0	*Katie Zelem missed pen 68 (saved by Hannah Reid)*	2,244	1
14.10	Charlton Athletic (h)	W	3-0	Katie Zelem 15, Jess Sigsworth 55, Lizzie Arnot 75	2,349	1
04.11	Tottenham H (h)	W	4-1	Lauren James 10, Jess Sigsworth 18, 41, Charlie Devlin 80	2,367	2
18.11	Crystal Palace (a)	W	5-0	Lizzie Arnot 17, 55, Mollie Green 59, 83, Alex Greenwood (pen) 75	975	2
25.11	Millwall L (h)	W	8-0	Lauren James 16, Mollie Green 32, 38, 49, Katie Zelem 36, Ella Toone 58, Jess Sigsworth 71, Alex Greenwood (pen) 79	1,467	1
02.12	Lewes (a)	W	2-0	Mollie Green 51, *Alex Greenwood missed pen 80 (saved by Faye Baker),* Ella Toone 80 (scored from pen rebound)	1,958	1
09.12	Durham (a)	L	1-3	Ella Toone 43	912	1
06.01	London Bees (h)	W	9-0	Charlie Devlin 2, 57, Ella Toone 28, 66, Lizzie Arnot 39, Mollie Green 41, Lauren James 68, 73, Katie Zelem (pen) 78	1,889	1
13.01	Charlton Athletic (a)		A-A	*Match abandoned after 11 minutes due to injury. United leading 1-0*		2
13.02	Leicester City W (a)	W	7-0	Ella Toone 14, 16, (pen) 65, 88, Kirsty Hanson 51, Alex Greenwood 53, Natalie Johnson (og) 82, *Katie Zelem missed pen 45 (saved Demi Lambourne)*	824	2
20.02	Sheffield Utd (a)	W	4-0	Katie Zelem 1, Lauren James 27, Ella Toone (pen) 41, Mollie Green 51	1,008	2
10.03	Leicester City W (h)	W	6-1	Mollie Green 16, Lauren James 22, Kirsty Hanson 43, Ella Toone 48, Jess Sigsworth 67, 84	1,554	2
24.03	Charlton Athletic (a)	W	2-1	Katie Zelem (pen) 56, Jess Sigsworth 63	732	1
31.03	Tottenham H (a)	W	5-1	Katie Zelem, 4, (pen) 12, Mollie Green 47, Jess Sigsworth 81, Leah Galton 87	1,607	1
17.04	Aston Villa (h)	W	5-0	Millie Turner 6, Alex Greenwood (pen) 21, Jess Sigsworth 34, Ella Toone 49, Charlie Devlin 74	1,401	1P
20.04	Crystal Palace (h)	W	7-0	Lauren James 8, 82, 85, 88, Lizzie Arnot 33, Leah Galton 35, Jess Sigsworth 46	2,500	1C
28.04	Millwall L (a)	W	5-0	Katie Zelem (pen) 7, Amy Turner 13, Charlie Devlin 23, Martha Harris (pen) 29, Jess Sigsworth 78	1,920	1C
11.05	Lewes (h)	W	5-0	Lauren James 11, Jess Sigsworth 33, Leah Galton 67, Aimee Palmer 74, Amy Turner 79	3,702	1C

MANCHESTER UNITED'S TRIUMPHANT CHAMPIONSHIP SQUAD

2018-19 FA CONTINENTAL TYRES LEAGUE CUP: GROUP TWO NORTH

19.08	Liverpool (a)	W	1-0	Lizzie Arnot 83	829	
25.08	Reading (h)	L	0-2		4,835	
05.12	Durham (h)	W	1-0	Mollie Green 1	686	
13.12	Everton (a)	W	3-0	Lauren James 12, Leah Galton 17, Katie Zelem 37	267	Q
09.01 QF	West Ham Utd (h)	W	2-0	Katie Longhurst (og) 17, Jess Sigsworth 53	1,029	
07.02 SF	Arsenal (a)	L	1-2	Mollie Green 83	1,836	

2018-19 FA CUP

03.02 R4	Brighton & H A (a)	W	2-0	Lauren James 51, 90+2, *Man Utd GK Siobhan Chamberlain saved pen 78 (Danielle Buet)*	764
17.02 R5	London Bees (h)*	W	3-0	Ella Toone 27, Mollie Green 32, Charlie Devlin 87	838
17.03QF	Reading (a)	L	2-3 aet	Alex Greenwood (pen) 98, Natasha Harding (og) 106	951

*Played at Ewen Fields, (Hyde FC)

2018-19 AS IT HAPPENS

13.01.19: Manchester United's match away to Charlton is abandoned after 11 minutes with United leading 1-0. Charlton's Charlotte Kerr is injured during a collision as United's Charlie Devlin scores the opening goal. It is almost an hour later that the game is eventually called off. (NB: The game is replayed on 24 March with United winning 2-1).

17.02.19: Manager Casey Stoney comes up against her former England team-mate in the opposing dugout. Rachel Yankey – named London Bees boss just a day before the match – brings her team to Ewen Fields (United's home for the day) for an FA Cup 5th Round tie. Fellow former England international Rachel Unitt is also an unused substitute for Bees who are beaten 3-0.

17.04.19: A 5-0 win at home to Aston Villa sees Manchester United seal promotion (pending the award of a WSL licence) by ensuring a top-two finish with three games remaining.

20.04.19: United clinch the Championship title with a 7-0 home win over Crystal Palace. Lauren James scores four with Lizzie Arnot, Leah Galton and Jess Sigsworth also on target.

10.05:19: The FA ratifies Manchester United's promotion to the WSL for 2019-20 along with Championship runners-up Tottenham Hotspur.

11.05.19: Manchester United men's manager Ole Gunnar Solskjaer is among a home crowd of 3,702 to witness a final day 5-0 win over the Lewes and the presentation of the Championship trophy.

MAN UNITED APPEARANCES & GOALS 2018-19

				CH		FAC		CC		Total	
				A	G	A	G	A	G	A	G
Arnot, Lizzie	F	SCO	01.03.96	17	6	2	-	4	1	23	7
Bentley, Fran	G	ENG	26.06.01	1	-	-	-	-	-	1	-
Chamberlain, Siobhan	G	ENG	15.08.83	18	-	3	-	6	-	27	-
Devlin, Charlie	M	ENG	23.02.98	16	5	2	1	2	-	20	6
Galton, Leah	F	ENG	24.05.94	14	3	2	-	5	1	21	4
Green, Mollie	M	ENG	04.08.97	18	13	3	1	6	2	27	16
Greenwood, Alex	D	ENG	07.09.93	18	4	3	1	6	-	27	5
Hanson, Kirsty	F	SCO	17.04.98	17	5	3	-	5	-	25	5
Harris, Martha	D	ENG	19.08.94	15	1	3	-	4	-	22	1
Hartley, Naomi	D	ENG	12.01.01	3	-	-	-	-	-	3	-
James, Lauren	M	ENG	29.09.01	18	14	3	2	6	1	27	17
Palmer, Aimee	M	ENG	25.07.00	13	1	1	-	1	-	15	1
Ramsey, Emily	G	ENG	16.11.00	2	-	1	-	-	-	3	-
Roberts, Lucy	D	ENG	11.05.01	-	-	-	-	-	-	-	-
Sigsworth, Jessica	F	ENG	13.10.94	19	17	3	-	6	1	28	18
Smith, Kirsty	D	SCO	06.01.94	16	-	2	-	5	-	23	-
Toone, Ella	F	ENG	02.09.99	20	14	3	1	5	-	28	15
Turner, Amy	D	ENG	04.07.91	16	2	2	-	6	-	24	2
Turner, Millie	D	ENG	07.07.96	20	2	3	-	6	-	29	2
Zelem, Katie	M	ENG	20.01.96	18	10	2	-	6	1	26	11

READING

FOUNDED: 2006 **NICKNAME: THE ROYALS** **2019-20: WSL (TIER 1)**

Honours:	No.	Competition name & year(s)
English Tier 2 Champions	1	WSL 2: 2015
Tier 3 Champions (Regional)	2	WPL Southern: 2013
		South West Combination: 2008
Tier 3 Runners-up (Regional)	1	WPL Southern: 2010
Tier 4 Champions (Regional)	1	Southern Regional Premier: 2007

Since winning promotion to the top-flight as Tier 2 champions in 2015, Kelly Chambers' Reading side have been steadily progressing and are now firmly established as a WSL club. After an 8th-place finish in 2016, a 6th-place finish in 2017's transitional WSL 1 Spring Series and an impressive 4th position in 2017-18, the Royals enjoyed another steady League campaign in 2018-19, placing 5th.

They also had a brush with glory in the 2018-19 FA Cup when they came within a penalty shootout of making it to the final for the first time. They were unable to capitalise on home advantage at Adams Park though with their opponents West Ham keeping their cool to book a place at Wembley following a shootout that went to sudden death.

Rachel Furness' header had given Reading the lead just after half time, but Alisha Lehmann pulled West Ham level before the Royals' vastly experienced midfielder Fara Williams was unfortunate to hit the post with a penalty as the home side searched for a winner.

Reading also progressed to the knockout stages of the Continental Cup thanks to group stage wins over Manchester United and Durham and a draw with Liverpool (although they missed out on the bonus point by losing the penalty shootout). They came up against an in-form Chelsea side in the quarter-finals though and were beaten 4-0 at Kingsmeadow.

From 1988 Reading men's FC had an association with a club called Reading Royals Ladies FC but severed that link in 2006 to set up their own club which is the current Reading. In 2014 Reading were among the founding members of WSL 2. The club's youth products include England and Chelsea star Fran Kirby, while their Tier 2 title of 2015 is the only high-profile silverware so far in the club's 13-year history.

WSL ERA FINAL LEAGUE POSITIONS (SS = SPRING SERIES)

SEASON	2011	2012	2013	2014	2015	2016	2017ss	2018	2019
TIER	T2	T2	T3	T2	T2	T1	T1	T1	T1
POSITION	3/8	9/10	1/10	3/10	1/10	8/9	6/9	4/10	5/11

2018-19 REVIEW

League:	WSL (Tier 1): 5th		
FA Cup:	SF	**Stadium:**	Adams Park, (Wycombe Wanderers FC)
Conti Cup:	QF	**Manager:**	Kelly Chambers (since Nov 2014)

FARA WILLIAMS HAD AMASSED 170 ENGLAND CAPS BY THE END OF 2018-19

2018-19 STAR PERFORMER – FARA WILLIAMS

Having turned 35 in January 2019, England's most-capped international Fara Williams continued to dictate games from midfield for the Royals throughout 2018-19 and was rewarded with a new contract in May.

Despite not playing as a striker, Williams finished the campaign as Reading's top scorer with 11 WSL goals. According to Opta she attempted the second highest number of shots on goal in the division (82), behind only Arsenal's 22-goal Golden Boot winner Vivianne Miedema (108).

At the end of 2018-19 Williams had 170 England caps to her name and despite missing out on the World Cup, manager Phil Neville insisted she still has a future at international level. Williams started out in Chelsea's youth team and played for Charlton and Everton before winning WSL titles with Liverpool in 2013 and 2014. She spent 2016-17 with Arsenal then moved to Reading.

2018-19 WSL RESULTS

					Att	Pos
09.09	Yeovil Town (h)	W	4-0	Gemma Davison 5, Fara Williams 11, Lauren Bruton (pen) 59, Remi Allen 61	464	2
19.09	West Ham U (a)	D	0-0		658	3
23.09	Birmingham C (h)	L	0-1		693	5
30.09	Liverpool (a)	W	1-0	Brooke Chaplen 36	382	4
21.10	Arsenal (a)	L	0-6		1,586	6
26.10	Manchester C (a)	D	1-1	Jade Moore 50	1,015	6
04.11	Bristol C (h)	W	3-0	Fara Williams 32, 50, Brooke Chaplen 65	482	6
18.11	Brighton & H A (a)	W	4-1	Marie Hourihan (og) 20, Fara Williams 65, Brooke Chaplen 58, Gemma Davison 81	335	5
25.11	Everton (h)	W	2-1	Brooke Chaplen 20, 77	285	5
02.12	Chelsea (a)	L	0-1		1,741	5
09.12	Liverpool (h)	D	2-2	Fara Williams 62, 84	582	5
06.01	Birmingham C (a)	L	1-2	Remi Allen 88	606	5
27.01	Arsenal (h)	L	0-3		1,619	6
20.02	West Ham U (h)*	L	1-2	Fara Williams (pen) 66	2,148	7
13.03	Manchester C (h)	L	3-4	Brooke Chaplen 4, Fara Williams (pen) 62, Kirsty Pearce 87	449	7
31.03	Bristol City (a)	W	1-0	Brooke Chaplen 55, *Fara Williams missed pen 47 (saved)*	391	7
17.04	Yeovil Town (a)	W	5-0	Fara Williams 31, Lauren Bruton 54, 83, Millie Farrow 81, 90	473	6
20.04	Brighton & H A (h)*	W	1-0	Rachel Furness 49	1,119	5
28.04	Everton (a)	L	2-3	Remi Allen 8, Fara Williams 77	174	5
05.05	Chelsea (h)	L	2-3	Natasha Harding 50, Fara Williams 52	612	5

*Played at Madejski Stadium, (Reading FC)

2018-19 FA CONTINENTAL TYRES LEAGUE CUP: GROUP TWO NORTH

19.08	Durham (h)	W	4-1	Kirsty Pearce 6, Fara Williams 13, 24, 81	246	
25.08	Manchester U (a)	W	2-0	Brooke Chaplen 56, Gemma Davison 90+4, *Molly Bartrip sent off 63*	4,835	
16.09	Everton (a)	L	2-3	Megan Finnigan (og) 24, Brooke Chaplen 79	143	
12.12	Liverpool (h)	D	1-1 (L4-5p)	Rachel Furness 64	323	Q
09.01 QF	Chelsea (a)	L	0-4		973	

2018-19 FA CUP

03.02 R4	Keynsham Town (h)		P-P		
10.02 R4	Keynsham Town (h)*	W	13-0	Fara Williams (pen) 21, 24, (pen) 29, (pen) 55, 59, Lauren Bruton 37, 53, Brooke Chaplen 48, 49, Charlie Estcourt 68, Rakel Honnudottir 78, 80, Gemma Davison 84	272

17.02 R5	Birmingham C (h)	W	2-1	Kirsty Pearce 69, Rakel Honnudottir 83	275
17.03 QF	Manchester U (h)	W	3-2 aet	Remi Allen 100, Rachel Furness 107, Rakel Honnudottir 120	951
14.04 SF	West Ham U (h)	D	1-1aet (L3-4p)	Rachel Furness 48, *Fara Williams missed pen 70*	2,334

*Played at Kingfield Stadium, (Woking FC)

2018-19 AS IT HAPPENS

10.02.19: Reading are 13-0 winners at home to Tier 4 Keynsham Town in the FA Cup 4th Round. Fara Williams scores a hat-trick of penalties as part of her five-goal haul, while January transfer window signing Rakel Honnudottir also bags a brace – her first goals for the club.

17.02.19: Rakel Honnudottir scores Reading's 83rd-minute winner against Birmingham in the FA Cup 5th Round just two minutes after coming off the bench.

17.03.19: Reading reach the semi-finals of the FA Cup for the first time in their history following a frenetic period of extra-time during their home quarter-final against Manchester United. The match is goalless after 90 minutes, before the Royals twice come from behind to win. Just as she did in the previous round Rakel Honnudottir comes off the bench to score the winner, this time doing so in the last minute of extra-time.

04.04.19: Reading striker Lauren Bruton, 26, signs a new contract with the WSL club. Bruton joined the Royals from Arsenal in September 2013 and has gone on to make more than 100 appearances for them. The length of the deal is not revealed.

14.04.19: Reading's bid to reach the FA Cup final for the first time ends in the cruellest possible fashion as they lose 4-3 on penalties to fellow WSL side West Ham after a 1-1 draw. Rachel Furness puts the Royals ahead just after half-time in front of the home crowd at Adams Park. Alisha Lehmann equalises and Reading's Fara Williams then hits the post with a penalty 20 minutes from the end of normal time. With no further goals the match progresses to extra-time and then penalties. Rakel Honnudottir, Lauren Bruton and Jade Moore all miss in a shootout which goes to sudden death.

26.04.19: Goalkeeper Grace Moloney extends her contract with Reading. The Republic of Ireland international, 26, has been with the Royals since she was nine.

READING APPEARANCES & GOALS 2018-19

				WSL		FAC		CC		Total	
				A	G	A	G	A	G	A	G
Allen, Remi	M	ENG	15.10.90	19	3	3	1	4	-	26	4
Bailey, Jade	M	ENG	11.11.95	6	-	3	-	-	-	9	-
Bartrip, Molly	D	ENG	01.06.96	14	-	4	-	4	-	22	-
Bruton, Lauren	F	ENG	22.11.92	17	3	4	2	4	-	25	5
Chaplen, Brooke	M	ENG	16.04.89	16	7	3	2	5	2	24	11
Davison, Gemma	M	ENG	17.04.87	14	2	2	1	4	1	20	4
Estcourt, Charlie	M	WAL	27.05.98	7	-	1	1	2	-	10	1
Farrow, Millie	F	ENG	03.06.96	5	2	-	-	1	-	6	2
Furness, Rachel	M	NIR	19.06.88	19	1	3	2	3	1	25	4
Harding, Natasha	F	WAL	02.03.89	19	1	3	-	5	-	27	1
Honnudottir, Rakel	F	ISL	30.12.88	5	-	4	4	-	-	9	4
Howard, Sophie	D	SCO	17.09.93	6	-	1	-	3	-	10	-
Jane, Rebecca	D	ENG	31.03.92	8	-	1	-	5	-	14	-

Laws, Rachael	G	ENG	05.11.90	-	-	-	-	2	-	2	-
Moloney, Grace	G	IRE	01.03.93	20	-	4	-	3	-	27	-
Moore, Jade	M	ENG	22.10.90	13	1	4	-	1	-	18	1
Pacheco, Mayumi	D	ENG	25.08.98	16	-	4	-	2	-	22	-
Pearce, Kirsty	D	ENG	16.04.87	18	1	2	1	4	1	24	3
Potter, Josanne	M	ENG	13.11.84	16	-	4	-	5	-	25	-
Rowe, Rachel	M	WAL	13.09.92	1	-	-	-	2	-	3	-
Williams, Fara	M	ENG	25.01.84	20	11	4	5	5	3	29	19
Woodham, Lily	D	WAL	03.09.00	4	-	-	-	2	-	6	-

TOTTENHAM HOTSPUR

FOUNDED: 1985 (AS BROXBOURNE) | **NICKNAME: SPURS** | **2019-20: WSL (TIER 1)**

Former Names: Broxbourne (1985-1992)

Honours:	No.	Competition name & year(s)
English Tier 2 Runners-up	1	Championship: 2019
English Tier 3 Play-off Winners	1	WPL National Play-off: 2017
Tier 3 Champions (Regional)	1	WPL Southern: 2017
Tier 3 / 4 League Cup Winners	2	WPL Cup: 2016, 2017
Tier 4 Champions (Regional)	2	1xLondon & SE Premier League: 2008 1xSouth East Combination: 2011

Tottenham won automatic promotion to the top-flight at the end of 2018-19 as they secured the runners-up position in the Championship, behind title-winners Manchester United. It was a magnificent way to end what was only their second season in Tier 2.

The North London club sealed 2nd place with a 1-1 draw at Aston Villa on 1 May. Spurs kicked off needing a point and took the lead through Jessica Naz. Amy West equalised for the hosts in a high-quality encounter, but the visitors held out for the draw. Nine days later the FA approved their licence request and ratified their promotion to the WSL.

Going up to the top division added to the growing list of achievements for respected manager Karen Hills and her coaching team. For Hills, who has been in charge since 2009, and head coach Juan Amoros (with the club since 2011) it represented a second promotion in three seasons having first brought Spurs up to Tier 2 as WPL Southern Premier champions at the end of 2016-17. Hills ended the season by being named LMA Championship Manager of the Year 2018-19.

Spurs made their mark early in the season with six wins from their opening six Championship games, including an 8-0 victory at home to Millwall Lionesses. They occupied top spot from late November to early December and again from mid-January to early March but eventual champions Manchester United often had games in hand.

With Charlton and Durham also involved in an intriguing four-way promotion battle, perhaps Spurs' most important win of the season was their 3-2 victory at Charlton in April when they had to fight back from 2-0 down. Come the end of the campaign they had won 15 of their 20 Championship matches and will now set about trying to establish themselves as a stable WSL outfit.

Having played as a predominantly part-time outfit in 2018-19 they have had to transition to the fully professional top-flight where they find themselves in the same division as local rivals and current WSL champions Arsenal. They began their acclimatisation to their new division with an announcement in May that they would be following modern fashion by changing their name from Tottenham Hotspur Ladies to Tottenham Hotspur Women.

Founded as Broxbourne Ladies in 1985 they were first given permission to use the Tottenham Hotspur name in 1991-92. They train at Hotspur Way in Enfield, the same world class venue as 2019 Champions League finalists Tottenham Hotspur men.

WSL ERA FINAL LEAGUE POSITIONS

SEASON	2011	2012	2013	2014	2015	2016	2017	2018	2019
TIER	T4	T3	T3	T3	T3	T3	T3	T2	T2
POSITION	1/12	6/10	8/10	8/11	5/12	6/12	1/11	7/10	2/11

2018-19 REVIEW

League: Championship (Tier 2): Runners-up

FA Cup: 5th Round **Stadium:** Theobalds Lane, (Cheshunt FC)

Conti Cup: Group **Manager:** Karen Hills (since Aug 2009)

ASHLEIGH NEVILLE SCORED FIVE GOALS IN ALL COMPETITIONS IN 2018-19

Wu's Photography'

2018-19 STAR PERFORMER – ASHLEIGH NEVILLE

Talented defender Ashleigh Neville came to the fore at a crucial time of the season and was voted the FA Championship Player of the Month for April. It was her late brace against Charlton that month that saw Spurs turn a 2-0 away deficit into a 3-2 win against their promotion rivals. Always composed, Neville is highly adept at bringing the ball out of defence. More at home on the right, she can play on either side as evidenced by a fine solo goal when she cut in from the left to score in February's FA Cup win away to Crystal Palace. That effort helped set up a huge 5th Round tie against Manchester City which gave Spurs the chance to test themselves against a WSL outfit in front of a big crowd at Cheshunt. City won 3-0 but Spurs took plenty of positives from the experience.

2018-19 CHAMP RESULTS

					Att	Pos
09.09	London Bees (h)	W	2-1	Coral-Jade Haines (pen) 73, Josie Green 80	362	5
19.09	Leicester City W (a)	W	3-0	Sarah Wiltshire 14, 39, Rianna Dean 21	412	2
23.09	Durham (h)		P-P			3
30.09	Crystal Palace (a)	W	2-1	Rianna Dean 14, Angela Addison 65	202	2
14.10	Lewes (a)	W	3-1	Bianca Baptiste 16, Rianna Dean 32, 45, *Tottenham Hotspur GK Chloe Morgan saved pen 45+3*	714	2
21.10	Millwall L (h)	W	8-0	Angela Addison 22, 84, Rianna Dean 30, (pen) 50, (pen) 73, Sarah Wiltshire 31, Ashleigh Neville 38, Bianca Baptiste 62	295	1
28.10	Aston Villa (h)	W	2-1	Ashleigh Neville 41, Rianna Dean (pen) 82	438	1
04.11	Manchester Utd (a)	L	1-4	Angela Addison 82	2,367	1
18.11	Charlton A (h)	W	1-0	Jessica Naz 23	376	1
02.12	Durham (h)	L	1-6	*Chloe Morgan sent off 17*, Angela Addison 53	206	4
09.12	Crystal Palace (h)	W	1-0	Rianna Dean 26	289	4
06.01	Sheffield Utd (a)	W	2-1	Rianna Dean 5, Sarah Wiltshire 51	470	2
13.01	Lewes (h)	W	3-0	Jessica Naz 30, Rianna Dean 52, Jenna Schillaci 60	320	1
27.01	Millwall L (a)	W	3-2	Sarah Wiltshire 36, Emma Beckett 84, Rianna Dean 90+5	426	1
10.02	London Bees (a)	W	3-0	Rianna Dean (pen) 14, Annabel Johnson (og) 22, Sarah Wiltshire 47	387	1
20.02	Leicester City W (h)	W	1-0	Angela Addison 90+6	318	1
12.03	Aston Villa (a)		P-P			1
24.03	Sheffield Utd (h)	L	1-2	Jessica Naz 54	502	2
31.03	Manchester Utd (h)	L	1-5	Jenna Schillaci 35	1,607	2
21.04	Charlton A (a)	W	3-2	Rianna Dean (pen) 54, Ashleigh Neville 71, 80	569	2
01.05	Aston Villa (a)	D	1-1	Jessica Naz 2	513	2P
11.05	Durham (a)	W	2-0	Anna Filbey 69, 90+2	533	2P

2018-19 FA CONTINENTAL TYRES LEAGUE CUP: GROUP ONE SOUTH

18.08	Crystal Palace (a)	D	1-1 (L 3-5p)	Josie Green 37, *Angela Addison missed pen 67*	372
26.08	Brighton & H A (h)	D	2-2 (W 10-9p)	Rianna Dean 7, Megan Wynne 35	144
16.09	Yeovil Town (a)	W	4-0	Sarah Wiltshire 7, Coral-Jade Haines 22, 39, 61	415
05.12	London Bees (a)	L	2-4	Rianna Dean 5, Sarah Wiltshire 40	146
12.12	Chelsea (h)	L	0-5		358

2018-19 FA CUP

03.02 R4	Crystal Palace (a)	W	3-0	Jessica Naz 41, Ashleigh Neville 45+3, Coral-Jade Haines 55	282
17.02 R5	Manchester C (h)	L	0-3	*Angela Addison missed pen 76 (saved Ellie Roebuck)*	1,158

TOTTENHAM CELEBRATE AS PROMOTION TO THE WSL IS CONFIRMED

Wu's Photography'

SPURS' DELIGHTED PLAYERS RACE TOWARDS CAPTAIN JENNA SCHILLACI

Wu's Photography'

2018-19 AS IT HAPPENS

21.10.18: It proves to be quite a 20th birthday for Rianna Dean as she scores a hat-trick in Tottenham's 8-0 win against Millwall Lionesses to help move her team top of the Championship for the first time this season.

17.02.19: Tottenham's FA Cup 5th Round match at home to Manchester City is watched by 1,158 – a club record for them for a match at Theobalds Lane, Cheshunt FC.

20.04.19: Tottenham's slim title hopes are ended on a day when they are not in action as Manchester United secure the title with a 7-0 home win against Crystal Palace.

21.04.19: Spurs keep alive their hopes of finishing as runners-up by coming from 2-0 down to win 3-2 away at promotion rivals Charlton. Rianna Dean sparks the comeback with a 54th minute penalty before Ashleigh Neville is on target twice in the final 20 minutes. Spurs remain 2nd while 3rd-placed Durham also win 1-0 at home to Millwall Lionesses.

01.05.19: Tottenham get the point they need to secure 2nd place and promotion to the WSL (subject to FA licence approval) with a 1-1 draw away to Aston Villa. Jessica Naz gives them the lead in the second minute before Amy West equalises early in the second half.

10.05.19: The FA ratifies the promotion of Championship champions Manchester United and runners-up Tottenham Hotspur to the WSL for 2019-20.

TOTTENHAM APPEARANCES & GOALS 2018-19

				CH		FAC		CC		Total	
				A	G	A	G	A	G	A	G
Addison, Angela	M	ENG	09.12.99	19	6	2	-	5	-	26	6
Baptiste, Bianca	F	ENG	15.01.92	15	2	2	-	3	-	20	2
Beckett, Emma	M	IRE	29.05.87	8	1	2	-	-	-	10	1
Dean, Rianna	F	ENG	21.10.98	19	14	2	-	5	2	26	16
Filbey, Anna	M	ENG	11.10.99	7	2	1	-	4	-	12	2
Gibbon, Emma	G	WAL	06.02.99	3	-	-	-	3	-	6	-
Green, Josie	M	WAL	25.04.93	16	1	2	-	4	1	22	2
Haines, Coral-Jade	M	ENG	21.06.96	18	1	2	1	5	3	25	5
Hector, Renee	D	ENG	21.06.95	19	-	1	-	4	-	24	-
Leon, Lucia	D	ESP	14.08.97	17	-	2	-	5	-	24	-
Martin, Wendy	F	ENG	25.08.82	4	-	-	-	2	-	6	-
Mclean, Sophie	M	ENG	11.02.96	17	-	1	-	3	-	21	-
Meiwald, Anne	D	ENG	15.03.95	4	-	2	-	2	-	8	-
Morgan, Chloe	G	ENG	19.12.89	18	-	2	-	2	-	22	-
Naz, Jessica	F	ENG	24.09.00	17	4	1	1	5	-	23	5
Neville, Ashleigh	D	ENG	29.04.93	19	4	2	1	4	-	25	5
Schillaci, Jenna	D	ENG	21.03.84	19	2	2	-	5	-	26	2
Vyse, Ryah	D	ENG	27.10.92	1	-	-	-	1	-	2	-
Wiltshire, Sarah	F	WAL	07.07.91	19	6	-	-	3	2	22	8
Wynne, Megan	M	WAL	21.01.93	19	-	2	-	5	1	26	1

WEST HAM UNITED

FOUNDED: 1991 **NICKNAME: THE HAMMERS** **2019-20: WSL (TIER 1)**

Honours:	No.	Competition name & year(s)
FA Cup Runners-up	1	FA Cup: 2019
Tier 3 / Tier 4 Plate Winners	1	WPL Plate: 2018
Tier 3 Champions (Regional)	1	South East Combination: 2005

The 2018-19 season was West Ham's first as a professional club. Having finished 7th in Tier 3 in 2017-18 they were promoted two divisions that summer when their licence application to join the WSL was accepted by the FA.

Matt Beard, who led Liverpool to consecutive WSL titles in 2013 and 2014, was appointed as the East London club's new manager, with England centre-back Gilly Flaherty leaving Chelsea and being named as Hammers captain in August 2018.

Experienced left-back Claire Rafferty and Manchester City and Scotland striker Jane Ross were among other new signings that summer, with teenager Jack Sullivan – whose father David Sullivan co-owns West Ham United FC – placed in charge of running the club as managing director. United also attracted new fans after the club and Sullivan Jr. agreed to become the subject of a behind-the-scenes BBC Three documentary called '*Britain's Youngest Football Boss*'.

It proved to be a memorable season as the Hammers reached the FA Cup final for the first time. A dramatic semi-final win on penalties against Reading sent them through to face Manchester City at Wembley. The match ended in a disappointing 3-0 defeat but there was much to be proud of in having reached the final and finished 7th in their first WSL season.

Founded in 1991, West Ham had never previously seen the levels of support from the fans that they witnessed in their first professional season, with a large proportion of the 43,264 fans at Wembley for May's final backing the Hammers. Some supporters left the West Ham men's game against Southampton at half-time to get to the national stadium in time to cheer on the women.

WSL ERA FINAL LEAGUE POSITIONS

SEASON	2011	2012	2013	2014	2015	2016	2017	2018	2019
TIER	T3	T3	T3	T3	T3	T3	T3	T3	T1
POSITION	3/10	3/10	6/10	10/11	6/12	10/12	9/11	7/12	7/11

2018-19 REVIEW

League: WSL (Tier 1): 7th

FA Cup: RU **Stadium:** Rush Green, (West Ham United FC Training Ground)

Conti Cup: QF **Manager:** Matt Beard (since Jun 2018)

West Ham United

CAPTAIN GILLY FLAHERTY LED WEST HAM TO THE 2019 FA CUP FINAL

2018-19 STAR PERFORMER – GILLY FLAHERTY

Captain Gilly Flaherty led West Ham by example in 2018-19 with her stoic defending endearing her to fans and team-mates alike. The former Arsenal and Chelsea centre-back, who turned 27 in August 2018, arrived at the club with a host of honours to her name. She was part of Arsenal's Champions League winning squad (then known as the UEFA Cup) in 2007 and won six League titles and five FA Cups while with the Gunners. Flaherty then went on to claim WSL and FA Cup Doubles with Chelsea in 2015 and 2018 as well as the 2017 WSL Spring Series. She put in a battling performance for West Ham in the FA Cup final at Wembley in May demonstrating her passion, dedication and commitment to the cause. She threw herself in front of multiple goal-bound efforts and slid in with perfect timing to deny Manchester City and England winger Nikita Parris in the first half.

West Ham United

FLAHERTY WON FIVE FA CUPS WITH ARSENAL AND TWO WITH CHELSEA

2018-19 WSL RESULTS

Date	Opponent	Res	Score	Scorers	Att	Pos
19.09	Reading (h)	D	0-0		658	7
23.09	Arsenal (a)	L	3-4	Kate Longhurst 9, 17, Claire Rafferty 86	1,081	7
30.09	Yeovil Town (h)	W	2-1	Leanne Kiernan 67, Rosie Kmita 79	367	7
14.10	Manchester C (a)	L	1-7	Esmee de Graaf 82	1,245	8
21.10	Liverpool (h)	L	0-1		1,966	8
28.10	Everton (a)	W	2-1	Jane Ross 27, Alisha Lehmann 45, *Jane Ross missed pen 55 (saved by Kirstie Levell)*	143	8
04.11	Chelsea (h)	L	0-2		962	8
18.11	Birmingham C (a)	L	0-3		663	8
25.11	Bristol City (h)	W	2-0	Alisha Lehmann 13, Jane Ross 89	562	7
02.12	Brighton & H A (a)	W	1-0	Jane Ross 64	376	6
09.12	Yeovil Town (a)	W	5-0	Alisha Lehmann 19, 27, Julia Simic 34, 59, Brianna Visalli 53	516	6
06.01	Arsenal (h)	L	2-4	Jane Ross 11, 43	913	6
13.01	Manchester C (h)	L	1-3	Jane Ross 57	640	7
28.01	Liverpool (a)	L	0-1		186	7
20.02	Reading (a)	W	2-1	Alisha Lehmann 21, 54	2,148	6
13.03	Everton (h)	L	0-1		607	6
31.03	Chelsea (a)	D	1-1	Gilly Flaherty 65	2,854	7
21.04	Birmingham C (h)	L	1-2	Adriana Leon 27, *Anna Moorhouse sent off 41*	663	7
28.04	Bristol City (a)	W	2-1	Leanne Kiernan 74, Jane Ross 89	602	7
11.05	Brighton & H A (h)	L	0-4		1,412	7

2018-19 FA CONTINENTAL TYRES LEAGUE CUP: GROUP TWO SOUTH

Date	Opponent	Res	Score	Scorers	Att	
19.08	Arsenal (a)	L	1-3	Brianna Visalli 48	834	
26.08	Lewes (h)	W	4-1	Jane Ross 25, (pen) 49, Leanne Kiernan 29, Julia Simic 32	255	
16.09	Millwall L (h)	W	4-0	Esmee de Graaf 6, 86, Brianna Visalli 10, Rose Kmita 12	557	
12.12	Charlton A (a)	W	2-0	Rosie Kmita 46, Alisha Lehmann 56	202	Q
09.01 QF	Manchester Utd (a)	L	0-2		1,029	

2018-19 FA CUP

Date	Opponent	Res	Score	Scorers	Att
03.02 R4	Blackburn R (h)	W	3-1	Adriana Leon 45, 79, Brianna Visalli 72	834
17.02 R5	Huddersfield T (h)	W	8-1	Kate Longhurst 22, Leanne Kiernan 27, 81, 84, Alisha Lehmann 37, Jane Ross 38, Rosie Kmita 66, Brianna Visalli 71	865
17.03QF	Aston Villa (a)	W	1-0	Jane Ross 26	609
14.04 SF	Reading (a)	D	1-1aet (W4-3p)	Alisha Lehmann 57	2,334
04.05 F	Manchester C (n)	L	0-3		43,264

(n)Played at Wembley Stadium

2018-19 AS IT HAPPENS

22.11.18: Russ Fraser is appointed as the club's new general manager. Fraser, who has spent the last three seasons with Reading Women will work alongside Hammers head coach Matt Beard.

29.03.19: Matt Beard, who took over as head coach last summer, signs a contract extension. The length of the deal is undisclosed.

06.04.19: Switzerland international forward Alisha Lehmann, 20, signs a new contract with WSL club West Ham who she joined last summer. The length of the deal is undisclosed.

14.04.19: West Ham reach the FA Cup final for the first time with a dramatic semi-final penalty shootout win away to fellow WSL side Reading. The Royals go ahead just after half-time through Rachel Furness, but Alisha Lehmann equalises for the Hammers within 10 minutes. Fara Williams misses a 70th minute penalty for Reading and with no further score the match progresses to extra-time and penalties with West Ham prevailing 4-3 in a shootout which goes to sudden death.

04.05.19: The Hammers are beaten 3-0 by Manchester City in the FA Cup final at Wembley. Matt Beard's side hold the 2017 winners until the 52nd minute when Keira Walsh puts them ahead from distance. Late goals from Georgia Stanway and Lauren Hemp add gloss to the score line and leave the Hammers having to be content with runners-up medals in their first final.

11.05.19: Claire Rafferty plays her final WSL match having announced her retirement yesterday. The England international won two WSL and FA Cup Doubles during 11 years with Chelsea before joining the Hammers last summer. Lucienne Reichardt captains the team in what is also her last game as a professional footballer. The match ends in a 4-0 home defeat to Brighton.

WEST HAM UTD APPEARANCES & GOALS 2018-19				WSL		FAC		CC		Total	
				A	G	A	G	A	G	A	G
Cho, So-hyun	M	KOR	24.06.88	7	-	5	-	-	-	12	-
De Graaf, Esme	F	NED	02.08.97	10	1	-	-	3	2	13	3
Flaherty, Gilly	D	ENG	24.08.91	19	1	5	-	5	-	29	1
Hendrix, Brooke	D	USA	06.05.93	14	-	4	-	5	-	23	-
Kiernan, Leanne	F	IRE	27.04.99	15	2	5	3	2	1	22	6
Kmita, Rosie	F	ENG	27.07.94	14	1	3	1	3	2	20	4
Leon, Adriana	F	CAN	02.10.92	6	1	4	2	-	-	10	3
Lehmann, Alisha	F	SUI	21.01.99	20	6	5	2	5	1	30	9
Longhurst, Kate	M	ENG	02.05.89	19	2	5	1	5	-	29	3
Middag, Tessel	M	NED	23.12.92	-	-	-	-	-	-	-	-
Moorhouse, Anna	G	ENG	30.03.95	10	-	5	-	1	-	16	-
Percival, Ria	D	NZL	07.12.89	16	-	4	-	5	-	25	-
Rafferty, Claire	D	ENG	11.01.89	13	1	4	-	5	-	22	1
Reichardt, Lucienne	M	NED	01.05.91	12	-	4	-	5	-	21	-
Ross, Jane	F	SCO	18.09.89	20	7	5	2	5	2	30	11
Sampson, Vyan	D	ENG	02.07.96	12	-	3	-	4	-	19	-
Simic, Julia	M	GER	14.05.89	11	2	-	-	4	1	15	3
Simon, Erin	D	USA	19.08.94	17	-	5	-	1	-	23	-
Spencer, Rebecca	G	ENG	22.02.91	12	-	-	-	4	-	16	-
Visalli, Brianna	M	ENG	17.04.95	20	1	5	2	5	2	30	5

West Ham United

WEST HAM MANAGER MATT BEARD LED LIVERPOOL TO THE WSL TITLE IN 2013 AND 2014

FA WOMEN'S CHAMPIONSHIP
TIER TWO

In 2014 the FA introduced a second 'elite' division for women's football in England. It was named WSL 2 until being rebranded ahead of 2018-19 as The FA Women's Championship, at which point more stringent criteria were introduced in order to obtain a licence to compete at that level.

The 2019-20 season is the second under the Championship banner. There have of course been some changes since the first season. Inaugural champions Manchester United and runners-up Tottenham Hotspur have been promoted out of the division up to the WSL. Millwall Lionesses' Tier 2 licence has been transferred to a new club, London City Lionesses. WNL Northern Premier champions Blackburn Rovers and their Southern Premier counterparts Coventry United have both been promoted into the Championship. While Yeovil Town – who finished bottom of the WSL in 2018-19 – were due to be relegated into the division, they failed to obtain a Championship licence and instead dropped to Tier 3.

Yeovil's absence means that the Championship continues as an 11-team division for 2019-20, consisting of: Aston Villa; Blackburn Rovers; Charlton Athletic; Coventry United; Crystal Palace; Durham; Leicester City Women; Lewes; London Bees; London City Lionesses; and Sheffield United.

At the end of 2019-20 the champions of the Championship will be promoted to the WSL if they satisfy the FA's licence criteria, and the bottom club in the WSL will drop into the Championship. The bottom club in the Championship will be relegated into the WNL with the champions of both the WNL Northern Premier and Southern Premier being promoted (again subject to satisfying licence criteria). This will bring the Championship to 12 teams for 2020-21.

From the end of 2020-21 the FA intends for there to be one up, one down between the Championship and the WNL. The promoted team from that point will be the winner of the traditional end-of-season play-off between the WNL Northern Premier and Southern Premier champions.

The inaugural 2018-19 Championship season perhaps unsurprisingly saw Manchester United – the only full-time team in a part-time division – crowned as champions. Tottenham followed them as runners-up, getting the better of Charlton Athletic and Durham in what had been a hugely entertaining four-way tussle for promotion.

At the other end Millwall Lionesses – who had placed 3rd the season before, after overcoming huge financial difficulties – finished bottom. They were spared the drop because the FA had decided ahead of the start of the season that there would be no relegation.

To obtain a Championship licence clubs must appoint full-time general managers and provide a minimum of eight hours' daytime contact per week (plus matches) for semi-professional players.

Four clubs have remained Tier 2 constants since the formation of WSL 2 in 2014: Aston Villa, Durham, London Bees and the entity that is now London City Lionesses (formerly Millwall Lionesses). The first season under the Championship banner saw a massive overhaul. The new criteria proved beyond four teams who had finished 2017-18 in WSL 2: champions Doncaster

Rovers Belles; Oxford United; Sheffield FC; and Watford, who all had to drop to Tier 3. There were six newcomers to the division: Manchester United (who had reformed, not having run a senior women's team since 2005); Charlton Athletic (who had finished 2017-18 as champions of the WPL Southern Premier); Crystal Palace (3rd in the WPL Southern Premier); Lewes (5th in the WPL Southern Premier); Leicester City Women (2nd in the WPL Northern Premier); and Sheffield United (promoted two divisions having finished 3rd in WPL Midlands 1).

This second club section of the book concentrates on the 11 teams who compete in Tier 2 in 2019-20. The clubs appear in alphabetical order: Aston Villa; Blackburn Rovers; Charlton Athletic; Coventry United; Crystal Palace; Durham; Leicester City Women; Lewes; London Bees; London City Lionesses; and Sheffield United.

The stadium listed is the main home ground the club played at in 2018-19 and the manager or managers are those who took charge of the team throughout 2018-19. Some clubs may have changed their stadiums and managers throughout the summer of 2019 after our publishing deadlines.

Results of each team's matches in the League, FA Cup and Continental Cup (which is the League Cup for teams in Tiers 1 and 2) for 2018-19 are listed. As Tier 3 clubs in 2018-19 Blackburn Rovers and Coventry United did not compete in the Continental Cup so their results for the WNL Cup (the League Cup for teams in Tiers 3 and 4) are listed, as are their County Cup results.

Where known the following information has been included for each game: scorers; goal times; penalties; missed/saved penalties; own goals; and attendances. The figure in the column on the far right is the club's League position after all that day's fixtures have been completed. This has been included from the second fixture onwards. It's important to note this isn't necessarily the position they were in when they kicked off their next match as other fixtures involving other clubs may have taken place in between. Where the home team uses a stadium other than their main home ground, this is denoted at the bottom of the results' table on the home team's pages.

In the tables showing player appearances, an appearance is any match in which that player started the game or came on as a substitute. Appearances are shown for the Championship, FA Cup and Continental Cup matches. In the case of promoted clubs Blackburn Rovers and Coventry United appearances are shown for the League, FA Cup, WNL Cup and County Cup.

ASTON VILLA

FOUNDED: 1973 NICKNAME: THE LADY VILLANS 2019-20: CHAMPIONSHIP (TIER 2) (AS SOLIHULL)

Former Names:
Solihull (1973-1989)
Villa Aztecs (1989-1996)

Honours:	No.	Competition name & year(s)
English League Cup Runners-up	1	WPL Cup: 1995 (as Villa Aztecs)
Tier 2 / 3 League Cup Winners	1	WPL Cup: 2013
Tier 2 Champions (Regional)	1	WPL Northern: 2003
Tier 3 Champions (Regional)	1	WPL Northern: 2011

In 2018-19 Villa finished in a respectable mid-table position as they placed 6th in the Championship. They have been in Tier 2 ever since the introduction of (what was then called) WSL 2 in 2014. Their highest finish to date is 4th, a position they achieved in that 2014 campaign and again in the half-season WSL 2 Spring Series of 2017.

Gemma Davies has shown that youth is no barrier to managerial success. She was just 25 when she became Villa boss in June 2018, combining the job with her role leading the women's football set-up at the nearby University of Birmingham. The UEFA A Licence coach has in the past held various posts behind the scenes at Birmingham City Women, Derby County Ladies and Coventry United Ladies during a coaching career that began when she was asked to help out at a newly formed club called Erdington Ladies at the age of just 15.

As well as navigating Villa though a solid League campaign Davies also led the team to the FA Cup quarter-finals. The Cup run began with a 2-1 win over strong Tier 3 opponents Stoke City. Then followed a remarkable 5th Round tie against Championship rivals Sheffield United. Villa trailed 3-1 with five minutes to play but 18-year-old Jodie Hutton, who had already scored, went on to complete a hat-trick and then slotted home the crucial penalty in a shootout. The Wembley dreams were ended by eventual FA Cup runners-up West Ham in the quarter-finals, but Villa pushed the WSL outfit all the way in a game which ended 1-0.

The club was founded as Solihull Ladies FC in 1973. In 1989, Aston Villa men's asked for help forming a ladies team. Solihull responded and changed their name to Villa Aztecs. Villa Aztecs reached the 1995 WPL Cup final where they were beaten 2-0 by Wimbledon. In 1996 they changed their name to Aston Villa Ladies and were officially recognised as the Premier League club's ladies' team, but it wasn't until 2007 that they were fully integrated into the Aston Villa FC family.

WSL ERA FINAL LEAGUE POSITIONS (SS = SPRING SERIES)

SEASON	2011	2012	2013	2014	2015	2016	2017ss	2018	2019
TIER	T3	T2	T2	T2	T2	T2	T2	T2	T2
POSITION	1/10	3/10	6/10	4/10	5/10	6/10	4/10	9/10	6/11

2018-19 REVIEW

League:	Championship (Tier 2): 6th		
FA Cup:	QF	**Stadium:**	The Trevor Brown Memorial Ground, (Boldmere St Michaels FC)
Conti Cup:	Group		
		Head coach:	Gemma Davies (since Jun 2018)

AMY WEST SCORED FOUR GOALS IN THE CHAMPIONSHIP IN 2018-19

2018-19 STAR PERFORMER – AMY WEST

A childhood fan of Aston Villa FC, Amy West fulfilled a lifelong dream when she broke into the Villa Ladies team in 2015. She scored her first goal in a 2-2 draw against Yeovil in May of that year. Her ambitions to pull on the famous claret and blue for the senior team began when she joined the club's Centre of Excellence at the age of eight in 2006.

West turned 22 in April 2019 and has become a fans' favourite having spent 13 years with the club. Her stylish midfield performances have won her an army of admirers and she is also renowned for her work ethic. That hardworking nature is also in evidence off the pitch as she continues her studies for a degree in Business Management at the University of Birmingham.

In the past her versatility has perhaps counted against her with managers knowing they could turn to her to play in any number of positions. Throughout 2018-19 she had a more settled midfield role and weighed in with four goals in her 17 Championship appearances.

NADINE HANSSEN PREPARES TO EMBRACE GOALSCORER JODIE HUTTON

2018-19 CHAMPIONSHIP RESULTS

Date	Opponent	Res	Score	Scorers	Att	Pos
09.09	Manchester Utd (h)	L	0-12		1,165	11
19.09	Charlton Athletic (a)	L	0-2		189	11
30.09	Sheff Utd (a)	L	1-4	Kerri Welsh 19	804	11
14.10	Durham (h)	D	0-0		185	11
21.10	Leicester City W (a)	D	1-1	Jodie Hutton 20	315	10
28.10	Tottenham H (a)	L	1-2	Kerri Welsh 7	438	10
04.11	Millwall L (h)	W	2-0	Kerri Welsh 28, Amy West 50	284	9
18.11	Lewes (a)	D	1-1	Jade Richards 16	536	9
24.11	London Bees (h)	L	1-3	Jodie Hutton 1	354	9
02.12	Crystal Palace (a)	W	3-1	Sophie Haywood 12, Nadine Hanssen 33, Amy West 36	242	9
09.12	Sheffield United (h)	W	5-1	Jodie Hutton 40, 63, 73, Sophie Haywood 42, Tanisha Smith 82	284	8
13.01	Durham (a)	D	2-2	Jodie Hutton 22, Kerri Welsh 45	454	8
27.01	Leicester City W (h) *	D	0-0		1,618	7
20.02	Charlton Athletic (h)	W	2-0	Sophie Haywood 14, Kerri Welsh 32, *Kerri Welsh sent off 70*	290	7
12.03	Tottenham H (h)		P-P			7
31.03	Millwall L (a)	W	3-1	Jodie Hutton 7, Tanisha Smith 45+3, Aoife Hurley 70	296	7
17.04	Manchester Utd (a)	L	0-5	*Sian Rogers sent off 52*	1,401	8
21.04	Lewes (h)	D	2-2	Asmita Ale 4, Jodie Hutton 34	323	
28.04	London Bees (a)	W	5-1	Jade Richards 35, Asmita Ale 38, Amy West 52, Tanisha Smith 80, 90	266	6
01.05	Tottenham H (h)	D	1-1	Amy West 50	513	6
11.05	Crystal Palace (h)	D	0-0		441	6

*Played at Villa Park, (Aston Villa FC)

2018-19 FA CONTINENTAL TYRES LEAGUE CUP: GROUP ONE NORTH

Date	Opponent	Res	Score	Scorers	Att
18.08	Sheff Utd (h)	L	1-2	Nadine Hanssen 54	251
26.08	Bir'ham City (a)	L	0-2		638
16.09	Leicester City W (a)	W	1-0	Kerri Welsh 17, *Aston Villa GK Aja Aguirre saved pen 67*	312
05.12	Bristol City (a)	L	2-5	Natasha Baptiste 60, Nadine Hanssen 89	218
13.12	Manchester City (h)	L	0-4		458

2018-19 FA CUP

Date	Opponent	Res	Score	Scorers	Att
03.02 R4	Stoke City (a)		P-P		
10.02 R4	Stoke City (a)	W	2-1	Kerri Welsh 58, Sophie Haywood 66	252
17.02 R5	Sheffield Utd (h)	D	3-3aet (W5-3p)	Jodie Hutton 74, (pen) 86, 90+6	252
17.03 QF	West Ham Utd (h)	L	0-1		609

2018-19 AS IT HAPPENS

08.08.18: Nadine Hanssen becomes the club's first ever overseas signing. The 24-year-old Dutch midfielder joins from Belgian club KRC Genk and has previously played in her home country for PSV Eindhoven and VVV-Venlo.

27.01.19: Aston Villa's home Championship match against Leicester City Women is played at Villa Park and attracts a club record crowd of 1,618. The match finishes in a goalless draw.

17.02.19: Jodie Hutton is the hero of a dramatic FA Cup 5th Round tie at home to fellow Championship outfit Sheffield United. The 18-year-old scores a hat-trick as Villa fight back from 3-1 down with five minutes to play. Her equaliser comes in the sixth minute of added time, and when the match eventually progresses to a penalty shootout, who should score the winner? Hutton of course.

16.03.19: Jodie Hutton signs her first professional contract with the club, putting pen to a deal that will run until June 2020 with the option to extend for a further year.

21.04.19: Seventeen-year-old Asmita Ale scores her first goal for the senior team to give Villa a fourth-minute lead at home to Lewes in a Championship match which ends 2-2.

11.05.19: Villa report that a crowd of 441 for today's final match of the season against Crystal Palace means their home attendances are up 100% on last season. The game ends in a goalless draw and Villa finish the season in 6th place, three places above last season's final position.

ASTON VILLA APPEARANCES & GOALS 2018-19				CH		FAC		CC		Total	
				A	G	A	G	A	G	A	G
Aguirre, Aja	G	CAN	18.11.91	2	-	-	-	1	-	3	-
Ale, Asmita	D	ENG	03.11.01	17	2	2	-	2	-	21	2
Baptiste, Natasha	F	ENG	29.07.91	1	-	1	-	1	1	3	1
Brown, Ashlee	D	ENG	04.08.96	11	-	3	-	3	-	17	-
Crackle, Hayley	D	NIR	13.05.95	1	-	-	-	2	-	3	-
Elsmore, Ria	D	ENG	07.02.99	1	-	-	-	2	-	3	-
Gane, Evie	D	WAL	10.12.99	3	-	-	-	1	-	4	-
Gibson, Hollie	D	ENG	07.03.99	17	-	2	-	3	-	22	-
Hall, Alison	F	ENG	30.03.96	16	-	2	-	4	-	22	-
Hanssen, Nadine	M	NED	07.10.93	17	1	3	-	5	2	25	3
Hassall, Alice	D	ENG	08.02.97	20	-	3	-	5	-	28	-
Haywood, Sophie	M	ENG	10.01.96	19	3	3	1	3	-	25	4
Hurley, Aoife	D	ENG	20.05.96	7	1	2	-	3	-	12	1
Hutton, Jodie	M	ENG	11.02.01	17	8	3	3	5	-	25	11
N'Dow, Elisha	D	ENG	13.10.96	20	-	3	-	4	-	27	-
Richards, Jade	D	ENG	13.11.92	20	2	2	-	3	-	25	2
Rogers, Sian	G	ENG	28.06.98	18	-	3	-	4	-	25	-
Smith, Tanisha	F	ENG	06.03.00	15	4	2	-	5	-	22	4
Warner, Phoebe	M	IRE	17.07.00	13	-	1	-	5	-	19	-
Welsh, Kerri	F	ENG	20.05.92	17	5	2	1	5	1	24	7
West, Amy	M	ENG	10.04.97	17	4	3	-	2	-	22	4

BLACKBURN ROVERS

FOUNDED: 1991 **NICKNAME: ROVERS** **2019-20: CHAMPIONSHIP (TIER 2)**

Honours:	No.	Competition name & year(s)
Tier 2 Champions (Regional)	1	WPL Northern: 2006
National Tier 3 Play-off Winners	1	WNL Play-off: 2019
Tier 3 Champions (Regional)	4	2xWPL Northern: 2017, 2018 1xWNL Northern: 2019 1xNorthern Combination: 2004
Tier 3 / 4 League Cup Winners	2	1xWPL Cup: 2018 1xWNL Cup: 2019

Rovers have been Tier 3 Northern champions in each of the last three seasons. At the end of 2016-17 they lost the play-off final to Southern counterparts Tottenham Hotspur and did so likewise to Charlton Athletic at the end of 2017-18. It had been decided ahead of 2018-19 that both Northern and Southern Premier champions would be promoted to the 2019-20 Championship but that the play-off would still go ahead. Rovers, who had become champions by winning all but one of their 24 League games, beat Coventry United 3-0 in the play-off at Bradford City FC's Valley Parade.

The win over Coventry saw Rovers complete a Quadruple for 2018-19 having already won the League, WNL Cup and County Cup. The magnitude of the achievement did not go unnoticed with Gemma Donnelly winning the WNL Manager of the Year award.

Since their formation in 1991, they have always had close support from the men's club. Within seven years they were playing in the Northern Combination, which was then the English game's third tier. In 2003-04 Rovers claimed the Northern Combination title without dropping a single point. They almost repeated the feat in the 2005-06 Women's Premier League Northern Division (Tier 2) campaign, claiming the title without losing a single game, winning 20 and drawing two of their 22 matches. On the back of that 2005-06 title success, manager Andy McNally became the first manager from outside the top-flight to win the FA Manager of the Year award.

WSL ERA FINAL LEAGUE POSITIONS

SEASON	2011	2012	2013	2014	2015	2016	2017	2018	2019
TIER	T2	T3	T3	T3	T3	T3	T3	T3	T2
POSITION	7/8	4/10	3/9	9/11	3/12	3/12	1/11	1/12	1/13

2018-19 REVIEW

League:	WPL Northern (Tier 3): Champions & WNL Play-off winners		
FA Cup:	4th Round	**Stadium:**	Sir Tom Finney Stadium, (Bamber Bridge FC)
WNL Cup:	Winners	**Manager:**	Gemma Donnelly
County Cup:	Winners		

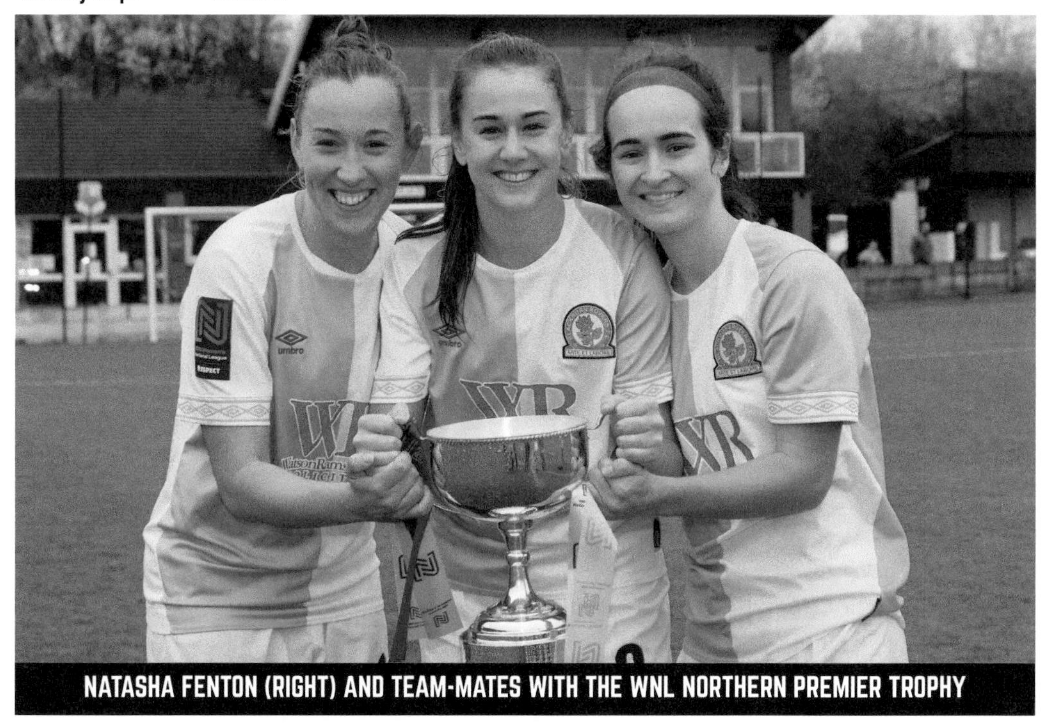

NATASHA FENTON (RIGHT) AND TEAM-MATES WITH THE WNL NORTHERN PREMIER TROPHY

2018-19 STAR PERFORMER – NATASHA FENTON

The fact that Rovers had so many stand out players in 2018-19 was in evidence at the club's end of season awards when Natasha Fenton and Jess Holbrook shared the Players' Player of the Year trophy. Central midfielder Fenton, who turned 20 in October 2018, started out playing for the club's youth team when she was 13 after arriving from Blackpool. A former England Under-17 international, she became the youngest player to make 100 appearances for Rovers during a season in which she helped the team complete a clean sweep of honours in 2018-19.

2018-19 AS IT HAPPENS

21.10.18: Saffron Jordan's appearance against Morecambe in the County Cup is her 100th for the club and she marks the occasion by scoring four goals. In the same match Eve Kennerley celebrates her first start for Rovers with a goal.

04.11.18: Natasha Fenton's appearance against Nottingham Forest in the League is her 100th appearance for the club. At 20-years-old she is the youngest Rovers player to reach that landmark.

10.02.19: Natasha Flint scores her 50th, and then 51st, goals for Rovers as they come from behind to beat Sunderland 2-1 in the League.

17.02.19: Saffron Jordan puts Rovers 2-0 up against Middlesbrough in the 41st minute of their League encounter. Two minutes later Rovers goalkeeper Danielle Hill is injured, and Jordan takes her place in goal. She helps preserve a clean sheet in what ends up as a 5-0 victory.

17.03.19: Having won their opening 15 League fixtures, Rovers drop points for the first time all season as they are beaten 3-0 away to 2nd-placed Sunderland. Sunderland are Rovers' nearest challengers in the table but remain seven points adrift having played three games more.

19.03.19: Captain Lynda Shepherd makes her 250th appearance for the club as Rovers win 5-0 at Guiseley Vixens. Sophie Charlton makes her debut as a substitute in the same match.

24.03.19: Sophie Charlton scores twice on her full debut as Rovers win 2-1 away to Hull City.

31.03.19: Rovers clinch their third Tier 3 title in a row with a 3-0 home win over Derby County. Saffron Jordan, Sophie Charlton and Jess Holbrook get the goals.

28.04.19: Rovers win the WNL Cup for the second year in a row as they beat Tier 4 Crawley Wasps 3-0 in the final at Burton Albion FC's Pirelli Stadium. Saffron Jordan scores her 100th and 101st goals for the club with Natasha Flint on target in between. The win means the club has completed a 'Double' by winning the League and League Cup in 2017-18 and 2018-19.

09.05.19: Blackburn win their fifth consecutive Lancashire FA County Cup with a 2-0 victory over WNL Northern Premier rivals Fylde. It's their 13th triumph in the competition overall.

10.05.19: The FA confirms that Blackburn, along with WNL Southern Premier champions Coventry United, have been granted a licence to play in the Championship in 2019-20.

17.05.19: At the end of season awards, Gemma Donnelly is named FA WNL Manager of the Year and Saffron Jordan receives the division's top scorer award for 32 goals in the regular League season.

18.05.19: Blackburn complete a Quadruple of trophies with a 3-0 win over Southern Premier champions Coventry United in the WNL Play-off final at Valley Parade, Bradford City.

2018-19 WNL N RESULTS

					Att	Pos
19.08	Doncaster R B (a)	W	9-0	Saffron Jordan 10, 69, 74, Natasha Flint 15, Lagan Makin 29, 71, Kayleigh McDonald 33, 85, Lynda Shepherd 38		
09.09	Hull City (h)	W	2-0	Natasha Flint 13, Hannah Walsh 44	198	2
12.09	Fylde (a)	W	1-0	Saffron Jordan 58	154	2
16.09	Sheffield FC (a)	W	7-0	Saffron Jordan 3, Ellie Stewart 5, 43, Lagan Makin 6, 81, Natasha Flint 31, 37	123	2
02.10	Bradford City (h)	W	10-0	Natasha Flint 6, 13, 18, 46, 81, Lynda Shepherd 8, Saffron Jordan 31, 74, Lauren Davies 33, Jess Holbrook 38	99	1
07.10	Middlesbrough (a)	W	2-1	Natasha Flint 46, Lynda Shepherd 86	94	1
28.10	Stoke City (h)	W	6-1	Saffron Jordan 1, 74, 84, Natasha Flint 20, 31, Ellie Stewart 68	186	1
04.11	Nottingham Forest (h)	W	7-0	Lagan Makin 13, 47, Ellie Stewart 23, Saffron Jordan 50, 87, Jess Holbrook 51, Natasha Flint 70	220	1
11.11	Derby County (a)	W	7-0	Natasha Fenton 5, Saffron Jordan 7, 52, 54, Lynda Shepherd 26, Eve Kennerley 47, Alex Taylor 83, *Lynda Shepherd missed pen 19*	216	1

25.11	Doncaster R B (h)	W	9-2	Natasha Flint 9, 13, 32, 40, 64, Lagan Makin 11, 54, Bethany Donoghue 22, Ellie Stewart 29	180	1
13.01	Huddersfield T (a)	W	4-3	Natasha Flint 2, Saffron Jordan 23, Lynda Shepherd (pen) 78, Jess Holbrook 83	97	1
27.01	Sheffield FC (h)	W	4-2	Natasha Flint 6, Jess Holbrook 25, Alex Taylor 40, Kayleigh McDonald 61	306	1
10.02	Sunderland (h)*	W	2-1	Natasha Flint 16, 22	133	1
14.02	Fylde (h)	W	3-0	Saffron Jordan 27, 36, 42	287	1
17.02	Middlesbrough (h)	W	5-0	Jess Holbrook 13, Saffron Jordan 41, Alex Taylor 61, 64, 65	178	1
10.03	Huddersfield T (h)		P-P			1
13.03	Bradford City (a)		P-P			1
17.03	Sunderland (a)	L	0-3		120	1
19.03	Guiseley Vixens (a)	W	5-0	Saffron Jordan 3, 29, 63, 66, Lagan Makin 33	40est	1
24.03	Hull City (a)	W	2-1	Sophie Charlton 14, 70		1
31.03	Derby County (h)	W	3-0	Saffron Jordan 8, Sophie Charlton 51, Jess Holbrook 89	436	1C
07.04	Nottingham F (a)	W	5-2	Saffron Jordan 56, 75, Lynda Shepherd (pen) 59, Natasha Flint 64, Sophie Charlton 90	203	1C
14.04	Stoke City (a)	W	4-0	Alex Taylor 4, Sophie Charlton 9, Lynda Shepherd (pen) 69, Saffron Jordan 79, *Natasha Flint missed pen 90+2*	120	1C
16.04	Huddersfield T (h)	W	4-0	Saffron Jordan 29, 50, Natasha Flint 42, 79	121	1C
01.05	Bradford City (a)	W	9-1	Sophie Charlton 6, 52, Natasha Fenton 43, Lagan Makin 50, 77, Natasha Flint 56, 70, 86, Carra Jones 79	42	1C
05.05	Guiseley Vixens (h)	W	5-1	Saffron Jordan 5, 86, Natasha Flint 13, 33, Natasha Fenton 37	276	1C

*Played at Accrington & Rossendale College

2018-19 WNL PLAY-OFF FINAL

18.05	Coventry Utd (n)	W	3-0	Saffron Jordan 41, Natasha Flint 54, Natasha Fenton 71	539

(n)Played at Northern Commercial Stadium, Valley Parade, (Bradford City FC)

2018-19 WNL CUP

02.09 DR	Liverpool Feds (h)	D	3-3aet (W 5-4p)	Bethany Donoghue 12, 77, *Natasha Fenton sent off 62*, Saffron Jordan 84	97
30.09 R1	Guiseley Vixens (a)	W	2-1	Saffron Jordan 3, 35	45
14.10 R2	Fylde (h)*	W	3-2	Saffron Jordan 52, Natasha Fenton 58, Jess Holbrook 76	154
09.12 R3	Sunderland (h)*	W	3-1	Saffron Jordan 54, Natasha Flint 74, 81	123

JOYOUS SCENES AS ROVERS CELEBRATE BECOMING WNL NORTHERN PREMIER CHAMPIONS

24.02 QF	Huddersfield T (a)	W	3-1	Own Goal 30, Lagan Makin 53, Saffron Jordan 69	
03.03 SF	Loughborough F (h)	W	4-0	Lagan Makin 57, 73, Natasha Flint 58, Saffron Jordan 67	283
28.04 F	Crawley Wasps (n)	W	3-0	Saffron Jordan 8, Natasha Flint 52, 81	227

*Played at Accrington & Rossendale College

2018-19 FA CUP

02.12 R2	Wolverhampton W (a)	W	4-0	Bethany Donoghue 35, Alexandra Taylor 41, Natalie Widal (og) 44, Jess Holbrook 71	60
06.01 R3	Oxford United (a)	W	2-1	Natasha Flint 66, 90	203
03.02 R4	West Ham United (a)	L	1-3	Natasha Flint 14	865

2018-19 LANCASHIRE FA COUNTY CUP

21.10 R2	Morecambe (h)	W	14-0	Lynda Shepherd (pen) 18, Natasha Flint 22, 32, 59, 61, Lagan Makin 27, 45, Saffron Jordan 30, 52, 57, 63, Eve Kennerley 51, Jess Holbrook 68, Kayleigh McDonald 77	53
18.11 QF	Fleetwood Town Wrens (a)	W	6-1	Eve Kennerley 8, Own Goal 17, Lagan Makin 31, Own Goal 59, Bethany Donoghue 75, Lynda Shepherd 80	150est
20.01 SF	Burnley (a)	W	3-0	Lagan Makin 28, Natasha Flint 63, Alex Taylor 74	550
09.05 F	Fylde (n)	W	2-0	Natasha Flint 15, Saffron Jordan 52	

(n) Played at the Lancashire FA County Ground

BLACKBURN ROVERS APPEARANCES & GOALS 2018-19

				WNL		FAC		WNLC		CouC		Total	
				A	G	A	G	A	G	A	G	A	G
Agger, Sarah	M	ENG	25.11.99	-	-	1	-	-	-	-	-	1	-
Brooks, Alex	G	ENG	19.01.95	4	-	-	-	1	-	-	-	5	-
Charlton, Sophie	F	ENG	26.07.00	8	7	-	-	-	-	-	-	8	7
Clarkson, Eve	D	ENG	19.01.01	2	-	2	-	-	-	-	-	4	-
Davies, Lauren	M	ENG	21.03.97	20	1	1	-	7	-	3	-	31	1
Donoghue, Bethany	F	ENG	21.07.94	8	1	2	1	2	2	2	1	14	5
Dykes, Megan	D	ENG	27.10.98	2	-	1	-	-	-	-	-	3	-
Fenton, Natasha	M	ENG	08.10.98	22	3	3	-	7	1	4	-	36	4
Fletcher, Serena	D	ENG	06.12.98	12	-	1	-	3	-	-	-	16	-
Flint, Natasha	F	ENG	02.08.96	21	30	3	3	5	5	4	6	33	44
Gibbons, Danielle	G	ENG	31.07.92	12	-	3	-	4	-	4	-	23	-
Hill, Danielle	G	ENG	15.04.88	2	-	-	-	-	-	-	-	2	-
Holbrook, Jess	M	ENG	01.08.92	24	6	3	1	7	1	4	1	38	9
Jones, Carra	F	ENG	03.09.01	1	1	-	-	-	-	-	-	1	1
Jordan, Saffron	F	ENG	27.11.93	22	32	2	-	7	8	4	5	35	45
Jukes, Chelsey	D	ENG	29.03.97	20	-	3	-	6	-	4	-	33	-
Kennerley, Eve	M	ENG	22.12.95	7	1	2	-	1	-	2	2	12	3
McDonald, Kayleigh	D	ENG	14.02.94	24	3	3	-	6	-	4	1	37	4
Makin, Lagan	M	ENG	10.05.91	21	11	2	-	6	3	4	4	33	18
Montgomery, Ria	F	ENG	18.05.99	1	-	-	-	-	-	1	-	2	-
O'Gara, Katie	M	ENG	n/a	1	-	-	-	-	-	-	-	1	-
Pacitto, Issy	M	ENG	06.06.01	2	-	1	-	1	-	1	-	5	-
Pearson, Kelsey	D	ENG	10.10.99	-	-	-	-	-	-	-	-	-	-
Redman, Charlotte	D	ENG	25.06.02	1	-	-	-	-	-	-	-	1	-
Shepherd, Lynda	M	NIR	05.05.85	24	7	2	-	7	-	4	2	37	9
Size, Amelia	G	ENG	07.10.00	5	-	-	-	1	-	-	-	6	-
Stenson, Fran	G	ENG	27.04.01	1	-	-	-	1	-	-	-	2	-
Stewart, Ellie	D	ENG	02.11.96	8	5	-	-	1	-	2	-	11	5
Stinson, Ebony	M	ENG	25.01.01	1	-	-	-	-	-	-	-	1	-
Stuart, Charlotte	D	ENG	28.05.90	12	-	3	-	5	-	1	-	21	-
Taylor, Alex	D	ENG	11.01.96	22	6	2	1	7	-	4	1	35	8
Walsh, Hannah	M	ENG	20.09.00	14	1	2	-	6	-	1	-	23	1

WNL apps/goals above do not include 18.05 WNL Play-off Final v Coventry United. Line-up: Gibbons, Jukes, Shepherd, Holbrook, Davies (Taylor 80), Fenton, Jordan, Flint, Makin, McDonald, Fletcher (Walsh 84). W 3-0 (Goals: Jordan, Flint, Fenton)

CHARLTON ATHLETIC

FOUNDED: 2000 (OUT OF CROYDON WFC) **NICKNAME: ADDICKS** **2019-20: CHAMPIONSHIP (TIER 2)**

Honours:	No.	Competition name & year(s)
FA Cup Winners	1	2005
FA Cup Runners-up	3	2003, 2004, 2007
English League Runners-up	2	WPL National: 2004, 2005
English Tier 3 Play-off Winners	1	WPL National Play-off: 2018
Tier 3 Champions (Regional)	1	WPL Southern: 2011, 2018
Tier 3 Runners-up (Regional)	1	WPL Southern: 2016
English League Cup Winners	2	WPL Cup: 2004, 2006
English League Cup Runners-up	1	WPL Cup: 2005
Tier 3/ 4 League Cup Winners	1	WPL Cup: 2015
Tier 3/ 4 League Cup Runners-up	1	WPL Cup: 2017

Of all six new teams awarded licences to join the rebranded Championship for 2018-19, Charlton Athletic were unique in that they earned their right to promotion to Tier 2 through their results on the pitch, as well as meeting the licence requirements off it. The Addicks topped the Southern Premier (Tier 3) table at the end of 2017-18 before overcoming Northern Premier counterparts Blackburn Rovers in the end of season play-off.

Having been one of England's most successful clubs in the 2000s, lifting the 2005 FA Cup in one of four appearances in the final, their promotion in 2018 saw them return to the elite of the game and they enjoyed a terrific inaugural campaign in the Championship. Manager Riteesh Mishra's side were unbeaten at home until 24 March and – alongside Durham – they mounted a serious challenge to Manchester United and Tottenham Hotspur's promotion hopes. Ultimately, the Addicks finished just outside the top two in 3rd spot, with 13 wins from a possible 20 and the second-best goal-difference (+28) in the division.

General manager Steve Adamson told The Women's Football Yearbook: "We were disappointed to miss out on the promotion positions but we can be proud that we held the bigger clubs down to the final few fixtures of the season and we became the side which clubs wanted to beat. Our aim has always been to return to the top levels of women's football and that aim continues in 2019-20. We want to have a strong season again and to push every team in every match of the season."

Charlton were formed in 2000 when Croydon – who had just won the Double – were controversially brought under the umbrella of the Addicks. However, they do not consider Croydon's honours (English League champions in 1995-96, 1998-99 and 1999-2000 and FA Cup winners in 1996 and 2000) to be part of their own history.

WSL ERA FINAL LEAGUE POSITIONS

SEASON	2011	2012	2013	2014	2015	2016	2017	2018	2019
TIER	T3	T2	T2	T3	T3	T3	T3	T3	T2
POSITION	1/10	5/10	7/10	5/11	3/12	2/12	4/11	1/12	3/11

2018-19 REVIEW

League:	Championship (Tier 2): 3rd		
FA Cup:	4th Round	**Stadium:**	The Oakwood, (VCD Athletic FC)
Conti Cup:	Group	**Manager:**	Riteesh Mishra (since 2016)

KIT GRAHAM (FAR RIGHT) TAKES THE ACCLAIM AFTER ANOTHER MATCH-WINNING PERFORMANCE

STAR PERFORMER – KIT GRAHAM

Kit Graham's performances for Charlton in 2018-19 saw her named as the Championship Player's Player of the Year at the FA's football awards in May and earned her a summer move to the WSL with Tottenham. She netted 12 times in 16 League appearances over the course of the season, including grabbing a hat-trick in the Addicks' final game as they beat Leicester City Women 4-0, but she is also renowned for her work-rate and movement off the ball. In 2017-18 she won the WPL (Tier 3) Golden Boot with 33 League goals in 23 appearances. Graham, who turned 23 in November 2018, scored her first goal for the Addicks when she was 16 and went on to net more than 200 for the club.

2018-19 CHAMPIONSHIP RESULTS

					Att	Pos
19.09	Aston Villa (h)	W	2-0	Gemma Bryan 12, 30	189	6
23.09	Durham (a)	D	2-2	Kit Graham 22, Amelia Ritchie 84	427	4
30.09	Lewes (h)	W	4-1	Charley Clifford 9, Charlotte Gurr 60, Lily Agg 79, Kit Graham 86	184	4
14.10	Manchester Utd (a)	L	0-3		2,439	5
21.10	Sheffield Utd (h)	W	2-0	Amber Stobbs 42, Charley Clifford 72	214	3
28.10	Millwall L (a)	W	8-0	Liz Ejupi 24, 30, 44, 57, Lily Agg 26, Charlotte Gurr 45, April Bowers 56, Kit Graham 85	200	3
04.11	London Bees (h)	W	2-0	Liz Ejupi 3, Gemma Bryan (pen) 42	208	3
18.11	Tottenham H (a)	L	0-1		396	4
25.11	Crystal Palace (h)	W	2-1	Liz Ejupi 14, Charley Clifford 90+6	471	3
02.12	Leicester City W (a)	W	4-0	Lily Agg 11, 50, Liz Ejupi 40, 49	240	2
09.12	Lewes (a)	W	2-0	Liz Ejupi 40, Lily Agg 69	330	2
06.01	Durham (h)	D	2-2	Ellie Bailes 20, Charlotte Gurr 86	279	3
13.01	Manchester Utd (h)		A-A	*Match abandoned after 11 mins due to injury. United leading 1-0.*		3
27.01	Sheffield Utd (a)	W	3-2	Kit Graham 26, Lily Agg 57, Charley Clifford 78	320	2
20.02	Aston Villa (a)	L	0-2		290	4
13.03	Millwall L (h)*	W	3-0	Kit Graham 35, Charlotte Gurr 39, Liz Ejupi 45	638	3
24.03	Manchester Utd (h)	L	1-2	Kit Graham 82	732	4
31.03	London Bees (a)	W	2-1	Liz Ejupi 33, Kit Graham 78	301	4
21.04	Tottenham H (h)	L	2-3	Liz Ejupi 41, Kit Graham 47	569	4
28.04	Crystal Palace (a)	W	4-1	Sara Eggesvik 24, Kit Graham 40, Liz Ejupi 75, Lily Agg 85	971	4
11.05	Leicester City W (h)	W	4-0	Kit Graham 1, 64, 90, Elizabeta Ejupi 49, *Hayley West sent off 80*	237	3

*Played at The Valley, (Charlton Athletic FC)

2018-19 FA CONTINENTAL TYRES LEAGUE CUP: GROUP TWO SOUTH

19.08	Lewes (a)	L	0-5		205
26.08	Millwall Lionesses (h)	W	4-2	Kit Graham 11, 48, Ellie Bailes 60, Gemma Bryan 83	204
05.12	Arsenal (a)	L	0-5		202
12.12	West Ham Utd (h)	L	0-2		202

2018-19 FA CUP

03.02 R4	Huddersfield T (h)		P-P		
10.02 R4	Huddersfield T (h)	D	3-3aet (L4-5p)	Kit Graham 6, 67, Charlotte Gurr 34	184

ELIZABETA EJUPI LEFT CHARLTON IN SUMMER 2019 FOR LONDON CITY LIONESSES

2018-19 AS IT HAPPENS

13.01.19: Charlton's match at home to Manchester United is abandoned after 11 minutes of play with United leading 1-0. Charlotte Kerr is injured during a collision as United's Devlin scores the opening goal. It is almost an hour later that the game is called off. The match is eventually replayed on 24 March with United winning 2-1.

13.03.19: Charlton's London derby at home to Millwall – which is played at The Valley – is dedicated to the memory of their former Regional Talent Centre goalkeeper Jordan Dawes who passed away at the age of 18 on 22 February having been diagnosed with liver cancer in November. Players wear T-shirts with her photo on during the warm-up and Dawes is listed as No.1 on the programme and team sheet. Fans are asked to wear something pink, which was Jordan's favourite colour and the colour of her goalkeeper top when she saved a penalty in a shootout in the 2018 Kent Cup final which helped her team Kent Football United to victory.

21.04.19: Charlton suffer a blow in the race for a top-two finish as they throw away a 2-0 lead at home to promotion rivals Tottenham to lose 3-2.

01.05.19: Tottenham's 1-1 draw away to Aston Villa ends Charlton's hopes of 2nd place and promotion to the WSL. Spurs have secured the runners-up spot behind champions Manchester United because they are now four points ahead of Durham and five ahead of Charlton with just a game to play.

11.05.19: Kit Graham opens the scoring after 48 seconds and goes on to complete a hat-trick as Charlton beat Leicester City Women 4-0 at home on the final day of the season to leapfrog Durham (who lose 2-0 at home to Tottenham) and finish their first campaign in the Championship in 3rd place.

CHARLTON ATHLETIC APPEARANCES & GOALS 2018-19

				CH		FAC		CC		Total	
				A	G	A	G	A	G	A	G
Agg, Lily	F	ENG	17.12.93	19	7	1	-	1	-	21	7
Bailes, Ellie	M	ENG	26.04.94	9	1	1	-	2	1	12	2
Bennett, Harley	D	ENG	14.07.90	16	-	1	-	2	-	19	-
Bowers, April	M	ENG	25.05.94	6	1	-	-	2	-	8	1
Brunton-Wilde, Chloe	D	ENG	07.01.98	-	-	-	-	1	-	1	-
Bryan, Gemma	F	ENG	14.08.87	10	3	-	-	4	1	14	4
Churchill, Hannah	M	ENG	15.02.93	6	-	-	-	2	-	8	-
Clifford, Charley	M	ENG	09.02.93	17	4	1	-	4	-	22	4
Coombs, Grace	D	ENG	25.11.90	20	-	1	-	4	-	25	-
Dorey, Ellie	F	ENG	04.12.95	3	-	-	-	-	-	3	-
Eggesvik, Sara	M	NOR	29.04.97	7	1	1	-	-	-	8	1
Ejupi, Elizabeta	F	ALB	21.04.94	20	14	1	-	4	-	25	14
Graham, Kit	F	ENG	11.11.95	16	12	1	2	2	2	19	16
Griffin, Georgia	F	ENG	03.06.00	3	-	1	-	2	-	6	-
Gurr, Charlotte	M	ENG	16.08.89	20	4	1	1	-	-	21	5
Kerr, Charlotte	D	ENG	26.11.94	19	-	-	-	3	-	22	-
Maple, Lilli	M	ENG	12.01.96	18	-	-	-	4	-	22	-
Nicol, Leigh	M	SCO	26.09.95	7	-	1	-	1	-	9	-
Parreno-Espinosa, Melanie	M	ENG	29.05.99	1	-	-	-	1	-	2	-
Pepper, Nicole	M	ENG	29.07.95	-	-	-	-	2	-	2	-
Ritchie, Amelia	D	WAL	09.05.99	15	1	-	-	3	-	18	1
Startup, Katie	G	ENG	28.01.99	20	-	1	-	4	-	25	-
Stobbs, Amber	M	ENG	21.10.92	18	1	1	-	-	-	19	1
West, Hayley	D	ENG	13.04.93	6	-	1	-	-	-	7	-

COVENTRY UNITED

FOUNDED: 1991 (AS COVENTRY CITY) **NICKNAME: COV UNITED** **2019-20: CHAMPIONSHIP (TIER 2)**

Former Names:
Coventry City (1991-2015)

Honours:	No.	Competition name & year(s)
Tier 3 Champions (Regional)	4	1xWPL Southern: 2014 (as Coventry City) 1xWNL Southern: 2019 2xMidland Combination: 2004, 2010 (as Coventry City)
Tier 3 Runners-up (Regional)	3	1xWPL Southern: 2017 2xWPL Northern: 2011, 2015 (both as Coventry City)
Tier 3 / Tier 4 Plate Winners	1	WPL Plate: 2016

It's believed the first Coventry Ladies team was founded in 1921, but the existing incarnation has been running since 1991 when they became affiliated with then top-flight men's side Coventry City FC. In July 2015 the team broke away from City and came under the umbrella of men's non-League outfit Coventry United. They have been Tier 3 champions (on a regional basis) four times, most recently in 2018-19 when they secured promotion to the Championship.

The FA had determined ahead of the season that the 2018-19 champions of both the WNL Northern Premier and the WNL Southern Premier would be eligible to go up to Tier 2 (subject to satisfying licence criteria) but that the traditional play-off between the two would nevertheless proceed. While United were beaten 3-0 by Blackburn Rovers in the play-off, held at Bradford City FC's Valley Parade, it did not detract from a magnificent season. Manager Jay Bradford's side led the table pretty much from start to finish and lifted the Birmingham FA County Cup with a 3-0 win over Tier 4 West Bromwich Albion in the final.

Chairman Peter Reynolds told The Women's Football Yearbook: "Emotions will be running high for some time after our title success. We are on the crest of a wave. The talent here has shone brightly this season and given renewed impetus to the activities of the whole club." On 24 May United announced a 10-year deal to play at Butts Park Arena, home of Coventry Rugby Club. United have played fixtures there in the past and considered it to be their official home ground in 2018-19, although they did not stage a match there throughout the season.

WSL ERA FINAL LEAGUE POSITIONS

SEASON	2011	2012	2013	2014	2015	2016	2017	2018	2019
TIER	T3	T2	T2	T3	T3	T3	T3	T3	T3
POSITION	2/10	6/10	5/10	1/11	2/12	4/12	2/11	4/12	1/12

2018-19 REVIEW

League:	WNL Southern (Tier 3): Champions		
FA Cup:	3rd Round	**Stadium:**	Communications Park, (Daventry Town FC)
WNL Cup:	QF	**Manager:**	Jay Bradford (since May 2016)
County Cup:	Winners		

Jeff Bennett

AMBER HUGHES IN ACTION IN THE WNL SOUTHERN PREMIER FIXTURE AGAINST QPR

2018-19 STAR PERFORMER – AMBER HUGHES

United striker Amber Hughes was a hugely influential figure in the club's title triumph. Recognised by her peers as Coventry's Players' Player of the Year she weighed in with 14 League goals during their successful promotion campaign. Manager Jay Bradford told The Women's Football Yearbook: "Amber had a superb season and was an integral part of the team's success. Winning the Players' Player of the Year award is a just reward for her hard work and dedication."

2018-19 AS IT HAPPENS

25.06.18: Reading and England player Jo Potter joins Coventry United as head coach working alongside existing manager Jay Bradford. Potter will continue to play for the Royals.

24.03.19: Coventry's 3-0 victory at Watford sees them complete a 14th League win in a row and a fifth without conceding a goal.

31.03.19: Coventry lose a League game for the first time all season as the leaders are beaten by their nearest challengers in the title race, Chichester City. It brings their 14-game winning run in the League to an end and is the first time they have dropped points since the opening game of the season.

14.04.19: A 4-1 win at home to Cardiff City Ladies – Coventry's nearest challengers in the title race at kick-off – sees United crowned WNL Southern Premier champions. Jade Brook puts Coventry ahead before Cardiff equalise. An Amy Wathan brace and a Marie Gauntlett goal seal the win.

COVENTRY UNITED CELEBRATE WINNING THE WNL SOUTHERN PREMIER TITLE

Jeff Bennett

30.04.19: Coventry secure their second trophy of the season as they beat newly crowned WNL Midlands 1 (Tier 4) champions West Bromwich Albion 3-0 in the Birmingham FA County Cup final. Amy Wathan, Beth Merrick and Amber Hughes score as United hold on to the Cup they won in 2017-18.

10.05.19: The FA confirms that Coventry, along with WNL Northern Premier champions Blackburn Rovers, have been granted a licence to play in the Championship in 2019-20.

18.05.19: Bradford City FC's Valley Parade plays host to the WNL play-off final between Coventry and Northern Premier champions Blackburn Rovers who run out 3-0 winners. At the FA awards the previous day, Coventry were named FA WNL Club of the Year 2018-19.

2018-19 MAIN HOME VENUE: COMMUNICATIONS PARK, (DAVENTRY TOWN FC)

2018-19 WNL SP

					Att	Pos
19.08	Gillingham (a)	D	0-0		70	
26.08	MK Dons (a)	W	3-0	Chenise Austin 19, Marie Gauntlett 33, Lois Jefferies 61		
09.09	Portsmouth (a)	W	2-1	Helen Dermody 5, Jade Brook 23, *Helen Dermody missed pen 44*	94	3
12.09	Loughborough F (h)	W	4-0	Marie Gauntlett 16, Amber Hughes 66, Helen Dermody (pen) 70, Lois Jefferies 73	75	2
16.09	Chichester City (a)	W	2-1	Jade Brook 8, 68	130	1
23.09	Plymouth A (h)		P-P			2
30.09	C&K Basildon (h)	W	4-1	Amber Hughes 9, Jade Brook 12, 59, Amy Wathan 81	165	1
02.10	Oxford United (a)	W	2-1	Jade Brook 62, Amy Wathan 73	56	1
21.10	Watford (h)	W	4-0	Amber Hughes 26, Chenise Austin (pen) 28, Marie Gauntlett 63, Amy Wathan 74	136	1
11.11	QPR (a)	W	7-1	Marie Gauntlett 15, Shannon O'Brien 19, Jade Brook 50, Lois Jefferies 64, Amber Hughes 65, Amy Wathan 77, 90	50	2

25.11	Plymouth A (a)	W	9-1	Shannon O'Brien 5, Natalie Haigh 6, Amber Hughes 11, Rosie McDonnell 31, 44, 77, Amy Wathan 63, Lois Jefferies 80, Chenise Austin (pen) 90+2	209	1
09.12	QPR (h)		P-P			1
27.01	Portsmouth (h)		P-P			2
03.02	Chichester City (h)		P-P			2
14.02	Loughborough F (a)	W	2-0	Amber Hughes 9, Amy Wathan 36	57	2
03.03	Portsmouth (h)	W	4-0	Amy Wathan 3, 54, Shannon O'Brien 43, Lois Jefferies 65	100	1
10.03	C&K Basildon (a)	W	6-0	Amy Wathan 14, Chenise Austin (pen) 26, (pen) 90+2, Shannon O'Brien 38, Beth Merrick 66, Own Goal		1
13.03	Oxford United (h)		P-P			1
17.03	Gillingham (h)	W	9-0	Lois Jefferies 4, 41, Amber Hughes 25, 46, Amy Wathan 42, 68, Marie Gauntlett 60, 90+1 Beth Merrick 62	90	1
24.03	Watford (a)	W	3-0	Marie Gauntlett 5, 90, Natasha Merritt 36	126	1
31.03	Chichester City (h)	L	2-3	Nikki Miles 9, Amy Wathan 71	90	1
03.04	Oxford United (h)	W	2-0	Amber Hughes 6, Beth Merrick 70	106	1
07.04	QPR (h)	D	1-1	Nikki Miles 32	106	1
10.04	MK Dons (h)	W	4-0	Amber Hughes 37, 46, Chenise Austin (pen) 68, Lois Jefferies 90	108	1
14.04	Cardiff City L (h)	W	4-1	Jade Brook 7, Amy Wathan 27, 90+2 Marie Gauntlett 90+3	206	1C
28.04	Plymouth A (a)	W	5-2	Amber Hughes 30, 67, 90+1, Amy Wathan 49, Rosie McDonnell 80	83	1C
05.05	Cardiff City L (a)	D	1-1	Beth Merrick 90+6	200	1C

2018-19 WNL PLAY-OFF FINAL

18.05	Blackburn R (n)	L	0-3	539

(n)Played at Northern Commercial Stadium, Valley Parade, (Bradford City FC)

2018-19 WNL CUP

02.09 DR	Norwich City (h)	W	7-0	Amy Wathan 9, 39, 59, Amber Hughes 17, 75, Jade Brook 57, Marie Gauntlett 90+1	93
R1	Bye				
14.10 R2	Watford (a)	W	3-2	Marie Gauntlett 20, Lois Jefferies 48, Jade Brook 74	65
13.01 R3	Chichester City (a)	W	2-0	Natasha Merritt 39, Amber Hughes 52, *Natasha Merritt sent off 69*	
24.02 QF	Crawley Wasps (h)	L	1-2	Beth Merrick	120

2018-19 FA CUP

02.12 R2	Plymouth A (h)	W	2-1	Chenise Austin (pen) 15, Amy Wathan 63	65
06.01 R3	Crawley Wasps (h)	L	1-2	Amber Hughes 26	90

2018-19 BIRMINGHAM FA COUNTY CUP

18.11 R2	Wolverhampton W (h)	W	5-1	Shannon O'Brien 16, Chenise Austin (pen) 24, Lois Jefferies 32, 60, Marie Gauntlett 36	141
16.12 R3	Bir'ham & WM (a)	W	w/o		
20.01 QF	Leafield Athletic (h)	W	8-0	Shannon O'Brien 15, Helen Dermody 24, Lois Jefferies 26, 44, 73, Amy Wathan 65, Bethan Merrick 85, Amber Hughes 87	50
17.02 SF	Stockingford AA Pavilion (a)	W	8-0	Amy Wathan 9, 68, Shannon O'Brien 17, 41, 90, Helen Dermody (pen) 20, Amber Hughes 54, Bethan Merrick (pen) 65	
30.04 F	West Brom Albion (n)	W	3-0	Amy Wathan 4, Beth Merrick 49, Amber Hughes 87	

(n)Played at The Lamb Ground, (Tamworth FC and Birmingham FA HQ)

COV UTD APPEARANCES & GOALS 2018-19			WNL		FAC		WNLC		CouC		Total	
			A	G	A	G	A	G	A	G	A	G
Austin, Chenise	D	ENG	21	6	2	1	4	-	3	1	30	8
Brook, Jade*	M	ENG	22	8	2	-	4	2	4	-	32	10
Buck, Alex	D	ENG	1	-	-	-	-	-	1	-	2	-
Dermody, Helen	M	ENG	16	2	1	-	2	-	3	2	22	4
Gauntlett, Marie	M	ENG	16	9	1	-	4	2	3	1	24	12
Haigh, Natalie	D	ENG	2	1	2	-	1	-	1	-	6	1
Hughes, Amber	M	ENG	21	14	2	1	4	3	4	3	31	21
Jefferies, Lois	F	ENG	22	8	2	-	3	1	3	5	30	14
Klucis, Yasmine	M	ENG	3	-	-	-	-	-	1	-	4	-
McDonnell, Rosie	D	ENG	13	4	1	-	2	-	2	-	18	4
McGlone, Laura	M	ENG	5	-	-	-	2	-	-	-	7	-
Merrick, Bethan	M	ENG	11	4	1	-	2	1	3	3	17	8
Merritt, Natasha	M	ENG	20	1	2	-	3	1	2	-	27	2
Miles, Nikki	D	ENG	22	2	2	-	3	-	1	-	28	2
O'Brien, Shannon	M	ENG	11	4	2	-	2	-	3	5	18	9
Riden, Erin	D	ENG	13	-	1	-	1	-	4	-	19	-
Roberts, Jenna	D	ENG	9	-	-	-	1	-	2	-	12	-
Shiner, Amelia	D	ENG	2	-	-	-	-	-	1	-	3	-
Slater, Emma	D	ENG	1	-	-	-	-	-	1	-	2	-
Stead, Lucy	D	ENG	3	-	-	-	1	-	-	-	4	-
Wathan, Amy	F	WAL	22	16	1	1	4	3	4	4	31	24
White, Ellie	M	ENG	6	-	-	-	-	-	-	-	6	-
Wood, Susan	G	ENG	22	-	2	-	4	-	4	-	32	-
Wright, Victoria	G	ENG	1	-	-	-	-	-	-	-	1	-

WNL apps above do not include 18.05 WNL Play-off Final v Blackburn Rovers (L 0-3). Line-up: Wood, Austin, Miles (Riden 63), McDonnell, Merritt, Merrick (Klucis 63), Formaston, Dermody, Hughes, Jefferies, Wathan

*also known as Formaston, Jade

CRYSTAL PALACE

FOUNDED: 1992 **NICKNAME: THE EAGLES** **2019-20: CHAMPIONSHIP (TIER 2)**

Honours:	No.	Competition name & year(s)
Tier 4 Champions (Regional)	1	WPL South East One: 2016
Tier 5 Champions (Regional)	1	London & SE Regional Premier: 2014

Crystal Palace had little time to prepare for their first season in Tier 2 when they received a last-minute call-up to the Championship for 2018-19. The Eagles initially had their application for a licence turned down by the FA but were awarded one of the vacant spots when Doncaster Rovers Belles and Sheffield FC relinquished their Championship berths due to financial constraints.

Having built a team for Tier 3 football, the Eagles now had to get ready to take on 10 Championship opponents who had all had longer to get ready for life in the new division. Cheered on by an always passionate support at Hayes Lane, Palace's never-say-die attitude saw them avoid the Championship wooden spoon. Highlights of the season included home wins over London rivals London Bees and Millwall Lionesses and a thrilling 3-2 win away to Leicester in February when they threw away a 2-0 lead only for Gemma Bryan to hit the winner six minutes from time.

There were also some impressive performances in the Continental Cup even though they didn't make it beyond the group stage. They opened the campaign with a 1-1 home draw against Tottenham and took the bonus point with victory in the penalty shootout. Later in the competition they won 1-0 at top-flight Yeovil with Jordan Butler scoring the winner and beat London Bees 7-2 in a game in which Ashlee Hincks scored four, including one from the spot.

Manager Dean Davenport told The Women's Football Yearbook: "From a standing start, after receiving notification of our place in the Championship six weeks after everyone else, the coaches and staff battled through with a team that had been built to win the WNL. It has shown us the strength of character in some of our players who have had to pull out all the stops for us to finish the season in 10th place in a hugely competitive division.

"We had some real bad luck with injuries which also put us behind where we wanted to be, but we have learnt a lot and we are confident that in 2019-20 we can finish at least mid-table. That is the Crystal Palace way, always the underdog, always the fighter and never to be underestimated."

The club was founded in 1992 and has enjoyed rapid progression in recent times with two promotions in the space of three seasons carrying them from Tier 5 to Tier 3 ahead of 2016-17. Their award of a Tier 2 licence for 2018-19 lifted them to the highest level in their history. In the summer of 2019, they announced they were dropping 'Ladies' from their name and will now simply be Crystal Palace FC, using Crystal Palace FC (Women) only where there could be confusion with the men.

WSL ERA FINAL LEAGUE POSITIONS

SEASON	2011	2012	2013	2014	2015	2016	2017	2018	2019
TIER	T4	T4	T4	T5	T4	T4	T3	T3	T2
POSITION	10/12	8/11	12/12	1/11	3/10	1/12	5/11	3/12	10/11

2018-19 REVIEW

League: Championship (Tier 2): 10th

FA Cup: 4th Round **Stadium:** Hayes Lane, (Bromley FC)

Conti Cup: Group **Manager:** Dean Davenport (since Jun 2013)

Tara Hook

ASHLEE HINCKS BATTLES IT OUT FOR PALACE AGAINST SHEFFIELD UNITED

2018-19 STAR PERFORMER – ASHLEE HINCKS

After making the switch across South London from Millwall Lionesses to Crystal Palace, Ashlee Hincks had a terrific first season in the famous red and blue shirt and ended up being named the club's Player of the Year. Including pre-season, the Palace No.10 hit 25 goals in her debut campaign for the Eagles. Hincks' game isn't just about finishing, she knows her way around Tier 2 defences and her astute passing and intelligent movement help bring her team-mates into the game.

2018-19 CHAMP

					Att	Pos
09.09	Leicester City W (h)	L	0-2		382	8
19.09	Lewes (a)	L	1-2	Ciara Watling 24	304	9
23.09	Millwall L (a)	D	1-1	Ashlee Hincks 10	117	8
30.09	Tottenham H (h)	L	1-2	Kallie Balfour (pen) 7	202	9
14.10	London Bees (h)	W	1-0	Ashlee Hincks 21, *Ashlee Hincks missed pen 60 (saved by Sarah Quantrill)*	148	7
21.10	Durham (a)	L	0-2		287	8
28.10	Sheffield Utd (h)	L	0-1		208	9
18.11	Manchester Utd (h)	L	0-5		975	10
25.11	Charlton Athletic (a)	L	1-2	Jordan Butler 43	471	10
02.12	Aston Villa (h)	L	1-3	Nikita Whinnett 45	248	10
09.12	Tottenham H (a)	L	0-1		289	10
05.01	Millwall L (h)	W	3-1	Chloe Burr 6, Hannah Mackenzie 52, Gemma Bryan 62	366	10
13.01	London Bees (a)	L	1-2	Andrea Georgiou 17	183	10
27.01	Durham (h)	L	0-2		138	10
10.02	Leicester City W (a)	W	3-2	Nikita Whinnett 57, Gemma Bryan 64, 84	478	9
21.02	Lewes (h)	L	0-3		786	10
10.03	Sheffield United (a)	L	0-2		434	10
20.04	Manchester Utd (a)	L	0-7		2,500	10
28.04	Charlton Athletic (h)*	L	1-4	Kallie Balfour (pen) 77	971	10
11.05	Aston Villa (a)	D	0-0		441	10

*Played at Selhurst Park, (Crystal Palace FC)

2018-19 FA CONTINENTAL TYRES LEAGUE CUP: GROUP ONE SOUTH

18.08	Tottenham H (h)	D	1-1 (W 5-3p)	Kallie Balfour 64	372
26.08	Yeovil Town (a)	W	1-0	Jordan Butler 82	301
16.09	Chelsea (h)	L	0-4		449
05.12	Brighton & H A (a)	L	1-5	Chloe Burr 85	204
13.12	London Bees (h)	W	7-2	Ashlee Hincks 11, 25, (pen) 45+2, 67, Chloe Burr 52, 70, Charmaine True 77	146

2018-19 FA CUP

03.02 R4	Tottenham H (h)	L	0-3	282

2018-19 AS IT HAPPENS

18.08.18: Kallie Balfour becomes the first player to score for Palace at Tier 2 level when she nets the 64th minute equaliser in a 1-1 Continental Cup draw at home to Tottenham.

19.09.19: Ciara Watling claims the honour of becoming the club's first goal scorer at Tier 2 level in a League match when she scores after 24 minutes in a 2-1 defeat to Lewes in the Championship.

05.03.19: Ciara Watling and Freya Holdaway help Northern Ireland win the 3rd Place Play-off at the Turkish Cup with a 2-1 win over Uzbekistan. The eight-team annual invitational event is won by France B who beat Romania 7-0 in the final.

Tara Hook

PALACE TAKE ON REIGNING WSL CHAMPIONS CHELSEA IN THE CONTINENTAL CUP

Tara Hook

THE EAGLES CELEBRATE A GOAL AGAINST CAPITAL RIVALS LONDON BEES

28.04.19: The South London derby at home to Charlton is staged at Selhurst Park, home of Crystal Palace men's, and is watched by a crowd of 971. The visitors win 4-1 with Kallie Balfour netting the Eagles' consolation goal from the penalty spot. Despite the result Palace know they will avoid the Championship wooden spoon because bottom club Millwall Lionesses lose 5-0 to Manchester United. Thankfully for Millwall there is no relegation from the Championship this season anyway.

CRYSTAL PALACE APPEARANCES & GOALS 2018-19				CH		FAC		CC		Total	
				A	G	A	G	A	G	A	G
Balfour, Kallie	F	ENG	13.10.92	15	2	1	-	2	1	18	3
Bryan, Gemma	F	ENG	14.08.87	5	3	-	-	-	-	5	3
Burr, Chloe	F	ENG	03.04.93	13	1	1	-	5	3	19	4
Butler, Jordan	D	ENG	14.09.92	13	1	-	-	3	1	16	2
Chandler, Megan	M	ENG	22.10.93	14	-	1	-	4	-	19	-
Chong, Dayna	M	ENG	06.11.95	-	-	-	-	1	-	1	-
Collins, Ria	D	ENG	15.03.93	8	-	-	-	2	-	10	-
Davenport, Jade	M	ENG	16.06.97	2	-	-	-	-	-	2	-
Georgiou, Andria	M	ENG	15.04.96	18	1	-	-	4	-	22	1
Gillett, Lucy	G	USA	28.10.93	8	-	1	-	-	-	9	-
Green, Amy	M	ENG	12.01.96	1	-	-	-	2	-	3	-
Haydock, Leesa	M	ENG	21.12.88	13	-	1	-	4	-	18	-
Hincks, Ashlee	F	ENG	04.12.88	16	2	1	-	4	4	21	6
Holdaway, Freya	D	NIR	12.04.89	13	-	1	-	3	-	17	-
Keogh, Jade	M	ENG	02.11.94	9	-	-	-	3	-	12	-
Lynch, Megen	G	ENG	03.09.91	4	-	-	-	3	-	7	-
Martin, Sandra	M	ENG	25.08.99	1	-	-	-	2	-	3	-
MacKenzie, Hannah	D	ENG	03.02.95	20	1	1	-	4	-	25	1
McKeag, Meghan	D	ENG	12.08.89	7	-	1	-	-	-	8	-
McRoberts, Pamela	D	NIR	15.07.86	10	-	1	-	3	-	14	-
Nash, Hope	D	ENG	08.10.97	15	-	1	-	5	-	21	-
Nuttall, Anneka	M	ENG	26.02.91	19	-	1	-	4	-	24	-
Salgado, Shanell	G	ENG	09.12.93	9	-	-	-	2	-	11	-
Stevens, Lily	D	WAL	29.09.98	5	-	-	-	1	-	6	-
True, Charmaine	F	ENG	29.12.93	1	-	-	-	2	1	3	1
Watling, Ciara	M	NIR	18.08.92	16	1	1	-	4	-	21	1
Whinnett, Nikita	F	ENG	17.03.91	16	2	1	-	2	-	19	2

DURHAM

FOUNDED: 2013 NICKNAME: THE WILDCATS 2019-20: CHAMPIONSHIP (TIER 2)

Honours: None

In 2018-19 Durham proved their success of the previous season was no fluke. For the second year in a row, the Wildcats secured both a 4th-place finish in Tier 2 and an FA Cup quarter-final berth. A 2-0 win away to Bristol City – their first ever victory against top-flight opponents – led to a home quarter-final against holders Chelsea. Durham themselves described that match at New Ferens Park as arguably the biggest in their history, and they pushed the Blues all the way.

Ultimately, they lost 1-0, going down to South Korea star Ji So-yun's winner. As part-timers against one of the strongest squads in the country, Durham were widely praised for a performance which saw them create several good chances themselves – they came close to forcing extra time when Zoe Ness' effort was cleared off the line in the closing stages.

In the Championship, Lee Sanders' side lost just three games. Only champions Manchester United conceded fewer than the 16 goals Durham let in during their 20 League matches. Durham were always in the thick of a four-way promotion race that also included Tottenham and Charlton, a race eventually won by United with Spurs following them up to the WSL for 2019-20.

Both United and Tottenham were left in no doubt of Durham's true quality in December with the Wildcats inflicting a 6-1 defeat on Spurs and then beating United 3-1. That proved to be the only League defeat, and one of only two matches United failed to win in the division, all season.

Durham are one of the youngest clubs in England's upper tiers, having been founded in 2013. They joined WSL 2 for the inaugural 2014 season and have always finished between 4th and 7th in the division. Formed as a collaboration between South Durham & Cestria Girls and Durham University, their first competitive match as Durham was an FA Cup 3rd Round tie which ended in a 4-0 win over Chichester City on 14 February 2014. South Durham & Cestria Girls had themselves been founded in 2007 by the man who went on to manage Durham – Lee Sanders. They quickly became one of the best teams in the region, competing in international events in Portugal, Ghana and the USA and winning a prestigious youth tournament, the World Peace Cup, in Oslo in 2010. In 2011 they were runners-up at the Gothia World Youth Cup. When Durham were founded as a WSL club, South Durham & Cestria Girls continued as a separate entity, Durham Cestria, who were promoted to Tier 4 at the end of 2018-19.

WSL ERA FINAL LEAGUE POSITIONS: (SS = SPRING SERIES)

SEASON	2014	2015	2016	2017ss	2018	2019
TIER	T2	T2	T2	T2	T2	T2
POSITION	6/10	7/10	4/10	5/10	4/10	4/11

2018-19 REVIEW

League:	Championship (Tier 2): 4th		
FA Cup:	QF	**Stadium:**	New Ferens Park
Conti Cup:	Group	**Manager:**	Lee Sanders (since Mar 2014)

George Ledger

BETH HEPPLE IN ACTION FOR DURHAM AGAINST SHEFFIELD UNITED

2018-19 STAR PERFORMER – BETH HEPPLE

Beth Hepple's displays in Durham's midfield saw her named as the North East Football Writers' Player of the Year in February 2019, an individual honour previously bestowed on current England captain Steph Houghton. Former England youth international Hepple featured in all 20 of Durham's Championship games in 2018-19 and finished as their top scorer with eight League goals and 10 in all competitions. She came through the ranks at Durham Cestria and is always one of the first names on the team-sheet. Her outstanding fitness has seen her miss very few games over the last four seasons, with her consistently high performances playing a key role in the Wildcats' progress.

2018-19 CHAMP

					Att	Pos
08.09	Sheff Utd (a)	W	2-0	Becky Salicki 57, Emily Roberts 90+4	412	3
23.09	Charlton Athletic (h)	D	2-2	Beth Hepple 23, Emily Roberts 26	427	5
30.09	Manchester Utd (a)	D	0-0	*Durham GK Hannah Reid saved pen 68*	2,244	6
14.10	Aston Villa (a)	D	0-0		185	6
21.10	Crystal Palace (h)	W	2-0	Emily Roberts 61, Ciara Watling (og) 83	208	5
28.10	London Bees (a)	W	1-0	Beth Hepple 19	107	4
04.11	Lewes (h)	W	5-0	Becky Salicki 18, Zoe Ness 20, Abi Cottam 23, 27, 34	417	4
18.11	Millwall L (a)	W	5-1	Beth Hepple 3, 11, Nicki Gears 5, Sarah Wilson 36, *Beth Hepple missed pen 53,* Zoe Ness 54	154	3
25.11	Leicester City W (h)	L	0-2	*Beth Hepple missed pen 77 (saved by Demi Lambourne)*	278	4
02.12	Tottenham H (a)	W	6-1	Emily Roberts 9, Beth Hepple 20, 30, Sarah Robson 47, Zoe Ness 48, Chloe Ryan 90+1, *Becky Salicki sent off 53*	206	3
09.12	Manchester Utd (h)	W	3-1	Amy Turner (og) 22, Beth Hepple (pen) 60, Zoe Ness 88	912	3
06.01	Charlton A (a)	D	2-2	Zoe Ness 42, 45	279	4
13.01	Aston Villa (h)	D	2-2	Lisa Robertson 21, Becky Salicki 75	454	4
27.01	Crystal Palace (a)	W	2-0	Emily Roberts 4, Nicki Gears 50	138	3
10.03	London Bees (h)	W	1-0	Kathryn Hill 68	353	3
31.03	Lewes (a)	W	1-0	Nicki Gears 43	343	3
14.04	Sheffield Utd (h)	L	1-2	*Becky Salicki sent off 60,* Beth Hepple 75	359	4
21.04	Millwall L (h)	W	1-0	Emily Roberts 69	355	3
28.04	Leicester City W (a)	D	1-1	Sarah Robson 45	264	3
11.05	Tottenham H (h)	L	0-2	*Beth Hepple sent off 18*	533	4

2018-19 FA CONTINENTAL TYRES LEAGUE CUP: GROUP TWO NORTH

19.08	Reading (a)	L	1-4	Beth Hepple (pen) 79	246
26.08	Everton (h)	W	1-0	Zoe Ness 21	284
16.09	Liverpool (h)	D	3-3 (L 4-5p)	Emily Roberts 3, 19, Abi Cottam 61	352
05.12	Manchester Utd (a)	L	0-1		686

2018-19 FA CUP

03.02 R4	Cardiff City L (h)		P-P		
10.02 R4	Cardiff City L (h)	W	5-1	Abby Holmes 9, Beth Hepple 43, Sarah Robson 54, Zoe Ness 81, 89, *Durham GK Megan Borthwick saved Cori Williams pen 19*	283
17.02 R5	Bristol City (a)	W	2-0	Lisa Robertson 66, 90+2	
17.03 QF	Chelsea (h)	L	0-1		1,629

George Ledger

2018-19 AS IT HAPPENS

09.12.18: A club record crowd of 912 watches Durham's 3-1 win against Manchester United in the Championship. *(NB: This record is itself beaten on 17.03 when 1,629 see the Wildcats take on holders Chelsea in the FA Cup quarter-finals, losing 1-0).*

10.02.19: Abby Holmes scores her first Durham goal in the club's 5-1 win against 3rd Tier Cardiff City Ladies in the FA Cup 4th Round.

17.02.19: Durham's FA Cup 5th Round win away to Bristol City is their first ever victory against top-flight opposition as well as their first ever win against City.

17.03.19: Durham stage what they describe as arguably the biggest game in their history as they host holders Chelsea in the FA Cup quarter-finals. Durham lose just 1-0 in front of a club record crowd of 1,629.

14.04.19: Durham's promotion hopes suffer a major blow as they lose 2-1 at home to Sheffield United. Becky Salicki is sent off on the hour mark with the Wildcats trailing 1-0, and United then double their lead. Beth Hepple pulls one back, but the visitors hold on to win. The result sees Durham slip a place to 4th with just three games remaining.

21.04.19: Durham keep alive their slim hopes of a top-two finish and promotion with a 1-0 home win over Millwall courtesy of Emily Roberts' goal. However, they trail 2nd-placed Tottenham (who come from 2-0 down to beat 4th-placed Charlton 3-2) by four points with just two games to play.

20.04.19: Durham's slim title hopes are ended as Manchester United secure the Championship title with a 7-0 home win over Crystal Palace.

28.04.19: A 1-1 draw away to Leicester City Women deals a severe blow to Durham's hopes of catching Tottenham in the race for 2nd place and promotion to the WSL. The Wildcats go 1-0 up through Sarah Robson just before half-time but Melissa Johnson equalises for Leicester with just eight minutes to go. The result means that Tottenham – who did not play today – can secure promotion if they get at least a point at Aston Villa on Wednesday.

01.05.19: Tottenham's 1-1 draw away to Aston Villa ends Durham's hopes of 2nd place and promotion to the WSL. Spurs have secured the runners-up spot behind champions Manchester United.

DURHAM PLAYER APPEARANCES & GOALS 2018-19

				CH		FAC		CC		Total	
				A	G	A	G	A	G	A	G
Borthwick, Megan	G	ENG	22.03.96	2	-	1	-	3	-	6	-
Briggs, Lauren	M	ENG	n/a	1	-	-	-	2	-	3	-
Christon, Ellie	D	ENG	21.09.93	20	-	3	-	4	-	27	-
Cottam, Abigail	F	ENG	13.12.90	11	3	2	-	3	1	16	4
Dixon, Caroline	D	ENG	27.07.87	7	-	2	-	-	-	9	-
Elliott, Megan	D	ENG	n/a	1	-	-	-	1	-	2	-
Gears, Nicki	F	ENG	n/a	19	3	3	-	3	-	25	3
Greenwood, Hannah	D	ENG	n/a	2	-	-	-	1	-	3	-
Hepple, Beth	M	ENG	15.09.96	20	8	2	1	4	1	26	10
Hill, Kathryn	D	SCO	21.06.94	17	1	3	-	4	-	24	1
Holder, Molly	M	ENG	n/a	2	-	1	-	-	-	3	-
Holmes, Abby	D	ENG	26.05.91	18	-	2	1	3	-	23	1
Knott, Chloe	M	NZL	n/a	6	-	-	-	1	-	7	-
Lee, Rachel	M	ENG	n/a	15	-	2	-	4	-	21	-
Ness, Zoe	F	SCO	24.03.96	18	6	3	2	4	1	25	9
Reid, Hannah	G	SCO	20.08.94	18	-	2	-	1	-	21	-
Roberts, Emily	F	ENG	07.04.94	19	6	3	-	4	2	26	8
Robertson, Lisa	D	SCO	15.05.92	11	1	3	2	1	-	15	3
Robson, Sarah	M	NIR	23.05.87	20	2	3	1	4	-	27	3
Ryan, Chloe	F	ENG	n/a	2	1	-	-	-	-	2	1
Salicki, Rebecca	D	ENG	30.07.92	17	3	3	-	2	-	22	3
Wilson, Sarah	D	ENG	01.07.91	20	1	3	-	4	-	27	1

LEICESTER CITY WOMEN

FOUNDED: 2004 **NICKNAME: THE FOXES** **2019-20: CHAMPIONSHIP (TIER 2)**

Honours:	No.	Competition name & year(s)
Tier 3/ 4 League Cup Runners-up	1	WPL Cup: 2018
Tier 3 Champions (Regional)	1	Midland Combination: 2008
Tier 3 Runners-up (Regional)	1	WPL Northern: 2018
Tier 4 Champions (Regional)	2	1xEast Midlands Premier: 2007 1xWPL Midlands One: 2016
Tier 4 Runners-up (Regional)	2	1xWPL Midlands One: 2015 1xMidland Combination: 2014
Tier 5 Champions (Regional)	1	East Midlands Southern League: 2006

Leicester City Women were among six newcomers to Tier 2 ahead of 2018-19 after proving to the FA that they could satisfy all licence criteria for a place in the Championship. The League campaign began in style with a 2-0 win away to Crystal Palace, a game in which Melissa Johnson achieved the honour of scoring the club's first ever Championship goal, a neat finish in the 18th minute.

The Foxes' most impressive result came at the end of November when Nicole Nymoen and Serena Fletcher struck early goals in a 2-0 win away to promotion contenders Durham. Goalkeeper Demi Lambourne preserved the clean sheet and thwarted Durham's hopes of a late comeback when she saved a penalty with 13 minutes to go.

There was also a League double to celebrate against Millwall Lionesses as well as 4-2 and 4-0 wins over London Bees and Lewes respectively. It all resulted in a respectable 7th place finish at the end of Leicester's first Championship season.

Captain Holly Morgan told The Women's Football Yearbook: "As a Club we learnt a lot from the 2018-19 season and in order to continue growing and developing we must use those experiences and lessons to realise our ambitions of competing at the highest level. There are highlights to reflect on, but we weren't consistent enough throughout the campaign and that is something we must look at going forward into 2019-20."

The club has made great strides on and off the pitch in recent years. They secured promotion to Tier 3 ahead of the 2016-17 season, going up as WPL Midlands 1 champions. The Foxes quickly acclimatised to their new level, finishing 3rd in 2016-17 and then 2nd in 2017-18.

Leicester were among the clubs bidding to join the WSL for the inaugural season of 2011, but their application was rejected. They were founded in 2004 and are officially affiliated to Leicester City FC – the men's surprise Premier League champions of 2015-2016. They are not to be confused with grassroots club Leicester City Ladies.

WSL ERA FINAL LEAGUE POSITIONS

SEASON	2011	2012	2013	2014	2015	2016	2017	2018	2019
TIER	T3	T4	T4	T4	T4	T4	T3	T3	T2
POSITION	3/10	3/10	9/9	2/11	2/12	1/12	3/11	2/12	7/11

2018-19 REVIEW

League:	Championship (Tier 2): 7th		
FA Cup:	4th Round	**Stadium:**	Farley Way, (Quorn FC)
Conti Cup:	Group	**Manager:**	Jonathan Morgan (since Feb 2015)

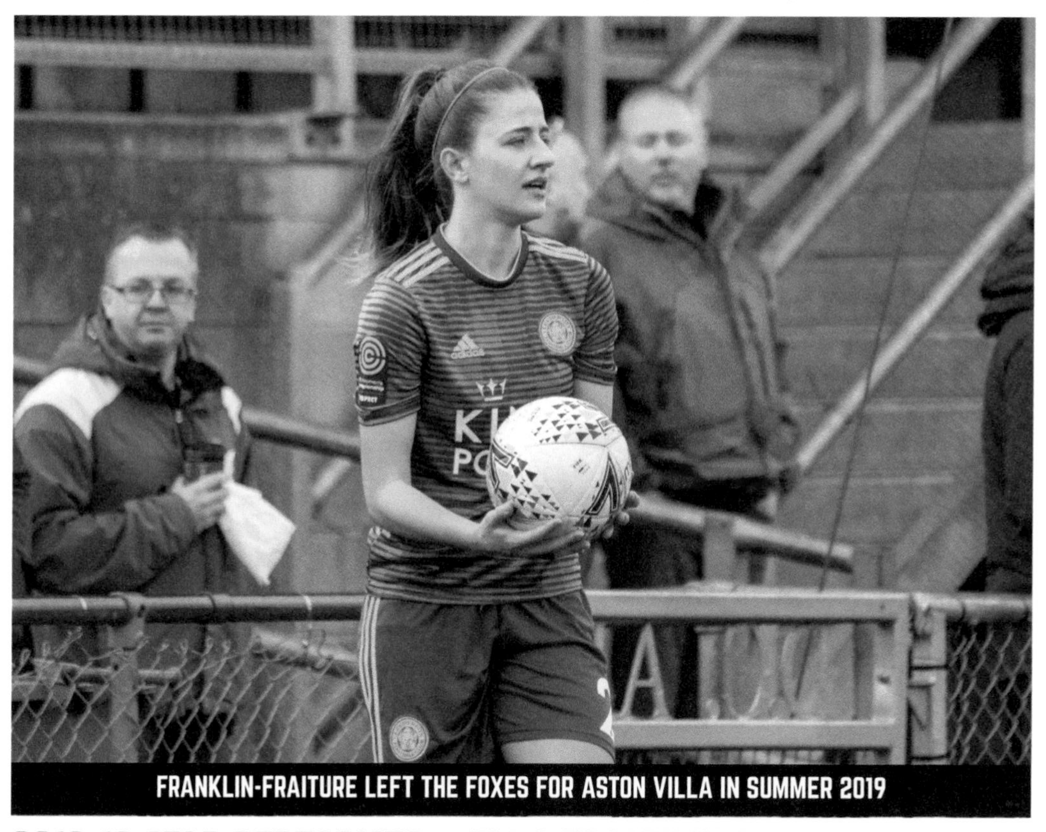

FRANKLIN-FRAITURE LEFT THE FOXES FOR ASTON VILLA IN SUMMER 2019

2018-19 STAR PERFORMER – ELLA FRANKLIN-FRAITURE

University of Birmingham student Ella Franklin-Fraiture left Leicester in the summer of 2019 for Championship rivals Aston Villa. She started out at Oxford United, playing for their youth teams from the age of 10 and breaking into their first team aged 16 in 2014. Franklin-Fraiture spent the next four years with the WSL 2 club before joining Leicester in summer 2018 ahead of their debut Championship season. The versatile defender, who can also play in midfield, overcame injury at the start of 2019 to finish the campaign with 14 Championship appearances while also studying for a degree in sports science. Her only goal of 2018-19 was an impressive and important one; she hit what proved to be the winner from 20 yards as Leicester won 3-2 at home to Millwall Lionesses in January.

2018-19 CHAMP

					Att	Pos
09.09	Crystal Palace (a)	W	2-0	Melissa Johnson 18, Holly Morgan 75	382	4
19.09	Tottenham H (h)	L	0-3		412	7
23.09	Lewes (a)	L	3-4	Melissa Johnson (pen) 8, 14, Fiona Worts 90	219	6
30.09	London Bees (h)	W	4-2	Rosie Axten 3, Freda Ayisi 33, Leigh Dugmore 40, Nicole Nymoen 83	174	5
14.10	Millwall L (a)	W	2-1	Rosie Axten (pen) 61, 76	163	3
21.10	Aston Villa (h)	D	1-1	Rosie Axten (pen) 43	315	4
04.11	Sheffield United (a)	L	0-1		458	5
25.11	Durham (a)	W	2-0	Nicole Nymoen 6, Serena Fletcher 18, *Leicester City W GK Demi Lambourne saved pen 77*	278	5
02.12	Charlton Athletic (h)	L	0-4		240	5
09.12	London Bees (a)	L	1-2	Melissa Johnson 27	157	6
06.01	Lewes (h)	W	4-0	Melissa Johnson 41, Fiona Worts 50, 55, Lucy Johnson 89	318	5
13.01	Millwall L (h)	W	3-2	Melissa Johnson 2, *Melissa Johnson missed pen 26 (saved by Charlotte Sansom),* Libby Smith (pen) 35, Ella Franklin-Fraiture 53	286	5P
27.01	Aston Villa (a)	D	0-0		1,618	6
10.02	Crystal Palace (h)	L	2-3	Hayley James 68, Leigh Dugmore 74	478	6
13.02	Manchester United (h)	L	0-7	*Leicester GK Demi Lambourne saved Katie Zelem pen 45*	824	6
20.02	Tottenham H (a)	L	0-1		318	6
10.03	Manchester United (a)	L	1-6	Libby Smith 59	1,554	6
31.03	Sheffield United (h)	L	1-2	Hayley James 73	604	8
28.04	Durham (h)	D	1-1	Melissa Johnson 82	264	7
11.05	Charlton Athletic (a)	L	0-4		237	7

2018-19 FA CONTINENTAL TYRES LEAGUE CUP: GROUP ONE NORTH

19.08	Bristol City (h)	D	2-2 (W 4-2p)	Melissa Johnson 1, Sophie Domingo 80	294
26.08	Manchester C (a)	L	0-4		1,609
16.09	Aston Villa (h)	L	0-1	*Freda Ayisi missed pen 67 (saved by Aja Aguirre)*	312
05.12	Birmingham C (h)	L	0-6		364
12.12	Sheffield U (a)	L	1-3	Ella Franklin-Fraiture 33	234

2018-19 FA CUP

03.02 R4	London Bees (h)	L	0-2	*Rosie Axten missed pen 75*	272

2018-19 AS IT HAPPENS

27.01.19: Leicester are the opponents for Aston Villa when the Birmingham club are watched by a club record home crowd of 1,618. The Championship match takes place at Villa Park, home of Aston Villa men's and finishes 0-0.

13.02.19: A record home crowd of 824 watches Leicester's Championship match against Manchester United with the Foxes going down 7-0.

28.02.19: Natalie Johnson becomes the first Leicester City Women player to win an international cap at senior level when she comes on with 10 minutes remaining of Northern Ireland's friendly at home to Jordan. Her team – leading 4-0 at that point – go on to win 6-0.

10.03.19: Nat Johnson becomes the third current Leicester City Women player to chalk up 100 appearances for the club when she is named in the starting line-up for the 6-1 defeat away to Manchester United.

LEICESTER CITY APPEARANCES & GOALS 2018-19				CH		FAC		CC		Total	
				A	G	A	G	A	G	A	G
Axten, Rosie	F	ENG	24.09.97	19	4	1	-	3	-	23	4
Ayisi, Freda	F	ENG	21.10.94	15	1	1	-	5	-	21	1
Brown, Rachel	D	SCO	24.10.00	4	-	-	-	2	-	6	-
Clarke, Charlotte	G	ENG	21.08.00	-	-	-	-	3	-	3	-
Cusack, Maddy	M	ENG	28.10.95	7	-	-	-	3	-	10	-
Domingo, Sophie	F	ENG	07.01.00	16	-	1	-	5	1	22	1
Dugmore, Leigh	F	ENG	15.06.90	18	2	1	-	4	-	23	2
Fletcher, Serena	D	ENG	06.12.98	6	1	-	-	3	-	9	1
Franklin-Fraiture, Ella	D	ENG	15.07.97	14	1	1	-	2	1	17	2
Greengrass, Charlotte	D	ENG	10.01.00	10	-	-	-	4	-	14	-
Hudson, Natasha	M	ENG	31.05.01	4	-	1	-	1	-	6	-
Jackson, Sarah	D	ENG	n/a	17	-	-	-	2	-	19	-
James, Hayley	D	ENG	07.07.95	9	2	1	-	3	-	13	2
Jhamat, Simran	M	ENG	22.01.01	3	-	-	-	-	-	3	-
Johnson, Lucy	D	ENG	06.01.02	8	1	-	-	1	-	9	1
Johnson, Melissa	F	ENG	11.08.91	19	7	-	-	5	1	24	8
Johnson, Natalie	M	ENG	12.11.93	19	-	1	-	2	-	22	-
Lambourne, Demi	G	ENG	30.04.96	20	-	1	-	2	-	23	-
McCue, Sherry	M	ENG	16.09.94	9	-	-	-	5	-	14	-
Moncaster, Mai	M	ENG	14.08.01	6	-	1	-	1	-	8	-
Morgan, Holly	D	ENG	10.02.93	18	1	1	-	4	-	23	1
Nymoen, Nicole	M	ENG	04.06.91	12	2	1	-	2	-	15	2
Oliver, Taome	M	ENG	11.05.96	1	-	-	-	1	-	2	-
Smith, Libby	F	ENG	03.11.01	11	2	1	-	1	-	13	2
Thomas, Freya	M	ENG	n/a	6	-	-	-	1	-	7	-
Worts, Fiona	F	ENG	n/	6	3	1	-	4	-	11	3

LEWES 

FOUNDED: 2002 NICKNAME: THE ROOKETTES 2019-20: CHAMPIONSHIP (TIER 2)

Honours:	No.	Competition name & year(s)
Tier 3 / 4 Plate Winners	1	WPL Plate: 2017
Tier 4 Champions (Regional)	1	South East Combination: 2012
Tier 4 League Cup Winners (Regional)	1	South East Combination League Cup: 2012

Lewes FC are much admired for their equal pay policy, introduced in the summer of 2017. It's believed they remain the only professional or semi-professional club in world football to award the same salary budget to their men's and women's teams. Admittedly they are perhaps aided in implementing the policy by the fact that their women play in Tier 2 and their men in Tier 7.

In February 2019 midfielder Shannon Moloney was the face of the club's campaign calling on the FA to look at redistributing the prize money disparity between the men's and women's FA Cup competitions, with the men's prize fund in 2018-19 standing at £30.25m compared to £250,000 for the women.

As well as their hard work off the pitch, they have made great strides on it in recent seasons. Having finished 5th in what was then known as the WPL Southern Premier in 2017-18 they found themselves elevated to the inaugural Championship when their application for a Tier 2 licence was accepted. They hit the ground running, with three consecutive wins over Millwall Lionesses, Crystal Palace and Leicester City Women. There then followed a run of 11 League games without a win, in the middle of which manager John Donoghue left after four years in charge.

His replacement was Spaniard Fran Alonso who had previously worked as an assistant coach under current Netherlands men's team boss Ronald Koeman at men's Premier League sides Everton and Southampton, and under Mauricio Pochettino at the Saints.

Alonso is also a former manager of Liverpool Feds Ladies but taking charge of Lewes was by far his highest-level managerial job so far. Following his arrival, Lewes won two and drew one of their remaining nine Championship fixtures and finished two places off the bottom of the table. Despite mixed results they attracted sizeable and lively crowds to their home ground at the Dripping Pan throughout the season.

Alonso told The Women's Football Yearbook: "The main achievement in 2018-19 was that we were able to implement our style, give the players a clearer picture on how to organise ourselves around the ball and make them familiar with our tactical concepts. We decided to look at the division as though two teams would be relegated from it and set out to achieve a points' target that would have kept us in the division if that was happening. We achieved our target.

"In 2019-20 we want to build on our achievements and play better football, that's our priority. We are building a well-balanced squad that is hungry for wins. We will be focusing on one game at a time, with the aim of winning every single one of them. Then in the last two months of competition we will see if we are in a position to fight for something or not."

WSL ERA FINAL LEAGUE POSITIONS

SEASON	2011	2012	2013	2014	2015	2016	2017	2018	2019
TIER	T4	T4	T3	T3	T3	T3	T3	T3	T2
POSITION	3/12	1/12	5/10	6 /11	7/12	7/12	7/11	5/12	9/11

2018-19 REVIEW

League:	Championship (Tier 2): 9th		
FA Cup:	4th Round	**Stadium:**	The Dripping Pan, (Lewes FC)
Conti Cup:	Group	**Managers:**	Jonathan Donoghue (Jun 2014-Nov 2018) Fran Alonso (since Dec 2018)

KATE McINTYRE IN ACTION FOR LEWES AGAINST MANCHESTER UNITED

James Boyes

2018-19 STAR PERFORMER – KATE McINTYRE

What's in a name? Lewes captain McIntyre is often referred to as Katie, but she insists to The Women's Football Yearbook that she prefers Kate. Most people call her Macca anyway, a nickname which perhaps better encapsulates the grit and determination with which she approaches every game. She played in every fixture of 2018-19 – all 20 Championship matches, all four Continental Cup matches, and Lewes' sole FA Cup tie. The central midfielder is a set-piece specialist and is also highly regarded for her accurate distribution across both short and long distances. McIntyre, who turned 32 in March 2019, has previously played for Fulham when they were in the top-flight and Lewes' Sussex rivals Brighton.

2018-19 CHAMP

					Att	Pos
09.09	Millwall L (a)	W	3-0	Samantha Quayle 3, Rebecca Carter 24, Avilla Bergin 45+1	153	2
19.09	Crystal Palace (h)	W	2-1	Avilla Bergin 48, Shannon Moloney 51	304	1
23.09	Leicester City W (h)	W	4-3	Rebecca Carter 32, 70, 76, Samantha Quayle 83	219	2
30.09	Charlton A (a)	L	1-4	Avilla Bergin (pen) 78	184	3
14.10	Tottenham H (h)	L	1-3	Sarah Kempson 14, *Avilla Bergin missed pen (saved by Chloe Morgan) 45+3*	714	4
21.10	London Bees (a)	L	2-3	Samantha Quayle 17, Sarah Kempson 26	182	6
04.11	Durham (a)	L	0-5		417	7
18.11	Aston Villa (h)	D	1-1	Sarah Kempson 72	536	6
25.11	Sheffield Utd (a)	L	2-3	Ellie Gilliatt (og) 34, Rebecca Carter 75	473	8
02.12	Manchester Utd (h)	L	0-2	*Lewes GK Faye Baker saved pen 80 (Manchester Utd scored rebound)*	1,958	8
09.12	Charlton A (h)	L	0-2		330	9
06.01	Leicester City W (a)	L	0-4		318	9
13.01	Tottenham H (a)	L	0-3		320	9
27.01	London Bees (h)	L	0-2		512	9
21.02	Crystal Palace (a)	W	3-0	Sarah Kempson (pen) 7, Jessica King 68, Katie Rood (pen) 84	786	9
17.03	Millwall L (h)	W	2-0	Jessica King 7, Charlotte Owen 87	404	9
31.03	Durham (h)	L	0-1		344	9
21.04	Aston Villa (a)	D	2-2	Katie Rood 45, 90+2	323	
28.04	Sheffield Utd (h)	L	0-3		543	9
11.05	Manchester U (a)	L	0-5		3,702	9

2018-19 FA CONTINENTAL TYRES LEAGUE CUP: GROUP TWO SOUTH

19.08	Charlton A (h)	W	5-0	Avilla Bergin (pen) 11, 44, Danielle Lane 22, Rebecca Carter 86, 90+1	205
26.08	West Ham Utd (a)	L	1-4	Danielle Lane 8	255
16.09	Arsenal (h)	L	0-9		945
05.12	Millwall L (a)	W	2-0	Rebecca Carter 68, Samantha Quayle 78	143

2018-19 FA CUP

03.02 R4	Millwall L (a)		P-P		
10.02 R4	Millwall L (a)	L	0-1	*Amy Taylor sent off 84*	326

2018-19 AS IT HAPPENS

14.12.18: Championship outfit Lewes name former Liverpool Feds Ladies boss Fran Alonso as their new manager. The 42-year-old Spaniard previously worked under Mauricio Pochettino at Southampton men and then Ronald Koeman at Southampton and Everton men. Lewes have been without a manager since sacking Jonathan Donoghue in mid-November.

19.01.19: Long-time servant of the club and fans' favourite Tash Wells announces her departure. The defender was with the Rookettes throughout their rise from the WPL to the Championship and fought back to fitness after missing most of 2017 through injury.

01.03.19: "Hardest decision I've had to make" writes midfielder Vicky Carleton on twitter as she announces she is leaving the club to return home to Northern Ireland in order "to find my happiness and love for the game again."

20.04.19: Lewes confirm the signing of striker Rachel Panting from Tier 3 Portsmouth. Panting has scored 14 goals in 22 appearances for Pompey this season.

LEWES APPEARANCES & GOALS 2018-19

				CH		FAC		CC		Total	
				A	G	A	G	A	G	A	G
Baker, Faye	G	ENG	10.06.90	16	-	1	-	4	-	21	-
Bergin, Avilla	M	NIR	01.08.91	9	3	1	-	2	2	12	5
Boswell, Charley	F	ENG	26.11.90	18	-	-	-	2	-	20	-
Bridge, Hayley	M	ENG	29.01.97	1	-	-	-	-	-	1	-
Carleton, Victoria	M	NIR	08.02.97	11	-	-	-	4	-	15	-
Carter, Rebecca	F	ENG	24.04.91	14	5	-	-	4	3	18	8
Kempson, Sarah	M	ENG	06.11.90	19	4	1	-	-	-	20	4
King, Jess	F	ENG	31.05.92	7	2	1	-	-	-	8	2
Lane, Danielle	M	ENG	09.08.93	19	-	-	-	4	2	23	2
Larkin, Kellie	M	ENG	07.02.97	1	-	-	-	2	-	3	-
McIntyre, Kate	M	ENG	10.03.87	20	-	1	-	3	-	24	-
Moloney, Shannon	M	IRE	24.11.88	11	1	-	-	4	-	15	1
Newman, Ella	D	ENG	15.12.00	1	-	-	-	-	-	1	-
O'Rourke, Sophie	M	ENG	03.06.99	11	-	1	-	1	-	13	-
Owen, Charlotte	F	ENG	23.11.95	5	1	-	-	4	-	9	1
Panting, Rachel	F	ENG	08.08.91	3	-	-	-	-	-	3	-
Paye, Rosie	D	ENG	30.05.96	8	-	1	-	3	-	12	-
Perry, Sophie	D	IRE	11.11.86	3	-	1	-	-	-	4	-
Quayle, Samantha	M	WAL	08.10.95	20	3	1	-	4	1	25	4
Robert, Georgia	D	ENG	06.06.95	8	-	1	-	1	-	10	-
Rood, Katie	F	NZL	02.09.92	7	3	1	-	-	-	8	3
Rowbotham, Ava	D	ENG	26.03.00	2	-	-	-	-	-	2	-
Rutherford, Leeta	M	ENG	14.12.87	20	-	1	-	3	-	24	-
Taylor, Amy	D	ENG	25.04.92	11	-	1	-	4	-	16	-
Thompson-Agbro, Rebecca	D	ENG	20.03.91	9	-	-	-	4	-	13	-
Wells, Natasha	D	ENG	07.09.86	11	-	-	-	3	-	14	-
Wilson, Nina	G	ENG	10.06.99	6	-	-	-	-	-	6	-

LONDON BEES

FOUNDED: 1975 (AS DISTRICT LINE LADIES) **NICKNAME: BEES** **2019-20: CHAMPIONSHIP (TIER 2)**

Former Names:

District Line (1975-1993)

Wembley (1993-1998)

Barnet (1998-2013)

Honours:	No.	Competition name & year(s)
FA Cup Runners-up	1	1997 (as Wembley)
English League Cup Winners	1	WPL Cup: 1996 (as Wembley)
Tier 2 / 3 League Cup Winners	1	WPL Cup: 2011 (as Barnet)
Tier 2 Champions (Regional)	2	WPL Southern: 1993 (as District Line), 2010 (as Barnet)
Tier 2 Runners-up (Regional)	1	WPL Southern: 2009 (as Barnet)

London Bees saw many changes during 2018-19, with manager Luke Swindlehurst leaving to take up a role in Barnet's boy's academy in February. He had been in charge for 19 months. His penultimate match saw the club win an FA Cup match for the first time under the London Bees name, beating fellow Championship outfit Leicester City Women 2-0 away.

Swindlehurst's successor was legendary former England winger Rachel Yankey – who had joined the club's coaching staff in June 2018. She stepped up to the position of head coach on a short-term deal, taking on her first managerial role.

Yankey, who won 129 caps for England, oversaw five League games but her team were unable to pick up any points in those fixtures, as they went on to finish 8th in Tier 2. Over the entire season, Bees did not draw any of their 20 League games, but did enjoy seven wins, including a double over Lewes and an away triumph at Aston Villa in November. In May, former Arsenal star Yankey – who also represented Great Britain at the 2012 Olympics – said she had turned down an offer to remain in charge of the Bees for 2019-20 and left the North London club.

The Bees are an independent entity but do have ties with Barnet FC's men's side, with whom they share their training facilities and home ground at The Hive. They were known as Barnet between 1998-2013 before becoming London Bees when their licence to join WSL 2 ahead of the competition's first season in 2014 was accepted. They have played in Tier 2 ever since with a highest finish of 6th under Swindlehurst in 2018.

The club started out as District Line Ladies in 1975 when they were formed by London Underground employees. They became Wembley FC in 1993 and reached the FA Cup final under that name in 1997 when they were beaten 1-0 by Millwall Lionesses at Upton Park.

WSL ERA FINAL LEAGUE POSITIONS (SS = SPRING SERIES)

SEASON	2011	2012	2013	2014	2015	2016	2017ss	2018	2019
TIER	T2	T2	T2	T2	T2	T2	T2	T2	T2
POSITION	5/8	4/10	10/10	10/10	8/10	7/10	7/10	6/10	8/11

2018-19 REVIEW

League:	Championship (Tier 2): 8th		
FA Cup:	5th Round	**Stadium:**	The Hive, (Barnet FC)
Conti Cup:	Group	**Managers:**	Luke Swindlehurst (Jul 2017-Feb 2019) Rachel Yankey (Feb-May 2019)

2018-19 STAR PERFORMER – SARAH QUANTRILL

Goalkeeper Sarah Quantrill became London Bees' first signing of the summer 2018 transfer window when she crossed the capital from Millwall Lionesses. She went on to have a fine season between the sticks. A WSL title winner with Liverpool in 2013, she was brought to The Hive by Luke Swindlehurst who had been part of the coaching staff during her days with the Reds. The former Chelsea shot stopper was a commanding presence behind the Bees defence throughout the 2018-19 campaign.

2018-19 CHAMP					Att	Pos
09.09	Tottenham H (a)	L	1-2	Paula Howells 22	362	7
19.09	Millwall L (h)	W	2-1	Emma Beckett 1, Lauren Pickett 87	224	6
23.09	Manchester Utd (h)	L	0-5		642	7
30.09	Leicester City W (a)	L	2-4	Ruesha Littlejohn (pen) 45+5, 70	174	8
14.10	Crystal Palace (a)	L	0-1	*London Bees GK Sarah Quantrill saved pen 60*	148	9
21.10	Lewes (h)	W	3-2	Emma Beckett 11, 43, Tricia Gould 62	182	7
28.10	Durham (h)	L	0-1		107	8
04.11	Charlton Athletic (a)	L	0-2		208	8
18.11	Sheffield Utd (h)	W	2-0	Ruesha Littlejohn 55, Nicola Gibson 76	192	8
24.11	Aston Villa (a)	W	3-1	Merrick Will 43, Rachel Unitt 57, Destiney Toussaint 86	345	7
09.12	Leicester City W (h)	W	2-1	Emma Beckett 52, Katie Wilkinson 70	157	5
06.01	Manchester United (a)	L	0-9		1,889	6
13.01	Crystal Palace (h)	W	2-1	Katie Wilkinson 6, Lauren Pickett 24	183	6
27.01	Lewes (a)	W	2-0	Brooke Nunn 64, Ruesha Littlejohn 67	512	5
10.02	Tottenham H (h)	L	0-3		387	5
20.02	Millwall L (a)	L	1-3	Daisy McLachlan 8	243	5
10.03	Durham (a)	L	0-1		353	5
31.03	Charlton Athletic (h)	L	1-2	Lauren Pickett 90	301	6
20.04	Sheffield United (a)	L	1-4	Ruesha Littlejohn 50	361	6
28.04	Aston Villa (h)	L	1-5	Daisy McLachlan 66	266	8

BEES CELEBRATE A GOAL IN THE FA CUP WIN OVER LEICESTER CITY

2018-19 FA CONTINENTAL TYRES LEAGUE CUP: GROUP ONE SOUTH

19.08	Yeovil Town (h)	D	1-1 (W 5-3p)	Ellie Wilson 28	246
26.08	Chelsea (h)	L	1-6	Lauren Pickett 44, (*Bees GK Sarah Quantrill saved Drew Spence pen 81, Chelsea scored rebound)*	374
16.09	Brighton & H A (a)	L	1-3	Paula Howells 22	171
05.12	Tottenham H (h)	W	4-2	Anne-Laure Davey 45+2, 47, Katie Wilkinson 64, Connie Forman 85	146
13.12	Crystal Palace (a)	L	2-7	Lauren Pickett 15, Anne-Laure Davey 21	146

2018-19 FA CUP

03.02 R4	Leicester City W (a)	W	2-0	Katie Wilkinson 8, Ruesha Littlejohn 59	272
17.02 R5	Manchester U (a)*	L	0-3		838

*Played at Ewen Fields, (Hyde FC)

2018-19 AS IT HAPPENS

19.08.18: Paula Howells makes her 100th appearance for London Bees at the age of only 21 when she faces Yeovil in a Continental Cup group stage tie which Bees win 5-3 on penalties after a 1-1 draw.

03.02.19: London Bees win 2-0 away to fellow Championship side Leicester City Women in the FA Cup 4th Round – it's their first win in the competition since rebranding as London Bees in 2014.

16.02.19: Manager Luke Swindlehurst stands down to take up the role of Under-18s academy coach at Barnet FC. It's announced that his assistant Rachel Yankey will take over until the end of the season. In her playing days Yankey won 129 caps for England. Her first match in charge of Bees comes the following day when her former Lionesses team-mate Casey Stoney is the opposing manager. Manchester United win the FA Cup 5th Round match 3-0. Rachel Unitt, who also played for England alongside Yankey and Stoney, is an unused substitute for Bees.

11.05.19: Having taken over in February, Rachel Yankey leaves her post as head coach saying she turned down the opportunity to sign an extended deal.

LONDONS BEES APPEARANCES & GOALS 2018-19

				CH		FAC		CC		Total	
				A	G	A	G	A	G	A	G
Beckett, Emma	M	IRE	29.05.87	11	4	-	-	5	-	16	4
Davy, Anne-Laure	F	FRA	30.01.92	10	-	-	-	5	2	15	2
Dench, Mollie	D	NIR	21.07.01	6	-	1	-	2	-	9	-
Forman, Connie	F	ENG	n/a	13	-	-	-	2	1	15	1
Gibson, Nicola	M	ENG	05.05.93	16	1	-	-	-	-	16	1
Gibson, Kelsey	M	SCO	02.04.01	4	-	1	-	3	-	8	-
Gould, Tricia	F	ENG	09.12.93	7	1	2	-	3	-	12	1
Howells, Paula	M	ENG	22.03.97	4	1	-	-	3	1	7	2
Johnson, Annabel	D	ENG	20.10.93	20	-	2	-	5	-	27	-
Lane, Rosanna	D	ENG	04.06.94	5	-	-	-	2	-	7	-
Lea, Danielle	D	ENG	10.08.94	3	-	-	-	1	-	4	-
Littlejohn, Ruesha	F	IRE	03.07.90	17	5	2	1	5	-	24	6
Loomes, Lucy	F	ENG	18.05.97	3	-	-	-	-	-	3	-
McLachlan, Daisy	M	ENG	n/a	6	2	-	-	-	-	6	2
Nunn, Brooke	M	ENG	04.02.93	10	1	2	-	2	-	14	1
O'Leary, Taylor	M	ENG	11.07.94	10	-	2	-	1	-	13	-
Pickett, Lauren	M	ENG	n/a	20	3	2	-	5	1	27	4
Quantrill, Sarah	G	ENG	21.07.90	20	-	2	-	5	-	27	-
Rolandsen, Ocean	D	ENG	31.01.98	18	-	2	-	4	-	24	-
Toussaint, Destiney	F	ENG	05.12.89	17	1	1	-	2	-	20	1
Unitt, Rachel	D	ENG	05.06.82	5	1	1	-	1	-	7	1
Wheeler, Hannah	D	ENG	14.11.97	5	-	2	-	-	-	7	-
Will, Merrick	M	ENG	21.12.96	18	1	2	-	5	-	25	1
Wilkinson, Katie	F	ENG	05.11.94	13	2	2	1	5	1	20	4
Wilson, Ellie	D	ENG	11.05.97	13	-	2	-	3	1	18	1

LONDON CITY LIONESSES

FOUNDED: 2019 **NICKNAME: THE LIONESSES**

At the end of 2018-19 the FA granted permission for the Championship licence held by Millwall Lionesses to be transferred to a new entity, a club called London City Lionesses. In practical terms this meant that the board and senior management of Millwall FC's women's team were breaking away to run the team on an independent basis under a new name.

Millwall FC – who had become the first men's club to officially partner with a women's club when they adopted Millwall Lionesses back in the 1980s – released a statement spelling out their disappointment at the decision: "Millwall FC regrets to announce that the board of directors and senior management at Millwall Lionesses have decided to become an independent entity from the end of this current campaign. This will mean the start of a new club, London City Lionesses; while Millwall Lionesses will go on to operate through Millwall Community Trust with its proud history and tradition intact."

With London City Lionesses taking their place in the Championship, the 'new' Millwall Lionesses were required to start life in 2019-20 in Tier 6. The London City Lionesses' directors initially stressed they considered the history of Millwall Lionesses – a club which won the FA Cup in 1991 and the FA Cup and WPL Cup 'Double' in 1997 – to be theirs, with a statement reading: "The management are not forming a new team, the Millwall Lionesses Football Club, which is a distinct legal entity from Millwall FC, has decided to move on from Millwall. They are renaming themselves London City Lionesses. It will take with it its own heritage of 48 years, including that part of their history that they affiliated with Millwall FC."

However, all those connected with Millwall FC and Millwall Lionesses insist they retain the heart, soul, history and honours of the original club. There was deep sadness and some anger at the breakaway given that it came just a year after Millwall supporters had helped raise money to keep the women's team alive as a Tier 2 club.

The 2018-19 campaign was a hugely difficult one in which Millwall Lionesses won just one of their 20 League matches while losing 17 and scoring less than a goal per game. Unsurprisingly, that form saw them finish bottom of the Championship, six points adrift of 10th-placed Crystal Palace, but Millwall were not relegated because the FA had confirmed before the start of the season that no teams would go down to the WNL.

The season was in stark contrast to their campaign of 2017-18, when – despite their financial difficulties – they finished 3rd in the final season that Tier 2 was known as WSL 2 under manager Lee Burch, before he left the club to take a job in the top-flight with Yeovil Town.

In the summer of 2018 former Arsenal Women boss Pedro Martinez Losa arrived at Millwall Lionesses as director of football, with Chris Phillips as manager, and local businesswoman Diane Culligan appointed chair. Losa left the club in the summer of 2019.

At the time of this book's publishing deadlines there was still some dispute over whether London City Lionesses or the 'new' Millwall Lionesses retain the history of the original club.

For the moment at least, we have taken the view that London City Lionesses is a new club formed in 2019 with Millwall Lionesses retaining the history and honours. However, for our readers' interest we have included the honours won by Millwall Lionesses, and their 2018-19 results, in these pages.

2018-19 MILLWALL LIONESSES REVIEW

League:	Championship (Tier 2): 11th		
FA Cup:	5th Round	**Stadium:**	Princes Park, (Dartford FC)
Conti Cup:	Group	**Manager:**	Chris Phillips (since Jul 2018)

MILLWALL LIONESSES HONOURS

Honours:	No.	Competition name & year(s)
FA Cup Winners	2	1991, 1997
English League Cup Winners	1	WPL Cup: 1997
English League Cup Runners-up	1	WPL Cup: 1992
Tier 2 Champions (Regional)	1	WPL Southern: 2009
Tier 2 Runners-up (Regional)	1	WPL Southern: 2008
Tier 3 Runners-up (Regional)	1	WPL Southern: 2013

2018-19 MILLWALL LIONESSES STAR PERFORMER – EVIE CLARKE

Netting six times in the League, forward Evie Clarke scored almost half of the club's 14 Championship goals in 2018-19. In February she hit a stunning brace, including an overhead kick, against her former club London Bees to help Millwall to their only League win of the season. The 5ft 4in striker can also play on the wing. A former Arsenal youth player, she was part of the Gunners squad that won the Continental Cup in 2015 although she wasn't involved in the final.

2018-19 CHAMP					Att	Pos
09.09	Lewes (h)	L	0-3		153	10
19.09	London Bees (a)	L	1-2	Lia Cataldo 41	224	9
23.09	Crystal Palace (h)	D	1-1	Gabby Ravenscroft 60	117	10
14.10	Leicester City W (h)	L	1-2	Beth Lumsden 20	163	10
21.10	Tottenham H (a)	L	0-8		295	11
28.10	Charlton Athletic (h)	L	0-8		154	11
04.11	Aston Villa (a)	L	0-2		284	11
18.11	Durham (h)	L	1-5	Evie Clarke 5	154	11

25.11	Manchester Utd (a)	L	0-8		1,467	11
02.12	Sheffield Utd (h)	D	1-1	Ylenia Priest 37	288	11
05.01	Crystal Palace (a)	L	1-3	Gabby Ravenscroft 53	366	11
13.01	Leicester City W (a)	L	2-3	Evie Clarke 30, (pen) 75, *Ellie Bailes sent off 90*	286	11
27.01	Tottenham H (h)	L	2-3	Evie Clarke 44, Beth Lumsden 90+1	426	11
20.02	London Bees (h)	W	3-1	Annie Rossiter 42, Evie Clarke 70, 78	243	11
13.03	Charlton Athletic (a)	L	0-3		638	11
17.03	Lewes (a)	L	0-2		404	11
31.03	Aston Villa (h)	L	1-3	Alice Hassall (og) 21	296	11
21.04	Durham (a)	L	0-1		355	11
28.04	Manchester Utd (h)	L	0-5		1,920	11
11.05	Sheffield Utd (a)	L	0-6	*Chantelle Mackie sent off 36*	1,010	11

2018-19 FA CONTINENTAL TYRES LEAGUE CUP: GROUP TWO SOUTH

26.08	Charlton A (a)	L	2-4	Gabby Ravenscroft 39, Evie Clarke 44	204
16.09	West Ham Utd (a)	L	0-4		557
05.12	Lewes (h)	L	0-2		143
12.12	Arsenal (h)	L	1-3	Gabby Ravenscroft 32	463

2018-19 FA CUP

03.02 R4	Lewes (h)		P-P		
10.02 R4	Lewes (h)	W	1-0	Grace Neville 90+1	326
17.02 R5	Liverpool (a)	L	0-2		412

2018-19 MILLWALL LIONESSES SEASON AS IT HAPPENS

10.02.19: Grace Neville's injury-time winner gives Millwall their first victory of the season in all competitions as they beat fellow Championship side Lewes 1-0 in the FA Cup 4th Round. Lewes have Amy Taylor sent off with six minutes remaining.

20.02.19: Millwall get their first League win of the season at the 14th attempt as they beat London Bees 3-1 thanks to a goal from Annie Rossiter and a brace from Evie Clarke.

28.04.19: A 5-0 home defeat to newly crowned champions Manchester United confirms that Millwall Lionesses will finish bottom of the Championship, however there will be no relegation this season.

13.05.19: Men's club Millwall FC announce that Millwall Lionesses have decided to break away from them and to continue under a new name – London City Lionesses. Millwall FC will continue a girls' and women's football programme as part of their community trust.

LEFT: EVIE CLARKE PREVIOUSLY PLAYED FOR ARSENAL

LIONESSES PLAYER APPEARANCES & GOALS 2018-19

				CH		FAC		CC		Total	
				A	G	A	G	A	**G**	**A**	**G**
Ali, Fran	M	ENG	09.03.93	10	-	1	-	1	-	12	-
Auguste, Jasmine	D	ENG	04.10.93	5	-	-	-	2	-	7	-
Bailes, Freya	M	ENG	13.09.00	10	-	2	-	4	-	16	-
Bailey, Eden	M	ENG	n/a	3	-	-	-	2	-	5	-
Casley, Riva	D	ENG	27.01.99	10	-	-	-	1	-	11	-
Cataldo, Lia	M	ENG	11.02.01	18	1	2	-	3	-	23	1
Charles, Asanteni	D	ENG	16.12.97	4	-	-	-	-	-	4	-
Clarke, Evie	F	ENG	17.10.97	20	6	2	-	4	1	26	7
Cowan, Leanne	D	ENG	01.02.96	11	-	2	-	3	-	16	-
Fitzgerald, Lucy	F	ENG	29.12.00	20	-	2	-	4	-	26	-
Giddings, Georgina	M	ENG	30.06.90	13	-	1	-	3	-	17	-
Guzowska, Sara	F	POL	07.04.02	1	-	-	-	-	-	1	-
Harford, Beth	F	ENG	16.09.99	5	-	2	-	1	-	8	-
Lumsden, Beth	F	ENG	n/a	15	3	2	-	2	-	19	3
Mackie, Chantelle	D	ENG	11.05.95	11	-	1	-	1	-	13	-
Neville, Grace	D	ENG	09.04.00	9	-	2	1	-	-	11	1
Peart, Kalani	D	ENG	16.07.99	3	-	-	-	1	-	4	-
Powell, Beth	D	ENG	17.01.99	9	-	-	-	2	-	11	-
Priest, Ylenia	D	ENG	23.10.01	20	1	2	-	4	-	26	1
Ravenscroft, Gabby	F	ENG	10.10.00	15	2	-	-	3	2	18	4
Robert, Georgia	M	ENG	n/a	2	-	-	-	-	-	2	-
Rossiter, Annie	F	ENG	05.09.01	18	1	2	-	4	-	24	1
Sansom, Chloe	G	ENG	17.10.96	12	-	2	-	3	-	17	-
Stenning, Ellie	M	ENG	09.04.91	6	-	-	-	2	-	8	-
Stewart, Rhiannon	G	ENG	n/a	6	-	-	-	-	-	6	-
Stovold, Sofia	M	ENG	n/a	1	-	-	-	-	-	1	-
Taylor, Grace	G	ENG	15.09.99	2	-	-	-	1	-	3	-
Young, Michelle	M	ENG	13.12.91	13	-	2	-	3	-	18	-

SHEFFIELD UNITED

FOUNDED: 1998 (AS SHEFFIELD UNITED COMMUNITY)

Former Names:

Sheffield United Community (1998-2016)

NICKNAME: THE BLADES

2019-20: CHAMPIONSHIP (TIER 2)

Honours:	No.	Competition name & year(s)
Tier 4 Champions (Regional)	1	2006 (as Sheffield United Community)
Tier 5 Champions (Regional)	2	2xEast Midlands Premier League: 2012 (as Sheffield United Community), 2017
Tier 4 League Cup Winners (Regional)	1	2006 (as Sheffield United Community)
Tier 5 League Cup Winners (Regional)	1	2012 (as Sheffield United Community)

Sheffield United finished 3rd in Tier 4 in 2017-18 but were promoted through two divisions that summer when their bid for a licence for the new Championship proved successful. They acquitted themselves well in their first Tier 2 season with a particularly strong end to 2018-19, when they won their final seven games in a row, helping them claim a 5th place finish.

It's been a rapid rise to the elite end of the game given that United were playing in Tier 5 as recently as 2016-17. They have proved to the authorities that they have the resources and financial backing to support part-time football at this level and their close links with the men's club – who were promoted to the Premier League at the end of 2018-19 – have no doubt played a part.

In the summer of 2018 United were among a growing number of clubs to change their name from Ladies to Women, a decision they said, "reflected the club's position as an emerging presence within the women's game" and described as being "representative of a modern view on language and equality".

Former Lincoln Ladies midfielder Carla Ward joined the club as assistant manager in November 2017 before stepping up to replace Dan O'Hearne as manager in 2018. Ward was named as the FA/LMA Championship Manager of the Month for March 2019 thanks to taking nine points from a possible nine as that brilliant end to the campaign gathered pace.

England defender Millie Bright and goalkeeper Ellie Roebuck are among the products of the club's youth pathway and their well-respected Regional Talent Club looks set to help the club thrive in the coming seasons.

Legendary Sheffield United men's player Tony Currie founded the club's girls' team which first entered the South Yorkshire League in 1998. The opportunity to play senior women's football arose in 2002 when local side Sheffield Inter looked set to fold and were taken over by Sheffield United who claimed their place in the East Midlands Premier League. The club was known as Sheffield United Community Ladies until being granted permission to change their name to Sheffield United Ladies in 2016.

WSL ERA FINAL LEAGUE POSITIONS

SEASON	2011	2012	2013	2014	2015	2016	2017	2018	2019
TIER	T5	T5	T4	T4	T4	T5	T5	T4	T2
POSITION	3/11	1/12	5/12	10/12	12/12	5/12	1/11	3/12	5/11

2018-19 REVIEW

League:	Championship (Tier 2): 5th		
FA Cup:	5th Round	**Stadium:**	Sheffield Olympic Legacy Park
Conti Cup:	Group	**Manager:**	Carla Ward (since Jan 2018)

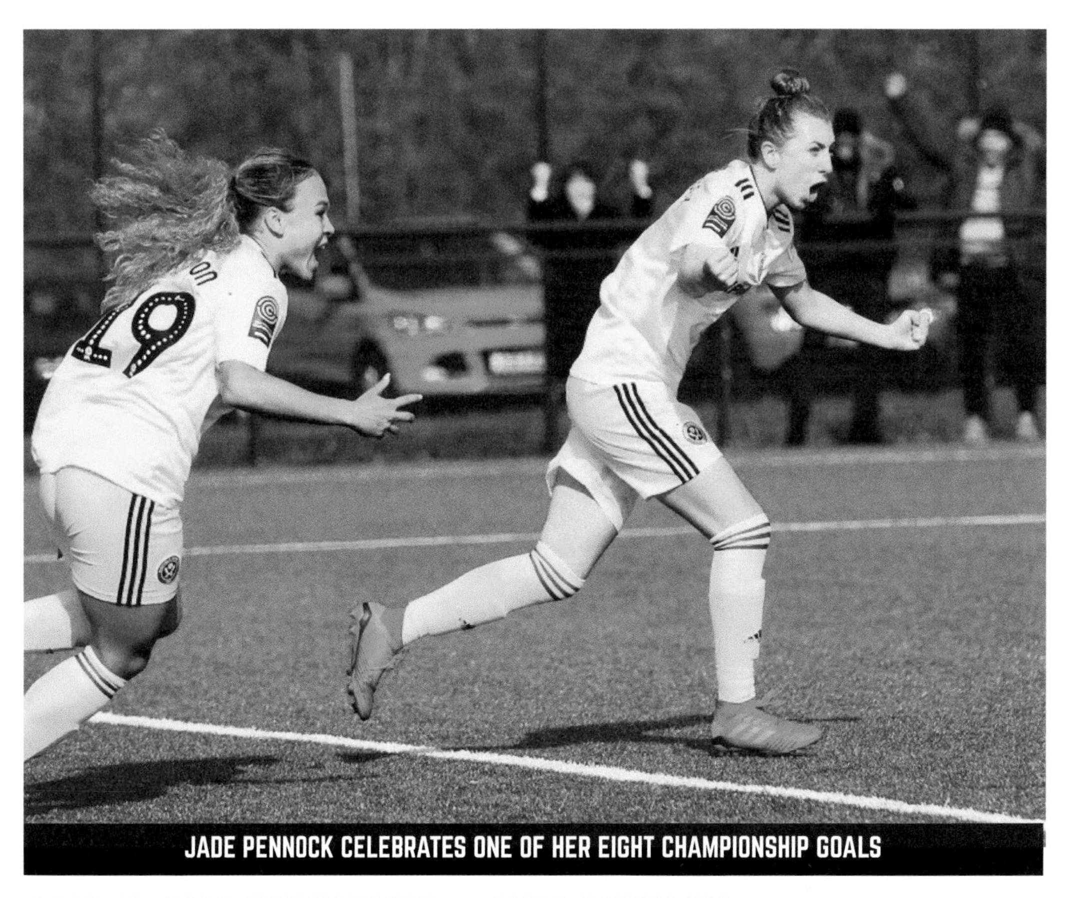

JADE PENNOCK CELEBRATES ONE OF HER EIGHT CHAMPIONSHIP GOALS

2018-19 STAR PERFORMER – JADE PENNOCK

Former Leeds United and Doncaster Rovers Belles midfielder Jade Pennock ended the campaign as the Blades' top scorer in the League with eight goals in 20 Championship appearances. Seven of her goals came in the club's seven-match winning streak at the end of the season. Her development was aided by six years spent studying and playing in the US. She graduated from the University of Montevallo in Alabama with a Bachelor of Science degree in Kinesiology. Away from the pitch she works in sports development and coaching at Leeds City College.

2018-19 CHAMP					Att	Pos
08.09	Durham (h)*	L	0-2		412	9
20.09	Manchester Utd (a)	L	0-3		2,003	10
23.09	Tottenham H (a)		P-P			10
30.09	Aston Villa (h)	W	4-1	Sophie Jones 4, 51, 74, Alethea Paul (pen) 35	804	7
21.10	Charlton Athletic (a)	L	0-2	*Sam Tierney sent off 70*	214	9
28.10	Crystal Palace (a)	W	1-0	Jade Pennock 35	208	7
04.11	Leicester City W (h)	W	1-0	Bex Rayner 83	458	6
18.11	London Bees (a)	L	0-2		192	7
25.11	Lewes (h)	W	3-2	Izzy Ford 17, Sophie Barker 66, Sophie Jones 80	473	6
02.12	Millwall L (a)	D	1-1	Sophie Jones 56	288	6
09.12	Aston Villa (a)	L	1-5	Sophie Jones (pen) 51	249	7
06.01	Tottenham H (h)	L	1-2	Jenna Schillaci (og) 6	470	7
27.01	Charlton A (h)	L	2-3	Bex Rayner 64, Ebony Salmon (pen) 90	320	8
20.02	Manchester Utd (h)	L	0-4		1,008	8
10.03	Crystal Palace (h)	W	2-0	Jade Pennock 69, Ebony Salmon 71	434	8
24.03	Tottenham H (a)	W	2-1	Ebony Salmon 64, Jade Pennock 90	502	7
31.03	Leicester City W (a)	W	2-1	Ellie Gilliatt 76, Jade Pennock 90	604	5
14.04	Durham (a)	W	2-1	Danielle Cox 16, Jade Pennock 69	359	5
20.04	London Bees (h)	W	4-1	Danielle Cox 36, Veatriki Sarri 52, Bex Rayner 76, Jade Pennock 88	361	5
28.04	Lewes (a)	W	3-0	Ebony Salmon 16, 60, Danielle Cox 35	543	5
11.05	Millwall L (h)+	W	6-0	Ellie Gilliatt 11, Bex Rayner 17, Ebony Salmon (pen) 37, 62, Jade Pennock 58, 84	1,010	5

*Played at Stocksbridge Park Steels +Played at Bramall Lane, (Sheffield United FC)

2018-19 FA CONTINENTAL TYRES LEAGUE CUP: GROUP ONE NORTH					
18.08	Aston Villa (a)	W	2-1	Danielle Cox 40, Tania Marsden 85	251
26.08	Bristol City (a)	L	1-3	Jade Pennock 11	156
16.09	Bir'ham City (h)	L	0-2		331
05.12	Manchester C (a)	L	0-6		1,079
12.12	Leicester City W (h)	W	3-1	Sophie Jones 7, Chloe Dixon 8, Danielle Cox 19	234

2018-19 FA CUP					
03.02 R4	Loughborough F (a)		P-P		
10.02 R4	Loughborough F (a)	W	2-0	Alethea Paul 14, Veatriki Sarri 54	202
17.02 R5	Aston Villa (a)	D	3-3aet (L3-5p)	Maddy Cusack 27, Ebony Salmon 59, Bex Rayner 84	252

2018-19 AS IT HAPPENS

05.12.18: Debate rages about 7pm midweek kick-off times for part-time teams when Sheffield United reveal that several members of their first team will be unable to leave work in time for the away match against full-time WSL outfit Manchester City in the Continental Cup. The Blades lose 6-0.

27.01.19: Ebony Salmon – who joined on loan from Manchester United in the January transfer window – scores her first goal for the club on her 18th birthday when she dispatches a last-minute penalty in the 3-2 defeat to Charlton.

01.02.19: The Blades say they hope work will begin within months to build their new £5m stadium at the Olympic Legacy Park on part of the site where they currently play. The venue will hold 3,900 fans and will also be used by Sheffield Eagles Rugby League Football Club.

10.03.19: Goalkeeper Fran Bentley, on loan from Manchester United, makes her Sheffield United debut and keeps a clean sheet in a 2-0 win at home to Crystal Palace.

31.03.19: Jade Pennock scores a last-minute winner for the second time in a week as United – just as they did against Tottenham in their last match – come from 1-0 down to win 2-1 against Leicester City Women.

11.05.19: A crowd of 1,010 cheers the team on in the final home game of the season, which is played at Bramall Lane, home of Sheffield United men. Tania Marsden comes off the bench to make her 300th appearance for the club in a 6-0 win over Millwall Lionesses which sees United clock up a 7th consecutive League win to end their debut campaign in the Championship in 5th place.

SHEFFIELD UNITED APPEARANCES & GOALS			CH		FAC		CC		Total	
			A	G	A	G	A	G	A	G
Barker, Hollie	D	ENG	17	-	1	-	1	-	19	-
Barker, Sophie	D	ENG	20	1	2	-	5	-	27	1
Bentley, Fran	G	ENG	6	-	-	-	-	-	6	-
Brooks, Alex	G	ENG	9	-	-	-	2	-	11	-
Cox, Danielle	D	ENG	19	3	2	-	4	2	25	5
Cresswell, Lauren	D	ENG	2	-	-	-	3	-	5	-
Cusack, Maddy	M	ENG	10	-	2	1	-	-	12	1
Davies, Nikki	G	WAL	4	-	2	-	2	-	8	-
Dixon, Chloe	F	ENG	16	-	1	-	3	1	20	1
Fletcher, Ellie	D	ENG	8	-	-	-	2	-	10	-
Ford, Izzy	F	ENG	8	1	2	-	2	-	12	1
Gilliatt, Ellie	D	ENG	19	2	1	-	4	-	24	2
Hartley, Jodie	M	ENG	1	-	-	-	1	-	2	-
Hartley, Naomi	D	ENG	7	-	-	-	-	-	7	-
Hobbs, Nicola	G	ENG	1	-	-	-	1	-	2	-
Housley, Autumn	D	ENG	-	-	-	-	1	-	1	-
Ibbotson, Beth	D	ENG	2	-	-	-	1	-	3	-
Jones, Sophie	F	ENG	8	6	-	-	2	1	10	7
Kemp, Nicole	D	ENG	3	-	1	-	3	-	7	-
Marsden, Tania	F	ENG	7	-	2	-	5	1	14	1
Merrick, Bethan	F	ENG	6	-	-	-	4	-	10	-
Michalska, Jodie	F	ENG	5	-	-	-	-	-	5	-
Paul, Alethea	M	ENG	11	1	2	1	4	-	17	2
Pennock, Jade	M	ENG	20	8	2	-	5	1	27	9
Rayner, Rebecca	F	ENG	17	4	2	1	4	-	23	5
Ryan, Lisa	D	ENG	2	-	-	-	2	-	4	-
Salmon, Ebony	F	ENG	9	7	2	1	-	-	11	8
Sarri, Veatriki	F	GRE	12	1	2	1	1	-	15	2
Stevens, Georgia	F	ENG	-	-	-	-	1	-	1	-
Tierney, Samantha	M	ENG	18	-	2	-	5	-	25	-

2019-20 WSL SQUAD NUMBERS & SUMMER 2019 TRANSFER WINDOW SIGNINGS

These are the squads that were lodged with the FA at the start of September 2019. However, there are circumstances under which transfers are possible after the transfer deadline, and clubs/players may also change squad numbers. Some youth players may also be introduced to the squad throughout the season. For transfers, we have listed each player's previous or next club even in cases when they have not moved directly between clubs but have seen their contracts expire first.

ARSENAL 2019-20 SQUAD NUMBERS

1	Manuela ZINSBERGER	G	19.10.95	AUT
2	Katrine VEJE	F	19.06.91	DEN
3	Emma MITCHELL	D	19.09.92	SCO
5	Jennifer BEATTIE	D	13.05.91	SCO
6	Leah WILLIAMSON	D	29.03.97	ENG
7	Danielle VAN de DONK	M	05.08.91	NED
8	Jordan NOBBS	M	08.12.92	ENG
9	Danielle CARTER	F	18.05.93	ENG
10	Kim LITTLE	M	29.06.90	SCO
11	Vivianne MIEDEMA	F	15.06.96	NED
13	Lia WALTI	M	19.04.93	SUI
14	Jill ROORD	M	22.04.97	NED
15	Katie McCABE	F	01.09.95	IRE
16	Louise QUINN	D	17.06.90	IRE
17	Lisa EVANS	F	21.05.92	SCO
18	Pauline PEYRAUD-MAGNIN	G	17.03.92	FRA
20	Leonie MAIER	D	29.09.92	GER
21	Tabea KEMME	D	14.12.91	GER
22	Viktoria SCHNADERBECK	M	04.01.91	AUT
23	Beth MEAD	F	09.05.95	ENG
24	Fran STENSON	G	27.04.01	ENG
26	Ruby GRANT	M	15.04.02	ENG
27	Melisa FILIS	M	30.07.02	ENG
28	Silvana FLORES	M	18.04.02	MEX

ARSENAL SUMMER 2019 TRANSFER WINDOW

In: Jill Roord (Bayern Munich), Manuela Zinsberger (Bayern Munich), Leonie Maier (Bayern Munich), Jennifer Beattie (Manchester City), Fran Stenson (Man City)

Out: Sari van Veenendaal (Atletico Madrid), Dominique Bloodworth (Wolfsburg), Paige Bailey-Gayle (Leicester City Women), Lachante Paul (Leicester City Women), Ava Kuyken (University of Florida), Abbie Roberts (Rutgers University), Amelia Hazard (London Bees), Janni Arnth (Fiorentina), Fran Stenson (Blackburn Rovers, loan)

BIRMINGHAM CITY 2019-20 SQUAD NUMBERS

1	Hannah HAMPTON	G	16.11.00	ENG
2	Sarah MAYLING	D	20.03.97	ENG
3	Harriet SCOTT	D	10.02.93	IRE
6	Kerys HARROP	D	03.12.90	ENG
7	Chloe ARTHUR	M	21.01.95	SCO
8	Rachel WILLIAMS	F	10.01.88	ENG
10	Brianna VISALLI	M	17.04.95	IRE
11	Abbi GRANT	M	11.12.95	SCO
13	Alex BROOKS	G	19.01.95	ENG
15	Adrienne JORDAN	D	30.01.94	USA
17	Heidi LOGAN	M	16.06.01	ENG
18	Connie SCOFIELD	M	20.05.99	ENG
19	Lucy WHIPP	F	12.11.95	ENG
20	Claudia WALKER	F	10.06.96	ENG
25	Rebecca HOLLOWAY	M	25.08.95	NIR
37	Lucy STANIFORTH	M	02.10.92	ENG

BIRMINGHAM CITY SUMMER 2019 TRANSFER WINDOW

In: Claudia Walker (Everton), Abbi Grant (Anderlecht), Brianna Visalli (West Ham), Rebecca Holloway (Nashville Rhythm), Lucy Whipp (St John's University), Adrienne Jordan (Atalanta)

Out: Ellen White (Manchester City), Charlie Wellings (Bristol City), Meaghan Sargeant (Bristol City), Hayley Ladd (Manchester Utd), Lucy Quinn (Tottenham), Aoife Mannion (Manchester City), Marisa Ewers (Aston Villa), Paige Williams (released), Shania Hayles (Aston Villa), Emma Follis (Aston Villa), Paris McKenzie (released), Hannah Kenny (released)

BRIGHTON & HOVE ALBION 2019-20 SQUAD NUMBERS

1	Megan WALSH	G	12.11.94	ENG
2	Bethan ROE	D	03.11.99	ENG
3	Felicity GIBBONS	F	09.07.94	ENG
4	Danielle BOWMAN*	M	31.10.88	ENG
5	Fern WHELAN	D	05.12.88	ENG
6	Laura RAFFERTY	D	29.04.96	NIR
7	Aileen WHELAN	F	18.08.91	ENG
8	Kirsty BARTON	M	29.05.92	ENG
9	Ini UMOTONG	F	15.05.94	NGA
10	Kate NATKIEL	M	24.09.92	ENG
11	Amanda NILDEN	M	07.08.98	SWE
12	Matilde LUNDORF Skovsen	D	19.01.99	DEN
13	Sophie HARRIS	G	25.08.94	ENG
14	Danique KERKDIJK	D	01.05.96	NED
15	Kayleigh GREEN	F	22.03.88	WAL
16	Ellie BRAZIL	F	10.01.99	ENG
17	Megan CONNOLLY	M	07.03.97	IRE
18	Jodie BRETT	M	09.03.96	ENG
19	Emily SIMPKINS	M	25.05.90	ENG
20	Victoria WILLIAMS	D	05.04.90	ENG
21	Maya LE TISSIER	D	18.04.92	ENG
27	Lea LE GARREC	M	09.06.93	FRA
	Laura HARTLEY	G	31.01.01	ENG
	Eleanor HACK	D	12.06.02	ENG

*born Danielle Buet

B&H ALBION SUMMER 2019 TRANSFER WINDOW

In: Danique Kerkdijk (Bristol City), Matilde Lundorf Skovsen (VSK Aarhus), Megan Walsh (Yeovil), Lea Le Garrec (Guingamp)

Out: Lucy Gillett (C Palace), Sophie Perry (released), Chloe Peplow (Tottenham), Marie Hourian (Braga), Jenna Legg (Charlton)

BRISTOL CITY 2019-20 SQUAD NUMBERS

1	Sophie BAGGALEY	G	29.11.96	ENG
2	Loren DYKES	D	05.02.88	WAL
3	Gemma EVANS	D	01.08.96	WAL
4	Jas MATTHEWS	D	24.03.93	ENG
5	Frankie BROWN	D	08.10.87	SCO
6	Vita VAN DER LINDEN	D	04.01.97	NED
7	Poppy PATTINSON	D	30.04.00	ENG
8	Carla HUMPHREY	F	15.12.96	ENG
9	Ebony SALMON	F	27.01.01	ENG
10	Yana DANIELS	F	08.05.92	BEL
11	Charlie WELLINGS	F	18.05.98	ENG
12	Flo ALLEN	D	21.01.99	ENG
13	Eartha CUMINGS	G	11.06.99	SCO
14	Kirsten REILLY	M	20.08.95	SCO
16	Meaghan SARGEANT	D	16.03.94	ENG
17	Ellie STRIPPEL	M	02.07.01	ENG
19	Katie ROBINSON	M	08.08.02	ENG
20	Ella RUTHERFORD	F	28.04.00	ENG
21	Abi HARRISON	F	07.12.97	SCO
25	Olivia CHANCE	M	05.10.93	NZL
27	Jess WOOLLEY	M	27.03.01	ENG

BRISTOL CITY SUMMER 2019 TRANSFER WINDOW

In: Charlie Wellings (Birmingham City), Meaghan Sargeant (Birmingham City), Jasmine Matthews (Liverpool), Yana Daniels (Liverpool), Vita van der Linden (Ajax), Ebony Salmon (Manchester United), Kirsten Reilly (Hibernian)

Out: Lucy Graham (Everton), Ali Johnson (Sheffield United), Juliette Kemppi (London City Lionesses), Danique Kerkdijk (Brighton), Julie Biesmans (PSV Eindhoven), Rosella Ayane (Tottenham), Heather Payne (Florida State University), Grace Riglar (Leicester City Women), Poppy Wilson (London City Lionesses), Ella Rutherford (Crystal Palace, loan)

CHELSEA 2019-20 SQUAD NUMBERS

2	Maria THORISDOTTIR	D	05.06.93	NOR
3	Hannah BLUNDELL	D	25.05.94	ENG
4	Millie BRIGHT	D	21.08.93	ENG
5	Sophie INGLE	M	02.11.91	WAL
6	Anita ASANTE	M	27.04.85	ENG
7	Jess CARTER	D	27.10.97	ENG
9	Bethany ENGLAND	F	03.06.94	ENG
10	JI So-Yun	M	21.02.91	KOR
11	Guro REITEN	M	26.07.94	NOR
14	Fran KIRBY	F	29.06.93	ENG
16	Magdalena ERIKSSON	D	06.09.93	SWE
17	Adelina ENGMAN	F	11.10.94	FIN
18	Maren MJELDE	M	06.11.93	NOR
20	Jonna ANDERSSON	D	02.01.93	SWE
21	Deanna COOPER	D	20.06.93	ENG
22	Erin CUTHBERT	F	19.07.98	SCO
23	Ramona BACHMANN	F	25.12.90	SUI
24	Drew SPENCE	M	23.10.92	ENG
28	Carly TELFORD	G	07.07.87	ENG
30	Ann-Katrin BERGER	G	10.10.90	GER
31	Charlotte FLEMING	M	09.01.02	ENG
32	Emily ORMAN	G	05.11.02	ENG

CHELSEA SUMMER 2019 TRANSFER WINDOW

In: Guro Reiten (LSK Kvinner)

Out: Hedvig Lindahl (released), Karen Carney (retired), Jade Bailey (Liverpool), Molly Pike (Chelsea Development Squad to Everton), Lizzie Durack (retired), Ali Riley (Bayern Munich), Maddie Phillips (Chelsea Development Squad to Charlton)

EVERTON 2019-20 SQUAD NUMBERS

1	Kirstie LEVELL	G	07.01.97	ENG
2	Taylor HINDS	D	25.09.99	ENG
3	Danielle TURNER	D	10.09.91	ENG
4	Georgia BROUGHAM	D	18.03.96	ENG
5	Kika van ES	D	11.10.91	NED
6	Gabrielle GEORGE	D	02.02.97	ENG
7	Chantelle BOYE-HLORKAH	F	08.09.95	ENG
8	Inessa KAAGMAN	M	17.04.96	NED
9	Elise HUGHES	F	15.04.01	WAL
10	Simone MAGILL	F	01.11.94	NIR
11	Chloe KELLY	F	15.01.98	ENG
13	Abbey-Leigh STRINGER	M	17.05.95	ENG
14	Esme MORGAN	D	18.10.00	ENG
15	Molly PIKE	M	22.01.01	ENG
16	Hannah CAIN	F	11.02.99	ENG
17	Lucy GRAHAM	M	10.10.96	SCO
20	Megan FINNIGAN	M	02.04.98	ENG
21	Maeva CLEMARON	M	10.11.92	FRA
22	Faye BRYSON	D	04.07.97	ENG
23	Tinja-Riikka KORPELA	G	05.05.86	FIN

EVERTON SUMMER 2019 TRANSFER WINDOW

In: Kika van Es (Ajax), Tinja-Riikka Korpela (Valerenga), Lucy Graham (Bristol City), Molly Pike (Chelsea Development Squad), Maeva Clemaron (FC Fleury 91), Esme Morgan (Man City, loan)

Out: Siri Worm (Tottenham), Dominique Bruinenberg (PEC Zwolle), Olivia Chance (released), Becky Flaherty (Sheffield United), Emma Brownlie (released), Angharad James (Reading), Emily Jones (Lewes), Claudia Walker (Birmingham City)

LIVERPOOL 2019-20 SQUAD NUMBERS

1	Anke PREUSS	G	22.09.92	GER
3	Leighanne ROBE	D	26.12.93	ENG
4	Rhiannon ROBERTS	M	30.08.90	WAL
5	Niamh FAHEY	D	13.10.87	IRE
6	Sophie BRADLEY-AUCKLAND	D	20.10.89	ENG
7	Jessica CLARKE	F	05.05.89	ENG
8	Jade BAILEY	M	11.11.95	ENG
9	Courtney SWEETMAN-KIRK	F	16.11.90	ENG
10	Christie MURRAY	M	03.05.90	SCO
11	Melissa LAWLEY	M	28.04.94	ENG
14	Ashley HODSON	F	05.05.95	ENG
17	Niamh CHARLES	F	21.06.99	ENG
18	Fran KITCHING	G	17.02.98	ENG
19	Amy RODGERS	M	04.05.90	ENG
20	Rinsola BABAJIDE	F	17.06.98	ENG
21	Missy Bo KEARNS	M	14.04.01	ENG
22	Becky JANE	D	31.03.92	ENG
23	Jemma PURFIELD	D	21.02.97	ENG
24	Kirsty LINNETT	F	24.09.93	ENG

LIVERPOOL SUMMER 2019 TRANSFER WINDOW

In: Becky Jane (Reading), Melissa Lawley (Manchester City), Jade Bailey (Chelsea)

Out: Leandra Little (Sheffield United), Laura Coombs (Manchester City), Jasmine Matthews (Bristol City), Yana Daniels (Bristol City), Aimee Everett (Leicester City Women), Annabel Blanchard (Leicester City Women), Satara Murray (Houston Dash), Ellie Fletcher (Sheffield Utd, loan)

MANCHESTER CITY 2019-20 SQUAD NUMBERS

1	Karen BARDSLEY	G	14.10.84	ENG
2	Aoife MANNION	D	24.09.95	ENG
3	Demi STOKES	D	12.12.91	ENG
4	Gemma BONNER	D	13.07.91	ENG
5	Megan CAMPBELL	D	28.06.93	IRE
6	Stephanie HOUGHTON	D	23.04.88	ENG
7	Laura COOMBS	M	29.01.91	ENG
8	Jill SCOTT	M	02.02.87	ENG
9	Pauline BREMER	F	10.04.96	GER
10	Georgia STANWAY	F	03.01.99	ENG
11	Janine BECKIE	F	20.08.94	CAN
12	Tyler TOLAND	M	08.08.01	IRE
15	Lauren HEMP	F	07.08.00	ENG
16	Jessica PARK	F	21.10.01	ENG
17	LEE Geum-min	F	07.04.94	KOR
18	Ellen WHITE	F	09.05.89	ENG
19	Caroline WEIR	M	20.06.95	SCO
24	Keira WALSH	M	08.04.97	ENG
25	Tessa WULLAERT	F	19.03.93	BEL
26	Ellie ROEBUCK	G	23.09.99	ENG
28	Emma BISSELL	F	21.12.01	ENG
24	Karima BENAMEUR	G	25.12.01	FRA
35	Matilde FILDAGO	D	15.05.94	POR
	Katie BRADLEY	F	25.12.01	ENG

MANCHESTER CITY SUMMER 2019 TRANSFER WINDOW

In: Ellen White (Birmingham City), Matilde Fidalgo (Sporting Braga), Laura Coombs (Liverpool), Aoife Mannion (Birmingham City), Lee Geum-min (Gyeongju KHNP), Tyler Toland (Sion Swifts)

Out: Nikita Parris (Lyon), Claire Emslie (Orlando Pride), Melissa Lawley (Liverpool), Jennifer Beattie (Arsenal), Abbie McManus (Manchester United), Fran Stenson (Arsenal), Esme Morgan (Everton, loan)

MANCHESTER UNITED 2019-20 SQUAD NUMBERS

1	Siobhan CHAMBERLAIN	G	15.08.83	ENG
2	Martha HARRIS	D	19.08.94	ENG
3	Lotta OKVIST	D	17.02.97	SWE
4	Amy TURNER	D	04.07.91	ENG
5	Abbie McMANUS	D	14.01.93	ENG
7	Ella TOONE	F	02.09.99	ENG
8	Mollie GREEN	M	04.08.97	ENG
9	Jessica SIGSWORTH	F	13.10.94	ENG
10	Katie ZELEM	M	20.01.96	ENG
11	Leah GALTON	F	24.05.94	ENG
12	Hayley LADD	M	06.10.93	WAL
13	Emily RAMSEY	G	16.11.00	ENG
14	Jackie GROENEN	M	17.12.94	NED
15	Aurora MIKALSEN	G	21.03.96	NOR
16	Lauren JAMES	M	29.09.01	ENG
17	Lizzie ARNOT	F	01.03.96	SCO
18	Kirsty HANSON	F	17.04.98	SCO
19	Jane ROSS	F	18.09.89	SCO
20	Kirsty SMITH	D	06.01.94	SCO
21	Millie TURNER	D	07.07.96	ENG
22	Fran BENTLEY	G	26.06.01	ENG
27	Mary EARPS	G	07.03.93	ENG

MANCHESTER UTD SUMMER 2019 TRANSFER WINDOW

In: Abbie McManus (Manchester City), Hayley Ladd (Birmingham City), Jane Ross (West Ham), Mary Earps (Wolfsburg), Jackie Groenen (Frankfurt), Lotta Okvist (Hammarby), Aurora Mikalsen (Kolbotn)

Out: Charlie Devlin (Charlton), Naomi Hartley (Sheffield United), Lucy Roberts (University of South Florida), Ebony Salmon (Bristol City), Alex Greenwood (Lyon), Aimee Palmer (Sheffield United, loan)

READING 2019-20 SQUAD NUMBERS

1	Grace MOLONEY	G	01.03.93	IRE
2	Kristine Bjordal LEINE	D	06.08.96	NOR
3	Mayumi PACHECO	D	25.08.98	ENG
4	Fara WILLIAMS	M	25.01.84	ENG
5	Molly BARTRIP	D	01.06.96	ENG
6	Angharad JAMES	M	01.06.94	WAL
7	Rachel FURNESS	M	19.06.88	NIR
8	Remi ALLEN	M	15.10.90	ENG
9	Amalie EIKELAND	F	26.08.95	NOR
10	Lauren BRUTON	M	22.11.92	ENG
11	Natasha HARDING	F	02.03.89	WAL
14	Millie FARROW	F	03.06.96	ENG
15	Rakel HONNUDOTTIR	F	30.12.88	ISL
18	Jade MOORE	M	22.10.90	ENG
19	Brooke CHAPLEN	M	16.04.89	ENG
21	Maxime BENNINK	F	21.06.97	NED
22	Josanne POTTER	M	13.11.84	ENG
23	Rachel ROWE	M	13.09.92	WAL
26	Sophie HOWARD	D	17.09.93	SCO
27	Rachael LAWS	G	05.11.90	ENG
29	Kiera SKEELS	D	20.11.01	ENG

READING SUMMER 2019 TRANSFER WINDOW

In: Kristine Bjordal Leine (Roa Il), Angharad James (Everton), Maxime Bennink (PEC Zwolle), Amalie Eikeland (IL Sandviken)

Out: Gemma Davison (Tottenham), Becky Jane (Liverpool), Kirsty Pearce (retired), Jaime Gotch (Charlton), Charlie Estcourt (Charlton, loan), Lily Woodham (Charlton, loan), Rachel Furness (Tottenham, loan)

TOTTENHAM HOTSPUR 2019-20 SQUAD NUMBERS

1	Chloe MORGAN	G	19.12.89	ENG
2	Lucia LEON	D	14.08.97	ESP
3	Ria PERCIVAL	D	07.12.89	NZL
4	Josie GREEN	M	25.04.93	ENG
5	Sophie MCLEAN	M	11.02.96	ENG
6	Anna FILBEY	M	11.10.99	ENG
7	Gemma DAVISON	F	17.04.87	ENG
8	Chloe PEPLOW	M	03.12.98	ENG
9	Rianna DEAN	F	21.10.98	ENG
10	Coral-Jade HAINES	M	21.06.96	ENG
11	Jenna SCHILLACI	D	21.03.84	ENG
12	Megan WYNNE	M	21.01.93	ENG
14	Angela ADDISON	M	09.12.99	ENG
15	Siri WORM	D	20.04.92	NED
16	Kit GRAHAM	F	11.11.95	ENG
17	Jessica NAZ	F	24.09.00	ENG
19	Lucy QUINN	F	29.09.93	ENG
22	Becky SPENCER	G	22.02.91	ENG
23	Rosella AYANE	F	16.03.96	ENG
25	Hannah GODFREY	D	17.07.97	ENG
27	Rachel FURNESS	M	19.06.88	ENG
29	Ashleigh NEVILLE	D	29.04.93	ENG

TOTTENHAM SUMMER 2019 TRANSFER WINDOW

In: Becky Spencer (West Ham), Ria Percival (West Ham), Siri Worm (Everton), Chloe Peplow (Brighton), Rosella Ayane (Bristol City), Gemma Davison (Reading), Lucy Quinn (Birmingham City), Hannah Godfrey (University of South Alabama/Pensacola FC), Kit Graham (Charlton), Rachel Furness (Reading, loan)

Out: Bianca Baptiste (Crystal Palace), Emma Beckett (Watford), Emma Gibbon (Crystal Palace), Renee Hector (Charlton), Wendy Martin (retired), Anne Meiwald (Watford), Ryah Vyse (Watford), Sarah Wiltshire (Yeovil), Megan Wynne (released), Grace Staunton (released), Maya Vio (retired), Rea Laudat (Crystal Palace)

WEST HAM UNITED 2019-20 SQUAD NUMBERS

1	Anna MOORHOUSE	G	30.03.95	ENG
2	Cecilie REDISCH KVAMME	D	11.09.95	NOR
3	Erin SIMON	D	19.08.94	USA
4	Brooke HENDRIX	D	06.05.93	USA
5	Gilly FLAHERTY	D	24.08.91	ENG
7	Alisha LEHMANN	F	21.01.99	SUI
8	Leanne KIERNAN	F	27.04.99	IRE
9	Martha THOMAS	F	31.05.96	USA
10	Julia SIMIC	M	14.05.89	GER
11	Katharina BAUNACH	D	18.01.89	GER
12	Kate LONGHURST	M	02.05.89	ENG
15	Jacynta GALABADAARACHCHI	F	06.06.01	AUS
17	Esmee DE GRAAF	F	02.08.97	NED
18	Courtney BROSNAN	G	10.11.95	USA
19	Adriana LEON	F	02.10.92	CAN
20	CHO So-hyun	M	24.06.88	KOR
21	Kenza DALI	M	31.07.91	FRA
23	Tessel MIDDAG	M	23.12.92	NED
24	Wiktoria KISZKIS	M	14.06.03	ENG
26	Laura VETTERLEIN	D	07.04.92	GER

WEST HAM UNITED SUMMER 2019 TRANSFER WINDOW

In: Laura Vetterlein (SC Sand), Martha Thomas (Le Havre), Jacynta Galabadaarachchi (Perth Glory), Kenza Dali (Dijon), Katharina Baunach (Wolfsburg), Courtney Brosnan (Le Havre), Cecilie Redisch Kvamme (Il Sandviken)

Out: Becky Spencer (Tottenham), Ria Percival (Tottenham), Jane Ross (Manchester Utd), Lucienne Reichardt (retired), Claire Rafferty (retired), Rosie Kmita (London Bees), Brianna Visalli (Birmingham City), Vyan Sampson (London City Lionesses, loan)

2019-20 CHAMPIONSHIP SQUAD NUMBERS & SUMMER 2019 TRANSFER WINDOW SIGNINGS

These are the squads that were lodged with the FA at the start of September 2019. However, there are circumstances under which transfers are possible after the transfer deadline, and clubs/players may also change squad numbers. Some youth players may also be introduced to the squad throughout the season. For transfers, we have listed each player's previous or next club even in cases when they have not moved directly between clubs but have seen their contracts expire first.

ASTON VILLA 2019-20 SQUAD NUMBERS

1	Sian ROGERS	G	28.06.98	ENG
2	Charlotte GREENGRASS	D	10.01.00	ENG
3	Asmita ALE	D	03.11.01	ENG
4	Ella FRANKLIN-FRAITURE	D	15.07.97	ENG
5	Elisha N'DOW	D	13.10.96	ENG
6	Jade RICHARDS	D	13.11.92	ENG
7	Alice HASSALL	D	08.20.97	ENG
8	Aoife HURLEY	D	20.05.96	ENG
9	Melissa JOHNSON	F	11.08.91	ENG
10	Kerri WELSH	F	20.05.92	ENG
11	Amy WEST	M	10.04.97	ENG
12	Jodie HUTTON	F	11.02.01	ENG
14	Emily SYME	M	23.07.00	ENG
15	Nat HAIGH	D	08.02.89	ENG
17	Sophie HAYWOOD	F	10.01.96	ENG
18	Daniela KOSINSKA	G	26.02.01	POL
20	Phoebe WARNER	M	17.07.00	IRE
21	Marisa EWERS	M	24.02.89	GER
22	Shania HAYLES	F	22.12.99	ENG
23	Nadine HANSSEN	M	07.10.93	NED
27	Emma FOLLIS	M	06.01.92	ENG

ASTON VILLA SUMMER 2019 TRANSFER WINDOW

In: Marisa Ewers (Birmingham City), Melissa Johnson (Leicester City Women), Ella Frankin-Fraiture (Leicester City Women), Emily Syme (Yeovil), Shania Hayles (Birmingham City), Charlotte Greengrass (Leicester City Women), Nat Haigh (Coventry United), Emma Follis (Birmingham City)

Out: Natasha Baptiste (released), Ria Elsmore (released), Aja Aguirre (N Forest), Hayley Crackle (Coventry United), Alison Hall (released), Hollie Gibson (released), Ashlee Brown (released), Tanisha Smith (released), Aoife Hurley (C Palace)

BLACKBURN ROVERS 2019-20 SQUAD NUMBERS

1	Fran STENSON	G	27.04.01	ENG
2	Chelsey JUKES	D	29.03.97	ENG
3	Alex TAYLOR	D	11.01.96	ENG
5	Kelsey PEARSON	D	10.10.99	ENG
6	Jess HOLBROOK	M	01.08.92	ENG
7	Lauren DAVIES	M	21.03.97	ENG
8	Natasha FENTON	M	08.10.98	ENG
9	Saffron JORDAN	F	27.11.93	ENG
10	Natasha FLINT	F	02.08.96	ENG
11	Rhema LORD-MEARS	M	18.06.94	ENG
12	Kayleigh McDONALD	D	14.02.94	ENG
13	Danielle HILL	G	15.04.98	ENG
14	Louise McDANIEL	M	24.05.00	NIR
15	Lauren THOMAS	M	10.01.00	ENG
16	Sophie CHARLTON	F	26.07.00	ENG

22	Serena FLETCHER	D	06.12.98	ENG
23	Carra JONES	F	03.09.01	ENG
28	Charlotte REDMAN	D	25.06.02	ENG
37	Ellie STEWART	D	02.11.96	ENG

BLACKBURN ROV SUMMER 2019 TRANSFER WINDOW

In: Rhema Lord-Mears (Anderlecht), Lauren Thomas (Liverpool), Fran Stenson (Arsenal, loan)

Out: Lynda Shepherd (retired), Danielle Gibbons (sabbatical), Lagan Makin, Charlotte Stuart

CHARLTON ATHLETIC 2019-20 SQUAD NUMBERS

1	Shanell SALGADO	G	09.12.93	GER
2	Charlotte KERR	D	26.11.94	ENG
3	Rachel NEWBOROUGH	D	19.11.96	NIR
4	Renee HECTOR	D	21.06.95	ENG
5	Maddie PHILLIPS	D	11.06.00	ENG
6	Grace COOMBS	D	25.11.90	ENG
7	Ellie DOREY	F	04.12.95	ENG
8	Charley CLIFFORD	M	09.02.93	ENG
9	Ellie LEEK	M	21.01.95	WAL
10	Charlie DEVLIN	F	23.02.98	ENG
11	Lily WOODHAM	M	03.09.00	WAL
12	Jaime GOTCH	D	30.03.00	ENG
14	Melanie PARRENO-ESPINOSA	M	29.05.99	ENG
15	Riva CASLEY	D	27.01.99	ENG
16	Georgia EVANS	M	16.10.95	WAL
17	Charlie ESTCOURT	M	27.05.98	WAL
18	Alice GRIFFITHS	M	22.01.01	WAL
19	Georgia GRIFFIN	F	03.06.00	ENG
20	Sara EGGESVIK	M	29.04.97	NOR
21	Jenna LEGG	M	23.06.97	ENG
23	Hannah CHURCHILL	M	15.02.93	ENG
24	Lilli MAPLE	M	12.01.96	ENG
25	Lois HEUCHAN	M	07.03.96	SCO
40	Katie STARTUP	G	28.01.99	ENG

CHARLTON ATHLETIC SUMMER 2019 TRANSFER WINDOW

In: Riva Casley (Millwall Lionesses), Georgia Evans (Yeovil), Ellie Leek (Le Havre), Lois Heuchan (Le Havre), Alice Griffiths (Cardiff Met), Jaime Gotch (Reading Development Squad), Rachel Newborough (Boston College), Renee Hector (Tottenham), Charlie Devlin (Manchester United), Charlie Estcourt (Reading, loan), Lily Woodham (Reading, loan), Shanell Salgado (C Palace), Maddie Phillips (Chelsea Development Squad), Jenna Legg (Brighton)

Out: Ellie Bailes (released), Chloe Brunton-Wilde (released), Amelia Ritchie (released), Hayley West (London Bees), Amber Stobbs (retired), Lily Agg (released), Harley Bennett (released), Kit Graham (Tottenham), Charlotte Gurr, Nicole Pepper (C Palace), Hannah Wheeler, Elizabeta Ejupi (London City Lionesses), Leigh Nicol

COVENTRY UNITED 2019-20 SQUAD NUMBERS

1	Sue WOOD	G
2	Chenise AUSTIN	D
3	Sian JOHNSON	M
4	Nikki MILES	D
5	Jodie BARTLE	D
6	Maz GAUNTLETT	M
7	Jade BROOK	M
8	Rosie AXTEN	F
9	Shannon O'BRIEN	M
10	Amy WATHAN	F
11	Amber HUGHES	M
12	Hayley CRACKLE	D
14	Dayna CHONG	M
15	Helen DERMODY	M
16	Yasmine KLUCIS	M
17	Erin SMITH	D
18	Bethan MERRICK	M
19	Fiona WORTS	F
20	Chelsea WESTON	D
21	Katy MORRIS	M
22	Becky ANDERSON	M
23	Jenna ROBERTS	D
24	Ffion MORGAN	D
25	Erin RIDEN	D
43	Lucy GARDNER	G

COVENTRY UNITED SUMMER 2019 TRANSFER WINDOW

In: Rosie Axten (Leicester City Women), Jodie Bartle (Loughborough Foxes), Katy Morris (Chorley), Becky Anderson (London Bees 2017-18, then sabbatical 2018-19), Erin Smith (Leafield Athletic), Sian Johnson (Leicester United), Hayley Crackle (Aston Villa), Ffion Morgan (Cardiff City Ladies), Fiona Worts (Leicester City Women), Chelsea Weston (London Bees 2017-18, then sabbatical 2018-19)

Out: Georgina Presswell (released), Alex Buck (released), Nat Haigh (Aston Villa), Lois Jefferies (released), Rosie McDonnell (released), Laura McGlone (released), Natasha Merritt (released), Amelia Shiner (released), Emma Slater (released), Lucy Stead (released), Amy Wathan (released), Ellie White (released), Victoria Wright (released)

CRYSTAL PALACE 2019-20 SQUAD NUMBERS

1	Lucy GILLETT	G	28.10.93	USA
2	Annabel JOHNSON	D	20.10.93	ENG
3	Nicole PEPPER	M	29.07.95	ENG
4	Amy GODDARD	D	16.12.98	ENG
5	Jordan BUTLER	D	14.09.92	ENG
6	Freya HOLDAWAY	D	12.04.89	NIR
8	Ciara WATLING	M	18.08.92	NIR
9	Magda MOSENGO	F	27.09.95	ENG
10	Ashlee HINCKS	F	04.12.88	ENG

11	Bianca BAPTISTE	F	15.01.92	ENG
12	Lizzie WALDIE	D	09.06.00	ENG
13	Cherelle KHASSAL	F	09.01.91	IRE
15	Andria GEORGIOU	M	15.04.96	ENG
16	Hannah MacKENZIE	F	03.02.95	ENG
19	Lily STEVENS	D	29.09.98	WAL
20	Emma GIBBON	G	06.02.99	WAL
21	Leeta RUTHERFORD	M	14.12.87	ENG
22	Ella RUTHERFORD	F	28.04.00	ENG
23	Ashleigh GODDARD	M	19.04.92	ENG
25	Rea LAUDAT	F	19.11.93	ENG
26	Aoife HURLEY	D	20.05.96	ENG

CRYSTAL PALACE SUMMER 2019 TRANSFER WINDOW

In: Leeta Rutherford (Lewes), Amy Goddard (Yeovil), Cherelle Khassal (Chichester), Lucy Gillett (Brighton), Bianca Baptiste (Tottenham), Emma Gibbon (Tottenham), Annabel Johnson (London Bees), Nicole Pepper (Charlton), Amy Goddard (Yeovil Town), Magda Mosengo (Carson Newman University), Lizzie Waldie (Kent Football United), Ashleigh Goddard (Apollon LFC Cyprus), Rea Laudat (Tottenham), Aoife Hurley (Aston Villa), Ella Rutherford (Bristol City, loan)

Out: Pamela McRoberts (sabbatical), Anneka Nuttall (Leicester City Women), Megen Lynch (London Bees), Nikita Whinnett (London Bees), Jade Davenport, Kallie Balfour (London City Lionesses), Chloe Burr (sabbatical), Francesca Ali, Jade Keogh, Amy Green, Megan Chandler, Dayna Chong, Ria Collins, Hope Nash, Mary Robinson, Leesa Haydock, Shanell Salgado (Charlton), Gemma Bryan

DURHAM 2019-20 SQUAD NUMBERS

1	Hannah REID	G	20.08.94	SCO
2	Kathryn HILL	D	21.06.94	SCO
3	Lauren BRIGGS	M		ENG
4	Lisa ROBERTSON	M	15.05.92	SCO
5	Sarah WILSON	D	01.07.91	ENG
6	Sarah ROBSON	M	23.05.87	NIR
7	Beth HEPPLE	M	15.09.96	ENG
8	Molly SHARPE	F		ENG
9	Nicki GEARS	F	05.03.93	ENG
10	Iris ACHTERHOF	F	09.05.97	NED
11	Megan BELL	M	17.04.01	NIR
12	Holly MANDERS	M		ENG
13	Megan BORTHWICK	G	22.03.96	ENG
14	Becky SALICKI	D	30.07.92	ENG
16	Ellie CHRISTON	D	21.09.93	ENG
17	Emily ROBERTS	F	07.04.94	ENG
19	Hannah GREEN-WOOD	D		ENG
20	Jordan ATKINSON	F		ENG
24	Abby HOLMES	D	26.05.91	ENG
96	Rachel LEE	M		ENG

DURHAM SUMMER 2019 TRANSFER WINDOW

In: Megan Bell (Linfield), Iris Achterhof (Old Dominion University), Molly Sharpe (Barry University, USA)

Out: Abi Cottam (Sunderland), Chloe Knott (released), Zoe Ness (Lewes), Caroline Dixon (retired)

LEICESTER CITY WOMEN 2019-20 SQUAD NUMBERS

1	Demi LAMBOURNE	G	30.04.96	ENG
2	Grace RIGLAR	D		ENG
3	Nat JOHNSON	M	12.11.93	ENG
4	Aimee EVERETT	M	02.08.01	ENG
5	Holly MORGAN	D	10.02.93	ENG
6	Lia CATALDO	M	11.02.01	ENG
7	Anneka NUTTALL	D	26.02.91	ENG
8	Simran JHAMAT	F	22.01.01	ENG
9	Libby SMITH	F	03.11.01	ENG
10	Annabel BLANCHARD	F	07.05.01	ENG
11	Lachante PAUL	F	06.08.01	ENG
12	Hayley JAMES	D	07.07.95	ENG
13	Scarlett FIELD	G	26.09.94	ENG
14	Leigh DUGMORE	F	15.06.90	ENG
16	Freya THOMAS	M	28.10.01	ENG
17	Paige BAILEY-GAYLE	F	12.11.01	ENG
18	Rachel BROWN	D	24.10.00	SCO
21	Annie TAYLOR	M	21.10.96	ENG
23	Lucy JOHNSON	D	06.01.02	ENG
25	Georgia POPPLE	D		ENG

LEICESTER WOMEN SUMMER 2019 TRANSFER WINDOW

In: Aimee Everett (Liverpool Development Squad), Lachante Paul (Arsenal Development Squad), Annabel Blanchard (Liverpool Development Squad), Paige Bailey-Gayle (Arsenal Development Squad), Lia Cataldo (Millwall Lionesses), Grace Riglar (Bristol City), Anneka Nuttall (Crystal Palace), Georgia Popple (Birmingham RTC), Paige Bailey-Gayle (Arsenal Development Squad)

Out: Rosie Axten (Coventry United), Ella Franklin-Fraiture (Aston Villa), Melissa Johnson (Aston Villa), Charlotte Greengrass (Aston Villa), Charlotte Clarke (Stoke City), Sarah Jackson (Derby County), Natasha Hudson (American University), Sherry McCue (released), Taome Oliver (released), Nicole Nymoen (West Bromwich Albion), Freda Ayisi (London City Lionesses), Sophie Domingo (Derby County), Fiona Worts (Coventry United) , Mai Moncaster (unattached)

LEWES 2019-20 SQUAD NUMBERS

1	Faye BAKER	G	10.06.90	ENG
2	Sammy QUAYLE	F	08.10.95	WAL
3	Rhian CLEVERLY	D	11.01.95	WAL
4	Kate McINTYRE	M	10.03.87	ENG
5	Caitlin HAYES	D	22.09.95	ENG
6	Amy TAYLOR	D	25.04.92	ENG
7	Emma JONES	F	10.10.94	WAL
8	Ellie NOBLE	M	12.09.99	ENG
9	Zoe NESS	F	24.03.96	SCO
10	Jess KING	F	31.05.92	ENG
11	Ella POWELL	F	01.02.00	WAL
12	Ava ROWBOTHAM	M	26.03.00	ENG
14	Emily JONES	F	17.08.01	WAL
15	Charley BOSWELL	D	26.11.90	ENG
16	Emily DONOVAN	F	16.02.97	ENG
19	Dani LANE	M	09.08.93	ENG
20	Sophie O'ROURKE	M	03.06.99	ENG
21	Filippa SAVVA	M	28.05.99	CYP
22	Katie ROOD	F	02.09.02	NZL
24	Issy FOSTER	G	19.09.93	ENG
26	Shannon MOLONEY	M	24.11.88	IRE
30	Annie TIMONEY	M	02.08.97	NIR
37	Molly PETERS	F	24.11.98	ENG

LEWES SUMMER 2019 TRANSFER WINDOW

In: Caitlin Hayes (Barcelona), Ella Powell (Georgia State University), Ellie Noble (Oxford United), Emily Jones (Everton Development Squad), Emma Jones (Cardiff City Ladies), Rhian Cleverly (Le Havre), Zoe Ness (Lewes), Filippa Savva (Liverpool Feds). Emily Donovan (Yeovil), Issy Foster (Southampton Women's), Annie Timoney (Marine Academy Plymouth), Molly Peters (Enfield)

Out: Leeta Rutherford (Crystal Palace), Victoria Carleton, Rebecca Carter (Crawley Wasps), Charlotte Owen (Crawley Wasps), Georgia Robert (London Bees)

LONDON BEES 2019-20 SQUAD NUMBERS

1	Sarah QUANTRILL	G	21.07.90	ENG
2	Ellie WILSON	D	11.05.97	ENG
3	Megan ALEXANDER	D	11.11.93	ENG
4	Hayley WEST	D	13.04.93	ENG
5	Georgia ROBERT	D		ENG
6	Billie BROOKS	D		ENG
7	Lauren PICKETT	F		ENG
8	Bonnie HORWOOD	M		ENG
9	Lucy LOOMES	F	18.05.97	ENG
10	Brooke NUNN	M	04.02.93	ENG
11	Rosie KMITA	F	27.07.94	ENG
12	Courtnay WARD-CHAMBERS	F		ENG
13	Taylor O'LEARY	M	11.07.94	ENG
14	Georgie GIDDINGS	M	30.06.90	ENG
15	Megen LYNCH	G	03.09.91	ENG
16	Nicola GIBSON	M	05.05.93	ENG
17	Nikita WHINNETT	F	17.03.91	ENG
19	Mollie DENCH	D	21.07.01	NZL
20	Connie FORMAN	F		ENG
21	Flo GAMBY	D		ENG
22	Amelia HAZARD	M	22.10.00	ENG
23	Merrick WILL	M	21.12.96	ENG

LONDON BEES SUMMER 2019 TRANSFER WINDOW

In: Amelia Hazard (Arsenal), Nikita Whinnett (C Palace), Rosie Kmita (West Ham), Courtnay Ward-Chambers (QPR), Hayley West (Charlton), Georgie Giddings (Millwall Lionesses), Megen Lynch (Crystal Palace), Flo Gamby (C&K Basildon), Billie Brooks (unattached), Megan Alexander (Yeovil), Georgia Robert (Lewes)

Out: Katie Wilkinson (Sheffield United), Annabel Johnson (C Palace), Destiney Toussaint (released), Rosie Parnell (born Lane) (Southampton FC), Ruesha Littlejohn (released), Danielle Lea (released), Paula Howells (released), Tricia Gould (released), Ocean Rolandsen (Watford), Emma Beckett (Watford), Kelsey Gibson (Luton Town), Rachel Unitt (released), Daisy McLachlan (released)

LONDON CITY LIONESSES 2019-20 SQUAD NUMBERS

1	Lucy THOMAS	G		
2	Chantelle MACKIE	D	11.05.95	ENG
3	Leanne COWAN	D	01.02.96	ENG
4	Poppy WILSON	M	06.08.99	ENG
5	Hannah SHORT	D	16.04.93	ENG
6	Ylenia PRIEST	D	23.10.01	ENG
7	Elizabeta EJUPI	M	21.04.94	ALB
8	Freda AYISI	M	21.10.94	ENG
9	Gabby RAVENSCROFT	F	10.10.00	ENG
10	Juliette KEMPPI	F	14.05.94	FIN
11	Evie CLARKE	F	17.10.97	ENG
12	Grace NEVILLE	D	09.04.00	ENG
14	Kallie BALFOUR	F	13.10.92	ENG
15	Vyan SAMPSON	D	02.07.96	ENG
16	Harley BENNETT	M	14.07.90	ENG
17	Lucy FITZGERALD	F	29.12.00	ENG
18	Ellie MASON	M	16.02.96	ENG
19	Lily AGG	F	17.12.93	ENG
20	Annie ROSSITER	F	05.09.01	ENG
21	Flo FYFE	F	19.05.98	ENG
22	Eden BAILEY	F		ENG
23	Amber GAYLOR	M	22.02.95	ENG
24	Ellie ARNOLD	M		

LONDON CITY LIONESSES SUMMER 2019 TRANSFER WINDOW

In: Poppy Wilson (Bristol City), Vyan Sampson (West Ham, loan), Elizabeta Ejupi (Charlton), Hannah Short (Yeovil), Freda Ayisi (Leicester City Women), Juliette Kemppi (Bristol City), Ellie Mason (Yeovil), Lily Agg (Charlton), Amber Gaylor (Yeovil), Florence Fyfe (Oxford United), Lucy Thomas (Oxford United), Harley Bennett (Charlton), Kallie Balfour (C Palace)

Out: Lia Cataldo (Leicester City Women), Riva Casley (Charlton), Grace Taylor (Kent Football United), Freya Bailes, Beth Lumsden (unattached), Chloe Sansom (unattached), Georgina Giddings (London Bees), Fran Ali (Leyton Orient), Ellie Stenning (Leyton Orient), Michelle Young (Leyton Orient), Kalani Peart, Beth Harford (Elon, USA), Sara Guzowska, Sofia Stovold

SHEFFIELD UNITED 2019-20 SQUAD NUMBERS

1	Becky FLAHERTY	G	06.03.98	NIR
2	Sophie BARKER	M	25.12.90	ENG
3	Sam TIERNEY	D	08.10.98	ENG
4	Leandra LITTLE	D	08.11.84	ENG
5	Naomi HARTLEY	D	12.01.01	ENG
6	Kasia LIPKA	M	26.05.94	ENG
7	Jade PENNOCK	F	08.01.93	ENG
8	Maddy CUSACK	M	28.10.95	ENG
9	Katie WILKINSON	F	05.11.94	ENG
10	Alethea PAUL	M	27.08.98	ENG
11	Chloe DIXON	F	12.07.96	ENG
12	Hollie BARKER	D	03.09.91	ENG
13	Emily BATTY	G	02.11.98	ENG
14	Keri MATTHEWS	F	02.12.02	ENG
15	Izzy FORD	M	29.06.02	ENG
16	Aimee PALMER	M	25.07.01	ENG
17	Veatriki SARRI	F	01.01.98	GRE
18	Ali JOHNSON	D	24.12.98	ENG
19	Olivia FERGUSSON	F	27.03.95	ENG
20	Megan TINSLEY	D	31.01.98	ENG
26	Ellie FLETCHER	D	16.06.99	ENG

SHEFFIELD UNITED SUMMER 2019 TRANSFER WINDOW

In: Katie Wilkinson (London Bees), Naomi Hartley (Manchester United), Leandra Little (Liverpool), Olivia Fergusson (Yeovil), Keri Matthews (York City RTC), Ali Johnson (Bristol City), Becky Flaherty (Everton), Emily Batty (Doncaster Rovers Belles), Kasia Lipka (unattached), Megan Tinsley (Sheffield FC), Aimee Palmer (Manchester United, loan), Ellie Fletcher (Liverpool, loan)

Out: Ellie Gilliatt (Derby County), Tania Marsden (Sheffield FC), Nikki Davies (retired), Danielle Cox (retired), Nicole Kemp (released), Georgia Stevens (Fylde), Jodie Hartley (released), Bex Rayner (N Forest)

FA WOMEN'S NATIONAL LEAGUE
TIERS THREE & FOUR

The FA Women's Premier League was renamed the FA Women's National League ahead of the 2018-19 season, but the format remained the same. The WNL represents Tiers 3 and 4 of the club game in England, with teams organised into regional divisions. Tier 3 consists of WNL Northern Premier (formerly WPL Northern) and WNL Southern Premier (formerly WPL Southern).

At the end of the season it has been traditional for the champions of each division to meet at a neutral venue in a play-off with the winner promoted to Tier 2 (now the Championship) so long as they satisfy the FA's licence criteria. It was decided ahead of 2018-19 that both the champions would be promoted but the play-off would still take place. WNL Northern Premier champions Blackburn Rovers beat WNL Southern Premier champions Coventry United 3-0 in the play-off with both clubs having already been notified by the FA that their licence applications to join the Championship for 2019-20 had been successful.

It will again be the case that at the end of 2019-20 both the Northern Premier and Southern Premier champions will be promoted (subject to meeting licence criteria) and that the play-off will still take place. The FA's original plan had been that it would be one up and one down between the Championship and WNL from the end of 2019-20, but Yeovil's inability to secure a Championship licence following their relegation from the WSL at the end of 2018-19 means there is an extra spot to fill. At the end of 2019-20 the bottom club in the Championship will be relegated to the WNL (either the Northern Premier or Southern Premier depending on geography).

Tier 4 consists of four regional divisions: WNL Division 1 North (formerly WPL North 1); WNL Division 1 Midlands (formerly WPL Midlands 1); WNL Division 1 South East (formerly WPL South East 1); and WNL Division 1 South West (formerly WPL South West 1). The Southern Premier relegates into, and grants promotion out of, Division 1 South East and Division 1 South West while the Northern Premier does likewise with Division 1 North and Division 1 Midlands.

The four divisions at Tier 4 level grant promotion from, and relegate into, the eight Regional Premier Leagues at Tier 5. The champions at regional level may sometimes opt against promotion, usually because of the additional expense and logistics of travelling for away games over a wider area. Throughout this section of the book all of the clubs competing in Tiers 3 and 4 in 2019-20 are listed alphabetically. Also included are the teams who were relegated from Tier 4 at the end of 2018-19. The head of each page appears like this:

ACTONIANS

2019-20: WNL DIVISION 1 SOUTH EAST (Tier 4)

Founded: 1998 (as Chiswick United)
Nickname: None

Season 2018-19:
WNL South East 1 (Tier 4): 4th
FA Cup: 2nd Qualifying Round
WNL Cup: Determining Round
WNL Plate: 2nd Round
Capital Cup: Winners

Underneath the club name is the division they compete in during 2019-20. Beneath that, to the right, is the club's form in each of the four main competitions in 2018-19 (League, FA Cup, WNL Cup/Plate, County Cup). Some teams also competed in other Cup competitions, but for reasons of space and uniformity of information presented, these have been excluded. For the teams who were promoted from Tier 5 (none of whom were eligible for the WNL Cup/Plate) we have included their regional League Cup results.

The following information – where known – is included for each game: scorers; goal times; penalties; missed penalties; sendings-off; attendances. Where goal times are unknown, if a player scored more than once it is listed such: (x2) or (x3) etc. Where an official attendance wasn't recorded, some clubs have provided us with an estimate which is denoted thus: 50est

The figure in the column to the far right is the club's position in the League at the end of all the matches played that day. This has been provided from the third or fourth League game of the season onwards. It's important to note that the team in question did not necessarily start its next match in that position as other games in their division may have been played in the interim.

The club's main home ground for 2018-19 is listed at the top of the results section. Where a club plays a home match at a ground other than its main home ground this information is listed in the pages dedicated to the home club, at the bottom of the results table. Some teams may have changed their main home venue for 2019-20. We have tried to include this information in the body of the text at the top of the page, but in many cases these changes will have been confirmed after our publishing deadlines.

We asked every club for a summary of the 2018-19 season from their captain, manager or another figure closely associated with the club. We are hugely grateful to those who had time to help us. In some cases, the people who provided us with their thoughts may have left the club since speaking to us.

Cup matches key: DR = WPL Cup determining round (losers go into WPL Plate)
PR = Preliminary Round RQ3 = 3rd Qualifying Round R3 = 3rd Round

FA WOMEN'S NATIONAL LEAGUE 2019-20 CONSTITUTION

TIER 3:	NORTHERN PREMIER	SOUTHERN PREMIER
	1.Burnley	1.Cardiff City Ladies
	2.Derby County	2.Chichester City
	3.Fylde	**3.Crawley Wasps**
	4.Huddersfield Town	4.Gillingham
	5.Hull City	5.Hounslow*
	6.Loughborough Foxes	**6.Keynsham Town**
	7.Middlesbrough	7.Milton Keynes Dons
	8.Nottingham Forest	8.Oxford United
	9.Sheffield FC	9.Plymouth Argyle
	10.Stoke City	10.Portsmouth
	11.Sunderland	11.Watford
	12.West Brom. Albion	**12.Yeovil Town**
		*formerly QPR

TIER 4:

DIVISION 1 NORTH	DIVISION 1 MIDLANDS	DIVISION 1 SOUTH EAST	DIVISION 1 SOUTH WEST
1.Barnsley	1.Bedworth United	1.Actonians	1.Brislington
2.Bolton Wanderers	2.Birmingham & W. M.	**2.AFC Basildon+**	2.Buckland Athletic
3.Bradford City	3.Burton Albion	3.AFC Wimbledon	3.Cheltenham Town
4.Brighouse Town	**4.Doncaster R. B.**	4.Billericay Town	4.Chesham United
5.Chester-le-Street T.	**5.Leafield Athletic**	**5.Cambridge City**	**5.Exeter City**
6.Chorley	**6.Leicester United ****	6.Cambridge United	6.Larkhall Athletic
7.Durham Cestria	7.Lincoln City*+	7.Enfield Town	7.Maidenhead United
8.Leeds United	8.Long Eaton United	8.Ipswich Town	8.Poole Town
9.Liverpool Feds	9.Solihull Moors	**9.Kent Football Utd**	**9.Southampton FC**
10.Newcastle United	10.Sporting Khalsa	10.Leyton Orient	10.Southampton Saints++
11.Norton & S. A.	11.The New Saints	11.Norwich City	11.Southampton Women
12.Stockport County	12.Wolverhampton W.	12.Stevenage	12.Swindon Town
	**formerly Leicester City Women Development	+formerly C&K Basildon	++folded July 2019
	*+formerly Nettleham		

Newcomers to each Tier in **bold**

NORTHERN PREMIER (TIER 3)

Burnley – Promoted as WNL Northern 1 (Tier 4) champions
Loughborough Foxes – transferred from WNL Southern (Tier 3) for geographical reasons
West Bromwich Albion – Promoted as WNL Midlands 1 (Tier 4) champions

SOUTHERN PREMIER (TIER 3):

Crawley Wasps – Promoted as WNL South East 1 (Tier 4) champions
Keynsham Town – Promoted as WNL South West 1 (Tier 4) champions
Yeovil Town – Relegated from WSL (Tier 1) and unable to attain Championship (Tier 2) licence

DIVISION 1 NORTH (TIER 4)

Bradford City – Relegated from WNL North 1 (Tier 3)
Durham Cestria ¬– Promoted as North East Regional Premier (Tier 5) champions
Stockport County – Promoted as North West Regional Premier (Tier 5) champions

DIVISION 1 MIDLANDS (TIER 4)

Doncaster Rovers Belles – Relegated from WNL Northern Premier (Tier 3)
Leafield Athletic – Promoted as West Midlands Regional Premier (Tier 5) champions
Leicester United – Promoted as East Midlands Regional Premier (Tier 5) champions

DIVISION 1 SOUTH EAST (TIER 4)

AFC Basildon – Relegated from WNL Southern Premier (Tier 3) (as C&K Basildon)
Cambridge City – Promoted as Eastern Regional Premier (Tier 5) champions
Kent Football United – Promoted as London & South East Regional Premier (Tier 5) champions

DIVISION 1 SOUTH WEST (TIER 4)

Southampton FC – Promoted as Southern Regional Premier (Tier 5) champions
Exeter City – Promoted as South West Regional Premier (Tier 5) champions

ACTONIANS

2019-20: WNL SOUTH EAST 1 (Tier 4)

Founded: 1998 (as Chiswick United)

Nickname: None

Season 2018-19:

WNL South East 1 (Tier 4): 4th

FA Cup: 2nd Qualifying Round

WNL Cup: Determining Round

WNL Plate: 2nd Round

Capital Cup: Winners

Everoy Johnson founded the club as Chiswick United in 1998 and they entered the Greater London League in Division Three West for their first season. They became known as Acton Sports Club when they moved to Acton in the summer of 2003. Then, finding themselves homeless in 2008, they were taken under the wing of existing club Actonians FC. A London & South East Regional League title and League Cup Double arrived in 2014-15. It was their title success that season that saw them promoted to Tier 4 where they have resided ever since. The 2018-19 campaign culminated in the club's highest Tier 4 finish to date – 4th – and a Capital Cup final triumph over Leyton Orient.

2018-19 AS IT HAPPENS

09.09.18: After beginning the season with back-to-back League defeats, Actonians pick up three points with a 3-0 win at home to Luton. Catherine Murphy and Carla Williams (x2) score.

30.09.18: Actonians become the first team to take a point off newly promoted Billericay Town in an entertaining 4-4 draw. Billericay almost nick a late winner but Actonians goalkeeper Paige Horsnell saves Jay Blackie's 88th-minute penalty.

02.05.19: Actonians win the Capital Cup with a 1-0 triumph over fellow WNL South East 1 side Leyton Orient. Jessica Byrne scores a long-range winner with 12 minutes left.

05.05.19: Despite a final-day defeat at AFC Wimbledon, Actonians finish 4th, their highest placing since entry into Tier 4.

17.05.19: Alessandra Barreca receives her top scorer award for League goals in WNL South East 1 this season (24gls).

2018-19 RESULTS: (HOME VENUE: RECTORY PARK, (MIDDLESEX FA), UNLESS STATED)

2018-19 WNL SE 1					Att	Pos
19.08	Stevenage (a)	L	2-5	Alessandra Barreca 35, 48	25	
26.08	Ipswich Town (h)	L	1-5	Mariko Engels 32	20	12
09.09	Luton Town (h)	W	3-0	Catherine Murphy 10, Carla Williams 73, 87	15	9
12.09	Denham United (a)	W	5-0	Alessandra Barreca 11, 59, Hannah Summers 26, 30, Carla Williams 22	45est	3
16.09	Norwich City (h)	W	5-2	Jennifer Laidlaw 10, Alessandra Barreca 27, 36, 65, Sara Lopez Ezzahiri 75	25	3
30.09	Billericay Town (h)	D	4-4	Jennifer Laidlaw 5, Sara Lopez Ezzahiri 32, Enya Collins 55, Carla Williams 68, Actonians GK Paige Horsnell saved pen 88	30	3
03.10	Crawley Wasps (a)	L	0-5		95	4
07.10	Leyton Orient (a)	L	2-3	Carla Williams 35, Jennifer Laidlaw 50	48	6
04.11	Enfield Town (h)	L	0-2		25est	7
02.12	Denham United (h)	W	5-1	Alessandra Barreca 30, 38, Sara Lopez Ezzahiri 44, Enya Collins 45, Sharon Odofin 53	15	7
16.12	AFC Wimbledon (a)	W	5-2	Naomi Graham 44, Jessica Byrne 48, 60, Alessandra Barreca 70, 75	50	5
06.01	Cambridge Utd (h)	D	1-1	Carla Williams 75	25est	5
13.01	Stevenage (h)	W	5-1	Alessandra Barreca 9, (pen) 41, 86, Mariko Engels 57, Melissa Jung 72	15	4
20.01	Ipswich Town (a)	W	5-0	Carla Williams 10, 67, Alessandra Barreca 77, 83, 90+1	20	3
10.02	Cambridge Utd (a)		P-P			3
24.02	Norwich City (a)	W	3-2	Carla Williams 5, Alessandra Barreca 21, 75	45	3
10.03	Billericay Town (a)		P-P			3
13.03	Crawley Wasps (h)	L	0-4		50	4
17.03	Cambridge United (a)	L	1-5	Alessandra Barreca 37	50	5
31.03	Enfield Town (a)	W	2-1	Alessandra Barreca 30, 90+3	23	4
07.04	Luton Town (a)	W	3-0	Alessandra Barreca 47, Carla Williams 53, Jennifer Laidlaw 65		3
14.04	Leyton Orient (h)	D	3-3	Carla Williams 6, 34, Alessandra Barreca 87		3
28.04	Billericay Town (a)	L	3-6	Mariko Engels 25, 33, Melissa Jung 50		3
05.05	AFC Wimbledon (h)	L	0-1			4

2018-19 FA CUP

23.09 RQ2	Enfield Town (a)	L	1-2	Alessandra Barreca 85	43

2018-19 WNL CUP

02.09 DR	Oxford United (h)	L	1-2	Alessandra Barreca 82	20

2018-19 WNL PLATE

R1	Bye				
14.10 R2	Chesham Utd (h)	L	1-2	Carla Williams 67	25est

2018-19 CAPITAL CUP*

R1	Bye				
09.12 QF	Enfield Town (h)	W	3-0	Sharon Odofin 35, Jenifer Laidlaw 71, 74	25est
17.02 SF	Fulham FC Foundation (a)	W	2-0	Sara Lopez Ezzahiri, Carla Williams	
02.05 F	Leyton Orient (n)	W	1-0	Jessica Byrne 78	

(n)Played at The Powerday Stadium, (Hanwell Town FC)

*The Capital Cup is the equivalent of a County Cup for teams in and around London. In 2018-19 it was run by the Surrey FA.

"Winning the Capital Cup capped off a very good season for the first team who, after a shaky start, finished 4th – the highest League position we've achieved so far. Manager Craig Brown took over in summer 2018 and led a small but talented squad who play for each other and keep pushing to improve. Going into 2019-20 we cannot afford to get complacent and must strive for even more both on and off the pitch as we do every season."

Linda Fox – Chairperson and Secretary

AFC BASILDON

formerly C&K Basildon
2019-20: WNL SOUTH EAST 1 (Tier 4)

Founded: 2004
(as Basildon Town Ladies)

Nickname: None

Season 2018-19 (competed as C&K Basildon):

WNL Southern Premier (Tier 3): 12th (R)

FA Cup: 2nd Round

WNL Cup: Determining Round

WNL Plate: 2nd Round

County Cup: Runners-up

Gary Reed

The 2019-20 season sees the club begin a new era as AFC Basildon following a turbulent 2018-19 campaign. The team started out as part of Basildon Town men's club in 2004 before founder Peter King changed the name to C&K Basildon, after his insurance company CKRE. In 2008 they were promoted out of the Essex County League with five League titles in seven seasons taking them into Tier 3 ahead of the 2015-16 season. There they flourished despite having far fewer resources than many of their rivals. In 2017-18 they won their fourth consecutive Essex FA County Cup (and fifth in six years) and finished as runners-up behind Charlton in (what was then) the WPL Southern Premier. King severed all ties with the club in the summer of 2018 and they finished 2018-19 bottom of the table. There was pride though in seeing 11 players from the U16 and U18 teams make their senior WNL debuts in 2018-19 and in reaching the County Cup final.

Gary Reed

2018-19 AS IT HAPPENS (COMPETED AS C&K BASILDON)

01.06.18: After a hugely successful 2017-18 season in which C&K finished as Tier 3 runners-up to Charlton, founder and former manager Peter King resigns from the club.

17.02.19: C&K advance to the Essex FA County Cup final for the sixth year in a row thanks to a 5-1 win away to Hutton.

25.03.19: First team coach Luke Pierre leaves the club by mutual consent with the team bottom of the table. The following day director of football Jason Stephens joins existing coach Les Thompson to take charge of first-team affairs until the end of the season.

14.04.19: C&K's relegation to Tier 4 is all but mathematically certain as they lose 4-1 away to the team immediately above them, QPR. Hollie Turner puts C&K ahead in the second minute, but Rangers come back for their first League win of the season to effectively send Basildon down.

17.04.19: The club confirms that from the start of 2019-20 it will be renamed AFC Basildon Ladies/Girls.

18.04.19: C&K finish as runners-up in the Essex FA County Cup after a 4-0 defeat to Tier 4 outfit Billericay Town in the final.

2018-19 RESULTS: (HOME VENUE: THE FROST FINANCIAL STADIUM, (CANVEY ISLAND FC) UNLESS STATED)

2018-19 WNL SP COMPETED AS C&K BASILDON

Date	Opponent	Res	Score	Scorers	Att	Pos
19.08	Portsmouth (h)	L	0-6		69	
26.08	Cardiff City L (h)*	L	0-5		33	12
09.09	Loughborough F (a)	D	1-1	Madelyn Thomas 35	47	10
12.09	Gillingham (h)	L	1-3	Raquel Murray		11
16.09	Plymouth A (a)	L	3-5	Raquel Murray, Patricia Gimenez (x2)	44	11
23.09	QPR (h)		P-P			11
30.09	Coventry United (a)	L	1-4	Katie Whitehead	165	12
03.10	Watford (h)	L	0-1			12
07.10	QPR (h)	D	3-3	Courtney Clarke, Katie Whitehead, Gemma Abela	55	12
28.10	Oxford United (h)	L	0-2			12
11.11	Chichester City (a)	L	2-4	Holly Turner 13, Courtney Clark 90	80	12
25.11	MK Dons (h)	L	1-2	Holly Turner 44		12
16.12	Cardiff City L (a)	L	0-7		80	12
13.01	Portsmouth (a)	L	0-2		93	12
27.01	Loughborough F (h)	L	0-2			12
14.02	Gillingham (a)	L	3-5	Courtney Clarke 4, Gemma Abela 15, Hollie Turner 83	60	12
03.03	Plymouth Argyle (h)	L	0-2			12
10.03	Coventry United (h)	L	0-6			12
14.03	Watford (a)		P-P			12
17.03	Chichester City (h)	L	0-8			12
24.03	Oxford United (a)	L	0-12		158	12
14.04	QPR (a)	L	1-4	Holly Turner 2	90	12
28.04	Watford (a)	L	1-3	Sophie Kelly 52	131	12
05.05	MK Dons (a)	L	0-4			12

*Played at Aspect Arena, (Concord Rangers FC)

2018-19 FA CUP: COMPETED AS C&K BASILDON

Date	Opponent	Res	Score
02.12 R2	Keynsham Town (a)	L	3-8

2018-19 WNL CUP: COMPETED AS C&K BASILDON

Date	Opponent	Res	Score	Att
02.09 DR	Cambridge U (a)	L	0-2	75

2018-19 WNL PLATE: COMPETED AS C&K BASILDON

Date	Opponent	Res	Score	Scorers	Att
R1	Bye				
14.10 R2	Ipswich Town (a)	L	2-4	Raquel Murray, Gemma Abela	35est

2018-19 ESSEX FA COUNTY CUP: COMPETED AS C&K BASILDON

Date	Opponent	Res	Score	Scorers	Att
20.01 QF	Harlow Town (h)	W	3-0	Sophie Rhodes 28, Holly Turner 48, Maddie Thomas	
17.02 SF	Hutton (a)	W	5-1	Holly Turner (x3), Maddie Thomas, Jodie Osborne	50est
18.04 F	Billericay Town (n)	L	0-4	Mollie Debell sent off 36	578

(n) Played at The Len Salmon Stadium, (Bowers & Pitsea FC)

AFC WIMBLEDON

2019-20: WNL SOUTH EAST 1 (Tier 4)

Founded: 1973 (as Friends of Fulham)

Nickname: The Dons

Season 2018-19:

WNL South East 1 (Tier 4): 6th

FA Cup: 4th Round

WNL Cup: Quarter-finals

County Cup: n/a

Female fans of men's side Fulham FC formed the team in 1973 as Friends of Fulham, starting out in the Hounslow & District League before progressing to the Greater London League and then the WPL. In 1984 Friends of Fulham won the Treble of FA Cup (beating Doncaster Belles in the final at Craven Cottage), the Home Counties League and the League Cup. They were FA Cup runners-up in 1989 (losing to Leasowe Pacific, who later became Everton) and 1990 (when they were beaten by Doncaster Belles). Friends of Fulham teamed up with Wimbledon FC men's in 1986, becoming Wimbledon Ladies. In 1993 a 3-2 win at Plough Lane saw them become the first team to beat Doncaster Belles in a League game for 15 years. When Wimbledon FC relocated to Milton Keynes in 2003 and became MK Dons, the ladies team joined forces with new men's club AFC Wimbledon.

2018-19 AS IT HAPPENS

02.12.18: The Dons shock Tier 3 Portsmouth in the FA Cup 2nd Round as Caroline Bisson and Georgia Heasman score in a 2-0 home win.

06.01.19: Higher tier opponents are toppled once more as the Dons knock out Hull City from the division above with a 3-0 win away in the FA Cup 3rd Round.

03.02.19: Having been handed a plum draw at home to WSL outfit Bristol City in the FA Cup 4th Round, the Dons put in a brilliant display but lose 3-0 to the Vixens in front of a crowd of 520.

2018-19 RESULTS: (HOME VENUE: WAR MEMORIAL SPORTS GROUND, (CARSHALTON ATH. FC), UNLESS STATED)

2018-19 WNL SE 1					Att	Pos
19.08	Cambridge United (h)	D	1-1	Katie Stanley 36	50	
26.08	Luton Town (a)	W	3-1	Sophie Manzi 24, 86, Sian Wylie 32	51	4
09.09	Billericay Town (a)	L	0-1	*Caroline Bisson missed pen 19*	163	6
12.09	Crawley Wasps (a)	L	2-5	Caroline Bisson 3, Jess Trimnell (pen) 75	100	8
16.09	Ipswich Town (h)	D	1-1	Caroline Bisson 26	100	8
03.10	Leyton Orient (a)	D	2-2	Jess Trimnell 36, Rebecca Sargeant 61	49	9
21.10	Stevenage (a)	W	2-1	Rebecca Sargeant 19, Katie Stanley 69		
28.10	Denham United (h)	W	4-0	Rebecca Sargeant 18, Jenny Nagle 45, Caroline Bisson 53, Jordanne Hoesli Atkins 71	50	3
04.11	Norwich City (h)	W	4-2	Jenny Nagle 5, 28, Caroline Bisson 9, Katie Stanley 48	50	4
25.11	Enfield Town (a)	W	3-0	Hannah Baptise 20, Katie Stanley 56, Jenny Nagle 60	53	3
16.12	Actonians (h)	L	2-5	Caroline Bisson 32, Bernice Tulley 90	50	3
13.01	Cambridge United (a)	L	0-3		75	6
10.02	Ipswich Town (a)		P-P			6
13.02	Crawley Wasps (h)	L	0-4		70	6
24.02	Luton Town (h)	L	1-4	Katie Stanley 65	30	6
03.03	Billericay Town (h)	W	2-1	Megan Kowalski 51, Hannah Baptiste 87	50	6
10.03	Denham United (a)	D	0-0		45	6
13.03	Leyton Orient (h)	L	1-3	Katie Stanley 25	50	6
24.03	Stevenage (h)	L	1-2	*Caroline Bisson missed pen 50 (saved),* Caroline Bisson 66	60	7
31.03	Norwich City (a)	D	1-1	Hannah Baptiste 32		7
07.04	Ipswich Town (a)	W	2-0	Georgia Heasman 55, Sophie Manzi 65	51	7
21.04	Enfield Town (h)*	W	3-2	Sian Wylie 5, Rebecca Sargeant 82, Rosie Russell 90+4	85	6
05.05	Actonians (a)	W	1-0	Becky McLaren-Johnson 81		6

*Played at Kingsmeadow, (Chelsea FC Women & AFC Wimbledon)

2018-19 FA CUP

23.09 RQ2	AFC Phoenix (h)	W	1-0 aet	Katie Stanley 108	100
07.10 RQ3	Goldalming Town (h)	W	4-0	Laura Quinn-Low 35, 38, Sophie Manzi 73, Own Goal 75	100
11.11 R1	New London Lionesses (a)		P-P		
18.11 R1	New London Lionesses (a)	D	3-3aet (W 4-3p)	Caroline Bisson 34, 40, 55	76
02.12 R2	Portsmouth (h)	W	2-0	Caroline Bisson 28, Georgia Heasman 57	95
06.01 R3	Hull City (a)	W	3-0	Katie Stanley 62, Jordan Hoesli-Atkins 69, Georgia Heasman 90+2	133
03.02 R4	Bristol City (h)	L	0-3		520

2018-19 WNL CUP

02.09 DR	Southampton Saints (a)	W	1-0	Jess Trimnell 87	25
30.09 R1	Buckland Athletic (h)	W	4-0	Bernice Tully 22, Laura Quinn-Low 29, Jenny Nagle 66, Georgia Heasman (pen) 85	100
14.10 R2	Larkhall Athletic (a)	W	3-2 aet	Katie Stanley 34, Caroline Bisson 47, Jess Trimnell 116	
09.12 R3	Cambridge United (h)	W	2-1	Jenny Nagle 39, Caroline Bisson 41	70
17.02 QF	Loughborough F (a)	L	0-3		86

BARNSLEY

2019-20: WNL NORTH 1 (Tier 4)

Founded: 1986

Nickname: The Reds

Season 2018-19

WNL North 1 (Tier 4): 4th

FA Cup: 2nd Qualifying Round

WNL Cup: Determining Round

WNL Plate: Quarter-finals

County Cup: Winners

Dean Bradford

Barnsley have made great strides in recent seasons, winning the Sheffield & Hallamshire FA County Cup for the first time in 2016 when they beat Huddersfield Town 4-2 in the final with 16-year-old Brittany Sanderson scoring a hat-trick. In 2016-17 they claimed the North East Regional Premier League title (Tier 5) and won their regional League Cup, beating Wallsend 3-2 in the final. Their promotion at the end of that season brought them into Tier 4 where they have been ever since. Fresh from leading Nettleham (now Lincoln City) to promotion, Chris Hamilton arrived as the Reds' new manager in the summer of 2018. His first season in charge was hugely impressive as he led Barnsley to a 4th place finish in the League and a County Cup final triumph over Tier 3 Huddersfield.

2018-19 AS IT HAPPENS

16.09.18: Barnsley's first League win of the season is a dramatic one as they beat Liverpool Feds 5-4 with goals from Melissa Woodhouse (x2), Amy Woodruff (x2) and a late Kathryn Smith penalty.

14.10.18: Barnsley beat Tier 3 Doncaster Rovers Belles in a thrilling WNL Cup 2nd Round match. Sophie Bell levels the scores at 2-2 in added time to take the match to extra-time. With a penalty shootout just two minutes away Mollie Crump nets the winner as The Reds prevail 3-2.

01.04.19: Midfielder Lindsey Tugby signs from WNL North 1 rivals Brighouse Town.

12.05.19: Despite playing the second half with a suspected broken finger goalkeeper Skye Kirkham saves two penalties in a shootout as The Reds beat Tier 3 Huddersfield Town 4-1 on spot-kicks following a 3-3 draw in the Sheffield & Hallamshire FA County Cup final. Barnsley go ahead early on when Drew Greene sets up twin sister Darcie for the opener. Their opponents come back from 2-0 and 3-2 down, but Barnsley eventually triumph on penalties.

2018-19 RESULTS: (HOME VENUE: BARNSLEY FC ACADEMY UNLESS STATED)

2018-19 WNL NORTH 1					Att	Pos
26.08	Chester-le-Street (a)	L	1-3	Annie Ward 82	40	
09.09	Bolton W (h)	L	0-1		50	11
12.09	Brighouse Town (a)	L	1-2	Sophie Bell 20	108	11
16.09	Liverpool Feds (a)	W	5-4	Melissa Woodhouse 36, 45, Amy Woodruff 67, 80, Kathryn Smith (pen) 87	40	9
30.09	Burnley (h)	L	0-1		50	10
04.10	Leeds United (h)		P-P			10
21.10	Crewe Alexandra (a)	W	3-2	Melissa Woodhouse 55, 83, Amy Woodruff 88	50	10
28.10	Chorley (h)	W	3-1	Melissa Woodhouse 3, Sophie Bell 52, Mollie Crump 75	50	9
11.11	Morecambe (h)	W	3-1	Drew Greene 42, Kathryn Smith (pen) 56, Amy Woodruff 57	50	9
18.11	Norton & Stockton (a)	W	4-3	Rebecca Hornsey 5, Melissa Woodhouse 20, Sophie Crosby 55, Kathryn Smith 88	80	5
20.11	Leeds United (h)	W	2-1	Melissa Woodhouse 8, 62	200est	4
02.12	Newcastle U (h)	D	0-0		50	4
06.01	Chester-le-Street (h)	W	2-0	Drew Greene 32, Danielle Whitham (pen) 77	50	2
13.01	Morecambe (a)	D	3-3	Darcie Kendall Greene 19, Kathryn Smith 37, Drew Greene 84	35	2
27.01	Brighouse Town (h)	D	1-1	Melissa Woodhouse 48	50	2
17.02	Liverpool Feds (h)	W	2-1	Drew Greene 29, Shannon Durkin 83, Danielle Whitham miss pen 45+2	100	2
10.03	Chorley (a)		P-P			4
13.03	Leeds United (a)	D	2-2	Sophie Bell 45, Own Goal 74	60	4
31.03	Burnley (a)	L	1-3	Danielle Whitham (pen) 90	88	6
07.04	Chorley (a)	W	5-1	Drew Greene 8, 19, Sophie Bell 17, Melissa Woodhouse 61, Shannon Durkin 77	107	5
14.04	Norton & Stockton (h)	W	2-1	Danielle Whitham 42, Kathryn Smith (pen) 58	50	4
21.04	Crewe Alexandra (h)	W	8-0	Annie Ward 14, Drew Greene 22, 24, 45, Shannon Durkin 27, Kathryn Smith (pen) 32, Ellie Brightmore 84, Sophie Bell 86	100	4

28.04	Bolton W (a)	D	2-2	Kathryn Smith 41, Darcie Kendall Greene 80		4
05.05	Newcastle U (a)	W	2-1	Drew Greene 41, Own Goal 72	110	4

2018-19 FA CUP

23.09 RQ2	Newcastle U (h)*	L	2-3 aet	Melissa Woodhouse 7, Amy Woodruff 41	50

*Played at Dorothy Hyman Sports Centre

2018-19 WNL CUP

02.09 DR	Bolton W (h)	L	3-4	Melissa Woodhouse 2, Amy Woodruff 15, Kathryn Smith 18, Lucy Turner sent off 85	50

2018-19 WNL PLATE

07.10 R1	Burton Albion (h)	W	5-1	Amy Woodruff 7, Mollie Crump 22, Emily Ward 62, Sophie Bell 71, Rebecca Hornsey 83	50
14.10 R2	Doncaster R B (a)	W	3-2 aet	Amy Woodruff 14, Sophie Bell 90+2, Mollie Crump 118	
09.12 R3	The New Saints (a)	W	9-0	Melissa Woodhouse 1, 60, 71, Darcie Kendall Greene 10, Annie Ward 16, Rebecca Hornsey 41, Amy Woodruff 69, 75, Sophie Bell 80	43
10.02 QF	West Bromwich A (h)	L	0-1		50

2018-19 SHEFFIELD & HALLAMSHIRE FA COUNTY CUP

16.12 R3	Doncaster Rovers (h)	W	w/o		
20.01 QF	Sheffield FC (h)	W	2-1	Danielle Whitham 16, Darcie Kendall Greene 19	
17.03 SF	Worksop Town (a)		P-P		
24.03 SF	Worksop Town (a)	W	3-0	Sophie Bell 33, Hannah Campbell 37, Drew Greene 65, Sophie Bell missed pen 65 (saved by Kathryn Wood - Greene scored rebound)	
12.05 F	Huddersfield Town (n)	D	3-3aet (W4-1p)	Darcie Greene 7, Melissa Woodhouse 11, Amy Woodruff 85	440est

(n)Played at New York Stadium, (Rotherham United FC)

"After a difficult start to 2018-19, I was hugely impressed with the way the players brought into what we were trying to do. Having lost four of our opening five League games everything clicked, and we lost just one of our remaining 17 games on our way to finishing 4th. The County Cup final in which we beat a strong Huddersfield Town team from the division above also showed what we can achieve. We will be aiming for promotion in 2019-20. In the past players who have grown up in this area, like Bethany England (Chelsea) and Amy Turner (Manchester United) have started out at bigger clubs, but we are putting in place a structure where players from the town can feel confident that beginning their development with us will give them every chance of success. We are also changing our name from Barnsley Ladies to Barnsley Women."

Chris Hamilton (Manager) & Steve Maddock (Chief Executive)

BEDWORTH UNITED

2019-20: WNL MIDLANDS 1 (Tier 4)

Founded: 2014

Nickname: United

Season 2018-19:

WNL Midlands 1: 5th

FA Cup: 2nd Qualifying Round

WNL Cup: Determining Round

WNL Plate: 3rd Round

County Cup: 2nd Round

Elisha Dunn

Bedworth were promoted into Tier 4 at the end of the 2017-18 season when they won the West Midlands Regional Premier League (Tier 5) title in dramatic style. United pipped Leafield Athletic by a solitary point. They acquitted themselves well at a higher level throughout 2018-19 rising to 2nd in the table at the start of December before finishing the campaign in 5th place.

2018-19 AS IT HAPPENS

26.08.18: Having been promoted as 2017-18 West Midlands Regional Premier champions Bedworth begin life in Tier 4 with a 2-1 away win against The New Saints.

21.10.18: After a run of four straight wins, Bedworth suffer League defeat for the first time all season as they lose 2-1 away to Long Eaton United.

24.03.19: Bedworth trail 3-0 at home to Long Eaton United with an hour played, but they hit back with goals from Xena Dhillon, Jessica Lundie and Kirsty Farnsworth to pull level at 3-3 with just 13 minutes left. However, one minute later Jade Arber completes her hat-trick for Long Eaton who win the WNL Midlands 1 encounter 4-3.

2018-19 RESULTS: (HOME VENUE: THE OVAL, (BEDWORTH UNITED FC) UNLESS STATED)

2018-19 WNL MIDLANDS 1

Date	Opponent	Res	Score	Scorers	Att	Pos
26.08	The New Saints (a)	W	2-1	Jessica Lundie 30, Amanda Whalley (pen) 42	26	6
09.09	Steel City W (h)	W	2-1	Amanda Whalley 73, Nicola Foskett 76	65	5
12.09	Bir'ham & W M (h)	W	2-1	Nicola Foskett, Lydia Hackney	60	4
16.09	Nettleham (a)	W	3-2	Kirsty Farnsworth 32, Jessica Lundie 60, 65	50	3
21.10	Long Eaton Utd (a)	L	1-2	Jessica Lundie 81	60	4
28.10	Burton Albion (h)	W	5-1	Jessica Lundie 17, Kirsty Farnsworth 22, Nicola Foskett 30, Sophie Wilson (pen) 40, Jessica Lundie 65	55	3
01.11	Solihull Moors (a)	W	4-1	Sarah Rowles 54, 75, Shanice Walsh 61, Lydia Hackney 77	30	3
04.11	Wolverhampton W (h)	W	2-1	Alice Belcher 18, Kirsty Farnsworth 89, *Amanda Whalley missed pen 74 (saved by Katie Clarke)*	80	3
25.11	West Brom Albion (a)	L	0-1		52	3
02.12	Sporting Khalsa (h)	D	3-3	Amanda Whalley 38, Shanice Walsh 75, Kirsty Farnsworth 85	35	2
20.01	The New Saints (h)	L	1-3	Kirsty Farnsworth 62	40	4
27.01	Bir'ham & W M (a)	L	0-4		27	4
03.02	Steel City W (a)	W	2-0	Kirsty Farnsworth 7, 29	35	4
24.02	Nettleham (h)	W	2-1	Sophie Wilson 50, 55	40	4
10.03	Burton Albion (a)	W	7-1	Jodie McGuckin 1, Xena Dhillon 6, Kirsty Farnsworth 20, Kirstie Deacon 21, Sophie Wilson 40, 65, 85	50	4
24.03	Long Eaton United (h)	L	3-4	Xena Dhillon 60, Jessica Lundie 65, Kirsty Farnsworth 77	40	4
31.03	Solihull Moors (h)	W	5-1	Jodie McGuckin 4, 44, Jessica Lundie 10, Kirsty Farnsworth 19, Tiarna Gilkes 50	35	4
07.04	West Brom Albion (h)	L	0-5	*Leanne Jones sent off 41*	60	4
14.04	Wolverhampton W (a)	L	1-9	Xena Dhillon 21	60	4
05.05	Sporting Khalsa (a)	L	1-4	Kirsty Farnsworth		5

2018-19 FA CUP

23.09 RQ2	Bir'ham & W M (h)	L	0-2		

2018-19 WNL CUP

02.09 DR	Derby County (a)	L	1-3	Shanice Walsh 29	110est

2018-19 WNL Plate

R1	Bye				
14.10 R2	Swindon Town (a)	W	2-1	Shanice Walsh 38, Kirsty Farnsworth 72	
09.12 R3	MK Dons (a)	L	1-2 aet	Jessica Lundie 68	120

2018-19 BIRMINGHAM FA COUNTY CUP

18.11 R1	Lye Town (h)	W	5-1	Sarah Rowles 22, Jessica Lundie 50, Amanda Whalley 55, 76, Jess Saunders 68	25
16.12 R2	Leafield Athletic (a)	L	3-6	Jessica Lundie 29, Amanda Whalley 76, Maisie Farr (og) 80	50est

BILLERICAY TOWN

2019-20: WNL SOUTH EAST 1 (Tier 4)

Founded: 1986 (as Basildon Ladies)

Nickname: The Blues

Season 2018-19:

WNL South East 1 (Tier 4): Runners-up

FA Cup: 3rd Round

WNL Cup: 2nd Round

County Cup: Winners

Nicky Hayes

The club started out as Basildon Ladies in 1986 and began life competing in the Greater London League, Division Three. They changed their name to Billericay Town ahead of the 1996-97 campaign. The Blues finished 2017-18 as Eastern Regional League Premier (Tier 5) champions when they pipped Acle United to the title by one point to secure promotion to the WNL. Their first season in Tier 4 was a success as they finished runners-up to fellow newly promoted side Crawley Wasps.

2018-19 AS IT HAPPENS

19.08.18: Having been promoted as 2017-18 Eastern Regional Premier champions, Billericay get their Tier 4 campaign under way with a 3-0 win away to Denham United.

03.10.18: After winning their opening five League games in Tier 3 and remaining unbeaten in six, Town suffer defeat for the first time all season as they lose 2-0 at Ipswich.

06.01.19: Billericay describe their FA Cup 3rd Rd tie against Tier 3 Loughborough Foxes as arguably their biggest match of all time. They put on a great show in a 4-3 defeat.

Nicky Hayes

27.01.19: Two players are on target eight times each as Billericay beat Rayleigh Town by an astonishing 31-0 in the Essex FA County Cup quarter-final. Zoe Rushen and Samantha Pittuck both hit eight goals. Rayleigh, who play four divisions below Billericay, are praised by Billericay manager Kim Coster who says: "They came, were competitive and never gave up."

31.03.19: Billericay become the first team in two years to beat WNL South East 1 leaders Crawley Wasps in the League. They prevail 1-0 courtesy of Danica Dougal's (née Revell's) first-half penalty.

14.04.19: Town's slim title hopes are ended despite a 2-1 home win against Cambridge. Leaders Crawley Wasps are champions with three games to go as they beat Enfield 1-0.

18.04.19: Billericay win the Essex FA County Cup for the first time in their history with a 4-0 victory over Tier 3 strugglers C&K Basildon 4-0 in the final at Bowers & Pitsea FC.

2018-19 RESULTS: (HOME VENUE: AGP ARENA, (BILLERICAY TOWN FC), UNLESS STATED)

2018-19 WNL SE 1

Date	Opponent	Res	Score	Scorers	Att	Pos
19.08	Denham United (a)	W	3-0	Lucy Jones 52, Lindsey Morgan 71, Samantha Pittuck 87	50	
26.08	Stevenage (h)	W	6-1	Samantha Pittuck 4, 74, Zoe Rushen 10, Jay Blackie 56, 66, Lucy Jones 82,	70	1
09.09	AFC Wimbledon (h)	W	1-0	Megan Jiggins 26	163	2
12.09	Leyton Orient (a)	W	3-1	Zoe Rushen 23, 80, Georgia Box 56	68	2
16.09	Luton Town (h)	W	2-1	Lucy Jones 18, Samantha Pittuck 35	102	2
30.09	Actonians (a)	D	4-4	Jay Blackie 10, 22, Georgia Box 20, 51, Jay Blackie missed pen 88 (saved by Paige Horsnell)	30	1
03.10	Ipswich Town (a)	L	0-2		70	2
21.10	Enfield Town (h)	W	3-2	Zoe Rushen 39, 43, 44	115	1
04.11	Crawley Wasps (h)	L	0-2		123	2
16.12	Norwich City (h)	W	1-0	Paris Smith 65	100	2
13.01	Denham United (h)	W	6-0	Jay Blackie (x2), Danica Dougal, Esme Lancaster (x2), Sophie Vale		2
10.02	Enfield Town (a)	D	2-2	Jay Blackie 57, Lindsey Morgan 62	58	2
13.02	Leyton Orient (h)	W	2-1	Zoe Rushen (x2)		2
24.02	Stevenage (a)	W	2-0	Zoe Rushen 60, Samantha Pittuck 90	28	2
03.03	AFC Wimbledon (a)	L	1-2	Lucy Jones	50	2
10.03	Actonians (h)		P-P			2
13.03	Ipswich Town (h)	D	1-1	Esme Lancaster 13		2
24.03	Cambridge Utd (a)	W	2-0	Zoe Rushen, Danica Dougal	73	2
31.03	Crawley Wasps (a)	W	1-0	Danica Dougal (pen) 38	280	2
14.04	Cambridge Utd (h)	W	2-1	Zoe Rushen, Danica Dougal		2
21.04	Luton Town (a)	W	4-2	Samantha Pittuck, Karissa Rodney, Karen Stephanou, Zoe Rushen		2
28.04	Actonians (h)	W	6-3	Jay Blackie, Danica Dougal, Zoe Rushen (x3), Freya Fuller		2
05.05	Norwich City (a)	L	2-4	Samantha Pittuck, Zoe Rushen	74	2

2018-19 FA CUP

Date	Opponent	Res	Score	Scorers	Att
23.09 RQ2	Colney Heath (h)	W	9-1	Lindsey Morgan 4, Megan Juggins 14, Zoe Rushen 60, 66, Nicole Farmer 62, Amy Nash 73, Jay Blackie 79, 85, Danica Dougal 88	78
07.10 RQ3	Wymondham Town (a)	W	4-3	Jay Blackie 14, Zoe Rushen 18, 85, Lindsey Morgan 80, Alex Baker sent off 40	
11.11 R1	Norwich City (a)	W	3-2 aet	Esme Lancaster, Zoe Rushen, Georgia Box, Karissa Rodney sent off 44, Nicole Farmer sent off 98	74
02.12 R2	Luton Town (h)	W	3-1 aet	Karen Stephanou, Broghan Kelly, Jay Blackie	70
06.01 R3	Loughborough F (h)	L	3-4	Samantha Pittuck 6, Zoe Rushen 81, 85	160

2018-19 WNL CUP

02.09 DR	Maidenhead Utd (h)	W	10-1	Jay Blackie 13, 45, Karissa Rodney 22, 52, 61, Samantha Pittuck 26, 39, 54, Zoe Rushen 59, Hayley Piggott (pen) 86	100
R1	Bye				
14.10 R2	Chichester City (h)	L	0-2		

2018-19 ESSEX FA COUNTY CUP

20.01	Rayleigh Town (h)		P-P		
27.01 QF	Rayleigh Town (h)	W	31-0	Zoe Rushen (x8), Samantha Pittuck (x8), Karissa Rodney (x5), Jay Blackie (x3), Paris Smith (x2) Esme Lancaster (x2), Lindsey Morgan (x2), Danica Dougal	
17.02 SF	Brentwood Town (h)	W	8-0	Lindsey Morgan (x4), Sophie Vale (x2), Zoe Rushen, Kerry Stimson	79
18.04 F	C&K Basildon (n)	W	4-0	Danica Dougal (pen) 9, Samantha Pittuck 45, Esme Lancaster 60, Zoe Rushen 62	578

(n) Played at The Len Salmon Stadium, (Bowers & Pitsea FC)

"I think we exceeded expectations as a club throughout 2018-19 with an amazing debut campaign at this level. Finishing 2nd in our first season in the WNL and winning the Essex FA County Cup for the first time in the club's history were both incredible achievements to be proud of. This is a special club that runs like one big family. Our hopes for 2019-20 are to push for promotion and build the profile of the club still further."

Lindsey Morgan – Captain

BIRMINGHAM & WEST MIDLANDS

2019-20: WNL MIDLANDS 1 (Tier 4)

Founded: 2001 (as Birmingham University)

Nickname: West Mids

Season 2018-19:

WNL Midlands 1 (Tier 4): 3rd

FA Cup: 3rd Qualifying Round

WNL Cup: 2nd Round

County Cup: 2nd Round

Founded in 2001 as Birmingham University, they became Birmingham Athletic and subsequently West Midlands Police before settling on Birmingham & West Midlands in 2014. The club have been in Tier 4 since being promoted to what was then known as WPL Midlands 1 by winning the 2014-15 West Midlands Regional Premier League. They also lifted the West Midlands Regional Premier League Cup in 2014-15 to complete the Double. There was further success in 2017-18 when they reached the Birmingham FA County Cup final. However, the match ended in a 15-0 defeat to Tier 3 heavyweights Coventry United. A 3rd place finish in 2018-19 bodes well for the future with excitement surrounding the club's move to the Trevor Brown Memorial Ground, the home of Boldmere St Michaels FC, for 2019-20.

2018-19 AS IT HAPPENS

13.12.18: Birmingham & West Midlands withdraw from their upcoming County Cup tie against Tier 3 Coventry United due to "excessive injuries and illness".

13.01.19: A run of seven League matches without defeat (W6 D1) comes to an end as Birmingham & West Midlands narrowly lose 1-0 at home to leaders West Brom.

19.02.19: The club announces that their stadium has been broken into overnight with all their match day equipment stolen. They thank the FA WNL for providing three new balls to last them until the end of the season.

05.05.19: Before the final match of the season against Solihull Moors, both teams give a guard of honour to long-term Birmingham players Emily Painter and Amy Eastwood who are hanging up their boots after over 25 years of service between them. Birmingham win the match 9-2 with Painter scoring twice.

2018-19 RESULTS: (HOME VENUE: THE VALE STADIUM, (CASTLE VALE FC) UNLESS STATED)

2018-19 WNL MIDLANDS 1					Att	Pos
19.08	West Brom A (a)	L	2-4	Stephanie Weston 13, Maimee Morris 41	58	
26.08	Nettleham (h)	W	2-1	Stephanie Weston 5, Natalie Gibson 80	22	7
09.09	Wolverhampton W (h)	L	1-3	Charlotte Fisher 78	67	8
12.09	Bedworth United (a)	L	1-2	Evangeline Gallop 13, *Chloe Evans sent off 34*	60	8
16.09	The New Saints (h)	W	4-1	Charlotte Fisher 8, Emily Painter 30, Giorgia Elizabeth Bracelli 58, Amy Eastwood 69	31	8
30.09	Long Eaton United (a)	W	4-1	Stephanie Weston 9, Lauryn Bryan 48, Charlotte Fisher 55, Christina Torkildsen 66	30	6
02.10	Sporting Khalsa (h)	W	2-1	Stephanie Weston 27, Lauryn Bryan 55	28	4
21.10	Burton Albion (a)	D	2-2	Stephanie Weston 57, Lauryn Bryan 73	61	3
04.11	Steel City Wanderers (h)	W	7-1	Stephanie Weston 4, 36, Ashlea Hargreaves 9, Nadia Bacciochi 66, Charlotte Fisher 76, 78, Natalie Gibson 85, *Birmingham & W M missed pen 43 (saved by Kirsty Johnson)*	17	4
02.12	Solihull Moors (a)		P-P			4
09.12	Nettleham (a)	W	4-0	Maimee Morris 11, Emily Painter 23, Stephanie Weston 43, Evangeline Gallop 58	50	4
06.01	Solihull Moors (a)	W	2-1	Shannie Jennings 16, Maimee Morris 72	30	3
13.01	West Brom A (h)	L	0-1		78	3
27.01	Bedworth United (h)	W	4-0	Emily Painter 32, Stephanie Weston 35, Evie Harms 48, Lyndsey Glover 52	27	3
10.02	Wolverhampton W (a)	W	3-1	Emily Painter 2, Lauryn Bryan 57, Evangeline Gallop 81	40	2
24.02	The New Saints (a)	W	5-1	Natalie Gibson 10, Evangeline Gallop 24, 49, Lauryn Bryan 38, Emily Painter 45	66	2
10.03	Long Eaton United (h)	D	2-2	Evangeline Gallop 1, Katherine Clarke (og) 87	43	3
13.03	Sporting Khalsa (a)	L	0-2		40	3
24.03	Burton Albion (h)	W	3-0	Emily Painter 64, 90, Evangeline Gallop 66	53	3
14.04	Steel City W (a)	W	11-0	Nadia Bacciochi 12, Maimee Morris 18, 44, Emily Painter 35, Evangeline Gallop 39, 58, 76, Elizabeth Steele (pen) 49, Stephanie Weston 74, Laura Cooper 69, Shannie Jennings 90	20	3
05.05	Solihull Moors (h)	W	9-2	Nadia Bacciochi 3, 35, Evangeline Gallop 10, 29, Emily Painter 15, 57, Stephanie Weston 17, 48, Shannie Jennings 88	42	3

2018-19 FA CUP

23.09 RQ2	Bedworth United (a)	W	2-0	Stephanie Weston 26, Shannie Jennings 50	
07.10 RQ3	Wolverhampton W (h)	L	0-2		54

2018-19 WNL CUP

02.09 DR	Nettleham (a)	W	2-1	Charlotte Fisher 72, Natalie Gibson 90+1	60
R1	Bye				
14.10 R2	Hull City (a)	L	1-2 aet	Evangeline Gallop (pen) 90	30

2018-19 BIRMINGHAM FA COUNTY CUP

18.11 R1	Burton Albion (h)	W	4-1	Lauryn Bryan 4, Maimee Morris 64, Evangeline Gallop 68, Emily Painter 68	23
16.12 R2	Coventry United (h)	L	w/o		

"Despite a transition in players and coaches before the start of 2018-19 everyone at Birmingham & West Midlands gelled really well which made the season a fantastic experience. We're a real family club where everyone involved goes above and beyond for the benefit of everyone else. In 2019-20 we hope to progress even further following the establishment of a three-way partnership with Boldmere St Michaels FC and the University of Birmingham. We will be pushing to better our 3rd-place finish of 2018-19 and hopefully enjoy a Cup run or two to match our great strides off the pitch."

Marcus Webber – Manager

BOLTON WANDERERS

2019-20: WNL NORTH 1 (Tier 4)

Founded: 1989

Nickname: Wanderers

Season 2018-19:

WNL North 1 (Tier 4): 8th

FA Cup: 3rd Round

WNL Cup: Semi-finals

County Cup: Quarter-finals

Bolton Wanderers Ladies officially became part of the Bolton Wanderers FC family in 2010. They won their first League title in 2016-17 and were thus promoted to Tier 4 as North West Regional Premier League champions. They secured the title with a game to spare thanks to a 3-0 win away to Blackpool when they needed only a point. Having been promoted, they then finished a highly creditable 4th in what was then known as WPL North 1 in 2017-18. The high points of 2018-19 were making the FA Cup 3rd Round for the first time and reaching the WNL Cup semi-finals.

2018-19 AS IT HAPPENS

21.10.18: Roisin Havelin and Ruby Howard both score four goals as Bolton beat lower League Burnley Belvedere 13-0 in the Lancashire FA County Cup 2nd Round.

09.12.18: Bolton beat WNL Midlands 1 outfit West Brom on penalties following a 2-2 draw to make it through to the FA Cup 3rd Round for the first time in their history.

06.01.19: Bolton put in a fine performance in their first ever FA Cup 3rd Round match but lose 2-0 away to Tier 3 high-flyers Cardiff City Ladies.

28.04.19: Bolton play their first game at the men's University of Bolton Stadium. The match ends in a 2-2 draw against Barnsley with Rosie Havelin and Nicola Worthington getting Wanderers' goals.

2018-19 RESULTS: (HOME VENUE: SKUNA STADIUM, (ATHERTON COLLIERIES FC) UNLESS STATED)

2018-19 WNL NORTH 1					Att	Pos
19.08	Newcastle United (h)	W	2-1	Ruby Howard 20, Kelly Halligan 55	60	
26.08	Chorley (h)		P-P			7
09.09	Barnsley (a)	W	1-0	Nicola Worthington 79	50	4
13.09	Burnley (h)	L	0-1			7
16.09	Leeds United (h)	W	4-0	Kelly Halligan 21, 71, Rosie Havelin 52, Katy Morris 55	65	5
03.10	Brighouse Town (a)	L	1-2	Safron Newhouse 3	56	6
28.10	Norton & Stockton Anc. (h)	W	3-0	Safron Newhouse 17, Ruby Howard 32, Rosie Havelin 60	50	5
04.11	Liverpool Feds (a)	L	0-5		50	8
25.11	Morecambe (h)	W	2-1	Safron Newhouse 30, Kelly Halligan 58	75	8
20.01	Chorley (a)	D	1-1	Rosie Havelin 16	102	8
27.01	Chorley (h)		P-P			8
10.02	Crewe Alexandra (h)	D	0-0		70	8
13.02	Burnley (a)	W	1-0	Kelly Halligan 85	77	6
24.02	Chester-le-Street T (h)	L	0-2		40	7
10.03	Chester-le-Street T (a)		P-P			8
13.03	Brighouse Town (h)		P-P			8
17.03	Newcastle United (a)	L	1-2	Safron Newhouse 55	37	8
20.03	Brighouse Town (h)	D	0-0		105	8
24.03	Liverpool Feds (h)	L	2-3	Rachel Hindle 8, Safron Newhouse 44		9
31.03	Norton & Stockton A (a)	L	1-2	Natalie Richardson 40	90	9
03.04	Chorley (h)	L	0-1			9
07.04	Leeds United (a)	D	0-0		100	9
14.04	Morecambe (a)	W	2-1	Nicole Johnston, Hayley Langford	35	8
21.04	Chester-le-Street T (a)	L	1-2	Rosie Havelin	40	8
28.04	Barnsley (h)*	D	2-2	Rosie Havelin 56, Nicola Worthington 63		8
05.05	Crewe Alexandra (a)	L	0-1		41	8

*Played at University of Bolton Stadium, (Bolton Wanderers FC)

2018-19 FA CUP

23.09 RQ2	Hartlepool United (h)	W	3-0	Nicola Worthington 25, Safron Newhouse 75, Ruby Howard 60	
07.10 RQ3	West Didsbury & Chorlton (a)	W	4-0	Kelly Halligan 20, 40, Safron Newhouse 55, Rachel Hindle 65	95
11.11 R1	Norton & Stockton Ancients (a)	W	1-0	Safron Newhouse 30	100
02.12 R2	West Brom (h)		P-P		
09.12 R2	West Brom (h)+	D	2-2aet (W 5-4p)	Safron Newhouse, Kelly Halligan	
06.01 R3	Cardiff City L (a)	L	0-2		

+Played at Little Lever School

2018-19 WNL CUP

02.09 DR	Barnsley (a)	W	4-3	Safron Newhouse 4, 60, Nicola Worthington 80, 88	50
R1	Bye				
14.10 R2	Derby County (a)	W	2-1	Safron Newhouse 3, 15	135
13.01 R3	Hull City (h)	W	3-1 aet	Safron Newhouse 55, 100, 118	
17.02 QF	Stoke City (h)	D	1-1aet (W5-3p)	Rosie Havelin 90+2	75
03.03 SF	Crawley Wasps (a)	L	0-1		120

2018-19 LANCASHIRE FA COUNTY CUP

30.09 R1	Barrow Celtic Jnrs Comets (h)	W	w/o		
21.10 R2	Burnley Belvedere (h)	W	13-0	Roisin Havelin 5, 20, 58, 76, Safron Newhouse 7, 55, Ruby Howard 10, 15, 35, 85, Rachel Hindle 63, Nicola Worthington 67, Caitlin Knowles 80	
18.11 QF	Fylde (a)	D	0-0 (L1-3p)		50est

"The team enjoyed two big Cup runs in 2018-19 but the weight of fixtures ended up counting against us in the League. We have six new signings planned for 2019-20 and with the current players having benefited from a year together we can hopefully push on. We fizzled out a bit towards the end of the campaign but, with a very young team, I think we can now get some stability and build for the future."

Chris Knights – Manager

,FORD CITY

ZU1.. /: WNL DIVISION 1 NORTH (Tier 4)

Founded: 1988

Nickname: The Bantams

Season 2018-19:

WNL NP (Tier 3): 13th (R)

FA Cup: 2nd Round

WNL Cup: Determining Round

WNL Plate: 2nd Round

County Cup: 3rd Round

In 1989 – a year after their formation – Bradford City were founder members of the Yorkshire and Humberside League. Their closest brush with major glory came in 1997-98 in the WNL Cup (or WPL Cup as it was then called). At the time the competition was the country's main League Cup competition and the Bantams reached the semi-finals only to lose on penalties to eventual winners Arsenal after a 2-2 draw. The 2018-19 campaign was a difficult one as they lost all their League matches and were relegated to Tier 4.

2018-19 AS IT HAPPENS

21.10.18: City get their first win of the season in any competition as they beat lower League side Farsley Celtic 4-1 in the West Riding FA County Cup 1st Round.

18.12.18: Manager Jamie Grand leaves the club with Bradford bottom of the table.

28.12.18: Bradford announce that Steve Winterburn will return to the club as interim first-team manager to work alongside existing coaches Meg Lawson and Toni Butcher. However, Lawson and Butcher quit five days later.

18.05.19: Retiring chairperson Sally Thackray is recognised for services to women's football at the WNL play-off final between Blackburn Rovers and Coventry United which is staged at Bradford City FC's Valley Parade.

2018-19 RESULTS: (HOME VENUE: PLUMPTON PARK, (ECCLESHILL UTD FC) UNLESS STATED)

2018-19 WNL NP

					Att	Pos
19.08	Nottingham Forest (a)	L	0-3		105	
26.08	Sunderland (h)	L	1-2	Olivia Taylor (pen) 33	120	12
09.09	Sheffield FC (a)	L	0-2		118	12
12.09	Guiseley Vixens (h)	L	1-7	Keegan Lambert 36, *Shirley Murphy sent off 60*	97	12
16.09	Stoke Ladies (a)	L	3-7	Shirley Murphy 22, Demi Wisher 33, Zoe Roberts 89	102	12
23.09	Huddersfield T (h)	L	0-8		125	12
30.09	Middlesbrough (h)	L	0-4		76	12
02.10	Blackburn Rovers (a)	L	0-10		99	13
04.11	Hull City (h)	L	1-3	Jessica Dunlop 80	53	13
11.11	Doncaster R B (a)	L	1-5	Shirley Murphy 20	86	13
25.11	Fylde Ladies (a)	L	0-9		47	13
09.12	Derby County (h)		P-P			13
13.01	Sunderland (a)	L	1-10	Falone Sumaili 78	124	13
20.01	Derby County (h)	L	0-10		65	13
27.01	Stoke City (h)	L	0-5		62	13
10.02	Nottingham F (h)	L	0-2	Bradford GK Aimee Routledge saved Ashleigh Edwards pen 73	39	13
12.02	Guiseley Vixens (a)		P-P			13
17.02	Sheffield FC (h)	L	0-5		37	13
24.02	Middlesbrough (a)	L	1-8	Harriet Jakeman 68	45	13
05.03	Guiseley Vixens (a)	L	0-9		81	13
10.03	Derby County (a)	L	1-2	Falone Sumaili 25	72	13
13.03	Blackburn R (h)		P-P			13
17.03	Hull City (a)	L	1-3	Falone Sumaili 11	72	13
31.03	Doncaster R B (h)	L	0-1		61	13
14.04	Fylde (h)	L	0-5		23	13
01.05	Blackburn Rovers (h)	L	1-9	Own Goal 10	42	13
05.05	Huddersfield T (a)	L	0-11		89	13

2018-19 FA CUP

02.12 R2	Huddersfield T (a)	L	1-7	Zoe Roberts 88	105

2018-19 WNL CUP

02.09 DR	Hull City (a)	L	1-2	Keegan Lambert 45+5	80

2018-19 WNL PLATE

R1	Bye				
14.10 R2	The New Saints (a)		P-P		
28.10 R2	The New Saints (a)	L	0-5		43

2018-19 WEST RIDING FA COUNTY CUP

21.10 R1	Farsley Celtic (a)	W	4-1	Shirley Murphy 6, 19, 32, Jess Dunlop 59	
18.11 R2	Thackley (h)	W	3-0	Jade Brindle (pen) 54, Sophie Moulden 69, 88	55
16.12 R3	Harrogate Town (a)	L	1-2	Hannah Shuttleworth 80	79

"The 2018-19 season was challenging as a young player, physically and mentally. We have learnt so many lessons though and are in a position to prepare ourselves better throughout pre-season ahead of 2019-20. The determination and resilience we demonstrated in the face of tough results all the way through 2018-19 will stand us in good stead as the new campaign unfolds."

Maisie Norde – Captain

BRIGHOUSE TOWN

2019-20: WNL NORTH 1 (Tier 4)

Founded: 2013

Nickname: Town

Season 2018-19:

WNL North 1 (Tier 4): Runners-up

FA Cup: 1st Round

WNL Cup: 2nd Round

County Cup: Winners

The club was established in 2013 when Brighouse men's were given the go-ahead to merge their ladies' team with Kirklees Ladies to create Brighouse Town Ladies. Town enjoyed a rapid rise going from Tier 6 to Tier 4 in three years after formation. They were crowned North East Regional League South champions in 2013-14 and then North East Regional League Premier Division champions in 2015-16, an achievement which saw them promoted to Tier 4 – the level at which they are now. In 2018-19 they finished as runners-up in the League and lifted the West Riding FA County Cup with a 3-2 win over Tier 3 side and holders Guiseley Vixens in the final.

2018-19 AS IT HAPPENS

20.01.19: Brighouse show no mercy against their lower League opponents Ripon City – who hail the West Riding FA County Cup quarter-final tie between the two teams as the biggest match in their history – by running out 5-0 winners.

10.02.19: Having scored a brace in five separate League matches so far this season, Charlotte Proud gets her first League hat-trick of the campaign in a 3-0 win away to Norton & Stockton Ancients.

24.03.19: Brighouse announce the signing of Chloe Wild from fellow WNL North 1 side Chorley. She makes her debut in a goalless draw with divisional leaders Burnley later in the day. Wild can play as a wide midfielder or forward.

30.04.19: Town cause something of a shock in the West Riding FA County Cup final with a 3-2 win over Tier 3 outfit and holders Guiseley Vixens.

05.05.19: Brighouse secure the runners-up spot on the final day of the WNL North 1 season with a 3-1 win away to Leeds. The three points sees them leapfrog Chester-le-Street Town who, after starting the day in 2nd place, suffer a shock 5-1 home defeat to strugglers Norton & Stockton Ancients.

2018-19 RESULTS: (HOME VENUE: YORKSHIRE PAYMENTS STADIUM, (BRIGHOUSE TOWN AFC) UNLESS STATED)

2018-19 WNL NORTH 1					Att	Pos
19.08	Liverpool Feds (h)	L	0-2	Aimi Beresford sent off 36	40	
26.08	Morecambe (a)	W	3-0	Charlotte Proud 5, 27, Stacey Buxton 59	45	6
09.09	Norton & Stockton A (h)	W	5-3	Charlotte Proud 14, 68, Annabelle Cass 45, Aimi Beresford 60, Lindsey Tugby 65	60	2
12.09	Barnsley (h)	W	2-1	Charlotte Proud 6, 14	108	2
16.09	Chester-le-Street T (h)	L	0-2		30	6
30.09	Crewe Alexandra (a)	W	4-0	Charlotte Proud 11, 36, Lauren Doyle 33, Stacey Buxton 84	70	3
03.10	Bolton W (h)	W	2-1	Lauren Doyle 30, Aimi Beresford (pen) 82	56	2
21.10	Chorley (h)	D	2-2	Charlotte Proud (pen) 42, Josephine Hewson 86	35	1
04.11	Newcastle United (h)	W	3-1	Charlotte Proud 42, 70, Lauren Doyle 48	25	1
25.11	Burnley (a)	L	0-1		40	3
02.12	Morecambe (h)	D	1-1	Lauren Doyle 51	20	2
13.01	Liverpool Feds (a)	D	2-2	Charlotte Blythe 62, Abigail Housecroft 90	50	3
27.01	Barnsley (a)	D	1-1	Emma Dobson 37	50	5
03.02	Norton & Stockton A (a)		P-P			5
10.02	Norton & Stockton A (a)	W	3-0	Charlotte Proud 26, 44, 86	50	3
24.02	Leeds United (h)	D	1-1	Charlotte Proud (pen) 85	70	3
03.03	Chester-le-Street T (a)	W	3-0	Annabelle Cass, Charlotte Proud, Lavinia Nkomo	50	2
10.03	Crewe Alexandra (h)		P-P			2
13.03	Bolton W (a)		P-P			2
20.03	Bolton W (a)	D	0-0		105	2

24.03	Burnley (h)	D	0-0		143	3
31.03	Newcastle United (a)	W	2-1	Lavinia Nkomo 16, Charlotte Blythe 60	96	3
07.04	Crewe Alexandra (h)	W	5-0	Charlotte Proud 3, 11, Danielle Brown 22, Annabelle Cass 75, Lavinia Nkomo 83, Annabelle Cass missed pen 75 (saved) – scored rebound	95	3
14.04	Chorley (a)	W	2-0	Charlotte Proud 44, Lavinia Nkomo 52	92	2
05.05	Leeds United (a)	W	3-1	Lavinia Nkomo 37, Emma Pilling 67, Kayleigh Bamforth 88	100	2

2018-19 FA CUP

23.09 RQ2	Penrith AFC (h)	W	5-0	Aimi Beresford 3, Kayleigh Bamforth 6, Abi Housecroft 32, Charlotte Proud 59, 67	60
07.10 RQ3	Burnley (h)	W	3-1	Charlotte Proud (pen) 38, Lauren Doyle 60, Lindsey Tugby 65	43
11.11 R1	Leeds United (a)	L	0-1		150

2018-19 WNL CUP

02.09 DR	Solihull Moors (a)	W	7-0	Charlotte Proud 13, 20, 49, 80, Jennifer Pearson 31, Hannah Poulter 58, Abigail Housecroft 70	45
R1	Bye				
14.10 R2	Leeds United (h)	L	1-2	Jennifer Pearson 55	112

2018-19 West Riding FA County Cup

18.11 R2	Ossett Town (h)	W	2-0	*Abi Housecroft missed pen 16,* Annabelle Cass (pen) 76, Lauren Doyle 89	100
06.01 R3	Harrogate Railway (a)	W	10-0	Kayleigh Bamforth 21, Lindsey Tugby 26, 68, Charlotte Proud 35, 49, 50, Stacey Buxton 65, Annabelle Cass 79, 86, Ellie Richardson 90	
20.01 QF	Ripon City (h)	W	5-0	Kayleigh Bamforth 20, 42, Lavinia Nkomo 28, 44, Emma Pilling 57	65est
02.04 SF	Harrogate Town (h)	W	3-2	*Charlotte Proud missed pen 15 (saved),* Amy Beresford 58, 80, Cara Mahoney 68	65est
30.04 F	Guiseley Vixens (n)	W	3-2	Annabelle Cass 44, Lavinia Nkomo 54, 59	200

(n) Played at Fleet Lane, (West Riding FA HQ)

"The 2018-19 season was one of ups and downs for us. The first half of the campaign, in particular, saw a mixed bag of results, where we were trying to get a settled team. We got there in the end with some good recruitment and then the results started to come. We ended the season with a 16-game unbeaten run in all competitions, which saw us lift the County Cup. In 2019-20 we look to build further with a few extra additions to the squad and the aim has to be promotion and retaining the County Cup."

Becky Alderson – Secretary

BRISLINGTON

2019-20: WNL SOUTH WEST 1 (Tier 4)

Founded: 2011

Nickname: None

Season 2018-19:

WNL South West 1 (Tier 4): 7th

FA Cup: 2nd Qualifying Round

WNL Cup: Determining Round

WNL Plate: 2nd Round

County Cup: Runners-up

In their first season after formation Brislington – with a team made up mostly of teenage players – won the 2011-12 Somerset County League Division Two title without dropping a point and with a goal difference of +186. They followed up by winning the South West Regional Premier League in 2015-16 to gain promotion to what is now WNL South West 1 for 2016-17. Since then they have secured a series of mid-table finishes, placing 6th in 2016-17 and 2017-18, then 7th in 2018-19.

2018-19 AS IT HAPPENS

19.08.18: Brislington play their part in a thoroughly entertaining opening-day goal-fest as they go down 7-4 at home to Cheltenham Town. Kim Maggs, Paige Saywer, Sophie Whelan and Abbie Kirby score their goals.

09.09.18: After losing their opening two League fixtures, Brislington pick up maximum points with a 5-2 win away to Maidenhead United. Paige Sawyer scores a hat-trick.

10.05.19: Brislington finish as runners-up in the Somerset FA County Cup after a 2-1 defeat to WNL South West 1 champions Keynsham Town in the final.

2018-19 RESULTS: (HOME VENUE: IRONMOULD LANE, (BRISLINGTON FC), UNLESS STATED)

2018-19 WNL SW 1

					Att	Pos
19.08	Cheltenham Town (h)	L	4-7	Kim Maggs 2, Paige Sawyer 8, Sophie Whelan 68, Abbie Kirby 88	74	
26.08	Southampton W (h)	L	0-3		42	
09.09	Maidenhead U (a)	W	5-2	Cheryl Baber 9, Paige Sawyer 24, 60, 72, Amy Ford 76	20	9
13.09	Keynsham Town (h)	L	0-7		78	9
16.09	Buckland Athletic (a)	L	1-2	Paige Sawyer, *Chelsea Heal sent off 75*	47	10
30.09	Chesham United (h)	W	3-2	Amy Ford 8, Polly Wardle 60, Paige Sawyer 85	43	6
25.10	Larkhall Athletic (a)	D	3-3	Polly Wardle 38, 51, 59	40	6
04.11	Poole Town (a)	W	5-3	Polly Wardle 5, Abbie Kirby 73, 80, Alice Kempski 76, Clarice White 86	20	6
11.11	Southampton S (h)	W	2-1	Polly Wardle 32, 75	48	4
25.11	Swindon Town (h)	W	2-1	Courtney Adams 10, Polly Wardle 88	38	4
09.12	Cheltenham Town (a)	D	2-2	Anusia Rourke 4, Polly Wardle 45	74	5
10.02	Southampton W (a)	L	2-4	Paige Sawyer 5, Polly Wardle 7	27	6
14.02	Keynsham Town (a)	L	0-6		75	6
24.02	Maidenhead U (h)	W	3-1	Abbie Kirby 33, Alice Kempski 62, Cheryl Baber 85	47	6
03.03	Buckland Athletic (h)		P-P			6
10.03	Chesham United (a)	L	0-3			6
14.03	Larkhall Athletic (h)		P-P			6
24.03	Southampton S (a)	L	2-4	Paige Sawyer 40, Chelsea Heal 80	15	6
28.03	Larkhall Athletic (h)	D	1-1	Paige Sawyer 5	64	6
31.03	Poole Town (h)	D	1-1	Anusia Rourke 18	41	6
07.04	Buckland Athletic (h)	L	1-6	Shannon Osman 84	39	6
05.05	Swindon Town (a)	L	2-3	Polly Wardle 30, Paige Sawyer 60	44	7

2018-19 FA CUP

23.09 RQ2	Cheltenham Town (a)	L	1-4	Paige Sawyer 30	76

2018-19 WNL CUP

02.09 DR	Buckland Athletic (a)	L	0-3	55

2018-19 WNL PLATE

R1	Bye			
21.10 R2	MK Dons (h)	L	0-3	53

2018-19 SOMERSET FA COUNTY CUP

21.10 R1	Bye				
20.01 QF	Ilminster Town (h)	D	2-2 (W7-6p)	Anusia Rourke 12, Amy Ford 25	
17.02 SF	Portishead (a)	W	2-1	Paige Sawyer, Anusia Rourke	50est
10.05 F	Keynsham Town (n)	L	1-2	Paige Sawyer 33	120est

(n) Played at Bishop Sutton, (Bishop Sutton AFC)

"The 2018-19 season didn't quite live up to expectations. We had a good run of six unbeaten games prior to Christmas, but several long-term injuries to key players then took their toll on League form. We did though have some dramatic ties in the Somerset FA County Cup to enjoy as we made it to the final. We beat Ilminster Town 7-6 on penalties in a shootout in which every player on the pitch took a kick. We then squeezed past Portishead 2-1 in the semis to take on our rivals Keynsham Town in the final. We had good early efforts from Paige Sawyer and Chez Barber that were saved. Sawyer went close again before putting us ahead. It was only a brilliant save from Keynsham's keeper that prevented us doubling our lead. Unfortunately, Keynsham equalised from a defensive error and won the game in added time, but we were proud of our efforts."

Bob Mewse – Press Officer and Programme Editor

BUCKLAND ATHLETIC

2019-20: WNL SOUTH WEST 1 (Tier 4)

Founded: 2015

Nickname: The Bucks

Season 2018-19:

WNL South West 1 (Tier 4): 3rd

FA Cup: 2nd Round

WNL Cup: 1st Round

County Cup: Runners-up

Buckland Athletic Ladies have enjoyed a rapid rise since being founded as part of men's non-League club Buckland Athletic FC ahead of the 2015-16 season. In that debut campaign, under manager Grant Fisher, they won the Devon Women's League Division One without dropping a single point and lifted their League Cup. That 2015-16 title took them into the South West Regional League in which they became 2017-18 Premier League champions to secure promotion to Tier 4. A fine debut season in WNL South West 1 culminated in a finishing position of 3rd.

2018-19 AS IT HAPPENS

19.08.18: Having been promoted as 2017-18 South West Regional Premier champions Buckland begin life in Tier 4 with a dispiriting 9-0 defeat away to Keynsham.

16.09.18: Buckland secure their first win at Tier 4 level in their third League match of the season as Alex Sheppard and Courtney Butt score in a 2-1 victory at home to Brislington.

17.02.19: An impressive crowd of 606 watches Buckland win 3-1 away to Exeter City in the Devon FA County Cup semi-final. The match is played at St James Park, home of Exeter City FC men.

07.04.19: Thierry Gauvain scores on her debut for Buckland as they go on to beat Brislington 6-1 in a League fixture.

12.04.19: Buckland go down 3-2 to Tier 3 Plymouth in an entertaining Devon FA County Cup final. Argyle lead 3-0 within 20 minutes but Athletic give themselves late hope when Leah Brooks scores with 19 minutes to play. Sarah Louise Stacey gets another in injury-time, but Plymouth hold on.

2018-19 RESULTS: (HOME VENUE: HOMERS HEATH, (BUCKLAND ATHLETIC FC), UNLESS STATED)

2018-19 WNL SW 1					Att	Pos
19.08	Keynsham Town (a)	L	0-9		50	
09.09	Cheltenham Town (a)	D	2-2	Courtney Butt 39, Natalie Warman 44	51	10
16.09	Brislington (h)	W	2-1	Alex Sheppard 48, Courtney Butt 81, *Laura Gough sent off 70*	47	6
14.10	Poole Town (h)		P-P			
28.10	Maidenhead U (a)	W	8-1	Natalie Warman, 4, 43, 50, 54, 57, Laura Gough 60, 88, Carla Staddon 65	15	5
04.11	Southampton S (a)	W	2-0	Sarah Louise Stacey 52, Laura Gough 53	20	5
25.11	Larkhall Athletic (h)*	D	3-3	Natalie Warman 10, 51, Laura Gough 89	15	6
16.12	Swindon Town (a)	W	6-1	Laura Gough 11, 25, 50, Maria Warman 41, 85, Sarah Louise Stacey (pen) 63	34	6
06.01	Chesham United (a)	L	3-4	Sarah Louise Stacey 58, Own Goal 76, Laura Gough 79	40	6
13.01	Keynsham Town (h)	L	1-4	Sarah Louise Stacey 72	42	6
20.01	Cheltenham Town (h)	W	3-2	Jana Richards 45, Sarah Louise Stacey (pen) 74, Laura Gough 86	39	5
27.01	Maidenhead U (h)		P-P			5
03.02	Southampton W (h)+	W	2-1	Sarah Louise Stacey 47, Leah Brooks 62	43	5
10.02	Poole Town (a)	W	5-0	Sarah Louise Stacey 5, 32, Laura Gough 23, 59, Alex Sheppard 55	25	4
24.02	Poole Town (h)	W	5-1	Sarah Louise Stacey 7, 28, 88, Laura Gough 41, Emily Hannaford 75	34	5
03.03	Brislington (a)		P-P			5
10.03	Maidenhead U (h)		P-P			5
17.03	Chesham United (h)+	W	8-4	Laura Gough 44, Sarah Louise Stacey (pen) 45, 65, 87, Kirsty Caunter 47, Jana Richards 51, 90+1, Sarah Smith 60	51	5
24.03	Larkhall Athletic (a)	L	1-2	Sarah Louise Stacey 72	25	5
31.03	Swindon Town (h)	W	2-0	Carla Staddon 33, Natalie Warman 52	30	4
07.04	Brislington (a)	W	6-1	Sarah Louise Stacey 7, 51, 64, Thierry Jo Gauvain 32, 61, Abigail Meyer 78	39	4

14.04	Southampton S (h)	W	w/o			4
28.04	Maidenhead U (h)	W	3-0	Sarah Louise Stacey 45+2, 49, 90	36	4
05.05	Southampton W (a)	D	0-0		38	4

*Played at Paignton Community College +Played at South Devon College

2018-19 FA CUP

23.09 RQ2	Ilminster Town (h)		P-P		
26.09 RQ3	Ilminster Town (h)	W	4-0	Sarah Smith 45, Sarah Louise Stacey (pen) 4, 7, (pen) 57	73
07.10 RQ3	Marine Academy Plymouth (h)	W	2-0	Natalie Warman 44, Sarah Louise Stacey 79	68
11.11 R1	Cheltenham Town (h)	W	2-0	Sarah Louise Stacey 20, Natalie Warman 67	74
09.12 R2	Watford (a)	L	0-1		70

2018-19 WNL CUP

02.09 DR	Brislington (h)	W	3-0	Courtney Butt, Sarah Louise Stacey (x2)	55
30.09 R1	AFC Wimbledon (a)	L	0-4		100

2018-19 DEVON FA COUNTY CUP

21.10 R1	Feniton Ladies (a)	W	6-1	Laura Gough, Maria Warman, Natalie Warman, Sarah Louise Stacey (x2), Leah Brooks	30
18.11 QF	Alphington (h)	W	5-0	Leah Brooks, Sarah Smith, Natalie Warman (x2), Sarah Louise Stacey	
17.02 SF	Exeter City (a)	W	3-1	Sarah Louise Stacey (pen) 1, 56, Jana Richards 89	606
12.04 F	Plymouth Argyle (n)	L	2-3	Leah Brooks 71, Sarah Louise Stacey 90+1	507

(n) Played at Coach Road, (Devon FA County HQ)

"Finishing 3rd in our first season in the WNL and reaching the 2nd Round of the FA Cup where we played former WSL side Watford, made 2018-19 a really special season. We travelled many miles together and always gave our best performance. The fight and determination that the players show makes this team a real family. There is only one way for us to approach things going forward, and that is to ensure we continue to give our all to try and do even better. Bring on 2019-20. We are one."

Grant Fisher – Manager

BURNLEY

2019-20: WNL NORTHERN PREMIER (Tier 3)

Founded: 1995

Nickname: The Clarets

Season 2018-19:

WNL North 1 (Tier 4): Champions (P)

FA Cup: 3rd Qualifying Round

WNL Cup: 2nd Round

County Cup: Semi-finals

John Lister founded Burnley FC Girls and Ladies in 1995, with the club being rebranded as Burnley FC Women at the end of 2017-18. Formally affiliated with men's Premier League club Burnley FC, the Clarets have just enjoyed back-to-back promotions, winning the North West Regional Premier League title in 2017-18 and the WNL North 1 title in 2018-19. The 2017-18 season also saw them enjoy their best run to date in the FA Cup when they made it all the way to the 3rd Round as a Tier 5 club before being beaten by Cardiff City Ladies of Tier 3.

2018-19 AS IT HAPPENS

19.08.18: Having won the 2017-18 North West Regional Premier title, Burnley begin life in Tier 4 with a 3-0 home defeat to Chester-le-Street Town.

09.09.18: After a defeat and a draw, the Clarets secure their first Tier 4 victory with a 3-0 away win over Liverpool Feds. Sarah Greenhalgh notches a brace and Evie Priestley is also on target.

24.02.19: Burnley play out a nine-goal thriller away to Norton & Stockton Ancients. Danielle Cooper puts the Clarets 5-3 up with what proves to be the winner late on before Norton get one back.

14.04.19: Evie Priestley hits a hat-trick as Burnley win 3-0 at bottom club Crewe to clinch the WNL North 1 title and seal back-to-back promotions. Goalkeeper Lauren Bracewell also saves a penalty after 58 minutes with Burnley leading 2-0.

17.05.19: Leah Embley is named FA WNL Division 1 Player of the Year across all four divisions of Tier 4.

2018-19 RESULTS: (HOME VENUE: ARBORIES MEMORIAL SPORTS GROUND, (PADIHAM FC) UNLESS STATED)

2018-19 WNL NORTH 1

					Att	Pos
19.08	Chester-le-Street T (h)	L	0-3		60	
26.08	Leeds United (h)	D	1-1	Sarah Greenhalgh 50	60	9
09.09	Liverpool Feds (a)	W	3-0	Sarah Greenhalgh 21, 74, Evie Priestley 26	40	6
13.09	Bolton W (a)	W	1-0	Lynette Craig 42		4
16.09	Norton & Stockton A (h)	W	2-1	Leah Embley 4, Evie Priestley 13	60	2
30.09	Barnsley (a)	W	1-0	Sarah Greenhalgh 34	50	1
03.10	Morecambe (h)	W	3-0	Evie Priestley 62, Lynette Craig (pen) 68, Leah Embley 82	70	1
28.10	Newcastle United (a)	W	1-0	Elizabeth Hamer 88	94	1
11.11	Crewe Alexandra (h)	W	4-0	Sarah Greenhalgh 59, 90+2 (pen), Leah Embley 79, Charlotte Banner 81	40	1
25.11	Brighouse Town (h)	W	1-0	Sarah Greenhalgh 65	40	1
16.12	Chorley (a)		P-P			1
06.01	Chorley (a)	W	1-0	Evie Priestley 50	98	1
13.01	Chester-le-Street T (a)	W	1-0	Sarah Greenhalgh 24	30	1
27.01	Liverpool Feds (h)	W	2-0	Leah Embley 36, Danielle Cooper 90+3	70	1
03.02	Leeds United (a)	W	1-0	Sarah Greenhalgh 27, Sarah Greenhalgh missed pen 90 (saved Georgia Wattam)	80	1
13.02	Bolton Wanderers (h)	L	0-1		77	1
24.02	Norton & Stockton A (a)	W	5-4	Sarah Greenhalgh 5, 33, Lynette Craig (pen) 6, Vikki Eastwood 44, Danielle Cooper 81	50	1
10.03	Newcastle United (h)		P-P			1
17.03	Morecambe (a)		P-P			1
24.03	Brighouse Town (a)	D	0-0		143	1
31.03	Barnsley (h)	W	3-1	Sarah Greenhalgh 43, (pen) 87, Evie Priestley 68	88	1
07.04	Morecambe (a)	W	3-2	Sarah Greenhalgh 26, 74, Elizabeth Hamer 69		1
14.04	Crewe Alexandra (a)	W	3-0	Evie Priestley 10, 16, 73, Burnley GK Lauren Bracewell saved pen 56	100	1C
28.04	Newcastle United (h)	W	2-1	Evie Priestley 42, Elizabeth Hamer 44	54	1C
05.05	Chorley (h)	W	1-0	Samantha Fleck 51	225	1C

2018-19 FA CUP

23.09 RQ2	Liverpool Feds (h)	W	3-2	Linny Craig 24, Sarah Greenhalgh 69, Lizzy Harmer 74	60
07.10 RQ3	Brighouse Town (a)	L	1-3	Danielle Cooper 15	43

Women's
National League

2018-19 WNL CUP

02.09 DR	West Bromwich A (a)	W	3-0	Courtney Murphy (og) 31, Leah Embley 51, 73, Justine Wallace missed pen 80	
R1	Bye				
14.10 R2	Huddersfield T (a)	L	0-1		47

2018-19 LANCASHIRE FA COUNTY CUP

21.10 R1	Wythenshawe Amateurs (a)	W	7-0	Katie Halligan 24, 73, Charlotte Banner 35, Leah Embley 48, 50, 66, Evie Priestley 70	58
18.11 QF	Chorley (a)	W	1-0	Burnley GK Lauren Bracewell saved pen 30, Lynette Craig 73	90
20.01 SF	Blackburn R (h)	L	0-3		550

"The celebrations at Crewe when the League title was secured will live long in the memory. At the start of 2018-19 our aim was to consolidate our position in the League, but to go on to become champions was phenomenal. As a huge Burnley FC fan and a player that played my first game for Burnley in 1998, to win back-to-back promotions two decades later and see this club having the opportunity to play at Tier 3 of the women's game is nothing short of amazing. Our manager Matt Bee left no stone unturned in preparing us for every single game and it will be exciting to see what the future holds for this team as we compete in the WNL Northern Premier."

Jo Holt – Captain

BURTON ALBION

2019-20: WNL MIDLANDS 1 (Tier 4)

Founded: 2000

Nickname: The Brewers

Season 2018-19:

WNL Midlands 1 (Tier 4): 9th

FA Cup: 2nd Qualifying Round

WNL Cup: Determining Round

WNL Plate: 1st Round

County Cup: 1st Round

Burton are recent newcomers to Tier 4, winning promotion to this level as 2016-17 West Midlands Regional Premier League champions. Prior to their debut season in Tier 4 in 2017-18 the club enjoyed a rapid rise to prominence, winning four League titles in a row, including League and Cup Doubles in 2014-15, 2015-16 and 2016-17. They finished as runners-up in their debut campaign in Tier 4 in 2017-18 but were unable to scale those heights again in 2018-19 when they placed 9th.

2018-19 AS IT HAPPENS

01.11.18: Albion appoint Ryan Hamilton as their new first team manager and Danny Bray as his assistant.

02.12.18: Burton come back from 2-0 down to draw 2-2 at home to TNS. However, the jubilation surrounding Paris O'Connor's 58th-minute equaliser is somewhat soured as O'Connor and two opposition players, Taylor Davis and Sarah Parkes, are all sent off for pushing each other as O'Connor goes to retrieve the ball from the net.

10.03.19: Managerial duo Ryan Hamilton and Danny Bray resign on the morning of the League match at home to Bedworth. They remain in charge for the game itself which ends in a 7-1 home defeat.

31.03.19: Kick-off for Albion's home match against Sporting Khalsa is delayed after their opponents turn up having forgotten their kit. The delay means the match is played over two halves of just 40 minutes. Burton lose 4-0.

2018-19 RESULTS: (HOME VENUE: THE LAMB, (TAMWORTH FC), UNLESS STATED)

2018-19 WNL MIDLANDS 1

Date	Opponent	Res	Score	Scorers	Att	Pos
19.08	Solihull Moors (h)	W	7-1	Jamie Leigh Fowler 25, Hayleigh Sutton 39, 82, (pen) 87, Paris O'Connor 42, Amelia Robb 49, Jordan Atkin 84	120	
26.08	Steel City W (a)	W	4-2	Paris O'Connor 32, (pen) 34, 47, Hayleigh Sutton 66	28	2
12.09	Long Eaton United (a)	L	0-3		50	5
16.09	Wolverhampton W (h)	L	1-4	Jamie Leigh Fowler 19	80	5
02.10	West Brom A (a)	L	1-2	Paris O'Connor 38	58	6
21.10	Bir'ham & W M (h)	D	2-2	Jordan Atkin 45+5, 55	61	7
28.10	Bedworth United (a)	L	1-5	Jamie Leigh Fowler 80	55	7
04.11	Sporting Khalsa (a)	D	2-2	Hayleigh Sutton 2, Amelia Robb 41	20	8
25.11	Nettleham (h)	L	2-3	Jordan Atkin 43, Portia Badach 84	64	9
02.12	The New Saints (h)	D	2-2	Jordan Atkin 51, Paris O'Connor 58, Paris O'Connor Sent Off 60	80	9
13.01	Solihull Moors (a)	W	2-0	Laura McQuilkin 22, Jordan Atkin 33	25	8
10.02	Steel City W (h)	W	4-1	Jordan Atkin 6, 7, Louisa Anderson 11, Hannah Baker 90	61	7
17.02	Wolverhampton W (a)	L	0-8		50	8
03.03	Long Eaton United (h)	L	0-4		33	8
10.03	Bedworth United (h)	L	1-7	Ellie Milsom 42	50	8
24.03	Bir'ham & W M (a)	L	0-3		53	9
31.03	Sporting Khalsa (h)	L	0-4		51	9
07.04	Nettleham (a)	L	0-3		50	9
28.04	West Brom A (h)*	L	0-6		60	9
05.05	The New Saints (a)	L	1-9	Lauren Brown (og) 7	60	9

*Played at NFU Sports Ground, (Ashby Ivanhoe FC)

2018-19 FA CUP

30.09 RQ2	Chesterfield (a)	L	0-1	103

2018-19 WNL CUP

02.09 DR	Fylde (a)	L	0-9	30est

2018-19 WNL PLATE

07.10 R1	Barnsley (a)	L	1-5	Charlotte Jarvis 18	50

2018-19 BIRMINGHAM FA COUNTY CUP

18.11 R1	Bir'ham W&M (a)	L	1-4	Amelia Robb 8	23

CAMBRIDGE CITY

2019-20: WNL SOUTH EAST 1 (Tier 4)

Founded: 2015

Nickname: The Lilywhites

Season 2018-19:

Eastern Reg Prem (Tier 5): Champions (P)

FA Cup: 1st Round

League Cup: Winners

County Cup: Runners-up

The Lilywhites have enjoyed a trophy-laden four years since their formation in 2015, lifting their first silverware that very year when they claimed the Cambridgeshire League Cup. Starting out in the Cambridgeshire Premiership they were promoted as champions at the end of 2015-16 and immediately went up again as Eastern Regional Division One champions 2016-17. City took barely any time to acclimatise to their new level, finishing as Eastern Regional Premier runners-up in 2017-18 and then claiming the title and promotion to the WNL at the end of 2018-19. A new era begins in 2019-20 as City move to Downham Road, the home of Ely City FC.

2018-19 AS IT HAPPENS

11.11.18: City pull off an FA Cup 1st Round shock against local rivals Cambridge United by beating the Tier 4 side 2-1 after extra-time. However, the result is voided by the FA following a complaint from their opponents that the pitch was below FA Cup regulation size. United insist they alerted the officials before kick-off. A replay is ordered which United win 2-0.

19.03.19: For the second year in succession City meet Cambridge United in the Cambridgeshire FA County Cup final. Their Tier 4 opponents go 2-0 up, but an injury-time goal from Megan Tonks for City sparks a frantic finish. United hold on to lift the trophy in front of a crowd of around 500 people at The Abbey Stadium, home of Cambridge United men.

12.05.19: The Lilywhites end the season with a Double, lifting the League Cup after coming from 2-0 down to win on penalties. Sarah Mosley, Shannon Shaw, Lauren Tomlinson and Megan Tonks all score their spot-kicks with goalkeeper Tafadzwa Mhundury saving Bedford's first effort. When Bedford captain Michelle Byrne sends her team's 4th effort wide, Cambridge can celebrate victory.

2018-19 RESULTS: (HOME VENUE: TRINITY OLD FIELD, GRANGE ROAD, UNLESS STATED)

2018-19 EASTERN REGIONAL PREMIER

19.08	Peterborough N S (a)	W	5-2	Laura Mills, Shannon Shaw, Carla Penny, Grace Stanley (x2)
09.09	Harlow Town (h)	W	3-1	Charlotte Gillies, Laura Mills, Isabella Simmons
16.09	Bedford (h)	W	3-2	Sofia Castiglione, Laura Mills, Isabella Simmons
30.09	Wymondham T (h)	W	2-1	Laura Mills, Own Goal
14.10	Haringey B (h)	W	w/o	
21.10	AFC Sudbury (a)	W	11-1	Anna Goggin (x2), Laura Mills (x4), Shannon Shaw, Erin Davies (x2), Carla Penny (x2)
28.10	AFC Dunstable (h)	W	4-0	Erin Davies (x2), Charlotte Gillies, Laura Mills
04.11	Harlow Town (a)	W	5-2	Laura Mills, Shannon Shaw, Isabella Simmons, Lauren Tomlinson, Erin Davies
09.12	Acle United (a)	W	2-1	Isabella Simmons, Lauren Tomlinson, *Sarah Mosley sent off*
16.12	Royston Town (h)	D	4-4	Erin Davies, Charlotte Gillies (x2), Shannon Shaw, *Laura Mills sent off*
06.01	Haringey B (a)	W	11-1	Erin Davies, Rebecca Fay, Charlotte Gillies, Anna Goggin, Isabella Simmons (x3), Lauren Tomlinson, Carla Penny (x3)
20.01	AFC Sudbury (h)	W	12-0	Hannah Bodily, Charlotte Gillies (x2), Anna Goggin, Laura Mills, Shannon Shaw (x2), Carla Penny (x2), Erin Davies (x2), Isabella Simmons
27.01	Colney Heath (h)	W	3-2	Hannah Bodily, Shannon Shaw, Isabella Simmons
03.02	Brentwood Town (h)	W	3-0	Shannon Shaw (x2), Isabella Simmons
10.02	AFC Dunstable (a)		P-P	
24.02	Acle United (h)	W	4-0	Shannon Shaw, Sarah Mosley, Isabella Simmons, Carla Penny
10.03	Colney Heath (a)	W	4-0	Erin Davies (x2), Lauren Tomlinson, Freya Standing
17.03	Brentwood Town (a)	W	3-1	Shannon Shaw (x2), Carla Penny
24.03	Wymondham T (a)	W	5-0	Lauren Tomlinson, Shannon Shaw (x3), Own Goal
31.03	Peterborough N S (h)	W	4-0	Erin Davies, Anna Goggin, Own Goal (x2)
07.04	Royston Town (a)	W	3-0	Shannon Shaw (x2), Freya Standing
21.04	AFC Dunstable (a)	W	w/o	
19.05	Bedford (a)	W	3-0	Hannah Bodily, Shannon Shaw, Lauren Tomlinson

2018-19 FA CUP

26.08 PR	Newmarket Town (a)	W	2-0	Carla Penny, Charlotte Gillies
02.09 RQ1	Riverside (h)	W	14-0	Hannah Bodily, Bronte Rapley (x2), Laura Mills, Erin Davies (x6), Sofia Castiglione (x2), Anna Goggin, Amy Reed
23.09RQ2	Leyton Orient (h)	W	5-4	Laura Mills (x2), Sarah Mosley, Shannon Shaw, Isabella Simmons
07.10 RQ3	Acle United (a)	W	1-0	Laura Mills
11.11 R1	Cambridge Utd (h)	W	2-1 aet	Isabella Simmons, Laura Mills **RESULT VOIDED BY FA**
25.11R1	Cambridge Utd (h)*	L	0-2	

*Technically a home tie but played at their opponent's home venue Mildenhall Town

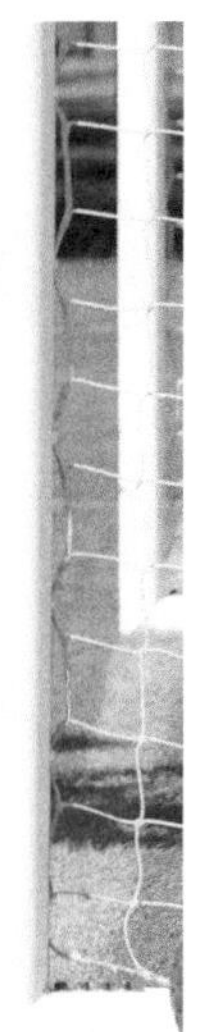

2018-19 LEAGUE CUP

13.01R1	Hutton (h)	W	8-1	Carla Penny (x2), Charlotte Gillies (x2), Isabella Simmons, Erin Davies, Shannon Shaw (x2)
03.03 QF	Colney Heath (h)	W	2-0	Amy Reed, Isabella Simmons
14.04 SF	Harlow Town (h)	W	3-1	Erin Davies, Bronte Rapley, Own Goal
12.05 F	Bedford (n)	D	2-2aet (W4-2p)	Megan Tonks, Hannah Bodily

(n)Played at The County Ground

2018-19 CAMBRIDGESHIRE FA COUNTY CUP

18.11 QF	Histon (a)	W	3-0	Erin Davies, Charlotte Gillies, Sarah Mosley
17.02 SF	Wisbech Town (a)	W	13-0	Erin Davies (x2), Laura Mills, Amy Reed, Shannon Shaw, Lauren Tomlinson (x2), Sarah Mosley (x2), Carla Penny (x4)
19.03 F	Cambridge United (n)	L	1-2	Megan Tonks

(n) Played at The Abbey, (Cambridge United FC)

"It is hard to imagine how we could have been any more successful in 2018-19. I am extremely proud to have worn the armband, but really it is about the team, not any individual. The whole club has such a great feeling about it. Everyone is pulling in the same direction. We will push on in 2019-20 and I am sure that together there is so much more we can achieve."

Becca Fay – Captain

CAMBRIDGE UNITED

2019-20: WNL SOUTH EAST 1 (Tier 4)

Founded: 2009 (as Cambridge Women)

Nickname: The U's

Season 2018-19:

WNL South East 1 (Tier 4): 8th

FA Cup: 2nd Round

WNL Cup: 3rd Round

County Cup: Winners

The current club technically began life as Cambridge Women in 2009 when Cambridge City Ladies and Cambridge United Ladies merged and were taken under the umbrella of the men's professional outfit Cambridge United FC, to become Cambridge United Women. However, they find their origins in a club called Pye Ladies which was set-up 30 years ago and which has evolved into the current club. Many of the original Pye Ladies committee members are still volunteering at Cambridge United Women today. A new Cambridge City Ladies also exists today and has been promoted to WNL South East 1 for 2019-20 meaning both teams can look forward to some local derbies.

2018-19 AS IT HAPPENS

11.11.18: Cambridge United lose 2-1 after extra-time away to Tier 5 Cambridge City in the FA Cup 1st Round. Four days later the FA rules the game must be replayed because the pitch at Trinity Fields was too small. United insist they lodged their complaint about their local rivals' pitch with the referee prior to kick-off. United win the replay 2-0.

10.03.19: Cambridge hold WNL South East 1 leaders Crawley Wasps to a goalless draw on a windy day at Mildenhall and become the first team to take points off Wasps – who have now played 13 League games – all season.

19.03.19: The U's meet Cambridge City in a repeat of last year's Cambridgeshire FA County Cup final. City ran out 3-1 winners in 2018, but this time the U's prevail 2-1 thanks to goals from Amy Howlett and Becky Shephard, with a penalty. The final is played at Cambridge United FC's Abbey Stadium for the first time and attracts a crowd of 500.

31.03.19: Cambridge announce they will be leaving Mildenhall at the end of 2018-19 to groundshare with Southern League Central Premier Division (Tier 7) men's side St Neots Town at The Premier Plus Stadium and The GESS 3G Arena.

07.04.19: Cambridge United boss Kevin Hooper is named FA WNL South East 1 Manager of the Month.

2018-19 RESULTS: (HOME VENUE: RECREATION WAY, (MILDENHALL TOWN FC) UNLESS STATED)

2018-19 WNL SE 1

					Att	Pos
19.08	AFC Wimbledon (a)	D	1-1	Kayleigh-Anne Burt 55	50	
26.08	Leyton Orient (a)	W	3-0	Kelley Blanchflower (x2), Becky Shephard	68	3
09.09	Denham United (h)	L	1-2	Vicky Neal 74	75	5
12.09	Stevenage (h)*	D	0-0	*Amy Howlett missed pen 65*	90	5
16.09	Enfield Town (a)	L	2-3	Amber Cantwell 69, 72	73	6
03.10	Norwich City (a)	L	0-3		65	7
04.11	Luton Town (h)	W	1-0	Becky Shephard 20	92	9
06.01	Actonians (a)	D	1-1	Mollie Coupar 68	25est	10
13.01	AFC Wimbledon (h)	W	3-0	Jade Bell, Kelley Blanchflower, Mollie Coupar	75	9
20.01	Leyton Orient (h)		P-P			10
27.01	Ipswich Town (a)	D	2-2	Becky Shephard 73, 78	40	9
10.02	Actonians (h)		P-P			9
13.02	Stevenage (a)	D	1-1	Vicky Neal	65	10
24.02	Leyton Orient (h)	L	1-2	Amber Cantwell		9
03.03	Denham United (a)	W	2-1	Kelley Blanchflower, Becky Shephard (pen)	40	7
10.03	Crawley Wasps (h)	D	0-0		40	7
13.03	Norwich City (h)	W	1-0	Amy Howlett 5	50	7
17.03	Actonians (h)	W	5-1	Kelley Blanchflower, Becky Shephard (x2, 1pen), Mollie Coupar (x2)	50	6
24.03	Billericay Town (h)	L	0-2		73	6
31.03	Luton Town (a)	W	4-2	Mollie Coupar 11, 35, 38, Becky Shephard 41		5
07.04	Crawley Wasps (a)	L	1-6	Mollie Coupar 70	95	6
14.04	Billericay Town (a)	L	1-2	Mollie Coupar		6
28.04	Enfield Town (h)	L	0-3		25	7
05.05	Ipswich Town (h)	L	2-3	Amy Howlett 4, Mollie Coupar 71	48	8

*Played at The Abbey Stadium, (Cambridge United FC)

2018-19 FA CUP

23.09 RQ2	Harlow Town (h)		P-P		
30.09 RQ2	Harlow Town (h)	W	6-0	Vicky Neal 34, Faith Hewitt 36, Kelley Blanchflower 40, Stephanie Gale 56, Kayleigh-Anne Burt 75, Gabrielle White-hurst 86	80

07.10 RQ3	Stevenage (h)	D	2-2aet (W4-2p)	Kelley Blanchflower 25, Mollie Coupar 71	82
11.11 R1	Cambridge City (a)	L	1-2 aet RESULT VOID	Jade Bell	
25.11 R1	Cambridge City (a)+	W	2-0	Amy Howlett (pen) 61, Mollie Coupar 81	
02.12 R2	Oxford United (a)	L	0-4		85

+Played at Cambridge United's Recreation Way, but Cambridge City technically home team

2018-19 WNL Cup

02.09 DR	C&K Basildon (h)	W	2-0	Kelley Blanchflower 21, Kayleigh-Anne Burt 56	75
R1	Bye				
14.10 R2	Leyton Orient (h)*		P-P		
28.10 R2	Leyton Orient (h)	W	3-0	Emma Jenkins 50, 61, 71	70
09.12 R3	AFC Wimbledon (a)	L	1-2	Emma Jenkins 77	70

2018-19 Cambridgeshire FA County Cup

21.10 R1	Fulbourn Bluebirds (a)	W	11-0	Amy Howlett (pen) 34, (pen) 74, Becky Shephard 40, Stephanie Gale 47, Kayleigh-Anne Burt 53, Kelley Blanch-flower 56, 81, 90, Chloe Smith 67, Victoria Neal 70, 85	70
18.11 QF	Newmarket Town (a)	W	3-0	Jade Bell 44, 68, Mollie Coupar 55	
17.02 SF	St Ives (h)	W	1-0	Millie Coupar	118
19.03 F	Cambridge City (n)	W	2-1	Amy Howlett, Becky Shephard (pen)	500

(n) Played at The Abbey, (Cambridge United FC)

"In 2018-19 we had a development side for the first time. They held their own in the FA WNL Reserve Division. We also had many young players featuring in the first team. CUWFC is a very special club. There are big changes ahead in 2019-20. Our link with St Neots Town FC will see both our first and development sides play their home games at the same venue – Rowley Park. We will have full use of their amazing facilities for training too. There will be stronger links with Cambridge United Girls' Development and Elite Development Centres providing a clear pathway into the women's game."

Vicky Hoover – Vice Chair

CARDIFF CITY LADIES

2019-20: WNL SOUTHERN PREMIER (Tier 3)

Founded: 1975 (as Llanedeyrn)

Nickname: The Bluebirds

Season 2018-19:

WNL Southern Premier (Tier 3): Runners-up

FA Cup: 4th Round

WNL Cup: 3rd Round

County Cup: n/a

Cardiff City Ladies are not to be confused with Cardiff City Women who play in the Welsh Premier League. Formed as Llanedeyrn in 1975, Cardiff City Ladies are the oldest women's club in Wales. They were formerly affiliated to the men's professional side Cardiff City FC between 2001 and 2003. It is now Cardiff City Women who are affiliated to Cardiff City men's club. Cardiff City Ladies were champions of the WPL Southern Division in 2005-06 and were promoted to the WPL National Division (which was then the top-flight in English football) for the first time. They survived their first season at that level but were then relegated at the end of 2007-08. With Welsh FA Cup success once providing entry into European competition, Cardiff City Ladies represented Wales in what is now the Champions League for seven consecutive seasons from 2003-04 until 2009-10. In 2018-19 they were on the fringes of the WNL Southern Premier (Tier 3) title race and finished as runners-up. It's unclear whether Cardiff would be eligible for promotion above Tier 3 with FA rules stating that only clubs with a "ground situated in England" can play in the WSL or Championship.

2018-19 AS IT HAPPENS

16.12.18: Cardiff's 7-0 win at home to C&K Basildon features seven different scorers with Grace Horrell, Kylie Nolan, Ffion Morgan, Chelsea Jumratie, Jordan Guard, Cori William and Jasmine Simpson all on target.

10.02.19: Cardiff put in a creditable performance away to Tier 2 side Durham in the FA Cup 4th Round but go down to a 5-1 defeat.

14.04.19: Cardiff's slim title hopes are ended as they lose 4-1 away to Coventry United who are crowned champions. The Bluebirds are in 2nd place at kick-off, trailing their hosts by 10 points with five games to play (while Coventry have played two games more). Jade Brook puts Coventry ahead before Cardiff equalise, but United go on to win comfortably.

21.04.19: A 3-2 win at home to Plymouth sees Cardiff secure the runners-up position in the WNL Southern Premier with one game still to play. The victory moves them one point above Chichester City who have already completed all their fixtures.

18.05.19: Wales international midfielder Jess Fishlock, who began her career with Cardiff, becomes a Champions League winner with Lyon who beat Barcelona 4-1 in the final in Budapest.

2018-19 RESULTS: (HOME VENUE: CCB CENTRE FOR SPORTING EXCELLENCE UNLESS STATED)

2018-19 WNL SP					Att	Pos
19.08	Watford (a)	L	2-5	Kylie Nolan 17, 87	151	
26.08	C&K Basildon (a)	W	5-0	Kylie Nolan 2, Hannah Miles 22, 26, Cori Williams 40, Alice Griffiths 62	33	5
09.09	QPR (h)+	W	5-1	Alice Griffiths, Kylie Nolan (x2), Cori Williams (x2, 1pen)	50	5
16.09	Loughborough F (h)*	W	3-1	Grace Horrell 74, Own Goal 76, Kelly Isaac 83	100	4
23.09	Chichester City (a)		P-P			4
28.10	Chichester City (a)	L	0-1		68	7
04.11	Oxford United (h)	D	1-1	Kylie Nolan 1	150	7
18.11	Loughborough F (a)	L	0-1	Nadia Lawrence sent off 90+2	30	7
25.11	Portsmouth (h)	W	2-1	Nia Rees 32, Jasmine Simpson 55	75	7
16.12	C&K Basildon (h)+*	W	7-0	Grace Horrell 15, Kylie Nolan 18, Ffion Morgan 33, Chelsea Jumratie 37, Jordan Guard 39, Cori Williams 51, Jasmine Simpson 74	80	5
13.01	Watford (h)	W	1-0	Cori Williams (pen) 20	175	5
27.01	QPR (a)	W	6-0	Kylie Nolan 26, 36, 82, Jordan Guard 44, Grace Horrell 51, Emma Jones 67	48	4
17.02	Gillingham (a)	W	2-0	Emma Jones 59, Kylie Nolan 90+6	50	3
24.02	Chichester City (h)	W	4-2	Emma Jones 6, 25, 31, Chloe Lloyd 86	150	3
10.03	Plymouth A (a)	W	3-2	Kelly Isaac 19, Cori Williams 82, Kylie Nolan 89	68	3
17.03	MK Dons (h)	W	2-1	Chloe Lloyd 69, Grace Horrell 84	175	3
24.03	Portsmouth (a)	W	3-0	Grace Horrell 20, Emma Jones 24, 27	131	2
31.03	Gillingham (h)	W	2-0	Emma Jones 24, 45+7	85	2
14.04	Coventry United (a)	L	1-4	Kylie Nolan 17	206	3
21.04	Plymouth A (h)	W	3-2	Cerys Jones 12, Kylie Nolan 29, Cori Williams 61	125	2
23.04	Oxford United (a)	W	3-2	Grace Horrell 60, Kylie Nolan 65, Gwennan Davies 72	101	2
28.04	MK Dons (a)	W	2-1	Nadia Lawrence 47, Jordan Guard 62		2
05.05	Coventry United (h)	D	1-1	Grace Horrell 51	200	2

+Played at University Sports Ground, Mendip Road *Played at The Met Coach Community Stadium +*Played at Llanrumney

2018-19 FA CUP

Date/Round	Opponent	Result	Score	Scorers	Attendance
02.12 R2	QPR (h)	W	4-0	Cori Williams 57, Nia Rees 64, Gwennan Davies 67, Grace Horrell 90+1	200est
06.01 R3	Bolton W (h)	W	2-0	Cori Williams 7, Kylie Nolan 15	200est
03.02 R4	Durham (a)		P-P		
10.02 R4	Durham (a)	L	1-5	*Cori Williams missed pen 19 (saved Megan Borthwick),* Kylie Nolan 21	283

2018-19 WNL CUP

Date/Round	Opponent	Result	Score	Scorers	Attendance
02.09 DR	Stevenage (a)	W	4-1	Cori Williams 9, Nadia Lawrence 13, Kelly Isaac 22, Grace Horrell 46	30
R1	Bye				
14.10 R2	Cheltenham T (h)	W	5-3	Grace Horrell 18, Kylie Nolan 25, 46, Cori Williams 90, 90+6	200est
09.12 R3	Loughborough F (h)	L	3-4 aet	Grace Horrell 38, Kylie Nolan (pen) 45, Cori Williams 52	115

"One of my highlights of 2018-19 was the 3-2 win against Oxford United away in April. It showed as a team and a group of players how far we had come over the season. The resilience to see the game out away from home against a strong team was hugely impressive. The MK Dons home game in March was the point in the season when we stood up and made ourselves recognised within the League. We were 1-0 down at half time knowing that only a win would do. The feeling that everyone had when Grace (Horrell) scored the winner showed how much of a team we had become. This club is so special to me because I have been playing here for 11 seasons since joining when I was 16. My hope for 2019-20 would be to go one place better and win the League."

Cori Williams – Wales international

CHELTENHAM TOWN

2019-20: WNL SOUTH WEST 1 (Tier 4)

Founded: 1989 (as Cheltenham YMCA)
Nickname: The Robins

Season 2018-19:
WNL South West 1 (Tier 4): 4th
FA Cup: 1st Round
WNL Cup: 1st Round
County Cup: Winners

The 2019-20 campaign represents Cheltenham Town Ladies' 30th anniversary season. They were formed out of a five-a-side team and began life as Cheltenham YMCA in the South West Combination League in 1989. The 2019-20 campaign is also their sixth consecutive season in Tier 4 and comes off the back of a highly successful 2018-19 in which they finished 4th in WNL South West 1 and won the Gloucestershire FA County Cup.

2018-19 AS IT HAPPENS

19.08.18: Cheltenham's 7-4 win over Brislington is their first ever opening-day victory at Tier 4 level.

13.01.19: Issy Newns scores her first ever goal for the club in the 3-0 win over Maidenhead – a game in which Annie Martin also chalks up her 20th of the season in all competitions.

16.02.19: Seventeen-year-old wide player Gipsy Viveash, the niece of former Reading and Walsall men's defender Adi, signs from Swindon where she made her WNL debut earlier this season.

25.03.19: Chairman Andy Liddle confirms he will stand down at the end of 2018-19 after seven years at the helm having overseen the rise from South West Regional Women's League strugglers to Tier 3.

11.04.19: Cheltenham lift the Gloucestershire FA County Cup with a 10-0 win over lower division FC Frampton in the final.

14.04.19: A crowd of 120 – a club record at the DN Fire Stadium – sees Cheltenham hold newly crowned champions Keynsham to a 1-1 draw, thus becoming only the second team all season to take points off the K's. It could have been even better but for the award of a last-minute penalty to the visitors which allowed them to cancel out the goal with which Sally Butterfield gave the Robins the lead. The result also guarantees Cheltenham their highest ever League finish and points return.

27.04.19: A club record crowd of 375 watches Cheltenham's 2-2 draw with Swindon Town which is played at Whaddon Road, home of Cheltenham Town men. The match takes place immediately after Cheltenham men have also played Swindon in League Two (a fixture which ends 3-2 to Cheltenham and is watched by 4,306 fans). The Ladies' match is also notable for Cerys Dolloway putting Cheltenham ahead with her first goal for the club and 16-year-old Georgia Brown netting their equaliser from the spot with four minutes to play.

2018-19 RESULTS: (HOME GROUND: DN FIRE STADIUM, PETERSFIELD PARK, (CHELTENHAM SARACENS FC), UNLESS STATED)

2018-19 WNL SW 1					Att	Pos
19.08	Brislington (a)	W	7-4	Annie Martin 1, 65, 72, 84, Ella Hitchcox 47, Sophie Wyatt 75, Eleanor Marie Briscoe 90+1	74	
26.08	Maidenhead Utd (h)	W	5-1	Samantha Morris 31, Annie Martin 62, 66, 86, Ella Hitchcox 63	68	2
09.09	Buckland Athletic (h)	D	2-2	Annie Martin 11, Ella Hitchcox 67	51	1
13.09	Swindon Town (a)	W	2-0	Annie Martin 4, Ella Hitchcox 45, *Sarah Walters missed pen 68*		1
16.09	Southampton S (h)	W	2-1	Louise Fensome 12, Ella Hitchcox 40	71	1
28.10	Poole Town (a)	W	7-0	Louise Fensome 2, Annie Martin 16, Rose Knuckey 41, 60, Georgia Brown 44, Sally Butterfield 83, Ella Hitchcox 89	30	2
04.11	Chesham U (h)*	L	0-1		79	3
25.11	Southampton W (h)	W	1-0	Annie Martin 76	76	3
09.12	Brislington (h)	D	2-2	Sally Butterfield 5, Georgia Brown 26	74	3
16.12	Larkhall Athletic (h)		P-P			3
13.01	Maidenhead U (a)	W	3-0	Isobel Newns 22, Eleanor Marie Briscoe 59, Annie Martin 76	20	3
20.01	Buckland Athletic (a)	L	2-3	Annie Martin 32, Rose Knuckey 62	39	3
27.01	Larkhall Athletic (h)	W	2-0	Annie Martin 48, Annabel Davies 55	91	3
03.03	Keynsham Town (a)	L	2-6	Georgia Brown (pen) 61, Ella Hitchcox 83	135	4
10.03	Poole Town (h)+	W	6-2	Georgia Brown 6, 27, (pen) 55, 62, Abby Bevan 8, Ella Hitchcox 74	61	4
24.03	Southampton W (a)	W	1-0	Natasha Angel (og) 65	34	3
31.03	Southampton S (a)	W	2-0	Ella Hitchcox 53, Annie Martin 79	27	3
07.04	Chesham United (a)	W	4-0	Annie Martin 10, 50, 90, Abby Bevan 25		3
14.04	Keynsham Town (h)	D	1-1	Sally Butterfield 67	120	3
27.04	Swindon Town (h)+*	D	2-2	Cerys Dolloway 3, Georgia Brown (pen) 86	375	3
05.05	Larkhall Athletic (a)	D	1-1	Annie Martin 28	70	3

*Played at Seasons, (Cheltenham Town FC Training Ground) +Played at Cheltenham Civil Service +*Played at Whaddon Road, (Cheltenham Town FC)

2018-19 FA CUP

23.09 R2	Brislington (h)	W	4-1	Ella Hitchcox 20, 43, Annie Martin 36, 78	76
07.10 RQ3	Exeter City (h)	W	1-0	Sarah Walters 43	116
11.11 R1	Buckland Athletic (a)	L	0-2		74

2018-19 WNL CUP

02.09 DR	Luton Town (a)	W	3-1	Annie Martin 33, 70, Amy Leask 47
14.10 R1	Cardiff City L (a)	L	3-5	Ella Hitchcox 2, 82, Annie Martin 87

2018-19 GLOUCESTERSHIRE FA COUNTY CUP

21.10 R1	St Nicholas Reserves (h)	W	13-1	Annie Martin 1, 73, Lucy Durham 14, 18, 33, Rose Knuckey 22, Georgia Brown 27, 40, 43, 57, 87, Ella Hitchcox 61, Kayleigh Hateley 61	75
18.11 R2	Downend Flyers (a)	W	4-0	Annabel Davies 26, Annie Martin 52, Ella Hitchcox 83, Kayleigh Hateley 88	35
17.02 QF	AEK Boco (a)	W	9-0	Rose Knuckey 3, Rebecca Wilkins 11, Louise Fensome 15, 63, 79, Ella Hitchcox 29, Sally Butterfield 50, Jade Wiltshire 73, Isobel Newns 82	40
17.03 SF	Almondsbury (a)	W	4-2	Lauren Ellis 3, Annie Martin 20, 85, Kayleigh Hateley 61	
11.04 F	Frampton Rangers (n)	W	10-0	Ella Hitchcox 2, Becky Wilkins 24, 34, 54, Georgia Brown 32, 73, Annie Martin 51, 62, 69, 82	

(n) Played at Almondsbury, Gloucestershire FA HQ

"Season 2018-19 was the most successful in the club's history. By claiming our highest ever WNL position and lifting the Gloucestershire FA County Cup we proved capable of getting the results to match all our hard work. I am sure that if we keep going, we can have even more success in 2019-20. Full credit must go to all our players and the management staff led by Alex Cheal."

Sarah Walters – Club Captain

CHESHAM UNITED

2019-20: WNL SOUTH WEST 1

Founded: 1995

Nickname: The Generals

Season 2018-19:

WNL South West 1 (Tier 4): 5th

FA Cup: 3rd Qualifying Round

WNL Cup: Determining Round

WNL Plate: 3rd Round

County Cup: Runners-up

Chesham were promoted to Tier 4 as 2017-18 Southern Regional Premier League champions. They completed that 2017-18 season without dropping a single point. The Generals won the League and Cup Double that season with Gemma Fraser scoring a hat-trick in the Southern Regional Premier League Cup final as they beat Bournemouth 3-0. The 2018-19 season was a successful debut campaign in the WNL as they finished in 5th place and reached the County Cup final.

2018-19 AS IT HAPPENS

19.08.18: Having been promoted as 2017-18 Southern Regional Premier champions, Chesham's first game at Tier 4 level ends in a 4-0 defeat away to Larkhall Athletic.

09.09.18: The Generals secure their first Tier 4 victory in style as they win 5-0 away to Southampton Saints with goals from Emma Bebbington, Kate Bowers, Gemma Fraser (x2) and Sarah Hazell.

02.05:19: Chesham put on a fine display against Tier 3 MK Dons in the Berks & Bucks FA County Cup final but are beaten 4-2 by opponents who lift the trophy for the second year in a row.

2018-19 RESULTS: (HOME VENUE: THE MEADOW, (CHESHAM UNITED FC), UNLESS STATED)

2018-19 WNL SW 1

					Att	Pos
19.08	Larkhall Athletic (a)	L	0-4		30	
09.09	Southampton S (a)	W	5-0	Emma Bebbington, Kate Bowers, Gemma Fraser (x2), Sarah Hazell	15	4
12.09	Maidenhead U (h)	W	5-0	Kate Bowers, Gemma Fraser (x2), Dawne Campbell, Natasha Smith	35	4
16.09	Keynsham Town (a)	L	1-7	Kate Bowers	65	4
30.09	Brislington (a)	L	2-3	Kate Bowers 29, Natasha Smith 41	43	4
21.10	Swindon Town (h)	W	1-0	Gemma Fraser, *Gemma Darvill sent off*	50	4
04.11	Cheltenham Town (a)	W	1-0	Natasha Smith 65	79	4
11.11	Southampton W (a)	L	1-2	Natasha Smith 31, *Chesham GK Lucia Delves saved pen 75*	41	5
25.11	Poole Town (a)	W	5-1	Gemma Fraser 29, 46, Niamh Euman 68, Lidia Niedertubbesing-Lopez 77, Natasha Smith 89	12	5
02.12	Swindon Town (a)	W	5-0	Gemma Fraser 36, 77, Emma Delves 40, Gemma Darvill 70, Emma Bebbington 85	23	4
06.01	Buckland Athletic (h)	W	4-3	Gemma Fraser 47, 52, 88, Emma Delves 60	40	3
13.01	Larkhall Athletic (h)	D	1-1	Gemma Fraser 71	40	4
13.02	Maidenhead Utd (a)	W	2-0	Natasha Smith 29, 51	20	4
24.02	Southampton S (h)	W	8-0	Kate Bowers, Gemma Fraser (x5), Jackie Hanson, Natasha Smith	40	3
10.03	Brislington (h)	W	3-0	Gemma Fraser 5, 21, Niamh Euman 69	35	3
17.03	Buckland Athletic (a)	L	4-8	Jacqueline Hanson 5, Livvi Harris 44, Gemma Fraser 70, 85, *Dawne Campbell sent off*	51	3
07.04	Cheltenham Town (h)	L	0-4			5
14.04	Southampton W (h)	L	2-3	Gemma Fraser 15, 40		5
28.04	Keynsham Town (h)	D	1-1	Gemma Fraser 14	80	5
05.05	Poole Town (h)	W	6-1	Jacqui Hanson 35, 55, Kate Bowers 60, Gemma Fraser 57, 65, 72		5

2018-19 FA CUP

23.09 RQ2	Peterborough U (h)	W	5-0	Gemma Fraser 5, 40, 70, Emma Delves 30, 52	60
07.10 RQ3	Crawley Wasps (h)	L	0-3		60est

2018-19 WNL CUP

02.09 DR	Enfield Town (h)	L	2-4	Niamh Euman, Gemma Fraser	35

2018-19 WNL PLATE

R1	Bye				
14.10 R2	Actonians (a)	W	2-1	Emma Delves 17, Gemma Fraser 90+3	25est
09.12 R3	Gillingham (a)	L	0-5		

2018-19 BERKS & BUCKS FA COUNTY CUP

18.11 QF	Ascot United (h)	W	w/o		
17.02 SF	Maidenhead United (a)	W	1-0	Sarah Hazell 30	37
02.05 F	MK Dons (n)	L	2-4	Kate Bowers 44, Gemma Fraser 82	200est

(n) Played at Arbour Park, (Slough Town FC)

CHESTER-LE-STREET TOWN

2019-20: WNL NORTH 1 (Tier 4)

Founded: 2009

Nickname: Town / The Cestrians

Season 2018-19:

WNL North 1 (Tier 4): 3rd

FA Cup: 2nd Round

WNL Cup: Determining Round

WNL Plate: 3rd Round

County Cup: Semi-finals

Chester-le-Street Town have been playing in Tier 4 since three successive promotions carried them up to that level ahead of the 2013-14 season. In 2018-19 they achieved their highest finish by coming 3rd, eclipsing their 4th place of 2016-17. The team is affiliated with men's Tier 10 side Chester-le-Street Town FC and play at the same Moor Park stadium.

2018-19 AS IT HAPPENS

23.09.18: Elizabeth Thompson-Clarke and Nichole Havery both score hat-tricks as Chester-le-Street Town beat Steel City Wanderers 8-1 in the FA Cup 2nd Qualifying Round.

18.11.18: Chester-le-Street Town win 6-0 at home to Morecambe with Nichole Havery scoring the side's first League hat-trick of the season.

02.12.18: Having successfully negotiated their way through three rounds, Chester-le-Street Town's FA Cup run comes to an end with a 2nd Round defeat away to Tier 3 side Stoke City.

05.05.19: Chester-le-Street kick-off the final game of the season in 2nd place but ultimately miss out on the runners-up spot in WNL North 1 as they suffer a shock 5-1 home defeat to strugglers Norton & Stockton Ancients while Brighouse Town win 3-1 at Leeds to leapfrog them in the table.

2018-19 RESULTS: (HOME VENUE: MOOR PARK, (CHESTER-LE-STREET TOWN FC) UNLESS STATED)

2018-19 WNL North 1

					Att	Pos
19.08	Burnley (a)	W	3-0	Rachel Mellor 38, Kacie Elson 40, Nichole Havery 44	60	
26.08	Barnsley (h)	W	3-1	Nichole Havery 10, Elizabeth Thompson-Clarke 23, Amy Kelly 86	40	1
11.09	Newcastle U (h)	L	0-1		100	1
16.09	Brighouse Town (a)	W	2-0	Nichole Havery 57, 79	30	3
21.10	Leeds United (h)	L	1-2	Elizabeth Thompson-Clark 13	50	6
28.10	Crewe Alexandra (h)	W	2-0	Kirsty Stafford (og) 4, Elizabeth Thompson Clarke 65	18	6
04.11	Chorley (a)	W	3-2	Nichole Havery 46, 72, Elizabeth Thompson-Clarke 80	85	3
18.11	Morecambe (h)	W	6-0	Elizabeth Thompson-Clarke 5, 78 Laura Hockaday 27, Nichole Havery 37, 60, 76	40	3
25.11	Liverpool Feds (h)	D	1-1	Laura Hockaday 10	40	2
06.01	Barnsley (a)	L	0-2		50	4
13.01	Burnley (h)	L	0-1		30	4
15.01	Norton & Stockton A (a)	W	2-1	Nichole Havery 23, 78	150	3
10.02	Leeds United (a)	W	3-1	Kacie Elson 53, 73, Nichole Havery 64	70	2
24.02	Bolton W (a)	W	2-0		40	2
26.02	Newcastle United (a)	D	2-2	Kacie Elson 50, Nichole Havery 80	94	2
03.03	Brighouse Town (h)	L	0-3		50	3
10.03	Bolton Wanderers (h)		P-P			3
17.03	Crewe Alexandra (a)	W	2-1	Nichole Havery (pen) 45, Laura Hockaday 58	43	2
24.03	Morecambe (a)	W	2-1	Elizabeth Thompson-Clarke 62, Laura Hockaday 86	20	2
31.03	Chorley (h)	W	1-0	Kacie Elson 78	30	2
21.04	Bolton W (h)	W	2-1	Nichole Havery 35, 50	40	2
28.04	Liverpool Feds (a)	D	2-2	Lucy Jackman 48, Kacie Elson 66	40	2
05.05	Norton & Stockton A (h)	L	1-5	Nichole Havery	50	3

2018-19 FA Cup

23.09 RQ2	Steel City W (a)	W	8-1	Elizabeth Thompson-Clarke 13, 33, 52, Laura Hockaday 58, 62, Nichole Havery 59, 86, 88	28
07.10 RQ3	Newcastle United (a)	W	2-0	Laura Hockaday 50, Nicole Havery 88, *Brogan Prudhoe sent off 59*	162
11.11 R1	FC United of Manchester (a)	W	5-0	Elizabeth Thompson-Clarke 55, Nichole Havery 58, 83, Jessica Ellison 63, Lucy Jackman 90	110
02.12 R2	Stoke City (h)	L	0-2	Kacie Elson sent off 55	60

2018-19 WNL Cup

02.09 DR	Guiseley Vixens (a)	L	2-4	Elizabeth Thompson-Clarke 18, Nichole Havery 41	40est

2018-19 WNL PLATE

R1	Bye				
14.10 R2	Long Eaton United (a)	W	1-0 aet	Nichole Havery 95	
09.12 R3	Liverpool Feds (a)	L	0-1		20

2018-19 DURHAM FA COUNTY CUP

16.12 R1	South Shields Reserves (a)	W	w/o	
20.01 QF	Hartlepool United (h)	W	3-0	Kelcie Elson (x2), Elizabeth Thompson-Clarke
17.02 SF	Durham Cestria (a)	L	1-2	Amy Lawson 55

CHICHESTER CITY

2019-20: WNL SOUTHERN PREMIER (Tier 3)

Founded: 1991

Nickname: Lilywhites / Green Army

Season 2018-19:

WNL Southern Premier (Tier 3): 3rd

FA Cup: 2nd Round

WNL Cup: 3rd Round

County Cup: Winners

Sheena Booker

Chichester City have been in Tier 3 since winning promotion ahead of the 2017-18 season as (what was then) WPL South West 1 champions. They had a steady first season in Tier 3, finishing 2017-18 in 9th place and making it through to the 5th Round of the FA Cup where they played arguably the biggest match in their history. Chi welcomed WSL side Liverpool to Oaklands Park where a crowd of 1,300 saw them acquit themselves well in a 3-0 defeat. They enjoyed an impressive 2018-19, topping the table between November and February and ultimately finishing 3rd as well as winning the Sussex FA County Cup final against WSL club Brighton & Hove Albion's Development team. Aaron Smith stood down as manager at the end of 2018-19 with Sadie Blakely taking over and heading up an all-female management team including head coach Kim Stenning.

2018-19 AS IT HAPPENS

11.11.18: Cherelle Khassal celebrates her 50th appearance for the club in style when she comes off the bench at half-time with Chichester trailing 1-0 to C&K Basildon. Within 17 minutes she has scored a hat-trick, with her team going on to win 4-2.

16.12.18: Sixteen-year-old Gemma White scores her first goal for the club in the 6-0 County Cup win away to Bexhill United – a stunning effort from 35 yards on her full debut for the senior team.

31.03.19: Chi keep their slim title hopes alive by winning 3-2 away at leaders Coventry United thanks to a Molly Clark brace and a goal from Kim Stenning.

10.04.19: Coventry United's 4-0 win at home to MK Dons ends Chichester's title ambitions on an evening when they themselves aren't in action. Cov are now 11 points clear with three games to play.

14.04.19: Chi beat Watford 1-0 on a day when Coventry are crowned WNL Southern champions with a 4-1 win at home to the only side who could have still caught them, Cardiff City Ladies.

18.04.19: Molly Clark's stunning 30-yard goal after just two minutes is enough for Chichester to beat Brighton & Hove Albion's Development team 1-0 in the Sussex FA County Cup final at Culver Road. It's the second time Chi have won the competition, with their first triumph coming in 2014.

2018-19 RESULTS: (HOME VENUE: OAKLANDS PARK, (CHICHESTER CITY FC) UNLESS STATED)

2018-19 WNL SP					Att	Pos
19.08	Oxford United (h)	W	2-1	Sara Tubby 36, Molly Clark 65	200	
26.08	Plymouth A (a)	W	3-0	Molly Clark 37, 40, Helen Ogle 84	61	
09.09	MK Dons (a)	W	1-0	Molly Clark 86		1
12.09	Portsmouth (h)	W	2-1	Holly Wride 12, Chloe Melton 52	272	1
16.09	Coventry United (h)	L	1-2	Cherelle Khassal 10	130	3
23.09	Cardiff City Ladies (h)		P-P			3
30.09	Loughborough F (a)	W	1-0	Molly Clark 47	27	3
21.10	QPR (a)	W	3-2	Hollie Wride 12, Jade Widdows 16, Cherelle Khassal 23	64	3
28.10	Cardiff City Ladies (h)	W	1-0	Molly Clark 40	68	2
04.11	Gillingham (h)	W	2-0	Cherelle Khassal 31, Molly Clark 47	105	1
11.11	C&K Basildon (h)	W	4-2	Cherelle Khassal 47, 53, 62, Alex Bailess (og) 59	80	1
18.11	Watford (a)	L	0-1		120	1
06.01	Plymouth A (h)	W	2-1	Helen Ogle 35, 70	150	1
27.01	MK Dons (h)	W	5-2	Molly Clark 45+2, Lauren Cheshire 47, Rebecca Barron 52, Sara Tubby 64, 66	90	1
03.02	Coventry United (a)		P-P			1
10.02	Oxford United (a)	L	0-1		167	1
13.02	Portsmouth (a)		P-P			1
24.02	Cardiff City L (a)	L	2-4	Cherelle Khassal 42, Jess Lewry 88	150	1
03.03	QPR (h)		P-P			2
10.03	Loughborough F (h)	L	1-3	Jess Lewry 17	80	2
17.03	C&K Basildon (a)	W	8-0	Jess Lewry (pen) 27, Kim Stenning 30, Molly Clark 33, 45+1, 63, 86, Sara Tubby 67, 90+1		2
27.03	Portsmouth (a)	L	1-3	Jess Lewry 22. *Jess Lewry missed 2 pens 80 & 85 (both saved)*	213	2
31.03	Coventry United (a)	W	3-2	Molly Clark 34, 44, Kim Stenning 64	90	3
14.04	Watford (h)	W	1-0	Lauren Cheshire (pen) 40	90	2
28.04	QPR (h)	W	3-0	Natasha Stephens 1, Lauren Cheshire 27, Tammy Waine (pen) 41, *Lauren Dolbear s/0 78*	50	3
05.05	Gillingham (a)	D	2-2	Laura Ingram 31, Kim Stenning 79	52	3

2018-19 FA Cup

02.12 R2	Crawley Wasps (a)		P-P		
09.12 R2	Crawley Wasps (a)	L	0-2		130

2018-19 WNL Cup

02.09 DR	Portsmouth (a)	W	4-2	Helen Ogle 1, Jade Widdows 42, Chloe Melton 50, 76	195
R1	Bye				
14.10 R2	Billericay T (a)	W	2-0	Hollie Wride 77, Molly Clarke 89	
13.01 R3	Coventry United (h)	L	0-2		

2018-19 Sussex County Cup

16.12 R2	Bexhill United (a)	W	6-0	Natasha Stephens, Gemma White, Laura Ingram, Helen Ogle, Gemma Simmonds, Rebecca Bell	30est
20.01SF	Crawley Wasps (a)	W	2-1	Tiffany Taylor 10, Jess Lewry (pen) 83	150est
18.04 F	Brighton & H A Development (n)	W	1-0	Molly Clark 2	240

(n) Played at Culver Road, (Sussex County HQ & Lancing FC)

CHORLEY

2019-20: WNL NORTH 1 (Tier 4)

Founded: 1978 (as Cumberland Rangers)

Nickname: The Magpies

Season 2018-19:

WNL Northern 1 (Tier 4): 7th

FA Cup: 1st Round

WNL Cup: 2nd Round

County Cup: Quarter-finals

Starting life as Cumberland Rangers in 1978, the team became New Longton in 1980. When Sheila Parker – the first captain of England's national team following the overturning of the FA ban – expressed an interest in playing for the team they moved their home ground to Astley Park in Chorley where she had been born and bred. Parker brought great experience having started out as a player for the legendary Dick, Kerr Ladies in 1963 when she was just 13. New Longton became Chorley in 1983 with Parker's husband taking over as manager. Chorley and Manchester City are the only clubs among the 42 founding members of the North West Women's Regional League in 1989 to still have the same name they had back then. The 2018-19 season was their fifth consecutive season in what is now WNL North 1 with their highest finish being the 3rd place they achieved in 2015-16. In summer 2018 they became formally affiliated with Chorley FC men's and changed their name from Chorley Ladies to Chorley FC Women.

2018-19 AS IT HAPPENS

19.08.18: The first League match of the season is a dramatic one with Chorley winning a nine-goal thriller against Norton & Stockton Ancients 5-4.

24.03.19: Chorley goalkeeper Rachel Darbyshire has an eventful afternoon. With Chorley leading 4-1 at home to Leeds, the visitors are awarded a penalty with two minutes remaining. Darbyshire flies to her left to keep out Emma Lee's spot-kick. In stoppage time Leeds win another penalty, Lee again steps up, and Darbyshire saves once more. The match ends 4-1.

31.03.19: One week after her double penalty save heroics, Darbyshire is sent off for handling outside her area just 18 minutes into the away match against Chester-le-Street Town. Ellie Mills goes between the posts and keeps the ball out until the 78th minute when Kacie Elson scores the only goal of the match for the hosts.

2018-19 RESULTS: (HOME VENUE: VICTORY PARK, (CHORLEY FC) UNLESS STATED)

2018-19 WNL North 1

					Att	Pos
19.08	Norton & Stockton A (h)	W	5-4	Scarlett Smith 4, 64, Rachel Wood 23, Rebecca Kemp 40, 82	59	
26.08	Bolton W (a)		P-P			
09.09	Newcastle U (a)	W	2-1	Lisa Topping 23, Chloe Wild 71	162	3
12.09	Morecambe (h)	W	3-0	Rebecca Kemp 59, 77, Laura Walker 82	73	1
16.09	Crewe Alexandra (h)	W	3-1	Chloe Wild 17, 87, Scarlett Smith 90+1	90	1
03.10	Liverpool Feds (h)	D	1-1	Grace Vella 56	95	3
21.10	Brighouse Town (a)	D	2-2	Chloe Wild 10, Grace Vella 62	35	3
28.10	Barnsley (a)	L	1-3	Katy Morris 47	50	3
04.11	Chester-Le-Street T (h)	L	2-3	Katy Morris 27, Megan Searson (pen) 63	85	4
25.11	Leeds United (a)	L	0-3		100	9
16.12	Burnley (h)		P-P			9
06.01	Burnley (h)	L	0-1		98	9
13.01	Norton & Stockton A (a)	L	1-2	Lisa Topping 77	75	10
20.01	Bolton W (h)	D	1-1	Danielle Bailey (og) 55	102	10
27.01	Bolton W (a)		P-P			10
03.02	Newcastle United (h)		P-P			10
13.02	Morecambe (a)	L	0-2		35	10
03.03	Newcastle United (h)	D	0-0		94	9
10.03	Barnsley (h)		P-P			10
14.03	Liverpool Feds (a)	W	2-1	Bethany Donoghue 37, Rebecca Kemp 43	50	9
24.03	Leeds United (h)	W	4-1	Katy Morris 29, Bethany Donoghue 31, 62, Rebecca Kemp 60, Chorley GK Rachel Darbyshire saved two Emma Lee penalties 88 & 90+2	105	8
31.03	Chester-le-Street T (a)	L	0-1	Rachel Darbyshire sent off 18	30	8
03.04	Bolton W (a)	W	1-0	Katy Morris 18		8
07.04	Barnsley (h)	L	1-5	Katy Morris 31	107	8
14.04	Brighouse Town (h)	L	0-2		92	9
28.04	Crewe Alexandra (a)	W	4-0	Ellie Mills 14, Bethany Donoghue 28, 70, Katy Morris 58	55	7
05.05	Burnley (a)	L	0-1		225	7

2018-19 FA Cup

23.09 RQ2	Farsley Celtic (h)	W	5-0	Scarlett Smith 9, 32, 53, 81, Rebecca Kemp 71, Laura Walker missed pen 37	93
07.10 RQ3	Crewe Alexandra (h)	W	2-1	Katy Morris 19, Megan Searson (pen) 43	90est
11.11 R1	Stockport County (h)	L	1-2	Melissa Ball 61	77

2018-19 WNL CUP

02.09 DR	Doncaster R B (a)	D	2-2aet (W4-3p)	Laura Walker 8, Rebecca Kemp 64	
30.09 R1	Newcastle Utd (a)	W	2-1 aet	Chloe Wild 5, Laura Walker missed pen 29 (saved by Grace Donnelly), Kerry Nickson 98	108
14.10 R2	Nottingham F (a)	L	0-2		

2018-19 LANCASHIRE FA COUNTY CUP

18.11 QF	Burnley (h)	L	0-1	Megan Searson missed pen 30 (saved by Lauren Bracewell)	90

"In 2018-19 we strengthened by introducing eight new first-team players to our squad, and our Development team were crowned champions in their first season. We also established a relationship with Chorley FC Men. Chorley FC Women is a self-funded family-friendly club. Our aim is to provide players with a pathway into women's football in an elite environment. Hopes for 2019-20 are to build on the solid foundation we have in place by introducing an U18s women's side allowing us to filter players through into our first-team and to grow our existing Development programme."

Andy Ramskill – Head Coach

CRAWLEY WASPS

2019-20: WNL SOUTHERN PREMIER (Tier 3)

Founded: 1991

Nickname: Wasps

Season 2018-19:

WNL South East 1 (Tier 4): Champions (P)

FA Cup: 4th Round

WNL Cup: Runners-up

County Cup: Semi-finals

All-female club Crawley Wasps were founded in 1991 and have just enjoyed their most successful two seasons to date with back-to-back promotions carrying them up to Tier 3 for 2019-20. Manager Paul Walker's side were crowned London & South East Regional Premier champions in 2017-18 and then immediately took Tier 4 by storm. They wrapped up the 2018-19 WNL South East 1 title with three games to spare, went all the way to the 4th Round of the FA Cup where they acquitted themselves well against the mighty Arsenal and reached their first national Cup final, losing 3-0 to WNL Northern Premier (Tier 3) champions Blackburn Rovers in the WNL Cup final.

2018-19 AS IT HAPPENS

09.12.18: Crawley pull off an FA Cup shock by beating Tier 3 Chichester City 2-0 to reach the 3rd Round for the first time in their history.

03.02.19: A crowd of 1,550 is at Oaklands to watch Crawley take on 14-time winners Arsenal in the FA Cup 4th Round. The Gunners eventually run out 4-0 winners.

03.03.19: Wasps reach their first national Cup final as they win 1-0 at home to WNL North 1 side Bolton in the WNL Cup semi-finals.

31.03.19: The People's Pensions Stadium – home of League Two men's team Crawley Town FC – hosts Wasps on a day when they could be crowned WNL South East 1 champions, but they go down 1-0 to 2nd-placed Billericay Town. Danica Dougal's 38th minute penalty ends a two-year run, spanning 32 games, without a League defeat.

14.04.19: Wasps are crowned WNL South East 1 champions in their first season at this level thanks to a 1-0 win at home to Enfield Town. Kemina Webber scores the goal which clinches the title.

28.04.19: Crawley are beaten 3-0 by newly crowned WNL Northern Premier (Tier 3) champions Blackburn Rovers in the WNL Cup final at Burton Albion FC's Pirelli Stadium.

2018-19 RESULTS: (HOME VENUE: TINSLEY LANE, (OAKWOOD FC), UNLESS STATED)

2018-19 WNL SE 1

Date	Opponent		Score	Scorers	Att	Pos
19.08	Ipswich Town (h)*	W	5-1	Ariana Fleischman 6, Sian Heather 42, 62, Faye Rabson 29, 59	74	
26.08	Enfield Town (a)	W	1-0	Rachel Palmer 84	58	2
09.09	Norwich City (a)	W	6-0	Sian Heather 24, 67, Kemina Webber 41, Emma Plewa 52, Naomi Cole 82, Suzy Davis 86	63	1
12.09	AFC Wimbledon (h)	W	5-2	Sian Heather 23, Emma Plewa 50, 64, Faye Rabson 51, 76, Naomi Cole missed pen 59	100	1
16.09	Stevenage (a)	W	7-2	Sian Heather 15, Kemina Webber 25, Faye Rabson 30, Megan Stow 40, 50, Suzy Davis 75, Naomi Cole 85	25	1
03.10	Actonians (h)	W	5-0	Rachel Palmer 13, Megan Stow 41, Darcey James 59, Faye Rabson 67, Charlotte Young 90+3	95	1
28.10	Luton Town (h)	W	6-0	Sian Heather 25, Naomi Cole (pen) 35, Ariana Fleischman 53, Darcey James 70, Megan Stow 77, Faye Rabson 84	60	1
04.11	Billericay Town (a)	W	2-0	Emma Plewa 64, Naomi Cole 81	123	1
25.11	Denham Utd (h)	W	9-0	Kemina Webber 6, 71, Sian Heather 20, 83, Emma Plewa 23, 29, Rachel Palmer 70, Megan Stow 72, Jenny Drury 86	50	1
27.01	Leyton Orient (h)	W	4-1	Kemina Webber 55, Rachel Palmer 82, Naomi Cole 87, Jenny Drury 90+2	65	1
13.02	AFC Wimbledon (a)	W	4-0	Rachel Palmer 2, Kemina Webber 12, Naomi Cole (pen) 36, (pen) 45	70	1
17.02	Stevenage (h)	W	7-0	Amy Woollard 38, Kemina Webber 45, 64, Megan Stow 58, Naomi Cole 62, 77, Charlotte Young 89	60	1
10.03	Cambridge U (a)	D	0-0		40	1
13.03	Actonians (a)	W	4-0	Megan Stow 12, Charlotte Young 33, Naomi Cole (pen) 43, Rachel Palmer 71		1
17.03	Norwich City (h)*	W	8-0	Megan Stow 8, 77, 79, Rachel Palmer 22, Kemina Webber 31, Naomi Cole 40, Darcey James 44, Jenny Drury 52		1
24.03	Luton Town (a)	W	3-0	Amy Green 12, Naomi Cole 16, Rachel Palmer 38	61	1
31.03	Billericay Town (h)+	L	0-1			
07.04	Cambridge U (h)**	W	6-1	Amy Green 21, Darcey James 40, Kemina Webber 59, Rachel Palmer 78, Megan Stow 49, 90+2	95	1
14.04	Enfield Town (h)++	W	1-0	Kemina Webber 83	135	1C

21.04	Ipswich Town (a)	W	2-1	Faye Rabson 64, Suzanne Davies 88, *Darcey James sent off 68*	67	1C
30.04	Denham United (a)	D	1-1	Kemina Webber 82	90	1C
05.05	Leyton Orient (a)	W	2-1	Darcey James 11, Naomi Cole (pen) 74		1C

*Played at The Haven, (Crawley Down Gatwick FC)

+Played at The People's Pensions Stadium, (Crawley Town FC)

**Played at Shooting Field, (Steyning Town FC)

++Played at Woodside Road, (Worthing FC)

2018-19 FA CUP

23.09 RQ2	Denham United (a)		P-P		
30.09 RQ2	Denham United (a)	W	3-1	Naomi Cole 15, Kemina Webber 50, Faye Rabson 58	35
07.10 RQ3	Chesham United (a)	W	3-0	Emma Plewa 67, 89, Megan Stow 90+3	60
11.11 R1	QPR Girls (h)	W	6-0	Kemina Webber 13, Emma Plewa 26, 49, 64, Megan Stow 59, Ariana Fleischman 69	80
09.12 R2	Chichester City (h)+	W	2-0	Kemina Webber 38, Darcy James 43	130
06.01 R3	Coventry United (a)	W	2-1	Ariana Fleischman 27, Darcy James 90+1	90
03.02 R4	Arsenal (h)	L	0-4		1,550

+Played at Woodside Road, (Worthing FC)

2018-19 WNL CUP

02.09 DR	Ipswich Town (h)	W	8-0	Sian Heather 14, Megan Stow 26, 90+2, Kemina Webber 23, 43, Faye Rabson 41, Charlotte Carter 73, Naomi Cole 89	60
R1	Bye				
14.10 R2	Oxford United (a)	W	3-1 aet	Naomi Cole 90+2, Emma Plewa 93, Sian Heather 100	
13.01 R3	Plymouth Argyle (a)	W	5-3 aet	Sian Heather 40, Kemina Webber 67, 95, 112, Faye Rabson 110	207
24.02 QF	Coventry United (a)	W	2-1	Kemina Webber 37, Darcey James 57	120
03.03 SF	Bolton W (h)	W	1-0	Own Goal 55	120est
28.04 F	Blackburn Rovers (n)	L	0-3		227

(n) Played at Pirelli Stadium, (Burton Albion FC)

2018-19 SUSSEX FA COUNTY CUP

21.10 R1	Eastbourne (a)	W	4-0	Suzy Davis, Ariana Fleischman (x2), Jenny Drury	
16.12 QF	Saltdean (a)	W	7-0	Megan Stow 10, Sian Heather 14, 45, Naomi Cole 16, 52, Ariana Fleischman 20, Jenny Drury 79	35
20.01 SF	Chichester City (h)	L	1-2	Charlotte Young 77	150

"Without question 2018-19 represented the most successful season in our club's 27-year history: League champions; promotion to the WNL Southern Premier; WNL Cup runners-up; and reaching the 4th Round of the FA Cup – eventually defeated by an Arsenal side who went on to win the WSL. It's all testimony to the quality of the first team squad assembled at the club. We chalked up five wins against Tier 3 clubs in 2018-19, so we head into 2019-20 looking forward to testing ourselves at that level every week. All last season's squad have been retained, and with some new additions our expectation is that we will prove capable of performing well in the Southern Premier."

Paul Walker – Manager

CREWE ALEXANDRA

2019-20: NORTH WEST REGIONAL PREMIER (Tier 5)

Founded: 2000 (as Crewe Vagrants)
Nickname: The Alex / Railway Women

Season 2018-19:
WNL North 1 (Tier 4): 12th (R)
FA Cup: 3rd Qualifying Round
WNL Cup: Determining Round
WNL Plate: 2nd Round
County Cup: Quarter-finals

The first club in the area, Crewe Ladies, joined the North West Regional League in 1985 before folding in 1992-93. At that point a new club was formed – Crewe Alexandra. They were elected into the North West Regional League for 1999-00 but folded in 2001. A rival club named Crewe Vagrants had been set up in 2000-01 and in 2005 they became the Crewe Alexandra Ladies that exists today. Early successes included winning the 2002-03 Midlands Regional Premier Division and the 2005-06 Midlands Combination. More recently they won the Cheshire FA County Cup three years in a row from 2015-16 to 2017-18. A difficult 2018-19 saw Alex finish bottom of WNL North 1 but there are reasons to be positive for the future with four players from the U18s progressing to the first team throughout the course of the season just gone.

2018-19 AS IT HAPPENS

22.10.18: Nick Pearce steps away from his role as first team manager with Matt Fisher being named as his replacement. Emma Lambourne is appointed Fisher's assistant manager while Jack Johnson continues in his role as first team coach.

01.02.19: Crewe announce that in 2019-20 their first team and development squad will play some home matches at the Reaseheath Training Complex, home of the Crewe Alexandra FC Academy. They are also to become incorporated into the men's club under the Community banner and will wear the same kit as well as play some matches at the men's Alexandra Stadium.

17.02.19: Crewe play out an entertaining 3-3 draw with Tranmere in the County Cup quarter-finals, but while both sides have no trouble finding the target during the 90 minutes the resulting penalty shootout is remarkably low-scoring with Tranmere winning 2-1.

28.04.19: Laura Goom makes her 200th appearance for the club in Alex's 4-0 home defeat to Chorley.

05.05.19: On the final day of the season Crewe get their first League win of the campaign as Amanda Fallon heads in the only goal of the game against Bolton.

2018-19 RESULTS: (HOME VENUE: CUMBERLAND ARENA, (CREWE FC) UNLESS STATED)

2018-19 WNL North 1					Att	Pos
19.08	Leeds United (a)	L	0-4		100	
26.08	Newcastle United (h)	L	1-3	Bethany Grice 34, Crewe GK Hannah Holloway saved Brooke Cochrane pen 39	35	12
09.09	Morecambe (a)	L	2-5	Laura Garner 10, Amanda Fallon 64	38	12
12.09	Liverpool Feds (h)	L	3-5	Michelle Saunders 59, 62, Meg Booth 70	48	12
16.09	Chorley (a)	L	1-3	Michelle Saunders 15	90	12
30.09	Brighouse Town (h)	L	0-4		70	12
21.10	Barnsley (h)	L	2-3	Meg Booth 35,75	50	12
28.10	Chester-Le-Street T (a)	L	0-2		18	12
04.11	Norton & Stockton A (h)	L	1-3	Amanda Fallon 63	40	12
11.11	Burnley (a)	L	0-4		40	12
18.11	Newcastle United (a)	L	0-2		72	12
02.12	Norton & Stockton A (a)	L	1-3	Beth Coppin 42	50	12
13.01	Leeds United (h)	L	0-1		28	12
03.02	Morecambe (h)		P-P			12
10.02	Bolton Wanderers (a)	D	0-0		70	12
21.02	Liverpool Feds (a)	L	0-5		75	12
24.02	Morecambe (h)	D	2-2	Bethany Grice 56, Loren Cooper 65	28	12
10.03	Brighouse Town (a)		P-P			12
17.03	Chester-le-Street T (h)	L	1-2	Laura Garner 72	43	12
07.04	Brighouse Town (a)	L	0-5	Crewe GK Hannah Holloway saved pen 74 (Brighouse score rebound)	95	12
14.04	Burnley (h)	L	0-3	Amanda Fallon missed pen (saved) 58	100	12
21.04	Barnsley (a)	L	0-8		100	12
28.04	Chorley (h)	L	0-4		55	12
05.05	Bolton W (h)	W	1-0	Amanda Fallon 32	40	12

2018-19 FA Cup

23.09 RQ2	Cammell Laird 1907 (a)	W	3-1	Laura Garner (pen) 19, Bethany Grice 50, Becky Garner 84	45
07.10 RQ3	Chorley (a)	L	1-2	Rachel Lever 11	90est

2018-19 WNL Cup

02.09 DR	Wolverhampton W (a)	L	0-1		98

2018-19 WNL Plate

R1	Bye				
14.10 R2	Liverpool Feds (a)	L	0-2		70

2018-19 Cheshire FA County Cup

R1	Bye				
R2	Bye				
17.02 QF	Tranmere Rovers (a)	D	3-3 (L1-2p)	Amanda Fallon 6, 47, Laura Garner 64	

"A number of long-term injuries made our third consecutive season in the WNL a difficult one. Fortunately, though we were able to strengthen the squad by tapping into the highly successful CALFC youth teams. Four 16-year-olds played for the first team in the final seven games of 2018-19. Another positive note is that the men's club have reached out to us. We will be working together more closely going forward, using the training ground and wearing the same kit."

Matt Fisher – Head Coach

DENHAM UNITED

2019-20: LONDON & SOUTH EAST REGIONAL PREMIER (Tier 5)

Founded: 1987

Nickname: None

Season 2018-19

WNL South East 1 (Tier 4): 11th (R)

FA Cup: 2nd Qualifying Round

WNL Cup: Determining Round

WNL Plate: 2nd Round

Capital Cup: Quarter-finals

Based in Uxbridge in North West London, Denham United are recognised as the largest all-female football club in the South East of England with teams from Under-9s up to seniors. They resided in Tier 4 from 2014-15, when they achieved a best finish of 6th, until the end of 2018-19 when they were relegated after finishing the season one place off the bottom of the table.

2018-19 AS IT HAPPENS

09.09.18: Denham secure their first League win of the season, at the third time of asking, thanks to a 2-1 victory away to Cambridge United. Denham's goals book-end the game with Emma Kern scoring in the first minute and Rae Roberts on target four minutes into added time.

10.02.19: Denham end a run of 11 League games without a win thanks to a 2-0 victory at Leyton Orient with Meila Rose D'Santos and Emma Kern scoring their goals.

30.04.19: Despite being just one place off the bottom of the table, Denham secure their best result of the season with a 1-1 draw at home to newly-crowned champions Crawley Wasps. United go ahead in the 21st minute through Lauren Cox and hold on until eight minutes from time. They are only the third team to take points off Wasps all season.

2018-19 RESULTS: (HOME VENUE: THE DEN, UNLESS STATED)

2018-19 WNL SE 1

					Att	Pos
19.08	Billericay Town (h)	L	0-3		50	
26.08	Norwich City (a)	D	2-2	Annie Hewitt 10, Joanne Torr 88	72	9
09.09	Cambridge United (a)	W	2-1	Emma Kern 1, Rae Roberts 90+4	75	8
12.09	Actonians (h)	L	0-5		40est	10
16.09	Leyton Orient (h)	D	1-1	Rachel Keightley 63	65	9
03.10	Luton Town (h)	D	0-0		50est	10
07.10	Ipswich Town (a)	L	0-4		45	10
28.10	AFC Wimbledon (a)	L	0-4		50	10
04.11	Stevenage (h)	L	1-2	Kayleigh Currivan 56	56	11
25.11	Crawley Wasps (a)	L	0-9		50	11
02.12	Actonians (a)	L	1-5	Holly Nicholls 54	15	11
06.01	Enfield Town (h)	D	0-0		50	11
13.01	Billericay Town (a)	L	0-6			11
20.01	Norwich City (h)	L	1-2	Lauren Cox	50	11
10.02	Leyton Orient (a)	W	2-0	Meila Rose D'Santos 47, Emma Kern 55	44	11
03.03	Cambridge United (h)	L	1-2	Rachel Keightley	40	11
10.03	AFC Wimbledon (h)	D	0-0		45	11
12.03	Luton Town (a)	D	1-1	Meila Rose D'Santos 55	91	11
24.03	Ipswich Town (h)	L	1-3	Kayleigh Currivan 25	60	11
31.03	Stevenage (a)	W	1-0	Lauren Cox 30	25	11
30.04	Crawley Wasps (h)	D	1-1	Lauren Cox 21	90	11
05.05	Enfield Town (a)	L	0-2		96	11

2018-19 FA Cup

23.09 RQ2	Crawley Wasps (h)		P-P		
30.09 RQ2	Crawley Wasps (h)	L	1-3	Livvie Thompson 64	35est

2018-19 WNL Cup

02.09 DR	Loughborough F (a)	L	0-4	40

2018-19 WNL Plate

R1	Bye			
14.10 R2	Maidenhead U (a)*	D	1-1aet (L 2-4p)	Rachel Keightley 88

*Waterlogged pitch saw match switched to home game and played at The Den

2018-19 Capital Cup*

R1	Bye			
18.11 QF	Fulham FC Foundation (a)	D	1-1 (L 2-3p)	Joanne Torr 71

*The Capital Cup is the equivalent of a County Cup for teams in and around London. In 2018-19 it was run by the Surrey FA.

"The 2018-19 season did not get off to a good start. After Christmas we had a change of management and following that we experienced an upturn in results. Our ethos has always been that we are one team, we go through the highs and lows together and will always be as one. That will always be the way we approach things even when results aren't going well."

Joanne Currivan – Secretary

DERBY COUNTY

2019-20: WNL NORTHERN PREMIER (Tier 3)

Founded: 1989

Nickname: Ewe Rams

Season 2018-19:

WNL Northern Premier (Tier 3): 3rd

FA Cup: 3rd Round

WNL Cup: 2nd Round

County Cup: n/a

Derby County's breakthrough season came in 2008-09 when they won the Midland Combination (Tier 3) for the first time in their history. The Ewe Rams sealed the title that season, (and promotion to Tier 2), in the final game of the campaign, beating Crewe 4-2 in a match that was played at Pride Park. When the FA created WSL 2 in 2014, Derby effectively dropped to Tier 3. After a series of respectable mid-table placings, they achieved their highest Tier 3 finish in 2018-19 when they came 3rd. Throughout 2018-19 they also strengthened their bonds with Derby County FC with the women's team present at every men's game to meet fans and conduct Q&A sessions.

2018-19 AS IT HAPPENS

09.09.18: Pride Park (home of Derby County FC) hosts the East Midlands derby against Nottingham Forest. The match attracts a Derby County Ladies club record home crowd of 2,109.

14.10.18: Cara Newton's goal against Bolton in the WNL Cup 2nd Round match makes her the club's record scorer with 74. She overtakes both Mel Johnson and Emily Jeffery who scored 73.

24.03.19: For the second time this season the East Midlands derby attracts an impressive crowd as 1,252 – a club record home attendance for Nottingham Forest Ladies – watches a 1-1 draw at Eastwood Community Football Club. Derby's equaliser is scored by Stephanie Smith in injury-time.

14.04.19: Derby's Development team (their first XI do not compete in the competition) win the Derbyshire FA County Cup with a 4-0 victory over Tier 4 side Long Eaton United.

05.05.19: A 3-0 win away to Doncaster Rovers Belles sees Derby finish 3rd with 48 points – their highest WNL finish and points tally. Hannah Ward opens the scoring with her 50th Derby goal while Cara Newton and Andrea Bell are also on target.

2018-19 RESULTS: (HOME VENUE: DON AMOTT LG ARENA, (MICKLEOVER SPORTS FC) UNLESS STATED)

2018-19 WNL NP					Att	Pos
19.08	Middlesbrough (a)	W	3-0	Nicole Ledgister 10, Andrea Bell 44, Jodie Redgrave 85	240	
26.08	Hull City (a)	D	2-2	Emily Joyce 10, Andrea Bell 40	50	3
09.09	Nott'm Forest (h)*	W	1-0	Amy Sims 45+3	2109	1
12.09	Stoke City (a)	D	1-1	Faye McCoy (og) 58	136	4
23.09	Doncaster R B (h)	W	4-2	Jodie Redgrave 15, 21, Cara Newton 41, Stephanie Smith 75, *Derby GK Lia Kellogg saved pen*	142	5
30.09	Sunderland (h)	W	1-0	Olivia Mitcham 72	146	3
07.10	Fylde (a)	L	1-3	Andrea Bell 74	150est	4
11.10	Sheffield FC (a)	W	1-0	Andrea Bell 30	141	3
21.10	Guiseley Vixens (h)	W	2-1	Cara Newton 75, Andrea Bell 78	99	2
11.11	Blackburn R (h)	L	0-7		216	4
18.11	Sunderland (a)	L	2-5	Emily Joyce 29, Cara Newton 73	102	4
25.11	Huddersfield T (a)	L	2-3	Cara Newton 15, 51	54	6
09.12	Bradford City (a)		P-P			6
13.01	Guiseley Vixens (a)		P-P			7
20.01	Bradford City (a)	W	10-0	Nicole Ledgister 15, Monique Watson 18, 87, Camilla Newton (pen) 22, Moriah McIntosh 50, Lauren Cresswell 51, Emily Joyce 65, Cara Newton 74, Andi Bell 89, 90	65	5
03.02	Middlesbrough (h)		P-P			7
10.02	Hull City (h)+	W	7-2	Monique Watson 5, Amy Sims 8, Andrea Bell 10, Camilla Newton 20, Cara Newton 70, 72, Stephanie Smith 87	93	6
14.02	Stoke City (h)	W	2-1	Stephanie Smith 40, Andrea Bell 44	81	4
17.02	Fylde (h)	L	0-1		96	5
10.03	Bradford City (h)+	W	2-1	Stephanie Smith 50, Grace Harrison 90+2	72	5
14.03	Sheffield FC (h)		P-P			5
17.03	Guiseley Vixens (a)	W	4-1	Cara Newton 1, Hannah James 21, Amy Simms 45+1, 54	40est	3
24.03	Nottingham F (a)	D	1-1	Stephanie Smith 90+1	1,252	4
31.03	Blackburn R (a)	L	0-3		436	4

07.04	Middlesbrough (h)	W	2-0	Monique Watson 59, Jodie Redgrave 81	203	4
14.04	Huddersfield T (h)	W	2-1	Kira Rai 10, Grace Harrison 25	141	4
28.04	Sheffield FC (h)	W	1-0	Cara Newton 76	117	3
05.05	Doncaster R B (a)	W	3-0	Hannah Ward 20, Cara Newton 30, Andrea Bell 46	140	3

*Played at Pride Park, (Derby County FC) +Played at Derby University Sports Centre

2018-19 FA Cup

02.12 R2	Guiseley Vixens (a)+	W	2-0	Nicole Ledgister 19, Stephanie Smith 77	40est
06.01 R3	Stoke City (h)	L	1-2	Nicola Hudson (og) 78	244

+Technically away tie but played at Mickleover Sports due to waterlogged pitch at Guiseley

2018-19 WNL Cup

02.09 DR	Bedworth Utd (h)*	W	3-1	Stephanie Smith 78, 80, Jodie Redgrave 85	110est
R1	Bye				
14.10 R2	Bolton W (h)	L	1-2	Cara Newton 78	135est

*Played at Etwall Leisure Centre

"The 2018-19 campaign was a really impressive one for the club. We worked tirelessly both on and off the field to work towards our goals. It's a whole-club effort from the players to the staff to the board and the support from our fans and our youngsters coming through shows why this club is special. We have the momentum going into 2019-20 and we really feel we can take that next step if we put the work in."

Sam Griffiths – Manager

DONCASTER ROVERS BELLES

2019-20: WNL MIDLANDS 1 (Tier 4)

Founded: 1969 (as Belle Vue Belles)

Nickname: Belles

Season 2018-19:

WNL Northern Premier (Tier 3): 12th (R)

FA Cup: 2nd Round

WNL Cup: Determining Round

WNL Plate: 2nd Round

County Cup: 3rd Round

One of England's most successful clubs find themselves in Tier 4 in 2019-20 despite having been crowned Tier 2 champions in 2017-18. Belles were WSL 2 champions by 10 points that season, but the FA restructure meant they were unable to secure a licence for either the 2018-19 WSL or the newly renamed Championship and instead dropped to Tier 3. They endured a difficult campaign in the WNL Northern Premier in 2018-19 and were relegated again after finishing 2nd from bottom.

Many have sympathy with the current predicament of a club that has done so much for women's football in England. They started out as Belle Vue Belles in 1969 before becoming Doncaster Belles and have lifted the FA Cup six times (only Arsenal (14) and the original Southampton Women (8) have won more). Belles were champions of the FA's inaugural national division – the Women's Premier League – in 1991-92 and again in 1993-94. They changed their name to Doncaster Rovers Belles when they formed a partnership with Doncaster Rovers FC, the men's professional club, in 2005. That partnership lapsed a few years later but was fully revived in 2019.

2018-19 AS IT HAPPENS

19.08.18: After failing to retain their Tier 2 licence following the FA restructure, Doncaster Rovers Belles begin life in Tier 3 with a 9-0 home defeat to reigning champions Blackburn Rovers. Having won the 2017-18 WSL 2 title many had hoped Belles would start the new season in the top-flight, but the new licensing criteria effectively saw them demoted to Tier 3.

17.02.19: Olivia Cook scores her first ever senior goal with one minute remaining to secure a 1-1 draw with Guiseley Vixens. There is even more late drama when Donny concede a penalty in the first minute of added time, but keeper Emily Batty saves it to preserve the point. Batty also saved a penalty in the shootout in the WNL Cup defeat to Chorley back in September.

27.03.19: It's confirmed that Belles will be taken under the umbrella of the Club Doncaster Group in a bid to eventually return them to the top division. Club Doncaster Group already incorporates Doncaster Rovers FC men, Doncaster Rugby League FC, Club Doncaster Foundation and Club Doncaster Sports College. Chair Faye Lygo says: "I have really enjoyed being the custodian of this club over the past few years but feel, for us to progress, we need to make this change."

2018-19 MAIN HOME VENUE: OXFORD STREET, (ROSSINGTON MAIN FC)

2018-19 WNL NP					Att	Pos
19.08	Blackburn R (h)	L	0-9			
26.08	Stoke City (a)	L	0-5		130	13
09.09	Middlesbrough (h)	L	0-2			13
12.09	Huddersfield T (a)	L	1-6	Ashleigh Edwards 26	102	13
16.09	Sunderland AFC (a)	L	0-5		160	13
23.09	Derby County (a)	L	2-4	Izzy Whittle, *Chloe Bethnall missed pen (saved by Lia Kellogg)* Nadia Khan *(scored from pen rebound)*	142	13
30.09	Nottingham F (h)	L	1-3	Izzy Whittle 26, *Emily Burgin missed pen (saved by Emily Hallam) 66*	121	13
03.10	Hull City (h)	L	0-2		110	12
07.10	Guiseley Vixens (a)	W	4-1	Chloe Bethell, Zoe Belding (x2), Izzy Whittle	80	
28.10	Fylde (a)	L	0-4		62	12
11.11	Bradford City (h)	W	5-1	Chloe Bethell, Emily Brett, Izzy Whittle, Abby Watkinson (x2)	86	12
25.11	Blackburn R (a)	L	2-9	Izzy Whittle 12, 39	180	12
09.12	Sheffield FC (h)	W	2-0	Izzy Whittle 21, 75		12
13.01	Stoke City (h)	L	1-2	*Georgia Marshall sent off 63,* Emily Burgin (pen) 86	130	12
20.01	Middlesbrough (a)	L	1-6	Emily Brett 67	54	12
27.01	Sunderland (h)	D	2-2	Abby Watkinson 83, 87		12
03.02	Nottingham F (a)	D	1-1	Lauren Breen	182	11
13.02	Huddersfield T (h)	D	2-2	Kirsty Smith 21, Chloe Bethell 31	122	11
17.02	Guiseley Vixens (h)	D	1-1	Olivia Cook 89, *Doncaster GK Emily Batty saved Charlotte Gill pen 90+1*	133	12

10.03	Fylde (h)		P-P			12
13.03	Hull City (a)	D	3-3	Chloe Bethell, Olivia Cook, Abby Watkinson	80	12
31.03	Bradford City (a)	W	1-0	Lauren Breen	61	12
14.04	Sheffield FC (a)	D	1-1	Chloe Bethell 44	202	12
28.04	Fylde (h)	L	2-3	Izzy Whittle 43, Abby Watkinson 85	141	12
05.05	Derby County (h)	L	0-3		140	12

2018-19 FA CUP

02.12 R2	Leeds United (a)	L	3-4 aet	Zoe Belding 4, Izzy Whittle 35, Emily Burgin 90+4	200

2018-19 WNL CUP

02.09 DR	Chorley (h)	D	2-2aet (L 3-4p)	Izzy Whittle 37, 90

2018-19 WNL PLATE

14.10 R2	Barnsley (h)	L	2-3aet	Izzy Whittle 70, 89

2018-19 SHEFFIELD & HALLAMSHIRE COUNTY CUP

16.12 R3	Sheffield United Development (a)	L	0-3		160est

DURHAM CESTRIA

2019-20: WNL NORTH 1 (Tier 4)

Founded: 2006

Nickname: Cestria

Season 2018-19:

North East Reg Prem (Tier 5): Champions (P)

FA Cup: 1st Qualifying Round

League Cup: Winners

County Cup: Runners-up

A 3-0 win over Farsley Celtic in mid-March saw Durham Cestria clinch the 2018-19 North East Regional Premier title and their third promotion since the 2013-14 season. They went on to complete the League campaign without dropping a single point and there was further reward for manager Gareth Smith when his team made it a Double by winning the North East Regional League Cup. Cestria are Championship (Tier 2) outfit Durham's 'Partner Side' with some of their players coming through the Wildcats' Regional Talent Club.

2018-19 AS IT HAPPENS

17.03.19: Lauren Robson, Gabrielle McConnell and Molly Holder are on target as Cestria win 3-0 at home to Farsley Celtic, a result which confirms their status as Northern Regional Premier champions.

04.04.19: Cestria come close to pulling off a shock against Tier 4 Norton & Stockton Ancients in the Durham FA County Cup final. They twice go ahead and lead 2-1 going into the last minute only for Norton to equalise. The match goes straight to penalties and Norton win the shoot-out 3-0.

07.04.19: Cestria win the North East Regional League Cup, beating Ossett United 4-0 in the final with a brace from Erin Nelson and goals from Jessica Clark and Jess Holder.

2018-19 RESULTS: (HOME VENUE: MAIDEN CASTLE, UNIVERSITY OF DURHAM, UNLESS STATED)

2018-19 NORTH EAST REGIONAL PREMIER

23.09	Wallsend Boys Club (a)	W	9-0	Molly Holder 26, Jess Holder 55, Lauren Robson 57, 82, 87, Sophie Hodgson 62, Michelle Brogden 77, Chloe Ryan 79, Georgia Richardson 87
30.09	Harrogate Town (h)	W	7-2	Alisha Miller 23, Lauren Robson 51, 80, 84, Jess Holder 65, Jessica Clark 67, Caroline Dixon 75
07.10	Hartlepool United (a)	W	7-1	Lauren Robson 6, 54, 90, Jessica Clark 13, Jennifer Jennings 20, Chloe Ryan 27, 69
14.10	Rotherham United (h)	W	17-0	Jess Holder 4, 28, Melissa Storey 7, Sophie Hodgson 15, 70, 73, Hannah Greenwood 31, 34, 63, Michelle Brogden 37, Molly Holder 43, Ellie Smith 61, Lauren Robson 79, 88, Chloe Ryan 79, Megan Elliott 87, Jennifer Jennings 90+1
21.10	Ryton & Crawcrook Albion Tynedale (a)	W	4-1	Lauren Robson 28, 75, Jess Holder 39, 60
28.10	South Shields (h)	W	3-0	Molly Holder 40, 73, Jennifer Jennings 55
04.11	Hartlepool United (h)	W	2-1	Caroline Dixon 71, Lauren Robson 74
11.11	Wallsend Boys Club (h)	W	10-0	Caroline Dixon 11, 46, 50, 73, Ellie Smith 28, 31, 33, 42, Chloe Ryan 37, Sophie Hodgson 62
18.11	Ryton & Crawcrook Albion Tynedale (h)	W	6-2	Ellie Smith 3, Sophie Hodgson 9, 30, 74, Lauren Robson 50, 83
25.11	York City (h)	W	10-1	Sophie Hodgson 1, 15, Jess Holder 6, 44, Michelle Brogden 9, Erin Nelson 23, 47, 61, Molly Holder 50, Chloe Ryan 88
09.12	Harrogate Town (a)	W	2-0	Lauren Robson 26, Hannah Greenwood 62
06.01	Rotherham United (a)	W	10-0	Erin Nelson 1, Ellie Smith 3, Lauren Robson 16, 23, 25, 46, 71, 77, Melissa Storey 83, Sophie Hodgson 84
27.01	York City (a)	W	6-0	Molly Holder 10, Lauren Robson 39, Erin Nelson 54, Chloe Ryan 62, 77, Sophie Hodgson 78
03.03	Farsley Celtic (a)	W	2-1	Chloe Ryan 8, Sophie Hodgson 18
17.03	Farsley Celtic (h)	W	3-0	Lauren Robson 62, Gabrielle McConnell 84, Molly Holder 87
31.03	Castleford White Rose (a)	W	w/o	
14.04	Castleford White Rose (h)	W	w/o	
21.04	South Shields (a)	W	5-1	Michelle Brogden 17, Ellie Smith 21, Sophie Hodgson 40, 47, Jessica Clark 85

2018-19 FA CUP

26.08PR	South Shields (h)	W	3-0	Lauren Robson 7, 65, Erin Nelson 39
02.09 RQ1	Alnwick Town (h)	L	1-2	Alisha Miller 1

2018-19 LEAGUE CUP

16.09	Alnwick Town (h)	W	3-1	Ellie Smith 7, Hannah Greenwood 52, Chloe Ryan 77
02.12	Norton & Stockton Ancients Reserves (h)	W	11-0	Michelle Brogden 7, 34, Lauren Robson 15, 25, Erin Nelson 28, 63, Jennifer Jennings 42, Hannah Greenwood 44, Bethany Wilson 47, Molly Holder 55, Sophie Hodgson 69
24.02	Consett (a)	W	6-0	Chloe Ryan 26, 28, Jessica Clark 29, Hannah Greenwood 44, Ellie Smith 71, Jennifer Jennings 76

24.03	Hartlepool United (a)	W	2-1	Erin Nelson 55, Hannah Greenwood 75
07.04 F	Ossett United (n)	W	4-0	Erin Nelson 8, 30, Jessica Clark 11, Jess Holder 67

(n) Played at the Storking Lane Ground, (AFC Wilberforce)

2018-19 DURHAM FA COUNTY CUP

PR	Bye			
16.12 R1	Lumley Ladies Pinks (a)	W	6-0	Jennifer Jennings 49, Michelle Brogden 60, Melissa Storey 70, Sophie Hodgson 78, 86, Lauren Robson 83
20.01 R2	Ryton & Crawcrook Albion Tynedale (a)	W	6-2	Alisha Miller 8, Jess Holder 13, 40, 41, Molly Holder 31, Ellie Smith 51
17.02 SF	Chester-le-Street T (h)	W	2-1	Own Goal 42, Own Goal 62
04.04 F	Norton & Stockton Ancients (n)	D	2-2 (L0-3p)	Mel Storey 3, Sophie Hodgson 45

(n) Played at Norton Sports Club

ENFIELD TOWN

2019-20: WNL SOUTH EAST 1 (Tier 4)

Founded: 1985 (as Merryhill Midgets)
Nickname: Town

Season 2018-19:
WNL South East 1 (Tier 4): 3rd
FA Cup: 3rd Qualifying Round
WNL Cup: 1st Round
Capital Cup: Quarter-final

When the club was founded in 1985 it was known as Merryhill Midgets. They then formed an alliance with Enfield men's and adopted the same name. In 2001, Enfield men's split as some fans formed a supporter-led club called Enfield Town. The ladies' team aligned with the latter. Enfield Town Ladies reached their first national Cup final in 2015-16 when they made it to the WPL Plate final under then manager Kyri Neocleous. They were beaten 5-1 by Coventry United at Keys Park in Hednesford. League form in 2018-19 was impressive as manager Billy Highton led the team to 3rd.

2018-19 AS IT HAPPENS

30.10.18: Enfield's away match at Luton attracts a crowd of 326 because it is played at Kenilworth Road, home of Luton Town men. Enfield win 2-0 with goals from Sasha Kelly and Nuala McKevitt.

04.11.18: Katherine Long scores just one minute after coming off the bench to put Town ahead against Actonians in a WNL South East 1 match which they go on to win 2-0.

27.02.19: Town come close to reaching a Cup final but lose 1-0 at home to fellow WNL South East 1 side Leyton Orient in the Isthmian Cup semi-final. *(NB: The Isthmian Cup is a secondary Cup competition for teams in the South East and results are not included in this book).*

05.05.19: A final day 2-0 home win against Denham sees Enfield Town finish the season in 3rd place thanks to goals from Molly Peters and Katherine Long.

2018-19 RESULTS: (HOME VENUE: QUEEN ELIZABETH II STADIUM, (ENFIELD TOWN FC), UNLESS STATED)

2018-19 WNL SE 1					Att	Pos
19.08	Norwich City (h)	W	5-1	Jodie Bellinger 37, 43, 55, Danielle Smith 63, Enfield GK Kerrie Marlborough saved Norwich pen 70, Isabella Agus 82	61	
26.08	Crawley Wasps (h)	L	0-1		58	5
09.09	Ipswich Town (a)	D	3-3	Sara Degooye 13, Molly Peters 43, 45+2, Tia Bailey sent off 90+3	45	4
12.09	Luton Town (a)		P-P			6
16.09	Cambridge United (h)	W	3-2	Isabelle Agus 44, Molly Peters 63, Claire Ford 83	73	4
03.10	Stevenage (h)	W	4-0	Molly Peters 3, 43, Sasha Kelly 7, 52	67	3
21.10	Billericay Town (a)	L	2-3	Molly Peters 17, Jodie Southby 42	115	5
30.10	Luton Town (a)	W	2-0	Sasha Kelly 21, Nuala McKevitt 31	326	3
04.11	Actonians (a)	W	2-0	Katherine Long 58, Sasha Kelly 69	25est	3
11.11	Leyton Orient (a)	L	0-5		57	3
25.11	AFC Wimbledon (h)	L	0-3		53	5
06.01	Denham United (a)	D	0-0		50	6
13.01	Norwich City (a)	D	2-2	Danielle Smith 28, Lily Bruno 90+2	54	5
03.02	Ipswich Town (h)	W	3-1	Molly Peters 61, Eliza Diaz 71, Sheryce Slater (pen) 90+3	58	4
10.02	Billericay Town (h)	D	2-2	Eliza Diaz 51, Leyla Yahioglu 80	58	4
20.02	Luton Town (h)	D	0-0		78	4
06.03	Stevenage (a)	W	1-0	Katherine Long 65	60	4
10.03	Leyton Orient (h)		P-P			4
17.03	Leyton Orient (h)		P-P			4
31.03	Actonians (h)	L	1-2	Katherine Long 4	23	6
07.04	Leyton Orient (h)	W	4-0	Molly Peters 16, 49, Claire Ford 66, Lily Bruno 82	63	5
14.04	Crawley Wasps (a)	L	0-1		135	5
21.04	AFC Wimbledon (a)	L	2-3	Molly Peters 17, 38	85	5
28.04	Cambridge United (a)	W	3-0	Nuala McKevitt 35, Claire Ford 50, Molly Peters 86	25	4
05.05	Denham United (h)	W	2-0	Molly Peters 57, Katherine Long 68	96	3

2018-19 FA Cup

23.09 RQ2	Actonians (h)	W	2-1	Sara Degooye 5, Molly Peters 85	43
07.10 RQ3	Norwich City (a)	L	0-4		95

2018-19 WNL Cup

02.09 DR	Chesham United (a)	W	4-2	Tia Bailey 25, Sara Degooye 75, 87, Molly Peters 90	35
30.09 R1	Southampton W (h)	L	3-4	Nuala McKevitt 6, Sara Degooye 53, Molly Peters 74	45

2018-19 Capital Cup*

18.11 R1	QPR Girls U18 (h)	W	4-1	Nuala McKevitt 7, 72, Danielle Smith 10, Molly Norman 28	49
09.12 QF	Actonians (a)	L	0-3		25est

*The Capital Cup is the equivalent of a County Cup for teams in and around London. In 2018-19 it was run by the Surrey FA.

"The 2018-19 season was a complete turnaround to the year before. Billy Highton came in as manager and made a lot of positive changes. A host of talented new young players settled in well and helped take us to a 3rd place finish which was a fantastic achievement. I loved being captain throughout 2018-19 and I hope in 2019-20 I can lead the team on to the success we deserve."

Nuala McKevitt – Captain

EXETER CITY

2019-20: WNL SOUTH WEST 1 (Tier 4)

Founded: 2000

Nickname: The Grecians

Season 2018-19:

South West Reg Prem (Tier 5): Champions (P)

FA Cup: 3rd Qualifying Round

League Cup: n/a

County Cup: Semi-finals

After relegation out of the WNL (or WPL as it was then) at the end of 2017-18, Exeter bounced back at the first attempt. They swept their way to the South West Regional Premier title by winning 18 of their 20 League games and clocking up 110 goals in the process. After two defeats in their opening eight League games they went on a run of 11 straight wins and did not drop points again until drawing 3-3 with Ilminster Town on the final day. Player-joint-manager Abbie Britton said: "Those early season losses really taught us a lot about ourselves and as a collective we regrouped and knew what we needed to work on, and we knuckled down and thankfully got that promotion."

2018-19 AS IT HAPPENS

07.10.18: Exeter come close to causing an FA Cup shock against Tier 4 outfit Cheltenham Town in the 3rd Qualifying Round but are beaten 1-0.

21.10.18: Sian Chapman and Sophie Gillies both score five goals as Exeter rack up a 16-0 win at home to Torquay Utd.

17.02.19: Exeter stage their Devon FA County Cup home semi-final against Buckland Athletic at the men's St James Park stadium and are watched by a crowd of 606. They put on a fine show against the Tier 4 side but are beaten 3-1.

14.04.19: A 3-1 win at home to title rivals Keynsham Town Development sees Exeter crowned champions of the South West Regional Premier League. A Sophie Gillies brace, including one from the spot, puts them 2-0 up by the break and Danielle Skinner adds a third before Town pull one back.

2018-19 RESULTS: (HOME VENUE: SPEEDS MEADOW, (CULLOMPTON RANGERS FC) UNLESS STATED)

2018-19 SOUTH WEST REGIONAL PREMIER

09.09	Middlezoy (a)	W	5-2	Sian Chapman (x2), Jana Richards, Zoe Watkins (x2)
16.09	Portishead (h)	W	6-1	Georgia Barbour-Gresham (x3), Sian Chapman, Sophie Gillies (x2)
30.09	Callington Town (h)	L	1-3	Sian Chapman
14.10	Downend Flyers (h)	W	12-0	Sophie Gillies (x3), Ella-Mae Miller, Carmen Morrison (x2), Kathryn Mundy (x2), Emily Toogood, Lannece Hole (x2), Zoe Watkin
21.10	Torquay United (h)	W	16-0	Sian Chapman (x5), Sophie Gillies (x5), Manfy Sharpe, Louise Ilsley, Hana Lily Bennett, Carmen Morrison, Erin Romanowski (x2)
28.10	Forest Green Rovers (a)	W	4-0	Sophie Gillies (x3), Kathryn Mundy
04.11	Ilminster Town (h)	W	4-0	Georgia Barbour-Gresham (x2), Sophie Gillies (x2)
11.11	Keynsham Town Dev. (a)	L	0-3	
25.11	Marine Academy Plymouth (a)		P-P	
30.11	Middlezoy (h)		P-P	
16.12	Bishops Lydeard (h)	W	5-2	Abbie Britton (x2), Sophie Gillies (x2), Daniella Tyson
06.01	Callington Town (a)	W	3-1	Georgie Barbour-Gresham, Sophie Gillies, Carmen Morrison
20.01	Downend Flyers (a)	W	13-0	Georgie Barbour-Gresham, Jessica Freeman-Roach, Sophie Gillies (x3), Carmen Morrison, Kathryn Mundy (x2), Daniella Tyson (x2), Hana Lily Bennett, Erin Romanowski (x2)
27.01	Middlezoy (h)	W	5-1	Abbie Britton, Sophie Gillies (x4)
10.02	Ilminster Town (a)		P-P	
24.02	Bishops Lydeard (a)	W	4-1	Sophie Gillies (x3), Kathryn Mundy
03.03	Marine Academy Plymouth (h)	W	5-2	Georgie Barbour-Gresham (x2), Sophie Gillies (x2), Emily Toogood
17.03	Torquay United (a)	W	6-1	Sian Chapman (x2), Sophie Gillies (x2), Danielle Skinner, Own Goal
24.03	Portishead (a)	W	6-1	Georgie Barbour-Gresham, Sian Chapman (x2), Sophie Gillies (x2), Lannece Hole
31.03	Forest Green Rovers (h)	W	4-0	Sian Chapman, Daniella Tyson (x2), Georgie Barbour-Gresham
07.04	Marine Academy Plymouth (a)	W	5-1	Sophie Gillies (x3), Ella-Mae Miller, Kelsie Miller
14.04	Keynsham Town Dev. (h)	W	3-1	Sophie Gillies (x2, 1pen), Danielle Skinner
21.04	Ilminster Town (a)	D	3-3	Sophie Gillies (x2), Sian Chapman

2018-19 FA Cup

26.08 PR	Callington Town (a)	W	5-2	Jana Richards (x2), Abbie Britton, Sophie Gillies, Jazz Hervin
02.09 RQ1	Frome Town (h)	W	5-0	Jana Richards, Georgie Barbour-Gresham (x2) Sian Chap-man, Zoe Watkins
23.09 RQ2	Keynsham Town Dev. (a)	W	8-1	Sophie Gilles (x3), Sian Chapman (x3), Abbie Britton (x2)
07.10 RQ3	Cheltenham Town (a)	L	0-1	

2018-19 Devon FA County Cup

R1	Bye			
18.11 QF	Torquay United (a)	W	13-0	Sophie Gillies (x2), Georgie Barbour-Gresham (x2), Kathryn Mundy (x2), Daniella Tyson (x2), Zoe Watkins, Own Gol, Carmen Morrison, Sian Chapman, Jazz Hervin, Jessica Freeman-Roach
17.02 SF	Buckland Athletic (h)*	L	1-3	Abbie Britton

*Played at St James Park, (Exeter City FC)

"Winning the League in 2018-19 was a tremendous achievement for everyone associated with the club. Everyone worked really hard on and off the pitch, and the desire to reach our pre-season target was achieved, whilst playing attractive passing football. Our aims for 2019-20 are to establish ourselves at the next level in the Women's National League, which we know will be a challenge."

Clive Watts – Joint Manager

FYLDE

2019-20: WNL NORTHERN PREMIER (Tier 3)

Founded: 1971 (as Duke of York)

Nickname: The Coasters

Season 2018-19:

WNL Northern Premier (Tier 3): 6th

FA Cup: 3rd Round

WNL Cup: 2nd Round

County Cup: Runners-up

Founded in 1971 as Duke of York, they became Preston Rangers in 1977 and reached the FA Cup semi-finals under that name in 1982-83 and 1989-90. In 1997 they formed an affiliation with men's club Preston North End and became known by the same name. Promotion to the WPL Northern Division (Tier 2) arrived at the end of 2005-06 when they won the Northern Combination. Their first national Cup triumph came in 2014-15 when they beat Huddersfield Town 3-0 in the WPL Plate final. In May 2016 they switched allegiance from Preston North End to AFC Fylde who made funds available to the team and offered them the chance to play at Mill Farm.

2018-19 AS IT HAPPENS

18.11.18: Goalkeeper Brittany Jackson is the hero against her former club Bolton as Fylde win the Lancashire FA County Cup quarter-final tie between the two sides 3-1 on penalties after a goalless draw. Jackson saves one while Bolton also hit a post with another.

25.11.18: Both Emily Hollinshead and Georgia Stevens score hat-tricks as Fylde beat WNL Northern Premier strugglers Bradford City 9-0. Sophie Charlton's goal is her 6th League goal of the season and her last before leaving for WNL Northern Premier leaders Blackburn Rovers.

10.05.19: Fylde finish as Lancashire FA County Cup runners-up after a 2-0 defeat to their divisional rivals and WNL Northern Premier champions Blackburn Rovers.

2018-19 RESULTS: (HOME VENUE: MILL FARM STADIUM, UNLESS STATED)

2018-19 WNL NP

Date	Opponent	Res	Score	Scorers	Att	Pos
19.08	Sunderland (a)	W	1-0	Emily Hollinshead 34	189	
26.08	Nottingham F (h)*	D	0-0		52	
12.09	Blackburn R (h)	L	0-1		154	8
16.09	Hull City (a)	L	2-5	Nikki Berko 55, Jenna Carroll (pen) 71	40	11
30.09	Sheffield FC (h)	W	4-1	Emily Hollinshead 12, Jenna Carroll 35, Hollie Kelsh, 51, Sophie Charlton (pen) 90	70	7
03.10	Huddersfield T (h)	W	2-1	Hollie Kelsh 2, Sophie Charlton 45	135	7
07.10	Derby County (h)	W	3-1	Sophie Charlton 11, Olivia Wild 45, Emily Hollinshead 88	150	6
28.10	Doncaster R B (h)+	W	4-0	Sophie Charlton 21, 74, Olivia Fuller 23, Emily Hollinshead 52, Jenna Carroll missed penalty 80	62	5
11.11	Middlesbrough (a)	D	2-2	Sasha Rowe 27, Jenna Carroll (pen) 63	146	6
25.11	Bradford City (h)+	W	9-0	Emily Hollinshead 2, 83, 87, Georgia Stevens 15, 17, 80, Georgia Payton 49, Sasha Rowe 59, Sophie Charlton 71	47	5
09.12	Guiseley Vixens (a)		P-P			5
13.01	Nottingham F (a)	L	0-1		78	5
27.01	Hull City (h)	W	1-0	Olivia Wild 20	100	5
03.02	Sheffield FC (a)		P-P			5
10.02	Guiseley Vixens (a)	W	3-1	Sasha Rowe 3, Olivia Fuller 25, Georgia Stevens 58	40	5
14.02	Blackburn Rovers (a)	L	0-3		287	6
17.02	Derby County (a)	W	1-0	Georgia Stevens 5	96	4
24.02	Sunderland (h)+	W	2-1	Sasha Rowe 16, Olivia Wild 75	80	3
03.03	Sheffield FC (a)	L	0-3			3
10.03	Doncaster R B (a)		P-P			4
13.03	Huddersfield T (a)		P-P			4
17.03	Stoke City (a)		P-P			5
24.03	Middlesbrough (h)	L	0-3		70	6
27.03	Huddersfield T (a)	L	1-4	Danielle Young 70	78	6
31.03	Guiseley Vixens (h)+	L	0-1		70	7
07.04	Stoke City (a)	D	2-2	Danielle Young 1, Emily Hollinshead 56	130	7
14.04	Bradford City (a)	W	5-0	Olivia Fuller 42, Danielle Young (pen) 46, Georgia Payton 55, Hollie Kelsh 72 Georgia Stevens 76	23	6
28.04	Doncaster R B (a)	W	3-2	Georgie Payton 36, Sadie Mitchell 47, Georgia Stevens 90+3	141	6
05.05	Stoke City (h)	W	3-1	Jenna Carroll 4, Sadie Mitchell 8, Emily Hollinshead 45+4	145	6

*Played at School Road, (Squires Gate FC) + Played at Kellamergh Park

2018-19 FA Cup

02.12 R2	Sunderland (a)	W	3-1	Danielle Young 15, Sophie Charlton 45, Emily Hollinshead 88	85
06.01 R3	Keynsham Town (a)	L	1-2	Sophie Charlton 43, Jenna Carroll sent off 75	80

2018-19 WNL Cup

02.09 DR	Burton Albion (h)*	W	9-0	Erin Staunton-Turner 16, Hannah Forster 46, Laura Merrin 60, Nikki Berko 72, 81, 83 Danielle Young 74, Emily Hollinshead 75, Sophie Charlton 89	30
14.10 R2	Blackburn Rovers (a)	L	2-3	Olivia Wild 12, Jenna Carroll (pen) 71	50

*Played at School Road, (Squires Gate FC)

2018-19 Lancashire FA County Cup

23.09 R1	Bury (a)	W	5-0	Olivia DaCosta, 19, 37, Hollie Kelsh 40, Sophie Charlton, 58, 90	
21.10 R2	Accrington FC (a)	W	w/o		
18.11 QF	Bolton W (h)	D	0-0 (W3-1p)	Danielle Young missed pen	50
20.01 SF	Blackburn Community Sports Club (h)	W	3-2	Sasha Rowe 4, Georgia Stevens 81, Unknown 82	
09.05 F	Blackburn Rovers (n)	L	0-2		

(n)Played at Lancashire FA County Ground

"We started off 2018-19 with a really good win at Sunderland who had just dropped down from the top-flight after the FA restructuring. We then went on a run of three games without a win but turned things round dramatically by losing only two of the next 12. That form saw us soar to the right end of the table and we were pushing leaders and eventual champions Blackburn Rovers hard at that point. It's a shame that we couldn't maintain it, ultimately a 6th place finish doesn't feel as good as we deserved. Our best moment of the season was our 3-1 win away to Sunderland in the FA Cup because they're a fantastic team. The mood in the dressing room and on the coach home summed it all up. We start 2019-20 with the aim of winning the League and getting promoted to the Championship. It will be a tough challenge, but we can be a real force."

Conrad Prendergast – Manager

GILLINGHAM

2019-20: WNL SOUTHERN PREMIER (Tier 3)

Founded: 1995

Nickname: The Gills

Season 2018-19:

WNL Southern Premier (Tier 3): 10th

FA Cup: 2nd Round

WNL Cup: Determining Round

WPL Plate: Semi-final

County Cup: Winners

Gillingham Ladies come under the umbrella of Gillingham FC, the men's professional outfit. It is the third link-up with the club in their history. The first came in 1995 when Gillingham FC chairman Paul Scally co-opted a local team called Borstal 88. After a period of independence, they were brought back into the Gillingham FC fold in 2008 and then again, after another break, in 2014. Gillingham were runaway WPL South East 1 champions (Tier 4) in 2016-17 and thus secured promotion to Tier 3. They finished 9th in 2017-18 and 10th in 2018-19 when they also won the County Cup.

2018-19 AS IT HAPPENS

14.02.19: Five different players score as Gillingham beat C&K Basildon 5-3. Alice Bussey, Ellie Manning, Grace Seely, Daisy Monaghan, and Samantha Booker are all on target.

14.03.19: Having reached the final, Gillingham are disqualified from the WNL Plate when the FA rules that they fielded two ineligible players in their 1-0 semi-final win against West Brom. Their beaten opponents will take their place in the final against MK Dons.

28.03.19: Gillingham win the Kent FA County Cup. Sharna Giordani scores the only goal in the seventh minute as the Gills beat their own Development side in a final played at Priestfield Stadium.

2018-19 RESULTS: HOME VENUE (THE SPORTS GROUND, (CHATHAM TOWN FC), UNLESS STATED)

2018-19 WNL SP					Att	Pos
19.08	Coventry United (h)	D	0-0		70	
26.08	Portsmouth (a)	L	1-4	Maddison Chamney-Farrand	90	9
09.09	Plymouth A (h)*	L	1-4	Maddison Chamney-Farrand (pen) 85	65	9
12.09	C&K Basildon (a)	W	3-1	Esmee Sword, Samantha Booker, Maddison Chamney-Farrand		8
16.09	Oxford United (h)	L	0-5		70	10
23.09	Watford (a)	L	2-6	Ellie Manning (pen) 19, Maddison Chamney-Farrand (pen) 75	93	10
30.09	MK Dons (a)	L	0-1			10
04.10	QPR (h)	W	2-0	Breon Grant 19, Ellie Manning (pen) 76	102	10
04.11	Chichester City (a)	L	0-2		105	10
25.11	Loughborough F (h)+	D	2-2	Samantha Booker 52, Breon Grant 79	65	10
16.12	MK Dons (h)		P-P			10
13.01	MK Dons (h)	W	2-0	Breon Grant 20, Alice Bussey 42	70	10
27.01	Plymouth Argyle (a)		P-P			10
14.02	C&K Basildon (h)	W	5-3	Alice Bussey 2, Ellie Manning 26, Grace Seely 62, Daisy Monaghan 78, Samantha Booker 87	60	9
17.02	Cardiff City L (h)	L	0-2		50	9
24.02	Oxford United (a)	L	0-1	*Ellie Manning missed pen 45 (saved by Lucy Thomas)*	107	9
10.03	Watford (h)		P-P			9
13.03	QPR (a)	W	3-1	Alice Bussey (x2), Maddison Chamney-Farrand	48	9
17.03	Coventry United (a)	L	0-9		90	9
24.03	Plymouth A (a)	D	1-1	Millie Waud	30	9
31.03	Cardiff City L (a)	L	0-2		85	9
07.04	Portsmouth (h)	L	0-2		50	9
21.04	Watford (h)	L	0-1			9
28.04	Loughborough F (a)	L	0-5		33	9
05.05	Chichester City (h)+*	D	2-2	*Maddison Chamney-Farrand missed pen 30,* Maddison Chamney-Farrand 65, Breon Grant 76	52	10

*Played at Priestfield Stadium, (Gillingham FC) +Played at Gallagher Stadium, (Maidstone Town FC) +*Played at Beechings Cross, (Gillingham FC Training Ground)

2018-19 FA CUP

02.12 R2	Loughborough F (a)	L	1-3 (aet)	Alice Bussey 65	48

2018-19 WNL CUP

02.09 DR	QPR (a)	L	1-3	Alice Bussey 71	

2018-19 WNL PLATE

R1	Bye				
14.10 R2	Luton Town (h)+	W	5-4	Sharna Giordani, Breon Grant, Alice Bussey, Emma Sherwood, Samantha Booker	
09.12 R3	Chesham Utd (h)++	W	5-0	Samantha Booker 21, 31, 78, Ellie Manning (pen) 29, Breon Grant 65	75
10.02 QF	Stevenage (a)	W	4-0	Grace Seely 23, 80, Breon Grant 33, Alice Bussey 52	
03.03 SF	West Brom (h)+	W	1-0	Chloe Fowler 49 *Gillingham disqualified from competition on 14.03 for fielding ineligible players*	

+Played at Meridian Sports & Social Club ++Played at Priestfield Stadium, (Gillingham FC)

2018-19 KENT FA COUNTY CUP

21.10 R1	Kent Football United (h)*	W	2-1	Ellie Manning (pen) 35, Grace Seely 49	83
18.11 QF	Margate (a)	W	6-0	Breon Grant 15, 28, Ellie Manning 67, Alice Bussey 68, (pen) 84, Vicky Ashton-Jones 72	70est
20.01 SF	Herne Bay (h)	W	3-0	Alice Bussey 11, Lydia Huntley 17, Maddison Chamney-Farrand 90	
28.03 F	Gillingham Development (n)*	W	1-0	Sharna Giordani 7	250

*Played at Priestfield Stadium, (Gillingham FC)

"The 2018-19 season was full of ups and downs, but our target was to retain our place in Tier 3 and thanks to a strong start and end to the campaign we managed to do that. We grabbed a shock point off eventual champions Coventry United on the opening day, and then also held one of the other strongest teams in the division – Chichester City – to a draw on the final day. To have an all-Gills final in the County Cup, in which our first team beat our development side 1-0, was also a real moment of pride. There is plenty to be positive about and I am sure we can set our goals higher in 2019-20."

Ellie Manning – Defender

GUISELEY VIXENS

Folded May 2019

Founded: 1993 (as Meanwood Vixens)

Nickname: The Vixens

Season 2018-19:

WNL Northern Premier (Tier 3): 8th

FA Cup: 2nd Round

WNL Cup: 1st Round

County Cup: Runners-up

Just days after the end of the 2018-19 season, in which Guiseley finished a creditable 8th in the WNL Northern Premier and reached the County Cup final for the second year in a row, the club announced that it was set to be liquidated. A statement read: "Since its inception, Guiseley Vixens has always been an independently run, and internally funded organisation. Despite all attempts to move to a more sustainable financial model, we have been unable to acquire the funding and infrastructure required to continue our football operations."

The club existed for 26 years: founded as Meanwood Vixens in 1993, then becoming Leeds City Vixens prior to an affiliation with men's non-League club Guiseley AFC in 2005. The Vixens were promoted to the WPL Northern Division (Tier 3) ahead of 2017-18 as champions of WPL North 1. Recent success in the West Riding FA County Cup saw them win the trophy in 2017-18 and finish as runners-up in 2018-19.

2018-19 AS IT HAPPENS

04.11.18: In an eventful WNL game 17-year-old Ellie Casper comes off the bench to score the winner against Sheffield FC with her first senior goal for the club. The Vixens trail 1-0 before Alarna Fuller equalises. They then win a penalty in an incident which sees Sheffield keeper Elizabeth Hobson sent off, only for her replacement Lauren Santoro to save it. Guiseley go on to win 2-1.

16.12.18: Guiseley beat Phoenix Juniors 11-0 in the 3rd Round of the County Cup. The scorers include Lauren Griffiths who nets her first goal since 22 November 2015. The club celebrate with the following tweet: "Barack Obama was president. Justin Bieber was top of the charts. We'd never heard of Brexit. Just a few things that were happening the last time @LozGriff7 scored a competitive goal for the club. 1120 days. 26680 hours. The wait is finally over."

17.02.19: Lauren Griffiths becomes the club's record appearance-maker when she plays for the 85th time in the 1-1 draw with Doncaster Rovers Belles.

14.04.19: Monika Estere Stube scores her first competitive goal for Vixens to pull her side back to 2-1 down against Sunderland in their final home game of the season, but it is not enough to avert defeat.

30.04.19: Vixens narrowly fail to defend the West Riding FA County Cup they won in 2017-18 as they are beaten 3-2 by Tier 4 outfit Brighouse Town in an entertaining final.

18.05.19: The club releases a statement confirming that they have had to fold due to financial difficulties.

2018-19 RESULTS: (HOME VENUE: NETHERMOOR PARK, (GUISELEY AFC) UNLESS STATED)

2018-19 WNL NP					Att	Pos
26.08	Huddersfield T (h)	L	1-2	Ella Hartley 14	40	10
09.09	Stoke City (h)	L	2-4	Ella Hartley 63, Ellie Olds 70	40	11
12.09	Bradford City (a)	W	7-1	Ella Hartley 2, Ellie Olds 34, Sophie Walton 61, Mercy Darkoah 70, Olivia Auker 73, Alarna Fuller 75, Kirstie Hunt 78	97	9
16.09	Nottingham F (h)	W	2-0	Olivia Auker 26, Eleanor Hall 78	40	7
04.10	Middlesbrough (a)	D	1-1	Ellie Olds 66	142	9
07.10	Doncaster R B (h)	L	1-4	Olivia Auker 50	80	11
21.10	Derby County (a)	L	1-2	Ellie Olds 54	99	11
28.10	Hull City (h)	W	3-1	Olivia Auker 33, Jodie Hunter 41, Emma Samways 62	30	8
04.11	Sheffield FC (a)	W	2-1	Alarna Fuller 41, Ellie Casper 86 *Sophie Walton missed a penalty 66 (saved by Lauren Santoro)*	87	7
09.12	Fylde (h)		P-P			9
06.01	Sheffield FC (h)	D	1-1	Ellie Casper 56	40	9
13.01	Derby County (h)		P-P			9
27.01	Nottingham F (a)		P-P			9
03.02	Hull City (a)	W	1-0	Charlotte Gill 28	50	8
10.02	Fylde (h)	L	1-3	Mariea Ledezma-Viso 66	40	8
12.02	Bradford City (h)		P-P			8
17.02	Doncaster R B (a)	D	1-1	Alarna Fuller 84, *Charlotte Gill missed pen 90+1 (saved by Emily Batty)*	133	9
24.02	Nottingham F (a)	W	3-1	Alarna Fuller 22, 44, Monika Stube 59	174	8
03.03	Stoke City (a)	W	2-1	*Guiseley GK Bethan Davies saved pen 30,* Olivia Auker 36, Charlotte Gill 57	85	8

05.03	Bradford City (h)	W	9-0	Olivia Auker 5, 57, Charlotte Gill 9, 28, Jodie Hunter 12, Maria Ledezma-Viso 19, 70, Alarna Fuller 35, Khloe Cooper (og) 83	81	8
17.03	Derby County (h)	L	1-4	Kirstie Hunt 41	40	8
19.03	Blackburn R (h)	L	0-5		40	8
24.03	Sunderland (a)	L	1-4	Sophie Walton 88	121	8
28.03	Middlesbrough (h)	D	0-0		40	8
31.03	Fylde (a)	W	1-0	Ellie Casper 58	70	8
14.04	Sunderland (h)	L	1-2	Monika Estere Stube 68	40	8
28.04	Huddersfield T (a)	L	2-5	Monika Estere Stube 9, Charlotte Gill 25, *Alarna Fuller sent off 55*	108	8
05.05	Blackburn R (a)	L	1-5	Charlotte Gill 65	276	8

2018-19 FA CUP

02.12 R2	Derby County (h)*	L	0-2		40

*Played at Derby County's Mickleover Sports ground because of waterlogged pitch

2018-19 WNL Cup

02.09 DR	Chester-le-Street T (h)	W	4-2	Olivia Auker 10, 32, Ellie Olds 16, Sophie Walton 85	40
30.09 R1	Blackburn R (h)	L	1-2	Shannon Durkin 19	45

2018-19 WEST RIDING FA COUNTY CUP

18.11 R2	Wetherby (h)	W	10-0	Olivia Auker 10, 15, 34, 45, Ellie Casper 28, 54, 73, 80, Iona Bennett 42, Milly Ash 84	42
16.12 R3	Phoenix Juniors (h)	W	11-0	Kirstie Hunt 5, Ellie Casper 13, Elisha Hardcastle 40, Jodie Hunter 44, Monika Estere Stube 45, 90, Olivia Auker 67, 88, Lauren Griffiths 70, Milly Ash 80, 86	40
20.01 QF	Altofts (h)	W	7-0	Charlotte Gill 3, Ellie Casper 20, 44, 86, Lauren Griffiths 22, 45+1, Maria Ledezma-Viso 70	40
11.04 SF	Leeds United (n)	W	1-0	Ellie Casper 22	120
30.04 F	Brighouse Town (n)	L	2-3	Beth Stanfield (pen) 9, Ellie Casper 67	200

(n) Played at Fleet Lane, (West Riding FA HQ)

HOUNSLOW (FORMERLY QPR)

2019-20: WNL SOUTHERN PREMIER (Tier 3)

Founded: 2001 (as QPR)

Nickname: The Tridents

Season 2018-19 (competed as QPR):

WNL Southern Premier (Tier 3): 11th

FA Cup: 2nd Round

WNL Cup: 2nd Round

Capital Cup: Semi-finals

Hounslow Women were reborn in the summer of 2019 when they took over the running of QPR Women. Rangers announced they would continue to operate a team lower down the football pyramid through their charitable arm. A merger between Wembley Mill Hill Ladies and a former QPR Women in 2001 led to the creation of the QPR Ladies club (reverting to the QPR Women name in 2018) that existed until 2019. They twice collected silverware; the Middlesex FA County Cup in 2009-10 and the South West Combination League Cup in 2006-07. Hounslow FC ran a men's team between 1885 and 1989 with a youth section remaining until 1995, but then continued to exist in name only without any teams. They have now been reborn as a women's and girls' club playing matches at Green Lane. Former QPR Women coach Miguel De'Souza is the club's first head coach.

2018-19 AS IT HAPPENS (COMPETED AS QPR)

16.09.18: After a four-game losing run QPR can celebrate their first League point of the season as Roschelle Shakes scores an injury-time equaliser in a 1-1 draw at home to MK Dons.

07.10.18: Jo Wilson, Roschelle Shakes and Whitney Locke all score in an entertaining 3-3 draw away to fellow strugglers C&K Basildon as QPR pick up their first away point of the season.

10.10.18: On World Mental Health Day, QPR player Courtnay Ward-Chambers speaks out about how QPR and football have helped her overcome her struggles.

17.02.19: QPR miss out on a place in the Capital Cup semi-final in heart-breaking fashion as they lose the semi-final 4-3 on penalties after a 1-1 draw with Leyton Orient.

14.04.19: Jo Wilson hits a hat-trick and Sue Kumaning is also on target as QPR come from behind to beat bottom club C&K Basildon to secure their first League win of the season.

22.05.19: QPR FC announce that their senior team will be breaking away to play independently under a new name, with Rangers set to continue to operate a team lower down the football pyramid.

2018-19 RESULTS: (HOME VENUE HONEYCROFT, (UXBRIDGE FC), UNLESS STATED)

2018-19 WNL SP				**COMPETED AS QPR**	Att	Pos
19.08	Loughborough F (a)	L	0-7		75	
26.08	Oxford United (h)	L	0-3		56	11
09.09	Cardiff City L (a)	L	1-5	Chontele Lawrence 5	50	12
12.09	Watford (a)	L	1-2	Mara Deluca 35	132	12
16.09	MK Dons (h)	D	1-1	Roschelle Shakes 90+1	78	12
23.09	C&K Basildon (a)		P-P			12
30.09	Plymouth A (h)	L	2-3	Whitney Locke 66, Roschelle Shakes 70	60	11
04.10	Gillingham (a)	L	0-2		102	11
07.10	C&K Basildon (a)	D	3-3	Jo Wilson 17, Roschelle Shakes 49, Whitney Locke 54	55	11
21.10	Chichester City (h)	L	2-3	Jo Wilson 44, Chontele Lawrence 90+4	64	12
11.11	Coventry United (h)	L	1-7	Jo Wilson 13	50	12
09.12	Coventry United (a)		P-P			12
16.12	Portsmouth (a)		P-P			11
06.01	Portsmouth (a)	L	0-1		84	11
13.01	Loughborough F (h)		P-P			11
20.01	Oxford United (a)	L	1-7	Stephanie Anes 24	157	11
27.01	Cardiff City L (h)	L	0-6		48	12
13.02	Watford (h)	D	1-1	Jo Wilson 2, *Hollie Hogan sent off 89*	90	11
24.02	Plymouth A (a)	L	3-4	Jo Wilson 14, 16, 80	50	11
03.03	Chichester City (a)		P-P			11
13.03	Gillingham (h)	L	1-3	Victoria Grieve 86	48	11
17.03	Loughborough F (h)	D	2-2	Courtnay Ward-Chambers 68, Jo Wilson 78	60	11
24.03	MK Dons (a)	L	2-3	Lauren Jordinson 25, Sue Kumaning 52	183	11
07.04	Coventry United (a)	D	1-1	Kasha Petit 68	106	11
14.04	C&K Basildon (h)	W	4-1	Jo Wilson 37, 51, 72, Sue Kumaning 82	90	11
28.04	Chichester City (a)	L	0-3		50	11
05.05	Portsmouth (h)	W	2-1	Courtney Ward-Chambers (pen) 25, Jo Wilson 73	135	11

2018-19 FA CUP: COMPETED AS QPR

02.12 R2	Cardiff City L (a)	L	0-4	

2018-19 WNL CUP: COMPETED AS QPR

02.09 DR	Gillingham (h)	W	3-1	Courtnay Ward-Chambers 19, 90+5, Sue Kumaning 70
R1	Bye			
14.10 R2	Loughborough F (h)	L	1-3	Jo Wilson 35, *Courtnay Ward-Chambers sent off 86*

2018-19 *CAPITAL CUP: COMPETED AS QPR

18.11 QF	Whyteleafe (h)	W	5-0	Jo Wilson 23, 79, Stephanie Anes 32, Whitney Locke 55, Roschelle Shakes 85
17.02 SF	Leyton Orient (h)	D	1-1 (L3-4p)	Jo Wilson 45

*The Capital Cup is the equivalent of a County Cup for teams in and around London. In 2018-19 it was run by the Surrey FA.

"We are so happy to become a part of Hounslow FC. The support the club has offered has been welcoming and their approach to, and enthusiasm for, women's football has been refreshing. The club's ethos means that we now have scope to look at programmes of development that we are keen to explore, allowing us to grow, improve and further increase the exposure to women's football in the local area. We cannot wait to have a well-motivated group to attack 2019-20 and start to develop a brand that can be recognised for generations to come. Here's to a new era."

Miguel De'Souza – Head Coach

HUDDERSFIELD TOWN

2019-20: WNL NORTHERN PREMIER (Tier 3)

H.T.L.F.C.

Founded: 1988 (as Huddersfield Ladies)

Nickname: Town

Season 2018-19:

WNL Northern Premier (Tier 3): 4th

FA Cup: 5th Round

WNL Cup: Quarter-finals

County Cup: Runners-up

Huddersfield Ladies became Huddersfield Town Ladies ahead of the 1993-94 season and went on to win the Treble of North East Regional Division 1, League Cup and what was then the Yorkshire FA County Cup in their first season. The 2018-19 season was Town's fifth consecutive campaign in Tier 4 and their most successful to date as they racked up their highest points total in the division. They have also had recent success in the Sheffield & Hallamshire FA County Cup winning it in 2016-17 and 2017-18 and finishing as runners-up in 2018-19.

2018-19 AS IT HAPPENS

20.01.19: Town hit double figures in their Sheffield & Hallamshire FA County Cup quarter-final tie against lower League Dronfield Town with Kate Mallin, Brittany Sanderson (x4), Sarah Danby, Lucy Sowerby (x2), Vicky Abbott and Laura Elford all on target.

10.02.19: With 74 minutes played Huddersfield trail 3-0 to Championship outfit Charlton in the FA Cup 4th Round. They then complete an amazing comeback with Brittany Sanderson, Laura Elford and Kate Mallin scoring three goals in the space of four minutes. The match eventually progresses to penalties with Town prevailing 5-4.

17.02.19: Huddersfield take a shock 14th minute lead against West Ham United in the FA Cup 5th Round. They put in a creditable performance away to the WSL side but eventually lose 8-1.

05.05.19: Sarah Dobby captains the side for the day in her retirement game and scores as Huddersfield beat Bradford 11-0 in the final WNL match of the season.

12.05.19: Huddersfield narrowly fail to win the Sheffield & Hallamshire FA County Cup final for the third year in a row as they go down 4-1 on penalties to Tier 4 Barnsley. It's the fourth consecutive year that these two teams have met in the final. Town battle back from 2-0 and 3-2 down but eventually lose on spot-kicks.

2018-19 RESULTS: (HOME VENUE: THE STAFFLEX ARENA, (SHELLEY FC) UNLESS STATED)

2018-19 WNL NP

					Att	Pos
19.08	Sheffield FC (h)	W	2-0	Katie Nutter 73, Brittany Sanderson 85	93	
26.08	Guiseley Vixens (a)	W	2-1	Katie Nutter 4, 74	40	2
09.09	Sunderland (h)	L	2-3	Charley Evans 50, Kate Mallin (pen) 55	92	4
12.09	Doncaster R B (h)	W	6-1	Katie Nutter 18, Kate Mallin 32, 78, 82, Kerry Hope 62, Shauna Legge 87	102	3
16.09	Middlesbrough (a)	L	2-3	Brittany Sanderson 13, Sarah Danby 90+1	163	4
23.09	Bradford City (a)	W	8-0	Own Goal 20, Sarah Danby 29, Kate Mallin 30, Katie Nutter 40, 45, Brittany Sanderson 46, 79, Anna Davis 85	125	4
30.09	Hull City (h)	W	4-1	Kerry Hope 1, Sarah Danby 31, Arianne Parnham 37, Kate Mallin 71	76	1
03.10	Fylde (a)	L	1-2	Amelia Turner 17	135	2
21.10	Stoke City (a)	W	4-3	Kate Mallin 47, Brittany Sanderson 54, 57, Lucy Sowerby 90+1	128	4
11.11	Nottingham F (a)	W	2-1	Brittany Sanderson 48, Kate Mallin (pen) 54	68	2
18.11	Sheffield FC (a)	W	3-2	Brittany Sanderson 45+1, Own Goal 48, Katie Nutter 65, *Shauna Legge sent off 90+4*	92	3
25.11	Derby County (h)	W	3-2	Brittany Sanderson 6, Kate Mallin (pen) 20, 90+1	54	2
13.01	Blackburn R (h)	L	3-4	Kate Mallin (pen) 38, Laura Elford 41, Brittany Sanderson 90+1	97	3
27.01	Middlesbrough (h)	W	4-2	Lucy Sowerby 6, Katie Nutter 23, Sarah Danby 49, Brittany Sanderson 90+4	76	2
13.02	Doncaster R B (a)	D	2-2	Lucy Sowerby 37, Sarah Dobby 71	122	2
03.03	Hull City (a)	L	1-2	Kate Mallin (pen) 90, *Cara Bickett sent off 90+1*	60	4
10.03	Blackburn Rovers (a)		P-P			6
13.03	Fylde (h)		P-P			6
24.03	Stoke City (h)	D	1-1	Kate Mallin 83	74	5
27.03	Fylde (h)	W	4-1	Brittany Sanderson 13, Laura Elford 36, Katie Nutter 24, 78	78	5
07.04	Sunderland (a)	W	2-1	Brittany Sanderson 25, Lucy Sowerby 48	110	5
14.04	Derby County (a)	L	1-2	Charley Evans 90	141	5
16.04	Blackburn R (a)	L	0-4		121	5
21.04	Nottingham F (h)	W	6-0	Kate Mallin 13, 55, Lucy Sowerby 41, Laura Elford 43, Lucy Roberts 45, Ellie White 64	77	5
28.04	Guiseley Vixens (h)	W	5-2	Lucy Sowerby 33, 35, (pen) 64, Laura Elford 46, Kate Mallin (pen) 55	108	4
05.05	Bradford City (h)	W	11-0	Laura Elford 4, 37, 81, Arianne Parnham 17, Lucy Sowerby 32, 58, Lucy Roberts 43, Kerry Hope 52, Kate Mallin 67, Lucy Sowerby 72, Phoebe Tomlin (og) 75	89	4

2018-19 FA CUP

02.12 R2	Bradford City (h)	W	7-1	Kate Mallin 2, 17, 38, Sarah Dobby 11, Laura Elford 18, Lucy Sowerby 34, Arianne Parnham 80	105
06.01 R3	Leeds United (h)	W	4-1	Britanny Sanderson 1, 17, Sarah Danby 55, Laura Elford 57	156
03.02 R4	Charlton Athletic (a)		P-P		
10.02 R4	Charlton Athletic (a)	D	3-3aet (W5-4p)	Brittany Sanderson 74, Laura Elford 75, Kate Mallin 78	184
17.02 R5	West Ham Utd (a)	L	1-8	Kate Mallin (pen) 14	865

2018-19 WNL Cup

02.09 DR	Middlesbrough (h)	W	3-0	Brittany Sanderson 12, 88, Sarah Danby 70	76
R1	Bye				
14.10 R2	Burnley (h)	W	1-0	Kate Mallin (pen) 90+2	47
09.12 R3	Nottingham Forest (h)	W	4-1	Lucy Sowerby 35, 90+2, Brittany Sanderson 53, Kate Mallin (pen) 58	95
24.02 QF	Blackburn R (h)	L	1-3	Lucy Sowerby 43	96

2018-19 SHEFFIELD & HALLAMSHIRE FA COUNTY CUP

16.12 R3	Steel City Wanderers (a)	W	w/o		
20.01 QF	Dronfield Town (a)	W	10-0	Kate Mallin 1, Brittany Sanderson 14, 17, 30, 40, Sarah Danby 24, Lucy Sowerby 26, 65, Vicky Abbott 48, Laura Elford 49	48
17.03 SF	Sheffield United Dev.(h)	W	4-0	Lucy Sowerby 16, 45, 54, Katie Nutter 17	
12.05 F	Barnsley (n)	D	3-3aet (L1-4p)	Kate Mallin 40, (pen) 89, Laura Elford 66	440est

(n)Played at New York Stadium, (Rotherham United FC)

"The 2018-19 season saw us reach all-time highs for the club. We enjoyed success in the League and Cups with our highest WNL League position and points total and our best ever runs in the FA Cup and League Cup as well as reaching the County Cup final. However, we never quite took the extra step to make it an outstanding season. We learnt lots along the way and in 2019-20 we will use the experience to push on. It's been a good summer of recruitment and we're ready to give our all."

Ashley Vickers – Manager

HULL CITY

2019-20: WNL NORTHERN PREMIER (Tier 3)

Founded: 2001

Nickname: City / The Tigresses

Season 2018-19:

WNL Northern Premier (Tier 3): 10th

FA Cup: 3rd Round

WNL Cup: 3rd Round

County Cup: n/a

Kevin Greene Photography

Hull City's recent progress is in part due to their merger with Beverley Town Ladies in 2011-12. The Tigresses were promoted to Tier 4 ahead of 2014-15 and in 2017-18 they were crowned WPL North 1 champions to claim promotion to their current level at Tier 3. They lost just two of their 22 League games in that 2017-18 campaign and scored 66 goals. The 2018-19 season was a challenging one although it did include wins over former WSL 2 sides Sheffield FC and Doncaster Rovers Belles who were both in transition following the FA's restructuring of the football pyramid.

2018-19 AS IT HAPPENS

19.08.18: Having been promoted as 2017-18 WPL North 1 champions, life in Tier 3 begins with a tough 4-0 home defeat to Stoke City.

16.09.18: In their fourth League match of the season, Hull secure three points for the first time as they win 5-2 at home to Fylde.

06.01.19: Katie Thompson re-signs for the club. Hull's twitter feed states that she is two appearances shy of her century for the club and 10 goals away from her half-century.

2018-19 RESULTS: (HOME VENUE: HULL UNIVERSITY SPORTS GROUND, UNLESS STATED)

2018-19 WNL NP

					Att	Pos
19.08	Stoke City (h)	L	0-4		60	
26.08	Derby County (h)	D	2-2	Misty Russell 69, Liberty Bott 71	50	9
09.09	Blackburn Rovers (a)	L	0-2		198	10
16.09	Fylde (h)	W	5-2	Joanna Symington 5, Emily Smith 25, 65, Misty Russell 33, Ellie Tanser 80	40	10
23.09	Nottingham F (a)	W	1-0	Hope Knight 84	82	10
30.09	Huddersfield T (a)	L	1-4	Emily Smith 24	76	9
03.10	Doncaster R B (a)	W	2-0	Ellice Jackman 58, Hope Knight 81	110	8
07.10	Sunderland (h)	L	2-4	Hope Knight 4, 60	40	9
28.10	Guiseley Vixens (a)	L	1-3	Hope Knight 3		10
04.11	Bradford City (a)	W	3-1	Amy Kay 9, Rachael Ackroyd (pen) 37, Hope Knight 67	53	9
11.11	Sheffield FC (h)	W	4-2	Ellice Jackman 15, 60, Harley Skinner 34, Amy Blinkhorn 86	50	7
18.11	Middlesbrough (h)	L	1-3	Joanne Symington 90	40	8
25.11	Stoke City (a)	L	1-4	Rachael Ackroyd 15	129	8
27.01	Fylde (a)	L	0-1		100	8
03.02	Guiseley Vixens (h)	L	0-1		50	9
10.02	Derby County (a)	L	2-7	Harley Skinner 3, Ellie Tanser 75	93	10
17.02	Sunderland (a)	L	2-6	Hope Knight 12, Amy Kay 31	210	10
03.03	Huddersfield T (h)	W	2-1	Hope Knight 10, Misty Russell 72	60	10
13.03	Doncaster R B (h)	D	3-3	Amy Kay, Joanna Symington (x2)	80	9
17.03	Bradford City (h)	W	3-1	Rebecca Beech 51, Amy Kay 60, Misty Russell 86	72	9
24.03	Blackburn R (h)	L	1-2	Hope Knight 17	60	9
31.03	Sheffield FC (a)	L	2-4	Harley Skinner 54, Joanna Symington 65	80	9
14.04	Middlesbrough (a)	L	0-3		233	9
05.05	Nottingham F (h)	L	3-5	Rebecca Beech 11, Hope Knight 63, Holly Johnson-Collier 90+2	126	10

2018-19 FA CUP

02.12 R2	Long Eaton United (a)	W	5-0	Misty Russell 14, Rachael Ackroyd 34, 44, Hope Knight 67, 82	60
06.01 R3	AFC Wimbledon (h)	L	0-3		133

2018-19 WNL CUP

02.09 DR	Bradford City (h)	W	2-1	Hope Knight (pen) 26, Rebecca Beech 59	80
R1	Bye				
14.10 R2	Birmingham & W M (h)	W	2-1aet	Rebecca Beech 36, Joanna Symington 103	30
16.12 R3	Bolton W (a)		P-P		
13.01 R3	Bolton W (a)	L	1-3 aet	Emily Smith	

Kevin Greene Photography

"Hull thoroughly enjoyed their first season in Tier 3 and achieved their main aim of survival. It was always expected that it would be an up and down season with the squad needing to blend some exciting youngsters into the side to complement the squad that won promotion in 2017-18. Manager Rachel Gay's team enjoyed some terrific victories over Bradford, Doncaster, Sheffield and Fylde, but the highlight was a 2-1 home win over Huddersfield at the beginning of March that turned the season around and went a long way to helping secure survival. That result showed what the side is capable of and in 2019-20 Hull will be looking to build on a solid debut in the division. Finishing higher than 10th would represent more success for a club that has progressed rapidly in recent years."

Sam Shepherd (@ferribyshep) – Editor of The Tigress matchday programme

IPSWICH TOWN

2019-20: WNL SOUTH EAST 1 (Tier 4)

Founded: Unknown

Nickname: Town / The Tractor Girls

Season 2018-19:

WNL South East 1 (Tier 4): 7th

FA Cup: 2nd Qualifying Round

WNL Cup: Determining Round

WNL Plate: 3rd Round

County Cup: Winners

Ipswich Town's formal association with the men's professional club of the same name was announced in February 2012. The 2018-19 campaign was Ipswich's fifth straight season in Tier 4 with their highest finish in that time being 3rd in 2017-18. The club's most recent successes have come in the Suffolk FA County Cup which they have won for the last five years in a row between 2014-15 and 2018-19.

2018-19 AS IT HAPPENS

14.02.19: Head coach Carla Dickinson stands down a day after a 3-0 defeat to Norwich in the East Anglian derby. Joe Sheehan is named as her replacement the following day. His first game is the County Cup semi-final against Brantham Athletic which Town win 14-0.

24.03.19: Goalkeeper Sian Fagg's 100th appearance for Town is a happy one as her side chalk up their first League victory of 2019 with a 3-1 win at Denham. Natasha Thomas opens the scoring within seconds of kick-off with what the Ipswich website describes as "perhaps the quickest goal in the club's history".

28.04.19: Ipswich come from 2-0 down at half-time to beat bottom-of-the-table Luton Town 5-2. Natasha Thomas scores a hat-trick, Paige Wakefield is also on target and Charlotte Kellett nets her first goal for the senior team. The result confirms Luton's relegation.

05.05.19: Abbie Lafayette scores an injury-time winner on her debut as Ipswich come from 1-0 down and 2-1 down to win 3-2 away to Cambridge United.

07.05.19: Ipswich win the Suffolk FA County Cup with an 8-0 victory over lower League Needham in the final, which is played at Portman Road, home of Ipswich Town men.

20.05.19: Joe Sheehan is named manager on a permanent basis having taken over temporarily in February. He won four, drew three and lost one of his eight matches in charge in 2018-19 and led Ipswich to Suffolk FA County Cup glory.

2018-19 RESULTS: (HOME VENUE: GOLDSTAR GROUND, (FELIXSTOWE & WALTON UTD FC), UNLESS STATED)

2018-19 WNL SE 1					Att	Pos
19.08	Crawley Wasps (a)	L	1-5	Amanda Crump 39	74	
26.08	Actonians (a)	W	5-1	Nicole Pannifer 64, Zoe Cossey 67, Paige Wakefield 73, Natasha Thomas (pen) 77, Laken Duchar-Clark 90	20	6
09.09	Enfield Town (h)	D	3-3	Amanda Crump (pen) 48, 50, Own Goal 90	45	7
12.09	Norwich City (h)	L	0-1		120	7
16.09	AFC Wimbledon (a)	D	1-1	Becky McLaren-Johnson (og) 30	100	7
30.09	Luton Town (a)	L	1-3	Paige Wakefield 32	43	9
03.10	Billericay Town (h)	W	2-0	Natasha Thomas 42, Natalie Richardson 52	70	5
07.10	Denham United (h)	W	4-0	Lindsey Cooper 17, Zoe Cossey 50, Natasha Thomas 55, 82	45	3
04.11	Leyton Orient (a)	D	2-2	Zoe Cossey 10, Paige Wakefield 48	62	5
25.11	Stevenage (a)	W	1-0	Kerry Stimson 74	20	6
20.01	Actonians (h)	L	0-5		20	7
27.01	Cambridge Utd (h)	D	2-2	Cassie Craddock 26, Toni-Anne Wayne 45	40	7
03.02	Enfield Town (a)	L	1-3	Paige Wakefield 45	58	7
10.02	AFC Wimbledon (h)		P-P			7
13.02	Norwich City (a)	L	0-3		230	8
03.03	Leyton Orient (h)	D	1-1	Paige Wakefield 53	40	8
10.03	Luton Town (h)		P-P			8
13.03	Billericay Town (a)	D	1-1	Paige Wakefield 85		8
24.03	Denham United (a)	W	3-1	Natasha Thomas 1, 88, Toni-Anne Wayne 44	60	8
07.04	AFC Wimbledon (h)	L	0-2		51	8
14.04	Stevenage (h)	D	2-2	Natasha Thomas 2, Lindsey Cooper 86, *Jordan Arnoup sent off 62*	61	8
21.04	Crawley Wasps (h)	L	1-2	Zoe Cossey 16	67	8
28.04	Luton Town (h)	W	5-2	Natasha Thomas 59, 73, 75, Paige Wakefield 63, Charlotte Kellett 85	60	8
05.05	Cambridge Utd (a)	W	3-2	Zoe Cossey 70, Natasha Thomas 85, Abbie Lafayette 90	48	7

2018-19 FA CUP

23.09 RQ2	New London Lionesses (a)	D	2-2aet (L2-4p)	Paige Wakefield 2, Cassie Craddock 41	

2018-19 WNL CUP

02.09 DR	Crawley Wasps (a)	L	0-8		60

2018-19 WNL PLATE

R1	Bye				
14.10 R2	C&K Basildon (h)	W	4-2	Zoe Cossey 15, Natasha Thomas 37, Toni-Anne Wayne 44, 45+1	35
02.12 R3	Stevenage (h)	L	1-2 aet	Natasha Thomas 61	26

2018-19 SUFFOLK FA COUNTY CUP

21.10 R1	Ipswich Wanderers (a)	W	2-1	Toni-Anne Wayne 77, 80	20
18.11 R2	Chantry Grasshoppers (a)	W	w/o		
17.02 QF	Brantham Athletic (h)	W	14-0	Georgia Box 4, 89, Toni-Anne Wayne 14, 80, Cassie Craddock 18, 27, 71, Paige Wakefield 23, 65, Jac Ball 35, Natasha Thomas 45, 81, Amy Nash 78, Amanda Crump 88	20
17.03 SF	AFC Sudbury (h)	W	w/o		
07.05 F	Needham Market (n)	W	8-0	Charlotte Kellett 27, Natasha Thomas 45, 47, Amanda Crump 48, 72, Amy Nash 58, Toni-Anne Wayne 67, Sophie Welton 70	

(n) Played at Portman Road, (Ipswich Town FC)

"In 2018-19 our League form made things a little underwhelming as we did not manage to hit the targets we had set. However, with the structure and plans we have in place, we are increasingly confident of achieving our goals in 2019-20. We are an incredibly ambitious club and we have our eyes fixed on eventually reaching the WSL. We have a tremendous WSL Academy set-up full of England youth internationals that will help our already talented first team grow into a formidable side and we believe that if we get it right, we can go on a special journey to the promised land."

Joe Sheehan – Manager

KENT FOOTBALL UNITED

2019-20: WNL SOUTH EAST 1 (Tier 4)

Founded: 2010

Nickname: United

Season 2018-19:

London & SE Regional Prem (Tier 5): 1st (P)

FA Cup: 1st Round

League Cup: Semi-finals

County Cup: 2nd Round

It was a fitting tribute to goalkeeper Jordan Dawes, 18, who tragically passed away in February 2019 within months of being diagnosed with liver cancer, that Kent Football United should go on to claim the London & South East Regional Premier title. Less than a year previously Dawes' penalty shootout heroics had helped United claim the Kent FA County Cup. Promotion to the WNL is the finest achievement in the club's short history.

2018-19 AS IT HAPPENS

22.02.19: The club announces that goalkeeper Jordan Dawes has sadly passed away at the age of just 18, four months after being diagnosed with liver cancer. Last season Dawes saved a penalty in the shootout to help her team win the 2017-18 Kent FA County Cup final. The club says it will retire the No.1 shirt in her honour.

14.04.19: Kent Football United secure the London & South East Regional Premier title and promotion to the WNL by winning their final match of the season 3-1 at home to QPR Girls (the club name for QPR's Development team). Amy Russ finishes as the division's Golden Boot winner with 37 goals in League and Cup matches. Team-mates Rachel Stevens (25) and Elizabeth Waldie (23) are second and third on the list.

2018-19 RESULTS: (HOME VENUE: GLENTWORTH EX-SERV. CLUB, LOWFIELD STREET, UNLESS STATED)

2018-19 London & SE RP

09.09	Parkwood Rangers (h)	W	5-1	Amy Russ (x2), Rachel Stevens, Elizabeth Waldie, Temilola Adeyemi
16.09	QPR Girls (a)	W	5-1	Rachel Stevens (x3), Amy Russ, Elizabeth Waldie
14.10	Whyteleafe (a)	W	2-0	Amy Russ (x2)
04.11	Fulham FC Foundation (h)	W	4-3	Amy Russ (x2), Rachel Stevens, Elizabeth Waldie
18.11	Eastbourne Town (h)	W	3-0	Rachel Stevens (x2), Shannon Burden
25.11	London Kent Football United (a)	W	2-1	Amy Russ, Elizabeth Waldie
09.12	Fulham FC Foundation (a)	W	9-1	Elizabeth Waldie, Rachel Stevens (x6), Amy Russ, Lucy Cockerill
16.12	AFC Phoenix (h)	L	1-2	Amy Russ
13.01	AFC Phoenix (a)		P-P	
20.01	Eastbourne Town (a)	L	0-2	
27.01	Whyteleafe (h)		P-P	
03.02	Parkwood Rangers (a)	W	5-1	Natasha Moloney, Amy Russ (x3), Elizabeth Waldie
10.02	Aylesford (h)	D	2-2	Megan Burrows, Elizabeth Waldie
24.02	London Kent Football United (h)		P-P	
03.03	Aylesford (a)	W	7-0	Chloe Francis, Amy Russ, Rachel Stevens (x2), Elizabeth Waldie, Bethany Smith (x2)
10.03	QPR Girls (h)		P-P	
17.03	AFC Phoenix (a)	W	2-1	Shannon Burden, Amy Russ, *Shannon Burden sent off, Megan Burrows sent off*
24.03	Whyteleafe (h)	W	5-1	Amy Russ (x3), Elizabeth Waldie, Rachel Stevens
07.04	London Kent Football United (h)	D	2-2	Shannon Burden, Elizabeth Waldie
14.04	QPR Girls (h)	W	3-1	Chloe Francis, Amy Russ, Elizabeth Waldie

2018-19 FA Cup

26.08 PR	Herne Bay (h)	W	8-0	Lucy Cockerill, Amy Russ (x4), Rachel Stevens (x2), Elizabeth Waldie
02.09 RQ1	Victoire (h)	W	8-0	Megan Burrows, Lucy Cockerill (x2), Rachel Stevens, Elizabeth Waldie (x3)
23.09 RQ2	Burgess Hill Town (h)		P-P	
30.09 RQ2	Burgess Hill Town (h)	W	9-0	Rachel Stevens (x3), Amy Russ (x4), Megan Burrows (x2)
07.10 RQ3	Ashford Town (a)	W	4-3	Rachel Stevens, Elizabeth Waldie (x3)
11.11 R1	Luton Town (a)	D	1-1aet (L1-3p)	Elizabeth Waldie

2018-19 League Cup

28.10 R1	Eastbourne Town (a)	W	3-1	Megan Burrows, Elizabeth Waldie, Elizabeth Cockerill
02.12 R2	London Kent Football United (h)	W	2-0	Amy Russ, Elizabeth Waldie
06.01 R3	Parkwood Rangers (h)	W	6-1	Amy Russ (x4), Rachel Stevens (x2)
13.01 QF	Aylesford (a)	W	8-0	Megan Burrows, Amy Russ (x5), Elizabeth Waldie (x2)
17.02 SF	AFC Phoenix (h)	L	0-4	

2018-19 Kent FA County Cup

R1	Bye			
21.10 R2	Gillingham (a)	L	1-2	Megan Burrows

KEYNSHAM TOWN

2019-20: WNL SOUTHERN PREMIER (Tier 3)

Founded: 1993 (as Super Strikers Girls)

Nickname: The K's

Season 2018-19:

WNL South West 1 (Tier 4): Champions (P)

FA Cup: 4th Round

WNL Cup: Determining Round

WNL Plate: Quarter-finals

County Cup: Winners

Initially formed as an U11s six-a-side team in 1993 by pupils of Chandag Junior School in Bristol as Super Strikers Girls. The name was later changed to Protel Super Strikers following sponsorship by a local telecoms company. At that point the club also adopted Celtic's green and white colours. In 1998-99 they became associated with Keynsham Town men's team and were granted use of their facilities. They changed their name to the same. The K's played in Tier 2 of English football (WPL Southern as it was then) between 2006-07 until 2010-11 with a highest finish of 3rd in 2009-10 above clubs including West Ham, Charlton and Brighton. Relegations at the end of 2011-12 and 2014-15 brought them down to Tier 4 where they remained until their title-winning success of 2018-19.

2018-19 AS IT HAPPENS

16.12.18: After taking a maximum 24 points from their opening eight League fixtures, the K's drop points for the first time all season when they lose 3-0 at home to title rivals Southampton Women.

06.01.19: Keynsham pull off an FA Cup shock as they beat Tier 3 Fylde 2-1 to make it into the 4th Round.

10.02.19: It was always going to be a tall order as Keynsham attempted to bridge the gap of 30 League places to WSL side Reading in the FA Cup 4th Round. The K's go down 13-0 and concede three penalties, all of which are scored by England international Fara Williams.

24.03.19: Keynsham win 14-0 away to Poole in a match featuring a hat-trick of hat-trick scorers as Laura Williams, Ellison Roberts and Kelly Aldridge bag three apiece.

07.04.19: Keynsham Town secure the WNL South West 1 title with a 5-0 win away to Southampton Saints. The victory also takes their goal difference for the season so far to 100.

10.05.19: The K's beat divisional rivals Brislington 2-1 in the Somerset FA County Cup final with Ellie Curson scoring both goals.

17.05.19: Kerry Bartlett receives her WNL South West 1 top scorer award having notched 40 League goals throughout 2018-19.

2018-19 RESULTS: (HOME VENUE: AJN STADIUM, (KEYNSHAM TOWN FC), UNLESS STATED)

2018-19 WNL SW 1					Att	Pos
19.08	Buckland Athletic (h)	W	9-0	Kerry Bartlett 34, 50, 67, 77, 83, Justine Lorton 46, 60, 70, Corinne Yorston 63	50	
09.09	Larkhall Athletic (a)	W	9-2	Ellie Curson 19, 59, Laura Williams 51, Corinne Yorston 52, Justine Lorton 57, 70, Kerry Bartlett 64, 78, 84	30	2
13.09	Brislington (a)	W	7-0	Michelle Munro 2, Justine Lorton 5, 24, Kerry Bartlett 20, 25, 35, Jade Radburn 70	78	2
16.09	Chesham United (h)	W	7-1	Kerry Bartlett 21, (pen) 58, (pen) 69, Corinne Yorston 23, 27, Ellie Curson 64, Laura Williams 46	65	2
04.10	Swindon Town (a)	W	5-0	Justine Lorton 10, 35, Kerry Bartlett 20, Ellie Curson 42, Hannah Davies 74	39	1
04.11	Maidenhead Utd (a)	W	5-2	Kerry Bartlett 7, Laura Williams 70, Corinne Yorston 71, Christina Vega Leandro 73, 83	10	1
18.11	Poole Town (h)	W	9-0	Justine Lorton 18, 40, Corinne Yorston 29, Kerry Bartlett 42, 46, 52, 82, Ellis Hillman 44, Laura Williams 45		1
25.11	Southampton S (h)	W	3-1	Ellie Curson 9, Laura Williams 57, Christina Vega Leandro 61	40	1
16.12	Southampton W (h)	L	0-3		75	2
13.01	Buckland Athletic (a)	W	4-1	Laura Williams 29, Ella Curson 55, Kerry Bartlett 58, Ellis Hillman 74	42	2
27.01	Southampton S (a)		P-P			2
14.02	Brislington (h)	W	6-0	Kerry Bartlett 7, Laura Williams 17, 66, 75, Justine Lorton 21, Kelly Aldridge 82	75	2
03.03	Cheltenham Town (h)	W	6-2	Kelly Aldridge 13, Kerry Bartlett 22, 32, 45+4, 72, Laura Williams 60	135	2

10.03	Southampton W (a)	W	5-1	Laura Williams 28, Kerry Bartlett 37, 82, Ellie Curson 55, 72	44	2
14.03	Swindon Town (h)	W	4-0	Kerry Bartlett 2, 28, Kelly Aldridge 61, Liberty Sims 86	60	1
17.03	Larkhall Athletic (h)	W	4-0	Kerry Bartlett 27, 42, Christina Vega Leandro 72, Justine Lorton 80	75	1
24.03	Poole Town (a)	W	14-0	Justine Lorton 8, Laura Williams 17, 23, 86, Liberty Sims 18, Kelly Aldridge 34, 77, 83, Ellison Roberts 56, 58, 76, Ellie Curson 60, Corinne Yorston 65, Own Goal	32	1
31.03	Maidenhead Utd (h)	W	11-0	Laura Williams 2, Kerry Bartlett 11, 22, 42, Kelly Aldridge 35, Christine Vega Leandro 64, 71, 78, 85, Justine Lorton 66, 80	60	1
07.04	Southampton S (a)	W	5-0	Laura Williams 8, Kerry Bartlett 18, 32, 43, 53	12	1C
14.04	Cheltenham Town (a)	D	1-1	Kerry Bartlett (pen) 90	120	1C
28.04	Chesham United (a)	D	1-1	Ellison Roberts 88	80	1C

2018-19 FA Cup

23.09 RQ2	Swindon Town (a)	W	8-0	Ellie Curson 6, Laura Williams 8, 53, Kerry Bartlett 40, 43, 66, Hannah Davies 70, Justine Lorton 81	
07.10 RQ3	Southampton S (h)	W	6-0	Ellie Curson 8, Kerry Bartlett 39, 41, Laura Williams 60, Justine Lorton 76, 78	45
11.11 R1	AFC Bournemouth CST (h)	W	8-1	Justine Lorton 5, 14, Jade Radburn 12, 37, Ellis Hillman 20, Christina Vega Leandro 52, Laura Williams 84, Kerry Bartlett	
02.12 R2	C&K Basildon (h)	W	8-3	Laura Williams 16, Kerry Bartlett 21, 33, 45+1, 60, Justine Lorton 53, Christina Vega Leandro 76, Ellis Hillman 78	60
06.01 R3	Fylde (h)	W	2-1	Kerry Bartlett 34, Christina Vega Leandro 80, Kirsten Rendall sent off 90	80
03.02 R4	Reading (a)		P-P		
10.02 R4	Reading (a)	L	0-13		272

2018-19 WNL Cup

02.09 DR	Larkhall Athletic (a)	L	2-3	Kerry Bartlett 29, Laura Williams 54

2018-19 WNL Plate

14.10 R1	Southampton Saints (h)	W	7-1	Kerry Bartlett 10, 35, 44, 55, Ellie Curson 80, Justine Lorton 60, Michelle Munro 75	
21.10 R2	Portsmouth (h)	W	2-1	Kerry Bartlett 39, Ellie Curson 90+2	90
09.12 R3	Maidenhead United (h)	W	7-1	Justine Lorton 21, 85, Kerry Bartlett 24, Christina Vega Leandro 33, Kirsten Rendall 57, Katie Jones 80, Laura Williams 90	40
24.02 QF	MK Dons (a)	D	2-2aet (L4-5p)	Laura Williams 26, Christina Vega Leandro 75	

2018-19 SOMERSET FA COUNTY CUP

21.10 R1	Bye				
20.01 QF	Middlezoy (a)	W	7-0	Laura Williams 3, 84, Kerry Bartlett 27, 49, 63, 74, Ellis Hillman 69	37
17.02 SF	Larkhall Athletic (a)	W	3-0	Kerry Bartlett 24, Laura Williams 32, Kirsten Rendall 88	
10.05 F	Brislington (n)	W	2-1	Ellie Curson (x2)	120

(n)Played at Bishop Sutton, (Bishop Sutton FC)

LARKHALL ATHLETIC

2019-20: WNL SOUTH WEST 1 (Tier 4)

Founded: 2008

Nickname: The Larks

Season 2018-19:

WNL South West 1 (Tier 4): 6th

FA Cup: 3rd Qualifying Round

WNL Cup: 2nd Round

County Cup: Semi-finals

The club was founded in 2008 when Larkhall Athletic men became formally affiliated with the Bath City Ladies team. The Larks have been in what is now WNL South West 1 every season since 2014-15 with their highest finish to date being 4th in 2015-16. In 2018-19 they finished in a respectable mid-table position and were beaten in the semi-finals of the County Cup by eventual WNL South West 1 champions Keynsham Town.

2018-19 AS IT HAPPENS

19.08.18: Larkhall begin the season in style with a 4-0 home win against newly promoted Chesham United. Katy-May O'Hara Nash nets a hat-trick and Mel Sartain is also on target.

14.10.18: Goals from Katy-May O'Hara Nash and Mel Sartain are not enough to save Larkhall from WNL Cup elimination as they go down 3-2 after extra-time in a 2nd Round tie away to fellow Tier 4 outfit AFC Wimbledon. Athletic also have Georgia Smith sent off.

07.04.19: Adele Hooper and Emily Harrington both notch a brace as Larkhall rack up their biggest win of the season so far, a 7-0 home triumph against Poole.

05.05.19: Larkhall end the season with a 1-1 draw at home to 3rd-placed Cheltenham on a day which marks the retirement of Nicki O'Connell after 20 years' service for the Larks.

2018-19 RESULTS: (HOME VENUE: PLAIN HAM, (LARKHALL ATHLETIC FC), UNLESS STATED)

2018-19 WNL SW 1					Att	Pos
19.08	Chesham United (h)	W	4-0	Katy-May O'Hara Nash (x3), Mel Sartain	30	
26.08	Poole Town (a)	L	3-6	Sarah Gregory, Katy-May O'Hara Nash, Own Goal	9	4
09.09	Keynsham Town (h)	L	2-9	Adele Hooper, Mel Sartain	30	9
16.09	Maidenhead U (a)	W	3-0	Adele Hooper (x2), Own Goal	18	5
21.10	Southampton W (h)	L	0-5		60	6
25.10	Brislington (h)	D	3-3	Kate German, Katy May O'Hara Nash, Jodie Sheppard	40	5
28.10	Southampton Saints (a)		P-P			6
04.11	Swindon Town (a)	D	0-0		38	7
25.11	Buckland Athletic (a)	D	3-3	Adele Hooper (x2), Jodie Sheppard, *Georgia Smith sent off*	15	7
02.12	Southampton Saints (h)		P-P			7
09.12	Southampton W (a)	L	0-3		23	7
16.12	Cheltenham Town (a)		P-P			7
06.01	Southampton S (h)	W	3-2	Kate German, Mel Sartain, Lizzie Barrett	30	7
13.01	Chesham United (a)	D	1-1	Kate German	40	7
27.01	Cheltenham Town (a)	L	0-2		91	7
03.03	Maidenhead United (h)		P-P			7
10.03	Southampton S (a)	L	0-1		18	8
13.03	Brislington (a)		P-P			8
17.03	Keynsham Town (a)	L	0-4		75	8
24.03	Buckland Athletic (h)	W	2-1	Kate German, Adele Hooper	25	8
28.03	Brislington (a)	D	1-1	Lily-May Withers	64	8
07.04	Poole Town (h)	W	7-0	Emily Harrington (x2), Adele Hooper (x2), Kate German, Carly Bryant, Lizzie Barrett	30	7
14.04	Swindon Town (h)	W	2-1	Lizzie Barrett, Katy-May O'Hara Nash	20	6
21.04	Maidenhead U (h)	W	3-0	Kate German, Mel Sartain, Own Goal	35	6
05.05	Cheltenham Town (h)	D	1-1	Amanda Blakely	70	6

2018-19 FA CUP					
23.09 RQ2	Weston-super-Mare (h)	W	7-2	Lizzie Barrett (x2), Carly Bryant, Kate German, Lucy Olde, Mel Sartain, Katy-May O'Hara Nash	50
07.10 RQ3	Southampton FC (a)	L	1-4	Kate German 25	121

2018-19 WNL CUP				
02.09 DR	Keynsham Town (h)	W	3-2	Lizzie Barrett (x2), Katy-May O'Hara Nash
R1	Bye			
14.10 R2	AFC Wimbledon (h)	L	2-3 aet	Katy - May O'Hara Nash, Mel Sartain, *Georgia Smith sent off*

2018-19 SOMERSET FA COUNTY CUP

21.01 R1	Bye			
20.01 QF	Keynsham Town Dev (h)	W	1-0	Kate German
17.02 SF	Keynsham Town (h)	L	0-3	

LEAFIELD ATHLETIC

2019-20: WNL MIDLANDS 1 (Tier 4)

Founded: 1997

Nickname: Athletic

Season 2018-19:

West Midlands Reg Prem (Tier 5): 1st (P)

FA Cup: 3rd Qualifying Round

League Cup: Runners-up

County Cup: Quarter-finals

Manager Gary Barrell's side were promoted back to Tier 4 as 2018-19 West Midlands Regional Premier League champions four years after their relegation. Leafield lost two of their opening four League fixtures but then went undefeated in the remaining 16 matches and secured promotion with one game to spare when they won 1-0 away to Goldenhill Wanderers. They also reached the League Cup final but were beaten 1-0 by Sutton Coldfield Town.

2018-19 AS IT HAPPENS

09.09.18: Athletic suffer a disappointing start to the season as they are beaten 1-0 at home by Stockingford AA Pavilion for whom Catherine Smith scores the winner.

07.10.18: A valiant FA Cup display sees Leafield push Tier 4 West Brom – who are currently 2nd in WNL Midlands 1 – all the way before losing 2-1. Samantha Berry scores Athletic's goal.

02.05.19: Leafield clinch the title and promotion with one game to spare thanks to a 1-0 win away to Goldenhill Wanderers. Lily Eustace scores the winner 11 minutes from time to send Athletic back to Tier 4 four years after their relegation.

2018-19 RESULTS: (HOME VENUE: DICKENS HEALTH SPORTS CLUB, UNLESS STATED)

2018-19 WEST MIDLANDS REGIONAL PREMIER

09.09	Stockingford AA Pavilion (h)	L	0-1	
12.09	Redditch United (a)	W	3-2	Maisie Farr, Georgia Harris, Sofi Liperis, *Sofi Liperis sent off*
16.09	Sutton C Town (a)	W	2-1	Maisie Farr, Sofi Liperis
30.09	Coundon Court (a)	L	4-6	Samantha Berry (x2), Georgina Conway, Lily Eustace
14.10	Crusaders (a)	W	3-1	Samantha Berry, Lily Eustace, Alice Rogers
21.10	Lye Town (a)	W	3-0	Leila Eminoglu, Lily Eustace (x2)
28.10	Goldenhill W (h)	W	3-0	Lily Eustace, Sofi Liperis (x2)
04.11	Knowle (a)	W	5-0	Lily Eustace (x2), Sofi Liperis, Georgia Harris (x2)
11.11	Worcester United (h)	W	5-0	Amy Kendall, Georgia Harris, Lily Eustace (x2), Alice Rogers
25.11	Lye Town (h)	W	6-0	Amy Kendall, Georgia Harris, Samantha Berry, Lily Eustace (x2), Alice Rogers
13.01	Coundon Court (h)	W	5-0	Ella Bridges, Lily Eustace (x2), Sofi Liperis, Alice Rogers
27.01	Crusaders (h)	D	2-2	Lily Eustace, Alice Rogers
17.02	Knowle (h)	W	4-0	Samantha Berry, Daisy-May Clements, Lily Eustace, Alice Rogers
24.02	Worcester United (a)	W	8-0	Amy Kendall, Danielle Miles-Ranger, Samantha Berry, Holly Biggs, Daisy-May Clements (x2), Lily Eustace, Alice Rogers
03.03	Redditch United (h)	W	2-0	Georgia Harris, Erin Smith
10.03	Coventry Sphinx (h)	W	6-0	Samantha Berry (x3), Georgia Harris, Sofi Liperis, Michelle McCormack
24.03	Coventry Sphinx (a)	W	7-0	Lily Eustace (x3), Michelle McCormack, Georgia Harris, Daisy-May Clements, Sofi Liperis
31.03	Sutton C Town (h)	D	0-0	
02.05	Goldenhill W (a)	W	1-0	Lily Eustace
19.05	Stockingford AA Pavilion (a)	W	7-0	Daisy-May Clements (x4), Georgia Kate Harris, Alice May Rogers (x2)

2018-19 FA CUP

02.09 RQ1	Shifnal Town (a)	W	7-0	Lily Eustace (x3), Alice Rogers (x2), McCormack (pen), Kerstin Ballard
23.09 RQ2	Lutterworth Athletic (h)	D	0-0aet (W4-2p)	
07.10 RQ3	West Brom Albion (h)	L	1-2	Samantha Berry

2018-19 WEST MIDLANDS REGIONAL PREMIER LEAGUE CUP

17.03 QF	Stockingford AA Pavilion (h)	W	3-1 aet	Samantha Berry, Daisy-May Clements, Lily Eustace
28.04 SF	Redditch United (h)	W	3-0	Georgia Harris, Erin Smith, Samantha Berry
05.05 F	Sutton Coldfield Town (n)	L	0-1	

(n)Played at Wellbeing Park, (Stone Dominoes FC)

2018-19 BIRMINGHAM FA COUNTY CUP

R1	Bye			
18.11 R2	Crusaders (h)	D	2-2 (W8-7p)	Lily Eustace, Sofi Liperis
16.12 R3	Bedworth United (h)	W	6-3	Samantha Berry (x3), Lily Eustace (pen), Georgia Harris, Amy Andrews
20.01 QF	Coventry United (a)	L	0-8	

"We had a fantastic 2018-19 season, securing promotion to the WNL. Having just missed out in 2017-2018, despite an unbeaten campaign, we were able to do it this time round and took the title with a game to spare. It was unfortunate that we didn't quite achieve the Double, narrowly losing 1-0 in the League Cup final. At junior level the club continues to go from strength to strength. The Under-16s were triumphant against the odds defeating Derby County 2-1 to lift the Open Cup. The Under-18s beat Leicester City 4-1 in the semi-finals of the Open Cup but fell short in the final against Derby County. In 2019-20 the first team squad will be looking to establish themselves quickly in Tier 4 and to build upon their recent success."

Dan Hearnden – Chairman

LEEDS UNITED

2019-20: WNL NORTH 1 (Tier 4)

Founded: 1989

Nickname: United

Season 2018-19

WNL North 1 (Tier 4): 6th

FA Cup: 3rd Round

WNL Cup: 3rd Round

County Cup: Semi-finals

Initially formed as Leeds United Ladies in 1989, they had intermittent funding from the men's club until 2013-14 when that support was withdrawn. At that point they became known as Leeds Ladies, but in June 2017 they re-established their association with Leeds United FC, an agreement which means they now currently have the Leeds United name again. They train at the men's Thorp Arch training ground which also became their main venue for home games in 2018-19. Former England forward Sue Smith, who won 93 caps for her country, is the best-known player ever to represent the club. She played for Leeds from 2002 to 2010 in an era when they reached the FA Cup final in 2006 and 2008 only to lose on each occasion to overwhelming favourites Arsenal. Ahead of 2019-20 they changed their name from Leeds United Ladies to Leeds United Women.

2018-19 AS IT HAPPENS

02.12.18: Leeds captain Bridie Hanson is stretchered off with a serious looking injury during the closing minutes of extra-time of a seven-goal FA Cup thriller at home to Doncaster Rovers Belles. Leeds win the match 4-3 but Hanson confirms the following day that she has broken her leg.

24.03.19: Emma Lee puts Leeds 1-0 up against Chorley but she, and the team, go on to have a difficult afternoon. Leeds trail 4-1 with two minutes to go when Lee has a penalty saved by Rachel Darbyshire. Leeds win another penalty in injury-time, but Lee's effort is again saved by Darbyshire. The match finishes 4-1.

31.03.19: A crowd of 980 turns up to watch Leeds play at Elland Road, home of Leeds men. Emma Lee scores the only goal of the game as United beat Morecambe to climb two places to 4th in the table.

2018-19 RESULTS: (HOME VENUE: THORP ARCH, (LEEDS UNITED ACADEMY) UNLESS STATED)

2018-19 WNL North 1					Att	Pos
19.08	Crewe Alexandra (h)	W	4-0	Abby Parkin (x2), Hannah Campbell, Rebecca Hunt	100	
26.08	Burnley (a)	D	1-1	Hannah Campbell 80	60	2
13.09	Norton & Stockton A (a)	W	3-0	Sophie Stamp 57, Hannah Campbell 75, 90+3	300	3
16.09	Bolton W (a)	L	0-4		65	7
04.10	Barnsley (a)		P-P			7
21.10	Chester-le-Street T (a)	W	2-1	Rebecca Hunt 16, Hannah Campbell 80	50	5
28.10	Liverpool Feds (a)	L	0-1		40	8
04.11	Morecambe (a)	W	4-1	Danielle Whitham 28, Emily Cassidy 45, Hannah Campbell 47, 81	35	6
20.11	Barnsley (a)	L	1-2	Hannah Campbell 89		8
25.11	Chorley (h)	W	3-0	Hannah Campbell 13, 69, Abby Parkin 44	100	5
13.01	Crewe Alexandra (a)	W	1-0	Rebecca Hunt 63	28	5
27.01	Newcastle United (h)	W	3-1	Emily Cassidy 11, Rebecca Hunt 67, Holly Findlay 79	180	4
03.02	Burnley (h)	L	0-1	Leeds United GK Georgia Wattam saved Sarah Greenhalgh pen 90	80	4
10.02	Chester-le-Street T (h)	L	1-3	Holly Findlay 10	70	5
13.02	Norton & Stockton A (h)	W	3-1	Rebecca Hunt 28, Holly Findlay 36, Catherine Hamill 44	40	4
24.02	Brighouse Town (a)	D	1-1	Emma Lee (pen) 38	70	5
10.03	Liverpool Feds (h)	L	1-2	Holly Findlay 15	60	5
13.03	Barnsley (h)	D	2-2	Bethanie Davies 59, Jemma White 90+1	60	5
24.03	Chorley (a)	L	1-4	Emma Lee 17, Emma Lee missed pen 88 (saved), Emma Lee missed pen 90+2 (saved)	105	6
31.03	Morecambe (h)*	W	1-0	Emma Lee 5	980	4
07.04	Bolton W (h)	D	0-0		100	6
14.04	Newcastle United (a)	W	1-0	Rebecca Hunt 59	131	5
05.05	Brighouse Town (h)	L	1-3	Rebecca Hunt 42	100	6

*Played at Elland Road, (Leeds United FC)

2018-19 FA CUP

23.09 R2	Alnwick Town Juniors (a)	W	3-2 aet	Rebecca Jeffels 26, Kitty Lindley (og) 85, Emma Lee 103	
07.10 RQ3	Boro Rangers (h)	W	8-0	Hannah Campbell 3, 39, Rebecca Hunt 9, Oda Sperra Tenffjord 13, Katie Thompson 22, Bethanie Davies 26, Sophie Stamp 64, Shelbey Morris 85	100
11.11 R1	Brighouse Town (h)**	W	1-0	Hannah Campbell 83	150
02.12 R2	Doncaster R B (h)	W	4-3 aet	Rebecca Hunt (pen) 26, 30, Hannah Campbell 36, Katie Thompson 102	200
06.01 R3	Huddersfield Town (a)	L	1-4	Katie Thompson 30	156

**Played at Garforth Town FC

2018-19 WNL CUP

02.09 DR	Sporting Khalsa (a)	W	2-1	Hannah Smith 40, Hannah Campbell 90+5	30
R1	Bye				
14.10 R2	Brighouse Town (a)	W	2-1	Sophie Stamp 36, Hannah Campbell 67	
09.12 R3	Stoke City (a)	L	3-6	Katie Thompson 5, Bethanie Davies 67, 74	115

2018-19 West Riding FA County Cup

18.11 R2	Tingley Athletic (a)	W	7-0	Holly Findlay 25, Rebecca Hunt 30, 90+4, Bethanie Davies 31, Hannah Campbell 82, 89, 90+3	
16.12 R3	Yorkshire Amateur (h)	W	8-2	Emily Cassidy 3, Shelbey Morris 38, Katie Thompson 41, 44, 75, Bethanie Davies 56, 66, Faye Boshell 88	80
20.01 QF	Brighouse Athletic (a)	W	3-0	Emily Cassidy 15, Rebecca Hunt 55, Holly Findlay 65	
11.04 SF	Guiseley Vixens (h)*	L	0-1		120

*Played at Woodlesford, (West Riding FA HQ)

"The 2018-19 season was about achieving stability, which we did. Our highlights included good FA Cup and County Cup runs. In both competitions we came up against opponents from the division above, beating Doncaster Rovers Belles in the FA Cup and only suffering a narrow defeat to Guiseley Vixens in the semi-finals of the County Cup. The 2019-20 campaign will be about pushing forward again to try and finish as high as possible in the League. We're excited about our name change from Leeds United Ladies to Leeds United Women and everything is in place off the field for the club to move forward. Leeds United FC are getting more involved behind the scenes and providing top class facilities for us to succeed. Much of our progress can be put down to the work of our dedicated general manager Julie Lewis who used to play for the club and has also worked for the FA."

Dan O'Hearne – Head Coach

LEICESTER UNITED

(formerly Leicester City Women Development)
2019-20: WNL MIDLANDS 1 (Tier 4)

Founded: 2015 (as Leicester City Women Development)

Nickname: United

Season 2018-19:

Competed as Leicester City Women Development

East Midlands Reg Prem (Tier 5): 1st (P)

FA Cup: 1st Round

League Cup: Winners

County Cup: Runners-up

The 2019-20 season is the first in which the team will compete under the name of Leicester United. They are now a separate entity entirely from the current Championship side Leicester City Women. It was in 2015 that Leicester City Women set up a third team alongside their first XI and reserves XI and named them Leicester City Women Development. The team started life in the Leicestershire Women's Senior League and enjoyed huge success on the pitch with back-to-back promotions. In 2017 the FA informed Leicester City Women – who were then in what is now the WNL Northern Premier – that the Development side would not be allowed promotion into the WNL. The decision was made that rather than fold the club they would become a separate entity. In 2018-19 they won promotion to WNL Midlands 1 (Tier 4) as East Midlands Regional League Premier champions.

2018-19 AS IT HAPPENS
(COMPETED AS LEICESTER CITY WOMEN DEVELOPMENT)

11.11.18: The FA Cup run comes to an end despite a brave performance away to Tier 4 high-fliers West Bromwich Albion who edge through to the 2nd Round as 2-1 winners.

03.02.19: After starting the season with 10 consecutive League victories, Leicester City Women Development drop points for the first time as they are beaten 3-1 by Mansfield Town.

17.02.19: A penalty shootout defeat to Loughborough Students sees Leicester City Women Development exit the County Cup at the semi-final stage, however the result is later overturned when it is ruled that Loughborough fielded an ineligible player.

19.05.19: Having already been crowned East Midlands Regional Premier League champions, Leicester City Women Development lift their second trophy of the season with a 7-1 win over Woodlands in the League Cup final.

24.05.19: The Leicestershire & Rutland FA County Cup final against Oadby & Wigston ends in a 1-1 draw and goes straight to penalties. Leicester City Women Development lose the shootout 4-3.

2018-19 RESULTS: (HOME VENUE: RIVERSIDE PAVILION, UNLESS STATED)

2018-19 EAST MIDLANDS REGIONAL PREMIER: COMPETED AS LEICESTER CITY WOMEN DEVELOPMENT

05.09	Leicester City Ladies (a)	W	3-0	Chantelle Amber (x2), Angel Craig-Tapper
09.09	Mansfield Town (a)	W	2-0	Chantelle Amber (x2)
12.09	Peterborough Utd (a)	W	3-2	Shanae Thomas, Chantelle Amber, Angel Craig-Tapper
16.09	Woodlands (h)	W	7-0	Angel Craig-Tapper, Natalie Hurst, Sian Johnson (x2), Lucie Mugridge, Chantelle Amber (x2)
14.10	Eastwood Community (a)	W	5-1	Katie Cropper, Chantelle Amber (x2), Courtney Cropper, Laura Allcock (og)
04.11	Ollerton Town (h)	W	6-2	Megan Kenney, Lucie Mugridge, Chantelle Amber, Courtney Cropper (x3)
18.11	Leicester City Ladies (h)	W	5-0	Katie Cropper, Megan Kenney (x2), Shanae Thomas, Courtney Cropper
02.12	Ride Park (h)	W	6-1	Lauren Bartle, Natalie Hurst, Chantelle Amber (x2), Courtney Cropper, Katie Cropper
16.12	Woodlands (a)	W	4-1	Megan Kenney, Natalie Hurst (x2), Lauren Bartle
13.01	Rise Park (a)	W	2-0	Courtney Cropper (x2)
03.02	Mansfield Town (h)	L	1-3	Natalie Hurst
10.02	Eastwood Community (h)	D	3-3	Jade Benford (x2), Lucie Mugridge
17.03	Ollerton Town (a)	W	4-2	Courteney Cropper (x2), Katie Cropper, Chantelle Robinson
24.03	Peterborough Utd (h)	W	8-0	Natalie Hurst (x2), Jade Benford, Megan Kenney, Chantelle Amber, Courtney Cropper, Sian Johnson (x2)
07.04	Kettering Town (h)	W	4-1	Katie Cropper, Natalie Hurst, Megan Kenney, Courtney Cropper
16.04	Loughborough Students (h)	W	6-3	Jade Benford, Chyna McIntosh, Chantelle Amber (x3), Courtney Cropper
21.04	Loughborough Students (a)	W	10-1	Jade Benford (x2), Katie Cropper (x2), Natalie Hurst, Chyna McIntosh, Chantelle Amber (x3), Courtney Cropper

28.04	Oughtibridge War Mem.(a)	L	1-5	Katie Cropper
07.05	Kettering Town (a)	W	5-4	Jade Benford (x2), Angel Craig-Tapper, Natalie Hurst (x2)
12.05	Oughtibridge War Mem. (h)	D	3-3	Lauren Bartle, Jade Benford, Megan Kenney

2018-19 FA CUP: COMPETED AS LEICESTER CITY WOMEN DEVELOPMENT

02.09 RQ1	Coalville Town Ravenettes (h)	W	15-0	Shanae Thomas, Megan Kenney (x2), Olivia Parrin, Lauren Bartle, Alana Cunningham, Chantelle Robinson (x4), Courtney Cropper (x4), Lucie Mugridge
23.09 RQ2	Solihull United (h)	W	6-3	Jade Benford, Chantelle Robinson, Natalie Hurst, Megan Kenney, Shane Thomas (x2)
07.10 RQ3	Oadby & Wigston (h)	W	2-1	Shanae Thomas (x2)
11.11 R1	West Brom Albion (a)	L	1-2	Chantelle Robinson

2018-19 EAST MIDLANDS REGIONAL PREMIER LEAGUE, LEAGUE CUP: COMPETED AS LEICESTER CITY WD

30.09 R1	Retford United (a)	W	17-0	Molly Boultbee, Angel Craig-Tapper (x3), Katie Cropper (x2), Natalie Hurst (x4), Lucie Mugridge (x2), Chantelle Amber (x5)
25.11 R2	Northampton Town (h)	W	1-0	Natalie Hurst
24.02 QF	Loughborough Students (h)	W	6-1	Jade Benford, Chantelle Robinson (x2), Courtney Cropper, Sinead Samarczuk, Natalie Hurst
31.03 SF	Oughtibridge War Memorial (a)	W	2-1aet	Lauren Bartle, Angel Craig-Tapper
19.05 F	Woodlands (n)	W	7-1	Jade Benford (x3), Courtney Cropper, Natalie Hurst, Georgia Gibson, Megan Kenney

(n)Played at Eagle Valley, (Arnold Town FC)

2018-19 LEICESTERSHIRE & RUTLAND FA COUNTY CUP: COMPETED AS LEICESTER CITY WOMEN DEV

20.01 QF	Loughborough Foxes Dev. (a)	W	4-2	Lauren Bartle (x3), Chantelle Robinson
17.02 SF	Loughborough Students (h)	D	2-2 (L3-4p)*	Lauren Bartle, Chantelle Robinson
24.05 F	Oadby & Wigston (n)	D	1-1(L3-4p)	Lauren Bartle

*Void result later overturned and Leicester City Women Development awarded a place in the final when it is ruled that Loughborough Students fielded an ineligible player. (n)Played at Holmes Park, (Leicestershire & Rutland FA HQ)

"The 2018-19 season was a hugely successful one for us. We managed to win the East Midlands Premier Division and gain promotion to the WNL. It is our third promotion in four years. We also managed to win the League Cup and reach the Leicestershire County Cup Final. We had another good run in the FA Cup, making it to the 1st Round where we got knocked out by a very strong West Brom team. We scored 151 goals in all competitions throughout 2018-19 and conceded only 49. In 2019-20 we hope to establish ourselves in Tier 4 and aim for a mid to top table finish, along with good FA Cup, County Cup and League Cup runs."

Natalie Hurst – Secretary

LEYTON ORIENT

2019-20: WNL SOUTH EAST 1 (Tier 4)

Founded: 2004 (as KIKK United)

Nickname: The O's

Season 2018-19:

WNL South East 1 (Tier 4): 5th

FA Cup: 2nd Qualifying Round

WNL Cup: 2nd Round

Capital Cup: Runners-up

The club began life as KIKK United in 2004, founded by a group of Swedish women who took the name from the Swedish expression Kick In Kulan I Krysset, which means 'scoring in the top corner'. KIKK United became officially affiliated with Leyton Orient men in the summer of 2015. They took the club's name and played their first League match as Leyton Orient Women on 23 August that year, beating Fulham 1-0. The O's won the London South East Regional Premier League title in 2016-17 to secure promotion to Tier 4. In 2018-19 – a season throughout which they played with Kick It Out logos on their shirts in honour of the anti-racism group's 25th anniversary – they finished 5th and won the Isthmian Cup. The 2019-20 season is the O's third consecutive season in Tier 4.

2018-19 AS IT HAPPENS

21.10.18: Lisa Fulgence scores a hat-trick as they beat AFC Phoenix 5-1 in the Capital Cup 1st Round.

06.01.19: After a run of six League games without defeat (W3 D3) Orient are beaten in a five-goal thriller as they go down 3-2 at home to Stevenage.

17.02.19: Goalkeeper Naomi Ogunde is the hero as the O's beat Tier 3 QPR 4-3 on penalties after a 1-1 draw to reach the final of the Capital Cup. Rangers' second spot-kick by Anya Kinnane is saved by Ogunde and when Sue Kumaning hits their final effort against the post the O's victory is confirmed.

17.04.19: The O's win the Isthmian Cup with a 2-0 victory over lower division Ashford Town (Middlesex). Hayley Barton gives them the lead in the 38th minute with Leyre Bastyr getting the second after the break.

02.05.19: Orient narrowly miss out on a Cup double for the season as they are beaten 1-0 in the Capital Cup final by WNL South East 1 rivals Actonians.

2018-19 RESULTS: (HOME VENUE: MILE END STADIUM, UNLESS STATED)

2018-19 WNL SE 1					Att	Pos
19.08	Luton Town (a)	W	1-0	Chanel Richards 81	33	
26.08	Cambridge Utd (h)	L	0-3		68	8
09.09	Stevenage (a)	W	2-0	Lisa Fulgence 11, 73	20	3
12.09	Billericay Town (h)	L	1-3	Lisa Fulgence 9	68	4
16.09	Denham United (a)	D	1-1	Rebecca Hirst 89	65	5
03.10	AFC Wimbledon (h)	D	2-2	Hayley Barton 47, Lisa Holmback 67	49	6
07.10	Actonians (h)	W	3-2	Hayley Barton 20, 85, Tara O'Halloran 90	48	4
04.11	Ipswich Town (h)	D	2-2	Egle Trizzi 81, Hayley Barton 90	62	6
11.11	Enfield Town (h)	W	5-0	Robin Reardon (og) 12, Tara O'Halloran 37, Hayley Barton 41, Chanel Richards 47, 61	57	5
25.11	Norwich City (a)	W	1-0	Sophie Le Marchand 74	58	4
06.01	Stevenage (h)	L	2-3	Chanel Richards 9, Hayley Barton 50	56	4
13.01	Luton Town (h)	W	3-0	Grace Stewart (og) 21, Chloe McNee 45+1, Camila Pescatore 65	59	3
20.01	Cambridge United (a)		P-P			4
27.01	Crawley Wasps (a)	L	1-4	Lisa Holmback 59	65	4
10.02	Denham United (h)	L	0-2		44	5
13.02	Billericay Town (a)	L	1-2	Egle Trezzi 64		5
24.02	Cambridge United (a)	W	2-1	Sophie Le Marchand 45, Suaila Cardoso Queni 68		4
03.03	Ipswich Town (a)	D	1-1	Sophie Le Marchand 73	40	4
10.03	Enfield Town (a)		P-P			4
13.03	AFC Wimbledon (a)	W	3-1	Hannah Porter 48, Lisa Holmback 69, Lisa Fulgence 89	50	3
17.03	Enfield Town (a)		P-P			3
24.03	Norwich City (h)*	W	4-1	Alice Parker (og) 26, Suaila Cardoso Queni 30, Hayley Barton 40, 46	188	3
07.04	Enfield Town (a)	L	0-4		63	4
14.04	Actonians (a)	D	3-3	Danielle Griffiths (pen) 5, Valeria Moreno 55, Sophie Le Marchand 58	20	4
05.05	Crawley Wasps (h)+	L	1-2	Lisa Holmback 31		5

*Played at The Breyer Group Stadium, Brisbane Road, (Leyton Orient FC) +Played at St Paul's Sports Ground, (Fisher FC)

2018-19 FA Cup

23.09 RQ2	Cambridge City (a)	L	4-5	Lisa Holmback 8, Sophie Le Marchand 27, 70, Tara O'Halloran 58	

2018-19 WNL CUP

02.09 DR	Swindon Town (a)	W	5-1	Lisa Fulgence 5, 65, Hayley Barton 30, Danielle Griffiths (pen) 35, Sophie Le Marchand 70	43
R1	Bye				
14.10 R2	Cambridge United (a)		P-P		
28.10 R2	Cambridge United (a)	L	0-3		70

2018-19 CAPITAL CUP*

21.10 R1	AFC Phoenix (a)	W	5-2	Sophie le Marchand 7, Lisa Fulgence 20, 63, 77, Danielle Griffiths 24	20
18.11 QF	Haringey Borough (h)	W	5-2	Hayley Barton 22, 54, 58, Danielle Griffiths (pen) 52, Chanel Richards 64	51
17.02 SF	QPR (a)	D	1-1 (W4-3p)	Suaila Cardoso Queni 1	
02.05 F	Actonians (n)	L	0-1		

(n)Played at The Powerday Stadium, (Hanwell Town FC)

*The Capital Cup is the equivalent of a County Cup for teams in and around London. In 2018-19 it was run by the Surrey FA.

"The 2018-19 season was another successful one for us, confirming our place as one of the top teams in our division and winning the Isthmian Cup. It's a brilliant club to be part of, with the camaraderie between the players evident. Lots of us have played here for many years and helped the club progress to where it is now. It's a club with huge potential for further development and, as a player, it's a really exciting place to be. Our primary aim for 2019-20 is to win the League and gain promotion to the WNL Southern Premier. If we could combine that with some more successful Cup runs and silverware, then all the better."

Danielle Griffiths – Captain

LINCOLN CITY
(formerly Nettleham)
2019-20: WNL MIDLANDS 1 (Tier 4)

Founded: (Unknown, as Nettleham)

Nickname: The Imps

Season 2018-19 (competed as Nettleham):

WNL Midlands 1: 7th

FA Cup: 1st Round

WNL Cup: Determining Round

WNL Plate: 2nd Round

County Cup: Winners

The 2019-20 season is Lincoln City's first under that name, having competed as Nettleham until the end of 2018-19. Promoted to Tier 4 ahead of 2018-19 as East Midlands Regional Premier League champions, Nettleham acquitted themselves well in their first season at a higher level. Under the management of former Sheffield United men's player Richard Cooper, they finished the season in mid-table and won the Lincolnshire FA County Cup for the sixth year in a row. The City of Lincoln has previously hosted women's football. A club called Lincoln Ladies was formed in 1995 and became founding members of the WSL in 2011. They were rebranded as Notts County ahead of the 2014 season, with County then folding in 2017.

2018-19 AS IT HAPPENS (COMPETED AS NETTLEHAM)

23.09.18: Abi Ringrose has an eventful match as Nettleham beat Stockingford AA Pavilion 2-1 in the FA Cup 2nd Qualifying Round. She misses a penalty, but then gives her side the lead with a goal scored directly from a corner. Abi Farrow hits the winning goal with just two minutes left.

17.02.19: Abbie Murrell receives high praise for passing up the opportunity for a hat-trick when she deliberately misses a penalty that Nettleham believe they have been incorrectly awarded. The Nettleham players briefly discuss what to do and then Murrell simply passes the penalty to the goalkeeper. The team go on to win the Lincolnshire FA County Cup semi-final match against Grimsby Borough 5-0.

05.04.19: Nettleham Ladies announce they will be rebranded as Lincoln City Ladies from June 1st and become part of the Lincoln City FC men's family. Lincoln City men's currently play in League Two. The home ground for Lincoln City Ladies will be The Sun Hat Villas and Resorts Stadium which is home to non-League men's side Lincoln United.

07.04.19: Heather Pettit and Olivia Leslie both score their first goals for the club in a 3-0 League win over Burton Albion.

14.04.19: Nettleham win the Lincolnshire FA County Cup for the sixth year in a row as they beat lower division side Lincoln Moorlands Railway 3-0.

2018-19 RESULTS; (HOME VENUE: MULSANNE PARK, (NETTLEHAM FC) UNLESS STATED)

2018-19 WNL MIDLANDS 1				COMPETED AS NETTLEHAM	Att	Pos
19.08	The New Saints (h)	W	4-1	Katie Williams 8, Abigail Ringrose 29, Abigail Murrell 38, Elise Keyworth 45	50	
26.08	Bir'ham & W M (a)	L	1-2	Tia Johnson 22	22	4
09.09	Sporting Khalsa (a)	W	3-2	Tia Johnson 4, Abigail Ringrose 6, Ella Thompson-Moulding 10	30	4
12.09	Steel City W (h)	W	6-2	Tia Johnson 3, 44, Abigail Ringrose 12, 29, 82, Katie Thornley 38	100	3
16.09	Bedworth United (h)	L	2-3	Tia Johnson 28, Abigail Ringrose (pen) 84	50	4
30.09	Wolverhampton W (a)	L	0-3		40	4
03.10	Long Eaton United (h)	L	1-2	Lucy Farrow 38	100	5
28.10	Solihull Moors (a)	W	2-1	Ella Thompson-Moulding 48, Daisy Marsh 50	40	5
04.11	West Brom Albion (h)	L	1-2	Daisy Marsh 62	70	5
25.11	Burton Albion (a)	W	3-2	Katie Thornley (pen) 3, Ella Thompson-Moulding 25, Abigail Murrell 58	64	5
09.12	Bir'ham & W M (h)	L	0-4		50	5
13.01	The New Saints (a)	W	1-0	Katie Thornley 48	31	5
03.02	Sporting Khalsa (h)		P-P			5
10.02	Sporting Khalsa (h)		P-P			6
12.02	Steel City W (a)	W	2-0	Abigail Ringrose 61, Imogen Burnley 80	70	5
24.02	Bedworth United (a)	L	1-2	Abigail Murrell 79	40	6
03.03	Sporting Khalsa (h)	L	2-3	Abigail Murrell 63, 64	50	7
10.03	Wolverhampton W (h)		P-P			7
13.03	Long Eaton United (a)		P-P			7
24.03	Solihull Moors (h)	W	5-1	Own Goal 11, Abigail Murrell 14, 81, Tia Johnson 35, Lucy Farrow 49	50	7

31.03	West Brom Albion (a)	L	1-7	Abigail Murrell 60, Abigail Murrell missed pen 85	48	7
07.04	Burton Albion (h)	W	3-0	Ella Thompson-Moulding 32, Heather Pettit 57, Olivia Leslie 81	50	6
09.04	Long Eaton United (a)	D	0-0		40	6
28.04	Wolverhampton W (h)	L	0-6		100	6

2018-19 FA CUP: COMPETED AS NETTLEHAM

23.09 RQ2	Stockingford AA Pavilion (a)	W	2-1	*Abigail Ringrose missed pen*, Abigail Ringrose 39, Lucy Farrow 88	
07.10 RQ3	Histon (h)	W	9-0	Own Goal 18, Lucy Farrow 19, 55, Katie Thornley 27, Ella Thompson-Moulding 32, 35, Abigail Ringrose 38, Holly Newman 58, Holly Wilson 87	30est
11.11 R1	Long Eaton United (h)	L	2-3	Abigail Murrell 32, 48	30est

2018-19 WNL CUP: COMPETED AS NETTLEHAM

02.09 DR	Bir'ham & W M (h)	L	1-2	Abigail Murrell 77	60

2018-19 WNL PLATE: COMPETED AS NETTLEHAM

R1	Bye		
14.10 R2	West Brom Albion (a)	L	0-5

2018-19 LINCOLNSHIRE FA COUNTY CUP: COMPETED AS NETTLEHAM

R1	Bye				
20.01 QF	Boston United (a)	W	4-1	Abigail Murrell 14, 33, Lucy Farrow 36, 42	40est
17.02 SF	Grimsby Borough (h)	W	5-0	Laura Saxby (og) 15, Abigail 46, 61, Holly Wilson 63, 69, Abigail Murrell missed pen	100est
14.04 F	Lincoln Moorlands Railway (n)	W	3-0	Olivia Leslie 18, Tia Johnson 47, Abigail Murrell (pen) 65	250est

(n) Played at Ashby Avenue, Lincoln United FC

"We have progressed as a club with a nucleus of home-grown players who have developed their talent in the Lincoln area. Following promotion at the end of 2017-18, our first season in the WNL provided a pleasing mid-table finish. We are also hugely proud of having defended the County Cup and having now won that trophy for six years in a row. We are a community-minded club that is always looking to help expand female football in Lincolnshire and are looking forward to a bright future as Lincoln City."

Richard Cooper – Manager

LIVERPOOL FEDS

2019-20: WNL NORTH 1 (Tier 4)

Founded: 1991

Nickname: Feds

Season 2018-19:

WNL North 1 (Tier 4): 5th

FA Cup: 2nd Qualifying Round

WNL Cup: Determining Round

WNL Plate: Runners-up

County Cup: Winners

Formed at the Liverpool Institute of Higher Education (now known as Liverpool Hope University) in 1991, where the sports teams competed as a Federation of the St Katherine's and Christ Notre Dame Colleges, hence the 'Feds' part of the name. A link-up with men's club Marshalls FC ahead of 2015-16 saw the team become known as Liverpool Marshall Feds. Under that name they won their first ever trophy in 2017-18 when Sasha Rowe's penalty with seven minutes left secured a 1-0 victory over Mossley Hill Athletic in the Liverpool FA County Cup final. In summer 2018 they broke away from Marshalls and dropped that part of the name. The 2018-19 season brought another County Cup triumph and a run to the WNL Plate final where they were beaten by a strong West Brom team.

2018-19 AS IT HAPPENS

15.10.18: Leanne Duffy and Colin Lewis are named joint first-team managers and heads of adult football.

05.11.18: Feds announce Heron Eccles Hub will be their main home ground for the remainder of 2018-19, but on 6 January they move again to Jericho Lane.

24.03.19: Molly Farley scores her first goal for Liverpool Feds in the 89th minute of an away match at Bolton. Her effort levels the scores at 2-2, with Feds having trailed 2-0 until the 73rd minute when Laura Bartup bought them back into the game. It got even better for Feds when Jennifer Rogers scored in the fourth minute of injury-time to seal a 3-2 win.

04.04.19: The FA confirms MK Dons have been stripped of their place in the WNL Plate final due to fielding an ineligible player in the semi-final against Liverpool Feds. Feds will take their place in the final against WNL Midlands 1 (Tier 4) leaders West Brom on 14 April.

14.04.19: Feds are beaten 5-1 by West Brom in the WNL Plate final which is played at the home of Rugby Town.

01.05.19: Feds defend the Liverpool FA County Cup (which they won for the first time last year) with a 4-1 win over North West Regional Premier League (Tier 5) side Merseyrail in the final.

05.05.19: Feds host second-to-bottom Morecambe on the final day of the season. They twice come from behind to head into half-time at 2-2, and then go on to rack up their biggest win of the season in the second half. Emily Douglas scores five, Laura Bartup claims a hat-trick and Jennifer Rogers hits two in a 10-2 victory.

2018-19 RESULTS: (MAIN VENUE: SOUTH LIVERPOOL FOOTBALL HUB, JERICHO LANE UNLESS STATED)

2018-19 WNL N1					Att	Pos
19.08	Brighouse Town (a)	W	2-0	Rosie Kinvig 17, Lynsey Longhurst 51	40	
26.08	Norton & Stockton A (a)	L	2-4	Rosie Kinvig 17, Jennifer Rogers 33	100	8
09.09	Burnley (h)*	L	0-3		40	10
12.09	Crewe Alexandra (a)	W	5-3	Laura Bartup 6, 74, Abby Pope 18, Jennifer Rogers 39, 50	48	6
16.09	Barnsley (h)	L	4-5	Chantelle Thompson (pen) 16, Amy Seagraves 62, Laura Bartup 70, 90+3	40	8
03.10	Chorley (a)	D	1-1	Emily Douglas 85	95	9
07.10	Morecambe (a)	D	3-3	Jodie Mortimer 22, Nicola James 27, Amy Seagraves 31	30	7
21.10	Newcastle United (h)	L	1-2	Laura Bartup 39	40	8
28.10	Leeds United (h)**	W	1-0	Emily Douglas 83	40	7
04.11	Bolton W (h)	W	5-0	Amy Seagraves 2, Jennifer Rogers 4, 83, Demi Devereaux 6, Carla Lee 80	50	5
25.11	Chester-le-Street T (a)	D	1-1	Emily Douglas 65	40	7
06.01	Norton & Stockton A (h)	W	3-2	Emily Douglas 4, 54, Jodie Mortimer 56	30	5
13.01	Brighouse Town (h)	D	2-2	*Caroline Charlton sent off 30,* Carla Lee 68, Demi Devereaux 74	50	6
27.01	Burnley (a)	L	0-2		70	7
17.02	Barnsley (a)	L	1-2	Carla Lee 39	100	7
21.02	Crewe Alexandra (h)	W	5-0	Jennifer Rogers 15, 43, Emily Douglas 60, Carla Lee 65, Jodie Mortimer 80	75	6
10.03	Leeds United (a)	W	2-1	Jennifer Rogers 25, Demi Devereaux 54	60	6
14.03	Chorley (h)	L	1-2	Chantelle Thompson 8	50	6
24.03	Bolton W (a)	W	3-2	Laura Bartup 73, Molly Farley 89, Jennifer Rogers 90+4		4
07.04	Newcastle United (a)	W	3-0	Rosie Kinvig 34, Nicola James 80, Amy Seagraves 85	80	4
28.04	Chester-le-Street T (h)	D	2-2	Jodie Mortimer 6, Emily Douglas 74	40	6
05.05	Morecambe (h)	W	10-2	Emily Douglas 23, 46, 57, 78, 90+2, Laura Bartup 36, 51, 71, Jennifer Rogers 52, 87	50	5

*Played at St John Bosco Arts College **Played at the Heron Eccles Football Hub

2018-19 FA Cup

23.09 RQ2	Burnley (a)	L	2-3	Laura Bartup 20, 47	60

2018-19 WNL Cup

02.09 DR	Blackburn R (a)	D	3-3aet (L 4-5p)	Jennifer Rogers 3, 23, Demi Devereaux 59, *Jennifer Rogers missed pen 65*	97

2018-19 WNL Plate

R1	Bye				
14.10 R2	Crewe Alexandra (h)+	W	2-0	Jennifer Rogers 72, Demi Devereaux 80	70
09.12 R3	Chester-le-Street T (h)	W	1-0	Demi Deveraux 3	20
10.02 QF	Middlesbrough (h)	W	2-0	Jodie Mortimer 30, Carla Lee 35	50
03.03 SF	MK Dons (a)	L	3-4 aet	Jodie Mortimer 9, Demi Devereaux 64, 99 *Result overturned on 04.04 due to MK Dons fielding ineligible player*	
14.04 F	West Brom A (n)	L	1-5	Molly Farley 18	342

+Played at Jeffrey Humble Hub (n)Played at Butlin Road, Rugby Town FC

2018-19 Liverpool FA County Cup

QF	Bye				
20.01 SF	Mossley Hill A (h)	W	5-0	Carla Lee 2, 80, Emily Douglas 22, Demi Devereaux 42, Jennifer Rogers 61	50
01.05 F	Merseyrail (n)	W	4-1	Emily Douglas (pen) 15, Jodie Mortimer 70, Molly Farley 74, Jennifer Rogers 90	

(n)Played at Walton Hall Park

"I am unbelievably proud of the team. We had to deal with a lot of upheaval throughout 2018-19 with several new players and a change of management half-way through the season. We really came together after that. To reach the final of the WNL Plate and to win the County Cup again are both huge achievements and I truly believe we will be title contenders in 2019-20."

Chantelle Thompson – Captain

LONG EATON UNITED

2019-20: WNL MIDLANDS 1 (Tier 4)

Founded: Circa 1996

Nickname: The Blues

Season 2018-19

WNL Midlands 1 (Tier 4): 6th

FA Cup: 2nd Round

WNL Cup: Determining Round

WNL Plate: 2nd Round

County Cup: Runners-up

Long Eaton United have been a Tier 4 club since the start of the 2016-17 season. They were promoted to this level for the first time in their history after winning the 2015-16 East Midlands Regional Premier League title with three games to spare. Their highest finish to date has been 6th place, achieved in 2017-18 and again in 2018-19. With 30 goals in 28 appearances in all competitions Jade Arber finished as the second highest scorer from WNL Midlands 1 in 2018-19.

2018-19 AS IT HAPPENS

09.09.18: After starting the season with two straight League defeats, United pick up their first three points of the campaign with a 3-2 victory away to Solihull Moors.

06.03.19: Long Eaton confirm the signing of former Derby County player Kate Wright.

24.03.19: Long Eaton lead 3-0 away to Bedworth with an hour played but then capitulate as their hosts pull back to 3-3 with just 13 minutes remaining. However, one minute later Jade Arber completes her hat-trick for Long Eaton who go on to win 4-3.

14.04.19: Long Eaton finish as Derbyshire FA County Cup runners-up after losing 4-0 in the final to Derby County's development team.

2018-19 RESULTS: (HOME VENUE: GRANGE PARK, (LONG EATON UNITED FC) UNLESS STATED)

2018-19 WNL MIDLANDS 1

Date	Opponent	Res	Score	Scorers	Att	Pos
19.08	Sporting Khalsa (a)	L	2-3	Jade Arber, Amy Pashley (pen)	30	
26.08	West Brom Albion (h)	L	1-4	Millie Fugler	42	8
09.09	Solihull Moors (a)	W	3-2	Jade Arber (x2), Amy Pashley	20	7
12.09	Burton Albion (h)	W	3-0	Ashleigh Evans 27, 64, Jade Arber 89	50	6
30.09	Bir'ham & W M (h)	L	1-4	Own Goal	30	7
03.10	Nettleham (a)	W	2-1	Laura Sears, Jade Arber	100	6
21.10	Bedworth United (h)	W	2-1	Millie Fugler, Laura Sears	60	5
04.11	The New Saints (a)	L	3-4	Ashleigh Evans, Jade Arber (x2)	21	6
09.12	Wolverhampton W (a)	L	0-7		40	7
06.01	Steel City W (h)	W	8-0	Jade Arber 5, 21, 37, 81, Ashleigh Evans 42, 63, Amy Pashley 62, Hannah Barber 83	40	5
13.01	Sporting Khalsa (h)	L	1-2	Ashleigh Evans		6
03.02	Solihull Moors (h)		P-P			6
10.02	Solihull Moors (h)	W	4-1	Laura Sears 19, Viktoria Adam 28, Jade Arber 62, 77	32	5
24.02	West Brom Albion (a)	L	1-2	Amy Pashley (pen) 90	58	7
03.03	Burton Albion (a)	W	4-0	Amy Pashley (pen) 21, 36, Laura Sears 57, Shannon Parkes 90	33	6
10.03	Bir'ham & W M (a)	D	2-2	Jade Arber 21, 82	43	6
13.03	Nettleham (h)		P-P			6
17.03	Wolverhampton W (h)	L	0-1		40	6
24.03	Bedworth United (a)	W	4-3	Jade Arber 4, 45, 78, Ashleigh Evans 33	40	6
31.03	The New Saints (h)	L	3-4	Hannah Barber 7, Jade Arber 81, Amy Pashley 90	32	6
09.04	Nettleham (h)	D	0-0		40	7
05.05	Steel City W (a)	W	4-0	Jade Arber, Laura Sears, Kate Wright, Viktoria Adam	65	6

2018-19 FA CUP

Date	Opponent	Res	Score	Scorers	Att
23.09 RQ2	The New Saints (h)	W	7-1	Jade Arber 5, 60, Ashleigh Evans 8, 28, Amy Pashley 33, Lucie Johnstone 67, Nicola Smyth 78	
07.10 RQ3	Sporting Khalsa (a)	W	6-1	Amy Pashley (x4), Kim Harford, Ashleigh Evans	30
11.11 R1	Nettleham (a)	W	3-2	Eden Pedersen (og) 46, Jade Arber 86, 90+2	30
02.12 R2	Hull City (h)	L	0-5		60

2018-19 WNL CUP

Date	Opponent	Res	Score	Scorers	Att
02.09 DR	Norton & Stockton Ancients (h)	L	3-4	Jade Arber (x2), Nicola Hereford-Smyth	42

2018-19 WNL Plate

R1	Bye		
14.10 R2	Chester-le-Street T (h)	L	0-1aet

2018-19 Derbyshire FA County Cup

18.11 R1	Woodlands (a)	W	6-1	Ashleigh Evans 9, Laura Sears 14, 85, Jade Arber 16, 36, 38	
20.01 QF	Ilkeston Town (a)	W	7-0	Laura Sears 7, Amy Pashley 9, (pen) 42, (pen) 88, Hannah Barber 35, Ashleigh Evans 65, Kim Hereford-Smyth 68	
17.02 SF	Chesterfield (a)	W	4-0	Jade Arber 10, Laura Sears 17, 72, Amy Pashley 58	103
14.04 F	Derby County Development (n)	L	0-4		

(n) Neutral tie, but played at Grange Park, (Long Eaton United FC)

LOUGHBOROUGH FOXES

2019-20: WNL NORTHERN PREMIER (Tier 3)

Founded: 2006

Nickname: The Foxes

Season 2018-19:

WNL Southern Premier (Tier 3): 7th

FA Cup: 4th Round

WNL Cup: Semi-finals

County Cup: Quarter-finals

The club started out playing in Shepshed before being reformed and renamed as Loughborough Foxes in 1999 in memory of player Rachael Fox who died that year. At that point they only had a junior team, but a ladies first team was added in 2006. The first team have been promoted six times in their 13-year history. Most recently they came up to Tier 3 as 2017-18 WPL Midlands 1 champions. They went through that entire League campaign without losing a game and only dropped two points. Foxes acquitted themselves well in their first season in Tier 3 in 2018-19, finishing 7th. In summer 2019 they were transferred across to the WNL Northern Premier to facilitate a more even geographical spread.

2018-19 AS IT HAPPENS

19.08.18: Following their promotion as 2017-18 WPL Midlands 1 champions, Foxes begin life in Tier 3 with a 7-0 home win against QPR.

09.12.18: With just 28 minutes of their WNL Cup 3rd Round match away to Cardiff City Ladies remaining, Foxes trail 3-0. Rebecca Matlock then pulls one back before Shauna Chambers makes it 3-2 with 10 minutes to play. Laura Dexter equalises with a minute remaining, and Rebecca Knight hits the winner in extra-time as Foxes complete a stunning comeback to win 4-3.

08.12.18: There is devastating news for the club as Loughborough release a statement confirming that captain Molly Webb has died at the age of 25. Media reports say that she passed away days after first experiencing 'flu-like symptoms'.

20.01.19: New manager Issy Martin's first game in charge proves to be a dramatic affair. Loughborough take on Leicester City Women Reserves in the quarter-finals of the County Cup. Leicester go 3-2 up with just two minutes to play but Rebecca Knight equalises two minutes into injury-time to take the match to a penalty shootout only for Loughborough to lose 6-5 on spot-kicks.

2018-19 RESULTS: (HOME VENUE: THE STADIUM PITCH, (LOUGHBOROUGH UNIVERSITY) UNLESS STATED)

2018-19 WNL SP					Att	Pos
19.08	QPR (h)	W	7-0	Rebecca McGrother 3, 47, Stephanie Anes (og) 20, Shauna Chambers 22, Charlotte Cooper 33, 77, Kate Lowder 38,	75	
26.08	Watford (a)	W	3-1	Rebecca Knight 22, Kate Lowder 28, Charlotte Cooper 79	75	1
09.09	C&K Basildon (h)	D	1-1	Kate Lowder 26	47	2
12.09	Coventry United (a)	L	0-4		75	4
16.09	Cardiff City L (a)	L	1-3	Kate Lowder 31, *Rebecca McGrother missed pen 90+3*	100	6
23.09	Oxford United (a)	L	2-4	Kate Lowder 6, Own Goal 57	76	8
30.09	Chichester City (h)	L	0-1		27	8
28.10	MK Dons (h)	W	6-0	Shauna Chambers 32, Charlotte Cooper 41, Eva Rogers 54, Ria Acton 55, Laura Steele (pen) 58, Millie Chandarana 75	95	6
04.11	Plymouth Argyle (a)	W	4-0	Rebecca McGrother 53, 62, 84 Chloe Young 55	33	5
11.11	Portsmouth (h)	W	2-1	Rebecca Knight 25, Eilidh Currie (og) 74	35	4
18.11	Cardiff City L (h)	W	1-0	Rebecca Knight 13	30	4
25.11	Gillingham (a)	D	2-2	Chloe Young 32, Charlotte Broad 53	65	4
13.01	QPR (a)		P-P			4
27.01	C&K Basildon (a)	W	2-0	Charlotte Cooper 58, Chloe Young 83		3
14.02	Coventry United (h)	L	0-2		57	5
24.02	Watford (h)	L	1-2	Rebecca McGrother 14	67	6
10.03	Chichester City (a)	W	3-1	Rebecca Knight 34, Chloe Young (pen) 40, Laura Steele 75	80	6
13.03	MK Dons (a)	W	3-1	Rebecca McGrother 17, Kate McLoughlin 81, Laura Dexter 90+3		4
17.03	QPR (a)	D	2-2	Tiana Hicks 44, Eva Rogers 67	60	5
31.03	Portsmouth (a)	L	0-2		73	6
14.04	Plymouth Argyle (h)	L	2-4	Rebecca Knight 33, Charlotte Cooper 79	40	7
28.04	Gillingham (h)	W	5-0	Eva Rogers 7, Rebecca McGrother 11, Rebecca Knight 17, 56, Katie McLoughlin 68	33	7
05.05	Oxford United (h)	D	1-1	Rebecca McGrother 78	67	7

2018-19 FA CUP

02.12 R2	Gillingham (h)	W	3-1 (aet)	Charlotte Broad 17, *Laura Steele missed pen 72,* Rebecca Knight 94, 104	48
06.01 R3	Billericay Town (a)	W	4-3	Rebecca Knight 7, Rebecca McGrother 8, 35, Eva Rogers 68	160
03.02 R4	Sheffield Utd (h)		P-P		
10.02 R4	Sheffield Utd (h)	L	0-2		202

2018-19 WNL CUP

02.09 DR	Denham United (h)	W	4-0	Eva Rogers 25, Laura Dexter 47, Charlotte Cooper 73, Shauna Chambers 79	40
R1	Bye				
14.10 R2	QPR (a)	W	3-1	Laura Steele (pen) 52, Eva Rogers 85, Rebecca McGrother 90+5	
09.12 R3	Cardiff City L (a)	W	4-3 aet	Rebecca Matlock 62, Shauna Chambers 80, Laura Dexter 89, Rebecca Knight 92	115
17.02 QF	AFC Wimbledon (h)*	W	3-0	Charlotte Cooper 39, Rebecca McGrother 48, 90+2	86
03.03 SF	Blackburn R (a)	L	0-4		283

*Played at Nanpanton Sports Ground, (Loughborough Dynamos FC)

2018-19 LEICESTERSHIRE & RUTLAND FA COUNTY CUP

20.01 QF	Leicester City W Reserves (h)	D	3-3 (L5-6p)	Eva Rogers 12, Rebecca McGrother 80, Rebecca Knight 90+2	150

"At Loughborough Foxes we always say we want to create memorable performances that we can look back on and be proud of. We can certainly do that at the end of our first season in the WNL Southern Premier, having taken points off every team in the division except eventual champions Coventry United. We're extremely proud to have proven ourselves in a competitive league whilst also reaching the semi-finals of the WNL Cup and the 4th Round of the FA Cup. There is such a strong culture at Loughborough Foxes, where the desire to improve and achieve together as a unit is second to none. We've built some strong foundations at this level now and are looking forward to coming back even stronger in 2019-20."

Shauna Chambers – Captain

LUTON TOWN

2019-20: EASTERN REGIONAL PREMIER (Tier 5)

Founded: 1997

Nickname: The Lady Hatters

Season 2018-19

WNL South East 1 (Tier 4): 12th (R)

FA Cup: 2nd Round

WNL Cup: Determining Round

WNL Plate: 2nd Round

County Cup: Runners-up

The club became officially affiliated with Luton Town men's in 2000 three years after their formation. The Lady Hatters suffered a difficult 2018-19 campaign when they finished bottom of WNL South East 1 and were relegated to Tier 5. That setback came after four successful years in Tier 4 in which they were 4th in 2014-15 and 2015-16, then 5th in 2016-17 and 2017-18.

2018-19 AS IT HAPPENS

06.01.19: In the 9-0 County Cup win over Sharnbrook there are eight different scorers including youngsters Olivia Abraham and Maddison Goodenough who score their first goals for the club.

27.01.19: The Hatters play their opening game at their new home venue, having left Stockwood Park Athletics Stadium for The Brache – which is Luton Town FC men's training ground. They beat Kempton Town & Bedford College 7-0 in the Bedfordshire FA County Cup semi-final.

17.03.19: Luton are beaten 1-0 by Tier 5 side Bedford in the Bedfordshire FA County Cup final.

28.04.19: Luton lead 2-0 at half-time away to Ipswich but go on to lose 5-2. The result confirms their relegation from WNL South East 1.

2018-19 RESULTS: (HOME VENUE: STOCKWOOD PARK ATHLETICS STADIUM UNTIL 27 JAN, THEN THE BRACHE (LUTON TOWN FC TRAINING GROUND, UNLESS STATED)

2018-19 WNL SE 1					Att	Pos
19.08	Leyton Orient (h)	L	0-1		33	
26.08	AFC Wimbledon (h)	L	1-3	Rachel Carter	51	11
09.09	Actonians (a)	L	0-3		15	12
12.09	Enfield Town (h)		P-P			12
16.09	Billericay Town (a)	L	1-2	Dione Manning	102	12
30.09	Ipswich Town (h)	W	3-1	Dione Manning 12, 51 Jess McKay 84	43	12
03.10	Denham United (a)	D	0-0		50	10
28.10	Crawley Wasps (a)	L	0-6		60	12
30.10	Enfield Town (h)*	L	0-2		326	12
04.11	Cambridge United (a)	L	0-1		92	10
09.12	Norwich City (a)	L	1-4	Amy Summerfield 90	65	12
13.01	Leyton Orient (a)	L	0-3		59	12
03.02	Actonians (h)		P-P			12
20.02	Enfield Town (a)	D	0-0		78	12
24.02	AFC Wimbledon (a)	W	4-1	Zara Carroll 3, Dione Manning 14, Remi Bains 43, Jess McKay 88	30	12
03.03	Stevenage (h)	L	0-1		94	12
10.03	Ipswich Town (a)		P-P			12
12.03	Denham United (h)	D	1-1	Rachel Kosky 27	91	12
24.03	Crawley Wasps (h)	L	0-3		61	12
31.03	Cambridge United (h)	L	2-4	Nicola Henman 2, Remi Bains 78		12
07.04	Actonians (h)	L	0-3			12
14.04	Norwich City (h)	W	2-1	Rachel Kosky 24, Remi Bains 31		12
21.04	Billericay Town (h)	L	2-4	Remi Bains, Kimberley Newns		12
28.04	Ipswich Town (a)	L	2-5	Remi Bains 22, Jess McKay 25	60	12
05.05	Stevenage (a)	L	0-3		70	12

*Played at Kenilworth Road, (Luton Town FC)

2018-19 FA CUP					
23.09 RQ2	AFC Dunstable (h)	W	7-0	Aurora Ryan, Jess McKay (x2), Zara Carroll, Nicola Henman, Erica Byron (x2)	94
07.10 RQ3	Oxford City (h)	W	5-2	Aurora Ryan 5, Nicola Henman 27, Dione Manning 29, Erica Byron 88, 90	45
11.11 R1	Kent Football United (h)	D	1-1 aet (W 3-1 p)	Nicola Henman 76	
02.12 R2	Billericay Town (a)	L	1-3 aet	Aurora Ryan 57	70

2018-19 WNL CUP

02.09 DR	Cheltenham Town (h)	L	1-3	Nicola Henman

2018-19 WNL PLATE

R1	Bye			
14.10 R2	Gillingham (a)	L	4-5	Jess McKay 47, 67, Rachel Carter 52, Aurora Ryan 80

2018-19 BEDFORDSHIRE FA COUNTY CUP

06.01 QF	Sharnbrook (a)	W	9-0	Aurora Ryan 11, 33, Dionne Manning 40, Olivia Abraham 52, Zara Carroll 62, Maddison Goodenough 64, Rachel Kosky 74, Remi Baines 79, Jess McKay 81
20.01	Kempston Town & Bedford College (h)		P-P	
27.01 SF	Kempston Town & Bedford College (h)	W	7-0	Dionne Manning 39, Erica Byron 40, (pen) 69, Jess McKay 57, 71, 90, Zara Carroll 87
17.03 F	Bedford (n)	L	0-1	

(n)Played at Ampthill Park, (Ampthill Town FC)

"To say I am devastated for us to get relegated is an understatement. Eighteen years ago, I captained the first team to the level we are at now and to lose that National League status is devastating. I have been first team manager for five years and we've been a top 4/5 team until this season. Something went wrong this year along with multiple injuries, but we will come back fighting. This will hurt for a long time, but Luton is in my heart and blood. Thanks to all our fans, staff and sponsors. We will be back."

Nikki Baker – Manager (writing on twitter after club's relegation at end of 2018-19)

MAIDENHEAD UNITED

2019-20: WNL SOUTH WEST 1 (Tier 4)

Founded: 2013

Nickname: The Magpies

Season 2018-19:

WNL South West 1 (Tier 4): 10th

FA Cup: 2nd Qualifying Round

WNL Cup: Determining Round

WNL Plate: 3rd Round

County Cup: Semi-finals

The club's first ever match was a friendly against WSL 2 side Reading in the summer of 2013 with around 100 fans attending the fixture at York Road which is the home venue they share with Maidenhead United men. The stadium is recognised by FIFA and the FA as being the oldest ground continuously used by the same club, with Maidenhead men having played there since 1871. In 2017-18 Maidenhead United Ladies came close to Berks & Bucks FA County Cup glory but were beaten by newly crowned WPL South East 1 champions MK Dons in a final played at Stadium: mk. In 2018-19 the U's celebrated climbing off the bottom of the table on the last day of the season.

2018-19 AS IT HAPPENS

08.02.19: Jamie Barratt announces he is stepping down as manager.

18.02.19: George Marsh and Liam Vaughan are confirmed as the club's new joint managers. The pair move into the role from their position as coaches for Magpies in the Community which is Maidenhead United FC's Community Trust.

17.03.19: At the 13th attempt, Maidenhead United win a League game for the first time this season as they beat Southampton Saints 3-0. Their record to this point reads P12, W0, D1, L11. Maidenhead joke on twitter: "This is not a typo. We have finally won our first League game of the season. Fantastic effort from every player."

05.05.19: Maidenhead pull off a great escape as they move off the bottom of the table for the first time all season on the final day. A 1-0 win away to Southampton Saints sees them pick up three points for only the second time in 2018-19 and finish above Poole who lose 6-1 at Chesham United. *(NB: In the summer it is confirmed that Poole will also remain in the division for 2019-20).*

2018-19 RESULTS: (HOME VENUE: YORK ROAD, (MAIDENHEAD UNITED FC), UNLESS STATED)

2018-19 WNL SW 1					Att	Pos
26.08	Cheltenham Town (a)	L	1-5	Sophie Modak 34	68	
09.09	Brislington (h)	L	2-5	Abigail Canvin, Kirsty Matthews	23	11
12.09	Chesham United (a)	L	0-5			11
16.09	Larkhall Athletic (h)	L	0-3		18	11
03.10	Southampton W (a)	L	0-5		34	11
07.10	Swindon Town (h)	D	2-2	Alex Dover 3, Natalie Barnes 23, Maidenhead *GK Ellie Parker saved penalty*	29	11
28.10	Buckland Athletic (h)	L	1-8	Natalie Barnes 28	15	11
04.11	Keynsham Town (h)	L	2-5	Kirsty Matthews 27, Lucy Casey 39	10	11
02.12	Poole Town (a)	L	0-3		20	11
16.12	Southampton S (h)		P-P			11
13.01	Cheltenham Town (h)	L	0-3		20	11
27.01	Buckland Athletic (a)		P-P			11
13.02	Chesham United (h)*	L	0-2		20	11
24.02	Brislington (a)	L	1-3	Simone O'Brien	47	11
03.03	Larkhall Athletic (a)		P-P			11
10.03	Buckland Athletic (a)		P-P			11
13.03	Southampton W (h)		P-P			11
17.03	Southampton S (h)+	W	3-0	Tina Brett (x2), Aine McKeever	10	11
24.03	Swindon Town (a)	L	1-2	Lucy Casey (pen) 51	49	11
31.03	Keynsham Town (a)	L	0-11		60	11
14.04	Poole Town (h)	D	0-0		20	11
17.04	Southampton W (h)	L	0-3		15	11
21.04	Larkhall Athletic (a)	L	0-3		35	11
28.04	Buckland Athletic (a)	L	0-3		36	11
05.05	Southampton S (a)	W	1-0	Aine McKeever 17	14	10

*Played at Mill Meadow, (Chalfont St Peter FC) +Played at Winklebury Stadium, (Basingstoke Town FC)

2018-19 FA CUP

23.09 RQ2	Whyteleafe (a)	L	0-2		

2018-19 WNL CUP

02.09 DR	Billericay Town (a)	L	1-10	Alex Dover 30	100

2018-19 WNL PLATE

R1	Bye				
14.10 R2	Denham U (h)*	D	1-1 aet (W4-2p)	Aine McKeever 57	23
09.12 R3	Keynsham Town (a)	L	1-7	Natalie Barnes 20	40

*Home tie but played at Denham United's The Den because of waterlogged match

2018-19 BERKS & BUCKS FA COUNTY CUP

18.11 QF	Abingdon United (a)	D	3-3 aet (W3-2p)	Shylla Carty Duhaney 2, Lucy Casey 69, Simone O'Brien 75	50
17.02 SF	Chesham United (h)	L	0-1		37

"The 2018-19 season was very tough, but we had reason to celebrate on the final day when we got a crucial win against Southampton Saints to stay up. With a new management team having come in half-way through the season we know that we have plenty to build on in 2019-20. We have shown just what a special club this is because in the toughest of circumstances we are able to stand together and pull through."

Alex Dover – Player and Social Media Admin

MIDDLESBROUGH

2019-20: WNL NORTHERN PREMIER (Tier 3)

Founded: 1976 (as Cleveland Spartans)

Nickname: Boro

Season 2018-19:

WNL Northern Premier (Tier 3): 5th

FA Cup: 3rd Round

WNL Cup: Determining Round

WNL Plate: Quarter-finals

County Cup: n/a

In their early days as Cleveland Spartans the team was coached by Middlesbrough FC men's players Mark Proctor and David Hodgson. Middlesbrough Women's central midfielder Marrie Wieczorek took charge in the early 1990s and remained at the helm for 20 years. More recently Boro have made an impression on Tier 3 since their promotion ahead of the 2016-17 campaign. They went on to finish that season as runners-up behind champions Blackburn and then followed that up with a 3rd place finish in 2017-18 and 5th in 2018-19.

2018-19 AS IT HAPPENS

13.02.19: A crowd of 300 watches the Tees-Wear derby which turns into a six-goal thriller as Middlesbrough and Sunderland play out a 3-3 draw at Bedford Terrace.

24.02.19: Boro rack up their biggest win of the season as they beat strugglers Bradford City 8-1 with goals from Emily Scarr (x2), Holly Manders (x2), Emma Foster, Leonie Hutchinson, Tyler Dodds, and Eve Marshall.

24.03.19: Eleanor Dale misses Boro's 3-0 win at Fylde because she is away on international duty. She scores a brace for England Under-17s as they beat Hungary 3-0 in the UEFA Women's Under-17s Euro Elite Round.

14.04.19: Middlesbrough complete their campaign with a 3-0 home win over Hull City to stay 3rd in the table. (NB: By the time all the other fixtures are completed on 5th May, they have slipped to 5th).

2018-19 RESULTS: (HOME VENUE: BEDFORD TERRACE, (BILLINGHAM TOWN FC) UNLESS STATED)

2018-19 WNL NP					Att	Pos
19.08	Derby County (h)	L	0-3		240	
26.08	Sheffield FC (a)	W	3-2	Emma Foster 9, Rebekah Bass 49, Emily Scarr 54	74	8
09.09	Doncaster R B (a)	W	2-0	Sarah Cramer 31, Eleanor Dale 76		6
13.09	Sunderland (a)	L	1-3	Eleanor Dale 86	175	7
16.09	Huddersfield T (h)	W	3-2	Holly Manders 9, 87, Emily Scarr 47	163	5
30.09	Bradford City (a)	W	4-0	Eleanor Dale 19, Holly Manders 42, Emma Kelly 48, Eve Marshall 60	76	6
04.10	Guiseley Vixens (h)	D	1-1	Tyler Dodds 47	142	6
07.10	Blackburn R (h)	L	1-2	Anna Birtwhistle 55	94	7
04.11	Stoke City (a)	L	1-4	Emily Scarr 53	130	8
11.11	Fylde (h)	D	2-2	Tyler Dodds 50, Emma Kelly 69	146	8
18.11	Hull City (a)	W	3-1	Rebekah Bass 60, 73, Eve Marshall 80	40	7
25.11	Nottingham F (a)		P-P			7
16.12	Nottingham F (a)		P-P			7
13.01	Sheffield FC (h)	W	5-1	Emma Kelly (pen) 11, Leonie Hutchinson 39, Eleanor Dale 41, 49, Holly Manders 80	72	6
20.01	Doncaster R B (h)	W	6-1	Eve Marshall 36, 70, Tyler Dodds 56, 75, 81, Emily Scarr 87	54	5
27.01	Huddersfield T (a)	L	2-4	Tyler Dodds 1, Emily Scarr 89	76	6
03.02	Derby County (a)		P-P			6
13.02	Sunderland (h)	D	3-3	Holly Manders 9, 53, Emma Kelly 33	300	7
17.02	Blackburn Rovers (a)	L	0-5		178	7
24.02	Bradford City (h)	W	8-1	Emily Scarr 2, 56, Holly Manders 25, 54, Emma Foster 38, Leonie Hutchinson 55, Tyler Dodds 58, Eve Marshall 76	45	7
03.03	Nottingham F (a)	W	2-1	Leonie Hutchinson 56, Ellie Dobson 62		5
10.03	Stoke City (h)*	W	4-2	Eleanor Dale 42, 52, 72, Tyler Dodds 77	31	3
24.03	Fylde (a)	W	3-0	Emily Scarr 35, 60, Tyler Dodds 40	70	3
28.03	Guiseley Vixens (a)	D	0-0		40	3
31.03	Nottingham F (h)	W	3-1	Emily Scarr 39, 48, Tyler Dodds 69	54	3
07.04	Derby County (a)	L	0-2		203	3
14.04	Hull City (h)	W	3-0	Leonie Hutchinson 14, Tyler Dodds 44, Emma Foster 85	233	3

*Played at Middlesbrough College

2018-19 FA Cup

02.12 R2	Stockport County (h)	W	1-0	Eleanor Dale 70	83
06.01 R3	Watford (h)	L	2-7	Emily Scarr 18, Eleanor Dale 28	92

2018-19 WNL Cup

02.09 DR	Huddersfield T (a)	L	0-3		76

2018-19 WNL Plate

R1	Bye				
14.10 R2	Solihull Moors (a)		P-P		
21.10 R2	Solihull Moors (a)	W	6-0	Anna Birtwhistle 8, Emily Scarr 16, 53, Tyler Dodds 36, 76, Eleanor Dale 84	30
09.12 R3	Morecambe (a)	W	3-2 aet	Emma Foster 17, Tyler Dodds 75, Eleanor Dale 102	
10.02 QF	Liverpool Feds (a)	L	0-2		50

MILTON KEYNES DONS

MK DONS

2019-20: WNL SOUTHERN PREMIER (Tier 3)

Founded: 2009

Nickname: The Dons

Season 2018-19:

WNL Southern Premier (Tier 3): 9th

FA Cup: 4th Round

WNL Cup: Determining Round

WNL Plate: Semi-finals

County Cup: Winners

MK Dons were promoted to Tier 3 ahead of 2018-19 after pipping AFC Wimbledon to the 2017-18 WPL South East 1 title. With three games to go MK Dons trailed AFC Wimbledon by three points and a vastly inferior goal difference, but they wiped that out within one game by beating bottom club Haringey Borough 16-1 to go top (on GD) for the first time all season and then saw out the campaign to take the sole promotion place. They managed to stay up in 2018-19 and almost tasted success in the WNL Plate. They beat Liverpool Feds 4-3 after extra-time in a dramatic semi-final, but the result was overturned when they were found to have fielded an ineligible player. They did though retain the Berks & Bucks FA County Cup with a 4-2 win over Tier 4 Chesham United in the final.

2018-19 AS IT HAPPENS

11.11.18: Leah Littlechild gives MK Dons the lead in their 3-0 win at Watford, scoring her first League goal for the club directly from a corner. Seventeen-year-old Ellie Gough then doubles the lead when she scores on her full debut.

06.01.19: Kim Farrow scores the only goal of the game in first-half injury-time as MK Dons win 1-0 at Nottingham Forest to reach the FA Cup 4th Round for the first time in their history.

16.01.19: Manager James Honeyman leaves after two-and-a-half years in the role to take up the position of women's technical talent coach at the FA. Under Honeyman the Dons won the 2017-18 Berks and Bucks FA County Cup, were promoted to Tier 3 for the 2018-19 season and reached the FA Cup 4th Round for the very first time. Following Honeyman's departure, Charlie Bill and Owen Evans are confirmed as joint managers, both stepping up from their existing roles with the MK Dons Sport and Education Trust.

04.04.19: The FA confirms MK Dons have been stripped of their place in the WNL Plate final due to fielding an ineligible player in the semi-final against Liverpool Feds. Feds will take their place in the final against West Brom on 14 April.

07.04.19: Despite a 3-1 defeat away to Plymouth, results elsewhere mean MK Dons know they will be staying up and can celebrate retaining their Tier 3 status in their first season at this level.

02.05.19: A 4-2 win over Tier 4 Chesham United in the Berks & Bucks FA County Cup final sees MK Dons win the trophy for the second year in a row, and for the fifth time in total.

2018-19 RESULTS: (HOME VENUE: STADIUM: MK, (MK DONS FC) UNLESS STATED)

2018-19 WNL SP					Att	Pos
19.08	Plymouth A (h)	L	3-4	Kimberley Farrow 40, 61, Zoe Boote 43	160	
26.08	Coventry U (h)	L	0-3			10
09.09	Chichester City (h)	L	0-1			11
11.09	Oxford U (a)	W	3-1	Leah Cudone 4, Alice Hughes 17, 25	100	9
16.09	QPR (a)	D	1-1	Kerry Newman 39	78	9
23.09	Portsmouth (h)	L	1-3	Charly Wright 42		9
30.09	Gillingham (h)	W	1-0	Kim Farrow 76		9
28.10	Loughborough F (a)	L	0-6		95	9
11.11	Watford (a)	W	3-0	Leah Littlechild 12, Eleanor Gough 29, Leah Cudone 82	137	8
25.11	C&K Basildon (a)	W	2-1	Charley Clarke 32, 56		8
16.12	Gillingham (a)		P-P			8
13.01	Gillingham (a)	L	0-2		70	9
27.01	Chichester City (a)	L	2-5	Charly Wright (pen) 4, Amy Gooderham 62	90	9
13.02	Oxford United (h)	L	0-3			9
10.03	Portsmouth (a)	L	0-4		88	10
13.03	Loughborough F (h)	L	1-3	Alice Hughes 38		10
17.03	Cardiff City L (a)	L	1-2	Leah Cudone 30, *Leah Cudone sent off 90+4*	175	10
24.03	QPR (h)	W	3-2	Leah Cudone 9, Kerry Newman 60, Kim Farrow 77	183	10
31.03	Watford (h)	L	1-2	Alice Hughes 90+1	90	10
07.04	Plymouth A (a)	L	1-3	Amy Gooderham 11	50	10
10.04	Coventry United (a)	L	0-4		108	10
28.04	Cardiff City L (h)*	L	1-2	Charley Clarke 31		10
05.05	C&K Basildon (h)	W	4-0	Leah Cudone 75, Louise Naylor 86, Alice Hughes 88, Kim Farrow 89		9

*Played at Weston Park, (Wootton Blue Cross FC)

2018-19 FA Cup

02.12 R2	Southampton FC (h)	W	4-0	Leah Cudone 4, 38, 86, Leah Littlechild 71	
06.01 R3	Nottingham F (a)	W	1-0	Kim Farrow 45+2	164
03.02 R4	Liverpool (a)		P-P		
10.02 R4	Liverpool (a)	L	0-6		394

2018-19 WNL Cup

02.09 DR	Plymouth A (a)	L	2-4	Kerry Newman 47, Kimberley Farrow 64	46

2018-19 WNL Plate

R1	Bye				
21.10 R2	Brislington (a)	W	3-0	Leah Littlechild 1, Leah Cudone 9, Alice Hughes 42	
09.12 R3	Bedworth U (h)	W	2-1aet	Leah Cudone 75, 95	120
24.02 QF	Keynsham T (h)*	D	2-2aet (W5-4p)	Leah Cudone, Amy Gooderham 90	
03.03SF	Liverpool Feds (h)	W	4-3aet RESULT VOID	Leanna Doyle 25, Kerry Newman (pen) 38, Kimberley Farrow 99, 111 *Result overturned 04.04 due to fielding ineligible player*	

*Played at Willen Road, (Newport Pagnell FC)

2018-19 Berks & Bucks FA County Cup

18.11 QF	Barton Rovers (a)	W	5-1	Vicky Barrett 14, Alice Hughes 35, 60, Kim Farrow 76, Zoe Boote (pen) 84
17.02 SF	Wycombe W (a)	W	3-0	Amy Gooderham 35, Charley Clark 78, Leah Cudone 88
02.05 F	Chesham United (n)	W	4-2	Leah Cudone 40, 69, Charley Clark 47, Vicky Holland 60

(n) Played at Arbour Park, (Slough Town FC)

"After winning promotion at the end of 2017-18 we always knew that 2018-19 would be a challenging season in Tier 3, but we thrived on the pressure. Our goal was to survive, and we did it. Not only that, we finished a respectable 9th. We were also victorious in the County Cup, winning it for the fourth time in five years. There's lots to look forward to in 2019-20 thanks to the confirmation that we will continue to play our home games at Stadium: mk and that we are changing our name from MK Dons FC Ladies to MK Dons FC Women."

Leanna Doyle – Captain

MORECAMBE

2019-20: NORTH WEST REGIONAL PREMIER (Tier 5)

Founded: 2005

Nickname: The Seagals

Season 2018-19:

WNL North 1 (Tier 4): 11th (R)

FA Cup: 2nd Qualifying Round

WNL Cup: Determining Round

WNL Plate: 3rd Round

County Cup: 2nd Round

Morecambe were promoted from the North West Regional Premier League (Tier 5) as champions ahead of 2014-15. They then finished 10th of 12 teams in what was their first ever season in Tier 4. Three consecutive 7th place finishes followed until the trials and tribulations of 2018-19 when the club ended the season second from bottom and were relegated to Tier 5. The Seagals have won two Cups over the years, lifting the Lancashire FA County Cup in 2009-10 and North West Regional League Cup in 2013-14.

2018-19 AS IT HAPPENS

14.10.18: Yasmine Swarbrick scores a hat-trick including a winner eight minutes from the end of extra-time as Morecambe beat Tier 3 Sheffield FC 4-3 in the WNL Plate 2nd Round.

17.02.19: Jess Tait's 66th minute goal in a 2-1 home win against Newcastle United is her ninth in nine League games.

31.03.19: Morecambe play in front of a crowd of 980 as their hosts Leeds stage the fixture at Elland Road, home of Leeds United men. The Seagals go down 1-0 to Emma Lee's 5th minute goal.

28.04.19: Morecambe play out an exhilarating 6-6 draw away to Norton & Stockton Ancients.

2018-19 RESULTS: (HOME VENUE: LANCASTER & MORECAMBE COLLEGE, UNLESS STATED)

2018-19 WNL North 1

					Att	Pos
26.08	Brighouse Town (h)	L	0-3		45	
09.09	Crewe Alexandra (h)	W	5-2	Carmel Daniel 10, Melissa Brown 78, Becky Whittingham 80, Rachel Warren 82, Natalie Broad 90	38	9
12.09	Chorley (a)	L	0-3		73	10
16.09	Newcastle United (a)	L	1-5	Rachel Warren 41	100	11
30.09	Norton & Stockton A (h)	L	1-4	Yasmin Swarbrick 32	41	11
03.10	Burnley (a)	L	0-3		70	11
07.10	Liverpool Feds (h)	D	3-3	Hannah Williamson 6, Beth Fisher 56, Jess Tait 59	30	10
04.11	Leeds United (h)	L	1-4	Jess Tait	35	11
11.11	Barnsley (a)	L	1-3	Jess Tait	50	11
18.11	Chester-Le-Street T (a)	L	0-6		40	11
25.11	Bolton W (a)	L	1-2	Jess Tait	75	11
02.12	Brighouse Town (a)	D	1-1	Jess Tait	20	11
13.01	Barnsley (h)	D	3-3	Yasmin Swarbrick, Jess Tait (x2)	35	11
03.02	Crewe Alexandra (a)		P-P			11
13.02	Chorley (h)	W	2-0	Jess Tait 8, 14	35	11
17.02	Newcastle United (h)	W	2-1	Jess Tait 66, Becky Whittingham 82	45	11
24.02	Crewe Alexandra (a)	D	2-2	Megan Doherty 75, Carmel Daniel 84	28	11
10.03	Norton & Stockton A (a)		P-P			11
17.03	Burnley (h)		P-P			11
24.03	Chester-le-Street T (h)*	L	1-2	Lottie Gray 22	20	11
31.03	Leeds United (a)	L	0-1		980	11
07.04	Burnley (h)*+	L	2-3	Jess Tait, Yasmin Swarbrick		11
14.04	Bolton W (h)+	L	1-2	Megan Doherty	35	11
28.04	Norton & Stockton A (a)	D	6-6	Natalie Broad (x2), Melissa Brown, Jessica Tait (x3), Megan Doherty sent off	120	11
05.05	Liverpool Feds (a)	L	2-10	Natalie Broad 1, Carmel Daniel 34	50	11

*Played at UCLAN Sports Arena   +Played at Giant Axe, Lancaster City FC   *+Played at Slyne FC

2018-19 FA Cup

23.09 RQ2	Norton & Stockton Ancients (h)	L	1-5	Yasmin Swarbrick (pen) 88	35

2018-19 WNL Cup

02.09 DR	Sunderland (h)	L	0-5		40

2018-19 WNL Plate

R1	Bye				
14.10 R2	Sheffield FC (h)	W	4-3 aet	Yasmine Swarbrick 16, 65, 112, Natalie Broad 81	35
09.12 R3	Middlesbrough (h)	L	2-3 aet	Melissa Brown, Emily Hutton	35

2018-19 LANCASHIRE FA COUNTY CUP

R1	Bye			
21.10 R2	Blackburn Rovers (a)	L	0-14	53

"Results in 2018-19 were disappointing but we had some good times too and took on new players like goalkeeper Katie McTague and midfielder Katherine Oldfield who were a joy to have around. We need to rethink our strategy ahead of 2019-20, building upon our strengths and recognising our weaknesses. We will have to look at our training policy, coaching team, recruitment, sponsors and facilities but I am confident we can have success in the future."

Nick Barrett – Chairman

NEWCASTLE UNITED

2019-20: WNL NORTH 1 (Tier 4)

Founded: 1989

Nickname: The Lady Magpies

Season 2018-19:

WNL North 1 (Tier 4): 9th

FA Cup: 3rd Qualifying Round

WNL Cup: 1st Round

County Cup: n/a

In 1996, seven years after formation, Newcastle United Women played Manchester United Women in an exhibition match at Wembley before the men's teams contested that year's Charity Shield (now known as the Community Shield). Their best FA Cup run came in 2006-07 when they reached the quarter-finals only to lose to Liverpool 9-8 on penalties after a 2-2 draw. The Lady Magpies became formally affiliated with the men's club in 2016.

2018-19 AS IT HAPPENS

16.09.18: Stephanie Ord scores the club's first hat-trick of the season (including one goal from the penalty spot) as Newcastle win 5-1 at home to Morecambe in the League.

23.09.18: Newcastle win a dramatic FA Cup 2nd Qualifying Round tie against Barnsley. The Magpies twice come from behind to take the tie to extra-time. With a penalty shootout just one minute away Abbey Joice scores their winning goal.

05.03.19: The Magpies end a run of five League games without a win as Jayden Maxwell scores the only goal at home to Norton & Stockton Ancients.

2018-19 RESULTS: (HOME VENUE: DRUID PARK, UNLESS STATED)

2018-19 WNL North 1

					Att	Pos
19.08	Bolton W (a)	L	1-2	Stephanie Ord (pen)	60	
26.08	Crewe Alexandra (a)	W	3-1	Nicole Dack 23, Megan McKenzie 31, Brooke Cochrane missed pen 38 (saved by Hannah Holloway), Jessica Foster 77	35	5
09.09	Chorley (h)	L	1-2	Megan McKenzie 73	162	7
11.09	Chester-le-Street T (a)	W	1-0	Jessica Foster 74	100	5
16.09	Morecambe (h)	W	5-1	Stephanie Ord 15, 57, (pen) 83, Rebecca Olley 53, Abbey Joice 58	100	4
02.10	Norton & Stockton A (a)	D	2-2	Stephanie Ord 20, Ellen Turnbull 51	120	5
21.10	Liverpool Feds (a)	W	2-1	Ellen Turnbull 22, Brooke Cochrane 65	40	4
28.10	Burnley (h)	L	0-1		94	4
04.11	Brighouse Town (a)	L	1-3	Jayden Maxwell 44	25	7
18.11	Crewe Alexandra (h)*	W	2-0	Stephanie Ord 67, 82	72	4
02.12	Barnsley (a)	D	0-0		50	5
27.01	Leeds United (a)	L	1-3	Jayden Maxwell 13	180	7
03.02	Chorley (a)		P-P			7
17.02	Morecambe (a)	L	1-2	Rebecca Olley 30	45	8
26.02	Chester-le-Street T (h)+	D	2-2	Stephanie Ord 28, 60	94	
03.03	Chorley (a)	D	0-0		94	8
05.03	Norton & Stockton A (h)*	W	1-0	Jayden Maxwell 54	102	7
10.03	Burnley (a)		P-P			7
17.03	Bolton W (h)**	W	2-1	Jayden Maxwell 60, Abbey Joice 77	37	8
31.03	Brighouse Town (h)	L	1-2	Abbey Joice 7	96	7
07.04	Liverpool Feds (h)*	L	0-3		80	7
14.04	Leeds United (h)	L	0-1		131	7
28.04	Burnley (a)	L	1-2	Stephanie Ord 57	54	9
05.05	Barnsley (h)	L	1-2	Rebecca Olley 5	110	9

*Played at Whitley Park +Played at Ashington Community FC **Played at Bullocksteads Sports Ground

2018-19 FA Cup

23.09 RQ2	Barnsley (a)	W	3-2 aet	Megan McKenzie 18, Jessica Foster 51, Abbey Joice 119	50
07.10 RQ3	Chester-le-Street T (h)	L	0-2		162

2018-19 WNL Cup

02.09 DR	Steel City W (a)	W	6-1	Own Goal, Rhiannon Gray, Megan McKenzie, Brooke Cochrane, Ellen Turnbull (x2)	38
30.09 R1	Chorley (h)	L	1-2 aet	Megan McKenzie 23, Newcastle GK Grace Donnelly saved pen 29	108

"The 2018-19 season was a mixed one leaving us, at times, very frustrated. One thing that shone throughout the campaign was that, no matter the result, every single player turned up week in week out, wanting to better themselves. I've seen us play some fantastic football, probably the best I've been involved with in my playing career. We have a great squad of players between two teams which is only getting stronger every year. The future is bright with young players being given the opportunity to shine and show their potential in the first team. The support we've received from the Newcastle Foundation and the crowds who have come to watch each week has been phenomenal."

Brooke Cochrane – Captain

NORTON & STOCKTON ANCIENTS

2019-20: WNL NORTH 1 (Tier 4)

Founded: 2006

Nickname: Ancients

Season 2018-19:

WNL North 1 (Tier 4): 10th

FA Cup: 1st Round

WNL Cup: 2nd Round

County Cup: Winners

Norton & Stockton Ancients were promoted to Tier 4 as 2017-18 North East Regional Premier League champions and ended that season by winning the Durham FA County Cup for the first time in four years. They successfully defended their County Cup trophy in 2018-19 when they beat Durham Cestria on penalties in the final following a 2-2 draw. They found acclimatising to life in Tier 4 a challenge but did well to retain their place in the division with a 10th place finish.

2018-19 AS IT HAPPENS

19.08.18: Having been promoted as 2017-18 North East Regional Premier champions, Norton begin life in Tier 4 in dramatic fashion as they lose a nine-goal thriller 5-4 away to Chorley.

21.10.18: Norton announce the retirement of their all-time top-scorer Nyci Thorns – who has been with the club since 2012. However, eight weeks later she comes out of retirement because she has missed playing for Norton so much.

24.10.18: The club announces the signing of Taylor Hebb From WNL Northern Premier outfit Middlesbrough.

25.11.18: Norton make another new signing as they reveal they have snapped up Faye Garside.

04.04.19: Maddy Atkinson's equaliser six minutes into injury-time saves Norton in the Durham FA County Cup final as they clinch a 2-2 draw with Durham Cestria and then win the resulting penalty shootout 3-0 to retain the trophy they won last season.

28.04.19: Norton play out an exhilarating 6-6 draw at home to Morecambe with Nyci Thorns scoring five.

17.05.19: Bianca Owens receives her award for finishing as the top scorer in WNL North 1 with 21 goals in 22 League appearances.

2018-19 RESULTS: (HOME VENUE: STATION ROAD, (NORTON & STOCKTON ANCIENTS FC) UNLESS STATED)

2018-19 WNL North 1					Att	Pos
19.08	Chorley (a)	L	4-5	Bianca Owens 16, 53, Sian Williams 34, Nyci Thorns 43	59	
26.08	Liverpool Feds (h)	W	4-2	Bianca Owens 29, 79, Nyci Thorns 88, 90+6	100	
09.09	Brighouse Town (a)	L	3-5	Nyci Thorns 35, Anna Mawston 76, 88	60	8
13.09	Leeds United (h)	L	0-3		300	10
16.09	Burnley (a)	L	1-2	Shannon Reed	60	10
30.09	Morecambe (a)	W	4-1	Bianca Owens, Shannon Reed (x2), Maddy Atkinson	41	8
02.10	Newcastle United (h)	D	2-2	Nyci Thorns 32, Maddy Atkinson 54	120	8
28.10	Bolton Wanderers (a)	L	0-3		50	10
04.11	Crewe Alexandra (a)	W	3-1	Vicki Burton 19, Bianca Owens 50 (pen), 67	40	9
18.11	Barnsley (h)	L	3-4	Maddy Atkinson 4, Bianca Owens 21, Courtney Corrie 73	80	10
02.12	Crewe Alexandra (h)	W	3-1	Katie Nuttall (og) 20, Maddy Atkinson 48, 55	50	10
06.01	Liverpool Feds (a)	L	2-3	Bianca Owens 2, 6	30	10
13.01	Chorley (h)	W	2-1	Bianca Owens, Victoria Burton	75	8
15.01	Chester-le-Street T (h)	L	1-2	Courtney Corrie	150	8
03.02	Brighouse Town (h)		P-P			9
10.02	Brighouse Town (h)	L	0-3		50	9
13.02	Leeds United (a)	L	1-3	Shannon Reed	40	9
24.02	Burnley (h)	L	4-5	Bianca Owens (x3), Lauren Bracewell (og) 54	50	9
05.03	Newcastle United (a)	L	0-1		102	10
10.03	Morecambe (h)		P-P			10
31.03	Bolton Wanderers (h)	W	2-1	Bianca Owens (x2)	90	10
14.04	Barnsley (a)	L	1-2	Bianca Owens (pen) 54	50	10
28.04	Morecambe (h)	D	6-6	Nyci Thorns (x5), Bianca Owens	120	10
05.05	Chester-le-Street T (a)	W	5-1	Louise Atkinson, Bianca Owens (x3), Shannon Reed	50	10

2018-19 FA Cup

23.09 RQ2	Morecambe (a)	W	5-1	Kate McSorley 12, Bianca Owens 16, 18, 39 Louise Atkinson 85	
07.10 RQ3	Redcar Town (h)	W	3-1	Nyci Thorns 23, 78, Bianca Owens 70	80
11.11 R1	Bolton Wanderers (h)	L	0-1		100

2018-19 WNL Cup

02.09 DR	Long Eaton Utd (a)	W	4-3	Bianca Owens 5, Maddy Atkinson 37, 43, Courtney Corrie 54	42
R1	Bye				
14.10 R2	Stoke City (a)	L	0-3		115

2018-19 Durham FA County Cup

RQ	Bye				
16.12 R1	Sunderland West End (a)	W	8-0	Bianca Owens 15, (pen) 28, (pen) 34, Nyci Thorns 12, 39 Maddy Atkinson 18, 20, 50	
20.01 QF	Bishop Auckland (h)	W	3-0	Victoria Burton, Bianca Owens (x2)	150
17.02 SF	Consett (h)*	W	4-1	Courtney Corrie, Bianca Owens (x3), *Rachel Chisnall sent off*	150
04.04 F	Durham Cestria (n)	D	2-2 (W3-0p)	Bianca Owens (pen), Maddy Atkinson	

*Played at Norton Teesside Sports Complex (n) Played at Norton Sports Complex

"The 2018-19 season was a record-breaking one. We secured our highest ever finish and record points total at this level, as well as retaining the Durham FA County Cup. Our junior section continued to thrive with our Under-18s winning the League and finishing as Cup runners up. In 2019-20 we will be aiming for a top three finish with both the first team and the reserves, as well as excitedly expanding our junior section to eight teams, including an Under-7 team for the first time."

Vicki Burton – Vice Captain

NORWICH CITY

2019-20: WNL SOUTH EAST 1 (Tier 4)

Founded: 1998

Nickname: The Canaries

SEASON 2018-19:

WNL South East 1 (Tier 4): 10th

FA Cup: 1st Round

WNL Cup: Determining Round

WNL Plate: 2nd Round

County Cup: 2nd Round

Officially affiliated to men's professional outfit Norwich City, the club proudly claims that 90% of its players have progressed through its youth ranks. Past honours include winning the South East Combination League Cup and Norfolk County Cup. The Canaries are also three-time winners of the Suffolk FA County Cup, beating Ipswich on penalties in the 2007 final, running out 5-0 winners over West Lynn in 2009 and defeating Ipswich 1-0 in 2010.

2018-19 As It Happens

12.09.18: After starting the campaign by going three League games without a win, Norwich pick up three points for the first time this season as Chelsea Garrett's 21st-minute goal proves enough to beat Ipswich in the East Anglian derby.

23.09.18: Kyla Love scores four and Chelsea Garrett hits a hat-trick as City beat Tier 6 outfit Boston United 11-3 in the FA Cup 2nd Qualifying Round.

31.03.19: Ellen Swift's goal with one minute remaining sees City avoid a fifth consecutive League defeat with a 1-1 draw at home to AFC Wimbledon.

28.04.19: Despite a valiant fightback from 3-0 down at half-time, Norwich lose 3-2 away to fellow strugglers Stevenage for whom the result ensures safety from relegation. The Canaries have one game left to play and remain one place and three points above the potential second relegation spot. Elsewhere Luton's relegation is confirmed after they throw away a 2-0 half-time lead to lose 5-2 at home to Ipswich.

05.05.19: Norwich secure their WNL South East 1 status in fine style on the final day as they come from 2-0 down to beat second-placed Billericay Town 4-2.

2018-19 RESULTS: (HOME VENUE: PLANTATION PARK, (NORWICH UNITED FC), UNLESS STATED)

2018-19 WNL SE 1					Att	Pos
19.08	Enfield Town (a)	L	1-5	Sasha Diston 7	61	
26.08	Denham United (h)	D	2-2	Chelsea Garrett 14, 79	72	10
09.09	Crawley Wasps (h)	L	0-6		63	11
12.09	Ipswich Town (a)	W	1-0	Chelsea Garrett 21	120	11
16.09	Actonians (a)	L	2-5	Natasha Snelling 12, Kate Parsons 40	25	11
30.09	Stevenage (h)	L	1-2	Laura Thacker 73, *Norwich GK Hope Armstrong saved Stevenage penalty*	49	11
03.10	Cambridge United (h)	W	3-0	Kate Parsons 16, Ellie Smith 30, Aimee Durrant 87	65	11
04.11	AFC Wimbledon (a)	L	2-4	Kathryn Stanley 28, Reeanna Cook 68	50	10
25.11	Leyton Orient (h)	L	0-1		58	10
09.12	Luton Town (h)	W	4-1	Aimee Durrant 27, Kathryn Stanley 46, Abbigail Tate 85, Rosie George 87	65	8
16.12	Billericay Town (a)	L	0-1		100	8
13.01	Enfield Town (h)	D	2-2	Aimee Durrant 11, Jodie Drake 49	54	10
20.01	Denham United (a)	W	2-1	Aimee Durrant 39, Rosie George 49	50	8
13.02	Ipswich Town (h)	W	3-0	Reanna Cook (x2), Chelsea Garrett	230	7
24.02	Actonians (h)	L	2-3	Chelsea Garrett 7, Kate Parsons 71	45	7
10.03	Stevenage (a)		P-P			9
13.03	Cambridge United (a)	L	0-1		50	9
17.03	Crawley Wasps (a)	L	0-8		125	9
24.03	Leyton Orient (a)	L	1-4	Chelsea Garrett 76	188	10
31.03	AFC Wimbledon (h)	D	1-1	Ellen Swift 89		10
14.04	Luton Town (a)	L	1-2	Kathryn Stanley 70		10
28.04	Stevenage (a)	L	2-3	Aimee Durrant 76, Natasha Snelling 87	35	10
05.05	Billericay Town (h)	W	4-2	Millie Daviss 49, Chelsea Garrett 59, 62, Sasha Diston 67	74	10

2018-19 FA CUP					
23.09 RQ2	Boston United (a)	W	11-3	Kyla Love 18, 20, 24, 85, Chelsea Garrett 28, 50, 55, Jodie Drake 39, Reanna Cook 43, Aimee Durrant 72, Kathryn Stanley 82	
07.10 RQ3	Enfield Town (h)	W	4-0	Chelsea Garrett 16, 30, 32, Laura Thacker 24	95
11.11 R1	Billericay Town (h)	L	2-3 (aet)	Chelsea Garrett, Ellie Smith *Kate Parsons sent off, Jodie Drake sent off*	74

2018-19 WNL Cup

02.09 DR	Coventry United (a)	L	0-7		93

2018-19 WNL Plate

R1	Bye			
14.10 R2	Stevenage (h)	L	w/o	

2018-19 Norfolk FA County Cup

R1	Bye			
18.11 R2	Acle United (a)	L	2-3	Natasha Snelling 10, Kathryn Stanley 61

"Our WNL status for 2019-20 was confirmed on the final day of the season in dramatic fashion as we beat Billericay – 2nd in the League – after being 2-0 down at half time. A result like that was testament to the fantastic attitude and spirit this group of players has. Doing the League double over our East Anglian rivals Ipswich was also a highlight. The 2018-19 season was full of highs and lows, all of which will make the players even stronger going forward. In 2019-20 we will be focusing our efforts on finishing higher in the League and having a good run in the Cups."

Greg Dimsey – Manager

NOTTINGHAM FOREST

2019-20: WNL NORTHERN PREMIER (Tier 3)

Founded: 1990

Nickname: The Reds

Season 2018-19:

WNL Northern Premier (Tier 3): 9th

FA Cup: 3rd Round

WNL Cup: 3rd Round

County Cup: Winners

Forest were founded in 1990 after advertising for players in the official matchday programme for Nottingham Forest men's Division One match against Everton. They applied to join WSL 2 when the division was introduced in 2014 but were unsuccessful in their application. The club's closest brush with national glory came in 2010-11 when they reached the WPL Cup final but lost on penalties to Barnet (now London Bees). Forest have enjoyed great success in the Nottinghamshire FA County Cup, winning it for a fourth year in succession (and 13th time overall) in 2018-19.

2018-19 AS IT HAPPENS

09.09.18: Forest take on Derby County away in a match which is played at Pride Park. The East Midlands derby attracts a Derby County Ladies club record crowd of 2,109.

28.10.18: A crowd of 3,914 is at the City Ground to watch Forest Ladies play Jamaica, who earlier this month became the first Caribbean team to qualify for the World Cup. Jamaica win 3-0.

11.02.19: Forest confirm they are leaving Carlton Town FC's CTFC Stadium to make Eastwood Community Football Club's 3G Arena their home for the remainder of 2018-19. They used the 5,000-capacity venue for last weekend's home match against Doncaster Rovers Belles.

24.02.19: Forest goalkeeper Rebecca Thomas takes, and successfully scores, a penalty to put her side 1-0 up in the 14th minute of their WNL match at home to Guiseley Vixens. Forest eventually lose 3-1.

04.03.19: Manager Graham Abercrombie announces his departure from the club on Twitter the day after a 2-1 home defeat to Middlesbrough leaves them 9th in the table.

06.03.19: Abercrombie's assistant Alena Moulton takes over as manager until the end of the season. Moulton is also technical director of the Nottingham Forest Female Regional Talent Club.

10.03.19: Beth Tyson – daughter of former Nottingham Forest men's player Nathan Tyson (currently with Wycombe Wanderers) – makes her debut for the club against Sunderland.

24.03.19: The East Midlands derby attracts a club record crowd as 1,252 see Forest host Derby in a 1-1 draw. Forest later report they have seen a 70% increase in home attendances this season.

26.04.19: Forest lift their fourth consecutive County Cup (and 13th in total) with a 1-0 win over lower League Ollerton Town. Helena Constantinou scores the winner early in the second half.

2018-19 RESULTS: (HOME VENUE: CTFC STADIUM, (CARLTON TOWN FC) UNTIL 03.02 THEN EASTWOOD COMMUNITY FOOTBALL CLUB 3G ARENA, UNLESS STATED)

2018-19 WNL NP					Att	Pos
19.08	Bradford City (h)	W	3-0	Charlotte Griffin 57, Amy Dicken (pen) 76, Georgia Hewitt 79	105	
26.08	Fylde (a)	D	0-0		52	4
09.09	Derby County (a)	L	0-1		2,109	7
13.09	Sheffield FC (h)	L	1-2	Sophia Bonser 68, *Rebecca Thomas sent off 85*	94	8
16.09	Guiseley Vixens (a)	L	0-2		40est	9
23.09	Hull City (h)	L	0-1		82	9
30.09	Doncaster R B (a)	W	3-1	Sophia Bonser 1, Charlotte Griffin 54, Lois Schole-field (og) 56, *Nottingham Forest GK Emily Hallam saved pen 66*	121	8
04.10	Stoke City (h)	W	3-1	Helena Constantinou 3, Viktoria Adam 27, Katie Middleton 75	166	7
21.10	Sunderland (a)	L	0-8		112	9
04.11	Blackburn Rovers (a)	L	0-7		220	10
11.11	Huddersfield T (h)	L	1-2	Ashleigh Edwards 8	68	10
25.11	Middlesbrough (h)		P-P			10
16.12	Middlesbrough (h)		P-P			10
13.01	Fylde (h)	W	1-0	Sammy Conroy 63	78	10
27.01	Guiseley Vixens (h)		P-P			10
03.02	Doncaster R B (h)	D	1-1	Trina Greaves 2, *Grace Walters sent off 43*	182	10
10.02	Bradford City (a)	W	2-0	Ashleigh Edwards 64, 76, *Ashleigh Edwards missed pen 73 (saved by Aimee Routledge)*	39	9
14.02	Sheffield FC (a)	W	2-1	Aimee Hickingbotham 29, Ashleigh Edwards 51, *Ashleigh Edwards missed pen 21*		8
24.02	Guiseley Vixens (h)	L	1-3	Rebecca Thomas (pen) 14	174	9

03.03	Middlesbrough (h)	L	1-2	Tina Greaves 39		9
10.03	Sunderland (h)	L	0-6		172	9
14.03	Stoke City (a)	D	1-1	Katie Middleton 84	85	9
24.03	Derby County (h)	D	1-1	Helena Constantinou 11	1,252	10
31.03	Middlesbrough (a)	L	1-3	Grace Walters 15	54	10
07.04	Blackburn R (h)	L	2-5	Katie Middleton 23, Precious Hamilton 26	305	10
21.04	Huddersfield T (a)	L	0-6		77	10
05.05	Hull City (a)	W	5-3	Precious Hamilton 12, 24, Aimee Hickingbotham 25, Grace Walters 28, Helena Constantinou 36	126	9

2018-19 FA CUP

02.12 R2	Sheffield FC (a)	W	3-2	Ashleigh Edwards 25, 74, 81	
06.01 R3	MK Dons (h)	L	0-1		164

2018-19 WNL CUP

02.09 DR	The New Saints (a)	W	3-0	Katie Middleton 13, 32, 64	53
R1	Bye				
14.10 R2	Chorley (h)	W	2-0	Viktoria Adam 13, Hazzana Parnell (pen) 82	
09.12 R3	Huddersfield T (a)	L	1-4	Katie Middleton 45	95

2018-19 NOTTINGHAMSHIRE FA COUNTY CUP

18.11 R2	Notts County (h)	W	5-0	Amy Dicken 25, (pen) 71, Hazzana Parnell 35, *Hazzana Parnell missed penalty 69*, Katie Middleton 41, Lauren Cresswell 47	179
20.01 QF	Clifton All Whites (a)	W	14-0	Hazzana Parnell 2, 41, Sarah Brown 8, 17, 78, 84, Sophia Bonser 20, 56, Nicola Emery 37, 50, Katie Middleton 66, 68, Ashleigh Edwards 80, (pen) 89	
10.02 SF	Arnold Town (h)	W	w/o		
26.04 F	Ollerton Town (h)	W	1-0	Helena Constantinou 54	

OXFORD UNITED

2019-20: WNL SOUTHERN PREMIER (Tier 3)

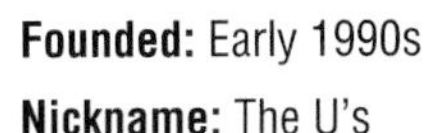

Founded: Early 1990s

Nickname: The U's

Season 2018-19:

WNL Southern Premier (Tier 3): 4th

FA Cup: 3rd Round

WNL Cup: 2nd Round

County Cup: Winners

Following their formation in the early 1990s, Oxford United had a loose affiliation with the men's club of the same name until 2008 when it became formal. At that point the men's club founded a girls' Centre of Excellence and fully integrated the women's team into the Oxford United FC set-up. The U's were among the original members of WSL 2 in 2014 and remained in that division until the FA restructuring in the summer of 2018. They were unsuccessful in their attempts to secure a licence for the newly renamed Championship and dropped down to Tier 3. The U's enjoyed a successful 2018-19 winning the County Cup and placing 4th in the WNL Southern Premier. Emily Allen finished as the division's joint top scorer with 16 League goals alongside Coventry United's Amy Wathan.

2018-19 AS IT HAPPENS

19.08.18: Having failed to retain their Tier 2 status after the FA's summer restructure, Oxford begin life in Tier 3 with a 2-1 defeat away to Chichester City.

21.10.18: Oxford rack up a club record County Cup win as they beat North Leigh 18-0 in the 1st Round. Laura Hennessy and Kerry Walklett both score four while Lauren Allison hits a hat-trick.

17.03.19: Gemma Sims scores her first goal for the club during Oxford's 4-2 WNL Southern Premier win away to Watford.

24.03.19: Emily Allen grabs two hat-tricks and Georgia Timms one as together they notch up nine goals in Oxford's 12-0 home win against WNL Southern Premier bottom club C&K Basildon.

21.04.19: United beat holders Oxford City (Tier 5) 2-0 in the Oxfordshire FA County Cup final. Ellie Noble gives them the lead midway through the second half with Flo Fyfe hitting a spectacular half-volley to double the lead with 11 minutes to play.

2018-19 RESULTS: (HOME VENUE: COURT PLACE FARM, (OXFORD CITY FC) UNLESS STATED)

2018-19 WNL SP					Att	Pos
19.08	Chichester City (a)	L	1-2	Ellie Noble 80	200	
26.08	QPR (a)	W	3-0	Georgia Timms (pen) 27, Kerry Walklett 43, Flo Fyfe 44	56	6
08.09	Watford (h)	L	1-2	Georgia Timms 19	163	7
11.09	MK Dons (h)	L	1-3	Own Goal 31	100	8
16.09	Gillingham (a)	W	5-0	Ellie Noble 23, Sophie Baker 45, Flo Fyfe 75, Lauren Haynes 81, Maddie Robertson 90	70	8
23.09	Loughborough F (h)	W	4-2	Flo Fyfe 13, 24, Catherine Beaver 75, Emily Allen 81	76	6
02.10	Coventry United (h)	L	1-2	Emily Allen 89	56	7
28.10	C&K Basildon (a)	W	2-0	Flo Fyfe 28, 90+2		5
04.11	Cardiff City L (a)	D	1-1	Georgia Timms 70	150	6
11.11	Plymouth A (h)	W	2-1	Sophie Baker 11, Georgia Timms (pen) 86	129	5
09.12	Portsmouth (a)		P-P			5
20.01	QPR (h)	W	7-1	Ellie Noble 15, Emily Allen 39, 67, (pen) 72, Evie Gane 69, Flo Fyfe 81, Madeleine Robinson 89, *Emily Allen missed pen 85*	157	6
27.01	Watford (a)		P-P			6
03.02	Portsmouth (a)		P-P			6
10.02	Chichester City (h)	W	1-0	Georgia Timms 66	167	6
13.02	MK Dons (a)	W	3-0	Flo Fyfe 44, Emily Allen 79, Cheryl Williams 90+1		3
24.02	Gillingham (h)	W	1-0	*Oxford GK Lucy Thomas saved Ellie Manning pen 45,* Flo Fyfe 50	107	4
13.03	Coventry United (a)		P-P			5
17.03	Watford (a)	W	4-2	Emily Allen 16, Gemma Sims 43, Haynes 57, Elle Richards (og) 78	70	4
24.03	C&K Basildon (h)	W	12-0	Emily Allen 21, 26, 44, 61, 78, 90, Georgia Timms 6, 24, 88, Flo Fyfe 43, 64, Imogen Lancaster 85	158	4
31.03	Plymouth A (a)	L	0-1		41	4
03.04	Coventry Utd (a)	L	0-2		106	4
14.04	Portsmouth (h)	W	2-1	Georgia Timms (pen) 49, Emily Allen 90		4
23.04	Cardiff City L (h)	L	2-3	Ellie Noble 32, Gemma Sims 75	101	4
28.04	Portsmouth (a)	W	2-0	Georgia Timms 29, Emily Allen 45+1	126	4
05.05	Loughborough F (a)	D	1-1	Emily Allen 80	67	4

2018-19 FA Cup

02.12 R2	Cambridge U (h)	W	4-0	Ellie Noble 30, Lauren Haynes 34, Flo Fyfe 46, Evie Gane 65	85
06.01 R3	Blackburn Rovers (h)	L	1-2	Evie Gane 45+4	203

2018-19 WNL Cup

02.09 DR	Actonians (a)	W	2-1	Ellie Noble 26, 63	20
R1	Bye				
14.10 R2	Crawley Wasps (h)	L	1-3aet	Sophie Baker 52	

2018-19 Oxfordshire FA County Cup

21.10 R1	North Leigh (a)	W	18-0	Laura Hennessy (x4), Stephaney Bent, Kerry Walklett (x4), Lauren Allison (x3), Sophie Baker, Georgia Timms (x2), Lena Stroem, Flo Fyfe, Emily Allen	81
18.11 QF	Banbury United (a)	W	6-0	Georgia Timms (pen) 7, 36, 73, Bobby Lynch 9, Lauren Allison 44, Catherine Beaver 72	80est
17.02 SF	Carterton (h)	W	8-0	Emily Allen 29, Evie Gane 32, 41, 73, Cheryl Williams 35, 46, Flo Fyfe 52, Georgia Timms 79	136
21.04 F	Oxford City (n)	W	2-0	Ellie Noble 67, Flo Fyfe 79	257

(n) Played at Court Place Farm (home venue of both clubs)

PLYMOUTH ARGYLE

2019-20: WNL SOUTHERN PREMIER (Tier 3)

Founded: 1975 (as Plymouth Pilgrims)

Nickname: The Lady Pilgrims / Argyle

Season 2018-19:

WNL Southern Premier (Tier 3): 6th

FA Cup: 2nd Round

WNL Cup: 3rd Round

County Cup: Winners

Following a five-a-side competition at Plymouth's Mayflower Leisure Centre, two teams joined forces in 1975 to create an 11-a-side team called Plymouth Pilgrims. With the team at the time playing their home matches at Saltash United's Kimberly Stadium, they changed their name to Saltash Pilgrims in the late 1990s. In 2001-02 they were invited to compete as part of the men's professional club, Plymouth Argyle, and changed their name to the same. They were promoted to Tier 3 at the end of 2017-18 as WPL South West 1 champions, having gone the entire League campaign unbeaten. Despite missing 100-goal striker Natasha Knapman through injury for six months of the 2018-19 campaign Argyle achieved their highest ever League finish of 6th in Tier 3 and won their 13th Devon County Cup. After having to use six different home venues in 2018-19, Argyle will move to Manadon Sports & Community Hub at St Peters Rd for 2019-20 and play on a new state of the art 3G pitch.

2018-19 AS IT HAPPENS

19.08.18: Following promotion, Argyle begin life in Tier 3 in style with a 4-3 win away to fellow promoted side MK Dons. Natasha Knapman scores all Argyle's goals.

13.01.19: Argyle play their part in a thrilling WNL Cup 3rd Round tie at home to Tier 4 high-flyers Crawley Wasps. The Pilgrims come from 2-0 down to force extra-time with an equaliser four minutes into injury time. Four goals are then scored in the extra half-hour with Wasps winning 5-3.

17.03.19: Leading striker Natasha Knapman returns after six months out with a knee injury. She scores the equalising goal as the 'Dockyard Derby' against Portsmouth finishes in a 2-2 draw in front of a crowd of 846 at Plymouth Argyle FC's Home Park.

25.03.19: Simon Hallett, chairman and majority shareholder of men's League One outfit Plymouth Argyle FC, says he hopes to one day bring Argyle Ladies under the control of the main club. Argyle Ladies are currently run by the Argyle Community Trust.

12.04.19: Argyle defend their Devon FA County Cup title with a 3-2 win over Tier 4 Buckland Athletic. Kayley Lane and Natasha Knapman (who hits a brace) send them into a 3-0 lead inside 20 minutes. Buckland hit back with two late goals, but Plymouth hold on.

2018-19 RESULTS: (HOME VENUE: HAYE ROAD, (ELBURTON VILLA FC) UNLESS STATED)

2018-19 WNL SP					Att	Pos
19.08	MK Dons (a)	W	4-3	Natasha Knapman 22, 34, 39, 68	160	
26.08	Chichester City (h)	L	0-3		61	8
09.09	Gillingham (a)	W	4-1	Zoe Cunningham 12, Helen Bleazard 16, Mollie Taylor 38, Katie Middleton 54	65	7
16.09	C&K Basildon (h)	W	5-3	Helen Bleazard 18, 68, Kayley Lane 40, Amber Pollock 64, Katie Middleton (pen) 86	44	5
23.09	Coventry United (a)		P-P			7
30.09	QPR (a)	W	3-2	Helen Bleazard 25, 45+2, Zoe Cunningham 83	60	4
07.10	Portsmouth (a)	W	3-0	Jessie Jones 15, 85, Kayley Lane 38	89	3
04.11	Loughborough F (h)+	L	0-4		33	4
11.11	Oxford United (a)	L	1-2	Katie Middleton 48	129	6
25.11	Coventry United (a)	L	1-9	Helen Bleazard 49	209	6
16.12	Watford (h)		P-P			7
06.01	Chichester City (a)	L	1-2	Rebecca Dandridge 9	150	7
20.01	Watford (h)*	W	3-2	Katie Middleton (pen) 31, Mollie Taylor 45, Jessie Jones 58	80	7
27.01	Gillingham (h)		P-P			7
24.02	QPR (h)+	W	4-3	Zoe Cunningham 12, 56, Jessie Jones 30, Mollie Taylor 83	50	7
03.03	C&K Basildon (a)	W	2-0	Helen Bleazard 2, Kayley Lane 39		6
10.03	Cardiff City L (h)+	L	2-3	Zoe Cunningham, Jessie Jones 61	68	7
17.03	Portsmouth (h)**	D	2-2	Kayley Lane 23, Natasha Knapman 70	846	7
24.03	Gillingham (h)*+	D	1-1	Zoe Cunningham 20	30	7
31.03	Oxford United (h)+	W	1-0		41	7
07.04	MK Dons (h)*+	W	3-1	Natasha Knapman 9, 66, Jessie Jones 33	50	5

14.04	Loughborough F (a)	W	4-2	Natasha Knapman 30, Helen Bleazard 46, Jessie Jones 66, 90	40	5
21.04	Cardiff City L (a)	L	2-3	Leah Burridge 65, Natasha Knapman 75	125	5
28.04	Coventry United (h)	L	2-5	Katie Middleton (pen) 45, Helen Bleazard 76	83	6
05.05	Watford (a)	L	2-3	Helen Bleazard 72, Zoe Cunningham 83	174	6

+Played at Coach Road, (Devon FA HQ) *Played at University of St Mark & St John **Played at Home Park, (Plymouth Argyle FC) *+Played at Mill Marsh Park, (Bovey Tracey FC)

2018-19 FA Cup

02.12 R2	Coventry U (a)	L	1-2	Helen Bleazard 17	65

2018-19 WNL Cup

02.09 DR	MK Dons (h)	W	4-2	Natasha Knapman 5, Amber Pollock 26, Kayley Lane 44, Rebecca Dandridge 52	46
R1	Bye				
14.10 R2	Southampton W (a)		P-P		
28.10 R2	Southampton W (a)	W	3-1	Helen Bleazard 36, Jessie Jones 84, 90+1	
13.01 R3	Crawley Wasps (h)	L	3-5 aet	Kayley Lane 79, Katie Middleton 90+4, Leah Burridge 100	207

2017-18 Devon FA County Cup

21.10 R1	Bideford (a)	W	13-0	Faye Ivall 17, 39, (pen) 65, Zoe Cunningham 21, 32, 62, 70, 80, Jessie Jones 54, Ebony Dover 60, Rebecca Dandridge 66, Tamsin Medd-Gill 79, 82	
18.11 QF	Marine Academy Plymouth (h)+	W	2-0	Panagiota Papaioannou 27, Jessie Jones 36	100
17.02 SF	Plympton (h)	W	w/o		
12.04 F	Buckland Athletic (n)+	W	3-2	Kayley Lane 9, Natasha Knapman 17, 20	507

+Played at Coach Road, (Devon FA HQ)

"The 2018-19 campaign was a very progressive first season in Tier 3 culminating in a respectable finishing position of 6th. The coaching staff and the players have gained a lot of experience throughout this season and have every confidence of moving forward successfully in 2019-20. We're extremely proud of the players' achievements and the personal dedication to make it happen."

Trevor Rodd & Dave Leonard – Joint Managers

POOLE TOWN

2019-20: WNL SOUTH WEST 1 (Tier 4)

Founded: 1980s

Nickname: The Dolphins

Season 2018-19:

WNL South West 1 (Tier 4): 11th

FA Cup: 1st Round

WNL Cup: Determining Round

WNL Plate: 1st Round

County Cup: Semi-finals

Back-to-back promotions carried Poole Town from Tier 6 to Tier 4 for the start of the 2017-18 season. They went up after finishing 3rd in the South West Regional Premier League in 2016-17, taking the promotion spot because champions Yeovil Town Intermediate were not eligible and runners-up Marine Academy Plymouth decided to continue competing in Tier 5. The Dolphins endured a difficult 2018-19 and slipped to the bottom of the table on the very last day of the season when they lost 6-1 at Chesham while Maidenhead beat Southampton Saints 1-0 to climb above them. They retained their Tier 4 status though with no relegation from the division.

2018-19 AS IT HAPPENS

26.08.18: After a heavy 8-1 defeat on the opening day of the season, Poole bounce back in style and win their second fixture 6-3 at home to Larkhall Athletic.

02.12.18: The Dolphins end a run of six straight League defeats with a 3-0 win at home to Maidenhead United – Kirstie Birmes, Samantha Gubb and Hollie Agombar get the goals.

31.03.19: After seven League defeats on the bounce Katherine Preston's goal secures a 1-1 draw and a welcome point away to Brislington.

05.05.19: Poole drop to the bottom of the table for the first time all season on the very last day. A 6-1 defeat at Chesham sees Maidenhead – who win 1-0 at Southampton Saints – leapfrog the Dolphins.

2018-19 RESULTS: (HOME VENUE: MILBORNE ST ANDREW FC, UNLESS STATED)

2018-19 WNL SW 1

					Att	Pos
19.08	Southampton W (a)	L	1-8	Hollie Agombar 76	46	
26.08	Larkhall Athletic (h)	W	6-3	Hollie Agombar 22, 39, Katie Marshallsay 44, Faye Rolfe-Hawkins 45+1, Hannah Gould 86, 89	9	
09.09	Swindon Town (a)	L	1-2	Rebecca Miles (pen) 76	44	8
04.10	Southampton S (a)	L	0-3		20	10
28.10	Cheltenham Town (h)	L	0-7		30	10
04.11	Brislington (h)	L	3-5	Faye Rolfe-Hawkins 17, 65, Hollie Agombar 52	20	10
18.11	Keynsham Town (a)	L	0-9			10
25.11	Chesham Utd (h)	L	1-5	Hollie Agombar 21	12	10
02.12	Maidenhead Utd (h)	W	3-0	Kristine Birmes 21, Samantha Gubb 22, Hollie Agombar 84	20	9
13.01	Southampton W (h)	L	0-5		18	9
03.02	Swindon Town (h)*	L	0-2		30	10
10.02	Buckland Athletic (h)*	L	0-5		25	10
24.02	Buckland Athletic (a)	L	1-5	Sacha Paynter 52	34	10
05.03	Southampton S (h)*	L	1-4	Katie Marshallsay 49	24	10
10.03	Cheltenham Town (a)	L	2-6	Samantha Gubb 25, Sacha Paynter (pen) 59	61	10
24.03	Keynsham Town (h)	L	0-14		32	10
31.03	Brislington (a)	D	1-1	Katherine Preston 43	41	10
07.04	Larkhall Athletic (a)	L	0-7		30	10
14.04	Maidenhead Utd (a)	D	0-0		20	10
05.05	Chesham Utd (a)	L	1-6	Hollie Agombar 82		11

*Played at Dorset FA County Ground

2018-19 FA CUP

23.09 RQ2	Frampton Rangers (h)	W	3-1	Hollie Agombar 14, 90, Rebecca Yeo 65	44
07.10 RQ3	Eastleigh (a)	W	2-1	Samantha Gubb 14, Hollie Agombar 90+1	55
11.11 R1	Southampton FC (h)	L	0-3		66

2018-19 WNL Cup

02.09 DR	Watford (h)	L	1-2	Faye Rolfe-Hawkins 33	40

2018-19 WNL Plate

30.09 R1	Portsmouth (h)	L	0-9		25

2018-19 Dorset FA County Cup

09.12 R2	Gillingham Town (h)	W	w/o		
20.01 QF	Wareham Rangers (h)*	W	12-1	Hollie Agombar, Lauren Fraser (x2), Sacha Paynter (x2), Faye Rolfe-Hawkins (x3), Katie Marshallsay (x2), Samantha Chrippes, Own Goal	10
17.03 SF	Sherborne Town (h)*	L	2-4	Katie Marshallsay 60, Sacha Paynter 90+3	48

*Played at Dorset FA County Ground

"We have an amazing club where everyone works hard together to achieve and develop to the best of their ability. The highlight for 2018-19 was the development of our youth and seeing players progress through our pathway into the first team. We had at least six players aged just 16 make their debuts, which is fantastic. It demonstrates that if you work hard then you can fulfil your dreams. In 2019-20 we will be introducing an Under-18 team to run alongside our first and reserves. We are also delighted to have the sponsorship support of MC Plan & Site Services; we couldn't do it without their amazing support."

Becca Witherington – Captain

PORTSMOUTH

2019-20: WNL SOUTHERN PREMIER (Tier 3)

Founded: 1987

Nickname: Pompey

Season 2018-19:

WNL Southern Premier (Tier 3): 8th

FA Cup: 2nd Round

WNL Cup: Determining Round

WNL Plate: 2nd Round

County Cup: Winners

Women's football has been played under the Portsmouth name for more than 100 years (except during the FA ban) with the original club believed to have been founded in 1917. The current incarnation was formed in 1987. They entered the Southern Regional League the following year and competed at that level for a decade. In more recent times Pompey were champions of the WPL Southern Division (Tier 3) in 2011-12 which saw them promoted to the WPL National Division (Tier 2) for 2012-13. Their only season at that level ended in relegation as they finished second-from-bottom. They have spent the subsequent six seasons competing in Tier 3, with their most successful season in that time being 2014-15 when they were crowned WPL Southern Premier champions. They missed out on promotion to WSL 2 by losing the play-off against Sheffield FC in the last minute.

2018-19 AS IT HAPPENS

18.11.18: Portsmouth begin the defence of their County Cup title with a 14-0 win over Eastleigh. Nine Pompey players score, and there is one own goal. Daisy McLachlan hits a hat-trick and Rachel Panting, who scores twice, tweets: "Don't think I've ever got six assists in one game before."

10.03.19: Jade Widdows makes her full debut and scores in the 36th minute to put her side 2-0 up. Pompey go on to win the home match against MK Dons 4-0.

17.03.19: A crowd of 846 watches Portsmouth's 2-2 draw away to Plymouth which is staged at Home Park, the home of Plymouth Argyle FC men. Pompey Women's boss Jay Sadler misses the match because his wife is imminently expecting their second child. Assistant James Wilson takes charge.

03.04.19: Portsmouth win the Hampshire FA County Cup by beating Tier 4 side Southampton Women's 3-1. It's the 11th year in a row, and 15th time over all, that Pompey have won the competition. The match, which is staged at Testwood Park – the home of AFC Totton – is watched by a competition record crowd of 577.

17.04.19: A 15-0 win over lower League side Horndean sees Portsmouth lift the Portsmouth District FA Cup. Alex Collighan scores five with Jade Widdows netting four. Katie James bags a brace, Caitlin Collighan grabs her first for the club while Emma Jane May, Shannon Albuery and an own goal complete the scoring. *(NB: Portsmouth District FA Cup results are not included in this book).*

2018-19 RESULTS: (HOME VENUE: PMC STADIUM, (BAFFINS MILTON ROVERS FC) UNLESS STATED)

2018-19 WNL SP					Att	Pos
19.08	C&K Basildon (a)	W	6-0	Hannah Geer 12, 38, Daisy McLachlan 45, 50, (pen) 63, Shannon Albuery 55	69	
26.08	Gillingham (h)	W	4-1	Shannon Albuery 46, Katie James 58, Jade Bradley 64, Daisy McLachlan 81	90	2
09.09	Coventry United (h)	L	1-2	Rachel Panting 9	94	4
12.09	Chichester City (a)	L	1-2	Daisy McLachlan 59	272	5
16.09	Watford (h)	L	2-4	Daisy McLachlan 16, Hannah Geer 70	118	7
23.09	MK Dons (a)	W	3-1	Rachel Panting 47, Daisy McLachlan 59, Katie James 76		5
07.10	Plymouth A (h)	L	0-3		89	7
11.11	Loughborough F (a)	L	1-2	Rachel Panting 27	35	9
25.11	Cardiff City L (a)	L	1-2	Danielle Rowe 72	75	9
09.12	Oxford United (h)		P-P			9
16.12	QPR (h)		P-P			9
06.01	QPR (h)	W	1-0	Rachel Panting (pen) 55	84	9
13.01	C&K Basildon (h)	W	2-0	Eilidh Currie 24, Jade Bradley 62	93	7
27.01	Coventry United (a)		P-P			8
03.02	Oxford United (h)		P-P			8
10.02	Watford (a)	L	4-5	Shannon Albuery 45, Rachel Panting 63, Rebecca Bath 65, Katie James 90+2	45	8
13.02	Chichester City (h)		P-P			8
03.03	Coventry United (a)	L	0-4		100	8
10.03	MK Dons (h)	W	4-0	Katie James 29, Jade Widdows 36, Alex Collighan 60, Rachel Panting 68	88	8
17.03	Plymouth Argyle (a)	D	2-2	Katie James 19, Jade Widdows 34	846	8
24.03	Cardiff City L (h)	L	0-3		131	8

27.03	Chichester City (h)	W	3-1	Katie James 11, Jade Bradley 21, Rachel Panting 90+1, *Portsmouth GK Hannah Haughton saved 2 Jess Lewry pens 80 & 85*	213	8
31.03	Loughborough F (h)	W	2-0	Rachel Panting (pen) 28, 35	73	8
07.04	Gillingham (a)	W	2-0	Katie James 52, Eilidh Currie 74	50	8
14.04	Oxford United (a)	L	1-2	Katie James 56		8
28.04	Oxford United (h)	L	0-2		126	8
05.05	QPR (a)	L	1-2	Alex Collighan 53, *Alex Collighan sent off 90*	135	8

2018-19 FA Cup

02.12 R2	AFC Wimbledon (a)	L	0-2		95

2018-19 WNL Cup

02.09 DR	Chichester C (h)	L	2-4	Shannon Albuery 38, Sarah Eadon 85	195

2018-19 WNL Plate

30.09 R1	Poole Town (a)	W	9-0	Katie James 8, Carla Perkins 16, 20, (pen) 58, Eilidh Currie 26, Rachel Panting 48, 71, 79, Hannah Geer 54	
21.10 R2	Keynsham T (a)	L	1-2	Katie James 11	90

2018-19 Hampshire FA County Cup

R1	Bye				
18.11 R2	Eastleigh (h)	W	14-0	Emma-Jane May 28, Daisy McLachlan 29, 33, 52, Esther Anu 46, Danielle Rowe 54, Rachel Panting 63, (pen) 90+1, Eilidh Currie 67, Jade Bradley 73, 83, Kat Littleboy (og) 76, Sarah Eadon 80, 86	170
20.01 QF	Southampton FC (h)	W	2-1	Shannon Albuery 70, Alex Collighan 82	546
27.01 SF	Southampton S (h)	W	1-0	Danielle Rowe 18	157
03.04 F	Southampton W (n)	W	3-1	Danielle Rowe 15, Shannon Albuery 17, Bradley 37	577

(n) Played at Testwood Park, (AFC Totton)

"The 2018-19 season started with a host of positives behind the scenes: a new board of directors; our formal incorporation into the Portsmouth FC family; our name-change from Ladies to Women and moving home to the PMC Stadium. Highlights during the season included beating our rivals from down the A27 (Southampton FC Women) in front of a crowd of 546 at the PMC and winning the Hampshire Cup for the 11th successive time in front of a crowd of 577."

Jay Sadler – Manager

SHEFFIELD FC

2019-20: WNL NORTHERN PREMIER (Tier 3)

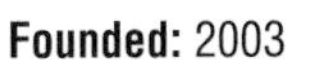

Founded: 2003

Nickname: The Club

Season 2018-19:

WNL Northern Premier (Tier 3): 11th

FA Cup: 2nd Round

WNL Cup: Determining Round

WNL Plate: 2nd Round

County Cup: Quarter-finals

Sheffield FC are officially recognized by FIFA as the oldest men's club in the world. In 2003 they took an existing team called Norton Ladies under their wing to form Sheffield FC Ladies. The ladies team began life in Division One East of the Yorkshire & Humberside League but rapidly rose up the football pyramid. They finished 2014-15 as WPL Northern Premier (Tier 3) champions and beat Southern Premier champions Portsmouth in the play-off final to secure promotion to WSL 2. They remained in Tier 2 until summer 2018 when they were casualties of the controversial new FA licensing criteria. Initially successful in their application for a place in the newly formed Championship, they took the difficult decision to withdraw and drop to Tier 3 stating the "move towards a full-time operation" in women's football was "no longer consistent" with their position. The 2018-19 campaign was a difficult transitional period as they finished two places off the bottom.

2018-19 AS IT HAPPENS

19.08.18: Having failed to retain their Tier 2 licence following the FA restructure, Sheffield FC begin life in Tier 3 with a 2-0 defeat away to Huddersfield Town.

04.11.18: Goalkeeper Lauren Santoro comes off the bench when first-choice keeper Elizabeth Hobson is sent off while conceding a penalty in a match against Guiseley Vixens. Santoro's first touch is to save the penalty keeping the score at 1-1. Unfortunately for Sheffield, Guiseley eventually win 2-1.

09.12.18: Manager Kyle O'Reilly resigns following a 2-0 defeat to Doncaster Rovers Belles. Chris Hames is appointed as his successor.

16.12.18: Molly Johnson and Molly Havard (x2) both score their first senior goals for Sheffield FC in the 7-0 County Cup win against Hepworth United which is new manager Chris Hames' first match in charge. The game represents Sheffield's first match in the competition for three years. They had been absent due to playing in Tier 2 prior to the FA restructuring in the summer of 2018.

03.03.19: Emma Johnson becomes the 10th player to make 150 appearances for the club as she starts the 3-0 home win against Fylde.

31.03.19: Samantha Conroy scores on her competitive debut to put Sheffield ahead for the third time during a match which they go on to win 4-2 against Hull.

2018-19 RESULTS: (HOME VENUE: DRONFIELD, (SHEFFIELD FC) UNLESS STATED)

2018-19 WNL NP					Att	Pos
19.08	Huddersfield T (a)	L	0-2		93	
26.08	Middlesbrough (h)	L	2-3	Lisa Giampalma 3, Ellie White 35	74	11
09.09	Bradford City (h)	W	2-0	Ellie White 18, Megan Tinsley 48	118	9
13.09	Nottingham F (a)	W	2-1	Ellie White (pen) 19, (pen) 86	94	6
16.09	Blackburn R (h)	L	0-7		123	8
23.09	Sunderland (h)	L	1-3	Millie Herbert-Clarke 39		8
30.09	Fylde (a)	L	1-4	Lisa Giampalma 45	70	11
07.10	Stoke City (h)	W	2-0	Ellie Hawcroft 73, Lisa Giampalma 75	126	10
11.10	Derby County (h)	L	0-1		141	10
21.10	Hull City (a)		P-P			10
04.11	Guiseley Vixens (h)	L	1-2	Ellie White 28, *Elizabeth Hobson sent off 66, Sheffield GK Lauren Santoro saved pen 66*	87	11
11.11	Hull City (a)	L	2-4	Lisa Giampalma 43, 90	50	11
18.11	Huddersfield T (h)	L	2-3	Milly Wortley 8, Holly Housley (pen) 82	92	11
09.12	Doncaster R B (a)	L	0-2			11
06.01	Guiseley Vixens (a)	D	1-1	Lisa Giampalma 62	40	11
13.01	Middlesbrough (a)	L	1-5	Megan Tinsley 89	72	11
27.01	Blackburn R (a)	L	2-4	Molly Havard 39, Ellie Hawcroft 79		11
03.02	Fylde (h)		P-P			12
14.02	Nottingham F (h)	L	1-2	Rhema Lord-Mears 83		12
17.02	Bradford City (a)	W	5-0	Holly Housley 40, (pen) 61, Milly Wortley 41, Jennifer Pearson 44, Lisa Giampalma 60	37	11
24.02	Stoke City (a)	D	2-2	Milly Wortley 54, Holly Housley (pen) 68	130	11
03.03	Fylde (h)	W	3-0	Rhema Lord-Mears 18, 77, Milly Wortley 74		

14.03	Derby County (a)		P-P			11
31.03	Hull City (h)	W	4-2	Rhema Lord-Mears 40, Holly Housley 64, (pen) 84, Samantha Conroy 68	80	11
14.04	Doncaster R B (h)	D	1-1	Millie Clarke 73	202	11
28.04	Derby County (a)	L	0-1		117	11
05.05	Sunderland (a)	L	2-5	Milly Wortley 60, Emma Johnson 85	124	11

2018-19 FA Cup

02.12 R2	Nottingham F (h)	L	2-3	Ellie Hawcroft 5, Ellie White 29	

2018-19 WNL Cup

02.09 DR	Stoke City (a)	L	0-3		134

2018-19 WNL Plate

R1	Bye				
14.10 R2	Morecambe (a)	L	3-4 aet	Jade Butcher 45, Ellie White 52, Megan Tinsley 62	

2018-19 Sheffield & Hallamshire FA County Cup

16.12 R1	Hepworth United (a)	W	7-0	Jade Butcher, Molly Johnson, Lisa Giam-palma, Millie Herbert-Clarke (x2), Molly Havard (x2)	32
20.01 QF	Barnsley (a)	L	1-2	Own Goal 39	

"Having been forced to withdraw from Tier 2 [due to the FA restructure] in the summer of 2018 after three very successful seasons in WSL 2, we faced a huge rebuilding exercise ahead of 2018-19. For the largely inexperienced squad, the aim was nothing more than to maintain a place in the WNL Northern Premier which was achieved thanks to a haul of 11 points from five straight games just before the end of the season. The turnaround was over-seen by new manager Calum Oakenfold, who was appointed in February 2019 with matches fast running out."

Helen Mitchell – General Manager

SOLIHULL MOORS

2019-20: WNL MIDLANDS 1 (Tier 4)

Founded: 1994 (as Shirley Town)

Nickname: Moors

Season 2018-19:

WNL Midlands 1 (Tier 4): 10th

FA Cup: 3rd Qualifying Round

WNL Cup: Determining Round

WNL Plate: 3rd Round

County Cup: 2nd Round

Founded as Shirley Town in 1994, ground relocations saw them change their name to Woodbourne United in 1996, Billesley United in 1998 and Solihull Glades in 2003 before becoming Solihull in 2005. In December 2016 they confirmed they would be joining up with men's National League side Solihull Moors from the start of the 2017-18 season. The club has won two League titles, finishing top of the West Midlands Division One Central during their days as Solihull Glades in 2003-04 and top of the West Midlands Premier Division as Solihull in 2012-13.

2018-19 AS IT HAPPENS

02.11.18: Manager Sarah Westwood leaves the club the morning after a 4-1 home defeat to Bedworth United with the team bottom of the table and still without a League win all season. Westwood joined the club when they were known as Solihull Ladies in 2015-16 and retained their WNL status in her three full seasons, finishing 4th, 9th and 7th.

13.11.18: Ross Thorpe is named as the new first-team manager and female development manager. The former Stratford Town Ladies manager has also previously enjoyed roles as an assistant manager at Nottingham Forest Ladies and Birmingham City Women.

03.01.19: Ross Thorpe stands down as manager.

08.01.19: Annie Zaidi is confirmed as new first-team manager. Zaidi, who has been part of the coaching set-up at the club since 2017 took over on a caretaker basis for Sunday's 2-1 League defeat to Birmingham & West Midlands and has now been given the job on a permanent basis. She is believed to be the only UEFA B coach in Europe who wears a hijab.

25.05.19: Following the departure of Annie Zaidi at the end of the season David Healey takes over as new manager with Dan Kembery continuing in his role as assistant manager.

2018-19 RESULTS: (HOME VENUE: WEST MIDLANDS SPORTS & SOCIAL CLUB, UNLESS STATED)

2018-19 WNL Midlands 1					Att	Pos
19.08	Burton Albion (a)	L	1-7	Phillippa Harmison (pen) 68	120	
26.08	Wolverhampton W (a)	L	0-7		110	11
09.09	Long Eaton United (h)	L	2-3	Emily Scott 63, (pen) 90	20	10
11.09	West Brom Albion (a)	L	0-8		56	10
16.09	Sporting Khalsa (h)	L	0-2		30	10
30.09	The New Saints (a)	L	0-3			10
28.10	Nettleham (h)	L	1-2	Jade Hewitt 28	40	11
01.11	Bedworth United (h)	L	1-4	Riann Hunt 85	30	11
25.11	Steel City W (a)	W	3-0	Chloe Bickley 10, 18, Abbie Taylor 23	28	10
02.12	Bir'ham & W M (h)		P-P			10
06.01	Bir'ham & W M (h)	L	1-2	Jade Hewitt 85	30	10
13.01	Burton Albion (h)	L	0-2		25	10
20.01	Wolverhampton W (h)	L	0-3		25	10
03.02	Long Eaton United (a)		P-P			10
10.02	Long Eaton United (a)	L	1-4	Abbie Taylor 40	32	10
12.02	West Brom Albion (h)	L	0-11		25	10
17.02	Sporting Khalsa (a)	L	2-6	Marianna Redmond-Lyon 18, 40	35	10
17.03	The New Saints (h)		P-P			10
24.03	Nettleham (a)	L	1-5	Chloe Bickley 37	50	10
31.03	Bedworth United (a)	L	1-5	Cherelle Archibald 60	35	10
07.04	Steel City W (h)	W	2-1	Hannah Vincent 75, Amelia Kirk 80	25	10
28.04	The New Saints (h)*	L	0-4		20	10
05.05	Bir'ham & W M (a)	L	2-9	Chante Douglas 65, Abbie Taylor 75	42	10

*Played at Studley Sports Centre

2018-19 FA Cup

23.09 RQ2	Loughborough Students (h)	W	3-2 aet	Alice Belcher 49, Amelia Kirk 75, Abbie Taylor 113	15
07.10 RQ3	Kidderminster H (a)	L	1-2	Samantha White 39	

2018-19 WNL Cup

02.09 DR	Brighouse Town (h)	L	0-7		45

2018-19 WNL Plate

R1	Bye				
14.10 R2	Middlesbrough (h)		P-P		
21.10 R3	Middlesbrough (h)	L	0-6		30

2018-19 Birmingham FA County Cup

18.11 R1	Stourbridge FC (h)	W	3-0	*Jade Hewitt missed pen 6 (saved by Amie Preston),* Catriona Stobie 55, Amelia Kirk 68, Natalie Dean 85	30
16.12 R2	Knowle (a)	D	1-1 (L2-4p)	Jade Hewitt 66	40

"Although 2018-19 was an extremely tough season, I feel our proudest achievement was the attitude and perseverance of every person involved in this team from players, managers and supporters. Every week the girls turned up to play the game that they love and stuck together through everything that happened. Everyone in the team has grown and shown real fight, grit and determination to keep the team together and stay in the division."

Abbie Taylor – Captain

SOUTHAMPTON FC

2019-20: WNL SOUTH WEST 1 (Tier 4)

Founded: 2018

Nickname: Saints

Season 2018-19:

Southern Regional Prem (Tier 5): 1st (P)

FA Cup: 2nd Round

League Cup: Winners

County Cup: Quarter-finals

Southampton FC Women are formally affiliated to the men's professional club Southampton FC who formed a senior women's team ahead of the 2018-19 season. They are not to be confused with Southampton Women's FC or Southampton Saints. As recently as 2017-18 Southampton FC were one of only two existing men's Premier League clubs, along with Manchester United, not to run a senior women's team. At that point both clubs reintroduced women's football and applied to join the new Championship. United were successful, but Southampton FC were not. They began life in Tier 5 but enjoyed immediate promotion to Tier 4 by winning the 2018-19 Southern Regional Premier League without dropping a point and completing the Double thanks to success in the League Cup.

2018-19 AS IT HAPPENS

16.07.18: Southampton FC announce the appointment of former England international Marieanne Spacey-Cale – who won 91 caps – as their new head of girl's and women's football.

02.12.18: Southampton FC lose for the first time in any competition this season as they go down 4-0 to Tier 3 side MK Dons in the FA Cup 2nd Round. It's their 13th game of 2018-19.

21.04.19: Southampton FC clinch the Southern Regional Premier title (Tier 5) with an 8-0 win at home to Barton Rovers and seal promotion to the FA WNL South West 1 (Tier 4) for 2019-20. It's their 17th straight League win of the season and they are yet to drop a point.

2018-19 RESULTS: (HOME VENUE: TESTWOOD STADIUM, (AFC TOTTON), UNLESS STATED)

2018-19 SOUTHERN RP

16.09	Newbury (h)	W	11-0	Ellie Chaffe (x2), Caitlin Collighan, Georgie Freeland (x4), Chloe Newton (x4)
30.09	Woodley United (a)	W	3-1	Ellie Chaffe, Georgie Freeland (x2)
21.10	Newbury (a)	W	9-0	Ellie Chaffe (x2), Georgie Freeland (x2), Ella Pusey (x3), Georgina Lowe, Own Goal
28.10	New Milton Town (h)	W	w/o	
04.11	Winchester City Flyers (h)	W	2-0	Ella Pusey (x2)
16.12	AFC Bournemouth CST (h)	W	3-1	Chloe Newton (x3)
06.01	Warsash Wasps (a)	W	5-0	Georgie Freeland, Caitlin Collighan, Emily Wernham, Ellie Chaffe, Shelly Provan
27.01	Ascot United (a)	W	4-1	Chloe Newton (x2), Caitlin Collighan. Ellie Chaffe
10.02	Oxford City (h)	W	5-0	Phoebe Williams, Shannon Sievwright (x2), Chloe Newton, Ellie Chaffe
17.02	New Milton Town (a)	W	3-0	Chloe Newton, Ella Morris, Phoebe Williams
10.03	Woodley United (h)	W	3-0	Chloe Newton, Ellie Chaffe, Ella Pusey
24.03	Winchester City Flyers (a)	W	6-0	Rachel Woods, Georgie Freeland (x2), Ella Pusey (x2), Ellie Chaffe
31.03	AFC Bournemouth CST (a)	W	4-1	Chloe Newton (x4)
07.04	Ascot United (h)	W	9-0	Ellie Chaffe, Chloe Newton, Georgie Freeland (x2), Shannon Sievwright, Ella Pusey (x2), Emily Wernham (x2)
14.04	Barton Rovers (a)	W	3-0	Shannon Sievwright, Rachel Woods, Ella Pusey
17.04	Warsash Wasps (h)	W	6-0	Ellie Chaffe, Ella Pusey, Emily Wernham (x2), Georgie Freeland (x2)
21.04	Barton Rovers (h)	W	8-0	Chloe Newton (x2), Ella Morris, Georgie Freeland, Emily Wernham (x2), Ellie Chaffe (x2)
28.04	Oxford City (a)	W	6-0	Ellie Chaffe, Phoebe Williams, Georgie Freeland, Ella Pusey (x2), Chloe Newton

2018-19 FA CUP

26.08 PR	Winchester City Flyers (a)	W	2-0	Ellie Chaffe, Emma Godden
09.09 RQ1	Swindon Spitfires (a)	W	6-0	Ellie Chaffe, Harriet Eastham, Georgie Freeland (x2), Shelly Provan, Shannon Sievwright
23.09 RQ2	New Milton Town (h)	W	5-0	Sam Burt, Ellie Chaffe, Caitlin Collighan, Kelly-Marie Fripp, Own Goal
07.10 RQ3	Larkhall Athletic (h)	W	4-1	Georgie Freeland, Rachel Woods, Ellie Chaffe (x2)
11.11 R1	Poole Town (a)	W	3-0	Georgie Freeland, Ella Pusey, Shannon Sievwright
02.12 R2	MK Dons (a)	L	0-4	

2018-19 League Cup

25.11 R1	Moneyfields (h)	W	4-0	Ella Pusey (x3), Georgie Freeland
13.01 QF	Wargrave (a)	W	9-0	Chloe Newton (x5), Caitlin Collighan (x2), Rachel Woods, Own Goal
24.02 SF	Wycombe Wanderers (a)	W	6-0	Ellie Chaffe (x3), Phoebe Williams, Chloe Newton, Georgie Freeland
19.05 F	Oxford City (h)	W	2-0	Phoebe Williams 61, Ella Pusey 68

2018-19 Hampshire FA County Cup

R1	Bye			
18.11 R2	Basingstoke Town (a)	W	11-1	Sam Burt, Chloe Newton (x4), Georgina Lowe (x3), Aliss Wheeler, Shelly Provan, Ellie Chaffe
20.01 QF	Portsmouth (a)	L	1-2	Chloe Newton

SOUTHAMPTON SAINTS

Folded in July 2019

Founded: 1979 (as Red Star Southampton)

Nickname: The Saints

Season 2018-19:

WNL South West 1 (Tier 4): 8th

FA Cup: 3rd Qualifying Round

WNL Cup: Determining Round

WNL Plate: 1st Round

County Cup: Semi-finals

The first club in the region – Southampton Women – was founded in 1970 and went on to win the FA Cup eight times before folding in 1985-86. At that point many of their players joined Red Star Southampton, which had been founded in 1979 and would go on to become Southampton Saints. Southampton Women then also reformed in 2003. Neither Southampton Saints nor Southampton Women should be confused with Southampton FC Women which is attached to men's Premier League club Southampton FC. However, in 1995 Southampton Saints did form an affiliation with Southampton FC, but that ended when the men's club withdrew its support after being relegated from the Premier League in 2005. On 3 July 2019 Southampton Saints sadly announced that due to a lack of financial support they had been forced to fold.

2018-19 AS IT HAPPENS

19.08.18: Saints get the new League campaign under way with a win as Catherine Browning scores twice in the space of two minutes to secure a 2-1 victory away to Swindon Town.

20.01.19: Alisha Buckingham scores five as Saints beat lower division Widbrook United 9-2 in the Hampshire FA County Cup quarter-final.

17.03.19: Saints become the first team to lose a League match to Maidenhead United all season as they go down 3-0 in what is United's 13th game of the campaign.

03.07.19: Saints tweet: "It is with great sadness and heavy hearts that we officially announce that this long standing and historic club has completely disbanded due to decreasing player numbers and a lack of financial support."

2018-19 RESULTS: (HOME VENUE: THE UNIVERSAL STADIUM, (SHOLING FC), UNLESS STATED)

2018-19 WNL SW 1

					Att	Pos
19.08	Swindon Town (a)	W	2-1	Catherine Browning 14, 16	52	
09.09	Chesham United (h)	L	0-5		15	7
12.09	Southampton W (a)	L	0-5		38	9
16.09	Cheltenham Town (a)	L	1-2	Catherine Browning 9	71	9
04.10	Poole Town (h)	W	3-0	Catherine Browning 1, 71, Sabrina Morris Manosalva 15	20	6
04.11	Buckland Athletic (h)	L	0-2		20	
11.11	Brislington (a)	L	1-2	Emma King 28	48	8
25.11	Keynsham Town (a)	L	1-3	Alisha Buckingham 87	40	8
02.12	Larkhall Athletic (a)		P-P			8
16.12	Maidenhead Utd (a)		P-P			8
06.01	Larkhall Athletic (a)	L	2-3	Alisha Buckingham 81, Krystal Whyte 85, Krystal Whyte sent off 90+1	30	8
13.01	Swindon Town (h)	W	3-1	Alisha Buckingham 48, 80, Lisa Gilham 89	15	8
27.01	Keynsham Town (h)		P-P			8
14.02	Southampton W (h)	L	1-7	Alisha Buckingham 38	54	8
24.02	Chesham United (a)	L	0-8		40	8
05.03	Poole Town (a)	W	4-1	Krystal Whyte (x2), Libby O'Dell, Alisha Buckingham	24	8
10.03	Larkhall Athletic (h)	W	1-0	Rhianne Parsons 35	18	7
17.03	Maidenhead Utd (a)	L	0-3		10	7
24.03	Brislington (h)	W	4-2	Catherine Browning, Emma Eldridge, Sabrina Morris Manosalva, Libby O'Dell	15	7
31.03	Cheltenham Town (h)	L	0-2		27	7
07.04	Keynsham Town (h)	L	0-5		12	8
14.04	Buckland Athletic (a)	L	w/o			8
05.05	Maidenhead Utd (h)	L	0-1		14	8

2018-19 FA CUP

23.09 RQ2	Warsash Wasps (h)		P-P		
30.09 RQ2	Warsash Wasps (h)	W	3-0	Sabrina Morris Manosalva 16, Catherine Browning 30, Alisha Buckingham 65	30
07.10 RQ3	Keynsham Town (a)	L	0-6		45

2018-19 WNL Cup

02.09 DR	AFC Wimbledon (h)	L	0-1		25

2018-19 WNL Plate

14.10 R1	Keynsham Town (a)	L	1-7	Alisha Buckingham 15	

2018-19 Hampshire FA County Cup

R1	Bye				
18.11 R2	AFC Bournemouth CST (h)	W	3-0	Krystal Whyte (pen) 34, Alisha Buckingham 49, 65	25est
20.01 QF	Widbrook United (h)	W	9-2	Libby O'Dell 1, Catherine Browning 3, 29, 57, Alisha Buckingham 6, 10, 36, 65, 75	20est
17.02 SF	Portsmouth (a)	L	0-1		157

SOUTHAMPTON WOMEN'S

2019-20: WNL SOUTH WEST 1 (Tier 4)

Founded: 2003

Nickname: None

Season 2018-19:

WNL South West 1 (Tier 4): Runners-up

FA Cup: 2nd Qualifying Round

WNL Cup: 2nd Round

County Cup: Runners-up

Southampton Women's have been in Tier 4 since winning promotion ahead of the 2017-18 season as champions of the 2016-17 Southern Regional Premier League. It's a matter of dispute as to whether the current Southampton Women's is a separate entity to the Southampton Women's that won eight FA Cups between 1971-1981, or a continuation of the club. The original Southampton Women's folded in 1985-86 with the current outfit founded in 2003. Only Arsenal (14) have won more FA Cups than the original Southampton Women's. Southampton Women's are not to be confused with Southampton FC Women, who are affiliated to men's Premier League club Southampton FC, or the now disbanded Southampton Saints.

2018-19 AS IT HAPPENS

15.12.18: The club announces that first team manager Simon Parker is leaving with immediate effect. Parker joined in 2014 taking the team from the Southern Regional League to the WNL, winning 37 of his 42 League matches. The following day Parker is confirmed as the assistant manager at Championship side Lewes who have recently appointed Fran Alonso as their manager. Parker has previously worked as assistant under Alonso at Southampton Women's.

13.01.19: Aimee Barnett makes her 200th appearance for the club in the 5-0 win away to Poole.

03.04.19: Southampton finish as runners-up in the Hampshire FA County Cup after a 3-1 defeat to Tier 3 Portsmouth at AFC Totton. Pompey race into a 3-0 lead inside 37 minutes with goals from Danielle Rowe, Shannon Albuery and Jade Bradley. Southampton pull one back through Natalie Bavister with 20 minutes left, but Pompey hold on for the victory. The match is watched by a competition record crowd of 577.

2018-19 RESULTS: (HOME VENUE: GREG WARILY REC, (BLACKFIELD & LANGLEY FC), UNLESS STATED)

2018-19 WNL SW 1					Att	Pos
19.08	Poole Town (h)	W	8-1	Roxanne Lee-Stewart 7, 27, Cassie Thorp 30, Lavinia Nkomo 40, Hannah Chalk (og) 52, Jane Yeates 74, 85, Kia Anteney 90	46	
26.08	Brislington (a)	W	3-0	Rachel Anderson 52, Jane Yeates 55, 90	42	3
12.09	Southampton S (h)	W	5-0	Laura Vokes 3, Manuela Naprta 7, Rachel Anderson 12, Emma Pinner 69, 84	38	1
16.09	Swindon Town (h)	W	5-0	Rachel Anderson 11, 40, Laura Vokes 20, 71, Kayleigh Tonks 60	18	3
03.10	Maidenhead U (h)	W	5-0	Emma Pinner 2, Natalia Bavister 10, Chelsie Hay 24, Jane Yeates 58, Kayleigh Tonks 86	34	1
21.10	Larkhall Athletic (a)	W	5-0	Jane Yeates 6, 39, 82, Emma Pinner 63, Kayleigh Tonks 90, Rosie Kirby sent off 87	60	1
11.11	Chesham U (h)	W	2-1	Chelsie Hay 44, 66, Chelsie Hay missed pen 75 (saved by Lucia Delves)	41	1
25.11	Cheltenham Town (a)	L	0-1		76	2
09.12	Larkhall Athletic (h)	W	3-0	Emma Pinner (x2), Kellie Warren	23	2
16.12	Keynsham Town (a)	W	3-0	Philippa Holden 15, Kellie Warren 68, Chelsie Hay 90+4	75	1
13.01	Poole Town (a)	W	5-0	Emma Pinner 16, 24, 38, Roxanne Lee-Stewart 52, Natalie Bavister 82	18	1
03.02	Buckland Athletic (a)	L	1-2	Philippa Holden 68	43	1
10.02	Brislington (h)	W	4-2	Jessica Werrett (og) 6, Roxanne Lee- Stewart 39, Emma Pinner 58, Natalie Bavister 79	27	1
14.02	Southampton S (a)	W	7-1	Roxy Lee-Stewart 6, Emma Pinner 9, 30, 50, Philippa Holden 46, Jane Yeates 68, Laura Da Silva 90	54	1
24.02	Swindon Town (a)	W	5-0	Manuela Naprta 2, Laura Da Silva 25, Natalie Bavister 65, Jane Yeates 70, Hannah Samuels 82	45	1
10.03	Keynsham Town (h)	L	1-5	Hannah Samuels sent off 21, Jane Yeates 34	44	1
13.03	Maidenhead Utd (a)		P-P			1
24.03	Cheltenham Town (h)	L	0-1		34	2
14.04	Chesham United (a)	W	3-2	Kirsty Whitton 56, Chelsie Hay 63, Julia Moulton 89		2
17.04	Maidenhead Utd (a)	W	3-0	Natalie Bavister 45, Kayleigh Tonks 66, Emma Pinner 68	15	2
05.05	Buckland Athletic (h)	D	0-0		38	2

2018-19 FA Cup

23.09 RQ2	Marine Academy Plymouth (h)	L	1-2	Jane Yeates 63	42

2018-19 WNL Cup

02.09 DR	St Nicholas (a)	W	w/o		
30.09 R1	Enfield Town (a)	W	4-3	Kayleigh Tonks 22, Natalie Bavister 38, Jane Yeates 47, Roxanne Lee-Stewart 87	45
14.10 R2	Plymouth A (h)		P-P		
28.10 R2	Plymouth A (h)	L	1-3	Natalie Bavister 59	45

2018-19 Hampshire FA County Cup

R1	Bye				
18.11 R2	Gosport Borough (a)	W	7-0	Chelsie Hay (x3), Emma Pinner, Roxanne Lee-Stewart (x2), Sophie Hall	
20.01 QF	Moneyfields (a)		P-P		
27.01 QF	Moneyfields (a)	W	4-1	Natalie Bavister 27, Roxanne Lee-Stewart 38, Kellie Warren missed pen, Emma Pinner 62, Philippa Holden 83	
17.02 SF	Warsash Wasps (h)	W	11-0	Jane Yeates 1, 33, 35, Emma Pinner 19, 51, Natalie Bavister 60, Chelsea Hay 66, 70, 87, Kayleigh Tonks 72, 82	51
03.04 F (n)	Portsmouth (n)	L	1-3	Natalie Bavister 70	577

(n) Played at Testwood Park, (AFC Totton)

"After three successive promotions we finished as runners-up in [what was called] WPL South West 1 at the end of 2017-18. It was very much our aim to go one better and win the title in 2018-19, but we just missed out at the end of a season of transition. We had plenty of challenges to deal with. Our manager left before Christmas and we had several long-term injuries to key players. We are confident that the appointment of manager Aaron Smith and his coaching team will bring an even higher level of professionalism to the club and offer a real pathway to girls in the area to make it into the WNL. We are increasing the number of youth teams to provide this opportunity and we are proud that our team of volunteer coaches and committee members share the passion to offer the best female football opportunities in Hampshire."

Emma Delaney – Chairman

SPORTING KHALSA

2019-20: WNL MIDLANDS 1 (Tier 4)

Founded: 2004 (as FC Reedswood)

Nickname: Sporting

Season 2018-19

WNL Midlands 1 (Tier 4): 4th

FA Cup: 3rd Qualifying Round

WNL Cup: Determining Round

WNL Plate: 3rd Round

County Cup: Runners-up

FC Reedswood Ladies were founded in 2004 and became integrated into Sporting Khalsa men's club in 2015, becoming Sporting Khalsa Women. Sporting Khalsa men's club began life as a grassroots team in 1991, competing in the Walsall & District Sunday Leagues. They quickly grew and between 1995 and 1997 they were playing at semi-professional level. The 2018-19 season was one of real progress for the women's team with the club finishing 4th in WNL Midlands 1 (four places higher than in 2017-18) and reaching the final of the Staffordshire FA County Cup.

2018-19 AS IT HAPPENS

16.12.18: Sporting rack up double figures against lower division Stafford Town in the Staffordshire FA County Cup quarter-final. Lauren Walker bags a hat-trick in a 10-0 win while Chloe Handy and Paige Kavanagh net two apiece and Jessica Keeling, Angelique Morley and Natalie Morris are all on target too.

31.03.19: Kick-off for the away match at Burton is put back after Sporting forget their kit. The delay leads to the match being played over two halves of just 40 minutes, with Sporting winning 4-0.

30.04.19: Sporting are beaten 8-1 by Tier 3 outfit Stoke City in the Staffordshire FA County Cup final. It's the 11th year in a row that Stoke have won the competition. A stunning equaliser from Natalie Morris in the 24th minute briefly has Khalsa level at 1-1, but Hannah Keryakoplis goes on to score seven for Stoke.

05.05.19: A 4-1 win over Bedworth United sees Sporting leapfrog their opponents to reach their highest position of the season on the final day. Paige Kavanagh scores twice, with Angelique Morley and Chloe Handy also on target to move Khalsa in to 4th place.

2018-19 RESULTS: (HOME VENUE: ASPRAY ARENA, (SPORTING KHALSA FC) UNLESS STATED)

2018-19 WNL Midlands 1

					Att	Pos
19.08	Long Eaton Utd (h)	W	3-2	Stephanie Kydd 50, Lauren Walker 70, Chloe Handy 88	30	
09.09	Nettleham (h)	L	2-3	Kiera Willdigg 66, 73	30	6
12.09	Wolverhampton W (a)		P-P			7
16.09	Solihull Moors (a)	W	2-0	Bethan Woolley, Donna Arrowsmith	30	6
19.09	Wolverhampton W (h)	L	2-10	Kiera Willdigg, Bethan Woolley	50	8
30.09	Steel City W (h)		P-P			8
02.10	Bir'ham & W M (a)	L	1-2	Rebecca Gill-Parsons 48	28	8
21.10	West Brom Albion (h)	L	0-3		30	9
28.10	Steel City W (a)	D	1-1	Natalie Morris	16	8
04.11	Burton Albion (h)	D	2-2	Lauren Walker 54, Chloe Handy 55	20	9
11.11	The New Saints (a)	W	4-0	Paige Kavanagh 27, Stephanie Kydd 44, Chloe Evans 70, Lou Anderson (og) 88	27	7
02.12	Bedworth United (a)	D	3-3	Jessica Keeling 18, Natalie Morris 23, Angelique Morley 56	35	7
13.01	Long Eaton United (a)	W	2-1	Chloe May Coldicott, Bethan Woolley		7
10.02	Nettleham (a)		P-P			8
17.02	Solihull Moors (h)	W	6-2	Angeliquie Morley 1, Julie Stirrup (pen) 35, Natalie Morris 52, Bethan Woolley 63, Paige Kavanagh 70, 78	35	7
24.02	Steel City W (h)	W	4-0	Chloe Handy, Kiera Willdigg, Bethan Woolley (x2)	30	5
27.02	Wolverhampton W (a)	L	1-3	Natalie Morris	40	5
03.03	Nettleham (a)	W	3-2	Paige Kavanagh 23, Angelique Morley 42, 71	50	5
10.03	West Brom Albion (a)	L	0-5		56	5
13.03	Bir'ham & W M (h)	W	2-0	Chloe May Coldicott, Chloe Handy	40	5
31.03	Burton Albion (a)	W	4-0	Bethan Woolley 24, Julie Stirrup 32, Angelique Morley 61, Paige Kavanagh 81	51	5
14.04	The New Saints (h)	W	3-0	Chloe Handy 55, 63, Lauren Walker 78	40	5
05.05	Bedworth United (h)	W	4-1	Paige Kavanagh (x2), Angelique Morley, Chloe Handy		4

2018-19 FA Cup

23.09 RQ2	Crusaders (a)	W	2-0	Kiera Willdigg 25, Chloe Handy 60	
07.10 RQ3	Long Eaton United (h)	L	1-6	Becky Parsons	30

2018-19 WNL Cup

02.09 DR	Leeds United (h)	L	1-2	Lauren Walker 30	30

2018-19 WNL Plate

R1	Bye				
14.10 R2	Steel City W (a)	W	6-4	Chloe Handy, Stephanie Kydd, Paige Kavanagh, Laura Quigley, Bethan Woolley, Lauren Walker	19
06.01 R3	West Brom Albion (h)	L	1-2	Paige Kavanagh 25	60

2018-19 Staffordshire FA County Cup

R1	Bye				
18.11 R2	Wyrley (a)	W	6-2	Gurj Dulay (x2), Paige Kavanagh, Julie Stirrup, Angelique Morley, Becky Parsons	
16.12 QF	Stafford Town (a)	W	10-0	Chloe Handy (x2), Paige Kavanagh (x2), Jessica Keeling, Angelique Morley, Natalie Morris, Lauren Walker (x3)	
20.01 SF	Stoke City Dev (h)	W	3-0	Jessica Keeling, Angelique Morley, Bethan Woolley	50
30.04 F	Stoke City (n)	L	1-8	Natalie Morris 24	336

(n) Played at Evans Park, (Stafford Town FC)

"The 2018-19 season was an improvement on the previous campaign. We finished four places, 10 points and nine goals better off. For 2019-20 we will remain at our own ground – The Aspray Arena – where we also train. Not many clubs at our level have that luxury so we are in a great position. We have a strong group, but we want to bring in more who like our project and can help us grow, develop and play a part in taking us forward."

Kelly Williams – Chairperson and First Team Assistant Manager

STEEL CITY WANDERERS

Folded summer 2019

Founded: 1993 (as Loxley Girls)

Nickname: Steels

Season 2018-19:

WNL Midlands 1 (Tier 4): 11th (R)

FA Cup: 2nd Qualifying Round

WNL Cup: Determining Round

WNL Plate: 2nd Round

County Cup: 2nd Round

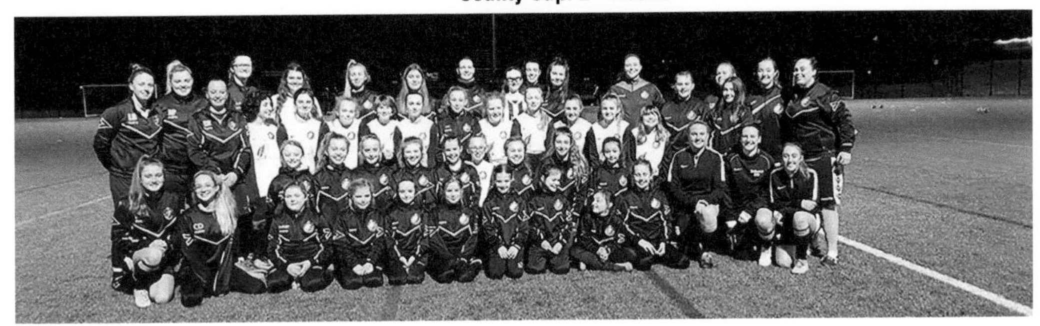

Based in Sheffield, the club took the name Steel City Wanderers in 1995, two years after forming as Loxley Girls. They were founded by Steve and Sue Odams who wanted their triplet daughters Cheryl, Johanna and Selina to have a place to play football. Having spent five consecutive seasons in Tier 4, injuries and work commitments hit hard in 2018-19 with Steel City Wanderers earning praise from their opposition for sometimes taking to the field with just eight players and always trying their best despite a string of poor results which ultimately led to their relegation out of the WNL. In summer 2019 they took the difficult decision to fold their senior team and continue with youth football only, with a view to hopefully reforming in "two to three years".

2018-19 AS IT HAPPENS

28.10.18: After starting the season with six straight League defeats, Wanderers can celebrate their first point thanks to a 1-1 draw at home to Sporting Khalsa.

04.11.18: Despite a 7-1 defeat at home to Birmingham & West Midlands, goalkeeper Kirsty Johnson puts in a commendable performance including saving a first-half penalty.

07.04.19: Lucy Ridley ends Wanderers' run of four League games without a goal, but it isn't enough to prevent a 10th consecutive League defeat as the team lose 2-1 away to Solihull Moors.

2018-19 RESULTS: (HOME VENUE: SGP THORNCLIFFE, HIGH GREEN, UNLESS STATED)

2018-19 WNL Midlands 1					Att	Pos
19.08	Wolverhampton W (h)	L	0-11		65	
26.08	Burton Albion (h)	L	2-4	Sarah Middleton, Libby Hallam	28	10
09.09	Bedford United (a)	L	1-2	Lucy Ridley	65	11

12.09	Nettleham (a)	L	2-6	Lucy Ridley, Claire Attrill	100	11
16.09	West Brom Albion (h)	L	1-18	Lucy Ridley 15	43	11
30.09	Sporting Khalsa (a)		P-P			11
07.10	The New Saints (h)	L	1-6	Lauren Brown	23	11
28.10	Sporting Khalsa (h)	D	1-1	Libby Hallam 40	16	10
04.11	Bir' ham & W M (a)	L	1-7	Lucy Blackburn 70, *Steel City GK saved pen 43*	17	10
25.11	Solihull Moors (h)	L	0-3		28	11
06.01	Long Eaton Utd (a)	L	0-8		40	11
13.01	Wolverhampton W (a)		P-P			11
03.02	Bedworth United (h)	L	0-2		35	11
10.02	Burton Albion (a)	L	1-4	Mia Ransom 40, *Clare Keats sent off 90+4*	61	11
12.02	Nettleham (h)	L	0-2		70	11
24.02	Sporting Khalsa (a)	L	0-4		30	11
03.03	Wolverhampton W (a)		P-P			11
17.03	West Brom Albion (a)		P-P			11
24.03	The New Saints (a)	L	0-14		20	11
31.03	Wolverhampton W (a)	L	0-11		60	11
07.04	Solihull Moors (a)	L	1-2	Lucy Ridley	25	11
14.04	Bir'ham & W M (h)	L	0-11		20	11
21.04	West Brom Albion (a)	L	0-7		33	11
05.05	Long Eaton United (h)	L	0-4		65	12

2018-19 FA Cup

23.09 RQ2	Chester-le-Street T (h)	L	1-8	Zoe Beresford 27	28

2018-19 WNL Cup

02.09 DR	Newcastle United (h)	L	1-6	Sarah Middleton	38

2018-19 WNL Plate

R1	Bye				
14.10 R2	Sporting Khalsa (h)	L	4-6	Libby Hallam, Lucy Ridley (x3)	19

2018-19 Sheffield & Hallamshire FA County Cup

R1	Bye		
16.12 R2	Huddersfield Town (h)	L	w/o

"It goes without saying that 2018-19 was a hard, gruelling season. Suffering from an endless list of injuries and work commitments, we sometimes took to the pitch with just eight players. For me every player who went out on to that pitch was Player of the Year. Most of the team stuck together, battled through and saw the season out with enjoyment regardless of the results. The club is without a doubt one of the friendliest, close knit groups you will find. It's not just a club, it's a family. We had to take the difficult decision this summer to fold the senior team, but we hope that in time we will be able to return."

Kirsty Johnson – Manager

STEVENAGE
2019-20: WNL SOUTH EAST 1 (Tier 4)

Founded: 2001

Nickname: Boro

Season 2018-19:

WNL South East 1 (Tier 4): 9th

FA Cup: 3rd Qualifying Round

WNL Cup: Determining Round

WNL Plate: Quarter-finals

County Cup: Runners-up

Stevenage Ladies were officially formed as Stevenage Borough Ladies in 2001 and moved under the umbrella of the men's professional outfit in 2014. Like the men's team the club's nickname remains Boro, despite the fact the 'Borough' part of the club's name was dropped in 2010. Although they have support from the men's club, they continue to fund themselves fully with player subs and fundraising. In 2017-18, under manager Reece Buck, Boro achieved their highest ever League finish as they secured 6th place in Tier 4. In 2018-19 they dropped to 9th and were County Cup runners-up.

2018-19 AS IT HAPPENS

18.11.18: Ashleigh Deacon and Amy Makewell both score four as Stevenage beat lower division Hitchin Belles 16-0 in the Hertfordshire FA County Cup 1st Round.

17.03.19: Stevenage are unable to hold onto the Hertfordshire FA County Cup that they won in 2017-18 as they are beaten 4-0 by Watford's U23s side in the final.

31.03.19: Stevenage club captain Paige Logie undergoes surgery after tearing her anterior cruciate ligament in January.

28.04.19: A 3-2 home win over fellow strugglers Norwich City ensures Stevenage are safe from relegation with a game to spare. An Ashleigh Deacon brace and a goal from Amy Makewell sees Stevenage lead 3-0 at half-time before Norwich hit back and almost rescue a point.

2018-19 RESULTS: (HOME VENUE: HERTINGFORDBURY PARK, (HERTFORD TOWN FC), UNLESS STATED)

2018-19 WNL SE 1

					Att	Pos
19.08	Actonians (h)	W	5-2	Nicole Emmings (x2), Amy Josland, Amy Makewell, Ellie Searle	25	
26.08	Billericay Town (a)	L	1-6	Nicole Emmings 30	70	7
09.09	Leyton Orient (h)	L	0-2		20	10
12.09	Cambridge U (a)	D	0-0		90	9
16.09	Crawley Wasps (h)	L	2-7	Nicole Emmings 45, 86	25	10
30.09	Norwich City (a)	W	2-1	Shona Chitate 20, Ashleigh Deacon 30, Norwich GK saved Stevenage pen	49	6
03.10	Enfield Town (a)	L	0-4		67	8
21.10	AFC Wimbledon (h)	L	1-2	Jodie Whitford Stark 50	30	9
04.11	Denham United (a)	W	2-1	Amy Makewell 22, Ashleigh Deacon 25	56	8
25.11	Ipswich Town (h)	L	0-1		20	8
06.01	Leyton Orient (a)	W	3-2	Nicole Emmings 12, 90, Ashleigh Deacon 80	56	8
13.01	Actonians (a)	L	1-5	Shona Chitate 10	15	8
03.02	Billericay Town (h)		P-P			10
13.02	Cambridge U (h)	D	1-1	Ashleigh Deacon 87	65	10
17.02	Crawley Wasps (a)	L	0-7		60	10
24.02	Billericay Town (h)	L	0-2		28	10
03.03	Luton Town (a)	W	1-0	Erin Pope 71	94	10
06.03	Enfield Town (h)	L	0-1		60	10
10.03	Norwich City (h)		P-P			10
24.03	AFC Wimbledon (a)	W	2-1	Ashleigh Deacon 2, Stevenage GK Gemma Biggadike saved pen 50, Shona Chitate 57	60	9
31.03	Denham United (h)	L	0-1		25	9
14.04	Ipswich Town (a)	D	2-2	Ellie Searle 21, Erin Pope 46	61	9
28.04	Norwich City (h)	W	3-2	Ashleigh Deacon 28, 38, Amy Makewell 30	35	9
05.05	Luton Town (h)	W	3-0	Erin Pope 1, Amy Makewell 24, Ellie Searle 46	70	9

*Played at The Abbey Stadium, (Cambridge United FC)

2018-19 FA CUP

23.09 RQ2	Peterborough Northern Star (a)	W	5-1	Amy Makewell 40, 50, Ashleigh Deacon 58, Ellie Searle 70, Erin Pope 80	30
07.10 RQ3	Cambridge United (a)	D	2-2aet (L2-4p)	Ellie Searle 73, Amy Makewell 79	82

2018-19 WNL Cup

02.09 DR	Cardiff City L (h)	L	1-4	Nicole Emmings	30

2018-19 WNL Plate

R1	Bye				
14.10 R2	Norwich City (a)	W	w/o		
02.12 R3	Ipswich Town (a)	W	2-1 aet	Ashleigh Deacon 90+4, Ellie Searle 94	26
10.02 QF	Gillingham (h)	L	0-4		

2018-19 Hertfordshire FA County Cup

18.11 R1	Hitchin Belles (h)	W	16-0	Ashleigh Deacon (x4), Amy Makewell (x4), Paige Logie (x2), Kristi Burling (x2), Nicole Emmings, Poppy Bennett, Dominique Godbeer, Ellie Searle	20est
09.12 QF	Royston Town (h)	W	7-2	Ellie Searle (x3), Hogan Coley (x2), Ashleigh Deacon, Erin Pope	45est
20.01 SF	Hoddesdon Town (a)	W	7-0	Shona Chitate (x2), Ashleigh Deacon (x2), Nicole Emmings (x2), Amy Josland	
17.03 F	Watford U23s (n)	L	0-4		

(n) Played at Letchworth County Ground

"In the main we had a good 2018-19 season. The first team made the final of the County Cup for the fifth season running but fell at the last hurdle, losing to a strong Watford Under-23 team. The reserves also went deep into a cup competition as they reached the semi-finals of the League Plate, only to cruelly lose to a goal in extra time. It was important that our first team retained their WNL status and we did so, finishing 9th and giving ourselves the chance to embark on a fifth consecutive season at this level in 2019-20. We will also be making a positive change by rebranding ourselves as Stevenage Women instead of Stevenage Ladies."

Dave Potter – Chairman and Reserve Team Manager

STOCKPORT COUNTY

2019-20: WNL NORTH 1 (Tier 4)

Founded: 1989-90

Nickname: The Hatters

Season 2018-19:

North West Reg Prem (Tier 5): Champions (P)

FA Cup: 2nd Round

League Cup: Runners-up

County Cup: Winners

A partnership with the local authority saw Stockport County FC become one of the first men's clubs outside of the top division to set up a women's team when they formed The Ladies Club in 1989-90. After initial success, problems in the running of the club led to members breaking away to set up a new team called Stockport Ladies. In 1999 County set out to re-establish a good relationship with Stockport Ladies with the clubs merging ahead of 2000-01. In 2018-19 County sealed promotion to the WNL as champions of the North West Regional Premier (Tier 5) and also won the County Cup.

2018-19 AS IT HAPPENS

28.10.18: The Hatters become the first team for three years to inflict a League defeat on FC United of Manchester as they win 4-1 away to make it five League wins from five this season.

11.11.18: Two late goals from Chloe Mapp and Claire O'Reilly (who scores a free kick with the last kick of the game) see the Hatters come from 1-0 down away to Tier 4 Chorley to win 2-1 in the FA Cup 1st Round.

07.01.19: Hanna Wilson – who has been a leading assist-maker over the last few years – scores her first goal for Stockport to put her team 3-0 up away to Chesterfield. The Hatters go on to win the 3rd Qualifying Round match 6-0.

31.03.19: Having won their opening 13 League matches, Stockport drop their first points of the season as they are held 2-2 away to struggling Sir Tom Finney FC.

28.04.19: County win their final League match of the season 3-0 at home to Manchester Stingers to finish the campaign on top of the table two points ahead of FC United of Manchester. However, they will have to await the outcome of an FA enquiry later to determine whether FC United (two points behind them) should be awarded extra points for another team allegedly fielding an ineligible player against them earlier this season.

29.04.19: Goalkeeper Lauren Blackett is the hero when she saves a penalty as the Cheshire FA County Cup final against Tranmere Rovers goes to a shootout following a 1-1 draw. Jeneyah Webb then converts the winning kick for County.

19.05.19: Stockport have to settle for runners-up medals in the North West Regional Premier League Cup as they are beaten 5-2 after extra-time by FC United of Manchester. They are though confirmed as League champions with an FA hearing deciding runners-up FC United of Manchester will not be awarded extra points despite allegations an opponent fielded an ineligible player against them earlier in the season.

2018-19 RESULTS: (HOME VENUE: STOCKPORT SPORTS VILLAGE 3G PITCH, UNLESS STATED)

2018-19 North West Regional Premier

09.09	Mossley Hill Athletic (h)	W	4-2	Chloe Mapp, Grace Wardle, Jade Parker (x2)
16.09	Penrith AFC (a)	W	3-2	Chloe Mapp (x2), Claire O'Reilly
14.10	Wigan Athletic (h)	W	4-2	Chloe Mapp 19, Claire O'Reilly 67, 90+2, Nicola Connor 86
21.10	Penrith AFC (h)	W	10-1	Sophie John, Chloe Mapp (x4, 1pen), Katie Brusell (x4), Claire O'Reilly
28.10	FC United of Manchester (h)	W	4-1	Jodie Hancock 5, Chloe Mapp 46, Katie Brusell 58, Shelby Wolstencroft 84
04.11	Fleetwood Town Wrens (a)	W	2-1	Chloe Mapp, Hanifa Douglas
25.11	Merseyrail (h)	W	2-0	Chloe Mapp, Holly Stokes
06.01	Accrington (a)	W	9-0	Abi Hayes (x3), Hanifa Douglas (x3), Chloe Mapp (x2), Sophie John
20.01	Tranmere Rovers (a)	W	4-2	Abi Hayes 42, Chloe Mapp 45+1, Nicola Connor 60, Chaneece Reeves 73
27.01	Accrington (h)	W	6-1	Chloe Mapp, Abi Hayes, Chaneece Reeves, Holly Stokes, Jodie Hancock, Hanifa Douglas
24.02	Merseyrail (a)	W	3-2	Jeneyah Webb, Hanifa Douglas (pen), Jodie Hancock, *Hanifa Douglas missed pen*
03.03	Fleetwood Town Wrens (h)	W	1-0	Chloe Mapp
24.03	Mossley Hill Athletic (a)	W	2-1	Hanifa Douglas 11, Chloe Mapp 90
31.03	Sir Tom Finney FC (a)	D	2-2	Chloe Mapp, Nicola Connor
10.04	FC United of Manchester (a)	L	1-2	Jeneyah Webb 11
14.04	Tranmere Rovers (h)	W	5-4	Chaneece Reeves, Chloe Mapp (x3), Abi Hayes
17.04	Manchester Stingers (a)	W	3-1	Chloe Mapp 55, Jeneyah Webb 67, 75
21.04	Wigan Athletic (a)	W	6-1	Jeneyah Webb 42, 55, 85, Nicola Connor 49, Chloe Mapp 53, 81, *Stockport GK Lauren Blackett saved pen 83 (Wigan scored rebound)*
24.04	Sir Tom Finney FC (h)	W	6-1	Chloe Mapp (x2, 1pen), Nicola Connor, Abi Hayes, Hanifa Douglas (x2)
28.04	Manchester Stingers (h)	W	3-0	Chloe Mapp 28, Chaneece Reeves 33, Jodie Hancock 38, *Chloe Mapp missed pen 30 (saved)*

2018-19 FA Cup

02.09 RQ1	Warrington Wolverines (a)	W	4-1	Chloe Mapp, Jade White, Nicola Connor, Katie Brusell
23.09 RQ2	Bishop Auckland (a)	W	8-0	Chloe Mapp 1, 20, 29, (pen) 45, Katie Brusell 2, 40, Jeneyah Webb 85, Shelby Wolstencroft 90
07.10 RQ3	Chesterfield (a)	W	6-0	Nicola Connor, Chloe Mapp (x2), Hanna Wilson, Hanifa Douglas, Emma Massey
11.11 R1	Chorley (a)	W	2-1	Chloe Mapp, Claire O'Reilly
02.02 R2	Middlesbrough (a)	L	0-1	

2018-19 League Cup

13.01 R1	Wigan Athletic (h)	W	4-2	Chloe Mapp (x2), Hanifa Douglas, Abi Hayes
10.02 R2	Bury (h)	W	2-1	Hanifa Douglas, Jeneyah Webb
10.03 QF	Sir Tom Finney FC (h)	W	w/o	
07.04 SF	West Didsbury & Chorlton (h)	W	4-0	Nicola Connor 21, Jeneyah Webb 53, Chloe Mapp (pen) 74, 80
19.05 F	FC United of Manchester (n)	L	2-5 aet	Chloe Mapp 8, 40

(n)Millbank Linnets Stadium, (Runcorn Linnets FC)

2018-19 Cheshire FA County Cup

18.11 R1	Ashville Youth (a)	W	w/o	
R2	Bye			
17.02 QF	Warrington Wolverines (h)	W	4-0*	Jasmin Limb 9, 32, Masa Butler 63, Abi Hayes 72
19.03 SF	Cammell Laird 1907 (h)	W	9-0	Chloe Mapp (x4), Abi Hayes, Chaneece Reeves, Jodie Hancock, Jasmin Limb (x2)
29.04 F	Tranmere Rovers (n)	D	1-1 (W4-3p)	Hanifa Douglas 53

*Match abandoned at 75 mins due to serious injury to Stockport's Melissa von Bargen. Result stands (n)Played at Vauxhall Motors Stadium, (Vauxhall Motors FC)

"The highlight of 2018-19 was probably winning away at Mossley Hill. Our nearest rivals, FC United of Manchester, had travelled there a few weeks prior and just scraped a 1-0 victory so we went in expecting a tough game on the heavily sloped pitch. After going ahead early, we conceded late in the first half. We missed a number of chances and it looked like we were set to drop our first points of the season, but Chloe Mapp hit a brilliant volley from a long ball over the top beyond the keeper and into the back of the net. The moment the ball hit the back of the net the final whistle blew. Had it not been for that one goal, County wouldn't have crossed the line as champions."

James Gill – Media Officer

STOKE CITY
2019-20: WNL NORTHERN PREMIER (Tier 3)

Founded: 2001

Nickname: The Potters

Season 2018-19:

WNL Northern Premier (Tier 3): 7th

FA Cup: 4th Round

WNL Cup: Quarter-finals

County Cup: Winners

The first known women's team in Stoke was founded in 1921 by Len Bridgett, a director at Stoke City men's football club. Known as Stoke United, they played against the legendary Dick, Kerr's Ladies side from Preston twice in April 1921 before beating French outfit Les Sportives de Paris in two exhibition matches which took place in Barcelona. The modern Stoke City Ladies team was formed in 2001 and enjoyed a breakthrough season in 2012-13 when they won a Treble of trophies and gained promotion to the WPL Northern Division (Tier 3). They are now formally affiliated with men's professional club Stoke City. In 2018-19 they won the Staffordshire FA County Cup for the 11th year in a row, beating Tier 4 outfit Sporting Khalsa 8-1 in a final which was notable for the fact that Hannah Keryakoplis scored seven goals.

2018-19 AS IT HAPPENS

18.11.18: Stoke set a new club record for margin of victory when they beat Black Country Fusion 20-0 in their Staffordshire FA County Cup 2nd Round tie. Faye Singleton scores five goals on her full debut, including a hat-trick inside six minutes.

06.01.19: Hannah Keryakoplis scores a brilliant goal with one minute remaining as Stoke win 2-1 away to Derby to reach the FA Cup 4th Round for only the second time in the club's history.

10.02.19: Stoke City's FA Cup 4th Round match at home to Championship (Tier 2) side Aston Villa is watched by 252 fans – their highest ever crowd at Community Drive. City take an early lead through Hannah Keryakoplis but eventually lose 2-1.

10.03.19: Roisin Kivel comes on as an 80th-minute substitute with Stoke trailing 4-0 away to Middlesbrough. One minute later she scores her first goal for the club, followed a minute later by her second. Stoke though are unable to claw Boro back and lose the match 4-2.

11.03.19: Management team Tim Dudding and Tom Davies leave the club by mutual consent along with reserve team manager Mike Harris. Three days later Chloe Jones, Ste Appleton, Lucy Ridgway, Jack Shirley and Tom Read are confirmed as the coaching team for the remainder of the season.

07.04.19: Stoke's reserve team are crowned FA WNL Midlands Reserve Division champions for the third season in a row.

30.04.19: Stoke win the Staffordshire FA County Cup for the 11th season in a row. Hannah Keryakoplis scores seven of their goals as they beat Tier 4 Sporting Khalsa 8-1 in the final. Five of her goals come in the space of 20 minutes in the first half. Amy Hughes is Stoke's other scorer. A competition record crowd of 336 watches the match at Evans Park, Stafford Town FC.

2018-19 RESULTS: (HOME VENUE: COMMUNITY DRIVE, (NORTON UTD FC) UNLESS STATED)

2018-19 WNL NP					Att	Pos
19.08	Hull City (a)	W	4-0	Faye McCoy 18, Kelsey Richardson 34, Holly Chipman 79, Hannah Keryakoplis 82	60	
26.08	Doncaster R B (h)	W	5-0	Meg Bowyer 33, Ashleigh Hayes 64, Hannah Keryakoplis 66, 86, Natasha Tezgel 84	130	1
09.09	Guiseley Vixens (a)	W	4-2	Faye McCoy 37, 45, Meg Bowyer 55, Ashleigh Hayes 83	40	1
12.09	Derby County (h)	D	1-1	Emily Owen 11	136	1
16.09	Bradford City (h)	W	7-3	Nicola Hudson 12, Faye McCoy 36, 38, 88, Ashleigh Hayes 48, Emily Owen 74, Hannah Keryakoplis 84	102	1
04.10	Nottingham Forest (a)	L	1-3	Emily Owen 45+1	168	5
07.10	Sheffield FC (a)	L	0-2		126	5
21.10	Huddersfield T (h)	L	3-4	Amy Hughes 31, Ashleigh Hayes 66, Own Goal 72	128	5
28.10	Blackburn Rovers (a)	L	1-6	Kelsey Richardson 89	186	6
04.11	Middlesbrough (h)	W	4-1	Emma Foster (og) 45+4, Hannah Keryakoplis 60, Amy Hughes 67, Cassie Hyde 74	130	5
11.11	Sunderland (a)	W	3-2	Amy Hughes 1, Ashleigh Hayes 6, Emily Owen 90+4		5
25.11	Hull City (h)	W	4-1	Natasha Tezgel (pen) 24, Amy Hughes 26, Ashleigh Hayes 30, Kelsey Richardson 40	129	4
13.01	Doncaster R B (a)	W	2-1	Hannah Keryakoplis 26, Amy Hughes 75	130	4

27.01	Bradford City (a)	W	5-0	Nicola Hudson 6, Natasha Tezgel 32, Faye McCoy 53, Hannah Keryakoplis 64, Amy Hughes 70	62	4
14.02	Derby County (a)	L	1-2	Jodie Redgrave (og) 79	81	5
24.02	Sheffield FC (h)	D	2-2	Kelsey Richardson (pen) 50, Ashleigh Hayes 61	130	5
03.03	Guiseley Vixens (h)	L	1-2	*Faye McCoy missed pen 30 (saved by Bethan Davies),* Amy Hughes 44	85	6
10.03	Middlesbrough (a)	L	2-4	Roisin Kivel 81, 82	31	7
14.03	Nottingham F (h)	D	1-1	Roisin Kivel 90+3	85	7
17.03	Fylde (h)		P-P			7
24.03	Huddersfield T (a)	D	1-1	Rosin Kivel 85	74	7
31.03	Sunderland (h)	D	4-4	Kelsey Richardson 20, 42, Faye McCoy (pen) 65, 90+2	108	6
07.04	Fylde (h)	D	2-2	Emily Owen 10, 50	130	6
14.04	Blackburn Rovers (h)	L	0-4		120	7
05.05	Fylde (a)	L	1-3	Amy Hughes 78	145	7

2018-19 FA Cup

02.12 R2	Chester-le-Street Town (a)	W	2-0	Natasha Tezgel 73, Faye McCoy 82	60
06.01 R3	Derby County (a)	W	2-1	Natasha Tezgel 15, Hannah Keryakoplis 89	244
03.02 R4	Aston Villa (h)		P-P		
10.02 R4	Aston Villa (h)	L	1-2	Hannah Keryakoplis 6	252

2018-19 WNL Cup

02.09 DR	Sheffield FC (h)	W	3-0	Hannah Keryakoplis 55, 73, Cassie Hyde 66	134
R1	Bye				
14.10 R2	Norton & Stockton A (h)	W	3-0	Nicola Hudson 12, Hannah Keryakoplis 37, 89	115
09.12 R3	Leeds United (h)	W	6-3	Cassie Hyde 10, Tash Tezgel 45+2, Faye McCoy 59, Hannah Keryakoplis 61, Ashleigh Hayes 72, Amy Hughes 90+4	115
17.02 QF	Bolton W (a)	D	1-1 aet (L3-5p)	Ashleigh Hayes 20, Tash Tezgel missed pen 81	75

2018-19 Staffordshire FA County Cup

18.11 R2	Black Country Fusion (a)	W	20-0	Amy Hughes 12, 19, 53, 55, 65, Faye Singleton 30, (pen) 35, 36, 79, 88, Leanne Robinson 31, Emily Owen 32, 40, 54, 59, 77, Lucy Jelf (og) 39, Natasha Tezgel (pen) 74, 84, Beth Roberts 85	30
16.12 QF	Leek Town (h)	W	4-0	Amy Hughes 13, 35, Leanne Robinson 15, 60	180
20.01 SF	Shenstone (h)	W	13-0	Hannah Keryakoplis 6, 16, 27, 45, 48, Cassie Hyde 10, Leanne Robinson 23, 41, Emily Owen 74, Ella Pemberton 76, Faye McCoy (pen) 78, Holly Chipman (pen) 88, Ashleigh Hayes 90	95
30.04 F	Sporting Khalsa (n)	W	8-1	Hannah Keryakoplis 22, 30, 34, 36, 42, 46, 58, Amy Hughes 31	336

(n) Played at Evans Park, (Stafford Town FC)

SUNDERLAND

2019-20: WNL NORTHERN PREMIER (Tier 3)

Founded: 1989 (as The Kestrels)

Nickname: The Lady Black Cats / The Lasses

Season 2018-19:

WNL Northern Premier (Tier 3): Runners-up

FA Cup: 2nd Round

WNL Cup: 3rd Round

County Cup: n/a

Sunderland were the inaugural champions of WSL 2 (now the Championship) in 2014, and thus went straight up to WSL 1. Their best finish at that level was 4th in 2015 but following the FA restructure in 2018 they were unable to secure a licence for either of the top two divisions and thus dropped to Tier 3 for 2018-19. The club began life as a five-a-side team called Kestrels in 1989. Over the next decade, competing in 11-a-side football in the Northern Premier League, they were variously known as Cowgate Kestrels, RTM Kestrels and Blyth Spartans Kestrels. In 1999 they merged with an existing Sunderland Ladies club to become Sunderland Women's. They had a fleeting relationship with Sunderland men at the start of the century, but that ceased in 2004. In 2013 they came back under the Sunderland men's umbrella and changed their name from Sunderland Women to Sunderland Ladies.

2018-19 AS IT HAPPENS

21.10.18: American goalkeeper Allison Cowling signs after a successful trial period at the club.

06.02.19: Maltese international forward Maria Farrugia joins the club, with defender Charlotte Potts also signing two days later.

13.02.19: Niamh McLaughlin scores on her full debut to put Sunderland 3-1 up at Middlesbrough, but they are eventually pegged back to a 3-3 draw in the Tees-Wear derby.

17.03.19: Sunderland become the first team to take League points off leaders Blackburn all season as they win 3-0, scoring all three in the opening 25 minutes. Sunderland are Rovers' nearest challengers in the table but remain seven points adrift having played three games more.

17.05.19: Captain Keira Ramshaw is named FA WNL Premier Player of the Season.

2018-19 RESULTS: (HOME VENUE: HETTON CENTRE UNLESS STATED)

2018-19 WNL NP					Att	Pos
19.08	Fylde (h)	L	0-1		189	
26.08	Bradford City (a)	W	2-1	Bridget Galloway (pen) 15, Keira Ramshaw 34	120	7
09.09	Huddersfield T (a)	W	3-2	Emily Hutchinson 6, Mollie Lambert 45+2, 81	92	5
13.09	Middlesbrough (h)	W	3-1	Keira Ramshaw 45+1, 54, Bridget Galloway 48	175	4
16.09	Doncaster R B (h)	W	5-0	Keira Ramshaw 28, Jordan Atkinson 32, Georgia Gibson 35, Emily Hutchinson 41, Own Goal 65	160	3
23.09	Sheffield FC (a)	W	3-1	Katie Barker 24, Keira Ramshaw 47, 66		3
30.09	Derby County (a)	L	0-1		146	2
07.10	Hull City (a)	W	4-2	Bridget Galloway 23, Keira Ramshaw 50, Emily Hutchinson 57, Georgia Gibson 86	40	2
21.10	Nottingham F (h)	W	8-0	Keira Ramshaw 3, 4, 36, Bridget Galloway (pen) 9, Anna Young 26, Emily Hutchinson 39, 67, Faye Mullen 56	112	1
11.11	Stoke City (h)	L	2-3	Bridget Galloway 4, Anna Young 17	97	3
18.11	Derby County (h)	W	5-2	Bridget Galloway 23, 45+1, 47, Mollie Lambert 30, Georgia Gibson 74	102	2
16.12	Fylde (a)		P-P		80	3
13.01	Bradford City (h)	W	10-1	Grace McCatty 5, 36, Emily Hutchinson 7, Bridget Galloway (pen) 28, 47, Keira Ramshaw 50, 55, 72, Mollie Lambert 53, 59	124	2
27.01	Doncaster R B (a)	D	2-2	Anna Young 9, Bridget Galloway 21		3
10.02	Blackburn R (a)	L	1-2	Keira Ramshaw 6	133	3
13.02	Middlesbrough (a)	D	3-3	Bridget Galloway 6, 17, Niamh McLaughlin 22	300	3
17.02	Hull City (h)	W	6-2	Keira Ramshaw 26, 40, 67, Bridget Galloway 44, Maria Farrugia 65, Katie Barker 79	210	2
24.02	Fylde (a)	L	1-2	Katie Barker 54		2
10.03	Nottingham F (a)	W	6-0	Niamh McLaughlin 42, 44, Keira Ramshaw 65, 87, Katie Barker 67, Bridget Galloway 90+1	172	2
17.03	Blackburn R (h)	W	3-0	Maria Farrugia 13, Niamh McLaughlin 21, Keira Ramshaw 25	120	2
24.03	Guiseley Vixens (h)	W	4-1	Bridget Galloway 5, Niamh McLaughlin 13, Keira Ramshaw 39, Grace McCatty 87	121	2
31.03	Stoke City (a)	D	4-4	Emily Hutchinson 12, Keira Ramshaw 45+2, 70, 83	108	2
07.04	Huddersfield T (h)	L	1-2	Niamh McLaughlin 20	110	2
14.04	Guiseley Vixens (a)	W	2-1	Keira Ramshaw 34, Georgia Gibson 67, Keira Ramshaw sent off 73	40	2
05.05	Sheffield FC (h)	W	5-2	Bridget Galloway 9, Niamh McLaughlin 25, Katie Barker 37, Maria Farrugia 53, Georgia Gibson 88	124	2

2018-19 FA Cup

02.12 R2	Fylde (h)	L	1-3	Katie Barker 78	85

2018-19 WNL Cup

02.09 DR	Morecambe (a)	W	5-0	Emily Hutchinson 4, Keira Ramshaw 34, Bridget Galloway 56, Louise Griffiths 67, Georgia Gibson 90+1	40
R1	Bye				
14.10 R2	Wolverhampton W (a)	W	4-1	Emily Hutchinson 5, Anna Young 28, Natalie Widdal (og) 58, Emma Cross (og) 66	90
09.12 R3	Blackburn R (a)	L	1-3	Emily Hutchinson 46	123

"The FA restructuring effectively saw us relegated from WSL 1 to Tier 3 for 2018-19. It was a huge shock to deal with. It was truly devastating, heart-breaking. I loved playing WSL football and feel we deserve to be there. Our coach, Mel Reay, stuck with us through thick and thin and is working so hard to get us back to where we belong. I have been a first-team player for nine years now. I was born and bred in Sunderland and my heart lies with the football club, and I so want us to have success again. Credit to Mel, all the coaching staff and all the players for finishing our first season in the WNL Northern Premier as runners-up. We beat the champions Blackburn along the way and know that we can achieve even more in 2019-20."

Keira Ramshaw – Captain and FA WNL Premier Player of the Season 2018-19

SWINDON TOWN

2019-20: WNL SOUTH WEST 1 (Tier 4)

Founded: 1993

Nickname: The Robins

Season 2018-19:

WNL South West 1 (Tier 4): 9th

FA Cup: 2nd Qualifying Round

WNL Cup: Determining Round

WNL Plate: 2nd Round

The first women's club to be established in the region were the Swindon Spitfires who were formed in 1967. Several players broke away from the Spitfires in 1993 to help set up Swindon Town who started life in the South West Regional League. Town have been in Tier 4 since 2014-15 and would have won the title that year but for a three-point deduction for fielding an ineligible player. The 2018-19 campaign was a difficult one with the Robins finishing two places off the bottom.

2018-19 AS IT HAPPENS

09.09.18: Swindon's 2-1 win against Poole is their first League victory for almost two years, having last taken three points when they beat QPR 7-0 in October 2016.

03.02.19: The Robins end a run of 10 League games without a victory thanks to a 2-0 win away to fellow strugglers Poole Town. Alice Smith and Sophie Barrett both score in the final 20 minutes.

24.03.19: Swindon make it two wins in four League matches as they prevail 2-1 at home to Maidenhead United. Milly Colford and Zoe Ridley are both on target.

29.04.19: The away match against Cheltenham is staged at Whaddon Road (home of Cheltenham Town men) straight after Swindon and Cheltenham men have also played each other in League Two. The men's match ends 3-2 to Cheltenham and is watched by 4,306. The women's match is watched by a Cheltenham Town record crowd of 375 and ends 2-2 after Swindon had come from behind to lead 2-1.

2018-19 RESULTS: (HOME VENUE: CINDER LANE, (FAIRFORD TOWN FC), UNLESS STATED)

2018-19 WNL SW 1

Date	Opponent		Score	Scorers	Att	Pos
19.08	Southampton S (h)	L	1-2	Polly New	52	
09.09	Poole Town (h)	W	2-1	Milly Colford 59, Abby Picton 73	44	5
13.09	Cheltenham T (h)	L	0-2		65	5
16.09	Southampton W (a)	L	0-5		18	8
04.10	Keynsham Town (h)	L	0-5		39	10
07.10	Maidenhead U (a)	D	2-2	Abby Picton 8, Gipsy Viveash 32, Polly New missed pen (saved by Ellie Parker)	29	9
21.10	Chesham U (a)	L	0-1		50	9
04.11	Larkhall Athletic (h)	D	0-0		38	9
25.11	Brislington (a)	L	1-2	Helena Diaz-Butcher 74	38	9
02.12	Chesham U (h)	L	0-5		23	10
16.12	Buckland Athletic (h)	L	1-6	Meghan Larkin 3	34	10
13.01	Southampton S (a)	L	1-3	Milly Colford 27	15	10
03.02	Poole Town (a)	W	2-0	Alice Smith 70, Sophie Barrett 85	30	9
24.02	Southampton W (h)	L	0-5		45	9
14.03	Keynsham Town (a)	L	0-4			9
24.03	Maidenhead U (h)	W	2-1	Milly Colford 45, Zoe Ridley 69	49	9
31.03	Buckland Athletic (a)	L	0-2		30	9
14.04	Larkhall Athletic (a)	L	1-2	Zoe Ridley 23	20	9
27.04	Cheltenham Town (a)	D	2-2	Alice Telling 9, Milly Colford 41	375	9
05.05	Brislington (h)	W	3-2	Polly New 35, Own Goal 40, Rianne Lewis 74	44	9

2018-19 FA Cup

				Att
23.09 RQ2	Keynsham Town (h)	L	0-8	28

2018-19 WNL Cup

					Att
02.09 DR	Leyton Orient (h)	L	1-5	Abby Picton (pen) 60	43

2018-19 WNL Plate

					Att
R1	Bye				
14.10 R2	Bedworth U (h)	L	1-2	Milly Colford 31	87

"The 2018-19 season didn't pan out the way we would have wanted it to but there were several positives throughout. New management and staff meant a change in style and approach and the players fully embraced what we were trying to do. We were also able to bring through several younger and development players who made their first team debuts. We would have liked to have been challenging at the top of the table, but we found ourselves in a period of transition and results were hard to come by in a very competitive League. In 2019-20 we are very much looking to building on what we have started."

Dan Jones – Manager (resigned July 2019 due to family illness)

THE NEW SAINTS

2019-20: WNL MIDLANDS 1 (Tier 4)

Founded: 2002

Nickname: The Saints

Season 2018-19:

WNL Midlands 1 (Tier 4): 8th

FA Cup: 2nd Qualifying Round

WNL Cup: Determining Round

WNL Plate: 3rd Round

County Cup: Winners

TNS have enjoyed their greatest successes in recent times. In 2017-18 they achieved their best League finish, placing 5th in Tier 4. They also went further than ever before in the FA Cup that season, reaching the 4th Round where they lost to Tier 3 Chichester City on penalties. Having had to rebuild ahead of 2018-19 it was always likely to be a season spent in transition. There was a trophy to celebrate though as new manager Lawrence Wilson's side claimed the Shropshire FA County Cup for the 11th time in the club's history with a 9-1 win over Shifnal Town in the final.

2018-19 AS IT HAPPENS

30.09.18: After beginning the season with four straight League defeats, TNS pick up their first three points of the campaign with a 3-0 win at home to Solihull Moors.

02.12.18: The 2-2 draw away to Burton is an eventful affair as three players are sent off in the immediate aftermath of Paris O'Connor's equaliser for Burton. O'Connor and TNS pair Sarah Parkes and Taylor Davis are all shown red cards after a melee.

24.03.19: The New Saints chalk up a club record League win as they beat bottom club Steel City Wanderers 14-0. Lia Lewis scores her first ever hat-trick for TNS while Emily Ridge also bags three. Young centre-back Erin Taylor nets her first TNS goal when she converts a penalty in the final minute to complete the scoring. According to the club website, TNS's previous record League win was a 13-0 defeat of the now defunct Wednesfield in the West Midlands Regional League in September 2014.

12.05.19: A 9-1 win over lower League Shifnal Town sees TNS lift the Shropshire FA County Cup for the 11th time. Emily Ridge scores a hat-trick in the final, which is played at the Montgomery Waters Meadow Stadium, the home of Shrewsbury Town FC.

2018-19 RESULTS: (HOME VENUE: PARK HALL STADIUM, (THE NEW SAINTS FC) UNLESS STATED)

2018-19 WNL Midlands 1					Att	Pos
19.08	Nettleham (a)	L	1-4	Taylor Davis 38	50	
26.08	Bedworth United (h)*	L	1-2	Kimberley Bebbington 4	26	9
09.09	West Brom Albion (h)	L	3-4	Laura Morris 34, Sarah Jackson 37, 75	37	9
16.09	Bir'ham & W M (a)	L	1-4	Laura Pennington 63	31	9
30.09	Solihull Moors (h)	W	3-0	Emily Ridge 40, Laura Morris 66, Stacey Garnham (pen) 72	35	9
03.10	Wolverhampton W (a)	L	0-3		115	9
07.10	Steel City W (a)	W	6-1	Emily Ridge (x2), Zoe Griffith, Lia Lewis, Laura Pennington, Own Goal	23	8
04.11	Long Eaton United (h)	W	4-3	Laura Morris 23, Kimberly Bebbington 58, Louisa Anderson (pen) 70, Sarah Jackson 90+1	21	7
11.11	Sporting Khalsa (h)	L	0-4		27	8
02.12	Burton Albion (a)	D	2-2	Emily Ridge 30, Laura Morris (pen) 40, *Sarah Parkes sent off 58, Taylor Davis sent off 58*	80	8
13.01	Nettleham (h)	L	0-1		31	9
20.01	Bedworth United (a)	W	3-1	Emily Ridge 1, Laura Pennington (pen) 25, Katie Doster 83	40	8
03.02	West Brom Albion (a)	L	1-4	Zoe Griffiths 9	58	8
24.02	Bir'ham & W M (h)	L	1-5	Emily Ridge 30	66	9
13.03	Wolverhampton W (h)	L	0-4		75	9
17.03	Solihull Moors (a)		P-P			9
24.03	Steel City W (h)	W	14-0	Kim Bebbington 6, 47, Zoe Griffiths 8, 49, Emily Ridge 10, 18, 69, Lia Lewis 22, 53, 84, Laura Pennington 44, 86, Laura Morris 75, Erin Taylor (pen) 90	20	8
31.03	Long Eaton United (a)	W	4-3	Katie Doster 1, 84, Kimberley Bebbington 18, Laura Morris 55	32	8
14.04	Sporting Khalsa (a)	L	0-3		40	8
28.04	Solihull Moors (a)	W	4-0	Jodie Bragan, Emily Ridge (x2), Kimberley Bebbington	20	8
05.05	Burton Albion (h)	W	9-1	Laura Morris (x3), Kimberley Bebbington, Laura Pennington, Erin Taylor, Emily Ridge, Jodie Bragan, Katie Doster	60	8

*Played at Foxen Manor, (Four Crosses FC)

2018-19 FA Cup

23.09 RQ2	Long Eaton United (a)	L	1-7	Millie Fugler (og) 11	

2018-19 WNL Cup

02.09 DR	Nottingham F (h)*	L	0-3		53

*Played at Foxen Manor, (Four Crosses FC)

2018-19 WNL Plate

R1	Bye				
14.10 R2	Bradford City (h)		P-P		
28.10 R2	Bradford City (h)*	W	5-0	Emily Ridge 6, 26, 32, Laura Morris 47, 75	43
09.12 R3	Barnsley (h)*	L	0-9		40

*Played at Foxen Manor, (Four Crosses FC)

2018-19 Shropshire FA County Cup

07.02 QF	Shrewsbury Juniors (a)	W	5-0	Kimberley Bebbington 9, 59, Laura Pennington 37, Zoe Griffiths 72, Courtney Ashworth 88	
10.03 SF	Ludlow (a)	W	5-0	Jodie Bragan (pen) 7, Zoe Griffiths (pen) 47, 55, Sarah Jackson 67, Kimberley Bebbington 89	50
12.05 F	Shifnal Town (n)	W	9-1	Kimberley Bebbington 13, 72, Laura Morris (pen) 15, 31, Emily Ridge (pen) 17, 41, 48, Laura Pennington 27, 65	230

(n)Played at Montgomery Waters Meadow Stadium, (Shrewsbury Town FC)

"We are proud of ourselves for what we achieved in 2018-19 after losing some key players in the summer and undergoing a complete change of coaching staff. We have a great dressing room atmosphere where all the girls want to work for each other to get the best possible outcome for the team. We finished the season by winning the County Cup for the 11th time and that was a just reward for all our efforts. In 2019-20 we will be looking to progress by competing with the top teams in the League and hopefully going on a good run in the FA Cup."

Phoebe Davies – Captain

WATFORD

2019-20: WNL SOUTHERN PREMIER (Tier 3)

Founded: 1970 (as Watford Supporters' Ladies Club)

Nickname: The Lady Hornets / The Golden Girls

Season 2018-19:

WNL Southern Premier (Tier 3): 5th

FA Cup: 4th Round

WNL Cup: 2nd Round

County Cup: n/a

Female fans of Watford FC formed their own team in 1970, calling it the Watford Supporters' Ladies Club. For a while the name was changed to the "Willy Walker Wonders" in homage to manager Doug Hewish and coaches John Williams and Mike Walker. In 1997 they merged with Watford Town Girls and then came their first link-up with Watford FC via the men's Community, Sports and Education Trust. It wasn't until early 2016 that Watford Ladies were formally brought under the Watford FC umbrella. The Golden Girls were among the founding members of WSL 2 in 2014 and competed at that level every year until the FA restructuring in the summer of 2018. At that point they were unable to secure a Tier 2 licence and dropped down to Tier 3. The 2018-19 campaign ended in a respectable 5th place finish and a run to the 4th Round of the FA Cup where they acquitted themselves well away to WSL giants and eventual winners Manchester City in a 3-0 defeat.

2018-19 AS IT HAPPENS

19.08.18: Having failed to retain their Tier 2 licence for 2018-19 after the FA's summer restructure, Watford begin life in Tier 3 with a 5-2 win at home to Cardiff City Ladies.

08.11.18: Former Watford Academy and Centre of Excellence player Grace Williams is named as the club's new general manager with Armand Kavaja continuing as head coach.

23.09.18: Captain and Wales international Helen Ward scores her seventh goal in the opening six League games of the season in a 6-2 win over Gillingham, five have come in the final 10 minutes.

10.02.19: A contender for WNL match of the season as Watford blow a 4-1 lead with 20 minutes to go at home to Portsmouth before Helen Ward completes her hat-trick to clinch a 5-4 win for the Golden Girls in the third minute of injury-time.

17.03.19: Watford's Under-23s are crowned Hertfordshire FA County Cup winners, beating Tier 4 outfit, and holders, Stevenage 4-0 in the final. The first team do not compete in the County Cup.

2018-19 RESULTS: (HOME VENUE: SADIKU STADIUM GAYWOOD PARK, (KINGS LANGLEY FC), UNLESS STATED)

2018-19 WNL SP					Att	Pos
19.08	Cardiff City L (h)	W	5-2	Helen Ward 7, (pen) 42, 84, Andrea Carid Cao 64, 75	151	
26.08	Loughborough F (h)	L	1-3	Leanne Bell 77	75	7
08.09	Oxford United (a)	W	2-1	Katie O'Leary 55, Helen Ward 87	163	4
12.09	QPR (h)	W	2-1	Linda Afuakwah 1, Helen Ward 83	132	3
16.09	Portsmouth (a)	W	4-2	Katie O'Leary 21, Anaisa Harney 79, 85, Helen Ward 89	118	2
23.09	Gillingham (h)	W	6-2	Katherine Huggins 48, Katie O'Leary 51, Laura Baker 59, Katie Akerman 65, Helen Ward 81, Leanne Bell 83	93	1
03.10	C&K Basildon (a)	W	1-0	Emily Hill 84		2
21.10	Coventry United (a)	L	0-4		136	3
11.11	MK Dons (h)	L	0-3		137	3
18.11	Chichester City (h)	W	1-0	Danielle Scanlon 15	120	3
16.12	Plymouth A (a)		P-P			3
13.01	Cardiff City L (a)	L	0-1	*Georgie Edwards sent off 67*	175	3
20.01	Plymouth A (a)	L	2-3	Adekite Fatuga-Dada 13, Leanne Bell 88	80	3
27.01	Oxford United (h)		P-P			5
10.02	Portsmouth (h)*	W	5-4	Helen Ward 21, 46, 90+3, Danielle Rowe (og) 27, Leanne Bell 48	45	3
13.02	QPR (a)	D	1-1	Helen Ward (pen) 28	90	4
24.02	Loughborough F (a)	W	2-1	Helen Ward 57, Alysha Stojko-Down 84	67	5
10.03	Gillingham (a)		P-P			5
14.03	C&K Basildon (h)		P-P			6
17.03	Oxford United (h)	L	2-4	Katherine Huggins 50, Danielle Scanlon 84	70	6
24.03	Coventry United (h)	L	0-3		126	6
31.03	MK Dons (a)	W	2-1	Helen Ward 84, Adekite Fatuga-Dada 87	90	5
14.04	Chichester City (a)	L	0-1		90	6
21.04	Gillingham (a)	W	1-0	Katie O'Leary 62		6
28.04	C&K Basildon (h)	W	3-1	Alysha Stojko-Down 69, Leanne Bell 71, Adekite Fatuga-Dada 78	131	5
05.05	Plymouth A (h)+	W	3-2	Alysha Stojko-Down 8, 56, Katie O'Leary 42	174	5

*Played at The County Ground, Letchworth, (Hertfordshire FA Headquarters) +Played at Gaywood Park

2018-19 FA Cup

02.12R2	Buckland A (h)		P-P		
09.12 R2	Buckland A (h)	W	1-0	Katie O'Leary 70	70
06.01 R3	Middlesbrough (a)	W	7-2	Danielle Scanlon 7, Helen Ward 10, 20, 81, 84, Katie O'Leary 39, Samantha Hallsworth 61	
02.02 R4	Manchester City (a)	L	0-3		883

2018-19 WNL Cup

02.09 DR	Poole Town (a)	W	2-1	Linda Afuakwah 25, Lauren Jones (og) 87	40
R1	Bye				
14.10 R2	Coventry U (h)	L	2-3	Helen Ward 64, Katie O'Leary 74	65

"The 2018-19 season was one of development and growth for us. Bringing together a largely new group of players in a new League takes time. The most important thing was that we stuck together through the hard times and knew we would see the good times return. We have seen what the men's first team has achieved recently and we want to emulate them. The high point of 2018-19 for me was our performance away to Manchester City in the FA Cup 4th Round. We kept our shape and organisation against one of the strongest teams in the land. It helped that our goalkeeper Weronika Baranowska had the game of her life. People expected a heavy defeat, but we only lost 3-0 and the occasion showed what we can achieve as a squad."

Helen Ward – Captain

WEST BROMWICH ALBION

2019-20: WNL NORTHERN PREMIER (Tier 3)

Founded: 1989

Nickname: Albion / Baggies

Season 2018-19:

WNL Midlands 1 (Tier 4): Champions (P)

FA Cup: 2nd Round

WNL Cup: Determining Round

WNL Plate: Winners

County Cup: Runners-up

West Bromwich Albion FC Women competed under the name Sporting Club Albion between 2009 and 2016. It was as Sporting Club Albion that they won the WPL Northern Premier (Tier 3) title in 2015-16 for the first time in their history. They met WPL Southern Premier champions Brighton & Hove Albion in a play-off for promotion to WSL 2, but were beaten 4-2 at Adams Park. In 2017-18 they suffered relegation to Tier 4 on the final day of the season. However, 2018-19 was hugely successful as they won immediate promotion by claiming the WNL Midlands 1 title and also lifted the WNL Plate thanks to victory over Liverpool Feds in the final.

2018-19 AS IT HAPPENS

19.08.18: Having suffered relegation from Tier 3 at the end of 2017-18, West Brom begin life back in Tier 4 with a 4-2 home win over Birmingham & West Midlands.

16.12.18: Kathryn Pagan scores her first goal for the club on her full debut. It proves to be the winner as West Brom beat Sutton Coldfield Town 1-0 away in the County Cup.

12.02.19: Imogen Sinclair and Bethany Jewitt both grab their first goals for the club as the Baggies run riot at Solihull Moors with an 11-0 win.

14.03.19: West Brom are informed by the FA that they are being restored to the WNL Plate despite having lost their semi-final on 3 March 1-0 to Gillingham. The Gills have been found guilty of fielding ineligible players and Albion will take their place in the final.

14.04.19: West Brom win the FA WNL Plate with a 5-1 victory over fellow Tier 4 side Liverpool Feds of WNL North 1.

21.04.19: The Baggies are promoted back to Tier 3 at the first time of asking as they clinch the WNL Midlands 1 title with two games to spare. Head coach Louis Sowe's team kick-off at home to Steel City Wanderers knowing they need just one point against the team who are bottom of the table and run out comfortable 7-0 winners with goals from Trina Greaves, Keeley Davies, Natalie Murray, Jessica Davies, Laura Davies, Fran Orthodoxou and an own goal.

30.04.19: West Brom are beaten by newly crowned WNL Southern Premier (Tier 3) champions Coventry United 3-0 in the Birmingham FA County Cup final. Goals from Amy Wathan, Beth Merrick, and Amber Hughes see the holders defend the Cup they won in 2017-18.

05.05.19: Albion's hopes of completing the season with maximum points are dashed as they slip to a final-day 3-1 defeat away to Black Country rivals and WNL Midlands 1 runners-up Wolves.

2018-19 RESULTS: (HOME VENUE: CHURCH ROAD, (BOLDMERE ST MICHAELS FC) UNLESS STATED)

2018-19 WNL Midlands 1					**Att**	**Pos**
19.08	Birm'ham & W M (h)	W	4-2	Francesca Orthodoxou 42, Reia Henry 58, Rachael Howard 79, Harriet James 82	58	
26.08	Long Eaton United (a)	W	4-1	Harriet James 56, Natalie Murray 65, 76, Keeley Davies 79	42	3
09.09	The New Saints (a)	W	4-3	Keeley Davies 16, 35, Harriet James 23, Kimberley Bebbington (og) 89, *Antonia Smith sent off, Nicole Dale sent off*	37	2
11.09	Solihull Moors (h)	W	8-0	Keeley Davies 48, 63, 79, 83, Natalie Murray 52, Gabriel Reid 57, Francesca Orthodoxou 64, Rachael Howard 68	56	1
16.09	Steel City W (a)	W	18-1	Harriet James (x4), Laura Davies (x3), Reia Henry (x3), Natalie Murray (x2), Abby Bevan (x2), Lauren Price, Gabriel Reid, Hannah George, Sarah Middleton (og)	43	1
02.10	Burton Albion (h)	W	2-1	Hannah George 23, Natalie Murray 70	58	2
21.10	Sporting Khalsa (a)	W	3-0	Keeley Davies 15, 90, Natalie Murray 24	30	2
04.11	Nettleham (a)	W	2-1	Reia Henry 90+5, Hattie James 90+8	70	1
25.11	Bedworth United (h)	W	1-0	Hannah Baines 90+6	52	1
13.01	Birm'ham & W M (a)	W	1-0	Keeley Davies 88	78	1
27.01	Wolverhampton W (h)	W	2-0	Keeley Davies 37, Natalie Murray 48	375	1
03.02	The New Saints (h)	W	4-1	Hannah Baines 17, Laura Davies 73, Keeley Davies 78, Jess Davies 80	58	1
12.02	Solihull Moors (a)	W	11-0	Hannah Baines 1, 46, Jess Davies 11, Bethan Jewitt 12, Imogen Sinclair 49, Laura Davies 55, 78, Natalie Murray 62, 67, Harriet James 74, 81	25	1
24.02	Long Eaton U (h)	W	2-1	Rachel Howard 26, Natalie Murray 58	58	1
10.03	Sporting Khalsa (h)	W	5-0	Natalie Murray 26, Hannah Baines 57, 61, 64, Keeley Davies 69	56	1
17.03	Steel City W (h)		P-P			1

31.03	Nettleham (h)	W	7-1	Jessica Davies 13, Laura Davies 15, 24, 26, Francesca Orthodoxou 23, Hannah Baines 56, Hannah George 67	48	1
07.04	Bedworth United (a)	W	5-0	Gabriella Reid 38, Lauren Price 65, Natalie Murray 76, Hannah George 74, 83	60	1
21.04	Steel City W (h)	W	7-0	Trina Greaves 3, Keeley Davies 8, Natalie Murray 18, Jessica Davies 34, Laura Davies 64, Fran Orthodoxou 78, Own Goal 81	33	1C
28.04	Burton Albion (a)	W	6-0	Fran Orthodoxou 24, 72, Hattie James 52, Keeley Davies 69, 90+2, Jessica Davies 90	60	1C
05.05	Wolverhampton W (a)	L	1-3	Natalie Murray 42, *Keeley Davies missed pen 90 (saved Madeline Elbro)*	500	1C

2018-19 FA Cup

23.09 RQ2	Rugby Town (a)	W	10-0	Gabriella Reid 2, Laura Davies 15, Francesca Orthodoxou 16, 47, 70, Reia Henry 32, Abby Bevan 37, Natalie Murray 60, Nicole Dale 87, 90	
07.10 RQ3	Leafield Athletic (a)	W	2-1	Laura Davies, Natalie Murray	283
11.11 R1	Leicester City W Dev. (h)	W	2-1	Chloe Harper 40, Gabriella Reid 88	
02.12 R2	Bolton Wanderers (a)		P-P		
09.12 R2	Bolton Wanderers (a)	D	2-2 aet (L4-5p)	Harriet James 6, Laura Davies 70	

2018-19 WNL Cup

02.09 DR	Burnley (h)	L	0-3

2018-19 WNL Plate

R1	Bye				
14.10 R2	Nettleham (h)	W	5-0	Keeley Davies (x2), Nicole Dale, Abby Bevan, Natalie Murray	
06.01 R3	Sporting Khalsa (a)	W	2-1	Hannah Price, Natalie Murray	60
10.02 QF	Barnsley (a)	W	1-0	Hannah George 83	50
03.03 SF	Gillingham (a)	L	0-1	Gillingham disqualified from competition on 14.03 for fielding ineligible players	
14.04 F	Liverpool Feds (n)	W	5-1	Hannah George 5, Jess Davies 39, Laura Davies 51, Ria Elsmore 75, Natalie Murray 89	342

(n) Played at Butlin Town, (Rugby Town FC)

2018-19 Birmingham FA County Cup

R1	Bye				
18.11 R2	Solihull (h)	W	w/o		
16.12 R3	Sutton Coldfield Town (a)	W	1-0	Kathryn Pagan 65	180
20.01 QF	Sandwell (a)	W	5-1	Gabriella Reid 5, 80, Hannah Baines 7, 75, Harriet James 90	
17.02 SF	Redditch United (h)*	W	4-1	Natalie Murray 19, Keeley Davies 26, 85, Reia Henry 86	
30.04 F	Coventry United (n)	L	0-3		

*Played at Bromsgrove Road, (Redditch United FC)   (n) Played at The Lamb Ground, (Tamworth FC)

WOLVERHAMPTON WANDERERS

2019-20: WNL MIDLANDS 1 (Tier 4)

Founded: 1975 (as Heathfield Rovers)

Nickname: The Wolfettes

Season 2018-19:

WNL Midlands 1 (Tier 4): Runners-up

FA Cup: 2nd Round

WNL Cup: 2nd Round

County Cup: 2nd Round

Wolves started out as Heathfield Rovers in 1975 and have also been known in the past as Wolverhampton & Wednesbury Tube and Wolverhampton Ladies. In 1993 they were granted permission from Wolverhampton Wanderers men's club to call themselves by the same name. Today they are officially affiliated to the men's club. At the end of 1993-94 they were promoted to the top-flight – the FA Women's Premier League National Division as it was then – where they spent two years before being relegated. Aston Villa men's 1982 European Cup-winning captain Dennis Mortimer was appointed manager in 2000 and narrowly missed out on promotion to the top-flight during his three seasons in charge. Wolves were promoted to Tier 3 as champions ahead of 2017-18 but suffered immediate relegation. In 2018-19 they almost bounced back at the first attempt but missed out on promotion, finishing as runners-up behind West Bromwich Albion.

2018-19 AS IT HAPPENS

19.08.18: Having suffered relegation from Tier 3 at the end of 2017-18, Wolves begin life back in Tier 4 with an 11-0 win away to Steel City Wanderers

04.11.18: After winning their opening seven League games of the season, and scoring 41 goals in the process, Wolves drop points for the first time as they lose 2-1 away to newly promoted Bedworth.

31.03.19: Wolves complete a League double over bottom club Steel City Wanderers and it's particularly notable because both victories were achieved with identical 11-0 score lines.

21.04.19: Wolves' faint title hopes are ended as West Brom beat Steel City Wanderers 7-0. Albion needed just a point against the bottom-of-the-table team to secure the title.

05.05.19: Two goals from Jade Cross and one from Lowri Walker see Wolves end the season in style with a 3-1 win over Black Country rivals and WNL Midlands 1 champions West Brom. It is the only League match West Brom have failed to win all season.

17.05.19: Jade Cross receives her WNL Midlands 1 top scorer award having hit 29 goals in 19 League appearances and 32 in 26 in all competitions. Twin sister and defender Emma wins Wolves' Player of the Season award.

2018-19 RESULTS: (HOME VENUE: QUEEN STREET, (BILSTON TOWN FC) UNLESS STATED)

2018-19 WNL Midlands 1

					Att	Pos
19.08	Steel City W (a)	W	11-0	OG 3, Lowri Walker 6, 38, 56, 70, Chloe Williams 15, Jess Jennings 29, 63, Jennifer Anslow 68, Billie Haynes 73, 81	65	
26.08	Solihull Moors (h)	W	7-0	Natalie Widdal 30, Anna Morphet 37, Billie Haynes 49, 61, Chloe Williams 51, Jennifer Anslow 66, 72	110	1
09.09	Bir'ham & W M (a)	W	3-1	Lowri Walker 3, Jade Cross 17, Chloe Williams 25	67	1
12.09	Sporting Khalsa (h)		P-P			2
16.09	Burton Albion (a)	W	4-1	Anna Morphet 13, Mai Butler 26, Lowri Walker 51, Jade Cross 63	80	2
19.09	Sporting Khalsa (a)	W	10-2	Billie Haynes 1, Jade Cross 4, 17, 34, 90, Lowri Walker 19, 72, Charlotte Wilkie 45, Jennifer Anslow 60, Anna Morphet 62	50	2
30.09	Nettleham (h)	W	3-0	Natalie Widdal 29, Jade Cross 44, Tammi George 65	40	1
03.10	The New Saints (h)	W	3-0	Jade Cross 39, 43, Charlotte Criddle 69	115	1
04.11	Bedworth United (a)	L	1-2	Jade Cross 45, Wolves GK Katie Clarke saved pen 75	80	2
09.12	Long Eaton United (h)	W	7-0	Jade Cross 1, 82, Anna Morphet (pen) 51, Chloe Williams 68, Billie Haynes 69, 71, Charlotte Criddle 83	40	2
13.01	Steel City W (h)		P-P			2
20.01	Solihull Moors (a)	W	3-0	Jade Cross 3, 57, Tammi George 40	25	2
27.01	West Brom A (a)	L	0-2		375	2
10.02	Bir'ham & W M (h)*	L	1-3	Charlotte Wilkie 6	40	3
17.02	Burton Albion (h)*	W	8-0	Jade Cross 8, 32, 40, 68, Chloe Williams 37, Jess Jennings 77, 84, Billie Haynes 86	50	2
27.02	Sporting Khalsa (h)*	W	3-1	Anna Price 31, Anna Morphet 35, Jennifer Anslow 42	40	2
03.03	Steel City W (h)		P-P			2
10.03	Nettleham (a)		P-P			2

13.03	The New Saints (a)	W	4-0	Jade Cross 24, 56, 84, Tammi George 41, Natalie Widdal sent off	75	2
17.03	Long Eaton United (a)	W	1-0	Jade Cross 50	40	2
31.03	Steel City W (h)+	W	11-0	Katie Johnson 5, Andrea Barnett 12, Hollie Hogan 14, Tammi George 23, 37, 39, Jennifer Anslow 33, Charlotte Wilkie 40, Jade Cross 48, 61, Billie Haynes 50	60	2
14.04	Bedworth United (h)*	W	9-1	Anna Morphet 10, (pen) 25, Billy Haynes 23, 33, Jennifer Anslow 31, 75, Jess Jennings 41, Tammi George 65, Anna Price 72	60	2
28.04	Nettleham (a)	W	6-0	Anna Price 37, Jess Jennings 64, Jade Cross 73, 85, 86, Billie Haynes 88	100	2
05.05	West Brom A (h)*	W	3-1	Jade Cross 24, 83, Lowri Walker 78, Wolves GK Madeline Elbro saved Keeley Davies pen 90	500	2

* Played at CKW/Castlecroft Stadium, (AFC Wulfrunians) +Played at The City Ground, (Darlaston FC)

2018-19 FA Cup

23.09 RQ2	Kingfisher (h)	W	6-0	Billie Haynes 14, Lowri Walker 26, 29 Charlotte Criddle 37, Charlotte Wilkie 68, Anna Morphet 83	75
07.10 RQ3	Bir'ham & W M (a)	W	2-0	Jade Cross 47, Chloe Shirley 81	54
11.11 R1	Kidderminster H (a)	W	6-1	Billie Haynes 28, Andre Barnett 53, Anna Price 58, Jess Jennings 76, 83, Nyah Edwards 87	330
02.12 R2	Blackburn Rovers (h)*	L	0-4		60

*Played at CKW/Castlecroft Stadium, (AFC Wulfrunians)

2018-19 WNL Cup

02.09 DR	Crewe Alexandra (h)	W	1-0	Jade Cross 16	98
R1	Bye				
14.10 R2	Sunderland (h)*	L	1-4	Charlotte Criddle 70	90

*Played at CKW/Castlecroft Stadium, (AFC Wulfrunians)

2018-19 Birmingham FA County Cup

R1	Bye				
18.11 R2	Coventry United (a)	L	1-5	Jade Cross 34	141

"The club has never been in a better position. The standard of girls coming through from our Regional Talent Club over the past two seasons has been unbelievable. It made a real difference in 2018-19, as did the signings of Lowri Walker and Anna Morphet from Aston Villa. They added real quality. Our target was promotion, and we didn't quite make it, but I feel we will be in a better position for 2019-20. The support from Wolverhampton Wanderers FC has been immense. In 2019-20 all senior training sessions will be held at the Sir Jack Hayward Training Ground, where the men train, no fees will be paid by any player from the RTC through to the first team, and the reserves team has been reintroduced to the WNL Reserve League. These changes have taken so much pressure off the players having to find sponsorship and means we will have the very best training facilities."

Anna Price – Captain

YEOVIL TOWN
2019-20: WNL SOUTHERN PREMIER (Tier 3)

Founded: 1990 (as Yetminster)

Nickname: The Lady Glovers

Season 2018-19:

WSL (Tier 1): 11th (R)

FA Cup: 4th Round

Continental Cup: Group

Yeovil's two-and-a-half-year stay as a top-flight club ended in the summer of 2019 when financial difficulties hit hard and saw them relegated two divisions to Tier 3. When the WSL expanded to embrace a second division in 2014 the Glovers were founding members of WSL 2. After finishing 5th, then 4th, they pipped Bristol City to the title on goal difference in 2016 and made their WSL 1 debut in the 2017 Spring Series. Life among the elite was far from easy and they won just two, drew four and lost 40 of their 46 top-flight matches before relegation at the end of 2018-19. Yeovil were docked 10pts in March 2019 after announcing their intention to go into administration, and even though they eventually avoided that fate they did not appeal the points' deduction. They intended to revert to part-time status in the Championship but were shocked when the FA rejected their application for a Tier 2 licence, a decision which saw them drop to the WNL Southern Premier.

2018-19 AS IT HAPPENS

04.11.18: At the 33rd time of asking Yeovil win a top-flight match for the very first time. They beat Everton 1-0 at home courtesy of Hannah Short's 21st minute goal. Their previous 32 WSL fixtures have resulted in 29 defeats and 3 draws.

10.02.19: Sixteen-year-old Erin Bloomfield scores with her very first touch of the match after coming on as a 76th-minute substitute against Birmingham. Her header proves to be a consolation goal in a 3-1 defeat which is watched by 523 fans – a club record for an FA Cup tie.

28.03.19: Yeovil announce they are set to go into administration and that they "recognise they will not be a WSL club next season." The Glovers – who are five points adrift of safety with just five games of the season remaining – will be docked 10 points with immediate effect.

31.03.19: Yeovil win a top-flight game for only the second time in their history, beating Everton 1-0 again just as they did when they won a WSL game for the first time back in November. Megan Alexander scores her first goal for the club with a cross-shot which evades Everton keeper Kirstie Levell for the only goal of the game.

16.04.19: Yeovil announce they have avoided going into administration but will not appeal the 10-point penalty they were hit with last month when they informed the FA of their intention to appoint an administrator. The Lady Glovers confirm they are to revert to part-time status and will apply for a Tier 2 licence for 2019-20.

17.04.19: A 5-0 home defeat to Reading confirms Yeovil's relegation to the Championship.

17.05.19: The FA confirms Yeovil's application for a Championship licence has been rejected, meaning the club will be relegated to Tier 3, or perhaps lower, ahead of the start of 2019-20.

2018-19 RESULTS: (HOME VENUE: THE AVENUE (DORCHESTER TOWN FC), UNLESS STATED)

2018-19 WSL

					Att	Pos
09.09	Reading (a)	L	0-4		464	10
19.09	Arsenal (h)	L	0-7		1,101	11
30.09	West Ham Utd (a)	L	1-2	Ellie Mason 78	367	11
14.10	Liverpool (a)	L	1-2	Annie Heatherson 28	423	11
21.10	Bristol City (h)	L	1-2	Amber Gaylor 34	583	11
28.10	Brighton & H A (a)	L	1-2	*Ellie Mason missed pen 69 (saved Marie Hourihan),* Ellie Mason 69 (scored pen rebound)	562	11
04.11	Everton (h)	W	1-0	Hannah Short 21	732	10
18.11	Chelsea (a)	L	0-5	*Nicola Cousins sent off 40*	1,484	10
25.11	Manchester C (h)	L	0-4		1,153	10
02.12	Birmingham C (a)	L	1-2	Emily Syme 90+3	662	11
09.12	West Ham Utd (h)	L	0-5		516	11
13.01	Liverpool (h)	L	1-2	Emily Donovan 52	984	11
27.01	Bristol City (a)	L	1-2	Annie Heatherson 46	616	11
20.02	Arsenal (a)	L	0-3		1,107	11
13.03	Brighton & H A (h)	D	1-1	Ellie Mason 64	408	11
31.03	Everton (a)	W	1-0	Megan Alexander 78	230	11
17.04	Reading (h)	L	0-5		473	11R
28.04	Manchester C (a)	L	1-2	Olivia Fergusson 1	1,369	11R
07.05	Chelsea (h)	L	0-8		843	11R
11.05	Birmingham C (h)	L	0-2		463	11R

2018-19 FA Continental Tyres League Cup: Group One South

19.08	London Bees (a)	D	1-1 (L 3-5p)	Olivia Fergusson 40	246
26.08	Crystal Palace (h)	L	0-1		301

16.09	Tottenham H (h)	L	0-4		415
05.12	Chelsea (a)	L	0-7		916
12.12	Brighton & H A (h)	L	1-4	Emily Syme 37	224

2018-19 FA Cup

03.02 R4	Birmingham C (h)		P-P		
10.02 R4	Birmingham C (h)	L	1-3	Erin Bloomfield 76	523

ENGLAND

RESULTS & LINE-UPS – ALL MATCHES 2018-19

Key: WCQ = World Cup Qualifier | F = Friendly | SBC = SheBelieves Cup
WCG = World Cup Group Stage | WC16 = World Cup Round of 16
WCQF = World Cup Quarter-final | WCSF = World Cup Semi-Final | WC3rd = World Cup 3rd Place Match

31.08 WALES (A) W 3-0 WCQ RODNEY PARADE, NEWPORT COUNTY FC 5,053

Toni Duggan 57, Jill Scott 60, Nikita Parris 69

Wales (3-4-2-1): Laura O'Sullivan (Cardiff City Ladies); Hayley Ladd (Birmingham City), Loren Dykes (Bristol City), Sophie Ingle (c) (Chelsea); Rhiannon Roberts (Liverpool), Angharad James (Everton), Jess Fishlock (Lyon), Natasha Harding (Reading) (sub 90 Ffion Morgan (Cardiff City Ladies)); Kylie Nolan (Cardiff City Ladies) (sub 61 Elise Hughes (Everton)), Helen Jane Ward (Watford)) (sub 73 Peyton Vincze (FC Wichita)); Kayleigh Green (Brighton & H A)

Unused subs: Gemma Evans (Bristol City), Alice Griffiths (Cardiff Met), Nadia Lawrence (Cardiff City Ladies), Claire Skinner (Cardiff City Ladies)

Head coach: Jayne Ludlow

England (4-2-3-1): Karen Bardsley (Man City); Lucy Bronze (Lyon), Steph Houghton (c) (Man City), Millie Bright (Chelsea), Alex Greenwood (Man Utd); Jill Scott (Man City) (sub 83 Keira Walsh (Man City)), Jordan Nobbs (Arsenal); Nikita Parris (Man City), Fran Kirby (Chelsea) (sub 88 Rachel Daly (Houston Dash)), Toni Duggan (Barcelona); Jodie Taylor (Seattle Reign) (sub 78 Isobel Christiansen (Lyon))

Unused subs: Abbie McManus (Man City), Carly Telford (Chelsea), Beth Mead (Arsenal), Melissa Lawley (Man City)

Head coach: Phil Neville

Referee: Katalin Kulcsar (HUN)

04.09 KAZAKHSTAN (A) W 6-0 WCQ ORTALIG STADIUM, ALMATY

Beth Mead (pen) 9, 62, Rachel Daly 35, Isobel Christiansen 54, Lucy Staniforth, 66, Lucy Bronze 87, *Beth Mead missed pen 69*

Kazakhstan (4-1-4-1): Oxana Zheleznyak; Kundyz Kozhakmet, Bibigul Nurusheva, Yulia Myasnikova, Alexandra Burova; Begaim Kirigizbaeva (c); Karina Zhumabaikyzy, Kamila Kulmagambetova (sub 74 Svetlana Bortnikova), Asselkhan Turlybekova, Saule Karibayeva (sub 43 Aida Gaistenova); Anastasia Vlasova (sub 52 Adilya Vyldanova)

Unused subs: Irina Sandalova, Batya Bagully, Mariya Demidova, Assem Zhaksymbay

Head coach: Razia Nurkenova

England (4-3-3): Mary Earps (Wolfsburg) (sub 67 Carly Telford (Chelsea)); Lucy Bronze (Lyon), Hannah Blundell (Chelsea), Abbie McManus (Man City), Gabby George (Everton); Lucy Staniforth (Birmingham City), Keira Walsh (c) (Man City) (sub 62 Lucy Bronze (Lyon)), Isobel Christiansen (Lyon); Lauren Bruton (Reading), Rachel Daly (Houston Dash), Beth Mead (Arsenal)

Unused subs: Jordan Nobbs (Arsenal), Steph Houghton (Man City), Millie Bright (Chelsea), Toni Duggan (Barcelona), Nikita Parris (Man City)

Head coach: Phil Neville

Referee: Hristiana Guteva (BUL)

06.10 BRAZIL (H) W 1-0 F MEADOW LANE, NOTTS COUNTY FC ATT: 7,864

Fran Kirby 2

England (4-2-3-1): Carly Telford (Chelsea); Lucy Bronze (Lyon), Steph Houghton (c) Man City), Millie Bright (Chelsea), Alex Greenwood (Man Utd); Jordan Nobbs (Arsenal) (sub 70 Fara Williams (Reading)), Isobel Christiansen (Lyon); Nikita Parris (Man City) (sub 75 Lucy Staniforth (Birmingham City)), Fran Kirby (Chelsea) (sub 75 Melissa Lawley (Man City)), Toni Duggan (Barcelona) (sub 61 Beth Mead (Arsenal)); Rachel Daly (Houston Dash)

Unused subs: Hannah Blundell (Chelsea), Mary Earps (Wolfsburg), Abbie McManus (Man City), Leah Williamson (Arsenal), Gabrielle George (Everton), Keira Walsh (Man City), Siobhan Chamberlain (Man Utd)

Head coach: Phil Neville

Brazil (4-4-2): Barbara (Kindermann); Leticia Santos (SC Sand), Bruna Benites (Houston Dash) (sub 41 Daiane Limeira (PSG)), Monica (Orlando Pride) (sub 75 Sousa Feitoza (Bordeaux)), Camila Martins (Orlando Pride) (sub 66 Tamires (Fortuna Hjorring)); Debinha (North Carolina) (sub 57 Kerolin (Ponte Preta)), Formiga (PSG) (sub 77 Andressinha (Portland Thorns)), Thaisa (Milan), Andressa Alves (Barcelona); Ludmila (Atletico Madrid), Marta (c) (Orlando Pride) (sub 22 Raquel (Sporting de Huelva))

Unused subs: Rilany (Atletico Madrid), Geyse Ferreira (Atletico Madrid), Aline Villares (Grenadilla Tenerife), Poliana (Orlando Pride), Darlene (Zaragoza)

Head coach: Vadao

Referee: Sandra Braz Bastos (POR)

09.10 AUSTRALIA (H) D 1-1 F CRAVEN COTTAGE, FULHAM FC ATT: 6,068

Fran Kirby 21; Clare Polkinghorne 84

England (4-2-3-1): Mary Earps (Wolfsburg); Lucy Bronze (Lyon), Steph Houghton (c) (Man City), Abbie McManus (Man City) (sub 86 Leah Williamson (Arsenal)), Alex Greenwood (Man Utd); Keira Walsh (Man City), Jordan Nobbs (Arsenal); Beth Mead (Arsenal) (sub 62 Nikita Parris (Man City)), Lucy Staniforth (Birmingham City) (sub 63 Rachel Daly (Houston Dash)), Toni Duggan (Barcelona); Fran Kirby (Chelsea) (sub 76 Fara Williams (Reading))

Unused subs: Siobhan Chamberlain (Man Utd), Carly Telford (Chelsea), Gabrielle George (Everton), Hannah Blundell (Chelsea), Isobel Christiansen (Lyon), Millie Bright (Chelsea)

Head coach: Phil Neville

Australia (4-2-1-3): Mackenzie Arnold (Brisbane Roar); Ellie Carpenter (Canberra United), Clare Polkinghorne (Brisbane Roar), Steph Catley (Melbourne City), Caitlin Foord (Sydney); Amy Sayer (Sydney) (sub 55 Emily Gielnik (Melbourne Victory)), Elise Kellond-Knight (c) (Melbourne City); Princess Ibini (Sydney) (sub 66 Larissa Crummer (Newcastle Jets)); Tameka Butt (Melbourne City), Chloe Logarzo (Sydney) (sub 81 Alexandra Chidiac (Atletico Madrid)), Lisa Da Vanna (Sydney) (sub 66 Mary Fowler (Bankstown City))

Unused subs: Aivi Luik (Levante), Jada Whyman (Western Sydney), Kyah Simon (Houston Dash)

Head coach: Alen Stajcic

Referee: Florence Guillemin (FRA)

08.11 AUSTRIA (A) W 3-0 F BSFZ-ARENA

Chioma Ubogagu 26, Georgia Stanway 71, Rachel Daly 81

England (4-3-3): Mary Earps (Wolfsburg) (sub 79 Ellie Roebuck (Man City); Hannah Blundell (Chelsea), Leah Williamson (Arsenal), Abbie McManus (Man City), Gabby George (Everton); Karen Carney (Chelsea), Lucy Staniforth (Birmingham City), Georgia Stanway (Man City); Melissa Lawley (Man City) (sub 65 Nikita Parris (Man City)), Toni Duggan (c) (Barcelona) (sub 79 Chloe Kelly (Everton)), Chioma Ubogagu (Orlando Pride – on loan at Brisbane Roar) (sub 59 Rachel Daly (Houston Dash))

Unused subs: Carly Telford (Chelsea), Jordan Nobbs (Arsenal), Millie Bright (Chelsea), Alex Greenwood (Man Utd), Jill Scott (Man City), Isobel Christiansen (Lyon), Beth Mead (Arsenal)

Head coach: Phil Neville

Austria (4-1-2-1-2): Manuela Zinsberger (Bayern Munich); Sophie Maierhofer (UMF Selfoss) (sub 55 Yvonne Weilharter (Sturm Graz)), Carinna Wenninger (Bayern Munich), Virginia Kirchberger (SC Freiburg), Verena Aschauer (Frankfurt); Sarah Puntigam (Montpellier); Laura Feiersinger (Frankfurt), Nadine Prohaska (SC Sand) (sub 55 Barbara Dunst (Duisburg)); Sarah Zadrazil (Turbine Potsdam); Nicole Billa (Hoffenheim) (sub 88 Jennifer Klein (Hoffenheim)), Nina Burger (c) (SC Sand) (sub 76 Viktoria Pinther (SC Sand))

Unused subs: Jasmin Eder (St Polten), Jasmin Pfeiler (SKV Altenmarkt), Sabrina Horvat (Werder Bremen), Laura Wienroither (Hoffenheim), Julia Fuller, Stefanie Enzinger (St Polten), Andrea Gurtner

Head coach: Dominik Thalhammer

Referee: Lucie Salkova (CZE)

NIKITA PARIS CELEBRATES SCORING AGAINST DENMARK IN MAY'S FRIENDLY INTERNATIONAL

11.11 SWEDEN (H) L 0-2 F NEW YORK STADIUM, ROTHERHAM UNITED FC ATT: 9,561

Sofia Jakobsson 20, Anna Anvegard 33

England (4-3-3): Carly Telford (Chelsea); Lucy Bronze (Lyon), Steph Houghton (c) (Man City), Millie Bright (Chelsea), Alex Greenwood (Man Utd); Isobel Christiansen (Lyon) (sub 73 Georgia Stanway (Man City)), Jordan Nobbs (Arsenal), Jill Scott (Man City) (sub Lucy Staniforth 83 (Birmingham City)); Nikita Parris (Man City), Rachel Daly (Houston Dash) (sub 73 Melissa Lawley (Man City)), Beth Mead (Arsenal) (sub 46 Toni Duggan (Barcelona))

Unused subs: Hannah Blundell (Chelsea), Mary Earps (Wolfsburg), Abbie McManus (Man City), Leah Williamson (Arsenal), Gabrielle George (Everton), Karen Carney (Chelsea), Ellie Roebuck (Man City), Chioma Ubogagu (Brisbane Roar – on loan from Orlando Pride)

Head coach: Phil Neville

Sweden (4-2-1-3): Hedvig Lindahl (Chelsea); Amanda Ilestedt (Turbine Potsdam), Linda Sembrant (Montpellier), Magdalena Eriksson (Chelsea), Jessica Samuellson (Arsenal) (sub 61 Nathalie Bjorn, (Rosengard), Elin Rubensson (Gothenburg) (sub 90+3 Julia Roddar (Koppabergs/Gothenburg)), Caroline Seger (Rosengard) (sub 79 Hanna Folkesson (Rosengard)), Jonna Andersson (Chelsea), Sofia Jakobsson (Montpellier) (sub 79 Lina Hurtig (Linkoping)), Kosovare Asllani (Linkoping) (sub 90+3 Olivia Schough (Koppabergs/Gothenburg)), Anna Anvegard (Vaxjo) (sub 61 Fridolina Rolfo (Bayern Munich))

Substitutes not used: Julia Karlenas (Pitea IF), Cajsa Andersson (Pitea IF), Mia Carlsson (Kristianstad), Zecira Musovic (Rosengard), Julia Spetsmark (NC Courage)

Head coach: Peter Gerhardsson

Referee: Petra Pavlikova (SVK)

27.02 BRAZIL (N) W 2-1 SBC TALEN ENERGY STADIUM, PHILADELPHIA ATT: 5,594

Ellen White 49, Beth Mead 75; Andressa Alves da Silva (pen) 16

England (4-3-3): Carly Telford (Chelsea); Lucy Bronze (Lyon), Steph Houghton (c) (Man City), Abbie McManus (Man City), Alex Greenwood (Man Utd); Keira Walsh (Man City), Fran Kirby (Chelsea) (sub 87 Lucy Staniforth (Birmingham City)), Isobel Christiansen (Lyon) (sub 66 Rachel Daly (Houston Dash)) ; Nikita Parris (Man City), Ellen White (Birmingham City) (sub 76 Toni Duggan (Barcelona)), Karen Carney (Chelsea) (sub 66 Beth Mead (Arsenal))

Unused subs: Karen Bardsley (Man City), Jodie Taylor (Seattle Reign), Demi Stokes (Man City), Gemma Bonner (Man City), Leah Williamson (Arsenal), Chioma Ubogagu (Orlando Pride), Georgia Stanway (Man City), Mary Earps (Wolfsburg)

Head coach: Phil Neville

Brazil (4-4-2): Aline Villares (Granadilla Tenerife); Leticia Santos (SC Sand), Erika (Corinthians), Monica (Orlando Pride) (sub 90+2 Kathellen (Bordeaux)), Jucinara (Valencia) (sub 83 Thaisa (Milan)); Ludmila (Atletico Madrid) (sub 35 Debora (North Carolina Courage)), Formiga (PSG), Andressa Alves (Barcelona), Adriana Leal da Silva (Corinthians); Marta (c) (Orlando Pride) (sub 70 Geyse Ferreira (Benfica)), Beatriz (Incheon Red Angels) (sub 69 Raquel Fernandes (Huelva))

Unused subs: Leticia Izidoro Lima da Silva (Corinthians), Tamires (Fortuna Hjorring), Tayla Pereira dos Santos (Benfica), Poliana (unattached), Juliana Ferreira (Flamengo), Luciana (Ferroviaria), Luana (Avaldsnes)

Head coach: Vadao

Referee: Ekaterina Kozyreva (RUS)

02.03 USA (A) D2-2 SBC NISSAN STADIUM, NASHVILLE ATT: 22,125

Megan Rapinoe 33, Tobin Heath 67; Stephanie Houghton 36, Nikita Parris 52

England (4-4-2): Karen Bardsley (Man City); Rachel Daly (Houston Dash), Steph Houghton (c) (Man City), Abbie McManus (Man City), Demi Stokes (Man City); Nikita Parris (Man City) (sub 88 Jodie Taylor (Seattle Reign)), Lucy Bronze (Lyon), Keira Walsh (Man City), Toni Duggan (Barcelona); Fran Kirby (Chelsea) (sub 73 Beth Mead (Arsenal)), Ellen White (Birmingham City) (sub 80 Georgia Stanway (Man City)

Unused subs: Carly Telford (Chelsea), Alex Greenwood (Man Utd), Isobel Christiansen (Lyon), Gemma Bonner (Man City), Leah Williamson (Arsenal), Chioma Ubogagu (Orlando Pride), Karen Carney (Chelsea), Mary Earps (Wolfsburg), Lucy Staniforth (Birmingham City)

Head coach: Phil Neville

USA (4-3-3): Adrianna Franch (Portland Thorns); Kelley O'Hara (Utah Royals) (sub 60 Becky Sauerbrunn (Utah Royals)), Abby Dahlkemper (North Carolina Courage), Tierna Davidson (Stanford), Crystal Dunn (North Carolina Courage) (sub 87 Carli Lloyd (Sky Blue FC)); Mallory Pugh (Washington Spirit) (sub 55 Christen Press (Utah Royals)), Julie Ertz (Chicago Red Stars), Rose Lavelle (Washington Spirit) (sub 64 Sam Mewis (North Carolina Courage)); Tobin Heath (Portland Thorns), Alex Morgan (Orlando Pride), Megan Rapinoe (Seattle Reign) (c)

Unused subs: Alyssa Naeher (Chicago Red Stars), Emily Sonnett (Portland Thorns), Andi Sullivan (Washington Spirit), Casey Short (Chicago Red Stars), Jessica McDonald (North Carolina Courage), Emily Fox (North Carolina Tar Heels), Ashlyn Harris (Orlando Pride), McCall Zerboni (North Carolina Courage)

Head coach: Jill Ellis

Referee: Marienela Araya (CRC)

05.03 JAPAN (N) W 3-0 SBC RAYMOND JAMES STADIUM, TAMPA ATT: 8,580

Lucy Staniforth 12, Karen Carney 23, Beth Mead 30

England (4-1-4-1): Carly Telford (Chelsea); Lucy Bronze (Lyon), Steph Houghton (c) (Man City), Leah Williamson (Arsenal), Alex Greenwood (Man Utd); Keira Walsh (Man City) (sub 60 Gemma Bonner (Man City)); Beth Mead (Arsenal) (sub 66 Chioma Ubogagu (Orlando Pride)), Lucy Staniforth (Birmingham City) (sub 81 Fran Kirby (Chelsea)), Isobel Christiansen (Lyon) (sub 39 Georgia Stanway (Man City)), Karen Carney (Chelsea) (sub 66 Toni Duggan (Barcelona)); Jodie Taylor (Seattle Reign) (sub 51 Ellen White (Birmingham City))

Unused subs: Karen Bardsley (Man City), Abbie McManus (Man City), Nikita Parris (Man City), Demi Stokes (Man City), Leah Williamson (Arsenal), Rachel Daly (Houston Dash), Mary Earps (Wolfsburg)

Head coach: Phil Neville

Japan (4-4-2): Erina Yamane (Real Betis); Risa Shimizu (Nippon TV Beleza) (sub 80 Asato Miyagawa (Nippon TV Beleza)), Risako Oga (Nojima Stella Kanagawa Sagamihara) (sub 46 Yuka Momiki (Nippon TV Beleza)), Moeka Minami (Urawa Reds), Aya Sameshima (c) (INAC Kobe Leonessa); Moeno Sakaguchi (Albirex Niigata) (sub 46 Rikako Kobayashi (Nippon TV Beleza)), Arisa Matsubara (Nojima Stella Kanagawa), Hina Sugita (INAC Kobe Leonessa), Yui Hasegawa (Nippon TV Beleza); Mayu Ikejiri (Suwon UDC WFC) (sub 46 Narumi Miiura (Nippon TV Beleza)), Jun Endo (Nippon TV Beleza) (sub 46 Kumi Yokoyama (Frankfurt))

Unused Subs: *Rei Takenaka, Rumi Utsugi (Seattle Reign), Saori Ariyoshi (Nippon TV Beleza).*

Head coach: Asako Takakura

Referee: Christina Unkel (USA)

05.04 CANADA (H) L 0-1 F ACADEMY STADIUM, MANCHESTER ATT: 5,682

Sinclair 81

England (4-2-3-1): Karen Bardsley (Man City); Rachel Daly (Houston Dash) (sub 73 Jill Scott (Man City)), Steph Houghton (c) (Man City), Abbie McManus (Man City), Demi Stokes (Man City); Lucy Bronze (Lyon), Keira Walsh (Man City); Nikita Parris (Man City), Toni Duggan (Barcelona) (sub 84 Georgia Stanway (Man City)), Karen Carney (Chelsea) (sub 64 Beth Mead (Arsenal)); Jodie Taylor (Seattle Reign) (sub 73 Ellen White (Birmingham City))

Unused subs: Millie Bright (Chelsea), Alex Greenwood (Man Utd), Leah Williamson (Arsenal), Jade Moore (Reading), Lucy Staniforth (Birmingham City), Chioma Ubogagu (Orlando Pride), Mary Earps (Wolfsburg), Ellie Roebuck (Man City), Carly Telford (Chelsea)

Head coach: Phil Neville

Canada (4-2-3-1): Stephanie Labbe (North Carolina Courage); Ashley Lawrence (PSG), Kadeisha Buchanan (Lyon), Shelina Zadorsky (Orlando Pride), Allysha Chapman (Houston Dash) (sub 56 Jayde Riviere (Vancouver Whitecaps)); Desiree Scott (Utah Royals), Sophie Schmidt (Houston Dash) (sub 75 Julia Grosso (Texas Longhorns)); Nichelle Prince (Houston Dash) (sub 81 Deanne Rose (Florida Gators)), Jessie Fleming (UCLA Bruins), Janine Beckie (Manchester City) (sub 90+3 Shannon Woeller (Eskilstuna United)); Christine Sinclair (c) (Portland Thorns)

Unused Subs: Erin McLeod (SC Sand), Sabrina D'Angelo (Vittsjo GIK), Jordyn Huitema (Vancouver Whitecaps), Gabrielle Carle (Florida State Seminoles), Lindsay Agnew (Houston Dash), Vanessa Gilles (Bordeaux), Jenna Hellstrom (KIF Orebro)

Head coach: John Herdman

Referee: Ivana Martincic (Croatia)

09.04 SPAIN (H) W 2-1 F COUNTY GROUND, SWINDON ATT: 13,856

Beth Mead 36, Ellen White 46; Aitana Bonmati 67

England (4-1-2-3): Ellie Roebuck (Man City) (sub 46 Mary Earps (Wolfsburg)); Rachel Daly (Houston Dash) (sub 68 Gemma Bonner (Man City)), Millie Bright (Chelsea), Leah Williamson (Arsenal), Alex Greenwood (Man Utd); Jade Moore (Reading) (sub 54 Lucy Staniforth (Birmingham City)); Jill Scott (c) (Man City), Georgia Stanway (Man City) (sub 68 Keira Walsh (Man City)); Beth Mead (Arsenal) (sub 84 Nikita Parris (Man City)), Ellen White (Birmingham City), Toni Duggan (Barcelona) (sub 54 Chioma Ubogagu (Orlando Pride)

Unused subs: Karen Bardsley (Man City), Jodie Taylor (Seattle Reign), Karen Carney (Chelsea), Demi Stokes (Man City), Abbie McManus (Man City)

Head coach: Phil Neville

Spain (4-4-2): Sandra Panos (Barcelona), Marta Corredera (Levante), Irene Paredes (c) (PSG) (sub 52 Ivana Andres (Levante)), Andrea Pereira (Barcelona), Maria Pilar Leon (Barcelona) (sub 52 Leila Ouahabi (Barcelona)); Victoria Losada (Barcelona) (sub 79 Angela Sosa (Atletico Madrid)), Silvia Meseguer (Atletico Madrid) (sub 39 Virginia Torrecilla (Montpellier)), Armanda Sampedro (Atletico Madrid) (sub 62 Aitana Bonmati (Barcelona)), Alexia Putellas (Barcelona); Mariona Caldentey (Barcelona), Jennifer Hermoso (Atletico Madrid) (sub 79 Esther Gonzalez (Atletico Madrid))

Unused Subs: Maria Asuncion Quinones (Barcelona), Celia Jimenez (Seattle Reig), Marta Torrejon (Barcelona), Barbara Latorre (Barcelona), Olga Garcia (Atletico Madrid), Irene Guerrero (Real Betis)

Head coach: Jorge Vilda

Referee: Stephanie Frappart (FRA)

25.05 DENMARK (H) W 2-0 F BANKS'S STADIUM, WALSALL ATT: 8,273

Nikita Parris 45+1, Jill Scott 59

England (4-3-3): Karen Bardsley (Man City); Rachel Daly (Houston Dash), Leah Williamson (Arsenal), Millie Bright (Chelsea), Demi Stokes (Man City); Jill Scott (c) (Man City), Jade Moore (Reading), Georgia Stanway (Man City) (sub 61 Fran Kirby (Chelsea)); Nikita Parris (Lyon) (sub 61 Karen Carney (Chelsea)), Ellen White (Man City), Beth Mead (Arsenal) (sub 80 Lucy Staniforth (Birmingham City))

Unused subs: Mary Earps (Wolfsburg), Lucy Bronze (Lyon), Alex Greenwood (Man Utd), Keira Walsh (Man City), Steph Houghton (Man City), Jodie Taylor (Seattle Reign), Abbie McManus (Man United)

Head coach: Phil Neville

Denmark (4-1-3-2): Katrine Abel (Brondby); Rikke Sevecke (Brondby), Stine Ballisager Pedersen (Valerenga Dalmer), Janni Arnth (Arsenal), Sofie Svava (Brondby); Sofie Junge-Pedersen (Juventus); Nicoline Sorensen (Brondby) (sub 75 Frederikke Thogersen (Fortuna Hjorring)), Sanne Trelsgaard Nielsen (Rosengard) (sub 75 Julie Tavlo Petersson (Brondby)), Emma Snerle (Fortuna Hjorring) (sub 41 Mille Gejl Jensen (Brondby)); Signe Bruun (PSG) (sub 64 Rikke Madsen (VSK Aarhus)), Pernille Harder (c) (Wolfsburg)

Unused Subs: Nanna Christiansen (Brondby), Sara Holmgaard (Fortuna Horring), Kathrine Ostergaard Larsen (Farum BK), Kamilla Lilhammer Karlsen (Bronby), Dajan Hashemi (Linkoping)

Head coach: Lars Sondergaard

Referee: Desiree Grundbacher (SUI)

01.06 NEW ZEALAND (H) L 0-1 F AMEX STADIUM, BRIGHTON & H A FC ATT: 20,076

Sarah Gregorius 50

England (4-2-3-1): Carly Telford (Chelsea); Lucy Bronze (Lyon), Steph Houghton (c) (Man City), Abbie McManus (Man Utd) Alex Greenwood (Man Utd); Lucy Staniforth (Birmingham City) (sub 68 Jill Scott (Man City)), Keira Walsh (Man City) (sub 89 Georgia Stanway (Man City)); Nikita Parris (Lyon) (sub 66 Beth Mead (Arsenal)), Fran Kirby (Chelsea), Toni Duggan (Barcelona) (sub 54 Karen Carney (Chelsea)); Jodie Taylor (Seattle Reign) (sub 75 Ellen White (Man City))

Unused subs: Karen Bardsley (Man City), Ellie Roebuck (Man City), Mille Bright (Chelsea), Leah Williamson (Arsenal), Hannah Blundell (Chelsea), Demi Stokes (Man City), Jade Moore (Reading), Rachel Daly (Houston Dash), Mary Earps (Wolfsburg)

Head coach: Phil Neville

New Zealand (4-4-1-1): Erin Nayler (Bordeaux); Rebecca Stott (Avaldsnes), Meikayla Moore (Duisburg), Abby Erceg (c) (North Carolina Courage), Ali Riley (Chelsea); Catherine Bott (Vittsjo GIK) (sub 84 Paige Satchell (SC Sand)), Ria Percival (West Ham), Katie Bowen (Utah Royals), Betsy Hassett (KR) (sub 73 Annalie Longo (unattached)); Rosie White (unattached) (sub 73 Olivia Chance (Everton)); Sarah Gregorius (AS Elfen Saitama) (sub 64 Hannah Wilkinson (Vittsjo GIK))

Unused Subs: Anna Green (Capital Football), Emma Kete (Canberra United), Sarah Morton (Western Springs), Katie Duncan (Onehunga Sports), Steph Skilton (Papakura City), Daisy Cleverley (Forrest Hill Milford United), Victoria Esson (Avaldsnes), Nadia Olla (Western Springs)

Head coach: Tom Sermanni

Referee: Monika Mularczyk (POL)

NB: For England's World Cup 2019 line-ups, see World Cup section

SHEBELIEVES CUP 2019 - FULL RESULTS AND STANDINGS

The SheBelieves Cup is an invitational event held in the US. It has been staged every year since 2016. The first three editions featured the same four teams, the USA, England, France and Germany. France and Germany were replaced by Brazil and Japan for the 2019 edition. The teams play each other once in a round-robin format. In common with regular friendly international matches, a maximum of six substitutions can be made in each match.

RESULTS

27.02	USA	2-2	Japan
27.02	England	2-1	Brazil
02.03	Brazil	1-3	Japan
02.03	USA	2-2	England
05.03	Japan	0-3	England
06.03	USA	1-0	Brazil

FINAL STANDINGS

Pos	Team	P	W	D	L	F	A	GD	Pts
1.	England	3	2	1	0	7	3	4	7
2.	USA	3	1	2	0	5	4	1	5
3.	Japan	3	1	1	1	5	6	-1	4
4.	Brazil	3	0	0	3	2	6	-4	0

If two or more teams are level on points, their rankings are decided by the following criteria in this order: 1) goal difference from all games; 2) goals scored in all games; 3) points from matches solely between the teams who are level on points; 4) goal difference from matches solely between the teams who are level on points; 5) goals scored in matches solely between the teams who are level on points; 6) FIFA Ranking

FIFA WOMEN'S WORLD CUP FRANCE 2019 QUALIFIERS

GROUP 1 RESULTS

17.09.17	Kazakhstan	0-1	Wales
19.09.17	England	6-0	Russia
21.10.17	Kazakhstan	0-2	Bosnia & Herzegovina
24.10.17	Russia	0-0	Wales
24.11.17	Wales	1-0	Kazakhstan
24.11.17	England	4-0	Bosnia & Herzegovina
28.11.17	Bosnia & Herzegovina	0-1	Wales
28.11.17	England	5-0	Kazakhstan
05.04.18	Bosnia & Herzegovina	1-6	Russia
06.04.18	England	0-0	Wales
09.04.18	Kazakhstan	0-3	Russia
10.04.18	Bosnia & Herzegovina	0-2	England
07.06.18	Wales	1-0	Bosnia & Herzegovina
08.06.18	Russia	1-3	England
12.06.18	Bosnia & Herzegovina	0-2	Kazakhstan
12.06.18	Wales	3-0	Russia
30.08.18	Russia	3-0	Kazakhstan
31.08.18	Wales	0-3	England
04.09.18	Kazakhstan	0-6	England
04.09.18	Russia	3-0	Bosnia & Herzegovina

GROUP 1 – FINAL STANDINGS

Pos	Team	P	W	D	L	F	A	GD	Pts	
1.	England	8	7	1	0	29	1	28	22	**Q**
2.	Wales	8	5	2	1	7	3	4	17	
3.	Russia	8	4	1	3	16	13	3	13	
4.	Bosnia & Herz.	8	1	0	7	3	19	-16	3	
5.	Kazakhstan	8	1	0	7	2	21	-19	3	

In total there were seven European qualifying groups for the FIFA Women's World Cup 2019. The winners of each group qualified automatically, namely: England; Scotland; Norway; Sweden; Germany; Italy and Spain. The four group runners-up with the best records against the teams which finish 1st, 3rd and 4th in their groups progressed to the play-offs, namely: Belgium; Denmark; Netherlands and Switzerland. The play-offs consisted of two semi-finals played over two legs in October 2018. Netherlands beat Denmark 4-1 on aggregate while Switzerland won on away goals after a 3-3 aggregate draw with Belgium. The play-off final also consisted of two legs with Netherlands winning 4-1 on aggregate to take the final European qualifying place for the World Cup. The FIFA Women's World Cup France 2019 finals took place 7 June – 7 July and included 24 teams from across the world. There were six groups of four teams. The top two in each group progressed to the knockout phase along with the four best 3rd-placed teams.

FIFA WOMEN'S WORLD CUP
FRANCE 2019

Bill Grant

WORLD CHAMPIONS USA LIFT THE TROPHY IN PARIS

The 2019 Women's World Cup saw 24 teams take part in the most entertaining, competitive and drama-filled staging of the tournament yet, as France hosted 52 matches and record-breaking television audiences watched the eighth staging of an event first held in 1991.

From the spine-tingling atmosphere that accompanied the host nation's blistering first half performance in their opening match against South Korea at a packed Parc des Princes on 7 June, to the United States' successful defence of their title 30 days later in Lyon, the finals more than lived up to expectations.

In the build-up to the big kick-off many predicted a wide-open competition, with more nations carrying realistic ambitions of winning the trophy than ever before. But despite facing tough tests throughout the knockout stages, the world champions and pre-tournament favourites, the USA, ultimately showed their superior strength to lift the title for a record fourth time, in their fifth final.

Led by Hampshire-born English boss Jill Ellis, who became the first coach to win the trophy twice, the Stars and Stripes beat the European champions the Netherlands 2-0 in front of a noisy, capacity crowd of 57,900 at the Stade de Lyon, thanks to Megan Rapinoe's penalty and Rose Lavelle's superb individual goal.

The ultimate triumph came after a run of three consecutive 2-1 wins in the knockout stages over battling European opposition in the shape of Spain, hosts France and England, who saw captain Steph Houghton's late penalty saved by Alyssa Naeher in a gripping semi-final.

Bill Grant

EXPECTANT DUTCH FANS PREPARE TO TAKE ON TEAM USA IN THE WORLD CUP FINAL

The Americans had opened the defence of their title with a World Cup record 13-0 victory against Thailand in Reims and went on to prove themselves unstoppable as winger Rapinoe and star striker Alex Morgan shone while they racked up seven wins from seven.

As well as lifting the World Cup, Rapinoe was also awarded the Golden Ball for the tournament's best player and the Golden Boot award for top scorer. While she finished level on six goals with team-mate Morgan and England's Ellen White, she took the accolade by virtue of having provided more assists than White and the same number as Morgan in less playing time.

As for England, their fourth-placed finish was their second-best result at a Women's World Cup, and 11.7 million TV viewers – a UK record for a women's match – watched their agonising semi-final loss to the USA, as the public's interest in women's football soared.

Phil Neville's side beat Scotland, Argentina and 2011 champions Japan to top Group D, before back-to-back 3-0 wins over Cameroon and Norway saw them reach the last four at a third consecutive major championship.

However, they suffered semi-final heartbreak once again and were then outdone by Sweden in the third-place play-off in Nice, a frustrating ending to a largely impressive campaign.

A major talking point of the tournament was the use of VAR which appeared more intrusive than it had done during its debut at the men's World Cup in Russia in 2018. That was in part due to law changes which came into effect on June 1, 2019 which included a stricter interpretation of what constitutes handball, with the world "deliberate" removed from the statutes.

At this tournament VAR was also used to enforce encroachment by goalkeepers at penalties. With the new laws also stating goalkeepers must be shown a yellow card for such an offence, there was the potential for chaos in the knockout stages before FIFA ruled just before the Round of 16 that cautions would not be issued during penalty shootouts.

While the new laws, and the way they were policed by video assistant referees, upset some players, fans and television viewers the overall tournament received favourable reviews and undoubtedly raised the profile of women's football across the globe.

ENGLAND RESULTS & LINE-UPS – FIFA WORLD CUP FRANCE 2019

09.06 SCOTLAND (N) W 2-1 WCG STADE DE NICE, NICE ATT: 13,188

Nikita Parris (Pen) 14, Ellen White 40; Claire Emslie 79

England (4-3-3): Karen Bardsley (Man City); Lucy Bronze (Lyon), Steph Houghton (c) (Man City), Millie Bright (Chelsea) (sub 55 Abbie McManus (Man City)), Alex Greenwood (Man Utd); Keira Walsh (Man City), Fran Kirby (Chelsea) (sub 82 Georgia Stanway (Man City)), Jill Scott (Man City); Nikita Parris (Lyon), Ellen White (Man City), Beth Mead (Arsenal) (sub 71 Karen Carney (Chelsea))

Unused subs: Jodie Taylor (Reign FC), Carly Telford (Chelsea), Leah Williamson (Arsenal), Jade Moore (Reading), Rachel Daly (Houston Dash), Mary Earps (Wolfsburg), Lucy Staniforth (Birmingham City), Toni Duggan (Barcelona – unavailable, injured), Demi Stokes (Man City – unavailable, injured)

Head coach: Phil Neville

Scotland (4-5-1): Lee Alexander (Glasgow City); Sophie Howard (Reading) (sub 75 Chloe Arthur Birmingham City)), Rachel Corsie (c) (Utah Royals), Jennifer Beattie (Arsenal), Nicola Docherty (Glasgow City) (sub 55 Kirsty Smith (Man Utd)); Lisa Evans (Arsenal), Christie Murray (Liverpool) (sub 87 Lizzie Arnot (Man Utd)), Kim Little (Arsenal), Caroline Weir (Man City), Claire Emslie (Orlando Pride); Erin Cuthbert (Chelsea)

Unused subs: Jo Love (Glasgow City), Hayley Lauder (Glasgow City), Leanne Crichton (Glasgow City), Shannon Lynn (Vittsjo GIK), Jane Ross (West Ham), Joelle Murray (Hibernian), Lana Clelland (Fiorentina), Fiona Brown (Rosengard), Jenna Fife (Hibernian)

Head coach: Shelley Kerr

Referee: Jana Adamkova (CZE)

14.06 ARGENTINA (N) W 1-0 WCG STADE OCEANE, LE HAVRE 20,294

Nikita Parris Missed Pen 28 (Saved Vanina Correa), Jodie Taylor 62

England (4-1-4-1): Carly Telford (Chelsea); Lucy Bronze (Lyon), Steph Houghton (c) (Man City), Abbie McManus (Man City), Alex Greenwood (Man Utd); Jade Moore (Reading); Nikita Parris (Lyon) (sub 87 Rachel Daly (Houston Dash)), Jill Scott (Man City), Fran Kirby (Chelsea) (sub 89 Karen Carney (Chelsea)), Beth Mead (Arsenal) (sub 81 Georgia Stanway (Man City)); Jodie Taylor (Reign FC)

Unused subs: Karen Bardsley (Man City), Keira Walsh (Man City), Millie Bright (Chelsea), Demi Stokes (Man City), Leah Williamson (Arsenal), Ellen White (Man City), Mary Earps (Wolfsburg), Lucy Staniforth (Birmingham City), Toni Duggan (Barcelona – unavailable, injured)

Head coach: Phil Neville

Argentina (4-5-1): Vanina Correa (Social Lux); Adriana Sachs (UAI Urquiza), Agustina Barroso (Madrid CFF), Aldana Cometti (Sevilla), Eliana Stabile (Boca Juniors); Florencia Bonsegundo (SC Huelva), Ruth Bravo (CD Tacon), Lorena Benitez (Boca Juniors) (sub 77 Vanesa Santana (EDF Logrono)), Miriam Mayorga (UAI Urquiza), Estefania Banini (c) (Levante UD) (sub 68 Mariana Larroquette (UAI Urquiza)); Sole Jaimes (Lyon) (sub 90 Yael Oviedo (Rayo Vallecano))

Unused subs: Gabriela Garton (Club Atletico Sol de Mayo), Virginia Gomez (Rosario Central), Maria Belen Potassa (Fundacion Albacete), Mariela Coronel (Granada CF), Gabriela Patricia Chavez (River Plate), Dalila Belen Ippolito (River Plate), Natalie Juncos (UAI Urquiza), Milagros Menendez (UAI Urquiza), Solana Peyreyra (UAI Urquiza)

Head coach: Carlos Borrello

Referee: Liang Qin (CHN)

19.06	JAPAN (N)	W 2-0	WCG	STADE DE NICE, NICE	14,319

Ellen White 14, 84

England (4-3-3): Karen Bardsley (Man City); Lucy Bronze (Lyon), Steph Houghton (c) (Man City), Millie Bright (Chelsea), Demi Stokes (Man City); Jill Scott (Man City), Keira Walsh (Man City) (sub 72 Jade Moore (Reading)), Georgia Stanway (Man City) (sub 74 Karen Carney (Chelsea)); Rachel Daly (Houston Dash), Ellen White (Man City) Toni Duggan (Barcelona) (sub 83 Nikita Parris (Lyon))

Unused subs: Alex Greenwood (Man Utd), Jodie Taylor (Reign FC), Fran Kirby (Chelsea), Carly Telford (Chelsea), Leah Williamson (Arsenal), Abbie McManus (Man City), Mary Earps (Wolfsburg), Beth Mead (Arsenal), Lucy Staniforth (Birmingham City)

Head coach: Phil Neville

Japan (4-4-2): Ayaka Yamashita (Nippon TV Beleza); Risa Shimizu (Nippon TV Beleza), Saki Kumagai (c) (Lyon), Nana Ichise (Mynavi Vegalta Sendai), Aya Sameshima (INAC Kobe Leonessa); Rikako Kobayashi (Nippon TV Beleza) (sub 62 Narumi Miura (Nippon TV Beleza)), Emi Nakajima (INAC Kobe Leonessa), Hina Sugita (INAC Kobe Leonessa), Jun Endo (Nippon TV Beleza) (sub 85 Saori Takarada (Cerezo Osaka)); Kumi Yokoyama (Nagano Parceiro) (sub 61 Yuika Sugasawa (Urawa Red Diamonds)), Mana Iwabuchi (INAC Kobe Leonessa)

Unused subs: Sakiko Ikeda (Urawa Red Diamonds), Rumi Utsugi (Reign FC), Mizuho Sakaguchi (Nippon TV Beleza), Moeka Minami (Urawa Red Diamonds), Yui Hasegawa (Nippon TV Beleza), Yuka Momiki (Nippon TV Beleza), Asato Miyagawa (Nippon TV Beleza), Chika Hirao (Albirex Niigata), Shiori Miyake (INAC Kobe Leonessa)

Head coach: Asako Takakura

Referee: Claudia Umpierrez (URU)

23.06	CAMEROON (N)	W 3-0	WC16	STADE DU HAINAUT, VALENCIENNES	20,148

Steph Houghton 14, Ellen White 45+4, Alex Greenwood 58

England (4-3-3): Karen Bardsley (Man City); Lucy Bronze (Lyon), Steph Houghton (c) (Man City), Millie Bright (Chelsea), Alex Greenwood (Man Utd); Keira Walsh (Man City), Fran Kirby (Chelsea), Jill Scott (Man City) (sub 78 Lucy Staniforth (Birmingham City)); Nikita Parris (Lyon) (sub 84 Leah Williamson (Arsenal)), Ellen White (Man City) (sub 64 Jodie Taylor (Reign FC)), Toni Duggan (Barcelona)

Unused subs: Demi Stokes (Man City), Carly Telford (Chelsea), Abbie McManus (Man City), Mary Earps (Wolfsburg), Beth Mead (Arsenal), Jade Moore (Reading), Rachel Daly (Houston Dash), Georgia Stanway (Man City), Karen Carney (Chelsea)

Head coach: Phil Neville

Cameroon (4-5-1): Annette Ngo Ndom (Amazone FAP), Yvonne Leuko (Strasbourg), Augustine Ejangue (Armar-Bjornar) (sub 64 Ysis Sonkeng (Amazone FAP)), Estelle Johnson (Sky Blue FC), Aurelle Awona (Dijon); Ajara Nchout (Valerenga), Michaela Abam (Paris FC) (sub 68 Ninon Abena (Louves Miniproff)), Raissa Feudjio (Granadilla), Jeannette Yango (Saint-Malo), Gabrielle Aboudi Onguene (c) (CSKA Moscow); Gaelle Enganamouit (unattached) (sub 53 Alexandra Takounda (Éclair))

Unused subs: Christine Manie (Nancy), Madeleine Ngono Mani (Ambilly), Claudine Meffometou (Guingamp), Charlene Meyong (Louves Miniproff), Isabelle Mambingo (Sunshine Queens), Henriette Akaba (Besiktas), Marlyse Ngo Ndoumbouk (Nancy), Genevieve Ngo Mbeleck (Amazone FAP), Marthe Ongmahan (AWA Yaounde)

Head coach: Alain Djeumfa

Referee: Liang Qin (CHN)

ENGLAND'S ELLEN WHITE FINISHED AS THE JOINT TOP-SCORER AT THE TOURNAMENT WITH SIX

27.06 NORWAY (N) W 3-0 WCQF STADE OCEANE, LE HAVRE 21,111

Jill Scott 3, Ellen White 40, Lucy Bronze 57, *Nikita Parris missed pen 83 (saved Ingrid Hjelmseth)*

England (4-3-3): Karen Bardsley (Man City); Lucy Bronze (Lyon), Steph Houghton (c) (Man City), Millie Bright (Chelsea), Demi Stokes (Man City); Keira Walsh (Man City), Fran Kirby (Chelsea) (sub 74 Georgia Stanway (Man City)), Jill Scott (Man City); Nikita Parris (Lyon) (sub 88 Rachel Daly (Houston Dash)), Ellen White (Man City), Toni Duggan (Barcelona) (sub 54 Beth Mead (Arsenal))

Unused subs: Alex Greenwood (Man Utd), Carly Telford (Chelsea), Abbie McManus (Man City), Mary Earps (Wolfsburg), Jade Moore (Reading), Karen Carney (Chelsea), Jodie Taylor (Reign FC), Leah Williamson (Arsenal), Lucy Staniforth (Birmingham City)

Head coach: Phil Neville

Norway (4-4-2): Ingrid Hjelmseth (Stabaek); Ingrid Moe Wold (LSK Kvinner) (sub 85 Synne Skinnes Hansen (LSK Kvinner)) , Maren Mjelde (c) (Chelsea), Maria Thorisdottir (Chelsea), Kristine Minde (Wolfsburg); Karina Saevik (Kolbotn) (sub 64 Lisa-Marie Utland (Rosengard)), Vilde Boe Risa (Kopparbergs/Goteborg), Ingrid Engen (LSK Kvinner), Guro Reiten (LSK Kvinner) (sub 74 Amalie Vevle Eikeland (Sandviken)); Caroline Graham Hansen (Barcelona), Isabell Herlovsen (Kolbotn)

Unused subs: Cecilie Fiskerstrand (LSK Kvinner), Oda Marie Hove Bogstad (Arna-Bjornar), Stine Hovland (Sandviken), Elise Thorsnes (LSK Kvinner), Therese Sessy Asland (LSK Kvinner), Frida Maanum (Linkoping), Cecilie Redisch Kvamme (Sandviken), Emilie Haavi (LSK Kvinner – unavailable), Emillie Nautnes (Arne-Bjornar)

Head coach: Martin Sjogren

Referee: Lucila Venegas (MEX)

02.07 USA (N) L 1-2 WCSF STADE DE LYON, LYON 53,512

Ellen White 19, *Steph Houghton missed pen 84 (saved Alyssa Naeher), Millie Bright sent off 86*; Christen Press 10, Alex Morgan 31

England (4-4-2): Carly Telford (Chelsea); Lucy Bronze (Lyon), Steph Houghton (c) (Man City), Millie Bright (Chelsea), Demi Stokes (Man City); Keira Walsh (Man City) (sub 71 Jade Moore (Reading)), Jill Scott (Man City), Beth Mead (Arsenal) (sub 58 Fran Kirby (Chelsea)), Rachel Daly (Houston Dash) (sub 89 Georgia Stanway (Man City)); Nikita Parris (Lyon), Ellen White (Man City)

Unused subs: Alex Greenwood (Man Utd), Karen Bardsley (Man City), Abbie McManus (Man City), Mary Earps (Wolfsburg), Karen Carney (Chelsea), Jodie Taylor (Reign FC), Leah Williamson (Arsenal), Lucy Staniforth (Birmingham City), Toni Duggan (Barcelona)

Head coach: Phil Neville

USA (4-3-3): Alyssa Naeher (Chicago Red Stars); Kelley O'Hara (Utah Royals) (sub 87 Ali Krieger (Orlando Pride)), Abby Dahlkemper (North Carolina Courage), Becky Sauerbrunn (Utah Royals), Crystal Dunn (North Carolina Courage); Lindsey Horan (Portland Thorns), Julie Ertz (Chicago Red Stars), Rose Lavelle (Washington Spirit) (sub 65 Samantha Mewis (North Carolina Courage)); Tobin Heath (Portland Thorns), Alex Morgan (c) (Orlando Pride), Christen Press (Utah Royals)

Unused subs: Mallory Pugh (Washington Spirit), Morgan Brian (Chicago Red Stars), Carli Lloyd (Sky Blue FC), Tierna Davidson (Chicago Red Stars), Emily Sonnett (Portland Thorns), Megan Rapinoe (Reign FC), Ashlyn Harris (Orlando Pride), Allie Long (Reign FC), Adrianna Franch (Portland Thorns), Jessica McDonald (North Carolina Courage)

Head coach: Jill Ellis

Referee: Edina Alves Batista (BRA)

06.07 SWEDEN (N) L 1-2 WC3RD STADE DE NICE, NICE 20,316

Fran Kirby 31; Kosovare Asllani 11, Sofia Jakobsson 22

England (4-3-3): Carly Telford (Chelsea); Lucy Bronze (Lyon), Steph Houghton (c) (Man City), Abbie McManus (Man City) (sub 83 Rachel Daly (Houston Dash)), Alex Greenwood (Man Utd); Fran Kirby (Chelsea), Jill Scott (Man City), Jade Moore (Reading); Nikita Parris (Lyon) (sub 74 Karen Carney (Chelsea)), Ellen White (Man City), Beth Mead (Arsenal) (sub 50 Jodie Taylor (Reign FC)

Unused subs: Karen Bardsley (Man City), Millie Bright (Chelsea – suspended), Mary Earps (Wolfsburg), Demi Stokes (Man City), Leah Williamson (Arsenal), Lucy Staniforth (Birmingham City), Toni Duggan (Barcelona), Keira Walsh (Man City), Georgia Stanway (Man City)

Head coach: Phil Neville

Sweden (4-3-3): Hedvig Lindahl (unattached); Hanna Glas (PSG), Nilla Fischer (Wolfsburg), Linda Sembrant (Montpellier), Magdalena Eriksson (Chelsea); Nathalie Bjorn (Rosengard) (sub 72 Amanda Ilestedt (Turbine Potsdam)), Kosovare Asllani (Linkoping) (sub 46 Julia Ziggioti (Kopparbergs/Goteborg FC)), Caroline Seger (c) (Rosengard); Sofia Jakobsson (Montpellier), Stina Blackstenius (Linkoping), Fridolina Rolfo (Wolfsburg) (sub 27 Lina Hurtig (Linkoping))

Unused subs: Jonna Andersson (Chelsea), Madelen Janogy (Pitea), Jennifer Falk (Kopparbergs/Goteborg FC), Julia Roddar (Goteborg), Anna Anvegard (Vaxjo DFF), Mimmi Larsson (Linkoping), Zecira Musovic (Rosengard), Olivia Schough (Djurgardens), Elin Rubensson (Kopparbergs/Goteborg FC)

Head coach: Peter Gerhardsson

Referee: Anastasia Pustovoytova (RUS)

FIFA WOMEN'S WORLD CUP FRANCE 2019 FULL RESULTS

GROUP A

07.06 Parc des Princes, Paris 8pm	**France**	**4-0**	**South Korea**
Att: 45,261	Le Sommer 9, Renard 35, 45+2, Henry 85		

Hosts comfortably win opening game in front of sell-out crowd. VAR makes its first intervention of tournament disallowing fine volley from France's Griedge Mbock Bathy at 1-0 for fractional offside.

08.06 Stade Auguste-Delaune, Reims 8pm	**Norway**	**3-0**	**Nigeria**
Att: 11,058	Reiten 17, Utland 34, Ohale (og) 37		

Nigeria's Onome Ebi appears in her fifth World Cup, only Japan's Homare Sawa (six) and Brazil's Formiga (for whom France 2019 is a seventh) have played in more.

12.06 Stade des Alpes, Grenoble 2pm	**Nigeria**	**2-0**	**South Korea**
Att: 11,252	Kim Do-yeon (og) 29, Oshoala 75		

Chelsea and South Korea midfielder Ji So-yun becomes first player booked for diving at Women's World Cup since Erika for Brazil v USA in the 2011 tournament.

12.06 Stade de Nice, Nice 8pm	**France**	**2-1**	**Norway**
Att: 34,872	Gauvin 46, Le Sommer (pen) 72		Renard (og) 54

Hosts are on verge of qualifying for knockout round following second win. VAR controversy as France awarded penalty on review with Syrstad Engen adjudged to have fouled Marion Torrent.

17.06 Roazhon Park, Rennes 8pm	**Nigeria**	**0-1**	**France**
Att: 28,267	*Ebere sent off 75*		Renard (pen) 79

VAR awards a penalty to France in an incident which sees Ngoze Ebere sent off. Wendie Renard hits the post but VAR orders a re-take for keeper Chiamaka Nnadozie stepping off her line. Renard scores.

NB: Nigeria qualify on 20.06 as one of the four best 3rd-placed sides

17.06 Stade Auguste-Delaune, Reims 8pm	**South Korea**	**1-2**	**Norway**
Att: 13,034	Yeo Min-ji 78		C. Graham Hansen (pen) 4, Herlovsen (pen) 50

Norway advance to last 16 with a penalty in each half. South Korea – who had to win to have any chance of going through – exit the tournament without picking up a point.

	P	W	D	L	F	A	GD	Pts	
1.France	3	3	0	0	7	1	6	9	**Q**
2.Norway	3	2	0	1	6	3	3	6	**Q**
3.Nigeria	3	1	0	2	2	4	-2	3	**Q**
4.South Korea	3	0	0	3	1	8	-7	0	

GROUP B

08.06 Roazhon Park, Rennes 2pm	**Germany**	**1-0**	**China**
Att: 15,283	Gwinn 66		

Giulia Gwinn, 19, scores winner in her first competitive appearance for Germany and substitute Lena Oberdof, 17 years 171 days, becomes youngest ever Germany player at Women's World Cup.

08.06 Stade Oceane, Le Havre 7pm	**Spain**	**3-1**	**South Africa**
Att: 12,044	Hermoso (pen) 69, (pen) 82, L.Garcia 89		Kgatlana 25, *Vilakazi sent off 81*

South Africa take shock lead through fine chipped finish from Thembi Kgatlana but Spain turn it round as Jennifer Hermoso becomes first player ever to score two penalties in one match at a Women's World Cup.

12.06 Stade du Hainaut, Valenciennes 5pm	**Germany**	**1-0**	**Spain**
Att: 20,761	Dabritz 42		

Germany all but through to knock-out stage after second consecutive 1-0 win. Two-time champions without Dzsenifer Marozsan who broke a toe in opening game.

13.06 Parc des Princes, Paris 8pm	**South Africa**	**0-1**	**China**
Att: 20,011			Li Ying 40

Brilliant Li Ying volley wins it for China and puts World Cup debutants South Africa on verge of elimination. Result also guarantees Germany's place in Round of 16.

17.06 Stade de la Mosson, Montpellier 5pm	**South Africa**	**0-4**	**Germany**
Att: 15,502			Leupolz 14, Dabritz 29, Popp 40, Magull 58

Melanie Leupolz scores her first goal for Germany for 1,048 days (since netting in the 2016 Olympics against Zimbabwe) to help her side wrap up top spot and eliminate South Africa.

17.06 Stade Oceane, Le Havre 5pm	**China**	**0-0**	**Spain**
Att: 11,814			

Spain – tournament debutants in 2015 – reach the knockout stages for the first time. The goalless draw also ensures China will go through as one of the best 3rd-place sides.

	P	W	D	L	F	A	GD	Pts	
1.Germany	3	3	0	0	6	0	6	9	**Q**
2.Spain	3	1	1	1	3	2	1	4	**Q**
3.China	3	1	1	1	1	1	0	4	**Q**
4.South Africa	3	0	0	3	1	8	-7	0	

GROUP C

09.06 Stade du Hainaut, Valenciennes 12pm	**Australia**	**1-2**	**Italy**
Att: 15,380	Kerr 22, Kerr missed pen 22 (saved Giuliani), scored rebound		Bonansea 56, 90+5

First shock of tournament as Italy (15th in world rankings), playing in first World Cup for 20 years, come from behind to beat Australia (6th in world) with two goals from Juventus' Barabara Bonansea.

09.06 Stade des Alpes, Grenoble 2:30pm	**Brazil**	**3-0**	**Jamaica**
Att: 17,668	Cristiane 15, 50, 64, *Andressa Alves missed pen 38 (saved Schneider)*		

Cristiane, 34 years 25 days, becomes oldest player to score hat-trick at men's or women's World Cup as Jamaica are first Caribbean country to play a game at the Women's World Cup. Brazil's Formiga becomes first player to appear in seven Women's World Cups. At 41yrs 98 days she also become the oldest player to appear (beating record of 40yrs 12 days held by USA's Christie Rampone). NB: Formiga ends France 2019 by extending the record to 41yrs 112 days when she plays against France in Brazil's Round of 16 defeat

13.06 Stade de la Mosson, Montpellier 5pm	**Australia**	**3-2**	**Brazil**
Att: 17,032	Foord 45+1, Logarzo 58, Monica (og) 66		Marta (pen) 27, Cristiane 38

Brazil's Marta becomes first player to score in five men's or women's World Cups but Australia come from 2-0 down. Winner awarded after VAR review – goal initially disallowed for offside.

14.06 Stade Auguste-Delaune, Reims 5pm	**Jamaica**	**0-5**	**Italy**
Att: 12,016			Girelli (pen) 12, 25, 46, Galli 71, 81

Cristiane Girelli scores a hat-trick including a re-taken penalty ordered after goalkeeper Sydney Schneider is adjudged to have moved off her line.

18.06 Stade des Alpes, Grenoble 8pm	**Jamaica**	**1-4**	**Australia**
Att: 17,402	Solaun 49		Kerr 11, 42, 69, 83

Sam Kerr becomes first Australian to score World Cup hat-trick as she grabs four to take her country through. Havana Solaun hits Jamaica's first ever World Cup goal but Reggae Girlz are eliminated.

18.06 Stade du Hainaut, Valenciennes 8pm	**Italy**	**0-1**	**Brazil**
Att: 21,669			Marta (pen) 74

Marta overtakes Germany's Miroslav Klose (16) to become highest-scoring man or woman in World Cup history with 17 goals. Italy top group, Brazil through as one of best 3rd-placed teams.

	P	W	D	L	F	A	GD	Pts	
1.Italy	3	2	0	1	7	2	5	6	Q
2.Australia	3	2	0	1	8	5	3	6	Q
3.Brazil	3	2	0	1	6	3	3	6	Q
4.Jamaica	3	0	0	3	1	12	-11	0	

GROUP D

09.06 Stade de Nice, Nice 5pm	**England**	**2-1**	**Scotland**
Att: 13,188	Parris (pen) 14, White 40		Emslie 79

Jill Scott and Karen Carney appear in record fourth World Cup for England. England penalty awarded after VAR review. Claire Emslie scores first ever World Cup goal for debutants Scotland.

10.06 Parc des Princes, Paris 5pm	**Argentina**	**0-0**	**Japan**
Att: 25,055			

Argentina cause a shock as they claim their first ever World Cup point by holding 2011 winners and 2015 runners-up Japan to a goalless draw.

14.06 Roazhon Park, Rennes 2pm	**Japan**	**2-1**	**Scotland**
Att: 13,201	Iwabuchi 23, Sugasawa (pen) 37		Clelland 88

Scotland are left on the brink of elimination as they lose to the 2011 champions and there is huge VAR controversy as three penalty appeals go against Scotland

14.06 Stade Oceane, Le Havre 8pm	**England**	**1-0**	**Argentina**
Att: 20,294	*Parris missed pen 28 (saved Correa),* Taylor 62		

England recover from Nikita Parris' first-half penalty miss as Jodie Taylor's winner sees them book their place in the last 16.

19.06 Stade de Nice, Nice 8pm	**Japan**	**0-2**	**England**
Att: 14,319			White 14, 84

England secure top spot with maximum points as new Manchester City signing Ellen White hits her second and third goals of the tournament. Japan qualify in 2nd place.

19.06 Parc des Princes, Paris	**Scotland**	**3-3**	**Argentina**
Att: 28,205	Little 19, Beattie 49, Cuthbert 69		Menendez 74, Alexander (og) 79, Bonsegundo (pen) 90+4

Scotland are heading through as they lead 3-0 with 16 minutes left only to throw it away. Lee Alexander saves an injury time penalty, but VAR rules a retake for encroachment; Argentina score.

	P	W	D	L	F	A	GD	Pts	
1.England	3	3	0	0	5	1	4	9	Q
2.Japan	3	1	1	1	2	3	-1	4	Q
3.Argentina	3	0	2	1	3	4	-1	2	
4.Scotland	3	0	1	2	5	7	-2	1	

JODIE TAYLOR CELEBRATES SCORING FOR ENGLAND AGAINST ARGENTINA

GROUP E

10.06 Stade de la Mosson, Montpellier 8pm	**Canada**	**1-0**	**Cameroon**
Att: 10,710	Buchanan 45		

Lyon defender Kadeisha Buchanan – voted best young player at the 2015 World Cup – scores the winning goal for Canada against one of the lowest-ranked teams in the tournament.

11.06 Stade Oceane, Le Havre 2pm	**New Zealand**	**0-1**	**Netherlands**
Att: 10,654			Roord 90+2

New Zealand come close to a first ever World Cup win in their fifth tournament but lose to the European champions. New Arsenal signing Jill Roord scores the only goal in injury time.

15.06 Stade du Hainaut, Valenciennes 2pm	**Netherlands**	**3-1**	**Cameroon**
Att: 22,423	Miedema 41, 85, Bloodworth 48		Onguene 43

Arsenal's Vivianne Miedema, 22, becomes the Netherlands' all-time leading scorer with her 59th and 60th goals on her 77th appearance (breaking Manon Melis' record). The Dutch qualify for the last 16.

15.06 Stade des Alpes, Grenoble 8pm	**Canada**	**2-0**	**New Zealand**
Att: 14,856	Fleming 48, Prince 79		

Canada qualify for the knockout stages with a comfortable win. New Zealand keeper Erin Nayler pulls off arguably save of tournament so far to tip away Nichelle Prince header with score at 1-0.

20.06 Stade Auguste-Delaune, Reims 5pm	**Netherlands**	**2-1**	**Canada**
Att: 19,277	Dekker 54, Beerensteyn 75		Sinclair 60

European champions top the group with three wins. Canada through in 2nd place as Christine Sinclair equals the achievement of Brazil's Marta by scoring at five World Cups.

20.06 Stade de la Mosson, Montpellier 5pm	**Cameroon**	**2-1**	**New Zealand**
Att: 8,009	Nchout 57, 90+5		Awona (og) 80

Cameroon are heading out with the scores at 1-1 until Ajara Nchout scores the latest winner (excluding extra time) in Women's World Cup history (94mins 49secs) to send them through.

	P	W	D	L	F	A	GD	Pts	
1.Netherlands	3	3	0	0	6	2	4	9	Q
2.Canada	3	2	0	1	4	2	2	6	Q
3.Cameroon	3	1	0	2	3	5	-2	3	Q
4.New Zealand	3	0	0	3	1	5	-4	0	

GROUP F

11.06 Roazhon Park, Rennes 5pm	**Chile**		**0-2**	**Sweden**
Att: 15,875				Asllani 83, Janogy 90+4

Play is suspended in the 72nd minute due to torrential rain and an electric storm. The players return after a 40-minute break before two late goals win the match for 2016 Olympic runners-up Sweden.

11.06 Stade Auguste-Delaune, Reims 8pm	**USA**	**13-0**	**Thailand**
Att: 18,591	Morgan 12, 53, 74, 81, 87, Lavelle 20, 56, Horan 32, Mewis 50, 54, Rapinoe 79, Pugh 85, Lloyd 90+2		

Defending champions, the USA, break the record for the biggest World Cup win, beating Germany's 11-0 victory over Argentina at the 2007 tournament.

16.06 Stade de Nice, Nice 2pm	**Sweden**	**5-1**	**Thailand**
Att: 9,354	Sembrant 6, Asllani 19, Rolfo 42, Hurtig 81, Rubensson (pen) 90+6		Sung-ngoen 90+1

Sweden book their place in the last 16 but minnows Thailand win praise for scoring their first goal of the tournament in injury time as Kanjana Sung-ngoen's strike sparks emotional scenes.

16.06 Parc des Princes, Paris 5pm	**USA**	**3-0**	**Chile**
Att: 45,594	Lloyd 11, 35, Ertz 26, *Lloyd missed pen 81*		

Holders comfortably through to last 16 despite heroic display by Chile keeper Christiane Endler. USA's Carli Lloyd misses chance for hat-trick when she hits 81st minute penalty wide.

20.06 Stade Oceane, Le Havre 8pm	**Sweden**	**0-2**	**USA**
Att: 22,418			Horan 3, Andersson (og) 50

USA take the lead with the quickest goal of the tournament so far and set a record for the most goals (18) in the Women's World Cup group stage. Sweden qualify in 2nd place.

20.06 Roazhon Park, Rennes 8pm	**Thailand**	**0-2**	**Chile**
Att: 13,567			Boonsing (og) 48, Urrutia 80, *Lara missed pen 86*

Requiring a 3-0 win to qualify, Chile fall just short, as Francesca Lara hits the crossbar with an 86th-minute penalty. The result sends Nigeria through as the final of the four best 3rd-placed sides.

	P	W	D	L	F	A	GD	Pts	
1.USA	3	3	0	0	18	0	18	9	**Q**
2.Sweden	3	2	0	1	7	3	4	6	**Q**
3.Chile	3	1	0	2	2	5	-3	3	
4.Thailand	3	0	0	3	1	20	-19	0	

ROUND OF 16

NB: On 21 June football's lawmakers IFAB announce a suspension of a new law (introduced on 1 June 2019) that states goalkeepers must be cautioned for encroaching at a penalty. The suspension is for shootouts only, with the law remaining in place for penalties awarded during the match itself.

22.06 Stade des Alpes, Grenoble 4:30pm	**Germany**	**3-0**	**Nigeria**
Att: 17,988	Popp 20, Dabritz (pen) 27, Schuller 82		

Popp header allowed to stand after VAR check for potential offside. Dabritz converts penalty awarded after lengthy VAR check. Schuller wraps up comfortable win for two-time champions late on.

22.06 Stade de Nice, Nice 8pm	**Norway**	**1-1 aet 4-1pens**	**Australia**
Att: 12,229	Herlovsen 31		Kellond-Knight 83 *Kennedy sent off 104*

Australia awarded penalty at 1-0 down but overturned after VAR check. Elise Kellond-Knight equalises direct from corner. Australia's Alanna Kennedy receives first straight red card of tournament in extra time. Sam Kerr skies Aussies' first penalty in shootout. Ingrid Hjelmseth saves their second from Emily Gielnik. Ingrid Systad Engen converts the decisive spot-kick for Norway.

23.06 Stade du Hainuat, Valenciennes 4:30pm	**England**	**3-0**	**Cameroon**
Att: 20,148	Houghton 14, White 45+4, Greenwood 58		

Cameroon players twice appear temporarily unwilling to restart the match. Firstly, they protest when VAR overturns the initial decision to disallow Ellen White's goal for offside. They do so again when VAR rules out Ajara Nchout's 'goal' for a marginal offside. Jill Scott sets a record for England World Cup appearances (men's and women's) with 18, over-taking Peter Shilton's 17.

23.06 Stade Oceane, Le Havre 8pm	**France**	**2-1aet**	**Brazil**
Att: 23,965	Gauvin 52, Henry 106		Thaisa 63

VAR rules out Valerie Gauvin opener with Brazil keeper Barbara adjudged to have had ball under control. Gauvin then puts France ahead. Brazil equaliser initially ruled out for offside, before VAR overturns decision. Henry hits extra time winner for hosts. Formiga extends her record for oldest player ever to appear at a Women's World Cup to 41yrs 112 days.

24.06 Stade Auguste-Delaune, Reims 5pm	**Spain**	**1-2**	**USA**
Att: 19,633	Hermoso 9		Rapinoe (pen) 7, (pen) 75

Holders and favourites USA take lead through early Megan Rapinoe penalty, but Spain equalise immediately as US concede for first time since April. Rapinoe scores again from spot to win it late on.

24.06 Parc des Princes, Paris 8pm	**Sweden**	**1-0**	**Canada**
Att: 38,078	Blackstenius 55		*Beckie missed pen 69 (saved Lindahl)*

Stina Blackstenius scores winner early in second half. Hedvig Lindahl makes superb save from Janine Beckie after Canada awarded penalty for handball following VAR review.

25.06 Stade de la Mosson, Montpellier 5pm	**Italy**	**2-0**	**China**
Att: 17,492	Giacinti 15, Galli 49		

The Azzurre reach the quarter-finals for the first time since 1991. Aurora Galli scores her third goal as a substitute in this tournament equalling the Women's World Cup record set by Australia's Lisa de Vanna in 2007.

25.06 Roazhon Park, Rennes 8pm	**Netherlands**	**2-1**	**Japan**
Att: 21,076	Martens 17, (pen) 90		Hasegawa 43

Reigning European champions win courtesy of a last-minute Lieke Martens penalty meaning a record seven sides from Europe in the quarter-finals.

QUARTER-FINALS

27.06 Stade Oceane, Le Havre 8pm	**Norway**	**0-3**	**England**
Att: 21,111			Scott 3, White 40, Bronze 57, *Parris missed pen 83 (saved Hjelmseth)*

Jill Scott (2mins 6secs) scores fastest goal of France 2019 and England's fastest ever Women's World Cup goal. Ellen White taps in her fifth goal of tournament before Lucy Bronze hammers home from outside box. Nikita Parris becomes first player to miss two penalties in one Women's World Cup.

28.06 Parc des Princes, Paris 8pm	**France**	**1-2**	**USA**
Att: 45,595	Renard 81		Rapinoe 5, 65

Hosts knocked out by holders. Result also ensures that England will finish as one of the top three European teams at the tournament, thus qualifying TeamGB for a place at the Tokyo 2020 Olympics.

29.06 Stade du Hainaut, Valenciennes 2pm	**Italy**	**0-2**	**Netherlands**
Att: 22,600			Miedema 70, Van der Gragt 80

European champions reach their first ever World Cup semi-final as Italy's fine showing in their first World Cup tournament since 1999 comes to an end. Result also sees Netherlands qualify for the Tokyo 2020 Olympics as one of the top three European teams at France 2019.

29.06 Roazhon Park, Rennes 5.30pm	**Germany**	**1-2**	**Sweden**
Att: 25,301	Magull 16		Jakobsson 22, Blackstenius 48

Sweden beat Germany for the first time in a major tournament since 1995 as they come from behind to shock the two-time world champions. The result also means Germany will not get a chance to defend their 2016 Olympic title with Sweden taking the final UEFA qualifying spot for Tokyo 2020 by finishing as one of the top three European teams at France 2019.

SEMI-FINALS

02.07 Stade de Lyon, Lyon 8pm	**England**	**1-2**	**USA**
Att: 53,512	White 19, *Houghton missed pen 84 (saved Naeher), Bright sent off 86*		Press 10, Morgan 31

Holders USA through to fifth final. England celebrate second equaliser from Ellen White in 69th minute but VAR rules goal out for marginal offside. Lionesses captain Steph Houghton sees late penalty – awarded after lengthy VAR review for foul on White – saved by Alyssa Naeher.

03.07 Stade de Lyon, Lyon 8pm	**Netherlands**	**1-0 aet**	**Sweden**
Att: 48,452	Groenen 99		

The 2017 European champions beat the 2016 Olympic runners-up in the first World Cup semi-final ever to progress to extra time. New Manchester United signing Jackie Groenen scores the only goal.

THIRD PLACE MATCH

06.07 Stade de Nice, Nice 4pm	**England**	**1-2**	**Sweden**
Att: 20,316	Kirby 31		Asllani 11, Jakobsson 22

England fail to repeat 3rd place finish of 2015 as Sweden take bronze for third time (also 1991 and 2011). Ellen White has equaliser ruled out for handball following VAR review. Karen Carney – who announced her retirement the day before the match – wins 144th and final England cap as substitute.

FINAL

07.07 Stade de Lyon, Lyon 4pm	**USA**	**2-0**	**Netherlands**
Att: 57,900	Rapinoe (pen) 61, Lavelle 69		

USA win the World Cup for a record-extending fourth time. They become only the second country (after Germany 2003 and 2007) to successfully defend the World Cup title. Captain Megan Rapinoe opens the scoring from a penalty awarded for a foul on Alex Morgan by Stefanie van der Gragt following a VAR review. Rapinoe thus becomes the first player to score a penalty in a women's World Cup final and the tournament's oldest scorer in a final (34 years and two days).

USA (4-3-3): Alyssa Naeher (Chicago Red Stars); Kelley O'Hara (Utah Royals) (sub 46 Ali Krieger (Orlando Pride)), Abby Dahlkemper (North Carolina Courage), Becky Sauerbrunn (Utah Royals), Crystal Dunn (North Carolina Courage); Samantha Mewis (North Carolina Courage), Julie Ertz (Chicago Red Stars), Rose Lavelle (Washington Spirit); Tobin Heath (Portland Thorns) (sub 87 Carli Lloyd (Sky Blue FC)), Alex Morgan (Orlando Pride), Megan Rapinoe (c) (Reign FC) (sub 79 Christen Press (Utah Royals))

Unused subs: Mallory Pugh (Washington Spirit), Morgan Brian (Chicago Red Stars), Tierna Davidson (Chicago Red Stars), Emily Sonnett (Portland Thorns), Ashlyn Harris (Orlando Pride), Allie Long (Reign FC), Adrianna Franch (Portland Thorns), Jessica McDonald (North Carolina Courage), Lindsey Horan (Portland Thorns)

Head coach: Jill Ellis

Netherlands (4-3-3): Sari van Veenendaal (c) (unattached), Desiree van Lunteren (SC Freiburg), Anouk Dekker (Montpellier) (sub 73 Shanice van de Sanden (Lyon)), Stefanie van der Gragt (Barcelona), Dominique Bloodworth (unattached); Jackie Groenen (Manchester United), Danielle van de Donk (Arsenal), Sherida Spitse (Valerenga); Lineth Beerensteyn (Bayern Munich), Vivianne Miedema (Arsenal), Lieke Martens (Barcelona) (sub 70 Jill Roord (Arsenal))

Unused subs: Merel van Dongen (Real Betis), Kika van Es (Everton), Victoria Pelova (Ajax), Renate Jansen (Twente), Inessa Kaagman (Everton), Lize Kop (Ajax), Ellen Jansen (Ajax), Danique Kerkdijk (Brighton & Hove Albion), Liza van der Most (Ajax), Loes Geurts (Koppaerbergs/Goteborg FC)

Head coach: Sarina Wiegman

Referee: Stephanie Frappart (FRA)

FIFA WOMEN'S WORLD CUP FRANCE 2019 INDIVIDUAL HONOURS

Top Scorer Awards	**Golden Boot**	Megan Rapinoe	USA	6 goals
	Silver Boot	Alex Morgan	USA	6 goals
	Bronze Boot	Ellen White	England	6 goals

Tie-breaker: Greater number of assists (Rapinoe 3, Morgan 3, White 0)

2nd Tie-breaker: Fewest minutes played (Rapinoe 428, Morgan 490)

Best Player Awards	**Golden Ball**	Megan Rapinoe	USA
	Silver Ball	Lucy Bronze	England
	Bronze Ball	Rose Lavelle	USA
Best Goalkeeper Award	**Golden Glove**	Sari van Veenendaal	Netherlands
Best Young Player Award		Giulia Gwinn	Germany
Fair Play Team Award			France

LEAGUE & CUP WINNERS 2018-19

CUP WINNERS 2018-19

Champions League	Lyon
FA Cup	Manchester City
Continental Cup	Manchester City
WNL Cup	Blackburn Rovers
WNL Plate	West Bromwich Albion

LEAGUE WINNERS 2018-19

Tier 1	**WSL**	Arsenal
Tier 2	**Championship**	Manchester United
Tier 3	**WNL Northern Premier**	Blackburn Rovers
Tier 3	**WNL Southern Premier**	Coventry United
Tier 3	**WNL Play-off**	Blackburn Rovers
Tier 4	**WNL Midlands 1**	West Bromwich Albion
Tier 4	**WNL North 1**	Burnley
Tier 4	**WNL South East 1**	Crawley Wasps
Tier 4	**WNL South West 1**	Keynsham Town

UEFA WOMEN'S CHAMPIONS LEAGUE 2018-19

Lyon's dominance continued as they swept to their fourth consecutive Champions League title with a 4-1 win over first-time finalists Barcelona. Their comfortable victory in Budapest was thanks in large part to a first-half hat-trick from 2018 Ballon d'Or winner Ada Hegerberg.

England defender Lucy Bronze and Wales midfielder Jess Fishlock were part of the triumphant French side's starting XI while Lionesses forward Toni Duggan was in the Barcelona side and almost put her team ahead early on only to fire wide.

Lyon – conquerors of Chelsea in the semi-final – came into their eighth European final since 2010 having already secured their 13th consecutive French League title. As the best-funded side in Europe, Lyon were heavy favourites for the final and went ahead when Netherlands winger Shanice van de Sanden crossed from the right for Germany's Dzsenifer Marozsan to open the scoring in the fifth minute. Nine minutes later Van de Sanden had laid on Hegerberg to make it 2-0. Norway's Hegerberg went on to become the first player to score a hat-trick in the final since the competition was rebranded as the Champions League in 2010. Amel Majri set up her second goal in the 19th minute before Bronze's whipped cross paved the way for her third.

With Lyon leading 4-0 inside half an hour the signs were ominous for Barca, but they managed to prevent any further damage and even claimed a late consolation when former Liverpool and Arsenal forward Asisat Oshoala netted with one minute to play.

PRELIMINARY STAGE

In the preliminary stage, 40 teams were split into 10 groups of 4. Each group has a host team. Most matches are played in the same stadium. Where that isn't possible, they are played close by. The final group games kick-off at the same time and thus take place in different stadiums.Teams played their group opponents once. Where teams were level on points the following tie breaker criteria are applied, in the order given:

Points in head-to-head matches among tied teams; b) Goal difference in head-to-head matches among tied teams; c) Goals scored in head-to-head matches among tied teams: d) If more than two teams are tied, and after applying all head-to-head criteria above, a subset of teams are still tied, all head-to-head criteria above are reapplied exclusively to this subset of teams; e) Goal difference in all group matches; f) Goals scored in all group matches; g) Penalty shoot-out if only two teams have the same number of points, and they met in the last round of group games and after applying all criteria above (not used if more than two teams have the same number of points, or if their rankings in the group are not relevant to qualification for the next stage; h) Disciplinary points (red card = 3pts, yellow card = 1pt, sending-off for two yellow cards = 3 points; i) UEFA club coefficient

The 10 group winners qualify for the Round of 32 as do the two runners-up with the best records against the teams finishing 1st and 3rd in their group.

GROUP 1
HOSTS: LINFIELD (NORTHERN IRELAND)

	P	W	D	L	F	A	Pts	
1.Ajax (NED)	**3**	**2**	**1**	**0**	**6**	**1**	**7**	**Q**
2.Thor/KA (ISL)	**3**	**2**	**1**	**0**	**5**	**0**	**7**	**Q**
3.Wexford Youths (IRL)	3	1	0	2	4	9	3	
4.Linfield (NIR)	3	0	0	3	2	7	0	

7 Aug	Ajax	4-1	Wexford Youths	224
7 Aug	Thor/KA	2-0	Linfield	331
10 Aug	Ajax	2-0	Linfield	360
10 Aug	Wexford Youths	0-3	Thor/KA	163
13 Aug	Thor/KA	0-0	Ajax	20
13 Aug	Linfield	2-3	Wexford Youths	267

GROUP 2
HOSTS: OLIMPIA LJUBLJANA (SLOVENIA)

	P	W	D	L	F	A	Pts	
1.Barcelona FA (CYP)	**3**	**3**	**0**	**0**	**10**	**0**	**9**	**Q**
2.FC Minsk (BLR)	3	2	0	1	7	2	6	
3.Slovan Bratislava (SVK)	3	1	0	2	1	3	3	
4.Olimpija Ljubljana (SVN)	3	0	0	3	0	13	0	

7 Aug	FC Minsk	6-0	Olimpija Ljubljana	200
7 Aug	Barcelona FA	2-0	Slovan Bratislava	80
10 Aug	FC Minsk	1-0	Slovan Bratislava	30
10 Aug	Olimpija Ljubljana	0-6	Barcelona FA	200
13 Aug	Barcelona FA	2-0	FC Minsk	40
13 Aug	Slovan Bratislava	1-0	Olimpija Ljubljana	300

GROUP 3
HOSTS: GLASGOW CITY (SCOTLAND)

	P	W	D	L	F	A	Pts	
1.Glasgow City (SCO)	**3**	**2**	**0**	**1**	**10**	**2**	**6**	**Q**
2.Anderlecht (BEL)	3	2	0	1	12	2	6	
3.Gornik Leczna (POL)	3	2	0	1	13	2	6	
4.Martve (GEO)	3	0	0	3	0	29	0	

7 Aug	Glasgow City	1-2	Anderlecht	180
7 Aug	Gornik Leczna	12-0	Martve	40
10 Aug	Glasgow City	7-0	Martve	180
10 Aug	Anderlecht	0-1	Gornik Leczna	150
13 Aug	Gornik Leczna	0-2	Glasgow City	220
13 Aug	Martve	0-10	Anderlecht	28

GROUP 4

HOSTS: MTK HUNGARIA (HUNGARY)

	P	W	D	L	F	A	Pts	
1.Slavia Prague (CZE)	**3**	**3**	**0**	**0**	**15**	**3**	**9**	**Q**
2.MTK Hungaria (HUN)	3	1	1	1	9	7	4	
3.Atasehir Belediyespor (TUR)	3	1	1	1	10	10	4	
4.Mitrovica (KVX)	3	0	0	3	2	16	0	

7 Aug	Slavia Prague	7-2	Atasehir Belediyespor	30
7 Aug	MTK Hungaria	6-1	Mitrovica	420
10 Aug	Slavia Prague	4-0	Mitrovica	35
10 Aug	Atasehir Belediyespor	2-2	MTK Hungaria	398
13 Aug	MTK Hungaria	1-4	Slavia Prague	519
13 Aug	Mitrovica	1-6	Atasehir Belediyespor	30

GROUP 5

HOSTS: BREZNICA PLJEVLJA (MONTENEGRO)

	P	W	D	L	F	A	Pts	
1.Spartak Subotica (SRB)	**3**	**3**	**0**	**0**	**10**	**0**	**9**	**Q**
2.Basel (SUI)	3	2	0	1	7	5	6	
3.Kiryat Gat (ISR)	3	0	1	2	4	8	1	
4.Breznica Pljevlja (MON)	3	0	1	2	4	12	1	

7 Aug	Spartak Subotica	1-0	Kiryat Gat	25
7 Aug	Basel	4-0	Breznica Pljevlja	75
10 Aug	Spartak Subotica	4-0	Breznica Pljevlja	30
10 Aug	Kiryat Gat	0-3	Basel	20
13 Aug	Basel	0-5	Spartak Subotica	70
13 Aug	Breznica Pljevlja	4-4	Kiryat Gat	20

GROUP 6

HOSTS: ZHYTLOBUD-1 KHARKIV (UKRAINE)

	P	W	D	L	F	A	Pts	
1.Zhytlobud-1 Kharkiv (UKR)	**3**	**3**	**0**	**0**	**16**	**3**	**9**	**Q**
2.Olimpija Cluj (ROU)	3	2	0	1	10	6	6	
3.Cardiff Met. (WAL)	3	0	1	2	6	10	1	
4.Birkirkara (MLT)	3	0	1	2	3	16	1	

7 Aug	Olimpija Cluj	3-2	Cardiff Met.	50
7 Aug	Zhytlobud-1 Kharkiv	8-0	Birkirkara	480
10 Aug	Olimpija Cluj	6-1	Birkirkara	75
10 Aug	Cardiff Met.	2-5	Zhytlobud-1 Kharkiv	400
13 Aug	Zhytlobud-1 Kharkiv	3-1	Olimpija Cluj	2,500
13 Aug	Birkirkara	2-2	Cardiff Met.	50

GROUP 7

HOSTS: RIGA FS (LATVIA)

	P	W	D	L	F	A	Pts	
1.BIIK Kazygurt (KAZ)	**3**	**3**	**0**	**0**	**9**	**1**	**9**	**Q**
2.Elpides Karditsas (GRE)	3	2	0	1	6	4	6	
3.Landhaus Vienna (AUT)	3	1	0	2	3	6	3	
4.Riga FS (LVA)	3	0	0	3	2	9	0	

7 Aug	BIIK Kazygurt	2-1	Elpides Karditsas	80
7 Aug	Landhaus Vienna	2-1	Riga FS	350
10 Aug	Elpides Karditsas	3-1	Landhaus Vienna	90
10 Aug	BIIK Kazygurt	5-0	Riga FS	200
13 Aug	Landhaus Vienna	0-2	BIIK Kazygurt	50
13 Aug	Riga FS	1-2	Elpides Karditsas	100

GROUP 8

HOSTS: SFK 2000 (BOSNIA & HERZEGOVINA)

	P	W	D	L	F	A	Pts	
1.SFK 2000 (BIH)	**3**	**3**	**0**	**0**	**12**	**1**	**9**	**Q**
2.Vllaznia Shkoder (ALB)	3	2	0	1	7	7	6	
3.Parnu (EST)	3	1	0	2	4	5	3	
4.Agarista-SS Anenii Noic (MDA)	3	0	0	3	1	11	0	

7 Aug	Parnu	2-0	Agarista-SS Anenii Noic	31
7 Aug	SFK 2000	5-0	Vllaznia Shkoder	200
10 Aug	Vllaznia Shkoder	3-1	Parnu	80
10 Aug	SFK 2000	5-0	Agarista-SS Anenii Noic	100
13 Aug	Parnu	1-2	SFK 2000	200
13 Aug	Agarista-SS Anenii Noic	1-4	Vllaznia Shkoder	20

GROUP 9

HOSTS: GINTRA UNIVERSITETAS (LITHUANIA)

	P	W	D	L	F	A	Pts	
1.Gintra Universitetas (LTU)	**3**	**2**	**1**	**0**	**17**	**1**	**7**	**Q**
2.Honka (FIN)	**3**	**2**	**1**	**0**	**13**	**1**	**7**	**Q**
3.NSA Sofia (BUL)	3	1	0	2	3	14	3	
4.EB/Streymur/Skala (FRO)	3	0	0	3	0	17	0	

7 Aug	NSA Sofia	3-0	EB/Streymur/Skala	125
7 Aug	Gintra Universitetas	1-1	Honka	450
10 Aug	Honka	5-0	NSA Sofia	120
10 Aug	Gintra Universitetas	7-0	EB/Streymur/Skala	315
13 Aug	NSA Sofia	0-9	Gintra Universitetas	512
13 Aug	EB/Streymur/Skala	0-7	Honka	35

GROUP 10

HOSTS: OSIJEK (CROATIA)

	P	W	D	L	F	A	Pts	
1.Avaldsnes (NOR)	**3**	**2**	**1**	**0**	**8**	**4**	**7**	**Q**
2.Sporting CP (POR)	3	2	0	1	9	3	6	
3.Osijek (CRO)	3	1	1	1	15	5	4	
4.Dragon 2014 (MKD)	3	0	0	3	0	20	0	

7 Aug	Avaldsnes	3-2	Sporting CP	35
7 Aug	Osijek	13-0	Dragon 2014	208
10 Aug	Avaldsnes	3-0	Dragon 2014	21
10 Aug	Sporting CP	3-0	Osijek	478
13 Aug	Osijek	2-2	Avaldsnes	273
13 Aug	Dragon 2014	0-4	Sporting CP	100

ROUND OF 32

The 10 group winners from the preliminary stage and two best runners-up were joined by 20 teams who qualified directly. They played over two legs with the winners advancing to the Round of 16.

Date	Home	Score	Away	Venue	Attendance
12 Sep	**Honka (FIN)**	**0-1**	**Zurich (SUI)** Moser 60	Telia 5G Arena Helsinki	572
27 Sep	**Zurich (SUI)** Humm 28, 45+1, 51, Moser (pen) 55	**5-1**	**Honka (FIN)** Rantala 90	Letzigrund Zurich	3,066
Agg:	Zurich win 6-1				

Date	Home	Score	Away	Venue	Attendance
12 Sep	**Fiorentina (ITA)** Mauro 9, 63	**2-0**	**Fortuna Hjorring (DEN)**	Stadio Artemio Franchi Florence	1,715
26 Sep	**Fortuna Hjorring (DEN)**	**0-2**	**Fiorentina (ITA)** Clelland 15, 25	Hjorring Stadium Hjorring	1,084
Agg:	Fiorentina win 4-0				

Date	Home	Score	Away	Venue	Attendance
12 Sep	**Ajax (NED)** Salmi 47, Zeeman 55	**2-0**	**Sparta Prague (CZE)**	Sportpark de Toekomst Duivendrecht	998
26 Sep	**Sparta Prague (CZE)** Burkenroad 27	**1-2**	**Ajax (NED)** Lewerissa 50, 52	Generali Arena Prague	558
Agg:	Ajax win 4-1				

Date	Home	Score	Away	Venue	Attendance
12 Sep	**Avaldsnes (NOR)**	**0-2**	**Lyon (FRA)** Henry 50, Majri 77	Haugesund Stadion Haugesund	2,319
27 Sep	**Lyon (FRA)** Majri 8, Le Sommer 22, 31 Hegerberg 55, 81	**5-0**	**Avaldsnes (NOR)**	Groupama Training Decines-Charpieu	1,214
Agg:	Lyon win 7-0				

Date	Home	Score	Away	Venue	Attendance
12 Sep	**Ryazan-VDV (RUS)**	**0-1**	**Rosengard (SWE)** Belomyttseva (og) 90	CSK Stadium Ryazan	4,500
26 Sep	**Rosengard (SWE)** Brown 18, Wieder 75	**2-0**	**Ryazan-VDV (RUS)**	Malmo IP Malmo	711
Agg:	Rosengard win 3-0				

12 Sep	**Juventus (ITA)**	**2-2**	**Brondby (DEN)**	Stadio Silvio Piola	1,001
	Bonansea 43, 84		Sorensen 60, Gejl 72	Novara	
26 Sep	**Brondby (DEN)**	**1-0**	**Juventus (ITA)**	Brondby Stadium	8,531
	Sorensen 33			Brondbyvester	
Agg:	Brondby win 3-2				

12 Sep	**SFK 2000 (BIH)**	**0-5**	**Chelsea (ENG)**	Asim Ferahtovic Stadium	2,200
			Bright 6, Spence 22	Sarajevo	
			Thorisdottir 36		
			Ji 87, Engman 89		
26 Sep	**Chelsea (ENG)**	**6-0**	**SFK 2000 (BIH)**	Kingsmeadow	667
	Spence 4, Kirby 31, 77			Kingston-upon-Thames	
	Mjelde 50, Blundell 86				
	Cuthbert 90				
Agg:	Chelsea win 11-0				

13 Sep	**Atletico Madrid (ESP)**	**1-1**	**Manchester City (ENG)**	Cerro del Espino	1,671
	Robles 89		Bonner 16	Majadahonda	
26 Sep	**Manchester City (ENG)**	**0-2**	**Atletico Madrid (ESP)**	Academy Stadium	1,178
			Meseguer 4, Ludmila 45+1	Manchester	
Agg:	Atletico Madrid win 3-1				

12 Sep	**Thor/KA**	**0-1**	**Wolfsburg (GER)**	Thorsvollur	1,529
			Harder 31	Akureyri	
26 Sep	**Wolfsburg (GER)**	**2-0**	**Thor/KA**	AOK Stadiun	1,213
	Harder 28, Masar 66			Wolfsburg	
Agg:	Wolfsburg win 3-0				

13 Sep	**Gintra Universitetas (LTU)**	**0-3**	**Slavia Prague (CZE)**	Savivaldybe Stadium	1,500
			M.Dubcova 63, 88	Siauliai	
			Szewieczkova 79		
27 Sep	**Slavia Prague (CZE)**	**4-0**	**Gintra Universitetas (LTU)**	FK Viktoria Stadion	651
	Kozarova 2, 28, (pen) 68, Herndon 73			Prague	
Agg:	Slavia Prague win 7-0				

12 Sep	**BIIK Kazygurt (KAZ)** Putellas (og) 45+6, Ikwaput 49 Gabelia 60	**3-1**	**Barcelona (ESP)** Duggan 66	BIIK Stadium Shymkent	2,800
26 Sep	**Barcelona (ESP)** Guijarro 4, Torrejon 48, Martens 90	**3-0**	**BIIK Kazygurt (KAZ)**	Mini Estadi Barcelona	1,667
Agg:	Barcelona win 4-3				

12 Sep	**Barcelona FA (CYP)**	**0-2**	**Glasgow City (SCO)** Lauder 3, Crichton 83	Tsirio Stadium Limassol	417
27 Sep	**Glasgow City (SCO)**	**0-1**	**Barcelona FA (CYP)** Freda 7	Petershill Park Glasgow	511
Agg:	Glasgow City win 2-1				

12 Sep	**Spartak Subotica (SRB)**	**0-7**	**Bayern Munich (GER)** Lewandowski 12, Roord 29, 39, Magull (pen) 64, Damnjanovic 82, Demann 87, Beerensteyn 90+3	Stadion na Somborskoj kapiji Subotica	600
26 Sep	**Bayern Munich (GER)** Beerensteyn 18, 53, Magull 55, Islacker 64	**4-0**	**Spartak Subotica (SRB)**	FC Bayern Campus Munich	662
Agg:	Bayern Munich win 11-0				

12 Sep	**St Polten (AUT)** Vago (pen) 65	**1-4**	**PSG (FRA)** Bruun 4, Diani 20, Katoto 86, Dudek 90	NV Arena St Polten	2,412
27 Sep	**PSG (FRA)** Katoto (pen 61), Pekel 84	**2-0**	**St Polten (AUT)**	Stade Jean-Bouin Paris	682
Agg:	PSG win 6-1				

12 Sep	**Zhytlobud-1 Kharkiv (UKR)** Voronina 70	**1-6**	**Linkoping (SWE)** Maanum 26, 60, 86, Hurtig 48, D'Anjou 74, Rasmussen 82	Metalist Oblast Kharkiv	6,000
26 Sep	**Linkoping (SWE)** Lantz 9, Angeldal 11, D'Anjou 78, Almqvist 84	**4-0**	**Zhytlobud-1 Kharkiv (UKR)**	Linkoping Arena Linkoping	518
Agg:	Linkoping win 10-1				

13 Sep	**LSK Kvinner (NOR)**	**3-0**	**Zvezda-2005 Perm (RUS)**	Jessheim Stadion	710
	Sonstevold 2, Kvernvolden 14, Haavi 80			Jessheim	
27 Sep	**Zvezda-2005 Perm (RUS)**	**0-1**	**LSK Kvinner (NOR)**	Sapsan Arena	100
			Haavi 52	Moscow	
Agg:	LSK Kvinner win 4-0				

ROUND OF 16

17 Oct	**Zurich (SUI)**	**0-2**	**Bayern Munich (GER)**	Letzigrund	4,376
			Herzog (og) 12 Skorvankova 31	Zurich	
31 Oct	**Bayern Munich (GER)**	**3-0**	**Zurich (SUI)**	FC Bayern Campus	652
	Dabritz 42, Roord 66, Skorvankova 73			Munich	
Agg:	Bayern Munich win 5-0				

17 Oct	**Wolfsburg (GER)**	**4-0**	**Atletico Madrid (ESP)**	AOK Stadion	1,523
	Harder 46, 67, Pajor 49, Hansen 61			Wolfsburg	
31 Oct	**Atletico Madrid (ESP)**	**0-6**	**Wolfsburg (GER)**	Cerro del Espino	652
			Popp 15, Hansen 46, Harder 61, 65, Minde 82, Pajor 90+3	Majadahonda	
Agg:	Wolfsburg win 10-0				

17 Oct	**Ajax (NED)**	**0-4**	**Lyon (FRA)**	Sportpark de Toekomst	1,783
			Majri 12, Bacha 27, Hegerberg 57, Christiansen 89	Duivendrecht	
31 Oct	**Lyon (FRA)**	**9-0**	**Ajax (NED)**	OL Training Centre	1,480
	Cascarino 4, 8, Renard 17, 22, Hegerberg 57, Mbock Bathy 62 Majri 69, Bakker (og) 89 Bronze 90+3			Decines-Charpieu	
Agg:	Lyon win 13-0				

Date	Home	Score	Away	Venue	Att
17 Oct	**Barcelona (ESP)** Hamraoui 12, Bonmati 38, Guijarro 41, Alves 68, Leon 81	**5-0**	**Glasgow City (SCO)**	Mini Estadi Barcelona	1,639
1 Nov	**Glasgow City (SCO)**	**0-3**	**Barcelona (ESP)** Duggan 13, 51, Putellas 48	Petershill Park Glasgow	795
Agg:	Barcelona win 8-0				

Date	Home	Score	Away	Venue	Att
17 Oct	**Linkoping (SWE)**	**0-2**	**PSG (FRA)** Katoto 42, Wang 80	Linkoping Arena Linkoping	1,639
31 Oct	**PSG (FRA)** Kildemoes (og) 30, Katoto 33, 50	**3-2**	**Linkoping (SWE)** Oskarsson 47, Lantz 71	Stade Jean-Bouin Paris	899
Agg:	PSG win 5-2				

Date	Home	Score	Away	Venue	Att
17 Oct	**Chelsea (ENG)** Carney (pen) 8	**1-0**	**Fiorentina (ITA)**	Kingsmeadow Kingston-up-on-Thames	804
31 Oct	**Fiorentina (ITA)**	**0-6**	**Chelsea (ENG)** Spence 4, Kirby 38, (pen) 53, 63, Cuthbert 57, Bachmann 67	Stadio Artemio-Franchi Florence	3,015
Agg:	Chelsea win 7-0				

Date	Home	Score	Away	Venue	Att
18 Oct	**Rosengard (SWE)** Utland 22, Mittag 52	**2-3**	**Slavia Prague (CZE)** Pincova 14, Kozarova 37, Divisova 57	Malmo IP Malmo	811
1 Nov	**Slavia Prague (CZE)**	**0-0**	**Rosengard (SWE)**	Eden Arena Prague	1,451
Agg:	**Slavia Prague win 3-2**				

Date	Home	Score	Away	Venue	Att
17 Oct	**LSK Kvinner (NOR)** Reiten 30	**1-1**	**Brondby (DEN)** Henriksen 35	Jessheim Stadion Jessheim	1,021
31 Oct	**Brondby (DEN)**	**0-2**	**LSK Kvinner (NOR)** Sonstevold 70, Hansen 78	Brondby Stadium Brondbyvester	2,975
Agg:	LSK Kvinner win 3-1				

QUARTER-FINALS

20 Mar	**Slavia Prague (CZE)**	**1-1**	**Bayern Munich (GER)**	Eden Arena	6,822
	Svitkova 73		Rolfo 62	Prague	
27 Mar	**Bayern Munich (GER)**	**5-1**	**Slavia Prague (CZE)**	FC Bayern Campus	1,040
	Rolfo 24, Leupolz 33, Islacker 41, 55, Roord 83		Svitkova 77	Munich	
Agg:	B. Munich win 6-2				

20 Mar	**Barcelona (ESP)**	**3-0**	**LSK Kvinner (NOR)**	Mini Estadi	5,563
	Duggan 3, 24, Caldentey (pen) 36			Barcelona	
27 Mar	**LSK Kvinner (NOR)**	**0-1**	**Barcelona (ESP)**	Arasen Stadion	5,655
			Martens 7	Lillestrom	
Agg:	Barcelona win 4-0				

20 Mar	Lyon (FRA)	**2-1**	**Wolfsburg (GER)**	Parc Olympique Lyonnais	17,840
	Le Sommer 11, Renard 18		Fischer 64	Decines-Charpieu	
27 Mar	**Wolfsburg (GER)**	**2-4**	**Lyon (FRA)**	AOK Stadion	4,445
	Harder 53, 56		Marozsan 8, Renard (pen) 25, Le Sommer 60, 80	Wolfsburg	
Agg:	Lyon win 6-3				

21 Mar	**Chelsea (ENG)**	**2-0**	**PSG (FRA)**	Kingsmeadow	2,616
	Blundell 73, Cuthbert 88			Kingston-up-on-Thames	
27 Mar	**PSG (FRA)**	**2-1**	**Chelsea (ENG)**	Stade Jean-Bouin	13,220
	Diani 47, Berger (og) 56		Mjelde 90+1	Paris	
Agg:	Chelsea win 3-2				

SEMI-FINALS

21 Apr	**Lyon (FRA)**	**2-1**	**Chelsea (ENG)**	Parc Olympique Lyonnais	22,911
	Eriksson (og) 27, Henry 38		Cuthbert 72, *Kirby missed pen 45 (saved Bouhaddi)*	Decines-Charpieu	
28 Apr	**Chelsea (ENG)**	**1-1**	**Lyon (FRA)**	**Kingsmeadow**	4,670
	Ji 34		Le Sommer 17	Kingston-up-on-Thames	
Agg:	Lyon win 3-2				

21 Apr	**Bayern Munich (GER)**	**0-1**	**Barcelona (ESP)** Hamraoui 63	FC Bayern Campus Munich	2,500
28 Apr	**Barcelona (ESP)** Caldentey (pen) 45+2	**1-0**	**Bayern Munich (GER)**	Mini Estadi Barcelona	12,764
Agg:	Barcelona win 2-0				

FINAL

18 May	**Lyon (FRA)** Marozsan 5, Hegerberg 14, 19, 30	**4-1**	**Barcelona (ESP)** Oshoala 89	Groupama Arena Budapest	19,487

Lyon (4-3-3): Sarah Bouhaddi; Lucy Bronze, Wendie Renard (c), Griedge M'Bock Bathy, Amel Majri; Jessica Fishlock (Saki Kumagai 72), Amandine Henry, Dzsenifer Marozsan; Shanice van de Sanden (Delphine Cascarino 63), Ada Hegerberg, Eugenie Le Sommer (Selma Bacha 82)

Unused subs: Lisa Weiss, Kadeisha Buchanan, Florencia Soledad Jaimes, Carolin Simon

Head coach: Reynald Pedros

Barcelona (4-4-2): Sandra Panos; Marta Torrejon, Andrea Pereira (Stephanie Van der Gragt 81), Maria Leon, Leila Ouahabi; Vicky Losada (c), Aitana Bonmati (Andressa Alves 69), Alexia Putellas, Mariona Caldentey; Lieke Martens, Toni Duggan (Asisat Oshoala 69)

Unused Subs: Gemma Font, Melanie Serrano, Patricia Guijarro, Natasha Andonova

Head coach: Lluis Cortes

SSE WOMEN'S FA CUP 2018-19

Manchester City completed a domestic Cup Double with a comfortable 3-0 victory over first-time finalists West Ham United. Manager Nick Cushing's team recovered from the disappointment of having missed out on the WSL title to Arsenal by adding to the League Cup they lifted after beating the Gunners in February's final.

The Hammers held out until early in the second half when England midfielder Keira Walsh put City ahead with a long-range effort which bounced beyond goalkeeper Anna Moorhouse. It took until nine minutes from time for City to double their lead when Georgia Stanway's low strike deflected in. Eighteen-year-old substitute Lauren Hemp completed the scoring with a composed finish two minutes from the end and almost grabbed a second when she hit the post in added time.

For West Ham there was pride in having reached the FA Cup final in their first season as a professional club. They also created the best chance in an even first half when Jane Ross' bouncing header forced a superb save from City keeper Karen Bardsley. City though went on to complete their second FA Cup triumph having picked up the famous trophy for the first time in 2017. The crowd of 43,264 at Wembley fell just short of the previous season's competition record of 45,423.

FORMAT

The 2018-19 competition consisted of one preliminary round, three qualifying rounds, and five proper rounds before reaching the quarter-final stage. The preliminary round was added by the FA after the publication of the original tournament schedule because of an increased number of clubs expressing an interest in competing. A total of 293 clubs entered the competition with clubs in Tier 4 (WNL Division 1) entering at the second qualifying round, those in Tier 3 (WNL Premier) coming into the competition in the second round proper, and those in Tiers 1 and 2 (WSL and Championship) beginning their involvement in the fourth round proper. As in previous years there were no replays with drawn matches progressing to 30 minutes of extra-time and then penalties if required.

KEY

The number in parentheses indicates the tier of English football the club plays its League football at. Attendances listed where known.

PRELIMINARY ROUND: SUN 26 AUG 2018

Lumley (7)	0-2	Boro Rangers (6)	41
Workington Reds (6)	1-3	Carlisle United (6)	
Durham Cestria (5)	3-0	South Shields (5)	
Altofts (6)	0-1aet	Tingley Athletic (7)	
Rotherham United (5)	14-0	Bradford Park Avenue (7)	
Dronfield Town (7)	0-8 *+	Ossett United (6)	48
Hepworth United (7)	0-4	Chesterfield (7)	42
Bridlington Rovers (7)	Hw/o	Leeds Medics & Dentists (7)	

Manchester Stingers (5)	3-1	Merseyrail (5)	
Tranmere Rovers (5)	7-0	Chester (6)	
Wythenshawe Amateurs (6)	5-1*+	Accrington Stanley Community Trust (7)	112
FC United of Manchester (5)	Hw/o	Blackburn Community Sports Club (6)	
Bury (6)	3-3aet (2-0p)	Mossley Hill Athletic (5)	
Burscough Dynamo (6)	3-3 aet (3-2p)	Fleetwood Town Wrens (5)	
Oadby & Wigston (6)	6-0	Sherwood (7)	
Mansfield Town (5)	3-2aet	Hykeham Town (6)	
Lincoln Moorlands Railway (6)	1-3	Loughborough Students (5)	
Leek Town (6)	3-0	Wyrley (6)	
Goldenhill Wanderers (5)	0-2aet	Sutton Coldfield Town (5)	230
AFC Telford United (6)	0-2**	Kidderminster Harriers (6)	116
Rugby Town (6)	2-1	Knowle (5)	
Crusaders (5)	4-2	Coundon Court (5)	
Shifnal Town (6)	1-0	Sedgley & Gornal United (6)	
Droitwich Spa (6)	1-2	Stockingford AA Pavilion (5)	
Wymondham Town (5)	Hw/o	Moulton (7)	
Newmarket Town (6)	0-2	Cambridge City (5)	
St Ives Town (6)	1-0aet	Corby Town (6)	65
Frontiers (7)	0-4	Brentwood Town (5)	
Beccles Town (7)	0-1	Chelmsford City (7)	
Colney Heath (5)	7-0*+	Hemel Hempstead Town (7)	
Royston Town (5)	7-1	Hertford Town (6)	
Queens Park Rangers Girls (5)	Hw/o	Barton United (7)	
Wantage Town (7)	2-2aet (0-3p)	Wycombe Wanderers (6)	39
Brentford (7)	1-2	New London Lionesses (6)	30
Woodley United (5)	Aw/o	Abingdon United (6)	
Ashford Ladies (6)	4-3	Eastbourne Town (5)	
Regents Park Rangers (6)	w/o	Carshalton Athletic (5)	
Kent Football United (5)	8-0	Herne Bay (7)	
Eastbourne (6)	1-2	Aylesford (5)	
Sutton United (7)	1-2++	AFC Phoenix (5)	
Newhaven (6)	6-3	Parkwood Rangers (5)	104
Oakwood (7)	0-4*+	Islington Borough (7)	
Saltdean (6)	4-1	Steyning Town (7)	
London Kent Football United (5)	11-0	Tonbridge Angels (7)	
Margate (7)	2-5	Thamesview (7)	
Moneyfields (6)	Aw/o*	Swindon Spitfires (6)	
Winchester City Flyers (5)	0-2	Southampton FC Women (5)	
Warsash Wasps (5)	5-1+	Bournemouth Sports (7)	

Callington Town (5)	2-5	Exeter City (5)	
Marine Academy Plymouth (5)	8-0	Purnell Sports (7)	
Bideford (6)	0-4	Portishead Town (5)	
Exeter & Tedburn Rangers (6)	Hw/o	Forest Green Rovers (5)	
Chipping Sodbury Town (7)	1-2	Downend Flyers (5)	

#*Moneyfield beat Swindon Spitfires 5-0 before being removed from the competition.
*+Played 19 Aug: Colney Heath v Hemel Hempstead Town, Oakwood v Islington Borough, Dronfield Town v Ossett United, Wythenshawe Amateurs v Accrington Stanley Community Trust. ++Played 23 Aug: Sutton United v AFC Phoenix played 23 August.
**Played 2 Sep: AFC Telford United v Kidderminster Harriers postponed on 26 Aug because of waterlogged pitch.
+Replayed on 2 Sep: Warsash Wasps v Bournemouth Sports after original game abandoned due to waterlogged pitch.

FIRST QUALIFYING ROUND: SUN 2 SEP 2018

South Park Rangers (7)	Aw/o	Redcar Town (6)	
Durham Cestria (5)	1-2	Alnwick Town (6)	
Boro Rangers (6)	8-1	Cramlington United (6)	83
Washington (6)	2-4	Hartlepool United (5)	
Carlisle United (6)	1-2	Bishop Auckland (7)	40
Penrith (5)	5-1	Wallsend Boys Club (5)	
Wakefield (6)	0-4	Sheffield Wednesday (6)	
Ossett United (6)	1-2	Farsley Celtic (5)	103
Tingley Athletic (7)	4-0	Harrogate Town (5)	
Oughtibridge War Memorial (5)	Hw/o	Malet Lambert (7)	
Rotherham United (5)	1-3	Bridlington Rovers (7)	
Chesterfield (7)	4-0	Yorkshire Amateur (7)	73
Warrington Wolverines (6)	1-4	Stockport County (5)	
Wythenshawe Amateurs (6)	1-3	Accrington Girls & Ladies (5)	142
Manchester Stingers (5)	2-5	West Didsbury & Chorlton (6)	105
Cammell Laird 1907 (6)	4-0	Burscough Dynamo (6)	
Tranmere Rovers (5)	6-3	Bury (6)	
FC United of Manchester (5)	6-0	Didsbury (6)	110
Leicester City Women Dev.(5)	15-0	Coalville Town Ravenettes (7)	
Oadby & Wigston (6)	4-2	Mansfield Town (5)	88
Grimsby Borough (6)	1-4	Boston United (6)	
Loughborough Students (5)	5-1	Rise Park (5)	
Leicester City Ladies (5)	2-5	Lutterworth Athletic (6)	45
Stockingford AA Pavilion (5)	2-0	Lye Town (5)	110
Stourbridge (6)	1-2	Solihull United (6)	100
St Johns (7)	5-4 aet	Sandwell (6)	
Shifnal Town (6)	0-7	Leafield Athletic (5)	
Leek Town (6)	1-2	Sutton Coldfield Town (5)	
Hereford Lads Club (7)	0-9++	Kidderminster Harriers (6)	76
Rugby Town (6)	5-1	Shenstone (7)	
Redditch United (5)	0-3	Kingfisher (6)	
Crusaders (5)	5-0	Solihull Sporting (6)	

Peterborough Northern Star (5)	4-4aet (3-1p)	Northampton Town (6)	
St Ives Town (6)	1-2	Peterborough United (5)	98
Wymondham Town (5)	Hw/o	Roade (7)	
Kettering Town (5)	1-3	Acle United (5)	25
Cambridge City (5)	14-0	Riverside (7)	
Histon (6)	2-1++	Thrapston Town (6)	
Leigh Ramblers (7)	2-0	Bowers & Pitsea (6)	
Corringham Cosmos (7)	Hw/o	Bungay Town (7)	
Brentwood Town (5)	1-2	Harlow Town (5)	
Chelmsford City (7)	0-1	AFC Sudbury (5)	55
AFC Dunstable (5)	5-0	Watford Ladies Development (6)	30
Bishop's Stortford (6)	0-11	Royston Town (5)	
Colney Heath (5)	2-0	Houghton Athletic (7)	
Ashford Town (Middx) (6)	15-0	Wargrave (6)	11
New London Lionesses (6)	4-0	Hampton & Richmond Borough (7)	
Queens Park Rangers Girls (5)	Hw/o*	Wealdstone (8)	
Sandhurst Town (6)	Aw/o	Newbury (5)	
Wycombe Wanderers (6)	1-3	Ascot United (5)	
Abingdon United (6)	1-3	Oxford City (5)	40
Newhaven (6)	2-1	Ashford Ladies (6)	112
London Kent Football United (5)	1-2	Godalming Town (6)	
Hassocks (7)	2-4	Islington Borough (7)	
Meridian (6)	1-4	Worthing (6)	20
Regents Park Rangers (6)	3-4	Whyteleafe (5)	
Kent Football United (5)	8-0	Victoire (6)	
Burgess Hill Town (7)	9-2	Thamesview (7)	
Abbey Rangers (7)	2-1aet	Saltdean (6)	
AFC Phoenix (5)	5-0	Phoenix Sports (6)	50
Aylesford (5)	1-3	Fulham (5)	
Basingstoke Town (6)	0-13	AFC Bournemouth (5)	15
Swindon Spitfires (6)	0-6	Southampton FC Women (5)	
Shanklin (6)	0-3	New Milton Town (5)	38
Warsash Wasps (5)	3-1+	Royal Wootton Bassett Town (6)	
Alton (6)	0-2	Eastleigh (6)	
Frampton Rangers (6)	4-3	Feniton (6)	
Exeter City (5)	5-0	Frome Town (7)	55
Ilminster Town (5)	4-0	Middlezoy Rovers (5)	
Marine Academy Plymouth (5)	13-1	Exeter & Tedburn Rangers (6)	
Portishead Town (5)	2-1	Downend Flyers (5)	
St Agnes (6)	1-3	Keynsham Town Development (5)	
Torquay United (5)	1-2	Weston-super-Mare (6)	50

*Wealdstone disqualified for not satisfying eligibility criteria

+Played 9 Sep: Hereford Lads Club v Kidderminster Harriers, Histon v Thrapston Town, Warsash Wasps v Royal Wootton Bassett Town

SECOND QUALIFYING ROUND: SUN 23 SEP 2018

Steel City Wanderers (4)	1-8	Chester-le-Street Town (4)	
Cammell Laird 1907 (6)	1-3	Crewe Alexandra (4)	11
Morecambe (4)	1-5	Norton & Stockton Ancients (4)	35
Redcar Town (6)	6-2	Sheffield Wednesday (6)	97
Bishop Auckland (7)	0-8	Stockport County (5)	110
Tingley Athletic (7)	0-5	West Didsbury & Chorlton (6)	
Bridlington Rovers (7)	4-1	Accrington Girls & Ladies (5)	35
Brighouse Town (4)	5-0	Penrith AFC (5)	
Oughtibridge War Memorial (5)	0-4	FC United of Manchester (5)	
Bolton Wanderers (4)	3-0	Hartlepool United (5)	
Barnsley (4)	2-3 aet	Newcastle United (4)	
Tranmere Rovers (5)	0-1	Boro Rangers (6)	60
Burnley (4)	3-2	Liverpool Feds (4)	
Alnwick Town Juniors (6)	2-3 aet	Leeds United (4)	
Chorley (4)	5-0	Farsley Celtic (5)	93
Oadby & Wigston (6)	2-0	Sutton Coldfield Town (5)	64
Crusaders (5)	0-2	Sporting Khalsa (4)	
Rugby Town (6)	0-10	West Bromwich Albion (4)	
Long Eaton United (4)	7-1	The New Saints (4)	64
Chesterfield (7)	1-0	Burton Albion (4)	103
Leicester City Women Dev.(5)	6-3	Solihull United (6)	
St Johns (7)	1-4	Kidderminster Harriers (6)	35
Wolverhampton Wanderers (4)	6-0	Kingfisher (6)	75
Bedworth United (4)	0-2	Birmingham & West Mids (4)	
Leafield Athletic (5)	0-0 (4-2p)	Lutterworth Athletic (6)	
Stockingford AA Pavilion (5)	1-2	Nettleham (4)	
Solihull Moors (4)	3-2 aet	Loughborough Students (5)	15
Billericay Town (4)	9-1	Colney Heath (5)	78
Wymondham Town (5)	17-1	Corringham Cosmos (7)	
AFC Sudbury (5)	0-7	Acle United (5)	
Chesham United (4)	5-0	Peterborough United (5)	60
Histon (6)	3-2	Leigh Ramblers (7)	
Cambridge City (5)	5-4	Leyton Orient (4)	
Luton Town (4)	7-0	AFC Dunstable (5)	94
Enfield Town (4)	2-1	Actonians (4)	43
Boston United (6)	3-11	Norwich City (4)	
New London Lionesses (6)	2-2aet (4-2p)	Ipswich Town (4)	
Peterborough Northern Star (5)	1-5	Stevenage (4)	30
Queens Park Rangers Girls (5)	5-1*	Royston Town (5)	
Cambridge United (4)	6-0*	Harlow Town (5)	
Worthing (6)	1-5	Islington Borough (7)	

Denham United (4)	1-3	Crawley Wasps (4)	35
AFC Wimbledon (4)	1-0 aet	AFC Phoenix (5)	100
Oxford City (5)	4-3	Fulham (5)	40
Newhaven (6)	3-1	Newbury (5)	112
Kent Football United (5)	9-0*	Burgess Hill Town (7)	
Godalming Town (6)	4-2	Abbey Rangers (7)	
Whyteleafe (5)	2-0	Maidenhead United (4)	
Ashford Town (Middx) (6)	11-2	Ascot United (5)	
Buckland Athletic (4)	4-0+	Ilminster Town (5)	73
Southampton FC Women (5)	5-0	New Milton Town (5)	213
Poole Town (4)	3-1	Frampton Rangers (6)	44
St Nicholas (n/a)	Aw/o	Eastleigh (6)	
Larkhall Athletic (4)	7-2	Weston-super-Mare (6)	50
Swindon Town (4)	0-8	Keynsham Town (4)	28
Cheltenham Town (4)	4-1	Brislington (4)	76
Southampton Saints (4)	3-0*	Warsash Wasps (5)	30
AFC Bournemouth (5)	4-1	Portishead Town (5)	
Southampton Women (4)	1-2	Marine Academy (5)	
Exeter City (5)	8-1	Keynsham Town Dev. (5)	

+Played 26 Sep after postponement on 23 Sep: Buckland Athletic v Ilminster Town

*Played 30 Sep after postponement on 23 Sep: Southampton Saints v Warsash Wasps, Cambridge United v Harlow Town, Denham United v Crawley Wasps, Chesterfield v Burton Albion, QPR Girls v Royston Town, Kent Football United v Burgess Hill Town

THIRD QUALIFYING ROUND: SUN 7 OCT 2018

West Didsbury & Chorlton (6)	0-4	Bolton Wanderers (4)	95
Leeds United (4)	8-0	Boro Rangers (6)	
Norton & Stockton Ancients (4)	3-1	Redcar Town (6)	80
FC United of Manchester (6)	13-0	Bridlington Rovers (7)	147
Chorley (4)	2-1	Crewe Alexandra (4)	90
Chesterfield (7)	0-6	Stockport County (5)	168
Brighouse Town (4)	3-1	Burnley (4)	43
Newcastle United (4)	0-2	Chester-le-Street Town (4)	162
Sporting Khalsa (4)	1-6	Long Eaton United (4)	30
Kidderminster Harriers (6)	2-1	Solihull Moors (4)	
Leicester City Women Dev. (5)	2-1	Oadby & Wigston (6)	
Birmingham & West Midlands (4)	0-2	Wolverhampton Wanderers (4)	
Leafield Athletic (5)	1-2	West Bromwich Albion (4)	283
Nettleham (4)	9-0	Histon (6)	30
Norwich City (4)	4-0	Enfield Town (4)	95
Acle United (5)	0-1	Cambridge City (5)	
Cambridge United (4)	2-2aet (4-2p)	Stevenage (4)	
Wymondham Town (5)	3-4	Billericay Town (4)	

Chesham United (4)	0-3	Crawley Wasps (4)	60
Islington Borough (7)	1-2 aet	New London Lionesses (6)	
Ashford Town (Middx) (6)	3-4	Kent Football United (5)	
AFC Wimbledon (4)	4-0	Godalming Town (6)	100
Whyteleafe (5)	1-2	Queens Park Rangers Girls (5)	
Luton Town (4)	5-2	Oxford City (5)	45
Newhaven (6)	0-8	AFC Bournemouth CST (5)	152
Buckland Athletic (4)	2-0	Marine Academy (5)	68
Eastleigh (6)	1-2	Poole Town (4)	55
Keynsham Town (4)	6-0	Southampton Saints (4)	45
Southampton FC Women (5)	4-1	Larkhall Athletic (4)	121
Cheltenham Town (4)	1-0	Exeter City (5)	116

FIRST ROUND: SUN 11 NOV 2018

FC United of Manchester (5)	0-4	Chester-le-Street Town (4)	
Chorley (4)	1-2	Stockport County (5)	77
Leeds United (4)	1-0	Brighouse Town (4)	150
Norton & Stockton Ancients (4)	0-1	Bolton Wanderers (4)	100
Nettleham (4)	2-3	Long Eaton United (4)	30
Kidderminster Harriers (6)	1-6	Wolverhampton W (4)	330
West Bromwich Albion (4)	2-1	Leicester City Women Dev. (5)	
Cambridge City (5)	0-2+	Cambridge United	
Norwich City (4)	2-3 Aet	Billericay Town (4)	
Luton Town (4)	1-1aet (3-1p)	Kent Football United (5)	
New London Lionesses (6)	3-3aet* (3-4p)	AFC Wimbledon (4)	76
Crawley Wasps (4)	6-0	QPR Girls (5)	80
Buckland Athletic (4)	2-0	Cheltenham Town (4)	74
Keynsham Town (4)	8-1	AFC Bournemouth (5)	
Poole Town (4)	0-3	Southampton FC Women (5)	

*Played 18 Nov: New London Lionesses v AFC Wimbledon

+Played 25 Nov: Tie originally took place on 18.11 with Cambridge City winning 2-1 (aet) but result declared void and replay ordered after City's pitch at Trinity Field was found to be too small. Replay took place at Mildenhall Town FC where United play their home matches, but City were still technically the home side.

SECOND ROUND: SUN 2 DEC 2018

Sheffield FC (3)	2-3	Nottingham Forest (3)	
Long Eaton United (4)	0-5	Hull City (3)	60
Leeds United (4)	4-3 aet	Doncaster Rovers Belles (3)	
Huddersfield Town (3)	7-1	Bradford City (3)	105
Sunderland (3)	1-3	Fylde (3)	85
Chester-le-Street Town (4)	0-2	Stoke City (3)	60
Middlesbrough (3)	1-0	Stockport County (5)	83

Bolton Wanderers (4)	2-2aet 5-4p+	West Bromwich Albion (4)	
Guiseley Vixens (3)*	0-2	Derby County (3)	
Wolverhampton Wanderers (4)	0-4	Blackburn Rovers (3)	
Keynsham Town (4)	8-3	C&K Basildon (3)	60
Loughborough Foxes (3)	3-1 (aet)	Gillingham (3)	48
Billericay Town (4)	3-1 aet	Luton Town (4)	70
MK Dons (3)	4-0	Southampton FC Women (5)	
AFC Wimbledon (4)	2-0	Portsmouth (3)	95
Oxford United (3)	4-0	Cambridge United (4)	85
Watford (3)	1-0+	Buckland Athletic (4)	70
Coventry United (3)	2-1	Plymouth Argyle (3)	
Crawley Wasps (4)	2-0+	Chichester City (3)	130
Cardiff City Ladies (3)	4-0	QPR (3)	200

*Played at Derby County's Mickleover Sports Ground due to waterlogged pitch at Guiseley

+Played 9 December after being postponed on 2 December: Bolton Wanderers v West Bromwich Albion; Watford v Buckland Athletic; Crawley Wasps v Chichester City

THIRD ROUND: SUN 6 JAN 2019

Cardiff City Ladies (3)	2-0	Bolton Wanderers (4)	
Derby County (3)	1-2	Stoke City (3)	244
Huddersfield Town (3)	4-1	Leeds United (4)	156
Middlesbrough (3)	2-7	Watford (3)	92
Billericay Town (4)	3-4	Loughborough Foxes (3)	160
Hull City (3)	0-3	AFC Wimbledon (4)	133
Coventry United (3)	1-2	Crawley Wasps (4)	130
Nottingham Forest (3)	0-1	MK Dons (3)	164
Oxford United (3)	1-2	Blackburn Rovers (3)	203
Keynsham Town (4)		Fylde (3)	80

FOURTH ROUND: SUN 3 FEB 2019

Manchester City (1)	**3-0+**	**Watford (3)**	883
Nikita Parris 62, 69, Pauline Bremer 86			
AFC Wimbledon (4)	**0-3**	**Bristol City (1)**	520
		Abi Harrison 1, Katie Robinson 24, Poppy Wilson 36	
Crawley Wasps (4)	**0-4**	**Arsenal (1)**	1,550
		Kim Little 17, Ruby Grant 43, 75, 86	
Reading (1)	**13-0***	**Keynsham Town (4)**	272
Fara Williams (pen) 21, 24, (pen) 29, (pen) 55, 59, Lauren Bruton 37, 53, Brooke Chaplen 48, 59, Charlie Estcourt 68, Rakel Honnudottir 78, 80, Gemma Davison 84			

Home	Score	Away	Att
Liverpool (1)	**6-0***	**MK Dons (3)**	394
Laura Coombs 31, Courtney Sweetman-Kirk 32, Leandra Little 60, Jemma Purfield 61, 86, Ashley Hodson 79			
West Ham United (1)	**3-1**	**Blackburn Rovers (3)**	834
Adriana Leon 45, 79, Brianna Visalli 72		Natasha Flint 14	
Durham (2)	**5-1***	**Cardiff City Ladies (3)**	283
Abby Holmes 9, Beth Hepple 43, Sarah Robson 54, Zoe Ness 81, 89		Cori Williams missed pen 19 (saved Megan Borthwick), Kylie Nolan 21	
Charlton Athletic (2)	**3-3* aet 4-5p**	**Huddersfield Town (3)**	184
Kit Graham 6, 67, Charlotte Gurr 34		Brittany Sanderson 74, Laura Elford 75, Kate Mallin 78	
Crystal Palace (2)	**0-3**	**Tottenham Hotspur (2)**	282
		Jessica Naz 41, Ashleigh Neville 45+3, Coral-Jade Haines 55	
Stoke City (3)	**1-2***	**Aston Villa (2)**	252
Hannah Keryakoplis 6		Kerri Welsh 58, Sophie Haywood 66	
Everton (1)	**0-2**	**Chelsea (1)**	560
		Drew Spence 66, Hannah Blundell 90	
Yeovil Town (1)	**1-3***	**Birmingham City (1)**	523
Erin Bloomfield 77		Aoife Mannion (pen) 38, Emma Follis 46, Charlie Wellings 58	
Brighton & H A (1)	**0-2**	**Manchester United (2)**	764
Danielle Buet missed pen 78 (saved by Siobhan Chamberlain)		Lauren James 51, 90+2	
Loughborough Foxes (3)	**0-2***	**Sheffield United (2)**	202
		Alethea Paul 14, Veatriki Sarri 54	
Millwall Lionesses (2)	**1-0***	**Lewes (2)**	326
Grace Neville 90+1		Amy Taylor sent off 84	
Leicester City Women (2)	**0-2**	**London Bees (2)**	272
Rosie Axten missed pen 75		Katie Wilkinson 8, Ruesha Littlejohn 59	

+Played 2 Feb: Manchester City v Watford

*Played 10 Feb after being postponed on 3 Feb: Reading v Keynsham Town; Liverpool v MK Dons; Durham v Cardiff City Ladies; Charlton Athletic v Huddersfield Town; Stoke City v Huddersfield Town; Yeovil Town v Birmingham City; Loughborough Foxes v Sheffield United; Millwall Lionesses v Lewes

FIFTH ROUND: 17 FEB 2019

Home	Score	Away	Att
Liverpool (1)	**2-0**	**Millwall Lionesses (2)**	412
Kirsty Linnett 57, Rinsola Babajide 67			
Bristol City (1)	**0-2**	**Durham (2)**	
		Lisa Robertson 66, 90+2	
Reading (1)	**2-1**	**Birmingham City (1)**	275
Kirsty Pearce 69, Rakel Honnudottir 83		Aoife Mannion (pen) 77	

Home	Score	Away	Att
Chelsea (1)	**3-0**	**Arsenal (1)**	2,232
Bethany England 5, 58, Jonna Andersson 40			
Manchester United (2)	**3-0**	**London Bees (2)**	838
Ella Toone 27, Mollie Green 32, Charlie Devlin 87			
West Ham United (1)	**8-1**	**Huddersfield Town (3)**	865
Kate Longhurst 22, Leanne Kiernan 27, 81, 84, Alisha Lehmann 37, Jane Ross 38, Rosie Kmita 66, Brianna Visalli 71		Kate Mallin (pen) 14	
Aston Villa (2)	**3-3aet (5-3p)**	**Sheffield United (2)**	252
Jodie Hutton 74, (pen) 86, 90+6		Maddy Cusack 27, Ebony Salmon 59, Bex Rayner 84	
Tottenham Hotspur (2)	**0-3**	**Manchester City (1)**	1,158
Angela Addison missed pen 76 (saved Ellie Roebuck)		Stephanie Houghton 37, Lauren Hemp 39, Gemma Bonner 51	

QUARTER-FINALS: SUN 17 MARCH 2019

Home	Score	Away	Att
Durham (2)	**0-1**	**Chelsea (1)**	1,629
		Ji So-Yun 28	
Manchester City (1)	**3-0**	**Liverpool (1)**	1,366
Janine Beckie 25, Georgia Stanway 69, 88			
Aston Villa (2)	**0-1**	**West Ham United (1)**	609
		Jane Ross 26	
Reading (1)	**3-2aet**	**Manchester United (2)**	951
Remi Allen 100, Rachel Furness 107, Rakel Honnudottir 120		Alex Greenwood (pen) 98, Natasha Harding (og) 106	

SEMI-FINALS: SUN 14 APRIL 2019

Home	Score	Away	Att
Reading (1)	**1-1aet (3-4p)**	**West Ham United (1)**	2,334
Rachel Furness 49		Alisha Lehmann 57	
Manchester City (1)	**1-0**	**Chelsea (1)**	1,763
Magdalena Eriksson (og) 90+1			

FINAL: SAT 4 MAY 2019

Manchester City (1)	**3-0**	**West Ham United (1)**	Wembley Stadium	Att: 43,264
Keira Walsh 52, Georgia Stanway 79, Lauren Hemp 87				

Manchester City: Karen Bardsley; Abbie McManus, Steph Houghton (c), Jen Beattie, Demi Stokes, Jill Scott, Keira Walsh, Tessa Wullaert, Caroline Weir (Claire Emslie 84), Nikita Parris (Lauren Hemp 84), Georgia Stanway.

Unused Subs: Ellie Roebuck, Gemma Bonner, Pauline Bremer, Janine Beckie, Megan Campbell

Manager: Nick Cushing

West Ham United: Anna Moorhouse; Erin Simon (Rosie Kmita 88), Gilly Flaherty (c), Brooke Hendrix, Claire Rafferty (Brianna Visalli 62), Ria Percival, Kate Longhurst, Cho So-hyun, Alisha Lehmann, Adriana Leon, Jane Ross (Leanne Kiernan 65).

Unused Subs: Becky Spencer, Vyan Sampson, Lucienne Reichardt

Manager: Matt Beard

Referee: Abigail Byrne

CONTINENTAL LEAGUE CUP 2018-19

In the eighth year of the Continental Cup the only two teams to have ever won this competition met in the final for the second season in a row. This time the result was reversed. In 2018 Arsenal had been 1-0 winners, but in 2019 City prevailed 4-2 on penalties after a goalless draw at Bramall Lane.

Heading into the game, City led the WSL by two points from Arsenal, although the Gunners had two games in hand. Both teams knew they could perhaps strike a psychological blow over their main title challengers by carrying off the first silverware of the domestic season.

Ultimately Nick Cushing's Manchester City were deserved winners having had the best chances during the game. Steph Houghton forced a decent save from Sari van Veenendaal in the first half with Nikita Parris and Janine Beckie both hitting the bar after the break.

Arsenal had been dealt a blow when they were forced to start with Vivianne Miedema – the standout WSL player so far this season – on the bench because of fatigue. The Gunners posed a greater threat when the Netherlands international came on midway through the second half.

With no goals in normal time, or the added 30 minutes, the Continental Cup final progressed to penalties for the first time in its history. It looked to be advantage Arsenal when 18-year-old substitute Lauren Hemp took City's second kick and saw it saved by van Veenendaal. However, England keeper Karen Bardsley then saved the next two kicks she faced from Arsenal's Leah Williamson and Danielle van de Donk.

The honour of converting the crucial winning kick eventually fell to Canada international Beckie who kept her cool as City won 4-2 on penalties to lift the trophy for the third time.

2018-19 FORMAT

The competition is exclusively for the teams in the top two tiers of English football, the WSL and the Championship. For 2018-19, the 22 teams were organised into four regional groups with each team playing the other teams in the group once. Winning a match is worth three points. When matches are drawn each team is awarded one point, with a penalty shootout then taking place (no extra time). The winner of the penalty shootout is awarded a bonus point. The top two teams in each group advance to the quarter-finals. Teams level on points are separated by goal difference and then goals scored. In the knockout stages, drawn matches progress to 30 minutes of extra-time and then penalties if required.

GROUP ONE NORTH

18.08	**Aston Villa (Ch)**	**1-2**	**Sheffield United (Ch)**	251
	Hanssen 54		Cox 40, Marsden 85	
19.08	**Leicester City W (Ch)**	**2-2**	**Bristol City (WSL)**	294
	M.Johnson 1, Domingo 77	(4-2p)	Graham (pen) 55, 86	
19.08	**Birmingham C (WSL)**	**0-0**	**Man City (WSL)**	574
		(4-5p)		

26.08	**Birmingham C (WSL)** Harrop 71, Wellings 88	**2-0**	**Aston Villa (Ch)**	638
26.08	**Man City (WSL)** Wullaert 53, 80, Beckie 72, Nadim 83	**4-0**	**Leicester City W (Ch)**	1,609
26.08	**Bristol City (WSL)** Graham 26, Dykes 58, Woolley 73	**3-1**	**Sheffield United (Ch)** Pennock 12	156
16.09	**Sheffield United (Ch)**	**0-2**	**Birmingham City (WSL)** Staniforth 72, Hayles 84	331
16.09	**Leicester City W (Ch)**	**0-1**	**Aston Villa (Ch)** Welsh 19	312
16.09	**Bristol City (WSL)**	**0-3**	**Man City (WSL)** Emslie 52, Nadim (pen) 66, Weir 72	451
05.12	**Man City (WSL)** Beckie 7, 25, 48, 79, Park 14, Stanway (pen) 53	**6-0**	**Sheffield United (Ch)**	1,079
05.12	**Bristol City (WSL)** Graham 7, 19, Kemppi 34, 52, Robinson 85	**5-2**	**Aston Villa (Ch)** Baptiste 60, Hanssen 89	218
05.12	**Leicester City W (Ch)**	**0-6**	**Birmingham City (WSL)** Hayles 3, 60, Staniforth 22, Arthur 31, Wellings 37, Mannion (pen) 73	364
12.12	**Birmingham C (WSL)**	**0-0 (1-3p)**	**Bristol City (WSL)**	363
12.12	**Sheffield United (Ch)** Jones 7, Dixon 8, Cox 19	**3-1**	**Leicester City W (Ch)** Franklin-Fraiture 33	234
13.12	**Aston Villa (Ch)**	**0-4**	**Man City (WSL)** Bonner 21, Beckie 27, Park 77, Hemp 82	458

GROUP ONE NORTH FINAL STANDINGS

	P	W	WP	LP	L	F	A	GD	Pts	
1.Manchester City	**5**	**4**	**1**	**0**	**0**	**17**	**0**	**+17**	**14**	**Q**
2.Birmingham City	**5**	**3**	**0**	**2**	**0**	**10**	**0**	**+10**	**11**	**Q**
3.Bristol City	5	2	1	1	1	10	8	+2	9	
4.Sheffield United	5	2	0	0	3	6	13	-7	6	
5.Aston Villa	5	1	0	0	4	4	13	-9	3	
6.Leicester City W	5	0	1	0	4	3	16	-13	2	

GROUP TWO NORTH

Date	Home	Score	Away	Att
19.08	**Reading (WSL)** Pearce 6, Williams 13, 23, 82	**4-1**	**Durham (Ch)** Hepple 79	246
19.08	**Liverpool (WSL)**	**0-1**	**Man Utd (Ch)** Arnot 84	829
25.08	**Man Utd (Ch)**	**0-2**	**Reading (WSL)** Chaplen 56, Davison 90+4, *Bartrip sent off 63*	4,835
26.08	**Durham (Ch)** Ness 21	**1-0**	**Everton (WSL)**	284
16.09	**Durham (Ch)** Roberts 3, 21, Cottam 57	**3-3 (4-5p)**	**Liverpool (WSL)** Bradley-Auckland 2, Babajide 71, Sweetman-Kirk 86	352
16.09	**Everton (WSL)** Walker 14, 27, Kaagman 56	**3-2**	**Reading (WSL)** Finnigan (og) 24, Chaplen 79	143
05.12	**Man Utd (Ch)** Green 1	**1-0**	**Durham (Ch)**	686
05.12	**Liverpool (WSL)**	**P-P**	**Everton (WSL)**	
12.12	**Reading (WSL)** Furness 64	**1-1 (4-5p)**	**Liverpool (WSL)** Sweetman-Kirk 66	323
13.12	**Everton (WSL)**	**0-3**	**Man Utd (Ch)** James 10, Galton 14, Zelem 36	267

16.12	**Liverpool (WSL)**	**1-3**	**Everton (WSL)**	207
	Fahey 14		Boye-Hlorkah 2, Magill 10, Hughes 18	

GROUP TWO NORTH FINAL STANDINGS

	P	W	WP	LP	L	F	A	GD	Pts	
1.Manchester United	**4**	**3**	**0**	**0**	**1**	**5**	**2**	**+3**	**9**	**Q**
2.Reading	**4**	**2**	**0**	**1**	**1**	**9**	**5**	**+4**	**7**	**Q**
3.Everton	4	2	0	0	2	6	7	-1	6	
4.Durham	4	1	0	1	2	5	8	-3	4	
5.Liverpool	4	0	2	0	2	5	8	-3	4	

GROUP ONE SOUTH

18.08	**Crystal Palace (Ch)**	**1-1 (5-3p)**	**Tottenham Hotspur (Ch)**	372
	Balfour 64		Green 37	
19.08	**London Bees (Ch)**	**1-1 (5-3p)**	**Yeovil Town (WSL)**	246
	Wilson 29		Fergusson 40	
19.08	**Chelsea (WSL)**	**3-1**	**Brighton & H A (WSL)**	1,095
	Spence 46, Kirby 68, England 87		A.Whelan 77	
26.08	**Tottenham H (Ch)**	**2-2 (10-9p)**	**Brighton & H A (WSL)**	144
	Dean 8, Wynne 36		Williams 52, Umotong 90+1	
26.08	**London Bees (Ch)**	**1-6**	**Chelsea (WSL)**	374
	Pickett 44		Bachmann 7, 45, Spence 9, 36, Kirby 79, England 81	
26.08	**Yeovil Town (WSL)**	**0-1**	**Crystal Palace (Ch)**	301
			Butler 82	
16.09	**Crystal Palace (Ch)**	**0-4**	**Chelsea (WSL)**	449
			Engman 10, England 56, 64, Spence 60	
16.09	**Brighton & H A (WSL)**	**3-1**	**London Bees (Ch)**	171
	Umotong 27, Brazil 36, A. Whelan 88		Howells 22	
16.09	**Yeovil Town (WSL)**	**0-4**	**Tottenham Hotspur (Ch)**	415
			Wiltshire 7, Haines 22, 39, 60	

Date	Home	Score	Away	Att
05.12	**Chelsea (WSL)** Engman 2, Spence 17, 63, England 24, 77, Cousins (og) 37, Cuthbert 75	**7-0**	**Yeovil Town (WSL)**	916
05.12	**Brighton & H A (WSL)** Perry 14, Natkiel 38, 64, Brett 40, Gibbons 72	**5-1**	**Crystal Palace (Ch)** Burr 85	204
05.12	**London Bees (Ch)** Davy 45+2, 47, Wilkinson 64, Forman 85	**4-2**	**Tottenham Hotspur (Ch)** Dean 5, Wiltshire 40	146
12.12	**Tottenham H (Ch)**	**0-5**	**Chelsea (WSL)** Cooper 11, Riley 19, Carney 46, England 60, 72	358
12.12	**Yeovil Town (WSL)** Syme 37	**1-4**	**Brighton & H A (WSL)** Brazil 15, Buet 45+2, Green 53, Roe 83	224
13.12	**Crystal Palace (Ch)** Hincks 12, 24, 45+2 pen, 67, Burr 52, 70, True 76	**7-2**	**London Bees (Ch)** Pickett 15, Davy 21	146

GROUP ONE SOUTH FINAL STANDINGS

	P	W	WP	LP	L	F	A	GD	Pts	
1.Chelsea	**5**	**5**	**0**	**0**	**0**	**25**	**2**	**+23**	**15**	**Q**
2.Brighton & H A	**5**	**3**	**0**	**1**	**1**	**15**	**8**	**+7**	**10**	**Q**
3.Crystal Palace	5	2	1	0	2	10	12	-2	8	
4.Tottenham Hotspur	5	1	1	1	2	9	12	-3	6	
5.London Bees	5	1	1	0	3	9	19	-10	5	
6.Yeovil Town	5	0	0	1	4	2	17	-15	1	

GROUP TWO SOUTH

Date	Home	Score	Away	Att
19.08	**Lewes (Ch)** Bergin (pen) 11, 43 Lane 22 Carter 86, 90+1	**5-0**	**Charlton Athletic (Ch)**	205
19.08	**Arsenal (WSL)** McCabe 12, 80, Mead 44	**3-1**	**West Ham United (WSL)** Visalli 48	834

26.08	**Charlton Athletic (Ch)** Graham 11, 48, Bailes 60, Bryan 83	**4-2**	**Millwall Lionesses (Ch)** Ravenscroft 39, Clarke 45	204
26.08	**West Ham U (WSL)** Ross 25, (pen) 49, Kiernan 28, Simic 31	**4-1**	**Lewes (Ch)** Lane 8	255
16.09	**West Ham U (WSL)** De Graaf 6, 82, Visalli 9, Kmita 12	**4-0**	**Millwall Lionesses (Ch)**	557
16.09	**Lewes (Ch)**	**0-9**	**Arsenal (WSL)** Van de Donk 6, Miedema 21, 27, 60, McCabe 26, Little (pen) 37, (pen) 45, 68, Evans 59	945
05.12	**Millwall Lionesses (Ch)**	**0-2**	**Lewes (Ch)** Carter 68, Quayle 78	143
05.12	**Arsenal (WSL)** Miedema 6, 76, McCabe 30, 81, Ritchie (og) 59	**5-0**	**Charlton Athletic (Ch)**	202
12.12	**Millwall Lionesses (Ch)** Ravenscroft 32	**1-3**	**Arsenal (WSL)** Miedema 55, Grant 56, Williamson 60	463
12.12	**Charlton Athletic (Ch)**	**0-2**	**West Ham United (WSL)** Rosie Kmita 46, Alisha Lehmann 56	202

GROUP TWO SOUTH FINAL STANDINGS

	P	W	WP	LP	L	F	A	GD	Pts	
1.Arsenal	**4**	**4**	**0**	**0**	**0**	**20**	**2**	**+18**	**12**	**Q**
2.West Ham United	**4**	**3**	**0**	**0**	**1**	**10**	**4**	**+6**	**9**	**Q**
3.Lewes	4	2	0	0	2	8	13	-5	6	
4.Charlton Athletic	4	1	0	0	3	4	14	-10	3	
5.Millwall Lionesses	4	0	0	0	4	3	12	-9	0	

QUARTER-FINALS

Date	Home	Score	Away	Att
09.01	**Arsenal (WSL)**	**2-1**	**Birmingham City (WSL)**	
	van de Donk 83, Miedema 90+1		Quinn 61, *Mannion had pen 18 saved by van Veenendaal*	
09.01	**Chelsea (WSL)**	**4-0**	**Reading (WSL)**	973
	Kirby 3, 86, Asante 37, Riley 90+1			
09.01	**Man Utd (Ch)**	**2-0**	**West Ham United (WSL)**	1,029
	Sigsworth 17, 53			
10.01	**Man City (WSL)**	**7-1**	**Brighton & H A (WSL)**	786
	Parris 6, Hemp 23, 86, Weir 59, Emslie 88, Stanway 90, Beckie 90+2		Buet 9	

SEMI-FINALS

Date	Home	Score	Away	Att
06.02	**Chelsea (WSL)**	**0-2**	**Man City (WSL)**	1,358
			Parris (pen) 49, 81	
07.02	**Arsenal (WSL)**	**2-1**	**Man Utd (Ch)**	1,836
	Miedema 18, 59		Green 81	

FINAL; 23RD FEBRUARY 2019

Arsenal (WSL)	**0-0aet (2-4p)**	**Man City (WSL)**	Bramall Lane, (Sheffield United FC)	Att: 2,424

Arsenal (4-2-3-1): Sari van Veenendaal; Janni Arnth (Vivianne Miedema 69), Louise Quinn, Leah Williamson, Katrine Veje (Amelia Hazard 71); Dominique Bloodworth, Danielle van de Donk, Kim Little (c); Lisa Evans, Beth Mead, Katie McCabe

Unused subs: Pauline Peyraud-Magnin, Ava Kuyken, Caterina Albuquerque

Manager: Joe Montemurro

Manchester City (4-4-2): Karen Bardsley; Gemma Bonner, Stephanie Houghton (c), Jen Beattie, Demi Stokes; Tessa Wullaert (Janine Beckie 65), Jill Scott, Keira Walsh, Caroline Weir (Claire Emslie 119); Georgina Stanway, Nikita Parris (Lauren Hemp 105)

Unused subs: Ellie Roebuck, Pauline Bremer, Megan Campbell, Abbie McManus

Manager: Nick Cushing

Referee: Lucy Oliver

PENALTIES: Manchester City took first

MAN CITY: Georgia Stanway, *Lauren Hemp (saved),* Claire Emslie, Stephanie Houghton, Janine Beckie

ARSENAL: Kim Little, Leah Williamson (saved), Danielle van de Donk (saved), Dominique Bloodworth

FA WNL CUP 2018-19

The FA WNL Cup is the League Cup for teams in Tiers 3 and 4. In 2018-19 the final was contested by two teams who had already been crowned champions of their respective divisions; Blackburn Rovers of the WNL Northern Premier and – operating a tier below them – Crawley Wasps of WNL South East 1.

Rovers came into the match keen to defend the WNL Cup they won in 2017-18, and in the end it proved to be a comfortable 3-0 victory. Saffron Jordan put Rovers ahead in the eighth minute with her 100th Rovers goal. They failed to add to their score until seven minutes after the break when Player of the Match Natasha Flint lifted the ball over advancing Wasps keeper Frankie Gibbs.

Jordan completed the scoring with a fine solo goal when she skipped her way round several challenges before rifling an effort into the top corner from a narrow angle.

The defeat didn't diminish Wasps' pride in becoming the first team from Tier 4 to make it to the WNL Cup final, nor detract from the successes of their debut season in the WNL in which they became champions of their division and also reached the FA Cup 4th Round where they took on Arsenal.

For Rovers' manager Gemma Donnelly this match ultimately proved to be the second part of a Quadruple of trophies for 2018-19 with the club going on to win the Lancashire FA County Cup (against Fylde) and WNL national play-off final (against Coventry United) in May, a month in which the FA also confirmed they had satisfied all necessary licence criteria for promotion to the Championship for 2019-20.

KEY

The letters in parentheses denote the division the team plays its League football in. (S) = WNL Southern Premier (Tier 3), (N) = WNL Northern Premier (Tier 3), (SE1) = WNL South East 1 (Tier 4), (SW1) = WNL South West 1 (Tier 4), (N1) = WNL North 1 (Tier 4), and (M1) = WNL Midlands 1 (Tier 4)

FORMAT

Matches that are drawn proceed to 30 minutes of extra-time and then penalties if required.

DETERMINING ROUND

The losing team in each Determining Round fixture drops into the 2018-19 WNL Plate.

02.09	Actonians (SE1)	1-2	Oxford United (S)
02.09	Barnsley (N1)	3-4	Bolton Wanderers (N1)
02.09	Billericay Town (SE1)	10-1	Maidenhead United (SW1)
02.09	Blackburn Rovers (N)	3-3aet (5-4p)	Liverpool Feds (N1)
02.09	Buckland Athletic (SW1)	3-0	Brislington (SW1)
02.09	Cambridge United (SE1)	2-0	C&K Basildon (S)
02.09	Chesham United (S)	2-4	Enfield Town (SE1)
02.09	Coventry United (S)	7-0	Norwich City (SE1)

02.09	Crawley Wasps (SE1)	8-0	Ipswich Town (SE1)
02.09	Derby County (N)	3-1	Bedworth United (M1)
02.09	Doncaster R B (N)	2-2aet (3-4p)	Chorley (N1)
02.09	Fylde (N)	9-0	Burton Albion (M1)
02.09	Guiseley Vixens (N)	4-2	Chester-le-Street Town (N1)
02.09	Huddersfield Town (N)	3-0	Middlesbrough (N)
02.09	Hull City (N)	2-1	Bradford City (N)
02.09	Larkhall Athletic (SW1)	3-2	Keynsham Town (SW1)
02.09	Long Eaton United (M1)	3-4	Norton & Stockton Ancients (N1)
02.09	Loughborough Foxes (S)	4-0	Denham United (SE1)
02.09	Luton Town (SE1)	1-3	Cheltenham Town (SW1)
02.09	Morecambe (N1)	0-5	Sunderland (N)
02.09	Nettleham (M1)	1-2	Birmingham & W M (M1)
02.09	Plymouth Argyle (S)	4-2	MK Dons (S)
02.09	Poole Town (SW1)	1-2	Watford (S)
02.09	Portsmouth (S)	2-4	Chichester City (S)
02.09	QPR (S)	3-1	Gillingham (S)
02.09	Solihull Moors (M1)	0-7	Brighouse Town (N1)
02.09	Southampton S (SW1)	0-1	AFC Wimbledon (SE1)
02.09	Sporting Khalsa (M1)	1-2	Leeds United (N1)
02.09	Steel City W (M1)	1-6	Newcastle United (N1)
02.09	Stevenage (SE1)	1-4	Cardiff City (S)
02.09	Stoke City (N)	3-0	Sheffield FC (N)
02.09	Swindon Town (SW1)	1-5	Leyton Orient (SE1)
02.09	The New Saints (M1)	0-3	Nottingham Forest (N)
02.09	West Brom (M1)	0-3	Burnley (N1)
02.09	Wolverhampton W (M1)	1-0	Crewe Alexandra (N1)
02.09	St Nicholas (SW1)	a/w	Southampton W (SW1)

FIRST ROUND

Of the winners from the Determining Round 28 were given byes to the 2nd Round, with the other eight teams contesting four 1st Round ties.

30.09	AFC Wimbledon (SE1)	4-0	Buckland Athletic (SW1)
30.09	Enfield Town (SE1)	3-4	Southampton W (SW1)
30.09	Guiseley Vixens (N)	1-2	Blackburn Rovers (N)
30.09	Newcastle United (N1)	1-2aet	Chorley (N1)

SECOND ROUND

14.10	Billericay Town (SE1)	0-2	Chichester City (S)
14.10	Blackburn Rovers (N)	3-2	Fylde (N)
14.10	Brighouse Town (N1)	1-2	Leeds United (N1)
14.10	Cardiff City (S)	5-3	Cheltenham Town (SW1)

14.10	Derby County (N)	1-2	Bolton Wanderers (N1)
14.10	Huddersfield Town (N)	1-0	Burnley (N1)
14.10	Hull City (N)	2-1aet	Birmingham & W M (M1)
14.10	Larkhall Athletic (SW1)	2-3aet	AFC Wimbledon (SE1)
14.10	Nottingham Forest (N)	2-0	Chorley (N1)
14.10	Oxford United (S)	1-3aet	Crawley Wasps (SE1)
14.10	QPR (S)	1-3	Loughborough Foxes (S)
14.10	Stoke City (N)	3-0	Norton & Stockton Ancients (N1)
14.10	Watford (S)	2-3	Coventry United (S)
14.10	Wolverhampton W (M1)	1-4	Sunderland (N)
28.10	Cambridge United (SE1)	3-0	Leyton Orient (SE1)
28.10	Southampton W (SW1)	1-3	Plymouth Argyle (S)

THIRD ROUND

09.12	AFC Wimbledon (SE1)	2-1	Cambridge United (SE1)
09.12	Blackburn Rovers (N)	3-1	Sunderland (N)
09.12	Cardiff City (S)	3-4aet	Loughborough Foxes (S)
09.12	Huddersfield Town (N)	4-1	Nottingham Forest (N)
09.12	Stoke City (N)	6-3	Leeds United (N1)
13.01	Plymouth Argyle (S)	3-5aet	Crawley Wasps (SE1)
13.01	Bolton Wanderers (N1)	3-1aet	Hull City (N)
13.01	Chichester City (S)	0-2	Coventry United (S)

QUARTER-FINALS

17.02	Bolton Wanderers (N1)	1-1aet 5-3p	Stoke City (N)
17.02	Loughborough Foxes (S)	3-0	AFC Wimbledon (SE1)
24.02	Coventry United (S)	1-2	Crawley Wasps (SE1)
24.02	Huddersfield Town (N)	1-3	Blackburn Rovers (N)

SEMI-FINALS

03.03	Blackburn Rovers (N)	4-0	Loughborough Foxes (S)
03.03	Crawley Wasps (SE1)	1-0	Bolton Wanderers (N1)

FINAL – 28.04

Crawley Wasps (SE1)	**0-3**	**Blackburn Rovers (N)**	Pirelli Stadium, Burton Albion FC
		Saffron Jordan 8, 81 Natasha Flint 52	Att: 227

Blackburn Rovers: Danielle Gibbons, Chelsey Jukes, Lynda Shepherd (c), Jess Holbrook, Lauren Davies, Natasha Fenton (Hannah Walsh 88), Saffron Jordan, Natasha Flint, Lagan Makin (Alexandra Taylor 67), Kayleigh McDonald, Serena Fletcher **Unused sub:** Amelia Size

Manager: Gemma Donnelly

Crawley Wasps: Frankie Gibbs, Rachel Palmer, Niamh Stephenson (Amy Woollard 89), Charlotte Young, Jenny Drury, Megan Stow, Kemina Webber (Suzanne Davies 80), Faye Rabson, Emma Plewa, Amy Green (Ariana Fleischman 58), Naomi Cole (c) **Unused subs:** Lauren Graves, Abbie Measures

Manager: Paul Walker

FA WNL PLATE 2018-19

The WNL Plate final was set to be contested by MK Dons and Gillingham only for the FA to find both clubs guilty of having fielded ineligible players in their semi-finals. As a result their respective opponents in the last four – Liverpool Feds and West Bromwich Albion – replaced them in the final. West Brom were comfortable 5-1 winners in a final staged at Rugby Town FC. Baggies skipper Hannah George fired them ahead with a free kick from 20 yards out but Feds quickly levelled through Molly Farley. Jess Davies restored Albion's advantage before half time with a powerful finish. After the break Laura Davies made it three with an exquisite chip, Ria Elsmore headed in number four and Player of the Match Natalie Murray completed the scoring with a cool finish. For Albion this proved to be the first trophy of a domestic Double with manager Louis Sowe's side going on to wrap up the WNL Midlands 1 title. Liverpool Feds went on to finish the season in 5th place in WNL North 1.

KEY

The letters in parentheses denote the division the team plays its League football in. (S) = WNL Southern Premier (Tier 3), (N) = WNL Northern Premier (Tier 3), (SE1) = WNL South East 1 (Tier 4), (SW1) = WNL South West 1 (Tier 4), (N1) = WNL North 1 (Tier 4), and (M1) = WNL Midlands 1 (Tier 4)

FORMAT

Matches that are drawn proceed to 30 minutes of extra-time and then penalties if required.

The WNL Plate is a competition for the 36 losing teams in the WNL Cup Determining Round. St Nicholas folded before the start of the competition meaning 35 teams took part in 2018-19.

FIRST ROUND

Three WNL Plate 1st Round fixtures took place with the other 29 teams given a bye to the 2nd Round.

30.09	Poole Town (SW1)	0-9	Portsmouth (S)
07.10	Barnsley (N1)	5-1	Burton Albion (M1)
14.10	Keynsham Town (SW1)	7-1	Southampton Saints (SW1)

SECOND ROUND

14.10	Actonians (SE1)	1-2	Chesham United (SW1)
14.10	Doncaster R B (N)	2-3aet	Barnsley (N1)
14.10	Gillingham (S)	5-4	Luton Town (SE1)
14.10	Ipswich Town (SE1)	4-2	C&K Basildon (S)
14.10	Liverpool Feds (N1)	2-0	Crewe Alexandra (N1)
14.10	Long Eaton United (M1)	0-1aet	Chester-le-Street Town (N1)
14.10	Maidenhead Utd (SW1)	1-1aet (4-2p)	Denham United (SE1)
14.10	Morecambe (N1)	4-3aet	Sheffield FC (N)
14.10	Steel City W (M1)	4-6	Sporting Khalsa (M1)

14.10	Swindon Town (SW1)	1-2	Bedworth United (M1)
14.10	West Brom (M1)	5-0	Nettleham (M1)
21.10	Brislington (SW1)	0-3	MK Dons (S)
21.10	Keynsham Town (SW1)	2-1	Portsmouth (S)
21.10	Solihull Moors (M1)	0-6	Middlesbrough (N)
28.10	The New Saints (M1)	5-0	Bradford City (N)
	Norwich City (SE1)	a/w	Stevenage (SE1)

THIRD ROUND

09.12	Gillingham (S)	5-0	Chesham United (SW1)
09.12	Ipswich Town (SE1)	1-2aet	Stevenage (SE1)
09.12	Keynsham Town (SW1)	7-1	Maidenhead United (SW1)
09.12	Liverpool Feds (N1)	1-0	Chester-le-Street Town (N1)
09.12	MK Dons (S)	2-1aet	Bedworth United (M1)
09.12	Morecambe (N1)	2-3aet	Middlesbrough (N)
09.12	The New Saints (M1)	0-9	Barnsley (N1)
06.01	Sporting Khalsa (M1)	1-2	West Brom (M1)

QUARTER-FINALS

10.02	Barnsley (N1)	0-1	West Brom (M1)
10.02	Liverpool Feds (N1)	2-0	Middlesbrough (N)
10.02	Stevenage (SE1)	0-4	Gillingham (S)
24.02	MK Dons (S)	2-2aet (5-4p)	Keynsham Town (SW1)

SEMI-FINALS

03.03	Gillingham (S)	Aw/o	West Brom (M1)
10.02	MK Dons (S)	Aw/o	Liverpool Feds (N1)

Gillingham beat West Brom 1-0 but were disqualified from competition on 14.03 for fielding ineligible players.

MK Dons beat Liverpool Feds 4-3 (aet) disqualified from competition on 04.04 for fielding an ineligible player.

FINAL – 14.04

West Bromwich Albion (M1)	**5-1**	**Liverpool Feds (N1)**
Hannah George 5, Jess Davies 39, Laura Davies 51, Ria Elsmore 75, Natalie Murray 89	Butlin Road, Rugby Town FC Att: 342	Molly Farley 18

West Bromwich Albion: Vanessa Kinnerley, Bethan Jewitt (Niamh Johnston 83), Hannah George (c), Fran Orthodoxou, Ria Elsmore, Imogen Sinclair, Natalie Murray, Keeley Davies, Gabriella Reid (Harriet James 76), Laura Davies, Jessica Davies (Lauren Price 76)

Unused Subs: Antonia Smith, Rachel Howard

Head Coach: Louis Sowe

Liverpool Feds: Meghan Pope, Rosie Kinvig, Caroline Charlton, Nicola James (Natalie Clark 70), Abby Pope, Jodie Mortimer, Carla Lee (c), Mollie Farley (Jen Rogers 70), Helen Griffiths (Emily Douglas 56), Laura Bartup, Demi Devereaux

Joint Managers: Colin Lewis & Leanne Duffy

2018-19 LEAGUE TABLES

WSL (TIER 1)

Pos	Team	P	W	D	L	F	A	GD	Pts	
1.	Arsenal	20	18	0	2	70	13	57	54	
2.	Manchester City	20	14	5	1	53	17	36	47	
3.	Chelsea	20	12	6	2	46	14	32	42	
4.	Birmingham City	20	13	1	6	29	17	12	40	
5.	Reading	20	8	3	9	33	30	3	27	
6.	Bristol City	20	7	4	9	17	34	-17	25	
7.	West Ham United	20	7	2	11	25	37	-12	23	
8.	Liverpool	20	7	1	12	21	38	-17	22	
9.	Brighton & H A	20	4	4	12	16	38	-22	16	
10.	Everton	20	3	3	14	15	38	-23	12	
11.	Yeovil Town	20	2	1	17	11	60	-49	-3*	R

*Yeovil docked 10pts after announcing intention to appoint administrators.

Champions Arsenal and runners-up Manchester City qualified for the 2019-20 Champions League. Yeovil Town relegated to Tier 2 by virtue of finishing bottom, and then relegated to Tier 3 after failing to satisfy Tier 2 licence critera.

CHAMPIONSHIP (TIER 2)

Pos	Team	P	W	D	L	F	A	GD	Pts	
1.	Manchester United	20	18	1	1	98	7	91	55	P
2.	Tottenham Hotspur	20	15	1	4	44	27	17	46	P
3	Charlton Athletic	20	13	2	5	49	21	28	41	
4.	Durham	20	11	6	3	37	16	21	39	
5.	Sheffield United	20	11	1	8	35	31	4	34	
6.	Aston Villa	20	6	8	6	30	39	-9	26	
7.	Leicester City Women	20	6	3	11	27	44	-17	21	
8.	London Bees	20	7	0	13	23	48	-25	21	
9.	Lewes	20	5	2	13	23	47	-24	17	
10.	Crystal Palace	20	3	2	15	14	44	-30	11	
11.	Millwall Lionesses	20	1	2	17	14	70	-56	5	

Champions Manchester United and runners-up Tottenham Hotspur promoted by virtue of finishing in top two positions and satisfying Tier 1 licence criteria

WNL NORTHERN PREMIER (TIER 3)

Pos	Team	P	W	D	L	F	A	GD	Pts
1.	Blackburn Rovers	24	23	0	1	115	18	97	69
2.	Sunderland	24	15	3	6	83	36	47	48
3.	Derby County	24	15	3	6	54	35	19	48
4.	Huddersfield Town	24	15	2	7	79	40	39	47
5.	Middlesbrough	24	13	4	7	60	41	19	43
6.	Fylde	24	13	3	8	48	33	15	42
7.	Stoke City	24	9	6	9	59	51	8	33
8.	Guiseley Vixens	24	9	4	11	45	48	-3	31
9.	Nottingham Forest	24	7	4	13	29	57	-28	25
10.	Hull City	24	7	2	15	41	65	-24	23
11.	Sheffield FC	24	6	3	15	37	55	-18	21
12.	Doncaster R Belles	24	4	6	14	32	75	-43	18
13.	Bradford City	24	0	0	24	12	140	-128	0

WNL SOUTHERN PREMIER (TIER 3)

Pos	Team	P	W	D	L	F	A	GD	Pts
1.	Coventry United	22	18	3	1	80	14	66	57
2.	Cardiff C. Ladies	22	16	2	4	58	26	32	50
3.	Chichester City	22	15	1	6	48	27	21	46
4.	Oxford United	22	13	2	7	56	24	32	41
5.	Watford	22	13	1	8	43	40	3	40
6.	Plymouth Argyle	22	11	2	9	50	54	-4	35
7.	Loughborough F.	22	10	4	8	48	32	16	34
8.	Portsmouth	22	9	1	12	41	38	3	28
9.	Gillingham	22	5	4	13	24	54	-30	19
10.	MK Dons	22	5	1	15	24	52	-28	16
11.	QPR	22	2	5	15	28	69	-41	11
12.	C&K Basildon	22	0	2	19	17	87	-70	2

WNL DIVISION 1 MIDLANDS (TIER 4)

Pos	Team	P	W	D	L	F	A	GD	Pts
1.	West Brom. Albion	20	19	0	1	97	15	82	57
2.	Wolverhampton W.	20	17	0	3	98	14	84	51
3.	Birmingham & WM	20	13	2	5	68	26	42	41
4.	Sporting Khalsa	20	11	3	6	49	40	9	36
5.	Bedworth United	20	11	1	8	46	46	0	34
6.	Long Eaton United	20	9	2	9	48	41	7	29
7.	Nettleham	20	9	1	10	38	43	-5	28

8.	The New Saints	20	8	1	11	57	49	8	25
9.	Burton Albion	20	4	3	13	30	71	-41	15
10.	Solihull Moors	20	2	0	18	18	88	-70	6
11.	Steel City W.	20	0	1	19	11	127	-116	1

WNL DIVISION 1 NORTH (TIER 4)

Pos	Team	P	W	D	L	F	A	GD	Pts
1.	Burnley	22	18	2	2	39	14	25	56
2.	Brighouse Town	22	12	7	3	44	20	24	43
3.	Chester-le-Street T.	22	13	3	6	40	27	13	42
4.	Barnsley	22	12	5	5	52	34	18	41
5.	Liverpool Feds	22	10	5	7	57	39	18	35
6.	Leeds United	22	10	4	8	34	28	6	34
7.	Chorley	22	8	4	10	33	35	-2	28
8.	Bolton Wanderers	22	7	5	10	24	27	-3	26
9.	Newcastle United	22	7	4	11	28	31	-3	25
10.	Norton & S. A.	22	7	2	13	51	57	-6	23
11.	Morecambe	22	3	5	14	35	69	-34	14
12.	Crewe Alexandra	22	1	2	19	15	71	-56	5

WNL DIVISION 1 SOUTH EAST (TIER 4)

Pos	Team	P	W	D	L	F	A	GD	Pts
1.	Crawley Wasps	22	19	2	1	88	11	77	59
2.	Billericay Town	22	15	3	4	54	29	25	48
3.	Enfield Town	22	10	5	7	41	29	12	35
4.	Actonians	22	10	3	9	58	53	5	33
5.	Leyton Orient	22	9	5	8	39	37	2	32
6.	AFC Wimbledon	22	9	5	8	36	39	-3	32
7.	Ipswich Town	22	7	7	8	39	42	-3	28
8.	Cambridge United	22	7	6	9	32	35	-3	27
9.	Stevenage	22	8	3	11	29	50	-21	27
10.	Norwich City	22	6	3	13	34	54	-20	21
11.	Denham United	22	3	7	12	15	53	-38	16
12.	Luton Town	22	3	3	16	19	52	-33	12

WNL DIVISION 1 SOUTH WEST (TIER 4)

Pos	Team	P	W	D	L	F	A	GD	Pts
1.	Keynsham Town	20	17	2	1	115	15	100	53
2.	Southampton W.	20	15	1	4	68	16	52	46
3.	Buckland Athletic	20	13	3	4	62	36	26	42
4.	Cheltenham Town	20	12	5	3	54	26	28	41
5.	Chesham United	20	11	2	7	57	38	19	35
6.	Larkhall Athletic	20	7	6	7	38	43	-5	27
7.	Brislington	20	6	4	10	39	62	-23	22
8.	Southampton Saints	20	6	0	14	23	53	-30	18
9.	Swindon Town	20	4	3	13	18	52	-34	15
10.	Maidenhead United	20	2	2	16	14	71	-57	8
11.	Poole Town	20	2	2	16	21	97	-76	8

EASTERN REGIONAL PREMIER LEAGUE (TIER 5)

Pos	Team	P	W	D	L	F	A	GD	Pts
1.	Cambridge City	22	21	1	0	94	18	76	64
2.	Acle United	22	15	2	5	65	28	37	47
3.	Royston Town	22	14	2	6	72	41	31	44
4.	Wymondham Town	22	13	4	5	66	30	36	43
5.	Peterborough N S	22	13	2	7	55	32	23	41
6.	Harlow Town	22	10	5	7	70	41	29	35
7.	Bedford	22	9	4	9	60	45	15	31
8.	Colney Heath	22	9	3	10	43	39	4	30
9.	Brentwood Town	21	9	0	13	46	44	2	27
10.	Haringey B	22	3	1	18	30	103	-73	10
11.	AFC Dunstable	22	1	3	18	18	85	-67	6
12.	AFC Sudbury	22	1	1	20	16	129	-113	4

EAST MIDLANDS REGIONAL PREMIER LEAGUE (TIER 5)

Pos	Team	P	W	D	L	F	A	GD	Pts	
1.	Leicester C W Dev	20	16	2	2	88	32	56	50	
2.	Peterborough Utd	20	15	3	2	77	29	48	48	
3.	Oughtibridge W M	20	15	2	3	68	25	43	47	
4.	Woodlands	20	10	4	6	65	50	15	34	
5.	Ollerton Town	20	9	4	7	43	38	5	31	
6.	Rise Park	20	7	3	10	32	40	-8	24	
7.	Loughborough S.	20	9	2	9	66	58	8	23	*
8.	Mansfield Town	20	7	1	12	31	49	-18	22	

9.	Kettering Town	20	5	3	12	40	52	-12	18	
10.	Leicester C Ladies	20	1	4	15	17	91	-74	7	
11.	Eastwood Comm.	20	1	2	17	24	87	-63	2	+

*Loughborough Students docked 3 points for failing to fulfil a fixture and 3 points for fielding an ineligible player.

+Eastwood Community docked 3 points for failing to fulfil a fixture.

LONDON & SOUTH EAST REGIONAL PREMIER LEAGUE (TIER 5)

Pos	Team	P	W	D	L	F	A	GD	Pts
1.	Kent Football Utd	16	12	2	2	57	19	38	38
2.	AFC Phoenix	16	11	2	3	58	23	35	35
3.	London Kent F Utd	16	9	2	5	38	25	13	29
4.	QPR Girls Dev.	16	9	0	7	37	33	4	27
5.	Whyteleafe	16	8	2	6	25	27	-2	26
6.	Eastbourne Town	16	7	1	8	23	23	0	22
7.	Fulham FC Found.	16	3	4	9	23	41	-18	13
8.	Aylesford	16	3	2	11	15	50	-35	11
9.	Parkwood Rangers	16	2	1	13	14	49	-35	7

NORTH EAST REGIONAL PREMIER LEAGUE (TIER 5)

Pos	Team	P	W	D	L	F	A	GD	Pts
1.	Durham Cestria	18	18	0	0	103	10	93	54
2.	Hartlepool United	18	14	1	3	82	34	48	43
3.	South Shields	18	12	1	5	59	31	28	37
4.	Harrogate Town	18	10	0	8	45	35	10	30
5.	Ryton & C A T	18	8	3	7	44	53	-9	27
6.	Farsley Celtic	18	8	1	9	34	36	-2	25
7.	York City	18	6	1	11	37	64	-27	19
8.	Wallsend B C	18	4	2	12	34	67	-33	14
9.	Rotherham Utd	18	4	0	14	20	81	-61	12
10.	Castleford W R *	18	1	1	16	19	66	-47	1

*Castleford White Rose docked 3 points for failing to fulfil fixture v Wallsend B C (a) on 20.01.19

NORTH WEST REGIONAL PREMIER LEAGUE (TIER 5)

Pos	Team	P	W	D	L	F	A	GD	Pts
1.	Stockport County	20	18	1	1	79	26	53	55
2.	FC Utd of Manc.	20	17	2	1	90	20	70	53
3.	Tranmere Rovers	20	12	3	5	68	42	26	39
4.	Mossley Hill Ath.	20	10	5	5	61	31	30	35

5.	Fleetwood T Wrens	20	10	2	8	42	39	3	32
6.	Merseyrail	20	7	7	6	46	42	4	28
7.	Wigan Athletic	20	9	1	10	40	46	-6	28
8.	Manchester S.	20	4	2	14	29	51	-22	14
9.	Sir Tom Finney	20	3	5	12	40	78	-38	14
10.	Penrith AFC	20	3	1	16	21	74	-53	10
11.	Accrington	20	2	1	17	19	86	-67	7

SOUTHERN REGIONAL PREMIER LEAGUE (TIER 5)

Pos	Team	P	W	D	L	F	A	GD	Pts	
1.	Southampton FC	18	18	0	0	90	4	86	54	
2.	AFC Bournemouth	18	16	0	2	93	16	77	48	
3.	Oxford City	18	13	0	5	63	38	25	39	
4.	Woodley United	18	8	3	7	31	39	-8	27	
5.	Warsash Wasps	17	7	1	9	34	47	-13	22	
6.	Ascot United	18	5	6	7	26	41	-15	21	
7.	Winchester City F	18	5	1	12	26	45	-19	16	
8.	Newbury	18	4	1	13	16	71	-55	13	
9.	New Milton Town	18	3	2	13	18	59	-41	10	*
10.	Barton Rovers	17	2	2	13	13	50	-37	8	

*New Milton Town docked 1 point for failing to fulfil a fixture

SOUTH WEST REGIONAL PREMIER LEAGUE (TIER 5)

Pos	Team	P	W	D	L	F	A	GD	Pts
1.	Exeter City	20	17	1	2	110	23	87	52
2.	Keynsham T Dev.	20	15	1	4	67	28	39	46
3.	Callington Town	20	12	4	4	66	25	41	40
4.	Marine Academy P	20	12	3	5	72	33	39	39
5.	Bishops Lydeard	20	10	4	6	77	38	39	34
6.	Portishead	20	9	3	8	26	32	-6	30
7.	Middlezoy	20	9	2	9	41	39	2	29
8.	Ilminster Town	20	8	3	9	37	38	-1	27
9.	Torquay United	20	3	2	15	26	98	-72	11
10.	Forest Green R.	20	3	1	16	15	65	-50	10
11.	Downend Flyers	20	0	0	20	8	126	-118	0

WEST MIDLANDS REGIONAL PREMIER LEAGUE (TIER 5)

Pos	Team	P	W	D	L	F	A	GD	Pts
1.	Leafield Athletic	20	16	2	2	76	13	63	50
2.	Sutton Coldfield T.	20	14	3	3	57	13	44	45
3.	Crusaders	20	14	2	4	70	31	39	44

4.	Coundon Court	20	14	1	5	56	34	22	43
5.	Redditch United	20	11	4	5	52	33	19	37
6.	Goldenhill W.	20	8	5	7	53	39	14	29
7.	Stockingford AA P.	20	8	2	10	39	48	-9	26
8.	Coventry Sphinx	20	7	2	11	34	43	-9	23
9.	Worcester United	20	3	1	16	19	79	-60	10
10.	Lye Town	20	2	1	17	18	79	-61	7
11.	Knowle	20	0	3	17	21	83	-62	3

2018-19 TOP SCORERS
LEAGUE GOALS ONLY

WSL

	Player	Club	Goals
1.	Vivianne Miedema	Arsenal	22
2.	Nikita Parris	Manchester City	19
3.	Beth England	Chelsea	12
=4.	Fara Williams	Reading	11
=4.	Georgia Stanway	Manchester City	11
=4.	Danielle van de Donk	Arsenal	11
7.	Courtney Sweetman-Kirk	Liverpool	10
=8.	Jordan Nobbs	Arsenal	9
=8.	Fran Kirby	Chelsea	9
=10.	Kim Little	Arsenal	8
=10.	Erin Cuthbert	Chelsea	8

CHAMPIONSHIP

	Player	Club	Goals
1.	Jess Sigsworth	Manchester United	17
=2.	Rianna Dean	Tottenham Hotspur	14
=2.	Elizabeta Ejupi	Charlton Athletic	14
=2.	Lauren James	Manchester United	14
=2.	Ella Toone	Manchester United	14
6.	Mollie Green	Manchester United	13
7.	Kit Graham	Charlton Athletic	12
8.	Katie Zelem	Manchester United	10
=9.	Jodie Hutton	Aston Villa	8
=9.	Jade Pennock	Sheffield United	8

WNL NORTHERN PREMIER

	Player	Club	Goals
1.	Saffron Jordan	Blackburn Rovers	32*
2.	Natasha Flint	Blackburn Rovers/Sunderland	30*
3.	Keira Ramshaw	Sunderland	24
=4.	Bridget Galloway	Sunderland	17
=4.	Kate Mallin	Huddersfield Town	17

*Totals do not include 1gl each scored in WNL Play-off final

WNL SOUTHERN PREMIER

	Player	Club	Goals
=1.	Emily Allen	Oxford United	16
=1.	Amy Wathan	Coventry United	16
3.	Kylie Nolan	Cardiff City Ladies	15
=4.	Molly Clark	Chichester City	14
=4.	Amber Hughes	Coventry United	14
5.	Helen Ward	Watford	13

WNL NORTH 1

	Player	Club	Goals
1.	Bianca Owens	Norton & Stockton Ancients	21
2.	Charlotte Proud	Brighouse Town	19
3.	Nichole Havery	Chester-le-Street Town	17
4.	Jessica Tait	Morecambe	14
5.	Sarah Greenhalgh	Burnley	13

WNL MIDLANDS 1

	Player	Club	Goals
1.	Jade Cross	Wolverhampton Wanderers	29
2.	Jade Arber	Long Eaton United	20
3.	Keeley Davies	West Bromwich Albion	16
4.	Natalie Murray	West Bromwich Albion	15
=5.	Evangeline Gallop	Birmingham & West Midlands	12
=5.	Emily Ridge	The New Saints	12
=5.	Stephanie Weston	Birmingham & West Midlands	12

WNL SOUTH EAST 1

	Player	Club	Goals
1.	Alessandra Barreca	Actonians	24
2.	Zoe Rushen	Billericay Town	16
=3.	Naomi Cole	Crawley Town	13
=3.	Molly Peters	Enfield Town	13

=5.	Megan Stow	Crawley Wasps	12
=5.	Kemina Webber	Crawley Wasps	12
=5.	Carla Williams	Actonians	12

WNL SOUTH WEST 1

	Player	Club	Goals
1.	Kerry Bartlett	Keynsham Town	40
2.	Gemma Fraser	Chesham United	28
3.	Sarah Louise Stacey	Buckland Athletic	21
4.	Annie Martin	Cheltenham Town	19
=5.	Justine Lorton	Keynsham Town	16
=5.	Laura Williams	Keynsham Town	16

AWARDS 2018-19

Award	Winner	Awarded
FIFA Best Player 2018	Marta (Orlando Pride)	Sep 2018
Ballon d'Or 2018 (awarded by *France Football*)	Ada Hegerberg (Lyon)	Dec 2018
BBC Footballer of the Year 2019	Ada Hegerberg (Lyon)	May 2019
FA WSL Players' Player of the Year 2018-19	Sophie Baggaley (Bristol C)	May 2019
PFA Players' Player of the Year 2018-19	Vivianne Miedema (Arsenal)	Apr 2019
FWA Player of the Year 2018-19	Nikita Parris (Man C)	Apr 2019
PFA Fans' Player of the Year 2018-19	Sophie Baggaley (Bristol C)	Jun 2019
LMA WSL Manager of the Year 2018-19	Joe Montemurro (Arsenal)	May 2019
FA Championship Players' Player of the Year 2018-19	Kit Graham (Charlton)	May 2019
LMA Championship Manager of the Year 2018-19	Karen Hills (Tottenham)	May 2019
FA WNL Manager of the Year 2018-19	Gemma Donnelly (Blackburn)	May 2019
FA WNL Premier Player of the Year 2018-19	Keira Ramshaw (Sunderland)	May 2019
FA WNL Division 1 Player of the Year 2018-19	Leah Embley (Burnley)	May 2019
FA WSL Club of the Year 2018-19	Man City	May 2019
FA Championship Club of the Year 2018-19	Man Utd	May 2019
FA WNL Club of the Year 2018-19	Coventry Utd	May 2019
FA WSL Goal of the Year 2018-19	Beth Mead (Arsenal)	May 2019
FA WSL Save of the Year 2018-19	Megan Walsh (Yeovil)	May 2019
FA Unsung Hero of the Year 2018-19	Sue Henson Green & Steve Shipway	May 2019
Special Recognition Award 2018-19	Patricia Gregory & Peter Hough	May 2019
Best Football Development Initiative in Women's & Girls' Football 2018-19	Blackburn Rovers Community Trust	May 2019

PFA = Professional Footballers' Association LMA = League Managers' Association FWA = Football Writers' Association

FA PLAYER OF THE MONTH AWARDS 2018-19 & FA/LEAGUE MANAGERS' ASSOCIATION MANAGER OF THE MONTH AWARDS 2018-19:

	WSL Player	WSL Manager	Champ. Player	Champ. Manager
Sep	Sophie Baggaley (Bristol City)	Tanya Oxtoby (Bristol City)	Lauren James (Man Utd)	Karen Hills (Tottenham H)
Oct	Vivianne Miedema (Arsenal)	Joe Montemurro (Arsenal)	Rianna Dean (Tottenham H)	Lee Sanders (Durham)
Nov	Danielle van de Donk (Arsenal)	Kelly Chambers (Reading)	Mollie Green (Man Utd)	Casey Stoney (Man Utd)
Dec	Georgia Stanway (Man City)	Nick Cushing (Man City)	Beth Hepple (Durham)	Lee Sanders (Durham)
Jan	Erin Cuthbert (Chelsea)	Tanya Oxtoby (Bristol City)	Sarah Wiltshire (Tottenham H)	Karen Hills (Tottenham H)
Feb	Bethany England (Chelsea)	Hope Powell (Brighton)	Ella Toone (Man Utd)	Casey Stoney (Man Utd)
Mar	Beth Mead (Arsenal)	Joe Montemurro (Arsenal)	Katie Zelem (Man Utd)	Carla Ward (Sheff Utd)
Apr	Beth Mead (Arsenal)	Marta Tejedor (Birmingham)	Ashleigh Neville (Tottenham H)	Casey Stoney (Man Utd)

NB: In some instances the manager's trophy was awarded to the club's management team, but for reasons of space this table only names the head of that management team.

PFA BRISTOL STREET MOTORS FANS' PLAYER OF THE MONTH 2018-19

	WSL Player
Sep	Sophie Baggaley (Bristol City)
Oct	Jordan Nobbs (Arsenal)
Nov	Megan Walsh (Yeovil Town)
Dec	Julia Simic (West Ham United)
Jan	Sophie Baggaley (Bristol City)
Feb	Sophie Harris (Brighton & H A)
Mar	Megan Walsh (Yeovil Town)
Apr	Aoife Mannion (Birmingham City)

THE NEWS 2019-20

Fri 17 Aug: In the draw for the Champions League Round of 32, Manchester City are paired with Spanish champions Atletico Madrid. Chelsea will face SFK 2000 Sarajevo of Bosnia & Herzegovina. The English duo – who both reached the semi-finals last season – will both be at home in the second leg. French side Lyon – who have won the last three tournaments – begin the defence of their title away to Avaldsnes of Norway. Ties to be played 12-13 and 26-27 September. This season's final will be held in Budapest, marking a split from the recent tradition of playing in the same city as the men's Champions League final. The 2019 men's final will be taking place in Madrid.

Sat 18 Aug: The 2018-19 season gets under way with two matches in the group stages of the WSL Continental Cup. Both ties are all-Championship affairs with Sheffield United winning 2-1 at Aston Villa and Crystal Palace drawing 1-1 at home to Tottenham. The Eagles pick up a bonus point by winning the penalty shootout after 90 minutes.

Sun 19 Aug: As the Continental Cup group stages continue, today's headline result is a 1-0 victory for Manchester United away to Liverpool at Prenton Park. It's United's first competitive fixture since their reformation (they last played in 2005) and Scotland international Lizzie Arnot scores the historic winner with just seven minutes remaining.

Mon 20 Aug: Mo Marley's Young Lionesses team are beaten 2-0 by Japan in the Under-20 World Cup semi-finals in France.

Chelsea's Sweden international left-back Magdalena Eriksson, 24, signs a new contract that will keep her at the club until 2021.

Tue 21 Aug: England manager Phil Neville recalls captain Steph Houghton of Manchester City and Manchester United newcomer Alex Greenwood for the upcoming 2019 World Cup qualifiers. Uncapped Gabby George of Everton is also named in the 23-player squad. The Lionesses face group leaders Wales in Newport on 31 August and Kazakhstan away four days later in their final two matches. If Wales win, they will claim the only automatic qualifying position, but a draw for England would mean a point away to Kazakhstan will see them take top spot.

Fri 24 Aug: England take the bronze medal at the Under-20 World Cup with a 4-2 penalty shootout win over hosts France after the 3rd/4th place play-off finishes 1-1. Georgia Stanway puts the Young Lionesses ahead during the match before an Emelyne Laurent equaliser from the penalty spot. Goalkeeper Sandy McIver makes two saves in the shootout after England's Alessia Russo had seen her effort stopped. Japan beat Spain 3-1 in the final later in the day.

Sat 25 Aug: Championship side Manchester United play their first competitive home game since their reformation as they take on WSL outfit Reading at Leigh Sport Village in their second Continental Cup group match. The Red Devils are unable to follow up last week's 1-0 win at Liverpool as they go down 2-0 to the Royals. A competition record crowd of 4,835 is in attendance, a figure which also beats the 4,096 who watched Manchester City seal their first WSL title against Chelsea in 2016. Reading are top of the group having beaten Durham 4-1 last week.

Fri 31 Aug: Wales host England in a crucial World Cup qualifier at Rodney Parade, home of Newport County FC. A victory for Wales, in what is their final group match, will seal them a World Cup place for the very first time and consign England to the play-offs. A draw will mean England will highly likely take top spot, given that they also still have one more game to play away to Kazakhstan. After a nervy goalless first-half, England come to life to win 3-0 with goals from Toni Duggan, Jill Scott and Nikita Parris. Wales' hopes of qualifying for the play-offs are hanging by a thread as they will need a series of results to go their way if they are to finish as one of the four best group runners-up.

England look set to host the 2021 European Championship as it is revealed that theirs is the only bid to have been received prior to UEFA's deadline. Rumoured bids from Austria and from Hungary fail to materialise. UEFA will now scrutinise England's bid and vote on whether to accept it on 3 December. As well as Wembley other proposed venues are Brighton's Amex Stadium, Brentford's new Community Stadium, which is set to open in 2020, MK Dons' Stadium:mk, Manchester City's Academy Stadium, Notts County's Meadow Lane, Peterborough's Abax Stadium, Rotherham's New York Stadium and Sheffield United's Bramall Lane.

Mon 3 Sep: Ada Hegerberg (Norway) and Dzsenifer Marozsan (Germany) of Lyon join Brazil and Orlando Pride forward Marta on the three-player short list for the Best FIFA Women's Player 2018 award. The men's nominees are Mo Salah (Liverpool and Egypt), Cristiano Ronaldo (Juventus and Portugal) and Luka Modric (Real Madrid and Croatia). The nominees were decided by a panel of FIFA legends and experts who drew up 10-player shortlists before a jury consisting of national team captains, coaches, journalists and fans choose the winner with each group accounting for 25% of the vote. The winners will be announced at London's Royal Festival Hall on 24 September. The Women's Coach of the Year shortlist consists of Reynald Pedros (Lyon), Asako Takakura (Japan) and Sarina Wiegman (Netherlands).

England manager Phil Neville names his starting line-up for Wednesday's World Cup qualifier away to Kazakhstan. With the Lionesses already safely through to France 2019 he will give full debuts to seven players: Gabby George (Everton); Lucy Staniforth (Birmingham City); Lauren Bruton (Reading); Mary Earps (Vfl Wolfsburg); Hannah Blundell (Chelsea); Leah Williamson (Arsenal) and Beth Mead (Arsenal). Also, in the team are Abbie McManus (Manchester City), Izzy Christiansen (Lyon), Rachel Daly (Houston Dash) and Keira Walsh (Manchester City).

Tue 4 Sep: Scotland qualify for the World Cup for the first time in the history. A 2-1 win in Albania is enough to clinch the only automatic qualifying spot because Switzerland – who led the group at kick-off – can only draw 0-0 away to Poland.

Wales' slim chances of sneaking into the play-offs as one of the four best group runners-up are extinguished. The Welsh – who weren't playing today – needed Belgium and Iceland both to lose, but Belgium beat Italy 2-1 and Iceland drew 1-1 with the Czech Republic.

An England side boasting seven full debutants win 6-0 in Kazakhstan. Phil Neville's side clinched qualification on Friday but end their campaign in style with two goals from full debutant Beth Mead (including one from the spot) and efforts from Rachel Daly, Izzy Christiansen, Mead's fellow debutant Lucy Staniforth, and Lucy Bronze. Mead also misses a penalty when England are 4-0 up as her strike cannons back off a post.

With the European qualifying campaign now over, joining England and Scotland in France will be Italy, Spain, Norway and Sweden. Norway consigned Euro 2017 winners Netherlands to the play-offs with a shock 2-1 win in Oslo, while Sweden did likewise to Euro 2017 runners-up Denmark with a 1-0 win. Belgium and Switzerland complete the four-team line-up for the play-offs.

Earlier in the day it's also confirmed that England will meet Brazil and Australia in October friendlies with the games taking place at Meadow Lane (6 October) and Craven Cottage (9 October) respectively.

Sat 8 Sep: The first game of the new FA Women's Championship takes place with Durham winning 2-0 away to Tier 2 newcomers Sheffield United at Stocksbridge Park Steels. Rebecca Salicki scores the division's first ever goal, a 57th-minute header before Emily Roberts wraps up the points in injury-time.

Sun 9 Sep: The new fully professional FA Women's Super League era begins. The lunch-time kick-off between Arsenal and Liverpool is the division's first ever game. Vivianne Miedema scores the division's first ever goal in the 6th minute as Arsenal romp into a 4-0 lead before eventually closing out a 5-0 victory. Miedema herself notches a hat-trick. Later in the day champions Chelsea draw 0-0 at home to last season's runners-up Manchester City. Charlie Wellings strikes after just 42 seconds for Birmingham City who beat Everton 1-0, Bristol City are 1-0 winners at top-flight newcomers Brighton & Hove Albion and Reading are 4-0 winners at home to Yeovil.

The headline score line of the day comes in the Championship though where Manchester United win 12-0 at Aston Villa raising questions about whether it was right to put a fully professional team into a part-time division. Lauren James notches United's first ever Championship goal after 10 minutes while Jessica Sigsworth goes on to score five. Divisional newcomers Lewes win 3-0 at Millwall Lionesses. Two promoted sides meet at Hayes Lane where hosts Crystal Palace are beaten 2-0 by Leicester City Women. Tottenham Hotspur come from behind at home to beat London Bees 2-1 in a North London derby.

In the WNL Northern Premier a club record attendance of 2,109 watches Derby's East Midlands derby against Nottingham Forest which is held at Pride Park, the home of Derby County men.

Wed 12 Sep: Chelsea begin their Champions League campaign with a comfortable 5-0 win away to SFK 2000 Sarajevo who have been champions of the Bosnian League for the last 17 years. Millie Bright sets the Blues on their way after six minutes with further goals from Drew Spence, Maria Thorisdottir, Ji So-yun and Adelina Engman. The goals from summer signings Thorisdottir and Engman are their first for the club. The only blot on their copy book is a missed penalty from Fran Kirby whose effort is saved by Envera Hasanbegovic when her side are already 3-0 up.

Thu 13 Sep: Manchester City are held to a 1-1 draw away to Atletico Madrid in the first leg of their Champions League Round of 32 tie. City go ahead through summer signing Gemma Bonner's first goal for the club but are denied the win by a deflected equaliser three minutes from time.

Fri 14 Sep: Neil Redfearn resigns as Liverpool manager after just 93 days and two matches in the job. Redfearn arrived in the summer following the departure of Scott Rogers at the end of last season. He was faced with the task of rebuilding the squad after a mass exodus of players. Liverpool began the season with a 1-0 defeat to Manchester United in the Continental Cup before their opening WSL match ended in a 5-0 drubbing at Arsenal. There are suggestions that Redfearn was not convinced Liverpool FC were fully committed to the women's team. Goalkeeping coach Chris Kirkland and development squad manager Vicky Jepson will take over as joint managers on a caretaker basis.

Tue 18 Sep: The husband of Manchester City captain Steph Houghton is forced to retire from professional football after being diagnosed with motor neurone disease. Stephen Darby, a 29-year-old Bolton Wanderers full-back, last played in December.

Mon 24 Sep: *France Football* magazine announces that a Ballon D'Or for the female Player of the Year will be awarded for the first time at the end of 2018. Stanley Matthews was the first male winner of the award which has been handed out every year since 1956. A list of 15 nominees (compared to 30 men) will be released in October with the award ceremony taking place in Paris on 3 December.

Tue 25 Sep: Reading's Fara Williams is recalled to the England squad for next month's friendlies against Brazil and Australia. With 168 Lionesses appearances to her name, the 34-year-old is her country's most-capped player but missed England's final two World Cup qualifiers. Manchester United's Alex Greenwood is the only player from outside the top-flight to be included in Phil Neville's 24-strong squad.

Wed 26 Sep: There's huge disappointment for Manchester City as they crash out of the Champions League at the first hurdle. After a 1-1 draw in Spain in the Round of 32 first leg, City go down 2-0 at home to Atletico Madrid to bow out 3-1 on aggregate. City had been semi-finalists in the last two seasons. Their exit leaves Chelsea as England's sole representatives. They follow up their 5-0 first leg win over SFK 2000 Sarajevo of Bosnia & Herzegovina with a 6-0 win at Kingsmeadow to prevail 11-0 on aggregate. Fran Kirby scores twice but – just as in the first leg – has a penalty saved by Envera Hasanbegovic. Her last-minute spot-kick is followed up by Erin Cuthbert who scores the rebound. The Blues' other goals come from Drew Spence, Maren Mjelde and Hannah Blundell.

Fri 28 Sep: England climb to third in the latest FIFA World rankings, overtaking France in the process. USA and Germany are the only teams placed above the Lionesses.

Sun 30 Sep: Manchester City's Abbie McManus scores a bizarre 50-yard-own goal as she attempts a long-range back-pass which bounces over goalkeeper Ellie Roebuck to put her side 1-0 down to Birmingham City after just eight minutes of their WSL match. Things get worse for Nick Cushing's side just after half-time when Meghan Sargeant doubles Birmingham's lead, but Manchester City rally to win 3-2 and end Birmingham's 100% record in the League so far this season.

Mon 1 Oct: Chelsea are drawn against Italian side Fiorentina in the Champions League Round of 16. England's only remaining European representatives are at home in the first leg with matches to be played 17/18 October and 31 October/1 November. The only other British team in the competition – Glasgow City – will face Barcelona, who have England's Toni Duggan in their side, with the first leg in Spain. Defending champions Lyon – who have won the title on the last three occasions – will take on Dutch champions Ajax. The French side have England's Lucy Bronze and Izzy Christiansen as well as Wales' Jess Fishlock among their squad.

Tue 2 Oct: The Football Associations of England, Northern Ireland, Scotland and Wales agree to allow a women's Great Britain team to compete at the Tokyo 2020 Olympics. FIFA confirms it has received written confirmation from the home associations. England have been nominated as the "qualification team". Should the Lionesses finish as one of the three best European teams at the 2019 World Cup, their qualification place will be handed to Team GB. It throws open the prospect of Scotland knocking England out of the World Cup, and therefore denying Great Britain an Olympic spot. Great Britain men's and women's teams competed as a 'one-off' at London 2012, but the Northern Irish, Scottish and Welsh FAs were opposed to plans to allow a Team GB women's team to compete in Rio in 2016. FIFA confirms there will not be a British men's team at the Olympics.

Sat 6 Oct: England meet Brazil for the very first time. The Lionesses win the friendly, which takes place at Meadow Lane – home of Notts County FC – 1-0 courtesy of Fran Kirby's 2nd-minute header. Fara Williams comes off the bench in the second half to extend her record number of England appearances to 169.

Sun 7 Oct: Sixth tier Kidderminster Harriers cause a shock in the 3rd Qualifying Round of the FA Cup as they come from 1-0 down to beat Tier 4 Solihull Moors 2-1. Kirsty Roberts and Amber Lawrence score the goals at Aggborough to take them into the 1st Round proper for the first time since the club reformed.

Mon 8 Oct: England internationals Lucy Bronze (Lyon) and Fran Kirby (Chelsea) are included on *France Football's* 15-player shortlist for their inaugural women's Ballon D'Or. The winner will be announced in December.

Bristol City's Tanya Oxtoby is the first ever winner of the League Managers' Association's WSL Manager of the Month award. She guided the Vixens through an unbeaten September. Tottenham's Karen Hills is the first winner of the LMA's Championship Manager of the Month award. The Player of the Month accolades go to Bristol City keeper Sophie Baggaley in the WSL and Manchester United midfielder Lauren James in the Championship.

Tue 9 Oct: England draw 1-1 with Australia in a friendly at Fulham's Craven Cottage. Fran Kirby scores her second goal in four days to put the Lionesses ahead in the 21st minute but Clare Polkinghorne heads in the equaliser from a corner with six minutes remaining. French referee Florence Guillemin comes in for scathing criticism after England have a Lucy Staniforth goal wrongfully disallowed for offside and two strong penalty appeals waved away. England also claim a Beth Mead effort crossed the line. As is the norm in men's and women's international friendlies, goal-line technology is not in operation. The performance of the officials sparks renewed calls for the video assistant referee (VAR) system to be used at next summer's World Cup. It was implemented at the men's 2018 World Cup in Russia, but FIFA is yet to confirm its use at France 2019. Fara Williams comes off the bench to extend her record number of England caps to 170.

FIFA launches its first global strategy which includes plans to double female participation to 60 million players by 2026. Other proposals include a women's Club World Cup – to mirror the men's tournament which was first held in 2000 – and the introduction of a FIFA Women's World League (of which there is no men's equivalent).

Sun 14 Oct: There's a huge shock in the WSL as Arsenal continue their 100% start to the season with a 5-0 win away to reigning champions Chelsea. It's the Blues' first League defeat since May 2017 and their first at home since July 2016.

Mon 15 Oct: UEFA says it will increase funding in women's football by 50% from 2020 in an attempt to make it Europe's biggest female sport. An extra 2.75m euros (£2.4m) will be made available with the money coming from the men's European Championship.

Bristol City goalkeeper Sophie Baggaley wins the first ever PFA Women's Player of the Month Award for her performances in September beating Birmingham City's Aoife Mannion in to second place. The award is voted for by fans.

Tue 16 Oct: It's revealed that Arsenal and Scotland striker Kim Little will be out for up to 10 weeks after fracturing her fibula in Sunday's 5-0 win at Chelsea. Little – who opened the scoring from the spot – was hurt in a tackle by Drew Spence who is cautioned. Media pundits suggest Spence should also have been booked for another tough challenge earlier in the match.

WSL club Yeovil Town announce that Gary Dawkins – who is managing director of the company that sponsors the club – will replace Steve Allinson as chairman with immediate effect. Allinson has been in the post since 2014.

Wed 17 Oct: Arsenal manager Joe Montemurro signs a new long-term contract. The Australian arrived in November 2017 and led the Gunners to the 2017-18 Continental Cup final where they beat Manchester City. His team currently sit top of the WSL having won 5-0 away to defending champions Chelsea at the weekend, a result which took his tally of wins to 21 from the 27 matches under his management so far.

Jamaica become the first Caribbean team ever to qualify for the FIFA Women's World Cup as they beat Panama on penalties in the CONCACAF Women's Championship third place match.

Thu 18 Oct: The FA calls on the police to tackle online abuse after vile posts aimed at Karen Carney on social media platform Instagram. The threats were made during last night's Champions League Round of 16 match in which Carney's penalty saw Chelsea win 1-0 at home to Fiorentina. England boss Phil Neville describes the message as "absolutely disgraceful".

Fri 19 Oct: Chelsea and the FA report the social media users who made threats to Karen Carney and teammates to the police.

Mon 21 Oct: Liverpool confirm that Prenton Park – home of Tranmere Rovers FC – will be their permanent home for the next three seasons. The Reds have played all three of their home matches so far in 2018-19 at the venue. Their main home venue prior to 2018-19 had been the Halton Stadium (most recently sponsored by Select Security) in Widnes.

Tue 23 Oct: The FA confirms England will play a friendly away to Austria on Thursday 8 November, three days before their home friendly against Sweden in Rotherham which was announced way back in September.

Fri 26 Oct: Vicky Jepson is named as Liverpool's new manager. Jepson and Chris Kirkland have been serving as joint caretaker managers since Neil Redfearn resigned on 14 September. Kirkland will continue as her assistant. Jepson has been with the Reds since 2009 and was development squad manager prior to Redfearn's departure.

FIFA announces that the prize fund for the 2019 World Cup will be $30m (£23.4m), double what was on offer for the 2015 tournament. The winners will take home $4m (£3.1m), twice the amount the USA banked when beating Japan in the most recent final. FIFA will also allocate $20m (£15.6m) for travel, training and to compensate players' club teams. Players' union Fifpro says the increase is insufficient with other critics pointing out that teams that exited the group stage of the men's 2018 World Cup in Russia collected double the amount that is on offer for the 2019 women's champions.

Sun 28 Oct: Leicester City Women's Championship match at home to Manchester United at Farley Way is postponed in the wake of last night's helicopter crash outside Leicester City FC's King Power Stadium. The helicopter, owned by the club's Thai owner Vichai Srivaddhanaprabha, crashed immediately after taking off from the pitch following City's 1-1 Premier League draw against West Ham United. While there has been no confirmation of who was on board, a source close to the family has told the BBC that Srivaddhanaprabha was among the passengers.

Tue 30 Oct: Former USA Under-23 international Chioma Ubogagu is a surprise inclusion in Phil Neville's squad for the upcoming friendlies away to Austria and at home to Sweden. The 26-year-old forward was born in England but moved to Texas as a youngster. She started her professional career in 2015 at Arsenal but now plays for Brisbane Roar in Australia where she is on loan from American side Orlando Pride. Also included for the first time are Manchester City forward Georgia Stanway and her club-mate, goalkeeper Ellie Roebuck. Missing through injury are goalkeeper Karen Bardsley, forward Melissa Lawley and midfielder Fara Williams.

Wed 31 Oct: The FA backs calls for Emma Clarke, England's first black female player, to be honoured. Women in Football co-founder Anna Kessel has called for a blue plaque to be placed on Clarke's childhood home in Bootle, Merseyside where she was born in 1875. She went on to play for the British Ladies team in 1895 at stadiums including St James' Park and Portman Road.

Chelsea reach the quarter-finals of the Champions League with a comprehensive 6-0 win away to Italian side Fiorentina to complete a 7-0 aggregate win. Fran Kirby scores her first hat-trick in the competition.

Sun 4 Nov: Nikita Parris scores twice in Manchester City's 3-0 win at home to Liverpool. Her second goal – an 84th minute penalty – takes her above former Chelsea player Eni Aluko onto 37 WSL goals (in 93 apps) to make her the competition's all-time leading goal scorer. Elsewhere leaders Arsenal win 3-1 at home to Birmingham to continue their 100% start to the season. Their seventh consecutive League win equals the best ever start to a WSL season.

History is also made in the south west as Yeovil win a top-flight WSL game for the very first time. Hannah Short scores the only goal after 21 minutes as they win at home to Everton. The victory also sees them climb off the bottom of the table and above their opponents. It's their first competitive win since 2016, ending a run of 41 matches without a victory.

Wed 7 Nov: Everton sack manager Andy Spence. His second spell in charge of the club ends just three days after a defeat to Yeovil Town that has left the club bottom of the WSL table. Goalkeeping coach Jennifer Herst is placed in temporary charge.

England manager Phil Neville confirms captain Steph Houghton will not play in Thursday's friendly against Austria so that she can be awarded her 100th cap in front of a home crowd against Sweden on Sunday. Neville insists Houghton wanted to play in Austria and jokes that he has effectively "banned" her from doing so.

Thu 8 Nov: England's friendly away to Austria ends in a 3-0 win. Chioma Ubogagu and Georgia Stanway both score on their debut while Rachel Daly adds a later third. With Steph Houghton rested, Toni Duggan captains her country for the first time. Goalkeeper Ellie Roebuck makes her debut when she replaces Mary Earps with 11 minutes remaining and helps preserve the clean sheet.

Argentina win 4-0 at home to Panama in the first leg of the South American play-off final for the continent's last qualifying berth for next summer's World Cup.

Fri 9 Nov: Netherlands beat Sweden 3-0 in Utrecht in the first leg of the World Cup qualifying play-off. Sheride Spitse, Lieke Martens and Arsenal's Vivianne Miedema get the goals.

Sun 11 Nov: England lose at home for the first time since 2015 as they are beaten 2-0 by Sweden in a friendly at Rotherham United FC'S New York Stadium. The defeat – which is manager Phil Neville's second since he took charge in January – mars the occasion of captain Steph Houghton's 100th cap.

Mon 12 Nov: Joe Montemurro of Arsenal is named the LMA's WSL Manager of the Month for October. His side remain unbeaten at the top of the WSL. Durham's management team of Lee Sanders (general manager), Chris Moore (head coach) and Steph Libbey (assistant head coach) win the Championship award.

Tue 13 Nov: Jonathan Donoghue leaves his position as manager of Championship side Lewes. Donoghue replaced Jacquie Agnew in 2014 and led the team through four seasons in the WPL South (Tier 3) before the club was awarded a Tier 2 licence for 2018-19.

The FA suspends referee David McNamara for "not acting in the best interests of the game". McNamara left his coin in the dressing-room prior to kick-off in the televised WSL match between Manchester City and Reading on Friday 26 October. Instead of returning to get it he improvised by asking captains Steph Houghton and Kirsty Pearce to play rock, paper scissors. The match finished 1-1. McNamara's ban will begin on 26 November.

Netherlands secure the final European qualifying place for next summer's World Cup as they draw 1-1 away to Sweden to complete a 4-1 aggregate win in the play-off. Argentina draw 1-1 in Panama to take the last South American qualifying place with a 5-1 aggregate win.

Arsenal's Vivianne Miedema is named WSL Player of the Month for October with Tottenham's Rianna Dean taking the Championship award.

Thu 15 Nov: The FA rules that last Sunday's FA Cup 1st Round tie between Cambridge City and Cambridge United must be replayed. Fifth tier City caused a shock by winning 2-1, but the pitch at their Trinity Fields venue had been found to be too small. United insist they lodged a complaint with the match officials prior to kick-off.

Mon 19 Nov: Arsenal midfielder Jordan Nobbs' World Cup availability is in jeopardy after the extent of the injury she sustained in yesterday's 4-0 WSL win against Everton becomes clear. The England international, who has 56 caps for her country, ruptured her anterior cruciate ligament with her club saying she could be out for the rest of the domestic season.

Thu 22 Nov: Manchester United manager Casey Stoney joins Juan Mata's Common Goal movement. Manchester United men's player Mata set up the scheme, which entails an individual donating 1% of their annual income to charitable causes, last year. Casey is the first individual (male or female) at Manchester United to join Mata in the initiative although goalkeeper Siobhan Chamberlain signed up before becoming a United player. Over 60 players across the globe participate so far.

Fri 23 Nov: Danish newspaper Politiken publishes copies of the standard FA contracts handed to WSL players which controversially includes a clause that players can be sacked with three months' notice as soon as they are diagnosed with an injury which will keep them out for more than three months. The BBC is told no club has ever activated the clause. Male Premier League players can only be sacked if they are injured for 18 out of 20 months, and the club must give them six to 12 months' notice.

CNN reports that FC Basel's women's team were not invited to a gala to celebrate the club's 125th anniversary but were instead asked to sell tombola tickets while the male players at the Swiss club were served a three-course meal. A club spokesperson says the players agreed to work at the event because some of the money raised would go to the women's team.

Sat 24 Nov: England internationals Fran Kirby and Carly Telford are among thousands of players, fans and administrators to tweet messages of support to 18-year-old Kent Football United goalkeeper Jordan Dawes after the Tier 5 club reveals their player has suffered a stroke.

Sat 1 Dec: Willie Kirk leaves his position as assistant manager at Championship club Manchester United to take up the role of manager at WSL strugglers Everton. Former Bristol City boss Kirk replaces Andy Spence who was sacked by the Toffees on 7 November.

Sun 2 Dec: Arsenal's 100% start to the WSL season ends as they drop their first points on match day 10 in a 2-0 defeat away to Manchester City for whom Georgia Stanway scores twice. City stay 2nd in the table and cut the gap to Arsenal to three points. Elsewhere Willie Kirk – who took over as Everton manager yesterday – leads the Toffees to their first win of the season as they beat Liverpool 2-1 in the Merseyside derby to move off the bottom of the table.

Mon 3 Dec: Norway and Lyon forward Ada Hegerberg becomes the first ever female winner of the *Ballon D'Or*. Hegerberg won the Champions League for the third time this year. The Ballon D'Or, an award created by *France Football* magazine, has been awarded to a male player every year since 1956. It was initially for European players only before becoming an award for players at European clubs, and then a global prize in 2007. It was briefly merged with FIFA's Player of the Year award from 2010-15.

This is the first time it has been a women's award. The moment is sullied by a French DJ asking Hegerberg whether she "knows how to twerk" while she is presented with the award. Twerking is a sexually provocative dance move.

Croatia and Real Madrid midfielder Luka Modric wins the men's award in a year in which he secured a third consecutive Champions League title with his club and finished as a World Cup runner-up. It is the first time neither Cristiano Ronaldo (five wins) nor Lionel Messi (five wins) have won it since 2007.

England – the only nation to bid for the tournament – are confirmed as the hosts of the 2021 European Championship having met all of UEFA's strict criteria. The final will be held at Wembley. The eight other venues are confirmed as The Amex Stadium (Brighton & Hove Albion FC), Stadium:mk (Milton Keynes Dons FC), The Community Stadium (Brentford FC's new ground which is currently under construction), The Academy Stadium (Manchester City FC Women's ground), The City Ground (Nottingham Forest FC), New York Stadium (Rotherham United FC), Bramall Lane (Sheffield United FC) and St Mary's (Southampton FC).

BBC Scotland reports that the Scottish Football Association may block plans for a Great Britain women's team to compete at the 2020 Tokyo Olympics. FIFA had previously announced that all four home nation FA's had agreed to the proposals. It's understood that Scotland's concerns centre around the nomination of England as the team through which qualification can be achieved should they finish as one of the top three European teams at the 2019 World Cup. That situation is complicated by the fact that Scotland have also qualified for the World Cup and could potentially face England. The World Cup draw is this coming Saturday.

Referee David McNamara drops his appeal against a 21-day ban for using a game of rock, paper, scissors instead of a coin toss at the kick-off of this season's WSL game between Reading and Manchester City on 26 October.

Wed 5 Dec: Some one-sided matches in the Continental Cup group stage reopens the debate about whether the competition should revert to the once-tried straight knockout format, especially in the wake of news this morning that up to six Sheffield United players would be unavailable for the trip to play Manchester City because they would be unable to get out of work in time for the 7pm kick-off. City win the game 6-0 to qualify for the quarter-finals with a game to spare. Arsenal – who are 5-0 winners at home to Charlton – and Chelsea who win 7-0 at home to Yeovil also make it into the last eight with one group stage match remaining. Birmingham are also 6-0 winners away to Championship outfit Leicester City Women. The Merseyside derby between Liverpool and Everton is postponed due to a waterlogged pitch at Prenton Park.

Thu 6 Dec: Visa signs a seven-year deal with UEFA to become the first ever sole sponsors of women's football. The contract means the payments company will be the main partner for the UEFA Women's European Championship and Champions League.

Fixtures for next year's SheBelieves Cup are revealed with England to face Brazil, Japan and USA in the annual Stateside tournament on 27 February, 2 March and 5 March respectively.

Fri 7 Dec: The Scottish FA says it will not block proposals for a Great Britain women's team to compete at the Tokyo 2020 Olympics, but that it will not actively support or promote it. If England finish as one of the top three European teams at next year's World Cup, then Team GB will be able to field a team. The SFA is believed to have been uncomfortable with those plans, since Scotland are also competing at the World Cup.

Sat 8 Dec: The draw for the 2019 World Cup pits England in the same group as former champions Japan, as well as Argentina and first-time qualifiers Scotland. Holders USA will begin their title defence against Thailand with Chile and Sweden also in the group. The opening game will be between hosts France and South Korea, with Norway and Nigeria completing their quartet. The other groups are Germany; China; Spain; South Africa and: Canada; Cameroon; New Zealand; Netherlands.

Wed 12 Dec: Birmingham City get the point they need to assure qualification for the quarter-finals of the Continental Cup as they draw 0-0 at home to Bristol City. The visitors needed to win by at least four goals if they were to pip Birmingham to the final qualifying place in their group but have the consolation of taking a bonus point by winning the penalty shootout 3-1. Also qualifying from their respective groups are Brighton who win 4-1 at Yeovil and West Ham who are 2-0 victors at Charlton.

Thu 13 Dec: Manchester United win 3-0 at Everton to finish top of their group and qualify for the Continental Cup quarter-finals. United will be the only Championship side in the last eight.

Fri 14 Dec: Championship outfit Lewes name former Liverpool Feds Ladies boss Fran Alonso as their new manager. The 42-year-old Spaniard has previously had roles as technical director and assistant coach to Ronald Koeman at both Southampton and Everton men's clubs. Lewes have been without a manager since sacking Jonathan Donoghue in mid-November.

Tue 18 Dec: The draw for the Continental Cup quarter-finals takes place. Group winners are automatically drawn at home against group runners up. Holders Arsenal will host Birmingham City, last season's runners-up Manchester City welcome Brighton, Reading travel to Chelsea and Manchester United – the only Championship club still in the competition – host West Ham. Ties will take place 9/10 January. The FA also confirms Bramall Lane, home of Sheffield United FC, will stage the final on 23 February.

Scotland international defender Lisa Evans signs a new long-term contract with Arsenal. At the point of inking her new deal Evans has made 41 appearances for the Gunners since signing from Bayern Munich in June 2017.

Wed 19 Dec: Denmark international Nadim Najim leaves Manchester City as the club agree to terminate her contract. The 30-year-old signed last January but requested a transfer in July saying she had "never felt at home in Manchester or Man City". She will become a free agent on 1 January.

Thu 20 Dec: Dutch international striker Vivianne Miedema signs a new long-term contract with Arsenal. As is common the club do not reveal the length of the deal.

Thu 27 Dec: London Bees captain Emma Beckett announces she is leaving after three years with the club.

Fri 28 Dec: Birmingham keeper Ann-Katrin Berger turns down the offer of a new contract with the club who are currently 4th in the WSL. The Germany international has been with the Blues since 2016 with her current deal set to expire on New Year's Eve.

Mon 31 Dec: Beth Merrick parts company with Championship club Sheffield United by mutual consent.

Wed 2 Jan: Arsenal sign Denmark winger Katrine Veje from French side Montpellier. The 27-year-old has been capped more than 100 times by her country.

WNL Southern Premier (Tier 3) leaders Coventry United sign Beth Merrick following her departure from Championship outfit Sheffield United.

Thu 3 Jan: Chelsea midfielder Jade Bailey signs a new one-year deal with the club, but it's announced she will spend the rest of this season on loan at fellow WSL side Reading. Bailey, who won the FA Cup with Arsenal in 2014, can also play in defence.

Former England Under-19 international midfielder Maddy Cusack joins Sheffield United from fellow Championship side Leicester City Women. The 22-year-old has previously played for Nottingham Forest, Aston Villa and Birmingham City. The Blades also announce that Greek international Veatriki Sarri has signed a permanent deal after impressing in their development team.

Fri 4 Jan: Goalkeeper Ann-Katrin Berger signs for Chelsea a week after leaving Birmingham City. The 28-year-old's deal runs until 2022. Crystal Palace re-sign former striker Gemma Bryan from fellow Championship side Charlton. Bryan left Palace for Charlton in June having scored more than 100 goals in three seasons with the Eagles. She says she only made that switch because at that time Palace had been told they would not be granted a Championship licence.

Striker Ebony Salmon joins Sheffield United on loan from fellow Championship side Manchester United. Salmon captained England at last May's European Under-17 Championship.

Sat 5 Jan: Grace Neville signs for her former club Millwall Lionesses in the Championship.

Sun 6 Jan: The WSL, Championship, and WNL campaigns resume after the winter break. Scotland international striker Kim Little returns earlier than expected from her broken leg as she plays the entire 90 minutes of Arsenal's 4-2 win away to West Ham. The Gunners remain top of the table and open a two-point gap on Manchester City who are held to a 1-1 draw at Bristol City. Arsenal also have a game in hand.

In the FA Cup, Tier 4 Crawley – who are playing in the 3rd Round for the first time in their history – reach Round 4 with a 2-1 win over WNL Southern Premier leaders Coventry United. MK Dons also reach Round 4 for the first time as they win 1-0 away to Nottingham Forest.

Leicester-born striker Libby Smith, 17, signs for Leicester City Women from Chelsea's Development side. Smith came through Leicester City FC's Regional Talent Club before leaving for Chelsea where she has been playing in the FA WSL Academy League.

Mon 7 Jan: The FA confirms it is investigating claims from Tottenham defender Renee Hector that she was racially abused by an opponent during her team's 2-1 win away to Sheffield United in the Championship yesterday.

Crawley Wasps' reward for reaching the FA Cup 4th Round for the first time is a home tie against record 14-time winners Arsenal. Wasps are one of three Tier 4 teams left in the competition with the other two also drawn against top-flight sides: AFC Wimbledon will host Bristol City while Keynsham Town will travel to Reading. Other notable ties from the draw – which is made live on BBC Radio 1Xtra – include holders Chelsea away to Everton, Manchester City at home to Tier 3 Watford and Championship leaders Manchester United away to WSL Brighton.

Tue 8 Jan: Annie Zaidi – who is believed to be the only hijab-wearing UEFA B coach in Europe – is appointed as the new manager of WNL Midlands 1 (Tier 4) outfit Solihull Moors, where she was already involved in the coaching set-up. She replaces Ross Thorpe who resigned five days ago.

Wed 9 Jan: Reports suggest that Marc Skinner is to leave WSL side Birmingham City to become manager at NWSL outfit Orlando Pride in the US. With rumours swirling, Skinner leads his City side out against Arsenal at Meadow Park for this evening's Continental Cup quarter-final. Blues come within six minutes of knocking out the holders through Lucy Quinn's goal only for Danielle van de Donk and Vivianne Miedema to turn the game round and send the Gunners through 2-1. City's Aoife Mannion had earlier seen her 18th minute penalty saved by Sari van Veenendaal with the match still goalless. In the other two quarter-finals played tonight Chelsea win 4-0 at home to Reading while Championship leaders Manchester United topple WSL opposition for the third time in this season's competition as they win 2-0 at home to Manchester United.

Manchester City's Georgia Stanway is named WSL Player of the Month for December while Durham's Beth Hepple takes the Championship award.

WNL Southern Premier (Tier 3) side Loughborough Foxes release a statement confirming tragic news that club captain Molly Webb died suddenly on Sunday afternoon at the age of 25. The statement adds: "Molly was a talented footballer and a fantastic role model and leader who was always smiling. Molly has played a huge part in the club's development and success since joining as a 13-year-old and our club will not be the same without her."

Thu 10 Jan: Manchester City complete the line-up for the semi-finals of the Continental Cup as they win 7-1 at home to Brighton. Among the scorers is Nikita Parris who gets the first goal of the evening - her 50th for the club. A Danielle Buet penalty briefly has Brighton level, but City go on to rack up a comfortable win.

Fri 11 Jan: Following days of speculation Birmingham City confirm that manager Marc Skinner is to leave the club after this Sunday's match against Bristol City. It's believed Skinner is to be named as boss of NWSL side Orland Pride in the US. The 35-year-old has been Blues boss since December 2016 and led the club to the 2017 FA Cup final.

Championship side Crystal Palace sign goalkeeper Lucy Gillett, 25, on loan from WSL outfit Brighton for the rest of the season.

Sat 12 Jan: The draw for the semi-finals of the Continental Cup is made at half-time in the men's EFL Championship match between Sheffield United and QPR at Bramall Lane which will host the final on 23 February. WSL leaders and holders Arsenal are drawn at home to Championship leaders Manchester United while Chelsea will host Manchester City in the other semi with ties to be played 5/6 February.

WSL side West Ham sign Canada international striker Adriana Leon. Championship outfit Tottenham sign defensive midfielder Emma Beckett, 31, who left London Bees earlier this month.

Sun 13 Jan: The Championship match between Charlton Athletic and Manchester United is abandoned after just 11 minutes of play when the Addicks' Charlotte Kerr is injured in a collision during the move which sees Charlie Devlin put United ahead. As she receives lengthy medical attention the rest of the players are told to return to the dressing rooms and an ambulance is called. The decision to call the match off is taken about an hour after the incident occurs.

West Ham sign South Korea captain Cho So-hyun. The 30-year-old midfielder has been capped 120 times meaning she is her country's all-time leading appearance-maker.

Mon 14 Jan: As expected, USA club side Orlando Pride confirm Marc Skinner as their new manager. Skinner took charge of Birmingham City for the final time yesterday, with the match ending in a 1-0 defeat at home to Bristol City.

Tue 15 Jan: Arsenal striker Beth Mead withdraws from England's upcoming training camp in Qatar after sustaining a knee injury in Sunday's defeat to Chelsea. Manchester City's Mel Lawley takes her place in the squad.

Wed 16 Jan: The BBC reports that Sunday's Championship match between Charlton Athletic and Manchester United at The Oakwood had to be abandoned because the home side did not have oxygen with which to treat injured players. League rules say clubs must have an oxygen supply on site, but when their defender Charlotte Kerr was seriously injured Charlton had to rely on United's oxygen to treat her. The referee was forced to abandon the game because there would have been no more oxygen available to treat any other injured players. Kerr was taken to hospital with a rib injury but released the next day. The punishment for failing to comply with medical rules is a £500 fine.

Fri 18 Jan: Liverpool sign England Under-23 international Gemma Purfield. The 21-year-old, who has recently graduated from Arizona State University, can play as an attacking full-back or on the wing.

Mon 21 Jan: Former Peru women's manager Marta Tejedor is named as the new Birmingham City boss. The 50-year-old has previously coached female youth sides for Chile and Atletico Madrid.

Arsenal rule out the possibility of manager Joe Montemurro leaving to become manager of his national team Australia. Australia Women head coach Alen Stajcic was sacked on Saturday – just five months before the World Cup – because of an "unsatisfactory team environment".

Thu 24 Jan: On January transfer deadline day Denmark international defender Mie Jans, 24, leaves Manchester City for Swedish side Rosengard. Jans struggled for game time during an injury-hit 18-month spell at City. Three players leave Scottish side Hibernian for WSL clubs: Scotland striker Abi Harrison, 21, joins Bristol City; Scotland winger Rachel McLauchlan, 21, signs for Yeovil Town and 25-year-old full-back Emma Brownlie moves to Everton. Championship side Lewes sign defender Sophie Perry on loan from WSL outfit Brighton until the end of the season. Birmingham snap up Everton forward Claudia Walker, 22, on loan until the end of 2018-19. Defender Rebecca Thompson-Agbro leaves Lewes and is now unattached. Some more transfer window signings are likely to be announced over the coming days since not all are made public on deadline day.

Fri 25 Jan: WSL side Reading confirm they have signed Iceland international striker Rakel Honnudottir, 30, from Swedish side IF Limhamn Bunkeflo 07. Championship outfit Lewes sign New Zealand striker Katie Rood, 26, on loan from Bristol City for the rest of the season.

Sat 26 Jan: Birmingham City announce that they have signed goalkeeper Alex Brooks, 24, from Championship side Sheffield United. City have been looking for a replacement for Ann-Katrin Berger who departed for Chelsea earlier this month. Brooks – who was once on Manchester City's books and is a former England Under-18 captain – will compete with Hannah Hampton to be Blues No.1.

Brighton confirm they have signed Republic of Ireland international midfielder Megan Connolly, 21, on a contract which runs until the end of the season. Connolly has returned to Europe having spent the last three years playing for Florida State University where she has been studying sports management.

Tue 29 Jan: Charlton are found guilty of failing to have the necessary medical equipment on site when their Championship match with Manchester United on 13 January was abandoned. They are hit with a mandatory £500 fine by the FA which says that the match will be rescheduled. The game was called off after Addicks defender Charlotte Kerr was seriously injured during the incident with which United took an 11th-minute lead. The home side did not have their own oxygen at The Oakwood stadium and had to use United's. The match was abandoned around an hour after play was halted following lengthy treatment and a delay in an ambulance arriving. The referee determined there was insufficient oxygen left for the game to continue safely.

Sat 2 Feb: WSL leaders Manchester City win 3-0 at home to Watford in today's only scheduled FA Cup 4th Round tie – the stage at which the WSL and Championship clubs enter.

Sun 3 Feb: The cold snap leads to the postponement of eight of today's scheduled 15 FA Cup 4th Round ties. In the matches that do go ahead, Championship side Manchester United are victorious in what is their first match in the competition since reforming, as they chalk up a 2-0 victory away to WSL outfit Brighton. Crawley Wasps put up a valiant effort at home to 14-time winners Arsenal before going down 4-0 while Wasps' fellow Tier 4 side AFC Wimbledon do themselves proud in a 3-0 home defeat to Bristol City.

Tue 5 Feb: The FA announces England will tour the country with four friendly games in the run up to this summer's World Cup. The Lionesses will face Canada at Manchester City Women's Academy Stadium on Friday 5 April, Spain at Swindon Town men's County Ground on Tuesday 9 April, Denmark at Walsall men's Banks's Stadium on Saturday 25 May and New Zealand at Brighton men's Amex Stadium on Saturday 1 June.

Wed 6 Feb: Manchester City take their place in the Continental League Cup final with a 2-0 semi-final win over Chelsea at Kingsmeadow. Nikita Parris opens the scoring with a penalty early in the second half and adds a second goal late in the game.

Chelsea's Erin Cuthbert is named WSL Player of the Month with Tottenham's Sarah Wiltshire collecting the Championship award.

Thu 7 Feb: Arsenal beat Manchester United 2-1 in the second Continental Cup semi-final. Vivianne Miedema strikes twice for the hosts before Mollie Green pulls one back with nine minutes to play. For the second season in a row the final will be between the Gunners and Manchester City. This year the match will take place at Bramall Lane, home of Sheffield United men's, on 23 February.

The head of the Danish FA tells BBC Sport that Denmark are keen to bid to host the 2025 Women's European Championship. The Danes were runners-up to hosts the Netherlands at Euro 2017.

Sheffield United forward Sophie Jones is charged by the FA with allegedly making racist comments towards Tottenham defender Renee Hector in the Championship match between the clubs on 6 January. Immediately after the game Hector claimed on social media that she had been subjected to monkey noises.

Sun 10 Feb: With eight of last week's postponed FA Cup 4th Round ties taking place today, there are just two matches in the WSL. Leaders Manchester City let a 2-0 lead slip at home to defending champions Chelsea. The 2-2 draw leaves City two points clear of Arsenal but having played two games more. Chelsea remain six points adrift. Bristol City draw 0-0 with Brighton in the other top-flight game. In the FA Cup, Tier 3 Huddersfield Town pull off a shock at Championship side Charlton. The Terriers are 3-0 down with 16 minutes to play but then score three times in four minutes and go on to win on penalties.

Sat 16 Feb: London Bees announce that manager Luke Swindlehurst is standing down from the position to take up the role of Under-18s academy coach at Barnet FC. His assistant Rachel Yankey, who won 129 England caps as a player, will take over until the end of the season.

Sun 17 Feb: There's one shock in the FA Cup 5th Round as Championship side Durham beat top-flight opposition for the first time in their history. Lisa Robertson scores a second-half brace as the Wildcats win 2-0 at Bristol City. Holders Chelsea inflict a 3-0 defeat on last year's runners-up Arsenal, WSL leaders Manchester City are 3-0 victors at Championship leaders Tottenham and Casey Stoney's Manchester United beat London Bees 3-0 as Stoney's former England team-mate Rachel Yankey takes charge of the North London side for the first time.

Mon 18 Feb: For the second round in succession the FA Cup draw is made live on the BBC News Channel's Sportsday programme at 6.30pm. The three remaining Championship sides will take on WSL teams in the quarter-finals with Durham welcoming holders Chelsea, Manchester United travelling to Reading and Aston Villa at home to West Ham. The only all-WSL affair is Manchester City v Liverpool.

Sheffield United say they will contest the FA charge against their forward Sophie Jones who is accused of racially abusing Tottenham's Renee Hector in January's Championship match.

Fri 22 Feb: Former Charlton youth player Jordan Dawes passes away at the age of 18. Dawes, who most recently played for fifth tier Kent Football United, had a stroke in November and was later diagnosed with liver cancer.

Sat 23 Feb: Manchester City win the first silverware of the season as they beat Arsenal 4-2 on penalties when the Continental Cup final finishes goalless after extra time. The Gunners appear to have the advantage when 18-year-old substitute Lauren Hemp takes City's second penalty and sees it saved by Sari van Veenendaal. However, City keeper Karen Bardsley then stops the next two kicks she faces from Leah Williamson and Danielle van de Donk before Janine Beckie ultimately goes on to score the decisive winning kick for Nick Cushing's side. It's the first Continental Cup final ever to have gone to penalties with City winning the trophy for the third time.

Wed 27 Feb: England win their opening match of the SheBelieves Cup as they come from behind to beat Brazil 2-1 in Philadelphia. Alves da Silva puts Brazil ahead with a 16th-minute penalty. Ellen White levels from a tight angle early in the second half before Beth Mead wins it with a long-range cross-shot with a quarter of an hour to play. Hosts USA later draw 2-2 with England's upcoming World Cup group opponents Japan.

Sat 2 Mar: England play out a thrilling 2-2 draw with hosts USA in their second game of the 2019 SheBelieves Cup. After Megan Rapinoe puts the world's No.1 ranked team into the lead, England hit back through Manchester City pair Steph Houghton and Nikita Parris. Tobin Heath then equalises for the US midway through the second half. Japan beat Brazil 3-1 in the other match, meaning they top the table on goal difference. England will meet Japan in the final game on Wednesday in a winner-takes-all match.

Sun 3 Mar: WNL South East 1 (Tier 4) leaders Crawley Wasps win 1-0 at home to WNL North 1 (Tier 4) team Bolton Wanderers to reach the WNL Cup final, their first ever national cup final. Holders Blackburn Rovers, the runaway leaders of WNL Northern (Tier 3), win 4-0 at home to WNL Southern (Tier 3) side Loughborough Foxes in the other semi-final. In the WNL Plate semi-finals both matches are won by WNL Southern (Tier 3) teams. Gillingham win 1-0 at home to WNL Midlands 1 (Tier 4) leaders West Brom while the other game is a thrilling affair at Stadium: mk. MK Dons come from 1-0 down and 3-2 down in extra-time to beat WNL Northern 1 (Tier 4) side Liverpool Feds 4-3.

Having reached the final, Gillingham are disqualified from the WNL Plate when the FA rules that they fielded two ineligible players in their 1-0 semi-final win against West Brom. Their beaten opponents will take their place in the final against MK Dons.

Mon 4 Mar: The organising committee of the 2019 World Cup officially recommends the implementation of VAR at this summer's tournament paving the way for its likely approval later this month.

Tue 5 Mar: England win the SheBelieves Cup for the first time as they beat Japan 3-0 in Tampa. All the goals come in the opening half an hour with Lucy Staniforth, Karen Carney and Beth Mead on target. Japan started the match knowing that a victory would secure the title for them. England have competed in all four editions of the round-robin tournament with their previous best finish being 2nd in 2018. In the final match of the competition hosts USA beat Brazil 1-0.

Liverpool forward Niamh Charles, 19, signs a new contract with the club. The length of the deal is not revealed.

The South Korean FA sends plans to its North Korean counterparts to consider a bid to co-host the 2023 Women's World Cup.

Sat 9 Mar: The FA confirms that England and Lyon midfielder Izzy Christiansen hopes to be fit for this summer's World Cup having undergone successful ankle surgery following the injury she sustained during last week's SheBelieves Cup match against Japan.

Sun 17 Mar: A crowd of 60,739 – believed to be a world record attendance for a women's domestic club fixture – watches Atletico Madrid host Barcelona at the Wanda Metropolitano in the Spanish League. The stadium is the new home ground of Atletico Madrid men's club. The women's team usually play their games at Atletico's training ground. Barca win the match 2-0 with England's Toni Duggan scoring one of their goals.

In the FA Cup quarter-finals, holders Chelsea are pushed all the way by Championship side Durham but win 1-0 courtesy of a Ji So-Yun goal. The Wildcats are watched by a club record crowd of 1,629 at New Ferens Park. Two other WSL sides come out on top against Championship opposition with West Ham winning 1-0 at Aston Villa and Reading twice coming from behind in extra-time to beat Manchester United 3-2 with a last-minute winner from substitute Rakel Honnudottir. Manchester City will complete the semi-final line-up after coasting to a 3-0 win over Liverpool.

Tier 5 Bedford cause a shock against Tier 4 Luton in the Bedfordshire FA County Cup final as they win 1-0 at Ampthill Park.

Mon Mar 18: The FA Cup semi-final draw takes place live on BBC Breakfast. Manchester City will host Chelsea with West Ham travelling to Reading.

England's upcoming pre-World Cup friendly against Canada is confirmed as a sell-out. The match, which will take place at Manchester City FC Women's 7,000-capacity Academy Stadium, is the opening game of four in what's been billed as The Lionesses' Road to France Series.

Tue 19 Mar: FIFA says a record nine countries have expressed an interest in hosting the 2023 World Cup, with Argentina, Australia, Bolivia, Brazil, Colombia, Japan, New Zealand and South Africa having formally done so and South Korea and North Korea in talks to submit a joint bid. The registration deadline is 16 April 2019.

The BBC reports that WSL bottom club Yeovil Town may revert to part-time status in 2019-20 meaning they would be forced to give up their top-flight licence even if they avoid relegation on the field.

It's confirmed that, just like last year, both this season's FA Cup semi-finals will be broadcast live by the BBC. Reading will take on West Ham at 12.30pm on Sunday 14th April on the BBC Red Button and iPlayer with Manchester City against Chelsea following at 3.30pm on BBC Two.

Cambridge United win the Cambridgeshire FA County Cup as they beat Cambridge City 2-1 at The Abbey Stadium.

Wed 20 Mar: It's a landmark day for women's football in England as Barclays becomes the first sponsors of the WSL. The three-year partnership, believed to be worth in excess of £10m, will run from the start of the 2019-20 season.

Three Champions League quarter-final first leg ties take place with Barcelona beating LSK Kvinner of Norway 3-0 at home, Slavia Prague drawing 1-1 at home with Bayern Munich and holders Lyon winning 2-1 at home to Wolfsburg,

Thu 21 Mar: Chelsea beat PSG 2-0 in the first leg of their Champions League quarter-final tie. Hannah Blundell and Erin Cuthbert both score late goals at Kingsmeadow to put the Blues in a commanding position ahead of next week's trip to Paris. Before the game around 50 PSG supporters were denied entry to the ground after weapons (including knives and knuckledusters), fireworks and class A drugs were found on their coach. Police were first called to reports of vandalism at the ground at 8am.

Fri 22 Mar: Twenty-year-old England international Georgia Stanway signs a new deal with Manchester City that will keep her at the club until 2022.

Sat 23 Mar: Former Liverpool men's goalkeeper Chris Kirkland resigns from his role as assistant manager at Liverpool Women's to concentrate on his own goalkeeping academy and developing his mental health app. Kirkland has been working on manager Vicky Jepson's staff since the pair initially took joint charge following Neil Redfearn's departure at the start of the season.

Sun 24 Mar: Juventus beat Fiorentina 1-0 in front of 39,000 fans, a record crowd for a women's match in Italy. Tickets for the fixture – which took place at the Allianz Stadium in Turin, home of Juventus men's team – were free. The previous record was 14,000. Former England international Eni Aluko features for Juve, whose winning goal is scored by Denmark midfielder Sofie Junge Pedersen.

Mon 25 Mar: The FA brings forward the final day of the 2018-19 WSL season to avoid clashing with the final day of the men's Premier League fixtures. The last round of games will now kick-off at 12.30pm on Saturday 11 May, instead of Sunday 12 May.

Tue 26 Mar: Chelsea defender Millie Bright and midfielders Jill Scott (Manchester City) and Jade Moore (Reading) return to the England squad as Phil Neville names his players for next month's friendlies against Canada and Spain. The trio missed out on the SheBelieves Cup earlier this month because of injury.

Republic of Ireland international Katie McCabe signs a new long-term contract extension with Arsenal. The length of the deal is not made public.

Wed 27 Mar: Maren Mjelde scores a crucial injury-time goal to send Chelsea into the semi-finals of the Champions League. The Blues kick-off the quarter-final second leg away to PSG leading 2-0 but concede twice early in the second half before Mjelde hits the late goal which wins the tie.

Arsenal confirm Swedish defender Jessica Samuelsson's appearance against Liverpool on Sunday was her final game for the club and that she has left to join Rosengard in her home country.

Thu 28 Mar: Yeovil announce they are set to go into administration and that they "recognise they will not be a WSL club next season." The Glovers – who are five points adrift of safety with just five games of the season remaining – will be docked 10 points with immediate effect.

Gillingham win the Kent FA County Cup. Sharna Giordani scores the only goal in the seventh minute as the Gills beat their own Development side in a final played at Priestfield Stadium.

Fri 29 Mar: Matt Beard, who took over as West Ham head coach last summer, signs a contract extension with the WSL club. The length of the deal is undisclosed.

Sun 31 Mar: Arsenal's 1-0 win at Birmingham keeps them top of the table and ensures them a top two finish meaning they will play Champions League football next season for the first time since 2013-14.

Blackburn Rovers win their third Tier 3 title in a row as they are crowned WNL Northern champions after a 3-0 home win over Derby County.

Wed 3 Apr: Tier 3 Portsmouth win the Hampshire FA County Cup by beating Tier 4 side Southampton Women's 3-1. It's the 11th year in a row, and 15th time overall, that Portsmouth have won the competition. Pompey race into a 3-0 lead inside 37 minutes with goals from Danielle Rowe, Shannon Albuery and Jade Bradley. Southampton pull one back through Natalie Bavister with 20 minutes left, but Pompey hold on for the victory. The match, which is staged at Testwood Park – the home of AFC Totton – is watched by a competition record crowd of 577.

Thu 4 Apr: The FA confirms MK Dons have been stripped of their place in the WNL Plate final due to fielding an ineligible player in the semi-final against Liverpool Feds. Feds will take their place in the final against West Brom on April 14th.

Reading striker Lauren Bruton, 26, signs a new contract with the WSL club. Bruton joined the Royals from Arsenal in September 2013 and has gone on to make more than 100 appearances for them. The length of the deal is not revealed.

Fri 5 Apr: England lose the first of their four World Cup warm-up matches 1-0 to Canada at Manchester City's Academy Stadium. Christine Sinclair scores the winner nine minutes from time.

Tier 4 side Nettleham announce they will be rebranded as Lincoln City Ladies from 1 June and become part of the Lincoln City men's FC family. Lincoln City men's currently play in League Two. The home ground for Lincoln City Ladies will be The Sun Hat Villas and Resorts Stadium which is home to non-League men's side Lincoln United. The City of Lincoln has previously hosted women's football. A club called Lincoln Ladies was formed in 1995 and became founding members of the WSL in 2011. They were rebranded as Notts County ahead of the 2014 season, with County then folding in 2017.

Sat 6 Apr: Switzerland international forward Alisha Lehmann, 20, signs a new contract with WSL club West Ham who she joined last summer. The length of the deal is undisclosed.

Sun 7 Apr: Keynsham Town seal the FA WNL South West 1 (Tier 4) title with a 5-0 win away to Southampton Saints. Kerry Bartlett scores four and Laura Williams is also on target.

Tue 9 Apr: A crowd of 13,856 sees England beat Spain 2-1 in their second World Cup warm-up match. Goals from Beth Mead and Ellen White are enough for victory in a fixture played at Swindon Town FC's County Ground.

Thu 11 Apr: Tier 4 outfit Cheltenham win the Gloucestershire FA Trophy final beating Tier 6 side Frampton Rangers 10-0 in the final at Almondsbury.

Fri 12 Apr: Tier 3 Plymouth Argyle win the Devon FA County Cup with a 3-2 victory over Tier 4 Buckland Athletic. Kayley Lane gives Argyle an early lead before Natasha Knapman strikes twice to send them into a 3-0 lead inside the opening 20 minutes. Buckland hit back with two late goals, but Plymouth hold on.

Sun 14 Apr: West Ham reach the FA Cup final for the first time in their history as they beat fellow WSL side Reading 4-3 on penalties at Adams Park following a 1-1 draw. Rachel Furness puts the Royals ahead early in the second half, but the Hammers equalise within 10 minutes through Alisha Lehmann. Fara Williams then misses a great chance for Reading when she hits the post from a 70th minute penalty. With no further goals the match progresses to extra-time and then penalties with Cho So-hyun eventually scoring the sudden death winner. In the other semi-final, holders Chelsea lose 1-0 away to Manchester City courtesy of an injury-time own goal by Magdalena Eriksson.

Coventry United seal the WNL Southern Premier title with a 4-1 win at home to Cardiff City Ladies. In Tier 4 two teams secure back-to-back promotions; Crawley Wasps are crowned WNL South East 1 champions with a 1-0 home win over Enfield while Burnley take the WNL North 1 crown with a 3-0 win away to Crewe.

The Derbyshire FA County Cup is won by Derby County's Development team (their first XI do not compete in the competition) who beat Tier 4 side Long Eaton United 4-0. Tier 4 outfit Nettleham win the Lincolnshire FA County Cup for the sixth year in a row, beating lower division Lincoln Moorlands Railway 3-0 in the final.

Tue 16 Apr: WSL club Yeovil announce they have avoided going into administration but will not appeal the 10-point penalty they were hit with last month when they informed the FA of their intention to appoint an administrator. The Lady Glovers confirm they are to revert to part-time status and will apply for a Tier 2 licence for 2019-20.

Wed 17 Apr: Nine member associations have now expressed an intention to bid to host the 2023 Women's World Cup says FIFA, insisting this is a record number for any tournament it has ever organised. The expressions of interest have come from Argentina, Australia, Bolivia, Brazil, Colombia, Japan, New Zealand and a joint bid from South Korea and North Korea.

Thu 18 Apr: The BBC announces its shortlist for its Women's Footballer of the Year award: Wolfsburg's Pernille Harder (Denmark); Lyon's Ada Hegerberg (Norway); Portland Thorns' Lindsey Horan (USA); Chicago Red Stars and Perth Glory's Sam Kerr (Australia); and Lyon's Saki Kumagai (Japan).

Tier 3 side Chichester City win the Sussex FA County Cup for the second time in their history. Molly Clark's stunning long-range effort in the second minute proves enough for them to beat Brighton & Hove Albion's Development team 1-0 as they lift the trophy for the first time since 2014.

Tier 4 outfit Billericay Town win the Essex FA County Cup with a 4-0 win over Tier 3 strugglers C&K Basildon 4-0 in the final at Bowers & Pitsea FC. Danica Dougal scores an early penalty before C&K have Mollie Debell sent off nine minutes before the break. Samantha Pittuck doubles the lead on the stroke of half-time before Esme Lancaster and Zoe Rushen complete the scoring in the second half.

Sat 20 Apr: Manchester United clinch the Championship title with a 7-0 home win over Crystal Palace. Lauren James scores four with Lizzie Arnot, Leah Galton and Jess Sigsworth also on target.

Championship outfit Lewes confirm the signing of striker Rachel Panting from Tier 3 Portsmouth. Panting, who has 14 goals in 22 appearances for Pompey this season, is available for tomorrow's game against Aston Villa.

Sun 21 Apr: A crowd of 22,911 – a record Champions League attendance outside of the final – watches Lyon beat Chelsea 2-1 in the semi-final first leg. The holders go 2-0 up through a Magdalena Eriksson own goal (her second in a week) and Amandine Henry's flick from a corner. Fran Kirby's penalty just before half-time is saved by Sarah Bouhaddi (her third penalty miss in this season's Champions League) but Erin Cuthbert grabs a crucial away goal in the 72nd minute.

In today's other semi-final second leg, Spanish giants Barcelona win 1-0 at Bayern Munich with both teams aiming to reach the final for the first time.

West Brom secure the WNL Midlands 1 title and promotion back to Tier 3 with two games to spare. Head coach Louis Sowe's side kick-off their home match against bottom club Steel City Wanderers needing just a point but rack up a comfortable 7-0 home win with goals from Trina Greaves, Keeley Davies, Natalie Murray, Jessica Davies, Laura Davies, Fran Orthodoxou and an own goal.

Southampton FC Women (the team formally affiliated to men's Premier League club Southampton FC and not to be confused with Southampton Women FC or Southampton Saints) win the Southern Regional Premier League (Tier 5) and promotion to the WNL for 2019-20. The result which clinches the title is an 8-0 home win over Barton.

Tier 4 Oxford United beat holders Oxford City (Tier 5) in the Oxfordshire FA County Cup final. Ellie Noble gives them the lead midway through the second half with Flo Fyfe hitting a spectacular half-volley to double the lead with 11 minutes to play.

Tue 23 Apr: The Premier League turns down a request from West Ham United FC to bring forward the kick-off time of the men's home match against Southampton on Saturday 4 May from 3pm to 12.30pm. The request was made to give supporters who also wanted to attend the Women's FA Cup final time to get from London Stadium to Wembley for the 5.30pm kick-off.

Reading goalkeeper Grace Moloney extends her contract with the WSL club. The Republic of Ireland international, 26, has been with the Royals since she was nine.

Fri 26 Apr: The PFA WSL Team of the Year is named: Sophie Baggaley (Bristol City, goalkeeper); Hannah Blundell (Chelsea, right-back); Aoife Mannion (Birmingham City, centre-back); Steph Houghton (Manchester City, centre-back); Demi Stokes (Manchester City, left-back); Kim Little (Arsenal, right midfield); Ji So-Yun (Chelsea, centre midfield); Lia Walti (Arsenal, left midfield); Nikita Parris (right attacker); Erin Cuthbert (Chelsea, centre forward); Vivianne Miedema (Arsenal, left attacker).

Championship side Tottenham Hotspur Ladies confirm they will change their name to Tottenham Hotspur Women at the start of next season. Spurs also appoint Heather Cowan as their first Head of Women's Football. Cowan previously undertook a similar role at Birmingham City.

WNL Northern Premier (Tier 3) side Nottingham Forest win their fourth consecutive County Cup (and 13th in total) with a 1-0 win over lower League Ollerton Town. Helena Constantinou scores the winner early in the second half.

Sun 28 Apr: Arsenal seal the title with a game to spare thanks to a 4-0 win away to Brighton & Hove Albion. The result means they can no longer be caught by Manchester City – who go on to beat Yeovil 2-1 later in the afternoon. It's the Gunners' first League title since 2012, their third of the WSL era and their 15th overall. The match – played at Brighton men's Amex Stadium – is watched by a WSL record crowd of 5,265, beating the previous of 5,052 for Arsenal v Chelsea at The Emirates Stadium in 2012. Vivianne Miedema opens the scoring and ends the day by being named PFA Player of the Year.

Chelsea's Champions League dream ends at the semi-final stage as they are held to a 1-1 draw by defending champions Lyon meaning they exit the competition 3-2 on aggregate. A crowd of 4,670 – the highest for a women's match at Kingsmeadow – sees Eugene Le Sommer's deflected shot put Lyon ahead before Ji So-yun equalises just after the half-hour mark. Barcelona beat Bayern Munich 1-0 in the other semi-final to complete a 2-0 aggregate win and reach their first final.

A 5-0 home defeat to newly crowned champions Manchester United means that Millwall Lionesses will finish bottom of the Championship. The result leaves them five points behind Crystal Palace (who are beaten 4-1 at home by Charlton) with just one game to play. There will be no relegation from the Championship this season though.

Tier 4 outfit Blackburn Rovers win the WNL Cup (the League Cup for Tier 3 and 4 sides) for the second year in a row as they beat Tier 4 Crawley Wasps 3-0 in the final at Burton Albion FC's Pirelli Stadium. Saffron Jordan scores her 100th and 101st goals for the club with Natasha Flint on target in between. The win means the club has completed a 'Double' by winning the Northern Premier title and WNL Cup in 2017-18 and 2018-19.

Luton Town's relegation from Tier 4 is confirmed as they throw away a 2-0 lead at Ipswich Town to lose 5-2 in WNL South East 1.

Mon 29 Apr: Manchester City forward Nikita Parris is named Football Writers' Association Player of the Year with club-mate Raheem Sterling winning the men's award. Arsenal forward Vivianne Miedema finishes one vote behind Parris.

Tue 30 Apr: Tier 4 side Brighouse Town cause something of a shock in the West Riding FA County Cup final with a 3-2 win over Tier 3 outfit and holders Guiseley Vixens. Annabelle Cass is on target and Lavinia Nkomo bags a brace for Brighouse.

Tier 3 Stoke City win the Staffordshire FA County Cup for the 11th season in a row. Hannah Keryakoplis scores seven of their goals as they beat Tier 4 Sporting Khalsa 8-1 in the final.

The Birmingham FA County Cup final is contested by two teams who have just won their respective divisions, Tier 3 Coventry United (of WNL Southern Premier) and Tier 4 West Bromwich Albion (of WNL Midlands 1). Amy Wathan, Beth Merrick and Amber Hughes score for United as they successfully defend the Cup they won in 2017-18.

Wed 1 May: Tottenham Hotspur get the point they need to secure 2nd place in the Championship and promotion to the WSL (subject to FA ratification) with a 1-1 draw away to Aston Villa. Jessica Naz gives them the lead in the second minute before Amy West equalises early in the second half, but Spurs hang on. The result also ends Durham's and Charlton's hopes of promotion, leaving them four points and five points adrift of Spurs respectively with just one game remaining.

Tier 4 outfit Liverpool Feds defend the Liverpool FA County Cup (which they won for the first time last year) with a 4-1 win over North West Regional Premier League (Tier 5) side Merseyrail in the final.

Thu 2 May: Jessica Byrne scores a long-range winner with just eight minutes remaining as Actonians beat their WNL South East 1 (Tier 4) rivals Leyton Orient 1-0 in the Capital Cup final.

Tier 3 outfit MK Dons win the Berks & Bucks FA County Cup for the second year in a row, and fifth time overall, as they beat Tier 4 Chesham United 4-2 in the final.

Sat 4 May: Manchester City win the FA Cup for the second time, beating first-time finalists West Ham United 3-0 at Wembley. The match is all-square until seven minutes after the break when Keira Walsh puts City ahead with a long-range strike. Georgia Stanway and Lauren Hemp add gloss to the score line late on. The crowd of 43,264 is just short of the record of 45,423 set at the 2018 final between Chelsea and Arsenal.

Mon 6 May: FIFA reveals there will be two new women's categories to go alongside FIFA Best Women's Player of the Year at the 2019 awards in September. For the first time a goalkeeper of the year and a team of the year will be recognised.

Tue 7 May: Tier 4 Ipswich win the Suffolk FA County Cup with an 8-0 win over lower League Needham in the final, which is played at Portman Road, home of Ipswich Town men.

Wed 8 May: England manager Phil Neville names his 23-player squad for France 2019 that includes 11 World Cup debutantes: Mary Earps; Millie Bright; Leah Williamson; Demi Stokes; Rachel Daly; Lucy Staniforth; Georgia Stanway; Keira Walsh; Nikita Parris and Beth Mead. Manchester City's Steph Houghton will captain the team while Karen Carney and Jill Scott will head to their fourth World Cup. The squad in full is:

Goalkeepers: Karen Bardsley (Man City), Mary Earps (Wolfsburg), Carly Telford (Chelsea)

Defenders: Millie Bright (Chelsea), Lucy Bronze (Lyon), Rachel Daly (Houston Dash), Alex Greenwood (Man Utd), Steph Houghton (captain, Man City), Abbie McManus (Man City), Demi Stokes (Man City) Leah Williamson (Arsenal)

Midfielders: Karen Carney (Chelsea), Jade Moore (Reading), Jill Scott (Man City), Lucy Staniforth (Birmingham City), Georgia Stanway (Man City), Keira Walsh (Man City)

Forwards: Toni Duggan (Barcelona), Fran Kirby (Chelsea), Beth Mead (Arsenal), Nikita Parris (Man City), Jodie Taylor (Seattle Reign), Ellen White (Birmingham City)

Thu 9 May: WNL Northern Premier (Tier 3) champions Blackburn lift the Lancashire FA County Cup after a 2-0 win over divisional rivals Fylde.

Fri 10 May: The FA confirms that Manchester United and Tottenham, who finished 1st and 2nd in the Championship, have been granted licences to play in WSL in 2019-20. Likewise, the WNL Northern Premier champions Blackburn and Southern Premier champions Coventry United have their promotions to the Championship ratified.

West Ham defender Claire Rafferty announces she will retire after tomorrow's final WSL match of the season against Brighton. The 30-year-old joined the Hammers last summer after 11 years at Chelsea where she won the WSL and FA Cup Double in 2015 and 2018.

Rachel Yankey leaves her role as head coach of Championship side London Bees. She succeeded Luke Swindlehurst back in February in a deal which ran until the end of 2018-19 and says she turned down the offer of a contract extension.

Keynsham Town beat WNL South West 1 (Tier 4) rivals Brislington 2-1 in the Somerset FA County Cup final with Ellie Curson scoring both goals.

Sat 11 May: England forward Nikita Parris posts on Instagram that she will leave Manchester City this summer. The 25-year-old, who won the Football Writers' Association Footballer of the Year award for 2018-19 has been linked with a move to French side Lyon.

The final round of WSL fixtures takes place with champions Arsenal winning 1-0 at home to runners-up Manchester City. The visitors are just two minutes away from completing the entire domestic season unbeaten only for Emma Mitchell to score from long range.

On the last day of the Championship season champions Manchester United win 5-0 at home to Lewes and runners-up Tottenham beat Durham 2-0 away.

Sun 12 May: Despite playing the second half with a suspected broken finger, goalkeeper Skye Kirkham saves two penalties in a shootout as Tier 4 Barnsley beat Tier 3 Huddersfield Town 4-1 on spot-kicks following a 3-3 draw in the Sheffield & Hallamshire FA County Cup final. Barnsley go ahead early on when Drew Greene sets up twin sister Darcie for the opener. Their opponents come back from 2-0 and 3-2 down, but Barnsley eventually triumph on penalties.

Tue 14 May: Millwall FC men's release a statement which reads: "(We) regret to announce that the board of directors and senior management at Millwall Lionesses have decided to become an independent entity. This will mean the start of a new club, London City Lionesses, while Millwall Lionesses will go on to operate through Millwall Community Trust with its proud history and tradition intact." The outgoing board of Millwall Lionesses later announce they will seek to retain their FA Championship licence for London City Lionesses, adding: "The management are not forming a new team, the Millwall Lionesses Football Club, which is a distinct legal entity from Millwall FC has decided to move on from Millwall. They are renaming themselves London City Lionesses. It will take with it its own heritage of 48 years, including that part of their history that they affiliated with Millwall FC."

Thu 16 May: Manchester City announce that England forward Ellen White will join them from Birmingham City on a two-year deal on 1 July.

Fri 17 May: Yeovil are shocked to discover that their application for a Championship licence has been turned down by the FA. The Glovers had been expecting to start 2019-20 in Tier 2 following their relegation from the WSL but will now need to begin again in Tier 3 or perhaps lower.

At the FA WNL end of season awards, the following prizes are handed out: Premier Division Player of the Year (Keira Ramshaw, Sunderland); Division 1 Player of the Year (Leah Embley, Burnley); Northern Premier Top Goalscorer (Saffron Jordan, Blackburn Rovers); Southern Premier Top Goalscorer (Emily Allen, Oxford United & Amy Wathan, Coventry United); Div 1 North Top Goalscorer (Bianca Owens, Norton & Stockton Ancients); Div 1 Midlands Top Goalscorer (Jade

Cross, Wolverhampton Wanderers); Div 1 South East Top Goalscorer (Alessandra Barreca, Actonians); Div 1 South West Top Goal Scorer (Kerry Bartlett, Keynsham Town); Manager of the Year (Gemma Donnelly, Blackburn Rovers); Club of the Year (Coventry United).

Sat 18 May: Lyon win the Champions League for the fourth year in a row with 2018 Ballon D'Or winner Ada Hegerberg scoring a hat-trick as they beat Barcelona 4-1 in Budapest. Germany's Dzsenifer Marozsan strikes early to give Lyon the lead before Hegerberg takes centre stage. Asisat Oshoala scores a late consolation for Barca who are appearing in their first final. England's Lucy Bronze and Wales' Jess Fishlock both start the game for Barca.

WNL Northern Premier (Tier 3) champions Blackburn Rovers beat Southern Premier counterparts Coventry United 3-0 in the play-off final in front of 539 fans at Valley Parade, Bradford City FC. The match traditionally decides which team is eligible for promotion to Tier 2 but it was decided at the start of 2018-19 that both participants would go up subject to satisfying the FA's licensing criteria, thus both teams started the match knowing they would be playing Championship football in 2019-20. The victory sees Blackburn complete a Quadruple of trophies for 2018-19 having also won the WNL Cup and County Cup.

Tue 21 May: England forward Nikita Parris, 25, signs for Champions League winners Lyon after leaving Manchester City.

Wed 22 May: Ada Hegerberg, 23, is named BBC World Footballer of the Year, claiming the award (which is voted for by fans across the globe) for the second time having also lifted it in 2017. The Norwegian striker, who plays her club football for Lyon, also won the inaugural Ballon D'Or in December 2018.

Thu 23 May: Manchester City goalkeeper Ellie Roebuck, 19, signs a new two-year deal with her club.

Fri 24 May: England defender Abbie McManus, 26, signs a pre-contract agreement with WSL newcomers Manchester United after leaving rivals Manchester City.

Liverpool captain and defender Sophie Bradley-Auckland, 29, signs a new contract with the Reds.

Sat 25 May: Goals from Nikita Parris and stand-in captain Jill Scott see England beat Denmark 2-0 in their penultimate World Cup warm-up match in front of a crowd of 8,273 at Walsall FC'S Banks's Stadium.

Sat 1 Jun: England suffer a dispiriting 1-0 home defeat to New Zealand (ranked 19th in the world) in their final World Cup warm-up match. Sarah Gregorius scores an early second-half winner in front of a crowd of 20,076 at The Amex Stadium as the Black Ferns chalk up their first ever win over England.

Mon 3 Jun: Former England defender Laura Bassett, 35, announces her retirement from football. Bassett made 61 appearances for the Lionesses and played for WSL clubs including Birmingham City and Chelsea.

Midfielder Laura Coombs, 28, signs a two-year deal with Manchester City after leaving Liverpool.

Following a successful loan spell, forward Claudia Walker makes a permanent move from Everton to Birmingham City signing a two-year deal.

Wed 5 Jun: Wales midfielder Hayley Ladd, who can also play in defence, signs for WSL newcomers Manchester United after leaving Birmingham City.

Scotland defender Jen Beattie, 28, leaves Manchester City to re-join Arsenal where she won the WSL title in 2011 and 2012 as well as two FA Cups and two Continental Cups.

The FA releases the following statement: "Following the withdrawal of Yeovil Town Ladies FC from Tier 2 of the women's football pyramid [FA Women's Championship], The FA Women's Football Board has agreed that at the conclusion of the 2019-20 season, two teams [champions of the FA Women's National League Northern and Southern Divisions respectively, subject to satisfying licence criteria] will be promoted from Tier 3 to Tier 2 and one team [bottom placed team in the FA Women's Championship] will be relegated from Tier 2 to Tier 3 [either the Northern or Southern Division of the FA Women's National League based on the geography].

Fri 7 Jun: The eighth FIFA Women's World Cup gets under way in France with the hosts beating South Korea 4-0 in the opening game in Paris.

Sun 9 Jun: Day three of the World Cup sees England play their opening game. The Lionesses beat Scotland 2-1 in what is the Scots' first ever World Cup fixture. Nikita Parris opens the scoring with a penalty awarded for handball after a VAR review. Ellen White doubles the lead before Claire Emslie's goal with 11 minutes to go ensures a nervy finish. The game is watched by a peak TV audience of 6.1m, a record for a women's match in the UK, beating the 4m who saw England lose 3-0 to the Netherlands on Channel 4 in the Euro 2017 semi-final.

Mon 10 Jun: Crystal Palace reveal they are to drop the 'Ladies' suffix and that their official name will now simply be Crystal Palace FC. They will use 'Women' only when there is potential for confusion with the men's team.

Tue 11 Jun: Holders the USA rack up a World Cup record 13-0 win in their opening game against minnows Thailand.

Manchester City forward Melissa Lawley tweets that she is leaving the club after two-and-a-half years.

Fri 14 Jun: England beat Argentina 1-0 in their second World Cup group match. Nikita Parris has a 28th-minute penalty saved by Vanina Correa but Jodie Taylor scores the winner just after the hour mark. The other game in the group earlier in the day ends in a 2-1 win for Japan against Scotland.

Tue 18 Jun: Brazil international Marta becomes the leading scorer in men's and women's World Cup finals as she converts her 17th goal in the tournament's history. The 33-year-old dispatches a 74th-minute penalty as Brazil beat Italy 1-0 to qualify for the knockout stages. The goal moves her ahead of Miroslav Klose who scored 16 goals for Germany's men's team.

Wed 19 Jun: England beat Japan 2-0 to finish the World Cup group stage with three wins from three. Ellen White scores both goals. Scotland are eliminated after throwing away a 3-0 lead with 16 minutes to go to draw 3-3 with Argentina. The South Americans have an injury-time penalty saved by Scotland goalkeeper Lee Alexander, but VAR spots that she has marginally moved off her line before the ball is kicked. Under a new law, which came in to force on 1st June, Alexander is booked. Florencia Bonsegundo scores the re-taken effort to knock Scotland out.

Thu 20 Jun: Defender Megan Campbell agrees a new one-year contract extension with Manchester City.

Sun 23 Jun: England beat Cameroon 3-0 in the World Cup Round of 16. Captain Steph Houghton puts England ahead after an indirect free-kick is awarded on the edge of the six-yard box when Cameroon goalkeeper Annette Ngo Ndom handles a back pass. The match descends into chaos when Cameroon twice appear unwilling to restart the game after two marginal offside decisions correctly go England's way following VAR reviews. First Ellen White's goal, which makes it 2-0, is allowed to stand after originally being chalked off, and then Ajara Nchout's effort is ruled out after having initially been given. Alex Greenwood makes it 3-0 just before the hour mark.

Mon 24 Jun: The BBC reveals a record-breaking peak UK TV audience of 6.9m viewers tuned into England's 3-0 victory over Cameroon yesterday making it the most-watched women's game ever, beating the 6.1m who watched England v Scotland earlier in the tournament.

Wed 26 Jun: FIFA opens disciplinary proceedings against Cameroon regarding their behaviour in Sunday's World Cup match against England.

Thu 27 Jun: England beat Norway 3-0 in the World Cup quarter-final with goals from Jill Scott, Ellen White and Lucy Bronze. Nikita Parris sees a late penalty saved – it's her second miss of the tournament. The match draws yet another record peak TV UK audience for a women's match with 7.6m tuning in (breaking the records of 6.1m who watched England v Scotland and 6.9m who watched England v Cameroon earlier in the tournament).

Fri 28 Jun: Holders the USA beat hosts France 2-1 in the World Cup quarter-final in Paris. Megan Rapinoe scores twice. Wendie Renard pulls one back with eight minutes remaining.

Sat 29 Jun: The final two World Cup quarter-finals take place with European champions the Netherlands beating Italy 2-0 and Sweden pulling off something of a shock against Germany as they beat the Olympic champions 2-1.

Mon 1 Jul: The FA releases the opening round of fixtures for the WSL and Championship seasons. Manchester City will host rivals and WSL newcomers Manchester United, with Tottenham Hotspur – who have also come up from the Championship – travelling to Chelsea. Champions Arsenal are at home to West Ham. The top-flight season gets under way on the weekend of 7/8 September which coincides with a break in the men's domestic calendar. The Championship begins on 17/18 August with newly promoted sides Blackburn Rovers and Coventry United away to Lewes and Crystal Palace respectively.

Tue 2 Jul: England's World Cup dreams are ended by holders the USA in the semi-finals. The States take a 10th-minute lead through Christen Press only for Ellen White to equalise nine minutes later. Alex Morgan puts the US 2-1 ahead just after the half-hour mark. White thinks she has equalised for England a second time in the 68th minute, but VAR correctly rules her effort out for a marginal offside. England have a great chance to make it 2-2 with six minutes to go after a lengthy

VAR review awards a penalty for a foul on White. With regular taker Nikita Parris having missed two penalties during the tournament, captain Steph Houghton steps up but sees her effort easily saved by Alyssa Naeher. England have Millie Bright sent off four a late challenge moments later to end any hopes of a comeback.

Wed 3 Jul: European champions the Netherlands beat Sweden 1-0 after extra time in the second World Cup semi-final. New Manchester United signing Jackie Groenen scores the winner.

The BBC reveals another record peak UK TV audience for a women's match with 11.7m watching last night's World Cup semi-final between England and the USA. The figure breaks the records of 6.1m (England v Scotland), 6.9m (England v Cameroon) and 7.6m (England v Norway) set earlier in the tournament.

Fri 5 Jul: Chelsea midfielder Karen Carney, 31, announces she will retire from all football after England's World Cup 3rd place match against Sweden tomorrow. Manager Phil Neville confirms that Carney will be involved at some point in the match, meaning she will win her 144th cap. Only Fara Williams has appeared more times for England. Carney made her first team debut for former club Birmingham City when she was 14 and went on to play in four World Cups and the 2012 Olympics.

WSL newcomers Tottenham announce they will play their home games in 2019-20 at The Hive, home of Championship outfit London Bees and men's National League side Barnet. Spurs have played their home game at Theobalds Lane, Cheshunt FC, in recent seasons.

Sat 6 Jul: England fail to match their 3rd-place finish at the 2015 World Cup as they are beaten 2-1 by Sweden in the 3rd place match. Kosovare Asllani and Sofia Jakobsson both strike early to put Sweden firmly in control before Fran Kirby pulls one back just after the half-hour mark. Ellen White has a second half 'goal' disallowed when VAR rules she handled the ball during the build-up. The handball law changed on 1st June with the word 'deliberate' removed. The new law means that any goal scored off the hand or arm, regardless of intent, is chalked off, as is any goal scored after the ball hits a hand or arm in the build-up.

Sun 7 Jul: The USA become the second team (after Germany 2003 and 2007) to defend the World Cup title as they win the tournament for a record-extending fourth time. Having scored in the opening 12 minutes of every game in the competition so far, the USA are made to wait by the European champions who keep them out until just after the hour-mark. At that point co-captain Megan Rapinoe opens the scoring from the spot after VAR awards a penalty for a foul by Stefanie van der Gragt on Alex Morgan. A sweet finish by Rose Lavelle eight minutes later completes the scoring as the US prevail 2-0.

After the match Rapinoe also wins the Golden Ball award for the tournament's best player and the Golden Boot award as the tournament's top scorer. She finishes level on six goals with team-mate Morgan and England's Ellen White, but takes the award by virtue of having assisted more goals than White and played for fewer minutes than Morgan (who also assisted three). Morgan takes the Silver Boot with White awarded the Bronze Boot. White's England team-mate Lucy Bronze wins the Silver Ball for the tournament's second-best player.

Mon 8 Jul: Manchester City and Chelsea switch their opening WSL fixtures of the season to the men's stadiums. City will take on Manchester United in the first WSL derby between the teams at the 55,000-capacity Etihad Stadium on Saturday 7 September with Chelsea hosting Tottenham at the 41,000-capacity Stamford Bridge the following day. The weekend coincides with an international break in the men's season.

The BBC reveals that 28.1m viewers watched some BBC coverage of this summer's World Cup.

Tue 9 Jul: Manchester City sign defender Aoife Mannion who left Birmingham earlier this summer.

Wed 10 Jul: The full fixture programme for the WSL and Championship seasons is released. The new 62,000-capacity Tottenham Hotspur Stadium will stage Tottenham's north London derby against champions Arsenal on 17 November. The match coincides with an international break in the men's calendar.

Thu 11 Jul: Everton sign France international midfielder Maeva Clemaron, 26, on a two-year deal following her departure from FC Fleury 91.

Fri 12 Jul: FIFA's latest rankings show World Cup winners and top-ranked side the USA now have a record 121-point lead. Germany are placed 2nd, World Cup runners-up Netherlands climb five places to 3rd, France remain 4th, and England slip two places to 5th.

The BBC wins exclusive rights to broadcast the 2021 European Championship on TV, radio and online. Euro 2021 is to be hosted by England.

WSL side West Ham sign former Champions League-winning defender Laura Vetterlein, 27, from German outfit SC Sand. Vetterlein helped Wolfsburg win back-to-back Champions League titles in 2013 and 2014.

Bristol City re-sign former players Yana Daniels, 27, and Jas Matthews, 26. Belgium international forward Daniels and former England Under-23 defender Matthews both left the club in the summer of 2018 to spend 2018-19 with fellow WSL outfit Liverpool.

Sat 13 Jul: England goalkeeper Mary Earps leaves German club Wolfsburg to sign for WSL newcomers Manchester United.

Mon 15 Jul: Striker Ebony Salmon joins WSL side Bristol City following her release by Manchester United. The 18-year-old spent part of last season on loan with Championship outfit Sheffield United.

Goalkeepers Anke Preuss, 26, and Fran Kitching, 21, both sign contract extensions with WSL side Liverpool. The lengths of the deals are not revealed.

Tue 16 Jul: WSL side West Ham sign forward Martha Thomas, 23, from French outfit Le Havre. Thomas was born in Dorset but grew up in the US.

Wed 17 Jul: Wales midfielder Angharad James, 25, joins Reading from fellow WSL side Everton.

Thu 18 Jul: Birmingham City sign 24-year-old former USA Under-23 international midfielder Brianna Visalli from West Ham.

New Zealand international wing-back Ali Riley leaves Chelsea for Bayern Munich.

Reading's Maz Pacheco and Sophie Howard sign one-year contract extensions with the club while team-mate Molly Bartrip agrees a new two-year deal.

Fri 19 Jul: West Ham sign 18-year-old forward Jacynta Galabadaarachchi from Perth Glory.

The Birmingham City exodus continues as defender Paige Williams and midfielder Shania Hayles become the eighth and ninth players to depart the club this summer.

Tue 23 Jul: Bristol City sign Netherlands Under-23 midfielder Vita van der Linden, 22, from Ajax. City goalkeeper Eartha Cumings also agrees a contract extension with the club.

Wed 24 Jul: Birmingham City sign Northern Ireland international Rebecca Holloway from American club Nashville Rhythm. Meanwhile, Tottenham make their eighth signing of the summer as centre-back Hannah Godfrey returns to England having spent four years in the US.

Thu 25 Jul: West Ham sign French international midfielder Kenza Dali, 27, from Dijon FCO.

Sun 28 Jul: Arsenal Women take part in Arsenal FC's annual pre-season tournament The Emirates Cup for the first time. Playing a double header with Arsenal men at The Emirates Stadium, they kick-off against Bayern Munich at 12:30pm prior to the men's match with Lyon. Arsenal announce a peak crowd of 28,500 in attendance for the women's match which Bayern win 1-0.

ACKNOWLEDGEMENTS

There are so many people to thank for helping me to bring to life 'The Women's Football Yearbook 2019-20'. Firstly, a huge thank you to my co-author Tom Garry and to Dave Lane at Legends Publishing for seeing the potential in this title and for the wonderful design and formatting. Tom and I are also extremely grateful to England head coach Phil Neville for agreeing to write the foreword to this third edition of 'The Women's Football Yearbook'.

I am hugely grateful to have been able to call on the diligent fact-checking of BBC Sport journalist Mark Mitchener and to Patricia Gregory, who co-founded the Women's Football Association in 1969, for some historical information and amendments.

Thank you to Olwen Davies at Opta for helping me verify the accuracy of goals and appearance data in the WSL section of this book and to Khalid Kharimullah for his assistance with the Championship information, as well as to BBC Sport journalist Owen Phillips.

Thanks also to Julian Barker for verifying the historical accuracy of some past honours and League positions via his copies of Women's Soccer Scene.

I am also extremely grateful for the efforts of the following second year students at the University Campus of Football Business based at Wembley Stadium for helping me keep across events in the WNL: Sam Bartlett-Clark; Eliott Brennan; Samuel Cross; Tony Fairbairn; Daniel Greene; Joshua O'Brien; Jake Sapsford and Axel Toudic. Elsewhere Middlesex University student Nana Acquaye thoroughly researched WNL South West 1 throughout 2018-19 and Liverpool John Moores student Michael Grimes did likewise with regards to WNL North 1. A huge thanks also to upcoming journalist Mitul Samji for keeping our associated website matchofherday.com updated with his insightful WSL match reports. With thanks also to all the clubs in the WSL, Championship, and WNL as well as to the FA and County FAs:

Actonians (Linda Fox); Arsenal (Rebecca James & Faye White); Aston Villa (Greg Styles & Amber Wildgust); Bedworth United (Tina Richards); Billericay Town (Kim Coster); Birmingham & West Midlands (Helen Carver); Blackburn Rovers (Sam Jones); Bolton Wanderers (Nicole Johnston); Bradford City (Matthew Kermode); Brighton & Hove Albion (James Hilsum); Brislington (Bob Mewse & Sharon Whelan); Buckland Athletic (Grant Fisher); Bristol City (George West); Burnley (Sinead Kennedy Peers & Matt Smith); C&K Basildon/AFC Basildon (Sean Eldridge); Burton Albion (Lucy Jelf); Cambridge United (Kevin Hoover, Victoria Hoover & Chris Walker); Cambridge City (Chris Mosley & Debbie Mosley); Cardiff City Ladies (Karen Jones); Charlton Athletic (Steve Adamson); Chelsea (Steve Bond & Jo Gaskell); Cheltenham Town (Ian Purvis); Chichester City (Mikki Collins); Chorley (Geoff Dawson, Janet Dawson, Janet Mitchell & Rod Prescott); Coventry United (Jay Bradford & Peter Reynolds); Crawley Wasps (Andrew Raeburn & Paul Walker); Crewe Alexandra (James Brown); Crystal Palace (Dean Davenport, Tara Hook & Paula Johnson); Denham United (Joanne Currivan); Derby County (Andy Moore); Durham (Mark Donnelly); Durham FA (Michael Bell); Enfield Town (Michael Bunyan); Exeter City, (Clive Watts & Exeter City Community Trust); Gillingham (Julian Hart); Ipswich Town (Kieren Standley); Leafield Athletic (Dan Hearnden & Tracie Clements); Leeds United (Dan O'Hearne); Leicester City Women (Dan Smith); Leicester United (Natalie Hurst); Lewes (James Boyes, Ash Head & Jack Heaselden); Leyton Orient (Chris Brayford); Liverpool (Kevin Guy & William Hughes); Liverpool Feds (Chantelle Thompson); London Bees (Aarron Pullen); London City Lionesses (Chris Phillips); Loughborough Foxes (Siobhan Eastham); Manchester United (Haylee Blease); Middlesbrough (Amy Cowan); Millwall Lionesses (Billy Taylor); Millwall Supporters Club (Tom Gale); Milton Keynes Dons (Owen Evans); Morecambe (Nick Barrett); Nettleham/Lincoln City Women (Jane Cooper, Richard Cooper & Bethany Pritchard); Newcastle United (Lisa Bell); Norton & Stockton Ancients (Victoria Burton & Kevin Waterworth); Norwich City (Louise Riseborough & Mel Swift); Nottingham Forest (Steven Gray); Oxford United (Kath Faulkner, Liam Gilbert, Shaun Ritchie & Chris Williams); Poole (Lisa Dootson Gill); Portsmouth (Bill Griffiths); Plymouth Argyle (Dave Potham); QPR (Andy Watkins); Sheffield FC (Helen Mitchell); Solihull Moors (Amador Cambra & Kerry Lenihan); Southampton FC; Southampton Saints (Tracey Wheeler); Southampton Women's (Amanda Burroughs); Sporting Khalsa (Kelly Williams); Steel City Wanderers (Ciara Douglas); Stevenage (Mark Dicker & David Potter); Stockport County (James Gill); Stoke City (James Knowles); Sunderland (Mark Craggs); Swindon Town (Dan Jones), The New Saints (Lawrence Wilson); The FA (Katie Brazier, Nick Frith, David Gerty, Emily Liles, Nick Smith & Wendy Taylor); Tottenham Hotspur (Rosie Bonass & Val Weaver); Watford (Andrew Waller, Helen Ward & Simon Wheeler); West Ham United (Samantha David & Mitchell Waddon); West Riding FA (Hannah Cottam); Wolverhampton Wanderers (Jenny Wilkes); Yeovil Town (Andy Bevins).

And of course, a huge thank you to my wonderful wife Sonja and my children Archie and Rosie for putting up with me spending so much time working on this book and to my Mum and Dad for all their help and support since the project began.

ENGLAND CELEBRATE JODIE TAYLOR'S WINNER AGAINST ARGENTINA AT THE 2019 WORLD CUP

WSL PHOTOS COURTESY OF:
Arsenal – The FA/Getty Images
Birmingham City – The FA/Getty Images
Brighton & Hove Albion – BHAFC and Paul Hazlewood
Bristol City – Bristol City Women via JMPUK
Chelsea – Darren Walsh
Everton – Everton FC & Emma Simpson
Liverpool – Liverpool FC/Getty Images
Manchester City – Manchester City Women Supporters Club
Manchester United – Manchester United
Reading – The FA/Getty Images
Tottenham Hotspur – Wu's Photography
West Ham United – West Ham United FC

CHAMPIONSHIP PHOTOS COURTESY OF:
Aston Villa – Aston Villa
Blackburn Rovers – Blackburn Rovers
Charlton Athletic – Keith Gillard
Coventry United – Jeff Bennett
Crystal Palace – Tara Hook
Durham – Durham
Leicester City Women – Leicester City Women
Lewes – James Boyes
London Bees – London Bees
Millwall Lionesses (London City Lionesses page) – Edward Payne
Sheffield United – The FA/Getty Images

WNL PHOTOS COURTESY OF:
Actonians – Linda Fox
Barnsley – Dean Bradford
Bedworth United – Elisha Dunn
Billericay Town – Nicky Hayes
Birmingham & West Midlands – Birmingham & West Midlands
Bolton Wanderers – Bolton Wanderers
Bradford City – Bradford City
Brighouse Town – Brighouse Town
Brislington – Brislington
Buckland Athletic – Buckland Athletic
Burnley – Burnley FC Women
Burton Albion – Burton Albion
Cambridge City – Cambridge City
Cambridge United – Cambridge United
Cardiff City Ladies – Cardiff City Ladies
Cheltenham Town – Cheltenham Town
Chesham United – Berks & Bucks FA
Chester-le-Street Town – Chester-le-Street Town
Chichester City – Sheena Booker
Chorley Women – Chorley FC Women
Crawley Wasps – Ben Davidson
Crewe Alexandra – Bev Lambourne
Derby County – Andy Clarke
Doncaster Rovers Belles – Steven Chicken
Durham Cestria – Durham Cestria
Enfield Town – Enfield Town
Exeter City – Exeter Community Trust
Fylde – Paul Melling
Gillingham – Gillingham Ladies
Guiseley Vixens – Alex Daniel
Hounslow – QPR Women & Ian Randall
Huddersfield Town – Huddersfield Town
Hull City – Kevin Greene Photography
Ipswich Town – Ipswich Town
Kent Football United – Kent Football United
Keynsham Town – Keynsham Town
Larkhall Athletic – Will Cheshire
Leafield Athletic – Leafield Athletic
Leicester United – Leicester United
Leeds United – Leeds United
Leyton Orient – Leyton Orient
Lincoln City – Lincoln City
Liverpool Feds – Liverpool Feds
Long Eaton United – @leufcladies
Loughborough Foxes – Loughborough Foxes
Maidenhead United – Maidenhead United
Middlesbrough – Colin Lock
Morecambe – Morecambe Ladies FC
MK Dons – MK Dons
Newcastle United – Newcastle United
Norton & Stockton Ancients – Norton & Stockton Ancients
Norwich City – Brian Coombes
Oxford United – Darrell Fisher & Jack Brown
Plymouth Argyle – Dave Potham
Poole Town – Andrew Orman
Portsmouth – Portsmouth FC
QPR – Ian Randall (on Hounslow page)
Sheffield FC – Sheffield FC
Solihull Moors – Tom King
Southampton FC – @SouthamptonFC
Southampton Saints – Southampton Saints
Southampton Women's – John Bilcliff, Bilcliff Photography
Sporting Khalsa – ThreeFiveThree Photography
Stevenage – Stevenage
Stockport County – James Gill Media
Stoke City – James Knowles
Sunderland – Sunderland AFC Ladies
Swindon Town – Swindon Town
The New Saints – The New Saints
Watford – Andrew Waller
West Brom – Ian Stevens
Wolves Women – Wolves Women

SOURCES
bbc.co.uk, fanatichull.com, fawsl.com, fifa.com, fulltime-league.thefa.com, matchofherday.com, midlandswoso.com, millwallsupportersclub.co.uk, Opta, sentherforward.wordpress.com, shekicks.net, thefa.com, uefa.com, womensfootballeast.com